Statue of Liberty—Ellis Island Centennial Series

BOARD OF EDITORS
Roger Daniels, Chair, University of Cincinnati
Jay P. Dolan, University of Notre Dame
Kathleen Conzen, University of Chicago

Books in the Series

The Immigrant World of Ybor City:
Italians and Their Latin Neighbors in Tampa, 1885–1985
Gary R. Mormino and George E. Pozzetta

The Butte Irish:
Class and Ethnicity in an American Mining Town, 1875–1925
David M. Emmons

The Making of an American Pluralism:
Buffalo, New York, 1825–60
David A. Gerber

The Making of an American Pluralism

THE MAKING OF AN AMERICAN PLURALISM

BUFFALO, NEW YORK, 1825–60

David A. Gerber

UNIVERSITY OF ILLINOIS PRESS
Urbana and Chicago

© 1989 by the Board of Trustees of the University of Illinois
Manufactured in the United States of America
C 5 4 3 2 1

This book is printed on acid-free paper.

Publication of this work was made possible in part by a grant from the Statue of Liberty–Ellis Island Foundation.

Library of Congress Cataloging-in-Publication Data

Gerber, David A.
 The making of an American pluralism.

 (Statue of Liberty—Ellis Island Centennial Series)
  1. Pluralism (Social sciences)—New York (State)—Buffalo.
2. Minorities—New York (State)—Buffalo—History—19th century.   3. Ethnicity—New York (State)—Buffalo—History—19th century.   4. Buffalo (N.Y.)—Ethnic relations.   I. Title.
II. Series.
F129.B89A24   1989   305.8'009747'97   88-20774
ISBN 0-252-01595-9

Permission to quote from the following articles is gratefully acknowledged by the author:
"Ethnics, Enterprise, and Middle Class Formation: Using the Dun and Bradstreet Collection for Research in Ethnic Social History," *Immigration History Newsletter*, 12 (May, 1980), 1–7.
"Modernity in the Service of Tradition: Ante-bellum Catholic Laymen and the Transformation of European Communal Traditions at Buffalo's St. Louis Church," *Journal of Social History*, 13 (Winter, 1980), 248–73.
"Cutting-Out Shylock: Toward a Reconceptualization of the Origins of American Anti-Semitism," *Journal of American History*, 69 (December, 1982), 615–37.
"Old Lutherans in Two Worlds: Religious Refugees in the United States and South Australia and the Pathos of Exile," *Comparative Studies in Society and History*, 26 (July, 1984), 498–522.
"Language Maintenance, Public Schools, and Ethnic Group Formation: Changing Patterns of German Concern, Buffalo, 1837–1874," *Journal of American Ethnic History*, 4 (Fall, 1984), 31–61.
"Ambivalent Anti-Catholicism: Buffalo's American Elite Faces the Challenge of the Catholic Church," *Civil War History*, 30 (June, 1984), 120–43.

For my parents, Joseph and Jeanette,
and my brother, Ken

Contents

Introduction xi

PART ONE
The Rise and Several Declines of Buffalo

1. "A Place of Immense Resort": From Frontier Village
   to Continental Entrepôt   3
2. Expansion, Speculation, and Collapse, 1825–38   22

PART TWO
The Formation of a Provincial Bourgeoisie

3. Commerce and Class Formation   43
4. Culture, Ethos, and Ideology in Class Formation   63
5. Clerks, Shopkeepers, and Artisans: Americans,
   Canadians, and Britons   92

PART THREE
The Rise of Ethnocultural Diversity and Pluralism

Introduction: Mass Immigration, Ethnicity, and
    Group Formation   113
6. Poverty, Catholicism, and Solidarity: The Formation
   of Irish Ethnicity   121
7. Buffalo's Germans: Foundations in Diversity   163
8. Buffalo's Germans: Leadership, Ideology, and the
   Struggle for Unity   211

9. Class and Ethnicity in the Rise of Labor   236
10. The Catholic Church and the Emergence of a New
    Interconfessional Order   280

PART FOUR
The Politics of Pluralism

Introduction: Politics, Pluralism, and Social
    Integration   321
11. Immigrant Political and Civic Integration: The
    Formative Decade, 1843–53   330
12. From Ethnic Polarization to Social and Political
    Realignment: 1854–60   371

Epilogue   410
Key to Abbreviations in the Notes   413
Notes   414
Index   515

Introduction

THIS book is not a community or local study as such, though it is infused with a sense of the singularity of Buffalo during the period of the city's commercial ascendence between the opening of the Erie Canal in 1825 and the Civil War. It is rather a study of the rise of social pluralism in a city ultimately much like many other new northern commercial cities located along the Great Lakes. By "social pluralism" I mean a form of society characterized by public competition, conflict, and cooperation among large, complex groups composed of overlapping social solidarities. (In the private sphere—everyday cultural matters such as family, household, kinship, friendship, sexuality, religion, and recreation—these groups enjoyed considerable communal independence, yet there was substantial interpenetration of public and private to the extent that the boundaries of the two not only never could be clearly articulated, but themselves became the subject of public controversy.) In the mid-nineteenth century northern city, two solidarities had special salience: social class, because of the intensity and scope of economic development, and ethnicity, because of the mass immigrations of Irish and Germans. Ethnicity, which in countless ways shaped the culture of daily life, the consciousness of individuals, and the patterns of human association, was frequently the vessel in which class (the social relations and groups formed by economic production) developed. Recognizing the interaction of class and ethnicity, as they then took shape in the environment of a new and dynamic commercial city, this study bases its conceptualization of the group components of an urban social system on an understanding of both the internal processes of group formation, such as language, religion, folk memory, and antecedent political experience, and the larger, external processes shaping the evolution of urban space, polity, and economy.

This book aims, therefore, not to study groups in isolation from one another, but rather as integral components of a common social system, which absorbs them pluralistically—as groups. Two different, but yet complexly related, phenomena led me in this direction. First, there was a movement within the popular culture, the so-called New Ethnicity, whose leading exponent, Michael Novak, suggested in his various writings that bitterness and alienation were the residue of the experience of the epic mass immigrations from Europe in the nineteenth and early twentieth centuries. In Novak's telling, immigrants were people of decent, conservative impulses who were needlessly alienated from mainstream American life because of the treatment they received at the hands of ethnocentric, condescending American elites.[1] Formed by the radical impulses in the culture of the 1960s, the second influence on my thought came from the new literature of American social history that has revolutionized scholarship in the last two decades. So much of this excellent literature has concentrated on groups in isolation from one another, as a way of seeing them narrowly in order to see them deeply, or in conflict (men versus women, workers versus employers, foreigners versus natives, etc.) as a reaction to the consensus history of the 1950s, that in a subtle way it seemed to reinforce, powerfully, because from the opposite ideological perspective, Novak's nonempirical and neoconservative contentions. It was easy to get the notion from both perspectives that our history is the story of vaguely related groups which inhabit the same space, fail to communicate, and often get in one another's way.[2]

I have always been impressed by the ability of the American social system, especially through the evolving institutions of politics and government, to defuse and absorb conflict and to integrate new and foreign groups. I do not celebrate this ability, for I take the United States to be a nation without messianic purposes and with a history replete with its own tragedies, injustices, and cruelties as well as its many successes and persistent efforts to correct its failures. In other words, a nation much like other nations, if now vastly more powerful, and hence dangerous, than most. But I do take these abilities to integrate groups and to diffuse conflict to be a fact of life; and one need not return to the pieties and cynicism of much of the old consensus history to reach such an understanding. For the other part of accepting the presence of conflict of every kind in our past is the obligation to see where conflict leads and what it becomes.

In the late 1970s, my analytical concern was the reception and integration of the first wave of mass immigration of the decades before the Civil War, a period in which the inception of northern commercial capitalism and urbanization, along with mass immigration, assisted in providing parameters for the development of new social groups and a new form of American society. I chose to attempt to understand this time period also because the new literature of American social history was largely concentrated in the late nineteenth century, and thus often seemed to claim for that period, with its dramatic industrialization, the inception of social processes and structures that in reality were present before the Civil War.

In its larger conceptualization, this work is deeply influenced by the long-established works of such historians as Oscar Handlin, Robert Weibe, and Roland Berthoff, whose interests in seeing society whole, understanding the role of immigration and immigrants in creating a distinctive American urban experience and public culture, and analyzing social processes as they exert different effects throughout a many-layered social system provide admirable models for historical synthesis.[3] Other almost as powerful influences have come from comparatively recent analytical concerns. As a historian of working-class, largely Catholic immigrants who settled in rapidly growing commercial and industrial cities where native white Protestants exercised significant economic, political, and social power, I touch bases with much of the new social history. The reader will find that my analysis is informed by recent historical literature on: the social patterning of urban space; the intricate web of relationships between economic development, family and kinship, the domestic economy, and family strategies for material security and economic mobility; the reformulation of preindustrial traditions and values into the weapons of working-class resistance by both native-born and foreign workers; the formation of American Catholicism; the roles of evangelical Protestantism in both the culture and society of white Americans; the transformation of bourgeois female roles under the impact of economic change and Victorian culture; and finally, from within the particular area of my own specialization, the process of ethnic group formation and the evolution of ethnic leadership. In addition, from the new political history, I derive my understanding of the ethnocultural bases of electoral politics and of the evolution of political culture (the values, beliefs, and symbols forming the context in which politics takes place). It has remained, however, the neo-Marxist political history of Ira Katznelson and Amy Bridges that has assisted me most in understanding the ways in which class and these ethnocultural dimensions of politics simultaneously worked to create a political system that was able to bring a high degree of social stability to northern cities, even in a time of intense class and ethnic conflict.[4]

Within the framework of contemporary social history this study does have a number of claims to being different. First, there is its concentration in the antebellum period, which has been even more neglected in the study of immigration, ethnicity, and pluralism than in other fields of concentration. Second, the analysis does not assume the existence of the ethnic group, but instead provides an analytical treatment of its formation (*ethnicization*). Third, politics—the pursuit of power and its frequent correlatives, authority and influence—is ultimately central to my analysis. I conceive of the pursuit both of power and of the opportunity to define the moral and practical ends of power, in all of power's myriad formal and informal varieties, as the principal integrating process of American pluralism. A social system that encouraged voluntary association and voluntary effort and a political system that encouraged a participatory public life across a broad spectrum of social groups, including even such disfranchised people as women, also encouraged the creation of a public culture of common forms of thought and behavior in pursuit of social resources, defense of traditions and values, individual and group self-determination, and justice. My biggest quarrel with some of the best of the new social history—especially that which focuses on the demography, family, residence, and mobility of ethnic groups—is its frequent neglect of the common public life, of the interpenetrations of the public, private, and group lives, and of the intragroup and pluralistic struggles for power, authority, and influence that swirl in and around the public life.

Fourth, and finally, my desire to analyze the pluralistic integration of groups on the road to social pluralism has led me to see the need for a top-down as well as bottom-up perspective on the power relations that shaped the integration process. Many readers attuned to the populist resonances in much contemporary social history may well find this an old-fashioned and somewhat implicitly conservative book, because my concern with power and its workings, in and outside politics, has led me to see the masses of immigrants, ethnics, and plebeian "little people" both as subjects making their history and as objects who were successfully manipulated and had their options narrowed by forces that, while not completely beyond their control, nonetheless had such significant power that they were difficult to resist. Which is only to say that the agency of the masses of ordinary folk had its limits precisely because they found themselves in a society in which profound inequalities were deeply embedded in the structure of society and the distribution of its resources. I hope that this recognition of the potency of power—and of its limitations—will be of benefit not only in furthering accurate social analysis of the direction of social changes, but also in accomplishing a related task: understanding the lives, aspirations, and desperations of Buffalo's American elite and its class allies and obscure retainers among coethnics and closely related peoples, such as British immigrants. Nothing was further from my mind than analysis of this elite group and the people variously related to it when I began my research, for I was then laboring under some false assumptions about its relevance to understanding ethnic group formation and ethnic self-understanding, not to mention class conflict itself. But I came increasingly to understand that while immigrant and ethnic workers and "little people" showed great resiliency and tactical virtuosity in forming their groups, and in the struggles they waged for the resources necessary to protect those groups and expand their power and opportunity, the directions those struggles had to assume (though not necessarily their outcomes) were often determined by the activities and interests of a powerful class of native-born Americans.

The existence of the power of this elite, and the bourgeois class from which it emerged, may be understood properly only if it is also recognized that its power had an explicitly moral component, one which conceived of the ultimate purposes of power as the definition of the standards and goals of an American civilization.[5] The circumstances of common culture, immigration experience, and resettlement in America amidst poverty, exploitation, and prejudice easily lent themselves, in the case of the immigrants, to the development of tight bonds within the comfortable, though hardly conflictless, boundaries of the ethnic group. But these same circumstances did not easily create the desire to achieve a vision of America or of the place of these new groups within it that was capable of mobilizing the nation's history, the spirit of its Constitution and its laws, and its historic values of republicanism, individual liberty, and decentralization, to serve the aspirations of a civilization in the making. That task fell logically to those descended from the nation's charter group—those whose forebears made the Revolution which gave the United States its central political myths, wrote its constitutions, and formed its institutions of government and politics. In contrast to immigrants, Americans possessed the national feeling and sense of social obligation, richly mixed with self-interest, to take up this challenge. Unlike immigrants, however, they were slow to develop an ethnic understanding of themselves as a people among peoples, and indeed it took exposure to foreign people unlike themselves, who seemed to frustrate their aims and challenge their social authority and aspirations, to prompt an increasingly *ethnic* self-understanding among them. This study then at times treats American Protestants as an emergent ethnic group. Relatedly, I analyze anti-Catholic and antiforeign nativism as a cultural phenomenon in the context of this American ethnicization, as well as—in the established view—an outgrowth of partisan politics and a reaction to mass immigration.

The period encompassing this study was a time of intense activity for those who aimed to create the foundations of an American civilization. The expansion of the scope and scale of commercial activities, creation of interregional markets, urbanization, rise of manufacturing, inception of mass politics through the new institution of political parties and in the context of frequent elections, and epic, mass immigrations from Europe all combined to necessitate reformulation of values and goals inherited from an earlier, simpler time. Nowhere perhaps was the need for the freeing of impulses attuned to this emerging age more acute than in Buffalo, which was known to contemporaries, at home and abroad, as one of the nation's original boomtowns. Little more than a village, privileged to be located at the head of the continuously navigable portion of the Great Lakes, it was chosen to be the terminus of the Erie Canal. In consequence of that decision, it soon would become the nation's principal inland port and the transshipment point that integrated the regional economies of the northern states. This unique locational asset provided the basis for dynamic economic and population growth. It also assisted in the rise of an ambitious American elite, which was occupied chiefly in facilitating that trade, but soon, too, became active in the larger tasks of attempting to impose order and meaning, on its own terms, for a rapidly changing city. The energies behind this impulse grew perceptibly after the devastating depression of 1837–43, which, following a decade of intense speculation and reckless expansion in new, postfrontier towns like Buffalo, necessarily proved a sobering experience to American professionals and entrepreneurs. After the depression in Buffalo and elsewhere, too, an emergent bourgeois class sought to bring to bear a degree of planning and a vision of orderly, quality urban life in their economic stewardship as capitalists and in public affairs as civic leaders.

Their vision, at once rationalist, materialist, and elitist, yet universalistic in many of its aspirations and moral in its yearnings, arose almost coterminously with mass immigration. The immigrants, principally German-speakers and the Irish, would come to interpret this program as an elite imposition which threatened their own cultures and their newly acquired American sense of rights. Moreover, they resented its reinforcement of deeply engrained inequalities, even if these existed at the higher standard of living afforded by the American economy. The only logical method of opposition involved organizing themselves for effective participation in the major institutions and social processes they found when they arrived. This, in turn, not only helped to give shape to their groups and to establish new parameters for the functions of these American institutions and processes, but integrated immigrants increasingly into a society whose principal public figures claimed a moral authority immigrants often came to regard with suspicion. The resulting public conflicts were played out in different contexts, none of them particularly unique to Buffalo, though given some shape and direction by the singular position of the city in the national economy and relatedly by the self-understandings and self-interest of the city's American bourgeois class and those who identified with its interests. We will observe these conflicts in the familiar terrain of partisan politics, labor-capital relations, denominational strife between American evangelical Protestants and the aggressive leadership of the newly established, multiethnic Catholic church, and in the ethnocultural strife over liquor, the Sabbath, and the language of primary instruction in the public schools. But we will also see them in such less familiar areas as the individual and group relations to government created by municipal services and consequently by taxation and the process of tax collection, and in the realm of popular entertainment and recreation.

Part One is an extended introduction; it sets the context of local economic growth and the city's spatial development. Part Two analyzes those Americans of all classes whose arrival preceded the immigrants of the mass migrations, and whose activities laid the foundations of much of the city's life that these thousands of newly resettled foreigners would encounter upon arrival. Part Three analyzes immigrant ethnic group formation among the Germans and Irish in its material, familial, political, cultural, and ideological aspects. It also evaluates both the interplay of class and ethnicity in the creation and organization of working-class protest and the rise and development of the most inclusive and formidable of immigrant institutions, the Catholic church. Part Four analyzes the political and civic interactions of Americans and immigrants in government and in electoral politics.

Institutions, librarians, and archivists, too numerous to list but no less appreciated, facilitated my research, and the following organizations provided financial assistance in support of that research: the American Philosophical Society, the Buffalo Foundation, the Cushwa Center for the Study of American Catholicism, the Fulbright Foundation, the National Endowment for the Humanities, and the Research Foundation of the State University of New York. Permission to quote from the records of the R. G. Dun and Company, which are located in the R. G. Dun and Company Collection at Baker Library of Harvard Business School, was given by the Dun & Bradstreet, Inc.

Carolyn, Chris, and Jonathan know just how much I need to thank them.

Part One

The Rise and Several Declines of Buffalo

CHAPTER 1

"A Place of Immense Resort": From Frontier Village to Continental Entrepôt

IN few of the new American cities of the first half of the nineteenth century was location more a factor in encouraging growth and development than in Buffalo. The town lay at the eastern head of the continuously navigable portion of the Great Lakes, twenty miles above Niagara Falls, which made waterborne passage between lakes Erie and Ontario impossible. Long before the 1823 decision to place at Buffalo the Erie Canal terminus, which would link the town to the populous seaboard and soon make it the North's principal transshipment point, the value of this location had been recognized. Joseph Ellicott, chief surveyor and supervisor of land sales for the Holland Land Company, the organization of Dutch capitalists who had purchased all of western New York State, predicted improbably as early as 1789 that the backwoods settlement someday would be "a place of immense resort."[1] With this in mind, Ellicott laid out an ambitious plan in 1803–4 for a town to be called "New Amsterdam" at the confluence of the Buffalo and Niagara rivers and Lake Erie. The town, which for the next fifteen years was little more than "a casual collection of adventurers,"[2] was to be built out from a central square. Occupying a high bluff up from the point of confluence, it would command a dramatic, panoramic view of the lake. Broad boulevards, which Ellicott named for the Amsterdam bankers and high officials of the company, radiated out from the square at regular intervals. The boulevards were then to be crossed by narrower, residential streets and enclosed, at points several blocks removed from the public square, by a gracefully curved avenue, which would provide access to the short streets along the dock and serve as the town's principal commercial avenue.[3]

A striking, symbolic statement, Ellicott's plan subordinated frontier realities to the rationalist ethos of the Enlightenment, and the individualizing force of commerce to the unifying force of government. The public square was to contain the company's western headquarters and the offices of local government, from both of which a sense of uniform and purposeful coherence, in the form of laws and regulations, would radiate outward down the spokes of the wheel of boulevards. Commerce formed a middle-range boundary for the hub. By no means denigrated, it was still not to interfere, by way of cluttered storefronts, clanging wagons, and cursing teamsters, with the dignified work of the offices along the central square. Nor did Ellicott envision that local commercial men would have much to do with the governing of New Amsterdam, unless, that is, they fully accepted the company's hegemony.

The Yankees and Yorkers who came to the western frontier in the next decade had other ideas. The Dutch names insulted their patriotism, and besides were unpronounceable. As soon as they formed a village government, they began to undo Ellicott's work. The curved commercial avenue now became plain "Main Street," and it was straightened to allow efficient passage both down to the river and north to the principal roads going across the state. Ellicott was so insulted he decided to keep the company's headquarters at Batavia rather than move it to the new village, the name of which, to make matters worse, was soon changed to "Buffalo."[4]

This was only the start of the residents' innovations, the sum total of which replaced Ellicott's vision with another, which was commercial, functionalist, and growth-oriented. Spurring them on were dynamic processes transforming western New York. The settlement of the country west of the eighteenth-century frontier in the Mohawk Valley constantly gathered force, deterred only briefly in the Niagara country by the War of 1812. Buffalo itself had been destroyed by the British, but with the return of peace, the small settlement again began to grow, as rural western New York's company lands were rapidly bought up and adjacent lands constantly alienated from their Indian inhabitants.[5]

A canal linking the agricultural towns of Upstate with the seaboard, and providing a jumping-off place for settlers going to the rich lands of the West, seemed a necessity. Begun in 1817, the Erie Canal by 1820 had reached the western New York counties without a decision on the location of its terminus. Buffalo and Black Rock, two miles north along the Niagara, were in competition as Governor DeWitt Clinton and the canal commissioners investigated their options. Black Rock had a fine natural harbor to provide passage to the lake and a safe haven from the unpredictable Great Lakes weather. Buffalo's lakefront was too exposed to offer safety and, little more than a creek, its river was too shallow, especially at the mouth where there was a sandbar, for ships of significant tonnage. But Buffalo had one distinct human advantage—superior and aggressive entrepreneurs. Under the leadership of some of the principal dock merchants a lobby was formed to sell Buffalo's case in Albany. Meanwhile, with the encouragement of state officials a partnership of Samuel Wilkeson, Charles Townsend, and Oliver Forward, all active in the lake trade, was formed to remove the sandbar and deepen the harbor. This, and the fact that water could be drawn from the Niagara to the canal at a higher elevation at Buffalo than at Black Rock, led to the 1823 decision to place the terminus at a site up a few hundred yards from the confluence of the Niagara and Buffalo rivers, west of the foot of Main Street. When the canal was dedicated on October 26, 1825, many of Black Rock's merchants had already removed to Buffalo, where they competed for commercial space at the increasingly congested lake-dock complex. Buffalo's victory was complete in 1854 when it annexed Black Rock.[6]

Though its harbor would never be adequate to the needs of its burgeoning trade, Buffalo soon would be recognized as "the great natural gateway between East and West."[7] Between 1826 and 1837 the number of vessels arriving there increased from 418 to 3,955 and the number of canal clearances from 1,100 to 4,755. In the 1820s and 1830s much of this commerce was intrastate in nature, stimulated by a tremendous decrease in travel time and freight rates across Upstate and by the construction of feeder canals tapping the rich hinterlands of central New York. Interstate commerce grew, too. At first, the canal's major interstate function was to bring westbound migrants to Buffalo, where they embarked for various Lake Erie ports to the west, and then to homesteads in Ohio, Indiana, and Michigan. Almost simultaneously came the flow of eastern and European finished goods, a trade reaching 36,000 tons shipped west from Buffalo by 1836. Within a few years, western produce, provisions (barreled pork), and grain began to find their way east.[8]

It was grain that became the source of much of Buffalo's dynamism and wealth. The town's strategic location allowed it to grow rich off grain at a time when advancements in milling technology and the opening of new grain lands democratized bread by lowering the cost of fine wheat flour.[9] By 1836, Ohio's grain crop had come to exceed New York's, and now grain, which had previously been shipped west from Buffalo, began to come east. While Upstate farms became increasingly oriented toward dairy farming, vegetables, and fruits, the Old Northwest became the North's breadbasket. With feeder canals in Ohio, Indiana, and Michigan pumping grain into Lake Erie ports, in 1838 Buffalo's flour and bulk wheat receipts exceeded those of the older port of New Orleans, marking a reorientation of northern trade away from the Ohio and Mississippi rivers toward the shorter, safer, and cheaper Buffalo–New York City passage. The opening of the Illinois-Michigan Canal, by which Buffalo was linked to the Illinois prairies, further solidified the northern route.[10] There was little competition, for other routes to the seaboard were longer, costlier, and more dangerous.[11]

Other events and processes further solidified Buffalo's position. In 1846, when thirteen million barrels and bushels of wheat came through Buffalo, the English Corn Laws were repealed, increasing the export trade, which British and continental short harvests and crop famines and disruptions of the Crimean War would further stimulate. Meanwhile technology, in the form of the grain elevator (first made operational at Buffalo in 1842), harbor improvements, steam-powered lake craft, the telegraph, and ultimately the railroad, facilitated the expansion of the trade. New types of business organization pioneered at Buffalo (uniform bills of lading, standardized weights and measures, and the placement of business agents in western grain regions and eastern credit markets) nationalized the trade as it grew more robust. By the mid-1850s, Buffalo was the world's largest grain port. Three-fourths of all grain and at least one-half of all rolling freight shipped in the United States in 1854 changed hands at Buffalo and went forward on the account of Buffalo commission and forwarding merchants. In 1860, even as it emerged from a short but severe depression, the city received an astonishing thirty-seven million bushels and barrels of wheat and flour.[12]

Buffalo's development was influenced profoundly by this rapid expansion of trade. Most evident perhaps was the steady expansion of population that accompanied a growing demand for labor. Twenty-five hundred people resided in the town in 1825; five years later, there were 8,668. Thereafter the population doubled or nearly doubled every decade, reaching 81,129 by 1860.[13] In that year Buffalo was the tenth-largest city in the nation, an excellent example, said one European traveler, of North America's "infant capitals and embryo cities."[14]

Less evident to the eye, but no less significant, was the impact of the expansion of commercial activity upon the city's economy, its social structure and its politics, and the use of its space. Before 1861, Buffalo's chief economic function was transshipment, and many of its economic activities would center around the development of commercial services linked to this task: commissioning grain and produce for sellers and buyers, forwarding cargoes between markets, warehousing, ship chandlering, breaking down bulk packaging, brokering in maritime insurance, and providing price and market information. The city would also develop a ship and canal boat building industry, catering to the needs of local forwarders and commission merchants, and by 1855 employing approximately 1,300 riggers, joiners, carpenters, painters, and finishers, and probably as many metal craftsmen making fittings, boilers, and engines for the lake and canal fleets. All of these activities created a vast, interconnected sector of managerial, lower white-collar, skilled, and unskilled, outdoor employment dependent for its livelihood on the lake and canal trade.[15]

The dynamism of this sector reinforced the structural limitations upon other lines of economic development. Unlike Rochester, which provided milling and mercantile services for its rich Genesee Valley hinterland, Buffalo could not substantially prosper from the economic pursuits or needs of either the marshy, grain-growing lands to its immediate north, or the stony grazing lands to its immediate south. Though Buffalo merchants organized plank road companies to tap the lands beyond this relatively poor hinterland, these areas did not even use Buffalo as a port, opting instead for Rochester and Dunkirk. Furthermore, Buffalo lacked convenient, cheap sources of fuel to provide a basis for heavy industry and milling. Again unlike Rochester, where the Genesee River fell sufficiently in a short distance to generate power, most of Buffalo lay on an almost flat area of lake plain, in which only one of the few sluggish streams was usable for industrial purposes. In a cumbersome manner, water was pumped from the Niagara as a source of steam power, but this was not viable as a basis for significant industrialization.[16]

While these natural disadvantages certainly helped to retard industrialization, so, too, did the widespread belief that Buffalo's location guaranteed it indefinite commercial supremacy and that little else was required to sustain local prosperity. This optimistic view was summarized by the editor of the 1836 *City Directory*. Buffalo, he said, "has no rival—it can have none—it is the medium through which all others, both East and West, must draw their wealth and resources; and so far from feeling distrust and jealousy at the prosperity of our neighboring cities, we look upon them as the most efficient auxiliaries of our own. The cities west of us may improve in wealth and importance, but they are our tributaries, their growth, our growth, their greatness, our greatness ... thus rendering Buffalo that which it may ever claim to be— the GREAT NATIONAL EXCHANGE."[17]

Convinced as they were, it was impossible for Buffalo's businessmen to come to the decision that business elites in other canal corridor cities were making to stimulate industrialization in order to avoid excessive reliance on commerce. When Utica merchants in the mid-1840s saw that western produce and grain, rather than New York State's, would dominate eastern markets, they diverted large amounts of capital from commerce to textile manufacturing.[18] There was little enthusiasm for such a development project in Buffalo for most of the period. Local banks agreed with this consensus and continually evinced a preference in granting credit for commerce, in which markets were more familiar and in which borrowers were long-established merchants, whose credit needs were relatively small and could be accommodated usually through short-term loans. What industry developed in the city, therefore, was usually begun not by merchant capitalists, but by masters and journeymen. They often were forced to obtain credit at high interest rates from money brokers, a matter about which advocates of local industrialization complained for years.[19]

Elite apathy on the question of economic diversification declined in the 1850s, however, as the long-term prospects for the Erie Canal for the first time appeared poor. The railroads, which had in the previous decade been seen as local routes ancillary to the great canal, now emerged with the consolidation of the new trunk lines as powerful competitors. None was a greater threat than the New York Central. In 1851, the last year that railroads like the New York Central running parallel to the canal were forced to pay canal tolls, the canal's receipts peaked, and they fell thereafter. Railroads now controlled east-west passenger traffic because of the rapid travel they afforded, and their speed, lower insurance rates, lack of transshipment costs, and business incentives for commercial shippers afforded them deep inroads into the flour and provisions trade. Ton-mileage on the canal was still greater than that on any other route, but the rate of increase of canal freight receipts slowed considerably, and increasingly it was only the heavier, bulkier goods, such as the 50 percent of the grain trade shipped in unprocessed form, that went by canal, largely because railroads had not yet found a cheap way to carry them. Within the era of the canal's "Golden Age," therefore, the successes of the railroads prefigured its decline and that of all of the interests dependent on it. Damaging, too, for Buffalo was the movement west to Chicago of the center of the grain trade, as wheat production itself moved further west. Based on deals made over vast distances by telegraph, flour was increasingly consigned directly to New York City from Chicago. It might arrive at Buffalo by lake craft as before, but there it was transferred directly onto New York Central trains at the railroad's western division headquarters in the city. Local forwarders, brokers, and commission merchants no longer could anticipate a share of this action. Even the lake craft themselves were increasingly owned by the railroads; in 1857 and

1858 the New York Central and the New York and Erie respectively established their own propeller lines.[20]

By the late 1850s, for the first time, many of Buffalo's entrepreneurs were asking why for three decades they had surrendered their fate to the barge canal, with its seasonal and spatial limitations and its constant need for improvement and repair. It was only then that the need for a new industrial strategy, based on massive imports of coal and lower taxes, and diversion of commercial capital to manufactures, was recognized by Buffalo's economic and political elites. It came to be institutionalized in the Buffalo Association for the Advancement of Manufactures.[21] It was too late to accomplish much by 1860, so the increase in industrial shops during the 1850s was more the result of individual activities than the realization of the new vision of the city's leadership.

Throughout the short period of Buffalo's antebellum preeminence, therefore, apart from transshipment and the various marketing services that facilitated it, the city's economy was narrowly developed and its much boasted prosperity shallow. Industry was weak. Some industrial linkages to commerce did develop, principally shipbuilding and the manufacturing of elevating and milling machinery. But flour milling, the potentially most fruitful linkage, was done solely for local consumption, largely because Rochester and even tiny Oswego, with their waterpower resources, came to control Upstate milling.[22] Efforts to develop an iron industry were retarded at first by a lack of convenient power. In the 1840s coal had to be brought by boat from northeastern Ohio mines to the forges at the Wilkeson family stove works. Smaller forges depended on charcoal, steam, and waterpower. Under these circumstances, metal work was limited until in 1851 and 1854 rail links to southern New York and Pennsylvania coalfields were established. By 1856 some 1,500 men were employed in the local iron industry, which at $1,250,000 had become the city's most capitalized industry. Even so, not until 1861 was there investment in blast furnaces, so that what became the largest antebellum industry was limited to some small and middle-sized foundries engaged in the secondary fabrication of metal made elsewhere. On the eve of the Civil War not enough iron goods were produced locally to meet local needs.[23] Tanning did develop early in the city's history, because of the local availability of stocks of hemlock, and it was the third-largest industry, employing 500 people, by the late 1850s. But the growth of this industry slowed as local bark stocks were depleted. The city remained a tanning center, but withal was slow to develop linkages to the production of leather goods. Some commercial men had struggled in the 1840s to get together bank loans to begin a shoe factory, but had failed. In the

1850s only one, middle-sized firm was established.[24] Outside these fields and shipbuilding, industry remained concentrated in small shops and capitalized at a low level. In 1850 only sixteen factories employed fifty or more workers, while the average shop had no more than fourteen. In 1860 Buffalo was the least industrialized of the six principal cities of the Erie Canal corridor, and most of its industry served either its home market or the local shipping industry.[25]

This narrow pattern of development made the city's economy especially vulnerable in the face of downturns in the business cycle. Both the 1837–43 and 1857–58 depressions were particularly severe in Buffalo. Moreover, so great a reliance on shipping and packaging agricultural goods made the city hostage to its harsh, variable Great Lakes weather. The most evident social effect of the long winter was routine unemployment for the large number of teamsters, boatmen, dockworkers, and sailors, and hence the underutilization of labor that resulted from the fact that most shipping on the lakes and canal stopped every winter for an average (between 1844 and 1856) of 137 days. The craftsmen employed in shipbuilding, which was done outdoors, also experienced a great deal of winter subemployment.[26] A persistent theme in the city's antebellum history was the family distress these seasonal patterns caused, both in good times and in bad in the general economy. The problem was exacerbated both by the rigors of the winter (a season in which long-term stays at the poorhouse were quite common, as were less dramatic forms of distress, such as visits to the pawnbroker) and by the rising cost of fuel as forest land receded from the city.[27]

A more subtle effect of this narrow development was the persistence of a preindustrial rhythm of worklife, which for many local people was dominated more by the seasons and the hours of daylight than by the clock. That Buffalo was not like, for example, Lowell, where the rhythms of the mills were geared to the clock and also became the basis for the regulation of much of life outside work, is illustrated by the fact that for four months in 1855, including the busy fall shipping season, the two principal downtown church clocks, by which many watches were set and schedules coordinated, were both incorrect. Only with the advent of greater industrialization in the late 1850s did it become possible to chart precisely correct time by observing daily habits of a large class of citizens, as the *Commercial Advertiser* noted in 1858 in observing the morning parade of factory hands past three principal street corners. In 1860, not coincidentally, clocks with the correct time were installed in the central business district.[28]

The structures of social and political relations that eventuated from this pattern of development, especially when coupled with the ethnic composition of the work force, contrast sharply not only with Ellicott's vision of New Amsterdam, but also with the social systems emerging in the industrial cities of the seaboard. In the latter, a gradual process of economic evolution saw the transformation of some local craftsmen and merchants into factory-owning capitalists, who increasingly were pitted against a native-born artisan class caught in the throes of deskilling, loss of job control, and relocation of production from home to factory, as well as competition from unskilled immigrants. Yet through it all in industrial cities like Newark the artisan ethos of craft skill, manly self-reliance, and republican liberty supplied the rhetoric of political discourse and the basis of the dominant ideology of craftsmen and employers alike.[29] In contrast, at Buffalo the ties formed by production were attenuated, and the position of the artisans far weaker. During the canal era Buffalo's forwarding and commission merchants were linked only indirectly and over vast distances to producers in the dominant transshipment sector. The dock merchants were instead tied directly principally to large numbers of professionals and lower white-collar workers, who provided commercial services, and to the city's own importing retail merchants, who siphoned off for local sale some of the goods passing through the city. The overwhelming majority of these individuals were native-born Americans. The dominant sector, compared to manufacturing, employed relatively few artisans. Its blue-collar employees were most often unskilled, casually employed immigrants in the secondary labor markets created by interregional trade: Irish dock laborers. With the exception of shipbuilding and the fabrication and maintenance of ships' engines and boilers and milling and elevator equipment, Buffalo's artisans were mostly absorbed by its internal economy and the comparatively small factory sector. The former was dominated after 1840 by ever larger numbers of German tailors, bakers, butchers, shoemakers, and building tradesmen, while Germans also provided a majority of the unskilled labor in construction. The underdeveloped industrial sector, especially iron and shipbuilding, was the only one which daily employed substantial numbers of male workers across ethnic and language lines in the same setting.[30]

The weakness of the artisan class that resulted from this segmentation combined with the dominance of the trade and transshipment sector to vault the position of the merchant yet further above the already high place that wealth and native birth usually gave him in American cities. Merchants and particularly the lawyers doing their legal work controlled the leadership of both major political parties and the most elevated positions in local government. For example, of the twenty-two mayors between the city's 1832 incorporation and 1860, eleven were lawyers (most with dock connections), eight merchants, and three doctors. Only one of these men claimed recent artisanal background. Franklin Allberger, a German-American Republican elected in 1859, had been a butcher, but in that year actually ran a large, lucrative wholesale meat business.[31]

To be sure, such mercantile dominance was hardly unusual. In Buffalo, however, it was intimately intertwined with a far more subtle pattern of dominance—that which set the economic agenda of local politics. Buffalo certainly had its share of artisans and unskilled workers, native-born and immigrant alike, with class grievances and a proven ability to organize, demonstrate, and strike. But these working-class grievances rarely entered local electoral politics. As we shall see, the reasons for this are complex. But one thing is clear: many people— and by no means only those who wore white collars—accepted the idea that without maintenance of the city's commercial preeminence, local prosperity would collapse. An American bookkeeper and an Irish dockworker alike could certainly come to the conclusion that their own prosperities, however unequal, would collapse. Thus, what were obviously the class interests of the dock merchants were so closely identified with the growth, development, and prosperity of the city and of the countless individuals given a livelihood by interregional trade that questions bearing on the future of commerce usually caught the attention of a wide spectrum of citizens and frequently dominated local politics, especially in the 1850s when threats to the city's prosperity loomed all around. It was commerce—the language of tolls, harbor improvement, and bonds for railroad construction—not worker grievances, that usually dominated local political discourse. Worker grievances were aired politically only during depression periods of mass unemployment or during the very occasional administration of a crusading mayor. While the two major parties disagreed strongly on many national and state issues, they both agreed on the commercial agenda of local politics. Indeed often they came to similar conclusions, though down different ideological paths, on what the needs of the city's commerce were. Of course, not every commercial issue was easily resolved, for while ends might be agreed upon, disagreements over means could be fierce. Moreover, least involved in the commercial sector and most ideologically at odds with the Whiggish political economy of the merchants, German immigrants were frequently opposed to plans to use their tax dollars to subsidize infrastructural improvements to aid commerce. Yet given the city's dependence on the canal, how surprising were the results of an 1854 referendum called by the legislature to determine whether state funds should be employed to enlarge the canal? Buffalo voted 10,239 to 3 in favor.[32]

The logic by which commerce came to dominate Buffalo was apparent to the eye in the spatial layout of social relations and economic functions. Ellicott envisioned a town in which the use of space was purposefully prioritized. The officials of the Holland Land Company, who saw themselves as an American squirearchy, were to dominate and structure space from their commanding position at the public square, while workaday commerce was to be restricted to the periphery of the inner town. What actually came to happen was the reverse. The requirements of commerce, as defined by many individual ambitions, became the dominant value in the utilization of space, and for a plan there was substituted the amoral logic of the real-estate market.

After 1825 the city grew around and out from the waterfront—its functional center. Then one of the world's most valuable pieces of land, the central docks, or "inner harbor," were located along the Buffalo River, which joined the canal terminus to Lake Erie via a number of narrow, north-south streets and an ever increasing number of ancillary private slips and public canals and channels. The dock area was a fascinating, congested, battered shambles of scenes and functions. The immediate environs of the docks soon contained elevators, warehouses, wholesale groceries, freight and passenger ticket offices, mercantile yards, drydocks, and small industrial workshops connected with waterborne commerce. The barrel-making, boiler, and engine shops and planing mills were especially heavily concentrated along Mechanic Street, one of the city's first areas of artisanal concentration. So many private slips and canals were eventually placed off the Erie Canal and river that the area was compared by more than one imaginative tourist to Venice. Commercial islands—really warehouses surrounded by shallow, narrow trenches just wide enough for canal boats—were thus formed. By 1845 this Venetian landscape had crossed to the east of Main Street.[33]

During the season of navigation, when boats so clogged the inner harbor that it was possible to walk from one bank to the other across their bows, the levels of activity and noise were formidable. Representatives of commissioning houses, generally young clerks serving commercial apprenticeships, ran to meet grain ships and inspect and grade their cargo. As quickly as sailors, longshoremen, and laborers could unload freight and place it on wagons, carters and teamsters sped down the narrow streets with goods in transshipment from one dock to the other. Eventually railroads would add a third element to the crosstown movement of goods. Yet barreled and boxed freight always was piled high on the docks—as high as thirty feet—because the volume of trade overwhelmed human capacities to inspect and move it. Grain was moved in similar ways until the advent of the elevator situated most of the activity indoors. Even then the grain trade continued to spill outdoors and to make its presence known, even in the distant reaches of the city. Wet grains and grains heated in the airless holds of boats were often spread out on the docks to cool or dry, creating a stench that found its way to the neighborhoods of rich and poor alike. Passengers faced other perils. "Runners" representing hotels and transportation lines created a dreadful din and personal nuisance with their attempts to manipulate exiting travelers, tourists, and even more defenseless immigrants to coaches, packets, and ships.[34]

Even though the harbor was eventually extended two miles inland and the number of manmade channels and slips continually grew, the river was never adequate before 1860 to accommodate all the lake craft wishing to find a berth, so dozens of ships waited near the lake shore (the "outer harbor") to off-load.[35] The canal was just as crowded, but this was not necessarily the source of its local reputation. Unlike the lake, it was filthy, both because of the droppings of the horses and mules that at the command of mostly young boys guided canal boats along the towpath and because of the use of canals to dump refuse and industrial wastes. Canal water was so foul food sellers went out of their way to assure patrons that Niagara ice alone was used in their freezers. Those who worked as navigators and deckhands on the filthy, congested waterway were called "canallers." Described by Melville as "abundantly and picturesquely wicked," with a "brigandish guise," set off by a "slouched and gaily-ribboned hat," they were widely known to be brawlers. Well earned, the reputation was nonetheless more a product of the circumstances of the work than the character of the men. They constantly competed for places in line at canal locks and along the docks, especially at the crowded Buffalo terminus, which witnessed some of their epic battles. Frequent breaks in the canal walls, all along the route, added to these delays. Once docked, canallers and their captains competed again for freight for the trip back east, for only the biggest carriers arranged such matters in advance.[36]

Interspersed with these commercial activities was the seamy, but for contemporaries fascinating, port culture, which joined laborers, sailors, canallers, vagabonds, and travelers to a number of services—cheap lodging houses and eateries, saloons (as plentiful as "the frogs of Egypt," it was said in 1850),[37] gambling dens, and brothels. The center of the port culture was what contemporary editors revealingly called "the infected district," a twelve-block area just up from the water, in the middle of which some streets formed a "five points" conjuncture, providing endless opportunities for comparison to the more notorious New York City slum. This area was a particular source of embarrassment for respectable folk, who found it necessary to pass through it when going between the docks, the central business district, and eventually the railroad stations. In 1850, the Ladies Temperance Union claimed, perhaps with some exaggeration, there were five hundred taverns and gaming houses here alone. These were widely reputed throughout the lakes, because tipsy sailors were frequently "shanghaied" into service from their backdoors. Violent crime was more associated with this area more than any other in the city, and bodies were found daily during the navigation season floating in the canal and river. Adopting the typical response of the time, police tolerated these conditions as necessary evils and became active against them only when they threatened to spill over into areas where higher-status people lived.[38]

There could be no doubt that moral conditions here were poor, but the neighborhood served, too, as the port's center of working-class social life. Taverns and eateries supplied not only victuals, drink, and vice, particularly to large numbers of transient, single men, but information about job opportunities, easy sociability, and cheap sleeping accommodations. Thus, while the bourgeois conception of the port area as all disorder, lawlessness, and drunken revelry was not entirely wrong, it was much too narrow to grasp the complexity of the area's functions in fulfilling the needs of the unskilled workers, whose labors made the viability of the port possible in the first place. Still, in 1851 and again in 1853, the chief organs of both the mercantile community, the *Commercial Advertiser*, and the evangelicals, the *Christian Advocate*, reported happily that fire had decimated the district. The location was too alluring, however, for moral rehabilitation, and before long the port culture vigorously reasserted itself.[39]

Neighborhoods of workers employed at the port bordered the central docks. Just beyond the wharves, along the river to the east, lay a number of shipyards opened in the 1830s and 1840s, and a few blocks up from these important employers were the principal residential neighborhoods of the Canadian, Irish, and American artisans employed in shipbuilding. This area of closely packed but comfortable frame cottages was not nearly as eye-catching for bourgeois contemporaries, however, as "the Flats," a shantytown nearby. Like the more distant areas of "the Beach," "the Hook," and "Sandytown," the Flats housed Irish dockworkers and their families. Housing here was cheap and inadequate. Most of the structures were one-room plank shanties with dirt floors. Furthermore, these were low-lying areas, which were surrounded by polluted waters and exposed to some of the continent's worst weather. During the months of changing seasons, the storms that wracked the lakes culminated here in all their ferocity, causing extensive flooding. Because of the inadequacy of the seawall in the outer harbor, and the fact that there were not yet enough auxiliary canals to absorb the flood, a tidal wave produced by the great windstorm of October 12, 1844, drove lake water right up over the Flats, killing fifty of the laboring poor and destroying the homes of countless others. In November of the next year another such storm, accompanied by gales of snow, again destroyed many shanties, though this time sparing human life. Still, to live in a jerrybuilt plank shanty was a triumph of sorts, for some residents of these waterfront locations lived aboard wrecked canal boats that had either been pushed up on the beach or floated precariously in shallow water.[40]

The spaces beyond the central docks also were to one extent or another shaped by the dictates of commerce. This influence was evident in the placement of much of the locally oriented commercial economy along the principal vehicular routes that came down to the canal terminus and the inner harbor several blocks beyond it. The most important of these was Main Street, the major thoroughfare to the canal terminus, down which for almost two miles buildings sprang up with astonishing rapidity in the decade after the canal opened. (Streets to the west, toward the Niagara, stopped at a scenic bluff called "the Terrace," which formed an abrupt southern border for the business district, while Main lay on flatland down to the water.) Main had asserted its preeminence prior to the opening of the canal, but that event sealed its position. One hundred and twenty feet wide, Main was often compared to New York's Broadway. In fact, it lacked Broadway's elegance, especially as one approached the canal, and it had along it the full spectrum of the city's workaday social and commercial life. Lower Main Street, below Seneca, was the location of many of those businesses and small, low-technology industrial shops that found it useful to be near the docks: factory outlets and warehouses, wholesale hardware stores, and the city's modest garment industry. Along Main, above Seneca Street, where a gently sloping rise crested, the ground was higher and healthier because better drained. Rents were high, and hence buildings, at five stories, were tall and tightly packed. But the hotels and the fancy shops of milliners, china dealers, merchant tailors, and dressmakers that dominated one side of the street here had a certain elegance, particularly in contrast to the other side, which was lined with dry goods stores.[41]

Both to the east of Main, along Seneca and Swan, and even more generally to the west of Main, lived the city's principal merchants and professionals, who resided in comfortable two- and three-story houses on substantial, cultivated lots within walking distance of their stores, warehouses, and offices, and of government buildings. The white-collar employees of these men lived here, too, but off the principal streets, in smaller homes and in boardinghouses. Also scattered about the streets near and off Main were the oldest and most prestigious Protestant churches and eventually, in a symbolic statement of Catholic claims to sectarian equality, the cathedral of the bishop of western New York. Ellicott's public square, known eventually as Niagara Square, was the heart of this area. It contained the city's most formidable concentration of elite residences. Nearby, up the boulevards that converged at the square, were the wealthiest Protestant congregations, such as First Presbyterian and St. Paul's Episcopalian. Above one of these boulevards, Genesee, Main Street itself became dominated by merchants' residences, which, the further north one traveled, seemed more like country estates. After 1840, the same was true of Delaware Avenue to the west, which became even more elegant and countrylike than Main Street. Delaware would also be compared to Broadway, especially in the 1850s, as elite shops increasingly chose to move north, because dry goods warehouses, garment factories, and even a stockyard were invading the lower precincts of Main Street.[42]

Outside the central business district and beyond the approximately five-block corridor of elite residences on either side of Main were the dwellings of Buffalo's nondockworking laborers and artisans. Located on the far West Side from the towpath and to the tracks of the Buffalo and Niagara Falls Railroad, which opened in 1836, were many native-born Americans, who were separated from the elite residences of the near West Side by a greensward. This neighborhood would also expand northward in the 1850s, and eventually it would merge with the working-class sections of Black Rock. Many smaller streets and lanes in affluent West Side areas also had workers' homes. On the East Side, north of Seneca and beyond Michigan, were the far larger numbers of German-speaking immigrants, along with their distinctive shops and social institutions—beer halls, churches, lodges, and theaters. The principal north-south streets in the densely populated *Deutschendörfchen* (German village)—Michigan, Ellicott, and eventually Main, too,—would contain, as time passed, the imposing residences of affluent German merchants, shopkeepers, and manufacturers, while the east-west boulevards—Genesee and Batavia—were packed with German groceries, artisan shops, and working-class residences.[43] With its foreign character, this area seemed exotic to Americans, a transplanted European town, "as little American," said the *Commercial Advertiser* in 1857, "as the duchy of Hesse Cassel."[44] Scattered among the Germans, however, was one of the oldest of American populations: a large percentage of the city's small, stable black population—about 704 persons in 1855. Though not ghettoized, blacks were never allowed, as gradually their German neighbors were, to enter the city's mainstream. They were in their own public school, barred from voting, unless able to meet a fifty-dollar poll tax, under state law, and able to find employment only as menials and service workers.[45]

East Side and West Side alike, a singular feature of the city's nonelite social landscape was the spatial and structural configuration of working-class housing. While rates of property ownership varied among the city's ethnic groups, most working-class households, outside the proletarian neighborhoods immediately adjacent to the docks and industrial areas near them, lived in frame or plank two-story houses or one-story cottages, each with a bit of yard where a vegetable garden and a fruit tree might be tended, and some chickens, pigs, or a dairy cow kept. In 1855 fully 57 percent of all families lived in single-family dwellings. Only a third of the laborers and skilled workers lived in dwellings with three or more families, while the majority were either owners or renters, often of an "upper" or "lower" in a house. Tenement dwelling was restricted to dockworkers and unskilled factory hands. In 1850 there were only twenty-five buildings in the city with more than twenty residents that were not hotels, and thirteen of these had only four or fewer families.[46] The visual effect was quite different than that to be found in more densely packed northern seaboard cities. As the city's leading nineteenth-century chronicler, Samuel Welch, observed: "A common remark of tourists and visiting strangers is that they have never seen a town before where so many private dwellings seemed each so to be separated and independent of its neighbors, each having its own special domain and adjacencies to ornament and embellish."[47]

Facilitating both this housing pattern and the rapid growth of the East Side's German immigrant population was the extensive, flat plain of the area east of Main Street. The East Side was unbroken by hills and water courses, with the exception of two creeks, and it was heavily wooded, providing an excellent, on-site source of both construction materials and fuel. The opportunity this area presented for a type of urban farming attracted German artisans and peasants to Buffalo. No more powerful inducement to leave Prussia was presented to the Old Lutherans, a large group of religious dissenters experiencing repression for refusal to accept the new state church, than the letter they received from a coreligionist, the Breslau shoemaker Johannes Züngler, who came to Buffalo in 1835. Speaking of the city, Züngler observed that within its boundaries "cattle wandered freely, and that there was plenty of wood and fodder enough that many pigs were kept and calves need not be slaughtered." Even "a family that cannot afford to buy a piece of ground keeps two or three cows and a few breeding sows," he said. Several years later in 1839, after receiving royal permission to emigrate as a group, some 700 Old Lutherans came to Buffalo, settling in the rustic upper reaches of the East Side, an area that came to be known as the "Fruit Belt" for its orchards.[48] The Old Lutherans were not the only group of German-speakers involved in rural pursuits on the East Side. So many of the poor immigrant men attached to St. Mary's Catholic parish, established in the early 1840s, worked as sawyers and wood haulers that the church became known as the *holzhackers Kirche* (woodcutters church). The comparative spaciousness of the East Side made it possible, as late as the 1850s, for German immigrants to continue to have the opportunity to live in a semirural setting, now close to the city's final boundaries.[49]

Yet settlement here was not without its problems. In contrast to the American West Side, which contained a series of low, gently sloping ridges and was adequately drained by the canal and the Niagara, the East Side was not only low-lying, but sat atop a thick clay cover. Drainage was quite poor, and the vast area was even more disease prone than the poorer neighborhoods around the docks. In 1854 seven of the more populous inner East Side streets accounted for nearly 30 percent of cholera deaths during a lethal epidemic. The East Side's location, relatively remote from the center of commerce, and its size as well as the poverty and recent immigration of many residents account for why it was usually the last area to profit from such infrastructural improvements as paving and fresh water pumped from the Niagara.[50]

The location of these working-class neighborhoods was not directly influenced by the demands of the city's interregional commerce. It was to be expected that those engaged in work outside the lake-canal complex would live and work furthest from the docks. Moreover, many artisanal occupations were practiced in workshops attached to or just behind the home, and this work pattern itself went along quite well with the city's preponderance, outside the dock area particularly, of detached dwellings on sizeable lots. By the late 1840s the East Side was filled with small artisanal shops of tailors, shoemakers, bakers, chairmakers, harnessmakers, and butchers, a reflection of German predominance in many traditional crafts. But the West Side, too, had its shops in the same crafts. The artisanal pattern continued to the extent that industrialization was retarded. In fact, it was not until the late 1850s that the local press began to note the extensive separation of work and home.[51] These neighborhoods were also within walking distance of the rapidly expanding central business district and the elite residential areas going up around it; and this, too, made them convenient for many craftsmen in the building trades. Finally, butchers, bakers, and other food craftsmen could live on the East or West Side and be near the municipally owned public markets that ringed the downtown. Many of them had stalls in these markets.[52]

Buffalo's three principal industrial areas also were not shaped directly by the spatial influences of the interregional trade. Their location reflected the effort to find a convenient source of power. Two of these sites were on the West Side, along the canal corridor. The largest of the two was located at Black Rock and utilized for power both steam and the force of water created by locks on the canal and by a dam along Scajaquada Creek, a narrow stream entering the Niagara at Black Rock. This area contained grain and lumber mills, a starch factory, and a number of ironworks, a few of which reached considerable size in the late 1850s when Pennsylvania coal became locally available. Two miles to the south along the towpath, on the northwestern fringe of the downtown, lay a second, smaller industrial area that contained by the mid-1840s several moderately sized factories (cotton and wool textile mills and a paint factory) and some small metal shops. These works depended upon steam from Niagara water, but their location was also stimulated by the adjacent Buffalo and Niagara Falls line.[53]

The location of the third area was a consequence of one of the few deliberate efforts made in antebellum Buffalo to create the preconditions for industrial development. In 1825, as the enormous economic potential of the canal began to make an impression on local merchants, a number of them raised $25,000 to develop the city's only significant waterpower source. Led by Reuben Heacock and the eminent Augustus Porter, the first judge of the county court of common pleas and later a congressman, they formed the Buffalo Hydraulics Association. Over the next two years, the association sponsored the damming of Big Buffalo Creek at an elevated site east of the city and the construction of a narrow channel to carry its waters until they merged with Little Buffalo Creek. At a point on Seneca Street, where the waters fell several feet, the new stream became the basis for the development of an industrial zone known as "the Hydraulics," which soon contained a flour mill, small metal shops, and tanneries. The height of the millrace was increased in 1850, allowing more industry to locate around the site.[54]

In the 1830s this emergent industrial zone was isolated enough from the centers of population in the city that the noxious odors and polluted waters that were an inevitable part of the tanning process were a problem to relatively few people. In the next decade, however, population spread east down Seneca Street, and this, combined with the creation of the state-financed ship basin, the Main-Hamburgh Canal, using the runoff waters of the millrace, brought the Hydraulics into the heart of the city. Soon, too, railroads linking the city with the coal regions would terminate east of the central business district in the same area. The Hydraulics thus merged with this newer industrial area to become the largest and one of the unhealthiest neighborhoods in Buffalo, with more than its share of cholera victims. It did not help either that the city's burgeoning meatpacking industry, also facilitated by the arrival of railroads in the 1850s, took root here. Now every spring thousands of hogs would arrive daily by lake craft. They would be driven up lower Main or Michigan, occasionally a few wayward swine stopping to root at the small Court House Park, and then on to East Side slaughterhouses to be packed and set aboard eastbound trains. The hogs fouled the streets and made travel on them impossible, while the slaughterhouses contributed to the foul smell of local air and along with the tanneries and a few distilleries and an oil refinery, dumped their wastes into the ship canal.[55]

George Washington Johnson was hardly a Buffalo booster. ("Buffalo—I hate it!" said an index entry in the 1848 volume of his diary.) The Massachusetts-born lawyer, dabbler in real estate, and social reformer disliked the city's filth, crudeness, and materialism and the indifference of most of its elite for many years to the evil of southern slavery. Haunted by the shame of the poverty of his early years, he remained only out of fear that he might fail elsewhere. Yet eventually Johnson had to admit that, in spite of everything, Buffalo possessed a certain alluring urban dynamism. "I realize now that Buffalo is size and hustle, is a city," he wrote in 1849. "It appears like Boston and New York."[56] Such a remark suggests how different the city had become from the one planned by Joseph Ellicott. With life and space sorted out according to material concerns, Ellicott's broad boulevards served less to integrate the lives of individuals and groups about a common social center than to separate them by sectorializing the immigrant poor and more affluent native-born. Indeed those boulevards contributed significantly to the fact that Buffalo had one of the most pronounced tendencies toward ethnic and class segregation among northern cities of the era.[57] It would take many years for the implications of such patterns to assert themselves in public ways that appeared to menace social stability. In the booming 1820s and 1830s, however, those who fancied themselves the town's leaders had their minds elsewhere—on making money in a situation that offered previously unimaginable and seemingly endless opportunities for wealth and high living.

Chapter 2

Expansion, Speculation, and Collapse, 1825-38

In 1830 the American merchants, attorneys, and other bourgeois men dominating Buffalo's public life had a curiously divided conception of the place. On the one hand, they possessed a vision of Buffalo as *the* up-to-date commercial entrepôt of the nation's vast interior, a cosmopolitan and sophisticated metropolis. In this view residents were impersonally bonded through a commitment to economic growth and the logic of the cash nexus. On the other hand, there was another, perceptible feeling about Buffalo that emphasized social cohesion and communality and gloried in the values not of material striving and laissez faire individualism, but of civic communalism. In this view Buffalo was a small, tradition-minded village, not unlike the fondly remembered New England and central and eastern New York towns from which many of its residents had recently come. Sharply at odds with one another, the two views expressed an emotional and ultimately an ideological division in the consciousness of those who saw it their responsibility to provide leadership in the emerging city.

In spite of the massive social, economic, and spatial changes being wrought by the canal, it was possible to think of Buffalo as an intimate village comprehensible within traditional experiential categories. Probably no more than 10 percent of the 8,000 inhabitants in 1830 were of foreign birth. They were too small in number, too recently arrived, too busy establishing their families and creating the bases of group life, and too "green" in every respect to take part in civic and political affairs. They were remembered, correctly it seems, by Samuel Welch not only for their purposeful efforts to make lives for themselves ("They were honest, industrious, economical, thrifty, and law abiding"), but equally for their civic quietism ("They were not exciters of strikes, disturbances, and rioting"). Thus, in stark contrast to the turbulent, pluralistic city of a quarter century later, with its vocal immigrant majority and its variety of ethnic cultures, this was a town in which the majority of inhabitants shared many common experiences and a common American Protestant background.[1]

They routinely had face-to-face encounters with people just like themselves. The promising young men who eventually would lead the city during the years of its commercial maturity all boarded at the popular Eagle Tavern and were working for one of the retail shops on Main Street, or reading law, or serving commercial apprenticeships on the docks. Some complained they were too busy during the season of navigation to attend one of the city's six American Protestant churches, partake of its small lending library, or attend the meetings of the debating society. But a number of haunts for casual conversation existed—Haskin's Bookstore, Perry's Coffee House, the Buffalo Hotel, the Eagle's taproom, and the corner of Main and Seneca, where men met going to and from work. The city had a number of small, intimate social circles in which an unpretentious spirit of conviviality was said to exist.[2]

The expanding economy offered significant opportunities for the city's artisans, whose American values and attitudes were similar enough to those of the merchants and professionals to create a general sense of common concerns and a common destiny. Strikes were unknown, and trade unions were rare. The reformist workingmen's movement had a presence, but it was gradually being absorbed into the national Democratic party. In addition some of its major goals, such as free public education, were often shared, with varying degrees of enthusiasm, across class lines. Under any circumstance, as elsewhere, the movement encompassed not only artisans but merchants and professionals. The lack of a feeling of fixed class distinctions, greatly at odds with the perception that held sway two decades later, especially among the foreign-born, was apparent in the early history of the Buffalo Apprentices Society, which was founded in 1832. Composed at first of poor boys, who were shop clerks, indentured apprentices, and journeymen working at trades, its motto was "Get wisdom and endeavor to acquire knowledge, for a good education is the best of all earthly possessions, the basis of power, and the foundation of rational enjoyment." But the society's debates, library, and essay contests grew so popular, and the valued experience it afforded in conducting meetings and business affairs was held in such esteem, that soon the sons of the affluent sought and gained admission, and the society became thoroughly socially mixed.[3]

Only sectarian rivalries and partisan politics proved divisive enough occasionally to blight this communal atmosphere. An annual Fourth of July parade, dinner, and ball was once called off because political feeling had rent the town. Too, Methodist and Unitarian ministers complained that Presbyterian colleagues spoke ill of their denominations and did not want them to gain a foothold. Yet inter-Protestant contentions rarely spilled over into public life, and what political partisanship there was seems to have involved recreation as much as ideology. The emerging national political parties had yet to achieve a strong representation in local affairs. Until the end of the 1830s, most local elections were without issues, often involved ad hominem contentions, and were nonpartisan because the parties had yet to establish permanent, local organizational structures.[4]

The expectation that Buffalo was a community that could possess one mind was especially clear in the town's first charter, which was drafted in 1832 during the process of municipal incorporation. The powers given the Common Council to regulate even minute aspects of daily life were founded upon pre-laissez faire concepts of commonwealth and positive government. The power to oversee both commerce and the work of tradesmen went far beyond the sort of regulation necessary for gathering licensing fees to raise money for the municipality. The council took on the regulation not only of the waterways, streets, and sidewalks, but of taverns, eating places, water pumps, gunpowder stores, slaughterhouses, and tanneries. Butchers, bakers, carters, and runners would be regulated, as would all who sold vegetables, eggs, poultry, fruit, pickled fish, hay, coal, and wood; and provision was made to appoint knowledgeable persons as inspectors. Exact measures for the weight of bread loaves were mandated, and each loaf was to have its weight and the baker's initials stamped on it. Food sellers were to be fined for withholding products from the market in order to raise prices. Public markets were to be established particularly to facilitate regulation of meats, which could be sold only at private shops in wholesale quantities. All butchers' scales were to be sealed and all their market stalls clean; and they were to be dressed at all times in clean white shirts and aprons. They and their apprentices were forbidden during market hours from playing quoits and using obscene language. With their low overhead, these markets were conceived not only as a way of safeguarding the public health, but of providing cheaper goods for the city's wage earners. The public markets were placed in locations convenient to the most densely populated working-class areas.[5]

These ambitious regulations almost immediately ran afoul of the tremendous growth of the city and its commerce, and most would be infrequently enforced before 1860. Perhaps, as Rev. George Hosmer of the city's First Unitarian Church said, Buffalo in 1832 was merely a "little city erected upon the substance of things hoped for rather than things seen," but the hopes and opportunities born of the canal era were then materializing with tremendous force. "From the opening of the canal," said Hosmer, "there was a rush of western emigration; the canal was crowded; hotels all full; warehouses groaned under their burdens; [and] vessels and steamers could not be built fast enough for the demands of the business." Toward the mid-1830s the pace of growth and the speculation that attended it reached fever pitch. As people, in the minister's words, "got wild with hope," the traditional-minded, moral center of community life buckled under the strain.[6] Individuals and institutions seemed swept up in a hurricane of expansion and innovation. Then in 1836–37 a sudden economic collapse brought it all crashing down around them, and led to the ruin of both individual fortunes and collective civic aspirations. Memory of the calamity would haunt the city's leadership for many years.

The unsettling impact of rapid growth on the social fabric was not always readily apparent, let alone easily remedied. A comparison with almost contemporaneous events in nearby Rochester suggests why. In that city large numbers of merchants and manufacturers and many craftsmen were responding to the challenge of industrialization in the early 1830s by embracing evangelical religion, through the medium of religious revivals, as a means of achieving social stability. Wage earners working for these entrepreneurs now had to give evidence of piety and good moral habits to obtain employment. Such was the case in other industrializing Upstate cities. But the Upstate commercial cities were different. It was not simply that Rochester experienced slower population and economic growth than Buffalo. Nor was it that a good portion of Buffalo's elite was Episcopalian, and thus on the fringe of the evangelical mainstream; just as many of Buffalo's leading citizens were Presbyterians. Rather the rise of milling and industrially organized shoemaking at Rochester brought such fundamental changes to the organization of work and to the social relations of employers and a new class of wage earners that a crisis of social authority resulted. It cried out for solutions within the framework of a common Protestant religious culture. The city's factory owners picked up the challenge, along with their new profits, and forged a new cultural base for the legitimation of their social authority. In Buffalo no such changes in the social relations of production took place. On the surface of life the relations between people and ways of accomplishing basic productive tasks remained the same. The city's crisis of growth lay not in the realm of relationships torn apart, but rather in the constant escalation of individual opportunities and aspirations on the foundation of a social morality too weakened to withstand the strain. While Rochester's entrepreneurs became pious bourgeois Christians, Buffalo's became speculators and freebooters widely known in the North for the refusal to make small plans, either individual or civic. While Rochester's entrepreneurs created a city in which the church aggressively sought to dominate social behavior, in Buffalo religion remained an individual matter, and beyond that limited sphere the church seemed ever on the defensive, as its local leaders admitted. "You have no idea," Buffalo's lone Presbyterian minister, Sylvester Eaton, wrote the famed revivalist Charles Grandison Finney in 1831, "of the awfully stultifying, hardening influence which prevails here."[7]

To the naked eye the disorganizing processes of growth were perhaps most apparent in the sudden establishment of the port culture, which provided a particular, local flavor to the city's urbanization. During the season of navigation, an ever circulating population of sailors, canallers, immigrants, dock laborers, travelers, peddlers, sharpers, and confidence men now appeared. "The rendezvous of all manner of persons—as undesirable a residence as any in the free states," scoffed Harriet Martineau as she observed Buffalo during this human flood.[8] The seasonal population increase crowded the waterfront and strained public and private services. "Vagabonds of all ages, colors, and moral statuses" were collecting around the docks, and especially at the various "resorts" at the Five Points.[9] The transshipment of people, too, encouraged the rise of the antebellum trade in bilking the unwary visitor. Indeed, the city hardly put on its best face for travelers, whose experience helped earn it the reputation as a "dirty, mean-looking, trunk-stealing, roguery sustaining sort of town."[10]

Buffalo did become a haven for those uncomfortable with conventional restraints, and they helped to develop the anything-goes atmosphere of dubious deals and rough amusements. That liquor flowed freely in the city hardly made Buffalo unique, but the city did develop an unusually large number of drinking places to cater to the thousands of travelers and sailors passing through. As early as 1828 the county legislature felt it necessary to establish a grand jury to investigate the rise of places giving root to drunkenness, gambling, and prostitution.[11] The pieties expressed in the first municipal ordinances regulating liquor were from the start largely unenforceable, and in turn, this provided an incentive for those struggling with an emerging, repressive moral climate in places like Rochester to relocate in Buffalo. S. P. Needham, a substantial Rochester grocer and liquor dealer, did just that. After three years of battling the local clergy and government, in 1833 he came to the "conviction that Church dominancy has such influence over this community that no honest man can do business in his own way." Needham reestablished his business in Buffalo.[12] Such men helped develop a wide range of amusements for the populace. In addition to the standard vices, for example, liquor dealers and tavern keepers, along with the stagecoach proprietors, organized one of the region's truly novel summertime entertainments—sending empty boats over Niagara Falls.[13]

This expansion of the realm of the acceptable was also seen in individual business practices and in the hodgepodge of civic and private plans projected to encourage further development. As commerce expanded, the docks and the central business district experienced a rapid increase in construction and an escalation of land values. The change was especially noticeable on Main Street. "All the buildings have the appearance of being run up in a great hurry, though everything has an air of great pretension; there are porticos, columns, domes, and colonnades, but all of wood," said Frances Trollope, for whom Buffalo was proof that "this country may be said to spread rather than to rise."[14] Yet the harbor grew ever more congested, streets went unpaved, the quasi-public schools charged a tuition many could not pay, and there was almost nothing in the way of organized charity besides public relief. What charity existed was limited mostly to the patronage of wealthy individuals like Dr. Cyrenius Chapin, who opened his home to beggars and vagabonds. Meanwhile, entrepreneurs focused on largely symbolic civic improvements, as grandiose as their imaginations. Merchants planned a $500,000 exchange, with a dome 225 feet high, to fill a large, new public square in the heart of downtown. The exact functions of the exchange had yet to be worked out in spite of the vast energies going into planning it. A few blocks away a $75,000 monument of white marble, dedicated to Commodore Perry, was to be raised from merchant subscriptions. Though Buffalo was still not more than a mile in any direction in concentrated population, the first tracks for an extensive intraurban street railway system were laid on Main Street in 1834. The capstone of these big plans was to create a world-class University of Western New York on a wooded site on Delaware Avenue. The initial desire for a university came from the region's Presbyterians, who conceived of it as a place to train ministers. But the project soon became ecumenical, and fell under the sway of the heady, expansive atmosphere then prevailing, so that the 1836 charter contained provision for four heavily endowed chairs.[15]

The principal backers of this frontier Oxford were prominent merchants and evangelical clergymen. They were led by Alanson Palmer. A dashing figure with no particular employment but a great deal of his wife's money, Palmer went by the purely honorific "Colonel" and was easily identified by the six-horse coach in which he traveled. He was, it was said, "a natural-born speculator." He had once attempted to purchase the city of Troy and its suburbs. He routinely bought out individuals—house, lot, business, stable, and even clothing. The university was only one of Palmer's civic enthusiasms. He financed construction of the first full-rigged sailing ships on the lakes; endowed for five years the only free school (for sixty orphans), and along with the region's principal contractor, Benjamin Rathbun, built the American Hotel, probably the largest such establishment west of the seaboard. Reputed to be worth $750,000, Palmer contributed most of the prime land for the new university, and pledged to endow a chair. Yet there was something insubstantial about men like Palmer. His origins were obscure, and he seemed little more than his money and life-style. This, however, was the level on which he was respected in an unsettled social environment in which, as David Grimstead has said of mid-nineteenth century urban America, it seemed that "individuals became who they said they were or who others accepted them as being."[16]

Land and the easy availability of credit to buy and develop it were the basis for this expansive local mood. Pressure on land had increased values astronomically. In the mid-1830s, prime land was selling at $125 per front foot in the central business district and $60 outside it; four decades later the same lots would go for only $8 to $12 a foot. Values were escalating daily. The merchant James Barton would remember how early in 1835 he had purchased two lots at Black Rock for $250 to find them worth $3,000 that fall. While walking down the street one day the next year, he was offered for them, in rapid succession, $6,000, then $7,500, and finally $20,000 with $2,000 offered as a down payment on the spot.[17]

The volume of real-estate transactions was staggering. In 1836 alone, said the merchant and editor Guy Salisbury, "there were some 12,000 deeds, mostly for city property, recorded ... about 3000 more than had been made in the entire county since its organization in 1812." Assuming, he continued, "that there were as many transfers by private contract as by deed—a low estimate—the aggregate number of conveyances must have reached nearly 25,000, and the entire amount of purchases could have been little less than $25,000,000." Thus, "a speculative mania seemed to come over the common sagacity of men who, in the ordinary affairs of life, had sense enough to look after their own interests," but in land transactions were losing all judgment. Most were engaging in complex, large transactions in which little or no money changed hands. Furthermore, these deals were all the more risky because little was known about either the buyer's or the property's history. Land, said Salisbury, was commonly being purchased by persons "whose responsibility was often unknown, without knowledge of title or protection against prior encumbrances. Men of straw bought blocks of credit, giving mortgages for the purchase price, and then sold them out in lots with no provision for releases from the lien which covered the whole." Soon much of Buffalo's property, commercial and residential alike, was tied up in one or more such mortgages. The recklessness prevailing in land transactions was characteristic, too, of the deals put together in the construction of commercial buildings and the $20,000 mansions that lined Delaware Avenue in the mid-1830s. Building contractors gathered funds on the inflated notes of local banks or on the personal notes of individuals who were themselves deeply involved in dubious land transactions and no wealthier than the notes signed over to them by the next man, whose own fate was equally dependent on some speculator's notes.[18]

Credit arrangements were increasingly pervasive throughout the entire economy, and these, too, lent themselves to speculation. Much of the grain and flour trade was developing a speculative outlook, for some traders worked for themselves as buyers rather than acting on behalf of others. They anticipated gains in price after the harvest, and they borrowed on their expectations in the months prior to it.[19] Though the U.S. Bank branch was a source of restraint until it closed in 1835, the three locally owned banks helped to fuel the expansion of credit. The mechanisms for regulation established by the legislature were inadequate, and all three were controlled by Buffalo merchants who were deeply involved in speculation. Within a short time each was far exceeding the legal limits of specie circulation defined by the extent of their capital stock. Yet much of that stock was itself worthless because it was based on the assets of local plungers.[20]

Even had local banks been less inclined to dubious practices, it might not have made a difference. Alongside the banking system chartered under law there arose a parallel, informal system based exclusively on the word of honor of merchants in what was still a small, intimate trading community. Three informal mechanisms absorbed a significant degree of the local demand for short-term credit. Because the banks met but once a week to decide discounts and loans, between meetings merchants were accustomed to sending their clerks up and down Main Street to ask mercantile colleagues if they could sign over a note. No records were ever kept, so great was their confidence in each other. Similar trust governed their relations with Rathbun's private bank, the second of these mechanisms. The bank issued small notes that were wholly unsecured. Their value rested solely on Rathbun's reputation, and they circulated freely and widely. Last, a system of brokerage existed for those who had been refused discounts by the banks. Bank directors frequently referred these disappointed individuals to money brokers, who would supply funds for a fee far in excess of bank rates. Among these brokers were prominent local mercantile and professional people, including some of the directors of the city's Commercial Bank. These directors routinely voted themselves bank loans, while refusing them to businessmen, and then used the loans in brokerage.[21]

With the costs of money and volume of credit escalating in the city and the nation, by 1834 prices began to spiral sharply upward, outstripping the wages of workers. In consequence the lingering sense of communal unity received a sharp blow in the form of militant working-class discontent. In February of that year the carpenters' Journeymen Operative Building Society, a small union, struck for higher wages, and promised support to any other building tradesmen who would strike for the same wage scale. Around the same time a union of stonecutters and masons was formed, which made similar demands, while stopping short of striking. The striking carpenters probably spoke for large numbers of wage earners when, in defending their actions, they denounced not only the steep rise in the price of essentials, but also the role of speculators in creating inflation. Framed in this way, the strike involved more than a conflict over the distribution of resources. It was a moral indictment of many of the city's principal men by those working for them.[22]

The striking carpenters were not alone in their condemnation of decadence and greed. Criticisms and dissenting ideologies came from several directions. Closest to the trade unions in spirit was the reformist workingmen's movement, which enjoyed a resurgence in the mid-1830s. With no stable organization, it depended heavily on articulate spokesmen, the most powerful of whom, Oliver G. Steele, could be heard increasingly denouncing the lag in wages.

Born in Connecticut in 1805, Steele was the son of a Jeffersonian editor of humble means but respectable lineage. Armed with the spirit his father had possessed in doing editorial battle with New England Federalists, and with his own generation's Jacksonian ideals, Steele, who worked as a bookbinder and kept a bookshop, took the lead in organizing many efforts in behalf of the local artisanry. None grew more in importance, as wage earners saw their standard of living eroded, than Steele's campaign to end tuition payments at the schools, and to establish free, tax-supported public schools.[23]

The city's committed Christians, as distinct from the much larger body of casual church attenders, also felt ill at ease. Like Dr. Bryant Burwell, they felt threatened by the irreligious atmosphere of a place where, as the doctor recorded during the 1837 municipal election campaign, a mayoral candidate and councilmanic candidates in three of four wards, all of them of well-established families, were charged with keeping mistresses.[24] At the beginning of the decade the pious had pinned their hopes on revivalism, and sought to obtain an appearance by the brilliant Charles Grandison Finney. The effort was an ecumenical one, with Episcopalians involved, but it was led by Sylvester Eaton. Eaton, whose entreaties to Finney were filled with an appraisal of his difficulties relative to those of the ministers of Rochester's three Presbyterian churches, understood the singular features of the local scene. Many of the prominent merchants, said Eaton, wanted Finney to come, too. Yet, he continued, "they cannot feel it their duty to leave business to attend prayer meeting," even frequently in the off-season. He warned that if Finney waited to visit Buffalo until the season of navigation commenced, he could never hope to combat the "awful wretchedness" that prevailed.[25]

But after months of preaching by Eaton and others and finally late in 1831 by Finney, the results were disappointing. A Young Men's Temperance Society was founded, but expressed alarm when politicians denounced as intolerant its report claiming a rise in intemperance and wholesale violations of liquor laws. Nor were there many conversions of important local citizens, in spite of the ministrations of many prominent ladies, who, as elsewhere, took a significant role in the 1831 revivals. These women, who were spiritually energized by the revivals, would one day exert an important influence in behalf of moral reform. But that would require a different moral climate than the one in the 1830s.[26]

The situation was not completely a loss for the evangelicals, however, for their belief that Buffalo's redemption could commence only with conversions among prominent men was given a boost when John Chase Lord and Samuel Wilkeson were saved. In separate but complexly overlapping spheres of life, both men were fated to exercise tremendous influence, constituting, to Steele's left-wing dissent, a conservative counterpoint that was fated to have even more influence before 1861. In the years before the depression, this influence was exerted largely by force of example and outspoken criticism of the reigning passions of the day. Both men functioned as the voice of the now submerged, other side of the elite's consciousness: that which urged strength of character, communal responsibility, courage of conviction, and skepticism of the blandishments of the world.

Born in western Pennsylvania to Scots-Irish immigrant parents, Wilkeson was already fifty-two when his conversion added new force to his commanding personality. A pioneer in the trade between western New York and Pittsburgh, he found himself at Buffalo during the War of 1812, in which he fought in the Niagara Frontier campaigns. After the conflict, he decided to remain, and began a business career and governmental service. He served as judge (1815–22), state assemblyman (1823–28), and finally, as mayor (1836–37), a position he aspired to out of concern for the deterioration of moral order. In office, he upheld a stern code of public behavior and inflexible regard for law and order that cared little for anything besides his own principles, particularly temperance, the sanctity of the Sabbath, and strict probity in money matters. Always satisfied with "the wisdom and rectitude of his own course," it was said, he was "habitually careless of the opinions of adversaries, and went boldly to his object." When demobilized soldiers appeared drunk on the streets in 1815, he adopted a single-minded course: "The dangerous he threw in jail; the turbulent and petty-larcenous he frightened out of town with a look and voice which few men could endure." As mayor, he adopted a similar course when Texas nationalists came to recruit for their army in contravention of neutrality laws. He did not limit his wrath to interlopers. Wilkeson worked successfully for the creation of a self-supporting county workhouse (which eventually became a penitentiary) in order that criminals be segregated from the worthy poor receiving indoor relief. It was testimony perhaps to the discomfort of many people over what the city was becoming that Wilkeson was chosen mayor. For his part, he was full of contempt for his own class. In 1834 he told his sons, who were seeking a city further west as a location for a new enterprise, not to settle in Louisville, because "the society" there might well be as bad as Buffalo's.[27]

In his entrepreneurial career, Wilkeson also took an independent course. He had almost single-handedly engineered the harbor improvement that won the canal terminus for Buffalo, and he continued to take an interest in the enlargement of the harbor. He and his sons worked privately among New York City capitalists to urge them to invest in western canals and road construction, so that Ohio grain areas might be better linked to Lake Erie. But he distrusted excessive reliance on commerce as the foundation of his fortune and the city's economy. Along with a few other merchant families, Wilkeson used mercantile profits to begin manufacturing. He opened a small cotton textile mill in 1836, and made two separate ventures in manufacturing iron goods. He tried to attract additional manufacturing to Buffalo, but was frustrated to find, he said, that capitalists were reluctant to establish enterprises requiring a disciplined work force because of Buffalo's reputation as a wide-open place. Though Wilkeson signed large notes for his merchant friends, he avoided debt, and while reckless land speculation went on around him, he put his money into the local, family iron business and two forges he opened in northeastern Ohio.[28]

For John Chase Lord, Wilkeson met the standards of a "valiant man," as Lord said at the time of Wilkeson's death in 1848. By this, Lord meant he possessed a stubborn courage and moral independence that rejected the easygoing morality around him and made God's judgment the ultimate test of conscience. By such criteria Lord, too, would have qualified, though there was little way to foretell this prior to his conversion. Born in 1805, he had been the sort of clergyman's son who caused his Presbyterian parents endless anxiety. Restless and impulsive, he seemed devoid of religious concern. He showed no seriousness of purpose until 1825 when, with but eighteen cents, he showed up in Buffalo and was allowed to read law at a prominent firm. In 1828 he was admitted both to the bar and to membership at First Presbyterian. Yet his old impulsiveness remained. He courted the daughter of Ebenezer Johnson, a physician who had gotten rich through land speculation and who served as the city's first mayor. Johnson did not approve of Lord, and refused to allow a marriage. The couple eloped, touching off a scandal. Though the Johnsons soon came to respect their new son-in-law, the young couple felt a remorse that made them receptive not long after to Finney's preaching. They were both saved during his Buffalo revival.[29]

Upon conversion Lord entered the ministry. Returning to Buffalo in 1835 after seminary training, he established a congregation composed of members of the overcrowded First Presbyterian and the much smaller Free Congregational Church. The new church was called Central Presbyterian, but it was a measure of his personal authority that until his death, while still its minister, in 1877, it was known as "Dr. Lord's Church." Located just off prestigious Niagara Square, it included within a decade many of the principal mercantile and professional families: Dr. Johnson, Samuel and William Wilkeson, the attorneys Thomas Love and Solomon Haven, and the merchants Ira Joy, George Tifft, A. S. Sprague, Stephen Lockwood, and Reuben Heacock. By 1852, there were 580 members, making it one of the largest Protestant churches in Buffalo.[30]

Lord liked to boast that in four decades in the ministry his theological position did not change, and that Central Presbyterian was ever "steadfast, conservative, and orthodox." Calvinist and theocratic in religion and antireform in politics, Lord was not a typical disciple of Finney. Indeed he personifies the conservative potential in the Presbyterian wing of the Puritan movement, and it is likely that the moral laxity of Buffalo, as much as retrospective disgust with his own undisciplined early life, overdetermined his course. For him humanity was innately depraved, while God was ever inscrutable and transcendent. One might be touched by the Holy Spirit, but could not initiate the process of regeneration. Though he himself had been saved at an essentially stage-managed revival, he rejected modern revivalism as a theatrical sham, just as he rejected other evangelical tactics—tracts, Bible societies, and missions. His religion mixed inward-looking self-scrutiny, piety, humility, and a sober, modest style of life. He rejected the worldly reform program of the evangelicals, charging that it was contrary to scripture and would merely patch up the surface of society, while leaving the individual sinful. The Bible sanctioned slavery, so abolitionists were not only fanatics, but heretics. Advocates of women's rights and opponents of capital and corporal punishment also held views contrary to scripture. Temperance was well-meaning, but naive, because the drinker could not reform merely through an act of will. The public schools were godless and materialist.[31]

From his entrenched position, however, he struggled to mediate between Calvinism and democracy, and entered into the ranks of those clerical Christian republicans who believed as deeply in America as they did in their religion. While he saw progress as finite without God, he espoused the Puritan idea of the national covenant between God and the nation. If the covenant were broken, along with the majority of the Protestant clergy he feared a national catastrophe. Democracy and affluence without God, he stated frequently, would surely degenerate into a majoritarian tyranny. Moreover, he greatly feared the growth of the Catholic church, which he found a threat to democracy and liberty as well as to America's mission to save the world for true Christianity. He spent many years opposing Catholicism, and assisted in paving the way ideologically and emotionally for the 1850s nativist reaction. The antidote he offered for threats to the national covenant was the cultivation through religion of those traits he found compelling in Wilkeson: civic courage, self-reliance, the willingness to assume responsibility, opposition to all material and spiritual corruption, and humility before God. The form of society in America and its Protestant culture made people capable at once of becoming "valiant" and more receptive to God.[32]

Lord's effort to reconcile religion and morality with a promising, yet problem-laden America gave his impassioned jeremiads significance for his congregants and led him to become a conservative voice of its collective conscience, a voice that demanded they exert their authority in the name of moral order. Perhaps it was the most representative voice, for the forces of millenialist, libertarian reform were weak in Buffalo during the period. In coming years, too, Lord's practical influence would grow. When the Presbyterian General Synod fell into schism in 1837, he was the only western New York preacher to remain within the orthodox Old School movement, his preference for which was determined by both its theological position and antiabolitionism. The Old School movement was mostly southern, and this gave Lord deep ties with the South, and an important role in interpreting and defending the South as sectional conflict intensified.[33] Buffalo's dockside merchants feared disunion would disrupt national markets, and Lord served to provide their essentially economic anxieties with the political ammunition they required to argue against sectional agitation. What compassion they felt toward blacks led people like Lord to support the American Colonization Society, which Wilkeson headed in the 1840s.[34] Another, indirect source of Lord's influence was friendship with his intellectual comrade, Dr. Thomas J. Foote, editor during much of the period of the Buffalo *Commercial Advertiser*, the principal organ of the mercantile interest. Foote, though an Episcopalian, shared Lord's Calvinist view of human nature and American society, and gave as articulate a commercial and political interpretation to local conservatism as Lord gave a religious one.[35]

What prepared a religiously apathetic, high-living, and speculating elite to contemplate the examples and ideas of Wilkeson and Lord was the catastrophic reversal of the city's bright prospects. The impact of this economic collapse was intensified because with it came the disgrace of the city's most successful entrepreneur, an icon of another sort, Benjamin Rathbun.

Inner and outer man were sharply at odds in Rathbun. As a contemporary remarked, "Of quiet, unassuming manners, Quaker in dress, moderate in all his expenses (except in charity wherein, assisted by his amiable wife, he was very liberal), he concealed under his apparent simplicity and goodness a mind capable of the vastest conceptions." Nothing in his past prior to settlement in Buffalo would have predicted anything but failure and obscurity. Born in 1790 in Connecticut of parents who found it difficult to make a living, he himself had already had two unsuccessful ventures in innkeeping before arriving in 1819. In Buffalo's precanal years his ventures were modestly successful. He bought the Eagle Tavern, opened a theater, managed the local section of the Albany coach, and ran an omnibus up Main Street. Under him the Eagle, which had had a disreputable clientele, became the principal local hotel for respectable travelers, while its taproom served as the location for civic events. With these successes he was able to overcome persistent rumors about the legitimacy of his first bankruptcy and the later business troubles of his brother and father. Indeed, so exemplary was his conduct he was elected a vestryman at St. Paul's Episcopal, the oldest elite congregation, and in 1827 and 1829, a village trustee.[36]

After the canal opened, Rathbun shifted his activities away from the Eagle toward land speculation and construction. He built many of the principal structures in the commercial district—the U.S. Hotel, the American House, the U.S. Bank branch, and a massive block of fourteen shops. It was later said, "Every structure worthy of observation in the whole town was projected by, contracted for, and executed by Mr. Rathbun." This record of accomplishment won him the contract for the block-square Merchants Exchange. At the same time his operations branched out to encompass development of Niagara Falls. With the Porters and Dr. Johnson he gathered the capital to build the Buffalo and Niagara Falls Railroad, the construction of which he supervised. After the road opened in 1834, the partners began to develop the industrial and commercial potential of the falls themselves, which were owned by the Porters. All of these operations together constituted the region's most extensive local business empire. By the mid-1830s, Rathbun owned warehouses, artisan shops, sawmills, quarries, and brickyards. The "Master Builder and Architect," his Ibsenian designation for himself, employed two thousand laborers and craftsmen and ninety-seven agents and bookkeepers in 1836, a year in which he spent $300,000 on supplies and had a *daily* payroll of $10,000. One-third of Buffalo worked for him, and he supervised almost half of the $1,130,000 in local construction in that same year.[37]

The funds to finance this empire at first came from Rathbun's other enterprises. But as his payroll grew, he ventured into the credit market. At first the local banks were cooperative, but his needs so escalated that bankers became wary. Rathbun then opened his own bank and issued unsecured notes, which circulated as if they were currency. But this merely satisfied short-term needs. For larger amounts he borrowed privately from men like Wilkeson or went to brokers, who asked for increasingly large percentages in fees and interest. He secretly took out first, second, and third mortgages and in 1835, through third parties, bought banks outside the state for use in his borrowing and discounting schemes. Nonetheless, he was now constantly facing crises over due notes, and he feared his mammoth indebtedness would be discovered.[38]

In 1836, in response to federal deflationary policies and a growing European distrust of American finances that led continental banking houses to call in their loans, American creditors demanded repayment of loans. In a state of desperation, Rathbun forged the signatures of thirty-five individuals and private firms on notes totaling $1,500,000, which he then marketed in his own banks, and in New York City. Around August 1 one of these "endorsers" was told that his signature was present on a Rathbun note. Benjamin Rathbun's, and many other people's, world began to unravel.[39]

The first impulse of the local bankers and merchants who heard of Rathbun's forgeries was to keep the matter secret in fear that the city would be ruined. Buffalo was, after all, said one visitor in 1836, "a splendid pyramid, but it is based on a peg"—i.e., Rathbun. But word leaked out beyond the circle of "endorsers," spread throughout the local trading community, and soon reached New York City and Rathbun's out-of-state banks. Shock waves were sent throughout financial markets and the local artisan community. Twelve hundred of his artisans and laborers went to Rathbun's countinghouse to demand their wages. When they did not get satisfaction, an attack on Rathbun's provisions warehouse seemed imminent. Not even the grim visage of Mayor Wilkeson, who read the riot act, succeeded in quelling the angry workers. Only the promise of a public meeting the next day with the recently appointed trustees of the Master Builder's property got the men to go home.[40]

Meanwhile Rathbun himself sat in jail, charged with fraud. There was substantial sympathy for him. Some attributed Rathbun's problems to the fact that he was "infatuated with previous success," but prominent men in the know conceded that local money brokers had "for years shaved the man most abominably."[41] The recently established German *Weltbürger* noted that, native and foreign alike, many now jobless artisans and laborers continued to believe that if only Rathbun could get back on his feet, prosperity would return.[42] It is not surprising that he was acquitted at his first trial, which was held in Buffalo. At his second, however, held at Batavia, Rathbun received five years at hard labor. Prominent local men petitioned for his release, but several governors would refuse him a pardon. After leaving prison, he managed a number of progressively shabbier hotels in New York City, and suffered one family tragedy after another until his death in 1873. Word of these reversals reached Buffalo, where they served to augment the cautionary tale his career inspired about how far the mighty could fall. Years after he died people were ruminating on the meaning of his life.[43]

The local economy was badly shaken in 1836, and the next year brought the national panic and the inception of a long depression. Henceforth the downward spirals of local and national crises would reinforce one another, heaping misery upon misery. All of the work on Rathbun's many projects ended, and thousands were out of work. The structure of local credit and debt collapsed. Because it was not clear which were Rathbun's forged notes and which the legitimate notes of the eleven most prominent "endorsers" whose names had been forged, the notes of all twelve were repudiated. A massive contraction of credit took place, and along with it the spread of debt and one business failure after another, with unemployment growing constantly. Land contracts were voided for nonpayment, mortgages foreclosed, land sold for taxes, and personal property sold at public and private auction.[44] In May, 1837, Dr. Burwell noted "the heart-rending situation of Buffalo today. . . . No business—no money; no confidence in men; rents failing; merchants in despair; the poor starving; streets thronged with beggars; mechanics idle for want of employment; much suing and no collections."[45]

The collapse of fortunes and reputations proceeded apace. In February, 1838, Ira Blossom, the last resident agent of the Holland Land Company, noted that "the general and distressing embarrassments of our entire community here have greatly diminished my confidence in everybody."[46] Doubtless that confidence was further shaken shortly thereafter when state authorities closed all three local banks, charging their prominent directors with gross malfeasance. Banking in Buffalo was dead for years to come; in 1843 not a bank existed.[47]

By 1840 many of the city's principal men faced ruin. Burwell reported in January, "The times are getting very bad among the higher and business part of our community. There is a great danger of our heretofore wealthiest merchants failing."[48] A number of large mercantile houses, especially those that had been tied directly to Rathbun, had already or were about to collapse. Some individuals, such as Hiram Pratt, the mayor that year and son of one of the first merchants, and Dr. Johnson, lost so much of their personal fortunes that they consequently experienced rapid physical decline and died. One ruined grain merchant committed suicide. Dr. John Clark, the wealthiest of the "endorsers," lost everything and had finally to be maintained by the charitable assistance of friends. And Lance Palmer, who had seemed to personify the boom, began the decline that would culminate with his death in the poorhouse. These were only the most dramatic stories. Countless individuals like Millard Fillmore, Wilkeson, and Burwell himself, though not ruined, would spend years quietly covering their friends' notes and adjusting to straitened circumstances.[49]

In the central business district all the great building projects had stopped, leaving in place scaffolds, frames, and piles of wood. The site of the exchange provided the most striking evidence of the catastrophe. An entire block had been razed for the building, and now it was bare except for the rotting pillars of the U.S. Bank branch which had been on the site. Plans for the university ceased. The buildings constructed during the depression were cheap and unpretentious. Thus, in the early 1840s there was a shabby, ramshackle quality about the commercial district that would be captured in all of its pathos in Edward Hildebrandt's painting, "Buffalo, New York, 1844," which depicts lower Main Street. (See illustration section.) The street is littered, in part with the debris left from a recent campaign rally, and unpaved; the buildings are decrepit and plain. The artist had attempted to render the essence of the city, and the city he painted, as Hugh Honour has said, looks ill used, "old in youth and 'blasted ere her prime.' "[50]

The road back from this collapse would be neither as long nor as tortured as one might have predicted from the depths of the depression. Recovery would depend on the canal and further building upon the city's locational advantage. But the approach toward exploiting these assets would now change markedly, as businessmen and their allies sought to apply the tragic lessons of Buffalo's past in building the foundations for its future. In the process they fashioned themselves into a self-conscious social group with aspirations to build a civilization.

Part Two

The Formation of a Provincial Bourgeoisie

CHAPTER 3

Commerce and Class Formation

DURING the years of Buffalo's decline, civic leaders had ample opportunity to contemplate the disaster. Those in their midst they looked to for moral guidance spared them no pain in laying the responsibility on them and on others with power and wealth throughout the country. In a nationally circulated jeremiad Rev. John Lord accused them of earning divine wrath by having indulged themselves in "pride, fullness of bread, and abundance of idleness."[1] Rev. George Hosmer was also unforgiving. "A grasping spirit of accumulation," he said, had "inflamed our acquisition desires" and caused men to "sink down into the coarse interests of money-getters and bond and mortgage holders."[2] Such thoughts posed a problematic for the age: prosperity might be dangerous to individual morality and the survival of republican society. If prosperity corrupted society's democratic elites and blinded them to their own decadence and irresponsibility, what moral claim would they have to authority and power?

Even before the return of prosperity these men appeared to be considering their collective culpability and attempting to make amends and to build better for the future. The immediate stimulus was the suffering born of the depression. Before the economic collapse, organized charity had taken a backseat to the often flashy private benevolence of the Palmers, Rathbuns, and others. ("I have looked in vain for the record of a single charitable association," said a local historian of the year of municipal incorporation, 1832.)[3] Now, however, even in the straitened circumstances of the depression, it increased dramatically with the creation of an orphan asylum, a home for destitute boys, a city medicine dispensary, a Fireman's Benevolent Association to care for injured firemen and their dependents, and an American

Bethel Society to provide for the spiritual and physical needs of sailors, canal boatmen, and juvenile towpath drivers.[4] Furthermore, in a symbolic, penitent embrace of sobriety, principal evangelical churches became active in support of temperance. In 1838 there was but one, small temperance society. In 1842 there were five, and one of them, the Young Men's Temperance Society, claimed 800 members. Not all of these efforts would survive the more relaxed mood that eventually came with prosperity, but they suggested a deepening moral concern.[5]

Education, too, profited from this concern. Plans for a much scaled-down university were set in motion. When the University of Buffalo opened its doors in 1846, it did so only as a medical school.[6] It was the creation of a tuition-free public school system that would touch the most lives and excite many imaginations. Prior to the panic, the city had a few private academies and a weak system of semipublic schools that charged a fee most could not pay. In 1836, in a city of nearly 10,000, only 179 children regularly attended school. The workingmen's movement had protested, but had not been able to overcome taxpayer objections and elite apathy. The creation in 1838 and 1839 of tuition-free public schools, complete with a plan to provide every district with a public school building, was a response to the inability of those who had been paying the fees to continue to do so and to the idleness of the growing number of children for whom there was neither school nor work. Quite soon, however, in the midst of the civic introspection of the depression, people began to endow the new school system with important social meanings. The schools, Hosmer told an Erie County teachers' meeting in 1840, must educate to safeguard society from all that imperiled virtue and self-government.[7]

Thoughts of social responsibility and civic concern among the affluent and influential took on other dimensions with the return of prosperity. The enormous expansion of trade that commenced in 1843[8] taxed the city's port and dock facilities, and demanded a thorough reevaluation and physical expansion of the public and commercial infrastructure serving waterborne trade. Furthermore there was a problem of prosperity itself—of finding a vision of civic development and social coherence broad and profound enough to give purpose to worldly ambitions and affluence. Both challenges were fundamentally ones requiring transformations of elite behavior, values, and beliefs. Such transformations were increasingly in evidence, on a number of different levels, as the depression gave way to a new period of prosperity. Indeed, many would look back on this time as a turning point in the character of the local American elite. As Oliver Steele said years later while reflecting on the greatly differing approach to business and civic affairs of local leadership before and after the depression, "The kind of men required to build a city are necessarily different from those who perfect and beautify it."⁹

The transformation to which Steele alluded was clear in the less flamboyant style and more single-minded absorption in commerce that characterized the postdepression public style of local businessmen. Gone were the Lance Palmers and Benjamin Rathbuns, with their protean public activities and free-spending benevolence. The postdepression entrepreneur retreated somewhat from the public sphere. He left charity to the county poor masters and to the often ineffectual private agencies created to deal with it. He left social reform to his wife and minister, while he remained absorbed in business. He took politics mostly as it touched upon his immediate class interests. It was above all an extension of business. Government must be cheap, honest, and efficient, and when necessary responsive to business, in order to create a good climate for investment. Politics was not recreation, let alone a path to prestige, and he left to others the day-to-day work of organizing the political sphere. To the extent he was active at all, it was not at city hall, let alone in the wards, but as a lobbyist at Albany and Washington. He did not see either his definition of his political concern or his occasional effort to get government to spend vast sums to facilitate private commerce as selfish. He saw himself as the center of an effort to build a new, progressive civilization and universalized his interests so that they became society's interests.

Coinciding with the mass immigration of the 1840s and the resulting decline in ethnocultural homogeneity, this concentration of so much of bourgeois energy in business helped create new processes for the distribution of social authority. It left an opening for new sources of leadership. It presented the Catholic church with an opportunity to dominate local charities to needy Catholic immigrants, and even at times to Protestant foreigners and Americans, and thus to extend its social position. It assisted in the emergence of mass political parties and, in the 1850s, the political boss. Both fashioned electoral victories by courting and organizing the immigrant vote. That the bases of local authority did shift perceptibly before 1861 was evident in many ways. It was telling, for example, that while in 1836 news of impending economic difficulties immediately led workingmen to march on Rathbun's offices, during the next depression (1857–58) suffering workingmen, largely immigrants, marched on City Hall to make demands upon Democratic Mayor Dr. Timothy Lockwood, the city's most powerful political boss before 1861, and visited the Sisters of Charity soup kitchens to feed themselves and their families.¹⁰

In place of the grandiose, uncoordinated civic projects of the past, local leadership now dedicated itself to practical efforts to enhance commerce: it sought new methods to rationalize the organization of trade and reform its practices along ethical lines; it mounted aggressive campaigns in Washington and Albany in behalf of harbor improvement and widening the canal; and it attempted informally to consolidate a sense of interconnectedness and interdependence among the wide spectrum of men whose interests directly or indirectly lay on the docks. Self-interest obviously guided these activities. This is clear after 1843 in the case of efforts made in behalf of the improvement of the canal and harbor, the installation of sewers, gas, lighting, sidewalks, and a fresh water system, the paving of streets, and the creation of a more professional fire department and police force. Most enhanced the quality of urban life, but simultaneously each served the needs of business and industry by providing power, waste disposal, and protection for business and by facilitating the orderly movement of goods and people.

But self-defining and hegemonic processes—the actualization of a class morality and social ideology worthy of their views of themselves and of emulation by others—also lay behind these strivings. Under the era's assorted pressures, and with the painful memory of the recent collapse on their minds, disparate businessmen and professionals were abandoning the irresponsible, hyperindividualistic entrepreneurial style of the 1830s that had placed profit above all else. In its place they were forging themselves into a self-conscious bourgeois class with an ideology, life-style, code of conduct, and body of individual and group aspirations of its own. While elements of the life-style and values of this class were of necessity rooted in the past, it was the growing awareness of its singular, historic role, as much as its daily strivings for power and profit, that gave the process of class formation its dynamism. That this was a national development which, as the scope of markets became continental, linked ever larger numbers of a bourgeois class in the making intensified the process.[11] Relations with the salaried, white-collar employees and wage earners who worked for them also formed a vital thread of the process, though less so in the case of a commercial than of an industrial bourgeoisie, whose interactions with factory labor were conflict-ridden, tradition-smashing, and transformative. We shall leave to later chapters these interclass relations, and concentrate on processes internal to the group.

Perhaps it is true that the nation's antebellum leadership saw itself living unheroically in the shadow of the Founding Fathers' achievements.[12] Still, the work of marshalling the nation's vast productive capacities and forging modern markets while attempting to bring stability to the disorderly processes of capitalist development and urbanization posed its own significant challenges, which constituted participation in another sort of revolution—one no less revolutionary for not being recognized as such even by those who led it. It was not a political but an economic upheaval that sealed capitalism upon American society, and in the process demanded that people on every level of society reevaluate what had been largely unquestioned. In this revolution the merchants of Buffalo and the larger class of which they were the local core had a considerable role, because they were the stewards of the interregional commerce that tied the northern states together. Often the historical role of the bourgeoisie is equated exclusively with industrialization, while merchant capitalism is dismissed as an interlude in the economic transformation of the West. The point is easily exaggerated. Limited to commerce by the seemingly endless potential of Buffalo's location, the marginality of its hinterland, and the lack of inexpensive local sources of power, it was true that the Buffalo merchants could not utilize labor as effectively as industrial capitalists. Hence their power to create capital was impaired. This was the historic weakness of merchant capital everywhere. Yet the Buffalo merchants were self-conscious modernizers in their own right. In the brief hour of their preeminence, with all the intensity created by greed, self-interest, ideology, and culture, they embraced technology, pioneered methods to rationalize business organization, created economic infrastructure, and sought to fashion a moral basis for capitalism. They formed one bridge between the agrarian past and industrial future that enabled modern America to emerge.[13]

Not until the 1842 harvest were there signs that offered some real hope for the future. Fueled by strong eastern demand, early November was the busiest time in the port's history. With confidence returning, the local dock merchants began to make new investments in warehouses and equipment.[14]

These were to pay off richly. The year of 1843 began a period of unprecedented and confident prosperity, broken only by brief recessions in 1847–48 and 1854, and lasting until the 1857–58 depression. The amount of wheat transshipped through Buffalo grew from 1.4 to 2.8 million bushels in 1845–46 alone, while corn expanded by 1.5 million bushels, and flour by 460,000 barrels. The boom sent multipliers throughout the local economy. Population increased by 121 percent in the 1840s, rising from 18,214 to 40,261 by 1850, and doubled again to reach 81,129 in 1860. By 1847 the Main Street commercial district had expanded a mile to the north. "An army of mechanics" enjoying high wages were at work in November, 1847, as winter approached, attempting to meet the demand for homes by white-collar workers, merchants, and professionals, some of whom were awaiting completion of houses before moving their families from the East.[15]

The sources of this sustained boom were both national and foreign. Western production was increasing with the settlement of Michigan, Indiana, Illinois, and Wisconsin, all of which increasingly loomed as large as Ohio in Buffalo's trade. Grain and flour remained the chief commodities, but livestock and provisions grew after 1850 and stimulated the rise of a local meatpacking industry. Eastern demand was high, especially as grain production declined in New York State. In addition, there were the European crop failures of 1846 and 1847, and the repeal of the British Corn Laws in 1846, with the immediate consequence that October, 1846, saw the highest receipts in the local dock trade before 1861.[16]

This expansion led to the fulfillment of two related processes that were barely perceptible between 1825 and 1836. These were rationalization of the functions comprising the transshipment business, and consolidation into a self-conscious dock interest of the merchants and all those supplying them with ancillary professional and commercial services.

At the center of the interregional trade were forwarding and commission merchants, the owners of Buffalo's principal means of production, numbering by 1855 about 110 firms, which were mostly family-owned or partnerships among no more than two or three men. The forwarders, about 100 owners in thirty-five firms in the mid-1850s, were engaged in shipping, transshipping, and outfitting ships engaged in the movement of commodities, finished goods, and personal possessions, and in passenger traffic. They were themselves divided between those on the canal and those on the lakes, though a few firms had craft on both. The commission merchants, in contrast, comprised some 100 brokers in seventy-five firms that were engaged in providing more comprehensive services. They facilitated the transfer of finished goods, produce, grain, flour, and provisions from buyers to sellers through arranging insurance, shipping, transshipping, and storage. Some also provided banking and exchange services, such as remitting, collecting, endorsing, and advancing. They were usually employed by purchasers (for example, eastern millers) rather than sellers (such as western farmers), in effect making them the purchaser's western agent.[17]

After the depression Buffalo's commission merchants, especially those in grain, were proud that in spite of tempting market conditions they themselves did not purchase goods. Beginning in the early 1840s, the grain elevator made possible withholding crops from the market in anticipation of future price rises. But, said Merwin S. Hawley, a leading commission merchant, he did not choose to become a wholesaler and court the impulse to speculate. Buffalo did have its speculative grain wholesalers, but theirs was often a casual occupation. It arose episodically out of extraordinary historical circumstances, like the great European crop failures of the 1840s, among men with a surplus of cash who could with certainty anticipate price increases.[18]

In other fields, such as iron, dry goods, hardware, and groceries, there were large numbers of wholesalers who bought in the East and sold to the West. Some were auctioneers selling large allotments of diverse goods to retailers from other regions who gathered periodically in Buffalo to bid on stock. Others simply arranged shipping with local forwarders for those ordering through the mails. A few wholesaler firms bought large quantities of goods and shipped them to lake ports where agents put them on the market. This practice was common in the 1840s as new western lake ports, without a mercantile distribution system, arose.[19]

Working outward from this core of dock-situated functions, we find many professionals and merchants involved in providing services for commerce. A large number of businesses and services, from insurance brokerage to ship chandlering, took root after 1843.[20] By 1850 there were ten insurance firms catering to the needs of the harbor commercial firms, whose owners had helped found several of them, for fire and marine coverage.[21] A dry dock and seven firms doing ship and boat construction were established by 1855, and attached to them were planing mills and boiler and machine shops. More than a hundred hotels, lodging houses, and inns catered to passengers breaking their journeys at Buffalo. Banking, too, revolved around the needs of commerce.[22] The small, closely regulated banks founded after 1843 were largely engaged in discounting commercial paper for forwarders and commission merchants, collecting western notes, and buying and selling Buffalo and New York exchange.[23] Of Buffalo's 106 attorneys in 1855, a large number, especially among prominent firms, practiced commercial law. Routine tasks included replevining cargoes, collecting commercial debts, recovering the value of undelivered orders,[24] and, especially lucrative, the management of both dockside real estate and grain elevators. Owners of large holdings about the harbor—about two dozen families, prominent among them the Wilkesons, Wadsworths, Rumseys, Tiffts, Fargos, LeCouteulxs, and Joseph Ellicott's relations, the Evans-Peacock clan—all generated large amounts of land sales and rights-of-way agreements when railroads came to build track up to the docks. Even mundane tasks, such as paying municipal taxes and assessments, took up a lawyer's time when the holdings were as extensive as those of the Wadsworths, who owned ninety-five dockside lots in the 1850s, and engaged two firms simultaneously to manage their holdings.[25]

Considering that each of these port-related functions employed lower white-collar workers, artisans, and transport workers, the numerical significance of the cohort of local workers dependent on the health of the docks becomes clear. While estimates are difficult, by the mid-1850s probably 260 firms comprised of 400 partners, all of them Americans, were engaged in transshipment and ancillary services. These firms employed perhaps 2,000 sailors, boatmen, teamsters, ship carpenters and joiners, clerks, bookkeepers, and copyists, and an untold number of "scoopers" (who off-loaded grain) and other unskilled harbor workers.[26] It was from the educated, prosperous, upper ranks of this cohort that the energies needed to defend Buffalo's commerce usually came, but joining such people were many others outside the "dock interest" who understood its importance. Thus, while the forwarders and commission merchants and their various retainers could always be depended on to step forward in their own behalf, so, too, could many editors, retailers, manufacturers, and before the rivalry between the railroad trunk lines and the canal became bitterly competitive in the 1850s, railroad executives, even when it came to relatively small matters. An 1858 public meeting called to recommend ways to make the canal more successful in its battle with the New York Central chose a committee to investigate building steam-powered canal vessels. On it were not only five dock merchants and several of their more senior clerks, but an innkeeper, two retailers, three bankers, six lawyers, an editor, three manufacturers, two insurance brokers, and two local managers of western railroads that used the canal to ship east from Buffalo.[27] Such men often traveled in the same social circles as, and served on civic and corporate boards with, the harbor merchants.

Routine defense of the interests that intersected at the docks was left to the harbor merchants themselves. It emerged as one of the processes transforming the organization of commerce that began as the depression waned, and it commenced on individual and group levels. Individual efforts at money-making led to an expansion of trade, which in turn placed heavy burdens on the port. These necessitated collective, not individual, solutions and thus stimulated the organization of the merchants and the mobilization of their allies in supporting roles. Simultaneously a reformulation of commercial behavior and values was taking place, and it, too, inspired the movement for formal organization among the merchants.

One of the principal objectives of individual merchants was maximizing the benefit of the city's locational assets by consolidating their ties to both West and East. Several methods were utilized. Commission merchants established western connections through springtime visits to farming areas, where they circularized farmers and shippers, whom they promised advances, forwarding, and storage. When it was gradually discovered that these visits alone could not cast a wide enough net, western offices were opened, chiefly at Toledo. Western business ties were often built on personal ones. Merwin S. Hawley's brother, who was also his partner, had lived in Indiana and had extensive ties among the grain dealers there, and other branches of the family were established in business in Ohio. Buffalo's three Hollister brothers, all grain and wholesale grocery merchants, had seven brothers in Ohio with whom they did business. Nor were eastern markets neglected. Buffalo merchants in every field went, as often as twice a year, to New York City and Philadelphia to contact suppliers and purchasers.[28] These contacts were enhanced by technological advancements in communication and transportation. Telegraphic connections with the East which were completed in 1848 made possible close monitoring of eastern grain markets.[29] Markets were also integrated by the establishment of short-distance feeder railroads that connected with the canal and the lakes. Local merchants and other capitalists invested heavily in the creation in 1843, 1852, and 1853 of these cooperative lines, tapping nearby areas of Pennsylvania and New York and, in 1852, Ontario. Substantial investments were also made in the improvement of the technology for lake navigation. Until the 1840s only sailing vessels operated in the grain trade because, though less reliable than paddlewheel steamboats, they had a deeper draught and deeper holds. After the depression, local capitalists backed Buffalo shipbuilders in the development of the screw propeller, of which there were twenty-two on Lake Erie by 1847. These craft were not only faster than the paddlewheel, but had holds as deep as sailing ships, and they quickly won a significant share of the grain trade.[30]

Another investment in technology, the grain elevator, vastly affected the port. As the grain trade grew, local facilities for transshipping grain became inadequate. The method of unloading lake grain vessels was cumbersome and increasingly untenable: by means of a block and tackle, grain barrels were raised to the surface, where they were put on the backs of longshoremen. If the grain was shipped in bulk, it had first to be "scooped" into barrels. Storage was difficult because similar methods were needed to lift grain into warehouses. There was significant loss and damage in the lifting process, and an additional 25 percent of all grain was lost due to rain, wind, and carelessness. Under good weather conditions, often working late into the night by lantern, one crew would take a day to unload a boat carrying 2,000 bushels.[31]

Facing these obstacles, the Buffalo commission merchant, Joseph Dart, applied steam power to grain elevating technology. In June, 1843, Dart opened the world's first steam-powered storage and transfer elevator at the juncture of the Buffalo River and the Evans Ship Canal, near the lakeshore. Steam power allowed for the off-loading by a crew of six scoopers of 10,000 bushels in about three hours under optimal conditions. By 1860, improvements in lifting equipment as well as in techniques for weighing, screening, and cleaning grain enabled dockworkers to remove 15,000 bushels in the same number of hours—a week's work in 1840. Since it was possible for ships to go right into the massive elevators to unload, both transfer and storage were now safer for workers and less wasteful. It was hoped in the late 1840s that the vast increase in storage capacity would allow the grain trade to be spread throughout the year, for railroads could continue to ship the stored grain East after the canal and lakes iced over. By the time this became possible in the late 1850s, however, railroads had grown so competitive that they threatened both the primacy of the canal and the livelihood of the dock merchants.[32]

The number of elevators increased as a direct consequence of the increase in trade in 1846 and 1847, jumping from two to eight. By 1867 there were twenty-seven, including two floating elevators in the harbor, with a total capacity of 5,850,000 bushels.[33] The elevators were owned in partnership by the principal dock merchants, who came to see this as a logical expansion of their operations. Soon, too, manufacturers, retail merchants, and lawyers were investing in them. This had the effect of extending inland from the harbor the scope of those directly involved in the dock interest. Owners leased elevators to operators, who received 10 percent of the receipts, a figure formally arrived at in 1850 after a bitter price war. This cooperation was extended further before the Civil War, for though elevators continued to be separately owned, a cartel formed in 1859 to manage most of them jointly. Outside this cartel, however, was the much feared New York Central, which began to build its own local elevators in the late 1850s.[34]

While the elevators increased the capacity of the port, the inadequacy of the narrow, winding, shallow inner harbor remained, and merged with another problem—the no longer adequate breadth of the last few miles of the canal from Tonawanda to Main Street. There was a severe berthing problem at the docks. Vessels were sometimes backed up a quarter of a mile into the lake awaiting the opportunity to enter the inner harbor, while the traffic inside the harbor created congestion worse than that at any other lake port.[35]

Not long before the depression, the council attempted to establish some measure of efficiency and safety at the port. The council-appointed harbor master for the first time was given a duty beyond simply keeping order: he was allowed jurisdiction over standards of warehouse construction. The council, however, seemed to be reluctant to go beyond this modest measure on its own initiative and to prefer, as it would for years to come, to let the merchants dispose of those routine problems that arose daily at the docks. The councilmen preferred to become involved only when asked directly by the merchants for assistance. Before the depression the mercantile men were too absorbed in getting rich quickly to think about the matter.[36]

With recovery their concerns shifted dramatically. Development of the infrastructure of the port, and the creation of a Board of Trade and other formal organizations involved in the harbor's affairs, were important aspects of the merchants' transition from narrow, individual self-interest to a socially comprehensive class ideology that sought to remake the world in its own image. Efforts to improve the capacity of the harbor began in earnest in 1842 with a debate over strategies for improvement. Some wished to improve the outer harbor (the lake) by renovating piers, dredging the sandbar at the mouth of the Buffalo River, extending the primitive seawall that federal engineers had begun in 1838 just outside the inner harbor and building a breakwater south from Black Rock, and creating a channel across a narrow spit of land separating the Buffalo River and the lake just south of the harbor entrance. The other strategy was associated with Samuel Wilkeson, who criticized the former approach for providing space but not protection from the fierce storms that plagued the port and said that the seawalls would prolong the life of the ice cover in the spring and increase the depth of water in the lower town during storms. He proposed expanding the capacity of the inner harbor through an extensive system of ancillary slips and basins off the Buffalo River. The excavated material would be used to raise the level of the lower town as a safeguard against flooding.[37]

The two plans were not mutually exclusive, but money was still tight, and neither seemed cheap enough. By the mid-1840s the two sides felt confident enough to combine their approaches and seek funds to implement a plan conceived by former Democratic mayor, George Clinton. From a local viewpoint, the plan had the merit of rejecting any local assessments for improvements, and instead depending on federal and state monies. The state legislature and the Canal Board were to be asked, in the name of strengthening the competitiveness of the canal, to construct a ten-acre basin near where the inner harbor met the lake, widen the Buffalo section of the canal, connect the canal and the inner harbor, and complete work already begun on the Main-Hamburgh Canal, a narrow interior basin about a half mile east of

Main Street. In the name of uniting the nation, populating the West, and safeguarding national defense along the border, the federal government was asked to improve the outer harbor.[38]

In effect, it was being argued that what was good for Buffalo was good for New York State and the United States, an argument advanced with complete self-confidence by the Board of Trade, the Steamboat Owners Association, the merchants' own organ, the *Commercial Advertiser*, and, in spite of its Jacksonian principles, the Democratic *Courier*. Its postdepression revenues swelling, the state was persuaded to begin to fulfill Clinton's program with a $150,000 down payment, appropriated in December, 1847. Persistent lobbying would be required, but the state, with local help, eventually finished the Main-Hamburgh canal and built two other basins.[39] Enlargement anywhere along the canal was a political football, however, that would be kicked around from one legislative session to another. As early as 1838, a Whig legislature had appropriated funds, but the project languished, at first because of the depression and then because of Democratic opposition, particularly from counties outside the canal corridor, to a project which would create massive public debt. To Whig arguments that western trade would become so extensive that tolls would more than equal costs, most Democrats answered that railroads would eventually render the canal obsolete. Only in 1854 did extensive widening and deepening of the Buffalo section begin. By then, Buffalo merchants, fearing railroad competition, felt it in the city's interest to have the entire length of the canal enlarged. When that work was completed in 1862, the railroads had already emerged the clear victor.[40]

If frustration with the state's handling of canal improvement deepened the solid Whiggery that emerged among the majority of the local bourgeoisie in the 1840s and embarrassed the small cohort of American Democrats, so, too, did the response of the federal government. Washington not only refused to undertake the work, but actually backed off tasks such as dredging and maintaining the seawall that it had done routinely before 1840. Though the Whiggish merchants had allies in the White House (not the least of them their townsman Fillmore during 1849–53) a succession of Democratic and southern congressmen continued to argue that the harbor was Buffalo's affair. As the Whig party disintegrated in the 1850s, prospects for federal aid faded further.[41] The continuing inadequacy of the outer harbor did impair the work of the port. Though the inner harbor was eventually deepened enough to accommodate large ships and extended two miles inland, and though the dockside property owners themselves paid to have an additional channel cut between the lake and inner harbor, ships still routinely waited to dock along the storm-tossed, unprotected lakeshore.[42]

The type of activity involved in the campaigns for harbor improvement had an important influence upon class formation. Not only did it unify the constituent social and economic fragments of the multifaceted local economic elite, but it assisted the local bourgeoisie in clarifying class aspirations. In pursuing interests that they said were not merely self-interested, but vital to the civic welfare and future prosperity, to the extent that they provided employment and the bases of future growth, the merchants and their allies like Wilkeson and Clinton were gaining the self-confidence as a group to exert leadership in society's name.

The merchants sought in another way to define the quality of that leadership by setting moral standards to guide its behavior. The clearest example of this effort lay in the harbor merchants' and elevator operators' Board of Trade, which was founded in January, 1844. One of the first in the nation, the local board was a prototype for others soon to be established in response to the same felt needs. Located at the docks on the corner of Prime and Hanover in the modest Merchants Exchange Building, the Board of Trade commanded a symbolic location. On one side, it looked toward the central business district to the professionals, bankers, retailers, and politicians who were the dock merchants' principal allies. On the other, it faced Prime Slip and commanded a panoramic view of the inner harbor, and, beyond that, of the lake.[43]

The goals of the board were just as clear-sighted as the social understanding suggested by this dual exposure. The board did not see itself simply as lobby. It certainly did engage in lobbying in behalf of port improvement and canal enlargement, and in 1854–55 it singlehandedly spearheaded the failed efforts of Great Lakes harbor merchants to persuade the Pierce administration to support the dredging of the dangerous narrows at St. Clair Flats. Also, it was the negotiator between the harbor merchants and the local common council.[44] Yet it had broader goals than the lobby-minded groups formed in the 1840s and 1850s: the canal boat owners' Forwarding Association, the commission merchants' Corn Exchange, and the lakecraft owners' and captains' Steamboat Owners Association.[45] Its larger purposes were the reformation of commercial behavior and the reconstruction of relations within the trading community on the bases of trust, friendship, and ethical business principles, which in turn would create order and predictability in Buffalo's central commodity market. Russell Heywood, a flour merchant and insurance executive who was the board's founder and first president, stated in 1845 that the board had no wish to limit itself to giving "force and character to any project that may be started for obtaining the enactment of laws for the benefit of trade." Instead it sought primarily "to elevate the character of each member and of the city; to promote fair dealing and kindly feeling toward each other; [and] to establish precedence, rules, and usages for governing trade."[46]

Several methods were employed. First, a social atmosphere was created at the board's rooms conducive to open dealing and friendly relations. Here the harbor men "might mingle together and become better acquainted with each other and rub off many sharp corners of jealousy and selfishness." In the reading room one found commercial papers from all over the nation. In the social rooms men could exchange information about markets in a congenial setting. Visiting commercial men, too, could use the facilities to exhibit samples, place notices on bulletin boards, and put their names and local addresses in the visitors' log. Second, the board sought to standardize and open to public view all aspects of trade that might be subject to abuse. Among its first tasks were the creation of standards for inspecting and grading grain, a uniform bill of lading for canal and lake shippers, and a uniform scale of fees and commissions for the grain trade. Committees were established to monitor the application of these measures and to make recommendations for changes.

Third, in the belief that cutthroat competition was ruinous to individual interests and debilitating to the morale of the trading community, the board created a committee that met daily in open session during the season of navigation to recommend grain and potato prices based on market information collected from eastern and western sources. Fourth, various mechanisms were established for hearing complaints against members accused of unethical practices and for adjudicating disputes among members. The board's own directors were charged with the responsibility of investigating all charges of unethical behavior and making recommendations, including dismissal. An elected committee of those "well-versed in trade and commerce" was charged with "hearing and deciding all matters of difference without delay." The purpose was to avoid lawsuits between members, not only because the average jury, Heywood said, was "ignorant of commercial usages," but because litigation engendered "ill-will toward each other, perhaps for life," and hence created social division and moral disorder.[47] Board members were expected to use their attorneys for litigation *outside* the local trading community.

The board, therefore, was concerned, as George S. Hazard said on assuming the presidency in 1855, with creating "by example and carefully established precedent and customs," "landmarks and beacons" to guide those fashioning their public characters while working in the upper reaches of the transshipment sector. In the act of exerting moral authority, it was also disciplining the local bourgeoisie as a class, clarifying its goals, and helping it to define itself.[48] It employed both positive and negative incentives to bring its members into compliance with its principles and cooperation with its aims. It was not the only influence working toward these ends. Moral influences quite obviously came from the Protestantism that the bourgeois class shared. But religious influences are not easily traced. Take, for example, the question of Sabbath observation, which was central to the social program of evangelical reformers. There were few local harbor merchants as pious as the elevator operator James D. Sawyer, who was so seized with a sense of Sabbatarian obligation that he wrote into business contracts "that no work except that of necessity and mercy may be done on the Sabbath." Though they might frequently denounce desecration of the Sabbath by immigrant tavern keepers and religious processions, most Buffalo harbor merchants opposed Sabbatarian attempts to restrict commerce on Sunday. They led the battle against efforts to close the canal locks on Sunday which would impede the growth of the revenues needed to enlarge the canal.[49] The local evangelical paper, the *Christian Advocate*, was frustrated by the lack of direct influence between religion and business behavior. It warned that absorption in business compromised the merchant's spiritual well-being and, to the extent he made his employees work on the Sabbath, those dependent on him. But the "merchant princes" showed little sign of becoming the "missionary princes" the *Christian Advocate* wished them to be. No doubt they brought to their mutual relations a sense of how Christians should treat one another, and as we shall see, religion and church membership played an important role in ordering their lives beyond work. But they showed little self-conscious piety in business.[50]

The positive and negative incentives provided by the new institution of credit-reporting played a more direct role in inculcating and disseminating the new business ethics. The creation of credit-reporting also owed its origins to the effort to apply the economic lessons of the 1830s. But while the board's membership and influence were limited to a segment, albeit a most important one, of the bourgeoisie, credit-reporting spread rapidly to affect the thought and behavior of a large number of men, from peddlers to commission merchants, engaged in interregional markets. Credit-reporting thus illustrates the means by which a new class morality, founded on practical business calculations and diffuse cultural influences, was generalized hegemonically beyond the commercial elite to encompass not only bourgeois businessmen, but more obscure and plebeian small traders.

After the 1837 panic, with its massive credit collapse and defaulting, many businessmen involved in interregional markets recognized the need for up-to-date information on creditor assets and personal trustworthiness to replace the increasingly inadequate reliance on face-to-face relations and word-of-mouth communication. To fill this need, in 1841 Arthur and Lewis Tappan, New York City merchants and evangelical reformers, founded the Mercantile Agency. Run as a subscription service for eastern wholesalers doing business with inland merchants and manufacturers, the agency provided individual profiles derived from reports from the field. Reports were prepared twice a year by local attorneys, who were unpaid and offered their labor as a type of public service. While begun solely to serve eastern markets, by 1860 the agency had become a national organization capable of gathering and organizing data on the character and solvency of thousands of individuals ordering goods on credit from outside their own localities (and occasionally within their own bigger cities, too).[51] In consequence, the agency acquired great power over the informal social selection of those who were to profit, through the enhanced position credit afforded, from national economic expansion. This gatekeeping function was reinforced by the fact that, although subscribers were sworn to secrecy, gossip inevitably circulated about credit reports throughout mercantile networks. No less important than the economic were the cultural functions of credit-reporting. Credit-reporting served as a mechanism by which boundary markers were formed around acceptable commercial behavior. As such, it furthered class formation by stimulating the consolidation of class morality and behavior. This was all the more true because not only most of those commissioning credit investigations, but the investigators themselves, who were recruited out of the ranks of American attorneys, were inevitably bourgeois—or aspired to be so.[52] As we shall see, evaluations of character were grounded in the deepest and not always conscious recesses of culture. Thus, credit reports on individuals were also an important, and highly subjective and biased, device by which powerful, ethnocentric Americans interpreted objective ethnic differences to the detriment of immigrant businessmen who often brought culturally distinctive styles to running their enterprises. In this way, credit-reporting helped to order interethnic relations as it simultaneously and relatedly shored up the boundaries of American commercial morality.[53]

The knowledge that credit reporters worked in semisecret around them, interviewing neighbors, business associates, and customers and checking property deeds and private debts, deeply impressed local merchants. In addition to the knee-jerk resentments about spying articulated from time to time, this knowledge precipitated a measure of fear and a desire at the very least to *appear* virtuous. In an editorial ominously titled "We Are Watched," the *Christian Advocate* warned merchants that its editor, Methodist minister Rev. John Robie, while visiting New York City, had seen one of the agency's folio-sized ledgers with reports on hundreds of local entrepreneurs. "The object," he said, "is to know the responsibility of each." Distance did not make one safe from moral scrutiny: "A man's means, standing, and reputation are known in one place as well as another. The reason why some are not trusted in New York City is that they are known here." The lesson was clear, as Robie advised later. Drunkards and gamblers always needing money, "profane swearers," "breakers of oaths," and "schemers or wrongdoers in the name of profit" all were at risk in the competition for credit, the lifeblood of enterprise.[54]

With the aid of these various incentives, negative and positive, habits of moral introspection increasingly entered into the merchants' business practice and guided their relations with one another. The indications of the shift are subtle, but quite tangible. One of them may be seen in the growing emphasis on gentility in the merchants' self-evaluation. Gentility, which Stow Persons has defined as "the imposition of manners upon conduct" in situations in which such strongly coercive restraints as law do not exist to govern behavior, was called upon by the commercial gentleman to provide self-discipline. He sought, in effect, to "soften the contours of his aggressiveness with manners" which might "ease the friction" of personal and commercial relations.[55] Buffalo merchants gave evidence of valuing gentility. Sawyer, for example, wrote into an agreement governing the rental of an elevator that "the parties ... show proper respect to each other's opinions in regard to business and treat each other in a gentlemanly manner."[56] In a eulogy given the dock merchant Jacob Barker, the elements of the (wholly secular) character of "a true Christian gentleman" in business were listed: "fine intellect and much cultivation, a calm temperament, an amicable simplicity of character, and the most perfect integrity."[57] Self-possession and ethical constancy were particularly valued when demonstrated in adversity. To this extent, the record of one's behavior during panics and depressions constituted the ultimate mark of manhood and decency, and followed one through a career. Years after both the 1836–37 and 1857 financial panics, the author of a biographical sketch on Edward L. Stevenson, a local stagecoach line manager, real-estate broker, and bank director, commented at length on his subject's grace and probity under pressure. Stevenson, it was said, was one of the handful of men "whose wisdom, prudence, and foresight carried him safely through the panic of 1836 and other fiscal revulsions, in which such a large portion of the businessmen of the country were overwhelmed."[58]

The business practices consistent with gentlemanly character were frequently reviewed in the press and in autobiographies and eulogies. For Hawley, who boasted of his reputation as a "faithful commission merchant" in both the East and the West, business integrity had three characteristics. First, there must be no speculation. Throughout three decades in the grain business, he said in his memoirs, he had been proud of "never buying for my own account nor in any way becoming interested in the profits or losses—and seldom executing an order to buy for others." Second, one's practices must always be available for inspection: "My books and accounts were always open to the examination of any correspondent who desired it." Third, debts must be paid promptly: "Never did my note or acceptance pass the day of its maturity without being paid." This last point, when interwoven with ethical and decisive conduct during business crises, was especially important. Hawley was proud that, as president of the city's International Bank in 1857, he did not have to suspend payments on deposits. When the bank's reserves declined, he personally borrowed against his capital, at a high rate of interest, to keep the bank active.[59] George Tifft, an industrialist, banker, and dock merchant, was given the same praise for his behavior in 1857 as an endorser of $100,000 in debts of the Buffalo Steam Engine Company. "Under his management and superior financing skill," Tifft's biographer tells us, "the whole indebtedness was paid off in two years."[60]

A staunch advocate of the dock merchants, the *Commercial Advertiser* was ready to believe that such "honor and probity" characterized the entire group. It stated in 1856 that deals for large shipments of grain were often consummated on the strength of no more than a signature on a blank sheet or a verbal agreement. Moreover, the paper said, the dock men were "as staunch in their bank accounts as in their honor." Thus, when prices fell in 1855–56 because of poor weather on the lakes and the end of the Crimean War, and the commission merchants' percentages fell, Buffalo merchants were said to have displayed their integrity in their accustomed manner. "Dishonest men fail, put up their property out of [creditors'] hands, and make a nice thing of it." But in Buffalo there was only one failure, and it was done "Buffalo style": no property was spared in the effort to repay all obligations, and as a result a new firm lost all $75,000 of its capital. Dan Morgan, the most recent chronicler of the history of the grain trade, agrees with this general assessment. He maintains that the ethics of the nineteenth-century trade were never higher than during the period of Buffalo's preeminence.[61]

While the absence of public business scandal after 1843 is noteworthy, it is too much to believe that such praise is due every harbor merchant. It is enough to establish that new standards of commercial morality were being established by which these men judged themselves and judged others, and by which they staked their claims to public power and social authority. The new standards existed as much as a means of self-discipline as a self-confident description of real behavior. Indeed, only through moral self-discipline and probity in business relations could the self-confidence be gained to assert aspirations to create a new economic and social order. Moreover, the high visibility of owners in the family firms and small partnerships typifying the organization of the dock trade doubtless added the impetus of personal honor—and shame—to the assimilation of the new standards. Still, there could be no doubt that circumspect, prudent men known for their gentility, such as James D. Sawyer, had replaced Lance Palmer and Benjamin Rathbun as leaders among, and models for, local entrepreneurs.

Yet it was testimony to their fragility that these standards reigned no longer than the hour of the Buffalo harbor merchants' national economic preeminence. Technology and war would create temptations that proved more appealing for some among the next generation of merchants than the cautionary messages provided by local memories of the catastrophe of 1837–43. After the mid-1850s, the powerful combination of elevators, railroads, and the telegraph nearly guaranteed huge profits from speculative decisions to withhold large commodity shipments from eastern markets in anticipation of price rises. In the few years before the Civil War, markets were too depressed and uncertain for the implications of this situation to become clear. But in the volatile markets of the war years, during which grain prices soared, buying bulk grain and flour for speculation became common. Too, by then the city's locational advantage among inland ports was no longer assured, so the quick profit was a logical calculation amidst the shifting balance of interregional market forces.[62]

For the older commission merchants (men in their sixties by the war's end), said Hawley, "the growing propensity to deal with staple articles directly and speculate for individual gain" destroyed the possibility of engaging in "a remunerative and legitimate commission business."[63] It was a tribute to his generation that Hawley thought to pair the two adjectives. During the war, men like Hawley increasingly opted for semiretirement and began to immerse themselves in creating local cultural institutions, a project begun in the 1850s out of a sense of class obligation and a desire to assert American cultural identity and authority in what was by then an immigrant city. These efforts eventuated in the establishment of the Buffalo Historical Society (1862), the Buffalo Fine Arts Academy (1862), the Buffalo Society of Natural Sciences (1863), the Old Settlers Society (1864), and the Grosvenor Library (1865), all established so closely in time that they were powerful evidence of a reorientation of energies among Hawley's generation.[64]

But this is to get ahead of ourselves. Hawley's brief swan song may provide us with a way back. Its key words are "remunerative" and "legitimate," profit and principle, both of which marked the path in the process of antebellum bourgeois class formation. Both contributed powerfully to the synthesizing of the class sensibility and ideology that will gradually unfold before us as we look at the ways in which the times came to test the decency and durability of the civilization the merchants and their class allies were attempting to build.

CHAPTER 4

Culture, Ethos, and Ideology in Class Formation

THE social transformation by which the collection of speculating entrepreneurs of the 1830s was replaced by an increasingly unified and self-aware bourgeois class was multifaceted. It was comprised of mutually reinforcing generational, social, cultural, and ideological processes, which worked their powerful influences at the same time that the various efforts in behalf of the expansion, rationalization, and reformation of commerce worked theirs. In reality, none of these processes may properly be separated from the others, though historians may choose to look at them individually for analytical convenience. We should remember, however, that what gave this process of class formation its dynamism in Buffalo and elsewhere during the antebellum commercial revolution was the powerful force and rapidity of developments taking place simultaneously across a broad front.

This chapter will describe the vital elements of the bourgeois way of life, the various mechanisms of social reproduction by which an emergent class simultaneously reinforced its unity and achieved the daily continuity necessary to retain its coherence, wealth, and power, and the ideologically and emotionally conditioned mentality through which it interpreted and sought to mold its world. The class we meet now begins to defy the terminology created for describing it. Though "bourgeois" in its ownership of capital and of Buffalo's principal means of production, it was essentially "middle class," relative to its European counterparts, in the modesty of its domestically oriented life-style and in its self-acknowledged and at times self-mocking provincialism. We may legitimately call these people by the term "bourgeois," with its rich historical and literary associations, to acknowledge their place in the era's social hierarchy and their historical role as capitalist modernizers.[1]

In the next chapter we will proceed to another facet of class formation—the relatively close interclass relationships among Americans. American lower white-collar employees and skilled craftsmen shared much in the way of culture and many social and political attitudes with the local bourgeoisie, and while in their mutual relations there were some sources of conflict, nonelite Americans were nonetheless important sources of much of the identity-enhancing power and cultural authority the bourgeoisie enjoyed outside its own ranks. So, too, though to a lesser degree, were the most culturally similar to Americans of the city's immigrants—the British and Canadian Protestants; and they will be discussed in the same context.

Class formation took shape amidst powerful social and demographic changes in the character of the local elite. Just as the economic crisis swept away many of the enterprises and fortunes created in the 1830s, so, too, did it assist in the passing of the generation known as "old settlers" and facilitate the rise of new people. Born in the last three decades of the previous century, the old settler had usually arrived between 1815 and 1825. He prospered greatly in the next decade. The next seven years were ones of crisis, and by the time of recovery the old settler was in social and physical decline. A symbolic turning point in this generation's public role was reached in 1846 with the end of the tenure in office of William Ketchum, a retail furrier who was the last mayor born before 1800. Thereafter, not a year would pass without the death of one of these men of affairs, who had set the foundations, however unstable, for the city and its commerce.[2]

Fewer social traces of these pioneers would be found in the future than one might assume from their prominence in establishing the American presence on the Great Lakes frontier. To be sure, some intergenerational transfer of wealth, status, and power was apparent. It was seen, for example, in the manner in which Sam Wilkeson, Jr., and his brothers John and William built on their father's business achievements and personal reputation and emerged among the city's important manufacturers, publishers, bankers, and spokesmen for local commercial interests.[3] It was also seen in the continuity of wealth and power of the three generations of retail hardware merchants, the Pratts, whose residence predated 1812, and whose prominence, though shaken by the depression, went beyond 1860.[4] But just as men of Merwin Hawley's generation of dock merchants would later find it difficult to pass their eminence on to the next generation because of the changing nature of interregional forces and the grain trade, so, after 1836, had the generation that came before them. The principal reason was that the depression propelled families like the Palmers into debt and decline, which led their children to settle elsewhere in search of a fresh start, particularly when the alternative was to remain under vastly reduced circumstances.

In any case, the local bourgeois class would have to have been composed of large numbers of new people. The city's population growth after 1843 was so enormous, the expansion of local opportunity so great, and the rate of residential persistence, however much it varied among class and ethnic groups, so low, that it was more than likely in-migration rather than natural increase would account for the growth of all groups in the 1840s and 1850s, and this, too, effected the circulation of the elite. Michael Katz, Michael Doucet, and Mark Stern found that in 1855 Buffalo's professional and entrepreneural heads of households had on average lived in the city only 9.1 years.[5] A sample based on biographical sketches of sixty-three prominent men who made their careers before 1860 yields a fuller, but similar picture.[6] Of the fifty men on whom data was found regarding date of arrival, only fifteen (30 percent) had been born in the city or come there before age twenty. Of thirty-five (70 percent) who had come when over age twenty, twenty-six had been between twenty-one and thirty, and nine over thirty. Since eight in ten of these men had been born in the first two decades of the century, this would place their time of arrival between 1825 and 1840, after that of the old settler. Even those arriving before the depression were too young to have lost money or status in the debacle.

There were two consequences for class formation of this foreshortened pattern of intergenerational succession. First, in contrast to older, seaboard cities, Buffalo lacked a deeply entrenched "high society"—an exclusive network of old families of especially strong social prestige—within the local bourgeoisie.[7] Reflecting on "Manners, Customs, and Fashions," Samuel Welch correctly surmised the situation of the old settler families that survived the depression with either financial security or real wealth. Although a "few families" did have "a certain precedence" within the upper strata and gave the parties to which everyone wished to be invited, "success" at one's occupation became the measure of social standing, and "sycophancy or towdyism" were strictly frowned upon. To be sure, as Welch failed to tell readers, "success" was circularly tied to American ethnicity, education, parental affluence, and some connections upon arrival that might help one get situated in a career. But the point in this context is that the boundaries of the upper strata were permeable enough to accommodate the constant circulation of population that took place amidst the era's massive demographic shifts. Welch unconsciously attested to this point by including among the most elite "few families" Millard Fillmore's law partners, Nathan K. Hall and Solomon Haven. Both men were born in 1810, and had come to the city in their early twenties to begin legal careers, while the local origins of the families mentioned above, such as the Wilkesons, predated the canal. Closely connected with this pattern is a second point. Inheritance of a prestigious name was less a source of bourgeois affiliation than participation in the formation of a common way of life, based on commonly shared experiences, culture, and ideology.[8]

It is useful to have an experiential portrait of Buffalo's bourgeois men before proceeding to analyze the culture, attitudes, and ideas that endowed experience with meaning for them. The typical bourgeois professional, merchant, or manufacturer of the 1840s and 1850s had come to the city from somewhere else. Approximately 50 to 60 percent of the sample had been born in New York State of parents who were themselves natives of the declining farm country of western New England. In the 1790s this parental generation had migrated to Upstate New York.[9] While often of rural origins, the parents settled in villages in the counties of the Hudson Valley or, in many more cases, of what became the Erie Canal corridor. The higher commercial or professional status of these families is attested to in several ways. Only eight (13 percent) of sixty-three had been apprenticed, while forty (63 percent) were identified as having had some education—fifteen in common schools, eleven at academies, and fourteen at college. Only seven of these biographies are presented in the familiar rags-to-riches mode. Much, therefore, points to parental subsidies in the launching of careers.

After leaving school and before settling in Buffalo, most had experienced several types of employment and one or more relocations. They worked commonly as commercial or legal clerks or schoolteachers in New York State. They came to Buffalo in their twenties or early thirties to take positions as white-collar apprentices. They were clerks in dockside mercantile houses or retail shops, or read law at the invitation of relatives or parents' friends or men they themselves had met through past employment. A substantial minority (thirteen of the thirty-four whose early career patterns could be discovered) established their own businesses upon arrival. Most ultimately entered business. Of the fifty-two who could be said to have distinguished themselves principally at one endeavor over the decades, thirty-eight were in business, almost all of them in commerce, while the rest were lawyers (four), journalists (two), and doctors (eight). The origins of the capital on which mercantile careers were eventually launched suggests the possibilities and limitations of parental support. Of thirty men for whom data was discovered on the origins of such capital, only one acquired a business through inheritance and two through sale of the parental farm, while six sold businesses elsewhere before moving to Buffalo, and twenty-one combined parental gifts or loans with other monies. However modest the degree of parental support, this material assistance, combined with the social connections parents helped to provide, placed these men in a privileged position at the start of their lives in Buffalo. But they were hardly privileged enough not to have to work hard in pursuit of their career goals, which is attested to, for example, by the fact that Buffalo's most successful, first-generation commercial firms were not corporations, but for the most part small partnerships and family enterprises. Thus, they could legitimately conceive of themselves as self-made men, for they were more makers than inheritors of their fortunes. Yet what subsidies their careers did enjoy were rooted in family and other primary social networks, and this casts a somewhat ironic light on the much mythologized individualism of the nineteenth-century bourgeois man of affairs.[10]

With the creation of an economic base came the setting down of familial and other personal roots. The young men working in white-collar occupations often came alone, even when married, which helps to account for the imbalance in the sex ratio in 1855 in the American-born population ages twenty to twenty-five (157) and twenty-six to thirty (139).[11] Men such as Merwin S. Hawley, who at twenty-six began his career as the dockside representative for a firm of Rochester millers, believed that Buffalo was a rather disreputable place to which wives must not be brought until suitable arrangements had been made for lodging and the company of respectable society. Several years would pass before Hawley felt secure enough financially and trusting enough of his living situation to bring his wife to live with him at a lodging house owned by an old school friend. The young couple would live in this homelike setting for five years before building a house on exclusive Niagara Square.[12]

The Hawleys' early residential experience was typical. Married or single, young bourgeois men frequently at first lived in the homes of employers, friends, or relatives. Hawley, however, was actually on the border of two experiences. Though he resided in rooms at a boardinghouse, it was a *friend's* house nonetheless. Only a small minority of Buffalo residents actually lived in commercial boardinghouses, which comprised only slightly less than 3 percent of American residences in 1855. Boarding was then not an impersonal matter, but rather living with family or friends.[13] That so many young, white-collar Americans found such housing accounts for the singular pattern of many American households. Americans had the city's most complex households, and this was especially evident in the case of the bourgeoisie, which often had coresident individuals beyond the nuclear family. Fully 43 percent of American households, compared to 28 percent for the Irish and 18 percent for Germans, fell into the categories of extended (coresident with kin), augmented (coresident with unrelated people), or augmented-extended. For American retailers the figure was 58 percent, for commission merchants, 65 percent, and for lawyers, 63 percent. In such households coresident relatives were likely to be young kin of working and marrying age rather than parents.[14] The Hawleys' experience is representative here, too, for Merwin's unmarried brother Elijah lived with him. The Hawley brothers brought the sons of a cousin and of a friend to Buffalo to groom them for partnership in the firm. If the data on the households of commission merchants is any indication, it is likely that these two young men for a time lived with the Hawleys.[15]

For those not married when they arrived, marriage became a growing possibility with stability of employment, which was guaranteed by the post-1842 boom. By age twenty-seven, over 50 percent of all American men were likely to be married. It should not be surprising that they married women who, though a few years younger (by twenty-four, over 50 percent of American women were married), were very much of the same status and background. Only 15 percent of Americans in 1855 were married to immigrants, and two-thirds of these marriages involved British or Canadian immigrants, probably of the same class.[16] From the young woman's perspective, the city was an ideal marriage market, and this helps to explain why many unmarried sisters and nieces came there to reside with friends and relatives contemporaneously with the migration of single men. More choice among eligible bachelors was possible than in the small towns in which they were reared.[17] Intraclass marriage over a period of decades created a complex web of relationships among bourgeois families.

The relationships between class, occupational stability, and optimism about the future are apparent in the extent of home ownership within the bourgeoisie. Property ownership among Americans grew with residential persistence. Thus, between two to five years, and ten to fourteen years of local residence, it reached 32.5 percent and 57.5 percent, respectively. In all, 43 percent of the American-born owned property. Among bourgeois people, the figure was much greater. Among professionals, 91 percent owned property, while from 75 to 80 percent of the various groups of merchants did. The point at which the powerful aspiration for a home could be realized for American men was in their late twenties or early thirties.[18] By then the couple had already had one child and were possibly contemplating another. During these years, therefore, the problem of raising children in another's home combined with a desire for privacy and domesticity, bright hopes for the future, and the desire for a long-term investment to stimulate bourgeois home-buying.

In turn, the pressure of these young families on the real-estate market widened the geography of bourgeois residence considerably. Also stimulating this spatial mobility was the expansion of all types of commerce, including the growing trade in livestock, into the elite neighborhoods immediately adjacent to the central business district. Now the boundaries of the elite corridor on the West Side were pushed north approximately a mile and a half into one of the city's remaining forests. Homes on exclusive Delaware Avenue and only slightly less prestigious Pearl, Franklin, and upper Main Street enjoyed large lots, tree-lined streets and stone sidewalks. New, narrower cross-streets, more intimate and cheaper with their smaller lots, developed in between the grand avenues to accommodate the demand among both elite and nonelite Americans for homes and land.[19] The concentration of Whiggish bourgeois householders on Delaware was so evident in 1853 that the *Courier*'s editor suggested that the street's name be changed to "Fillmore Avenue."[20]

The ideal world of the bourgeois neighborhood and home as conceived in the imaginations of their inhabitants contrasted markedly with the image of Buffalo found increasingly in the Whig press, which daily served up a disturbing mix of violent crime, poverty, prostitution, drunkenness, and hellish scenes of depravity and destitution, especially among the immigrant poor. Behind the neat white fences and well-kept front lawns in the semiruralized precincts of these new elite neighborhoods, home was, in one guise, a private retreat from the dangers, disorder, and competition of the city. The juxtaposition of street, home, and neighborhood, as we see them in contemporary prints, suggests this desire for a private haven. These were neighborhoods intended for limited casual street interaction. Picket fences and trees stood guard over the front door, and the most habitable outside spaces were not in front, but in the wooded and high-fenced back gardens. The large frame homes of two and often three stories were also built as if to provide a sense of interior spaciousness and diverse visual options to combat winter's claustrophobic malaise.[21]

Home was also a focus for those bourgeois perfectionist energies bent on establishing what seemed so illusive in the city-at-large: order and stability within a framework of mutual regard and self-restraint.[22] In this way, domestic ideology offered a private analogue to the public and entrepreneural ideology being established by the Board of Trade and the other agencies of commercial reconstruction.

The composition of these households was tailor-made to allow each of the principal members to play a role closely fitted to the requirements of domestic ideology. Large houses and large, complex households, composed frequently of a nuclear family, relatives, and unrelated lodgers such as business apprentices, presented considerable demands regarding laundry, shopping, cleaning, and food preparation. Such a setting was surely a challenge to the bourgeois woman in her well-defined capacities as a "true woman"[23]—mother, wife, nurse, perhaps aunt or sister-in-law, and, in the case of fully 40 percent of American households, overseer of a staff of servants, almost all of them Irish or German immigrant girls.[24] For his part, the *pater familias* commanding this microcosmic patriarchy might exercise enlightened authority, in line with new strictures requiring love, patience, self-control, and mutual respect in familial and social relations, when he returned from the office each night.[25] Nothing so warmed the hearts of these Buffalonians as the image of a winter's evening on which mother and father convened the family circle before the hearth in a parlor offering fine, leatherbound books, a checkerboard, and children's toys for amusement.[26] The particular amusements might change, but such scenes could be anticipated for many years to come for new families. Male and female alike, the children of American bourgeois families remained resident at home longer than children of any other group or class, and thus prolonged the coherence of the family circle and the opportunity for parental surveillance.[27]

Doubtless many a bourgeois family attempted to, and perhaps actually did, live this scenario of tranquil domesticity, as the very occasional glimpses afforded us by the Hawley or Burwell diaries and the Fillmore papers suggest. Yet, like other utopian schemes, the idealized bourgeois family and household proved more successful in theory than practice. Perhaps the weakest link in the chain of perfect domesticity was the bourgeois woman. Such local domestic ideologists as Rev. John Lord, Dr. Foote, and Charles E. West, the first principal of the exclusive Buffalo Female Academy, which opened in 1851 to provide bourgeois girls with their first local opportunity for secondary education,[28] saw the "true woman" as bound by duty to family and home, with no social outlets beyond church and church-based charitable work. These private and public activities were linked, because in diverse ways they realized woman's purpose: to be, in Lord's words, "a hand ever ready to succor the needy and minister to the world." But open to women the world of civic affairs, West said, "of politics [and] caucus meetings, with all their concomitants, tobacco and profanity," and they would be unsexed. "We shall have," he warned, "female governors, female legislators, judges, sheriffs, to say nothing of generals and commodores." "Amazons," huffed the usually subdued *Commercial Advertiser*, commenting on an 1852 women's rights convention. The young girl must be instructed to direct her ambitions outside the public sphere. As West said, girls must be "encouraged to exercise self-control and to cultivate all those graces of heart and manner which give luster to the cultivated and refined woman." They must look upon the world only "to study its matchless beauty" and look within themselves "to see a miniature deity, a living soul, and train it for the skies."[29] A number of bourgeois women gave evidence of finding this sentimental idealism wanting, and through temperance activism and welfare work among the poor, they reached out beyond household, family, and church to save an unregenerate world for the values they were taught to believe they exemplified.[30] These women thus also gave evidence of understanding the limitation of any categorical distinction between public and private of the type regularly made by West, Lord, and others. Behind the public displays of good-humored indulgence, their menfolk probably were more than a little vexed by the muted, mannerly criticisms of the world they were fashioning by women of their own class. These women pointedly threw back at them the pious rhetoric of a common Christian, bourgeois culture to justify their claims to greater social influence. They seemed willing also to risk neglecting the home, the one social environment, unlike the marketplace, immigrant neighborhoods, and mass politics, that actually seemed amenable to practical control. Worse perhaps, female activism made politics a subject for discussion, or worse still, debate, in the sacred precincts of the home.

Other household members proved as restless as the bourgeois helpmeet. Whatever their outward compliance, children may well have resented the close scrutiny to which they were subject in such households. Enough young men of this class moved away from Buffalo during the early years of their careers that their rate of residential persistence, in spite of the great opportunities they enjoyed, was little different from that of less affluent Americans.[31] Some of them must have been seeking opportunities to get out from under the parental thumb, which may well have included supervision by father at the office, as well as looking for new career opportunities. And enough bourgeois young men raised hell in the brothels and taverns of the docks that the matter became a subject for commentary in the *Christian Advocate*.[32] With many bourgeois girls remaining at home years beyond Irish and German peers,[33] doubtless more than a few looked eagerly to marriage to free them from parental observation and to provide the opportunity to run their own households.

Domestics, too, could be a problem. Some servants, such as the Hawley's Bridget O'Brien, integrated themselves deeply into the emotional life of the family and were left handsome sums in their employers' wills. (O'Brien got $1,000.)[34] But not all domestic servants were tractable or good-humored, and those who hired servants frequently seem to have recognized that inherent in employing them was an untenable combination of market and personal relations. We shall see that bourgeois employers of domestics, especially of Irish servant girls, complained incessantly about their haughtiness, ingratitude, and insubordination.

While family and household might have fallen short of fulfilling all the idealized emotional functions, both ultimately had meaning beyond those functions. Seen not from the experiential perspective of contemporaries, but from the perspective of class formation, both successfully served the needs of social reproduction by providing a basis for continuity in daily life, personal security, and socialization of the young in the behavior and aspirations of the group into which they were born.

The same may be said, too, of bourgeois social and recreational life, which were usually practical extensions of the household and family. The rhythms by which both developed were tied to the seasonal cycle of commerce as well as the life cycle of individuals. The former was probably most directly at the center of consciousness during the canal era. The months from the opening of navigation to the icing up of the canal and lakes were ones of intense labors for those engaged in any aspect of commerce. Men regularly worked to nine in the evening six days a week, at a pace which was most intense just after shipping resumed in April and during the six-week harvest season, when farm commodities and the last orders of eastern finished goods were shipped. The pace was intensified for the merchant who took an annual business trip west or east in May or June to visit suppliers and shippers. Vacation came during a few weeks in August when, in anticipation of the busy fall season and in fear of cholera, many bourgeois families went to Upstate spas and mountain retreats.[35]

When navigation closed in November or early December, however, what contemporaries called the "gay season"[36] began. This was a period of several months of intense socializing made possible by the slowing down of business activity. It loomed as large a source of excitement as the image of a snowy winter evening before the hearth was one of security, and in the normal course of things, one alternated with the other to set the winter's agenda, along with the occasional lecture, revival, and other types of tonic for the spirit and mind. Among the many things lost when the railroad triumphed and commerce became a twelve-month affair were the cozy isolation of the long winter and this intense winter social schedule.[37]

The "gay season" consisted of "parties, balls, soirees, musical and otherwise private entertainments, theatricals, and tableaux vivants," given once or twice a week.[38] Preachers, such as the Presbyterian minister Grosvenor Heacock, urged moderation in the name of mind, body, and morals, and decried the intensity of the season as an unhealthy reaction to the obsessive work routines of the balance of the year. For its part, the *Commercial Advertiser* urged moderation on the grounds of expense. By October, the paper said, "Pa" had already begun to contemplate up to $1,500 for "giving an evening," complete with catered supper and fine wines. "Ma," it was said, was deciding on new clothes and jewels for her and the daughters. As an antidote to conspicuous consumption, the paper suggested smaller guest lists, light refreshments, and at-home parties rather than those in rented halls.[39]

But the festivities were often kept at an extravagant level that displeased press and pulpit. The reasons for this indulgence go beyond status-seeking, the desire to compensate for months of hard work, or a need to break up the colorless, long winter, though all are relevant. Also involved was the need for creating continuities that sustained the group. In the winter the social networks that constituted informal, face-to-face communities within the bourgeoisie were revitalized after suffering some because of the press of business. Just as the winter's evening before the hearth reinvigorated commitment to each other and to common values and attitudes, so did the activities of the "gay season." This was, furthermore, a time for courting and making those matches that formed the basis of new families and households. No less is suggested by the number of visits during the winter from small-town nieces, granddaughters, and other young female friends and relatives. These seasonal visits simultaneously served to strengthen the tight networks of female friendship, spanning space and decades, that were a conspicuous part of nineteenth-century women's culture.[40]

Seasonal rhythms also had a profound influence on the spiritual activities of the evangelical Protestant churches attended by all classes of Americans. In their early history, revivals were assumed to arise spontaneously. Yet it soon became clear that winter was the best time for them in the cities, because of the increase in leisure. (As a local minister said of Buffalo in the winter of 1831, there is nothing to do "but attend to preaching and pleasure.")[41] In spite of clerical efforts, however, not every winter saw revivals. In the 1850s the various pressures and moods that led to revival activity asserted themselves, with greatly uneven intensity, only in 1851, 1856, and 1858.[42] Among the bourgeoisie and middling Protestants who shared the lessening of work and increase in leisure in the winter, revivals in these years were scheduled not to interfere with work or the social calendar. The 1858 revival was by far the most popular and emotional of the decade—one which drew in even the Episcopal churches, the most uniformly higher-status denomination. The depression caused its particular intensity. But the economic crisis had begun in August, 1857, six months before the first revival activity. It seems apparent that the preoccupation with financial trends and end-of-the-year shipping, and then with the Christmas-New Year's heart of the "gay season," put off until mid-January the religious confrontation with human materialism and arrogance, the usual ministerial explanation of "financial revulsions." It was perhaps with these thoughts in mind that Rev. John Robie of the *Christian Advocate* editorialized bitterly as the 1858 revival waned at winter's end, "Our people have been accustomed to thinking that religion is something for winter months," and would now unreflectively return to business as usual.[43]

Robie's warning provides a suggestion about the role not simply of revivals, but of religion generally in the lives of bourgeois Buffalonians. Though diffuse religious influences entered into their conception of business ethics, we are not likely to find many examples of genuine piety in most bourgeois men, especially in prosperous times. Indeed, few are the extant biographies and memoirs of these men that suggest deep and abiding religious concern. The *Christian Advocate* spoke of this lack of profound religiosity so frequently that it is worthwhile attempting to ascertain the quality of religious belief among bourgeois men. The evangelical paper, which gave high praise routinely to those whose piety led them to leadership in local Bible and missionary societies, did not say that the rest were steeped in greed or vice, let alone that they were unregenerate sinners, but it did claim that "their religion and Christian obligation lessen in proportion as the responsibilities of trade and pecuniary interest advance." "Immersed as they are and must be necessarily in their chosen and accustomed pursuits of life, they give themselves little time for self-examination and those devotions which are so essential to a sound and healthful Christian experience." Thus, many exhibited that dangerous spiritual apathy that Robie claimed was caused by materialism. The best that could be said was that they "simply go to church and dispense charity with little reflection."[44]

There could be no doubt of the centrality of the social and cultural, as distinct from the spiritual, functions of religion in these male lives, or in the life of the group itself. It was the social maturation of the generation of bourgeois families formed after the return of prosperity that accounted for the rapid expansion of elite congregations. The older church buildings in and around the central business district proved too small to accommodate the rapid influx of single men ("young, enterprising businessmen," the *Courier* said, characterizing the overflow population at First Presbyterian) and new families desiring admission. These churches also were too distant from the new, northerly neighborhoods. Satellite congregations were now being formed in these areas, and they were said, in the case of both the Presbyterians and Episcopalians, to account for the growth of the former from three to ten, and the latter from two to seven, churches between 1842 and 1860. While it did not choose to establish satellites, First Unitarian, Fillmore's congregation, required extensive enlargements as its numbers grew. Though less elite, both Baptists and Methodists, among whom there were nonetheless such prominent men as manufacturers William Dobinson, Sherman Jewett, and Francis Root and dock merchants S. H. Fish and Pearl Sternberg, also increased their numbers of bourgeois and less elite congregants alike, and they, too, established churches in new neighborhoods.[45]

Laying aside the *Christian Advocate*'s disapproving, if partly true, view that the affluent attended church only because it was customary and fashionable, it is not difficult to understand the sources of their religious impulses. Many men doubtless followed their wives to church, for it was "a common situation," Robie said, for women to be pious and avid after religion, while the men were apathetic.[46] For many bourgeois women, in addition, church was not only the focus of spiritual striving, but one of the few opportunities for activity and responsibility outside the confines of the home. Moreover, it was the ideal place to reach out after those values of piety, purity, and self-abnegation proclaimed by "true womanhood." Even if some men simply accompanied their wives, or were made to do so, and shrewdly saw going as a way of hedging their bets against eternal damnation, church also had its strong symbolic functions for them. More than other branches of Christianity, Protestantism stimulated commitment to the values of individualism, self-reliance, and temperate, rationalistic behavior that girded the bourgeois character. Even Dr. Lord's more world-denying, Old School Presbyterianism embraced worldly prosperity as a sign that America was favored by God.[47] Furthermore, the more disciplined commercial capitalism that emerged in the 1840s depended upon a certain degree of decency and humility in social and personal relations. Protestantism encouraged this behavior, and in bad times amplified the message, as ministers and revivalists alike told people they must be self-effacing and contrite before a God they had angered. Humane mutual relations among men daily competing for status, wealth, and power were also encouraged by attendance at the same churches, or simply by participation in a common religious exercise every Sunday within separate but historically related denominations. Thus, in diverse ways, religion at once bound the bourgeoisie together, while etching more deeply the contours of its self-definition.

Sectarian animosities, however, did tend to impair the fullest realization of these unifying, intraclass functions of religion. The principal intraclass denominational cleavage was between evangelicals, especially Presbyterians, and Episcopalians. Probably as a result of complex patterns of chain migration that began in the precanal era, Buffalo was one of the few new, interior cities where Episcopalians were present in large enough numbers to be competitive with Presbyterians in elite circles. The lists of wardens, vestrymen, and ordinary congregants of St. Paul's (1817), Trinity (1836), St. John's (1845), St. James (1854), and Church of the Ascension (1855) read like a roster of the members of the Board of Trade, bench and bar, and medical profession.[48] The Episcopalian presence was a disturbing one for some evangelicals. Dr. Burwell reported that at a dinner party in 1846 at the home of a fellow Presbyterian, the prestigious attorney Heman Potter, much abuse was heaped upon Episcopalians, even to the point of lumping them with Catholics. The *Christian Advocate* often baited Episcopalians. It accused them of being uncharitable beyond their own denominational borders, guilty of Romanist doctrinal errors, and "none too liberal in their views of other Christians."[49] These tensions were probably exacerbated at the time because in doctrine Episcopalians were moving somewhat further from the evangelical sects. Buffalo's Episcopal churches, especially the eminent St. Paul's, were mildly touched by the High Church influences associated with the Oxford Movement. They displayed growing interest in the sacraments and in ritual, at the expense of preaching. All the while, however, like the evangelical churches, they participated in the major 1858 revival, and had strong traditions of congregational self-government and collective endeavor that were especially manifested in the establishment of new congregations.[50]

Denominational feeling was not limited to this one cleavage. Methodists lived with memories of the efforts of Presbyterians in the 1820s and 1830s to block them from becoming established in the city. Unitarian minister George Hosmer, who arrived in the city to take his pulpit in 1836, said that his church also for some years felt the hostility of the local Presbyterian establishment. Dr. Lord, who himself battled against his New School coreligionists, did a great deal to make Hosmer and his liberal, rationalistic church unwelcome. Nor was the temporary organization of a Congregational church, because of a schism among some Presbyterians over the great revival of 1833–34, a happy day for relations among Protestants. It fractured the national Plan of Union by which the two denominations had promised to cooperate rather than compete.[51]

How far such cleavages actually stretched beyond doctrinal matters and congregational rivalries to poison business relations, draw exclusive boundaries around communal social networks, or influence civic affairs is difficult to say. Hosmer claimed that they did. He charged that Oliver Steele, a Unitarian, was dismissed from his position as the first school superintendent because of prejudice stirred up by, he said, "Trinitarians." But it seems more likely that partisan feeling and party needs divided the outspoken Jacksonian Democrat Steele and a new Whig city administration, which coincidentally might have contained a disproportionate number of Episcopalians.[52] Certainly political and civic affairs seem to have been conducted without reference to interdenominational Protestant rivalries. Civic boards and bourgeois charities, such as the Buffalo Orphan Asylum, regularly contained large numbers of Episcopalians.[53] It would have been unthinkable to run either the city or a charity without them. As we shall see, too, when presented by mass immigration and the subsequent growth of the Catholic church, which represented a more disturbing pluralism than the multiplicity of Protestant sects, bourgeois Protestants made very deliberate ecumenical efforts in the name of Protestant unity.

Bourgeois participation in voluntary associations, like their religious activity, also evolved in patterns related to the life and seasonal cycles. Young bourgeois men, most newly arrived, created a number of associations during the antebellum years. These, as Mary Ryan has said of similar organizations at Utica, were "based on common interest, age, and status," and nourished "warm, democratic, mutually supportive ties." They provided many men with a surrogate family before they could afford to start their own. These ties, and ones made simultaneously through church, followed men through the life cycle, helping to provide them with a routine of activities and lifelong networks of friends.[54] The Young Men's Association was founded in 1836 by "the young men employed in our commerce" to stimulate mental culture and fight "dissipation" during the winter through an active program of lectures, debates, and exhibitions and the maintenance of a library. The concern of the lectures was usually close to the hearts of members. Speakers explored the relationships between self-help, self-culture, and success. The organization proved so popular that its maturing founders were reluctant to resign. In the early 1850s about one-fifth of its four hundred members were middle-aged bourgeois men, such as Fillmore, Haven, and Hall, who were considerably above forty, the age defined by the bylaws as the upper limit. These "life members" contributed heavily to the association's treasury, and helped through their extensive contacts to maintain its excellent programs, which nonetheless continued to cater mostly to young professionals and businessmen.[55] Also mixed by age, but catering particularly to young, well-connected bourgeois men were the Odd Fellows' lodges, which were established after 1843. The Odd Fellows' mutual benefit, recreational, and home-away-from-home features, such as reading and club rooms, appealed to single (hence, "odd") men. The schedule of activities was most complete in the winter. But, as in the case of the Young Men's Association, the young men who pioneered the order proved reluctant to leave as they aged. By 1852, among the approximately 1,000 Odd Fellows, the *Courier* said, were "many of our most valuable citizens."[56]

There were a number of voluntary associations less integrated by age. By virtue of the vigorous nature of the efforts required, the voluntary fire companies were comprised exclusively of young men, though sponsored by older, wealthy ones. At least two of the twenty companies were composed solely of bourgeois young men—or those closely connected to the class: Red Jacket Engine Company #6 was made up of bookkeepers, clerks, and younger partners of Main Street retail shops; and Washington Engine Company #5 had a similar social base, but was recruited out of the dockside mercantile houses. The latter had the distinction of owning its own pews at Dr. Lord's church.[57] The Young Men's Christian Union, founded in 1852 and forerunner of the YMCA, was another activity solely for young white-collar men. Founded by sons of very prestigious families, it provided a library and reading rooms and a supportive, Christian atmosphere for new residents, and within two years had 600 members.[58] Other voluntary associations catered exclusively to older men. The Masons were the most socially exclusive fraternal, and the older lodges and the upper ranks of the order generally were constituted of the principal bourgeois professionals, merchants, and manufacturers, who affiliated in large numbers as the order regrouped after the collapse of the anti-Masonic politics of the 1830s.[59] The same cohort of older bourgeois men dominated the civic boards constituted after 1842 to govern new institutions and organizations—the University of Buffalo, the Buffalo Orphan Asylum, the Buffalo Association for Relief of the Poor, Buffalo General City Hospital, the City Temperance Union, the American Bible Society, the American Seamen's Bethel Society, and the City Missionary Society.[60]

Charity and much of the practical work of moral reform, however, were the province of bourgeois women. They had substantial assistance from young, unmarried women, who, unlike men of the same age, lacked their own voluntary associations and participated in those of older, married women. Two activities preoccupied bourgeois women and served with church and literary societies to round out their activities outside the home: in both temperance and poor relief, women were more active than men of their class, and were guided by a rather different vision. To be sure, like women's efforts, men's activities were guided by an impulse to do good and spread virtue, according to bourgeois definitions, while curbing social disorder, especially when it was rooted in the lower classes. Men were constrained by capitalist ideology and by the practical realities of the workaday world, and such constraints created a certain cynicism or resignation in the face of acknowledged moral evils. Women did not encounter these realities directly, and the constraints on their efforts were mostly imposed by patriarchal gender ideology, which they ordinarily accepted. Yet "true womanhood" could be redefined in activist ways that led women, in the name of spreading female virtues to the world beyond the home and making the world safe for the home, to a reformism that men shunned.

Though individual women in the 1840s were involved in church temperance work, not until 1850 did women have their own temperance organization. In that year the bourgeois Ladies Temperance Union was formed. The wives of all clergymen, editors, and physicians, professions judged potent at influencing public opinion, were automatically vice presidents, if their husbands would pledge not to use alcohol. A number did, including almost all the Protestant clergy. While the male City Temperance Union had done little more up to then than seek to establish individual moral examples, and infrequently to ask for enforcement of the local alcohol laws, the women now established a larger field of action. In addition to employing public education and moral suasion to reform drinking men of their class, beginning in 1851 they campaigned vigorously through petitions and public letters for enforcement of the long-dormant municipal licensing laws. Knowing the opposition to such laws in the politically potent immigrant majority, which possessed drinking cultures that did not see alcohol as immoral, and respecting the right to make a living of the approximately five hundred men engaged by 1855 in distilling, brewing, and selling alcohol, most bourgeois politicians and men of affairs were loath to enforce these laws, whatever their own personal attitudes toward alcohol.[61] The women's initial campaign thus got nowhere,[62] and they began with some male allies to shift their focus toward a statewide prohibition law.

Women's multifaceted activities in behalf of the poor had a common denominator—concern for children. Women managed and raised money for the Buffalo Orphan Asylum, the most successful Protestant charity, though men had founded and continued to govern it.[63] Women themselves created and maintained the Industrial Association and School (1853). Its purposes were markedly different from male efforts for the poor. The men's Buffalo Association for the Relief of the Poor (BARP) had been organized in 1850 to prevent street begging, but sought to help, through noncash home relief, only the "worthy" poor, whose worthiness was determined through home visitations and various tests of means. The women's school, on the other hand, lacked a punitive edge; it made no effort to sort out poor people by moral criteria. Moreover it was proactive; its intention was to teach useful skills and stimulate self-help. The school opened early each winter. Its purpose was to instruct young girls to do sewing for their mothers, who, it was assumed, were too busy to undertake the same activities. The girls were taught to make and mend winter garments, using donated clothing and fabrics. From twenty-five girls and two teachers the first winter, by 1857 five hundred girls and fifty teachers were involved. About 75 percent of the pupils were Americans, for though the vast majority of the poor were Catholics, the women claimed that priests discouraged parishioners from attending out of fear of Protestant proselytism.[64]

The social functions of women's welfare work for the creation of a world in the bourgeois image cannot be underestimated. Like the BARP, the women's school helped to check poverty, disease, and crime without public expense, and thus assisted the work of capital accumulation by keeping taxes low. Moreover, women's welfare work itself, the equivalent of social work in a society that had little conception of it, was unpaid, and thus it, too, aided in bourgeois capital accumulation.[65] Finally, this work functioned hegemonically to instill bourgeois values in the poor, and thus to create the internal basis of social order within the population. In all her varied roles then, the bourgeois woman helped to shape the social world her class aspired to create.

Within this bourgeois world, social prestige was linked intimately to one's success within the trading community or in one's profession, to the status of one's communal social networks, voluntary association affiliations and church membership, and to more intangible qualities, such as gentility and cultivation, that became evident in everyday dealings with people of all classes. Yet if social prestige was largely determined locally, Buffalo's bourgeois men and women nonetheless continually manifested the need to gain a sense of their own class legitimacy by comparing themselves favorably to, and modeling their behavior after, people of equivalent social position at what were widely deemed the true centers of bourgeois civilization. This feeling of living at the periphery of the bourgeois world expressed itself in many ways, from imitation of European and eastern fashions to the association of the very unrepublican Old World with true high culture. Defensive at times, these comparisons were also a source of good-hearted and gentle self-mockery, by which provincials learned to admit the limitations of their prestige beyond their own city and to laugh at their own cultural insecurity. In the boom years after 1843, as prosperity spread throughout the local bourgeoisie and it strained after self-definition, it increasingly took on, according to the *Courier* in 1847, "the fashionable airs" and "conveniences and luxuries" of New York City, Boston, and Philadelphia, and even, it was claimed, Paris and London. The paper proudly noted the latest sign: after a long hiatus caused by the depression, omnibuses had again made an appearance on the principal mercantile and residential streets, giving them the appearance of Broadway or Fifth Avenue, to which they were frequently compared.[66] Fashion, too, the paper said around the same time, had been affected by high-toned external influences: "Nothing takes 'the upper ten' that has not a foreign stamp to it. Our women are all French-a-fied and our gents are made up in Regent Street style."[67]

Soon, too, similar influences would be brought to the education of bourgeois children. No more evident sign existed than the enthusiastic reception of new private school opportunities presented in the 1850s when European teaching orders were invited to establish schools by the city's first Catholic bishop, John Timon. When the Sisters of the Sacred Heart opened a private academy for girls, a correspondent of the *Commercial Advertiser*, which would soon emerge as an organ of bourgeois anti-Catholicism, raved that the sisters conducted "the best female school in the city," and that they had the advantage of being "of high birth, great merit, and ... French." In order to attract bourgeois Protestant students, who were, practically speaking, the only ones able to pay the tuition, these new Catholic academies promised to teach no theology or religion. But the curriculum, as was the case, for example, at St. Joseph's College, which opened to high-school-aged students in 1851 under the direction of the French Oblates of St. Mary, promised immersion in high culture: classical and modern European languages, the fine arts, and the history of Western civilization. The attraction of such academies for local bourgeois families was great enough that Millard Fillmore, the anti-Catholic American party's 1856 presidential candidate, sent his daughter to the school of the Sisters of the Sacred Heart.[68]

In the 1850s this quest for a feeling of connection with the centers of their civilization asserted itself in the European "grand tours" Millard Fillmore and others took.[69] These tours brought them to most of the same areas of Catholic Europe which had been the homes of the immigrants whose presence in Buffalo made them so uncomfortable. But such ironies were lost amidst the opportunities for personal cultivation and for cure of the cultural "blahs" infecting those living in the provinces.

Though willing to admit there was much of what is called "humbug" in European travel, the *Commercial Advertiser* expressed empathy for these tourists in their quest for "enlarged ideas and correct tastes."[70] But the local bourgeoisie were just as accustomed to chiding themselves for their nouveau riche qualities. Some, it was said, had conveniently forgotten they began life in the back room of a country store, and had made their local appearance a generation ago as country bumpkins stepping off a canal boat with little more than an invitation from a merchant cousin and homespun clothing packed in a carpetbag. The souvenir program at the 1868 annual festival of the "Old Settlers of Buffalo" mocked a fictitious, wealthy local family for changing its name from the plebeian "Doolittle" to "De Le Telle" and attempting to pass themselves off as art collectors, world travelers, and friends of Old World aristocrats.[71] They were not, however, so good-natured about the charge that they had become pretentious when it came from outside their local ranks. When the New York City *News* belittled the Buffalo *Republic* as a journal in "a country town about one-fourth as large as Brooklyn" for its criticisms of two actresses well received in London and New York, the *Republic*'s editor was furious. People in Buffalo had just as good taste as those in New York, and anyway—somewhat contradictorily—that city's press made its "bread . . . currying favor with humbugs and monstrosities of every kind" that typically thrived in the metropolis.[72]

The feeling of provinciality had two potent historical sources. First, it suggested a yearning for aesthetic transcendence of the workaday functionalism of a city in which commerce determined the rhythms of life, and the beautification of the civic environment was subordinated to bottom-line fiscal considerations and political wrangling. Second, it betrayed a lack of cultural and social self-confidence at the root of which was not merely the class's lack of historical seasoning, but also its lack of control over its own destiny. As long as Buffalo's prosperity depended ultimately on both the calculations of capitalists in those same eastern and even European cities that its bourgeois citizens so ambivalently regarded, and on its own increasingly tenuous locational advantage, it would be impossible for its men of affairs to escape recognition of their own vulnerability.

Gender and denominational cleavages, self-consciousness about provinciality, and lack of class confidence, all give evidence that the worldview of the Buffalo bourgeoisie contained unresolved inner tensions. These were not limited to the areas of social existence we have been analyzing. They were present in the attitudes and ideological formulations evolved by the group for interpreting all the realities around it and for guiding its efforts to gain social ascendancy. The precise nature of these intraclass fissures will emerge in later chapters in discussions of ethnocultural, political, and class struggles. For now, it is enough to establish the boundaries in which bourgeois thinking, and the tensions within it, evolved. Approached in this way, our concern is not so much the particular tenets of a social ideology, but instead a generalized bourgeois mentality, within which various competing ideas took shape.

The bourgeois mentality was a curious blend of traditional and antitraditional elements derived from Anglo-American cultural chauvinism, Protestantism, capitalist ideology, and republican political thought, all coexisting in states of shifting tension. It could well be described as a series of potentially contradictory propositions about the requirements for the survival, prosperity, and moral improvement of the contemporary social order. At the heart of these propositions was a belief in moral progress through capitalist economic development and technological innovation, which combined with a deep-seated fear of the disorder and social instability inevitably accompanying that development. (Of course, the problem was rendered yet more difficult to the extent that, from a strictly individual perspective, so much money was being made in the new economy.) In reviewing the wondrous productivity of American agriculture, and speculating on its potential for liberating the peoples of the world from want, the *Commercial Advertiser* effused, "Every year exhibits the work of improvement as going on more rapidly than before. Every year leaves the world in a better state than it found it. Every month and every day finds on earth a happier population. . . . It may then be said of each succeeding day: 'This is the happiest day the world ever saw.' " The *Courier* heartily agreed. The age, it stated several years later, was "marked by humanizing progress" and "a rainbow of promise [was] spanning the world."[73]

Yet both papers noted, too, that for all the evident progress—the increased food production, the growth of medical and scientific knowledge, and the development of labor-saving technology of which the bourgeoisie of western nations was so justly proud[74]—great suffering coexisted alongside growing prosperity. Furthermore, it was also agreed that the widening gap between rich and poor, "the morbid love of money," and the "depressed and downtrodden" status of labor were somehow intimately linked with this progress.[75] In fact, capitalism, which unleashed the era's material dynamism, was also responsible for unprecedented derangements in the affairs of human beings, who were torn loose by powerful, impersonal market forces from traditional social arrangements and cultural moorings. Even in its more disciplined, post-1843 form, capitalism destroyed many of the impediments to its development, whether villages bypassed by canals or production processes and occupations rendered obsolete by machines. It uprooted the failed farmer and pushed the dependent peasant from the land, and then impelled them to a proletarianized existence in the emergent slums and shabby working-class neighborhoods of burgeoning cities.[76] While not always conscious, this suspicion that progress and misery were inseparable, that there could not be one without the other, was a dagger poised at the heart of the moral claims of bourgeois civilization. And on a more practical level, it boded ill for the hopes for order and stability which were linked not only to self-interested but disciplined profit-taking and the prospect of affluence, but to the claim that the world was growing less dangerous, more predictable and secure, every day.

There were three central ideological and emotional stances that arose to confront this paradox. One was denial, and it manifested itself commonly in a reflexive blaming of the poor for their miseries. As in the case of the BARP, this led inevitably to the always self-defeating effort to separate the "worthy" and "unworthy" poor—those who could not work from those who would not and wished to live off charity.[77] The *Commercial Advertiser* and the *Christian Advocate* frequently expressed views to the effect that "when the muscle is stout and the mind free to labor, it is hard to suffer for the necessarys of life"; and that "virtuous poverty seldom ever begs in the street, but suffers at home."[78] Such sentiments were most often expressed publicly when the sufferings of the immigrant poor were brought to light, and hence their articulation mixed ethnocultural with class prejudices. They were, therefore, an amalgam of biases based on nationality, language, and religion and on contempt for prebourgeois work habits, the seeking of charity, the refusal to accept wages that could not maintain subsistence, and the unwillingness to relocate to find work. Seeing poverty as Irish or German rather than a product of the new economy, moreover, allowed bourgeois commentators to escape having to question the justice of the social order they were creating. But there is also no doubt that they believed in the rightness of that order, for the assumptions undergirding their reaction to the poor ultimately derived from political and economic ideology. "Work is a market commodity, and must seek its market," said the *Commercial Advertiser* in commenting on demands for relief of the unemployed. Nowhere were the opportunities for finding that market and thriving in it greater than in America, "a land of equal laws and equal rights and an excess of cheap land," said Dr. Austin Flint in a well-attended lecture on poverty.[79]

Thus, while progress and poverty might occur simultaneously, the latter could conveniently be seen as the product of group cultural inadequacy and individual character flaws. From this followed logically a second stance in the problematization of progress and poverty: the attempt to remake the poor in the bourgeois image. In the belief that the poor and their relatives, the vice-ridden, might be reformed, and in the meanwhile, in a defensive effort to get them off the street, fed, and soon out looking for work (instead of demanding charity or high-wage jobs on the public works), the bourgeoisie advocated the development of welfare and penal institutions. With all its difficulties, remaking the poor was considerably more promising than reforming the market economy, which was conceived as a finely tuned machine governed by immutable natural laws that could not abide tinkering.[80] Thus, at the very time some bourgeois men began to demand that the state contract its role in regulating economic affairs and give free reign to the market, they called on it to regulate and reform personal behavior, particularly of the working and poor classes. Beginning with Samuel Wilkeson's 1843 advocacy of a quasi-penal reformatory workhouse for prostitutes and drunkards within the state-mandated poorhouse, several such schemes were discussed and a few realized. Out of its original workhouse origins, the Erie County Penitentiary was continually and vastly expanded.[81] The BARP attempted to ferret out those sturdy beggars who refused to work and those comfortable knaves who sent their children out to beg.[82] A juvenile asylum, intended to remove young beggars, street "arabs," towpath boys who had strayed from the canal, and juvenile petty offenders from public circulation, while feeding, clothing, and educating them, was incorporated. But it failed to become a reality because of both the opposition of Catholics, who feared the asylum would be a front for Protestant conversion efforts, and the tightness of money during the 1857–58 depression.[83] Since it was increasingly believed that only the unworthy poor ended up there, the poorhouse was a mainstay for most such efforts. Its regime actually grew harsher during the period, a process fueled by the increasing percentage of much-loathed Irish Catholic immigrants in its rapidly growing population, and by the bourgeois contention, articulated frequently by such influential men as Dr. Austin Flint, that such places must be made vile and uncomfortable so that poor folk would only fall back on, rather than aspire to, residence in them.[84]

A third stance derived from having to face the all too real and immediate sufferings of the poor. Although they did not doubt the justice of social inequalities and most often saw the difficulties faced by the poor as a consequence of their own failings rather than of the social system, they often rejected for religious, moral, and practical reasons the actual consequences of poverty for the individual. Though their ideological assumptions and individualistic ethic made them slow to act, especially in comparison with the Catholic church, after 1835 they did develop various systematic charities to replace the dependence on random giving by wealthy individuals that characterized the boom decade after 1825. They created the women's industrial school, the Buffalo Association for the Relief of Poverty, a sailors' home and chapel, and a public dispensary for medicines, as well as the Buffalo Orphan Asylum. (The desire of some, especially in the medical establishment, for a Protestant-controlled hospital to provide in-patient care for the poor and nonpoor alike was stalled for almost two decades because of lack of interest.) As the work of the relief association suggests, the charitable enterprise need not necessarily be completely divorced from the hope of reforming the poor or even the desire to punish them. Yet neither moral reform nor fear of disorder, nor for that matter simple humanitarian impulses to relieve suffering, accounts completely for charitable endeavors. The soul of the affluent was also thought to be at stake. "Property" might indeed need charity to protect itself, because charity was "better than crime, prisons, and expensive courts," the *Commercial Advertiser* stated, but even that paper's hardhearted editorialists at times allowed that giving might be a cure for "the curse of wealth." Charity, the paper once contended, checked the tendency of affluence to "crust the better nature with corroding selfishness, and shut out the purest, most enduring sources of happiness."[85]

The desire for order and stability had a tension at its heart deeper still than the problem of poverty amidst plenty. This tension lay in a commitment to the political economy of individualism. After 1845, only when the interests of the port and the maintenance of law and order were at stake did the principal organs of bourgeois opinion predictably and with a high degree of unity endorse an increase in the scope of government involvement in society. But the consensus rapidly broke down when the target of government involvement left the docks, jails, and poorhouses to make its way toward the neighborhoods in the form of, for example, public parks, ornamental fountains, and public markets. One finds, therefore, a segment of bourgeois opinion, which crossed party lines, combining to block government activity in society in the name of individual rights and private enterprise, and to argue perhaps most vociferously that taxation impeded capital accumulation. Yet the atomized, profit-seeking individual whom such arguments struggled to liberate was just as potent a potential source of instability as the underclasses or the fragile economy itself. Benjamin Rathbun's career might well have stood as proof for thoughtful people.

To counter this source of disorder was a separate work of intraclass reform. It involved the molding of the bourgeois character in the family and through such institutions as the church and Board of Trade. For some, it also involved a commitment to evangelically oriented moral reforms, such as temperance and Sabbatarianism. To the extent it had any success in propagandizing for these reforms, the bourgeoisie had greater success in its own ranks than outside them. But whether inside or out, their own commitment to individual property rights and entrepreneural freedom also made it difficult for them to attain consistency. Social control of liquor and protection of the Sabbath, for example, had an unsettling effect on commerce and enterprise if taken to their logical conclusion—state regulation.

In spite of these inconsistencies and contradictions, after the tragic collapse of the mid-1830s, there is evidence nonetheless of the growth among the bourgeoisie of a sense of civic responsibility that worked to tame the potentially destabilizing spirit of individual enterprise and to effect something of a compromise on the role of government in society's affairs. The growing concern of thoughtful bourgeois opinion leaders, such as the editors of all the principal newspapers, for civic improvement—for paving streets and sidewalks, pumping fresh water from the lake and the Niagara, developing sewers, and creating parks—was only in part based on the class interests of shippers, merchants, and manufacturers needing infrastructure to facilitate commerce. Of course paved streets did facilitate trade; sewers removed industrial waste; fire companies protected business property; and water converted to steam-powered engines. Yet civic improvement also was a product of the ongoing process of class self-definition, by which the bourgeoisie came to understand how it should behave responsibly in order to establish its claims to social authority.

Bourgeois support for the public schools demonstrates this. With the exception of such dogmatic sectarians as Dr. Lord, who joined Old Lutheran immigrant pastors and the Catholic church's local leadership in criticizing the public schools,[86] bourgeois people came quickly to understand their value. No reform was more eclectic in the expectations brought to it: public schools, it was argued, would work to counter excess materialism, political corruption, religious sectarianism, and antisocial behavior. As if to prove this faith, although bourgeois neighborhoods did account for about half of the nineteen private schools in 1849, no bourgeois enclave, no matter how affluent, was without its own well-attended public school, to which bourgeois parents like more humble ones sent children for the social and cultural conditioning they believed was needed for responsible public and private behavior, as well as for acquisition of skills conducive to cultivation and mobility. Under such circumstances, no matter how much dispute there might be about other government expenditures, public funding of the schools, which after all began during the worst depression in the city's antebellum history, almost always escaped criticism by bourgeois leaders. Indeed, providing well for the public schools became the mark of enlightened, responsible civic leadership. Both parties would compete for many years to win credit for the establishment of the school system.[87]

Internal tensions also pervaded the bourgeois conception of democracy and politics. While they possessed different notions of the exact qualifications for voting, especially in the case of black and immigrant men, bourgeois Buffalonians had a basic commitment to something approaching universal male suffrage. But they also possessed a deep-seated fear of democracy, which seemed to them always on the edge of degenerating into a majoritarian tyranny. This fear, which was associated intimately with a lack of confidence in the ability of the party system to provide a politically ethical and a probusiness civic assimilation for new immigrants, was a potent source of nativist efforts to curb immigrant political power. Their loss of confidence was hardly complete, for they maintained a republican faith that representative government could be sustained through the inculcation of civic virtue in the public schools. Still the essence of the government in which they took pride was the clash of legitimate opinion. So great was the identification of their own welfare with the welfare of the city, that bourgeois men often angrily rejected politics on any other terms than their own, no matter how much it was informed by a loyalty to American values and methods of civic participation.[88]

The extent to which the bourgeois ethos was ridden with internal tensions helps account for a frequently labored and inconsistent approach to important questions the class manifested. This apparent confusion led the *Christian Advocate*, from its evangelical perspective, to hold bourgeois leadership up to scorn. The paper at times characterized it as "cautious, amoral, defensive," fearful of "agitation," and composed of "unsexed men" who shied away from applying the Gospel to the world because of expedient material and political considerations.[89] There was enough truth in the charge to cause pain. But it was equally true that when convinced of their position, bourgeois people displayed that single-minded intensity, intolerance, and self-righteousness long identified with the Protestant temperament. Protestantism taught that order and virtue were the choices of morally responsible individuals, and not imposed by external authorities. Each Protestant must struggle for self-definition and validate the claims of the self by living according to a moral code. In so doing, one could be brought to immobilizing introspection or an uncompromising, condescending arrogance.[90]

Nowhere was this more evident than in the process by which the bourgeoisie shored up the boundaries of their beliefs by rejecting what they deemed morally unfit and socially unacceptable. It was a habit of mind that time and again they brought to appraising aspects of immigrant culture. But it also manifested itself in the rejection across partisan lines of the era's radical ideas, which were often conceived by dissidents within their own class. The *Courier* in 1846, in tones worthy of its partisan rival, the *Commercial Advertiser*, saluted Rev. John Lord for his sermonic "warnings against the revolutionary and almost infidel schemes of the day," which on this occasion were the abolition of capital punishment and Charles Fourier's socialism.[91] Woman suffrage might well have been added to the list; of all the local newspapers, only the *Republic*, and then cautiously, voiced support for the idea.[92] But bourgeois women apparently gave it no organized support either. Both the *Courier* and the *Commercial Advertiser*, and other papers, too, took stands for labor on the dominant local wage earner's grievance, "storepay," the payment of wages in scrip useable only at certain stores and groceries, but not in cash. But with the exception of the again cautious *Republic*, all opposed strikes and labor unions. The *Courier*, which had been successor to the *Bulletin* of the local, 1830s Workingmen's party, boasted of its friendship for the workingman. One of its editors, however, as secretary of the Board of Trade, was a pillar of the local trading community. Under such influences, it is not surprising that the paper regularly criticized unions as restraints on trade and curbs on progress, and offered a typically Democratic package of free-trade proposals and antibank rhetoric to local workers.[93]

Class consensus was evident, too, particularly in the 1840s, on slavery, increasingly the national issue of the day. The dominant approach in wide circles of the class was cautious and moderate, rejecting abolition and radical formulations of antislavery, but maintaining, via colonization and schemes for voluntary, compensated emancipation, a mild, if largely implicit, criticism of slavery. Slavery did, of course, contradict many of the tenets of bourgeois economic and political ideology, and in upholding that ideology, they indirectly helped to divorce North from South, politically and ideologically. But the prospect of the disruption of national markets and political disorder that might accompany constant criticism of slavery, let alone efforts to end it, created the cautious and compromising state of mind that their townsman Millard Fillmore displayed during his presidency. While colonization and voluntary emancipation continued to have advocates (such as Rev. John Robie) in the 1850s, the escalation of the sectional controversy began inexorably to chip away at consensus and paved the way for a significant political cleavage within the bourgeoisie. Even then, only Almon Clapp's *Express* embraced antislavery enthusiastically. No sizeable fragment of the class would come to espouse abolitionism.[94]

The existence of a broad consensus rejecting radicalism does not imply that the relatively few ideological dissenters within the bourgeoisie "lost caste" for views at variance with the mainstream. Surely this was true in the case of bourgeois Democrats, whose partisan affiliations may have placed them at political odds with the Whig majority of their class, but hardly barred them from either its social circles or its civic activities. But the same was true for the occasional radical, if he was deeply embedded in the way of life of his class by virtue of marriage, residence, church membership, voluntary association activities, and occupational success and reputation. One need only compare two prominent local abolitionists, Thomas C. Love and George Washington Johnson, to grasp the point. For many years an articulate foe of slavery, Love was also a brilliant attorney, respected judge, and member of Central Presbyterian, with whose minister he no doubt had some lively discussions. An affluent man of dignified, genteel bearing, he was a participant in prestigious social circles, and his daughter married the eminent physician Dr. Walter Cary. Unconnected as it was to any broader radicalism or departure from the life-style of his class, his abolitionism was perhaps seen as a sincere, if misguided, commitment. Thus, when he died in 1853, Lord preached the funeral sermon; and along with other prominent men, ex-president Fillmore, hated by abolitionists for engineering the 1850 Compromise, was a pallbearer.[95] George Washington Johnson was, like Love, a New Englander by heritage and an affluent attorney. But his abolitionism was part of a generalized nineteenth-century bourgeois radicalism that included outspoken agnosticism, feminism, antievangelicalism, anticlericalism, and anti-Sabbatarianism. If this did not limit his access to prestigious social circles, then his lack of attention to his profession, successful real-estate speculation (after the time when it was considered appropriate for one with pretensions to respectability), a host of personal eccentricities, and reclusive bachelor life-style certainly did. Moreover, his single-minded moral intensity led him frequently, and with little concern for gentility, to politicize everyday, casual encounters on the city's crowded streets.[96]

But there were few Johnsons probing the boundaries of bourgeois intraclass tolerance. Moreover, in themselves the tensions within the bourgeois ethos provoked sufficient controversy to deflect attention away from narrowly socially based radicalisms that lay outside the class consensus. And more important, the tensions within the bourgeois mentality were contained by a framework of overarching common interests and values and of communal, emotional ties. These served to mediate intraclass conflict. In the last analysis, the social cement that held bourgeois Buffalo together usually proved far more powerful than the forces that threatened to tear it apart.

CHAPTER 5

Clerks, Shopkeepers, and Artisans: Americans, Canadians, and Britons

BROAD congruence in many areas of daily life enabled Buffalo's bourgeoisie to form mutually sustaining relationships with nonbourgeois Americans and with British and Canadian immigrants. These relations provided bases for bourgeois social authority and assisted the class to make its values, social aspirations, and standards of respectability a matter of belief and practice beyond its social boundaries. Yet such hegemonic strivings were never completely fulfilled even here, with groups which shared a great deal with the bourgeoisie. They remained a process, ever in the midst of becoming. In these relationships, therefore, we see both the limits and possibilities of bourgeois leadership. For example, congruence often became a basis for consent only through emotionally charged negotiations, as was the case at times between American artisans and employers. Under any circumstance, the majority of the population by the 1850s was comprised of Irish and German immigrants, whose cultures were too vastly different from those of Americans and British and Canadian immigrants to present many opportunities for congruence, and whose communities found authority in their own ethnic leadership and institutions.

In 1855 approximately 12 percent (1,772) of Buffalo's household heads were immigrants from England (1,093), Canada (416), and Scotland (263). Some small percentage of the 2,723 household heads born in Ireland, who were 18 percent of the population, were Scots-Irish Protestants, who were Anglo-Saxon, not Celtic, in their conception of themselves and distinctive from their Irish neighbors in vital elements of culture, particularly religion.[1] Because these peoples, to varying degrees, had a weak group life, they blended into the American population at various class levels, usually the higher ones. Contemporary British immigration was largely comprised of skilled craftsmen and men in white-collar occupations in search of economic opportunity. In Buffalo, Scots, Canadians, and Englishmen were often retail merchants, wholesalers, and shopkeepers, and ship carpenters and joiners. So comparatively affluent were the Scots and English that their economic position, measured by the value of their dwellings, was well above that of the Irish and Germans, and just below native white Americans.[2]

Three of these four groups (the Scots, English, and Scots-Irish) did possess ethnic awareness and a semblance of organized group life, while the fourth, Canadians, had neither. Canadians in America were as slow to develop ethnic awareness as Canada was to develop a national identity. Moreover, many Canadian immigrants were probably the children of British or Irish immigrants to Canada, and like their parents continued to see themselves, in relation to Canada, as colonials loyal to the British mother country. Perhaps, therefore, they looked to the Irish Catholics, Scots, English, and Scots-Irish for their identities.[3] The last three were able, episodically, but in organized fashion, to offer identity. Their ethnic awareness was manifested principally in the Englishman's St. George Society, and the Scot's St. Andrew's Society. The Scots-Irish enjoyed communal relations in "Orange lodges" with the far larger number of their countrymen across the Canadian border. They also occasionally fraternized with Catholic Irish in ethnic societies, though sectarian distrust probably prevented such contacts from becoming common.[4]

Both St. George's (1845) and St. Andrew's (1840) societies were composed of several dozen merchants, craftsmen, shopkeepers, and professionals.[5] They were organized for the dual purpose of aiding poor coethnics and keeping alive memories of the homeland. Yet because the number of both groups in Buffalo was small and few among them seem to have been needy, charity took a distinctly second place to stimulating ethnic awareness. To this end, both societies did little more than sponsor a yearly banquet on their saint's day. The Scots' society also organized occasionally a dinner on the birthday of Robert Burns, and it raised money for Scottish famine relief in 1847. The St. George Society briefly sponsored a cricket club in the 1850s; it was comprised of both Englishmen and Americans.[6]

The annual banquets showed the nature and limits of the largely symbolic ethnicity, "primarily ephemeral, sporadic, and nostalgic," that characterized the English and Scots.[7] These feasts were the scene of hours of after-dinner toasts by members and eminent guests such as the mayor. In an atmosphere of inebriated fellowship toasts grew ever more emotional in conjuring up highly selective images of the ancestral village that were quite at variance with the poverty and proletarianization from which many had fled. Simultaneous with the recreation of memories was an affirmation of loyalty to American institutions that was as aggressively patriotic as the other toasts were emotionally nostalgic.[8] The mixture of the two themes suggests a need to justify reminiscence even while engaged in it, as if the participants felt the strain of abstracting themselves from their American lives to reenter a world they had left years ago. The members themselves admitted that the evening required a good bit of fantasy. When in 1843 the St. Andrew's Society drew criticism for toasting Queen Victoria before the American president, Joseph Stringham, the editor of the *Courier* and a St. George's member, explained, "The English on St. George's Day and the Scotch on St. Andrew's assume, in fancy, their original national character; they are again British subjects, and bound by the rules of etiquette to pay first honors to the sovereign of Great Britain." In effect, as he had said on a previous occasion, "For a short time, the gentlemen . . . went back, in imagination, to their lands of birth . . . forgetting the present and living only in the past."[9]

Such ethnic awareness *qua* nostalgia served no end but itself. It never became the basis for creating a communal life of the sort enjoyed by the Catholic Irish or the Germans. Unlike the latter, for example, the various British and Canadian peoples never mobilized themselves politically as groups. Yet their various subnational identities were strong enough at the same time to impede their consciously joining together to form a unified British-American group in politics.[10] Local political parties never recognized the existence of a "British vote," as opposed to the vote of various individuals who happened to be from Britain.

Possessing a language and broad religious orientation in common with Americans and a similar socioeconomic position, the British and Canadian residents had little desire to maintain ethnic ghettoes and possessed no institutions of their own. They lived, worshiped, and played alongside Americans, and shared most of their standards of respectability and some of their prejudices. Indices of residential dissimilarity for Buffalo's wards in 1855 reveal that while, in their spatial proximity to Americans, Germans and Irish (including the indeterminate number of Scots-Irish) had indices of 59.0 and 45.3 respectively, the figure for British and Canadians was lower: 31.3; or for each of the three: 22.8 for the English, 29.4 for Scots, and 41.9 for Canadians (a composite group including such non-Anglo-Saxon peoples as Irish Catholics and some Quebecers.) Their place of residence was determined not by ethnicity but by occupation: they lived where ship artisans, skilled craftsmen, and merchants found it convenient to live, and hence often among Americans.[11] None of the British or Canadian peoples had a communal religious life. No congregations were associated with them. They affiliated with churches composed largely of Americans, because these churches were often closely related, by history and ritual, with denominations in the British Isles. American Episcopalianism was the child of British Anglicanism, and the principal American evangelical churches—Methodists, Presbyterians, and Baptists—originated in British dissenting churches. Even at the local level transatlantic intradenominational relations continued well into the century. Buffalo's Episcopalians were influenced by the Oxford Movement.[12] Its Presbyterians, many of whom were probably of distant Scottish origins, were concerned enough about the sectarian conflicts in Scotland that speakers from the Old Country, representing one side or another, were invited to Buffalo in 1844. Furthermore, the austerity of Dr. Lord's Presbyterianism would have had a strong appeal to lowland Scots, with their strong Calvinist bent. Lord's anti-Catholicism would have probably appealed to many Scots-Irish.[13] British and Canadians found a place also in American secular institutions. No British or Canadian fraternal lodges existed in the two orders most popular among Americans—the Masons and the Odd Fellows, which English immigrants had established in America. Americans were attracted to British and Canadian activities. Prominent Americans attended the annual saint's day banquets, and played cricket on immigrant club teams.[14]

The acceptability to Americans of the British and Canadians is demonstrated by an absence of hostile stereotypes. With the very occasional exception of a newspaper joke at the expense of, or the appearance of a stage "delineator" of, English or Scottish national character, there is little evidence of publicly articulated, generalized images, let alone hostile ones. In the case of the Scots, what there was of a stereotype was rather positive. The typical Scot came across as shrewd in business and suspicious of clerical activity in nonreligious affairs.[15] The "stage Englishman," on the other hand, was usually an upper-class dandy, whose affectations and aversion to work were as objectionable to the average English immigrant as to Americans, and who could never be taken to represent the former. Americans did possess a nationalistic hostility to England. But as we shall see, this was declining by the 1850s.[16] It is not surprising then that though subject to some criticism by American nativists as parts of the general population of foreigners, none of these groups became special targets in the mid-1850s, as did the Germans and particularly the Irish. On the other hand, the Scots-Irish, and probably many English and Scots, shared the American Protestant hostility to Catholicism. ("If you will give this a place in your paper," said a Scots-Irish correspondent of the *Express* announcing joint American and Canadian Orangemen's celebration of the Battle of the Boyne in Ontario, "it will post the Romans up in something they don't like.")[17]

The sum total of all these relationships was that British, Canadians, and Americans at various class levels shared significant links and bonds. In order to examine the consequences of this for the authority of American bourgeois leadership, therefore, we must examine the relations between bourgeois and Americans of other classes and understand the bases of American group life.

Americans lacked a strong, ethnocultural sense of themselves as a unique people, so that while they were an ethnic group by such objective criteria as language, birthplace, and the habits of daily life, a subjective feeling of ethnicity was not an important source of those connections that bound them together. They lacked a common homeland, a common church, and deep roots on the American continent. As Arthur Mann has said, they created a nation-state before they were a people.[18] Rather than ethnicity, what Americans did possess in common was an abstract, ideological loyalty to and pride in the American state and its basic law, the Constitution, as embodiments of republican liberty. This was evident in such civic festivals as the Fourth of July and in the ritualized demonstrations that attended the deaths of their political leaders. Occasions such as Andrew Jackson's death provided, in symbolicized form, historical reference points for American ideology. In consequence, Americans defined "American" in terms of both the rights possessed by and the obligations of ideal republican citizenship. In the spirit of their laws, one became a citizen not through cultural seasoning or honorific award, but through allegiance to standards deemed universal. Such allegiance is precisely what was required by the oath of citizenship.[19] This understanding of the meaning of "American" did not provide a basis for a particularistic sense of peoplehood, i.e., ethnicity. As long as Americans saw themselves as the cultural personification of the nation, they could not easily also see themselves as one people among many, nor even look to one another as a way of defining their identities. American ideology did provide, however, an understanding of "American" sufficiently cosmopolitan to embrace, with widely varying degrees of enthusiasm, millions of immigrants.[20]

Other subjective sources of ethnic awareness were not much stronger than nationality for most of the period in creating a sense of peoplehood among Americans. Though across class lines the large majority of the city's Americans shared a common recent background in the New England diaspora, a symbolically conceived vision of their history as a people was not common during the period, though it would grow. Here and there musings that seemed to try to synthesize the powerful elements of this history into a legend of migration, from the bucolic, stable order of the New England village to a dangerous pioneer existence on the western frontier, could be found in private thoughts and public expressions. In 1838, for example, Dr. Burwell struggled to describe the meanings of the experience of his parents' generation: "They were the first settlers of a new and wilderness country; they were poor but enterprising, and after years of privation and fatigue—of increasing industry and rigid economy, they began to realize a more comfortable existence."[21] Groping for a symbolicized basis for peoplehood greatly increased in the following years. After 1845, as the pioneering generation died and the country they claimed as their own was filling up with foreigners, native Protestants reflected more on themselves and their roots. There was a growth of interest in local history that began in 1847, when the Young Men's Association formed a committee to collect artifacts, preserve old buildings and create monuments, and gather testimonies of pioneer days.[22] Newspapers, too, now published heavily nostalgic articles pondering the Yankee pioneering experience on the occasion of the razing of a historic building or the discovery that the gravesite of some local notable was neglected.[23]

These efforts would culminate, as we shall see, in a process of cultural vitalization that in the 1850s and early 1860s was evident along several fronts. There was the creation of filiopietistic societies (the New England Pioneers of Western New York, and Old Settlers associations) and of the Buffalo Historical Society.[24] There were signs in the late 1850s of a desire for an emotional reconciliation with Great Britain, the ultimate source of American roots, when a local British consulate was established amidst conspicuous good feeling, when the trans-Atlantic cable was completed, and when the Prince of Wales came to Fort Erie.[25] And most dramatic of all, there was political nativism—with its secret societies and elaborate symbolic evocation of Americanism, a cultural phenomenon as well as an artifact of a process of political party realignment. But these conscious and unconscious strivings toward a symbolically conceived past actually were quite tentative. They hardly created a group life like that of Irish and Germans. Among the bourgeois merchants and professionals, as the press observed in noting the desultory leadership usually given to organizing patriotic anniversaries, they often took second place to the demands of business and moneymaking.[26] Moreover, they served other functions and had other sources, too. They were also the product of an essentially negative, boundary-drawing impulse, which was informed by prejudice and functioned to exclude the immigrants from the mainstream of society and from political power. Furthermore, coinciding as they did with a period of local economic crisis in the history of the bourgeoisie, they were also comforting, compensatory activities that soothed a painful transition.

Americans also lacked a strong sense of shared interests to serve as a basis for ethnic mobilization across class lines, which, in turn, would heighten ethnic communal awareness. Nowhere was this clearer than in politics and relatedly in competition for public resources, such as patronage. Americans were the only one of the city's major descent groups that regularly split their vote among political parties. This was in sharp contrast to the Irish and Germans. Both usually could be counted on to vote overwhelmingly Democratic and hence found in politics a strong sense of communal feeling. Until its demise in the mid-1850s, the local Whig party, which could claim the support of the majority of American voters during most elections,[27] did in one sense function as a type of American machine, and hence a vehicle for American group competition for public resources, to the extent that its patronage appointments were always largely American. They could not have been otherwise, because so few foreigners voted Whig, even as a significant minority of Americans voted Democratic. Moreover, there were ideological constraints on the development of an American ethnic politics. American Whigs increasingly criticized politics based on personal or group gain, which they associated with foreign-born Democrats, rather than on abstract calculation of principle and the common good.[28] Under any circumstance, Americans controlled so many of society's *private* resources, that its public ones were of less practical importance to them. Beginning in the mid-1840s, nativists increasingly deplored what they took to be American apathy in recognizing and protecting both their group interests and national stewardship.[29] Under the influence of appeals to self-interest and pride, Americans did become more self-conscious about the need to work together to compete for public resources and power. This was, for example, evident in the organization of the local militia. In 1854, at a time of growing American clannishness and prejudice, two American companies left the German-dominated Sixty-fifth Regiment to form a new regiment in which they controlled leadership positions.[30] Also briefly in the mid-1850s, under the influence of nativism, there was a near unification of the American vote and an effort to make politics a source of American communal feeling.[31] But party realignment based on the growing intensity of the slavery issue soon would again divide Americans in new electoral patterns. Furthermore, the military exigencies and mood of unity during the Civil War produced a considerable degree of ethnic reintegration in the local militia.[32]

If Americans were usually not linked across class lines by a strong, subjective awareness or by a feeling of possessing group interests that required defense or enlargement through mobilization, they nonetheless had other bases for ethnic linkages. These were less matters of ideology, cultural identity, and group interests than similarities in habits, attitudes, and standards of behavior that manifested themselves in practical, daily interactions. It was through such similarities that Americans may be said to have gradually formed the bases of an ethnic group, even while they continually fell short on group awareness and lacked a propensity to organize as a group. The linkages these similarities created functioned simultaneously to enhance bourgeois cultural authority. This was the case not merely because the social prestige attached to the bourgeoisie encouraged imitation of its manners and mores, though something of a prestige-effect probably did take place. Instead, it was true because the bourgeoisie's control of so many of society's private resources made it impossible for many nonbourgeois Americans to achieve their socioeconomic aspirations without deferring, consciously or not, to bourgeois values and practicing bourgeois modes of behavior. When such behavior worked effectively to fulfill nonbourgeois aspirations, the structure of the world the bourgeoisie was creating was further reproduced. This is not to say that nonbourgeois American life was merely a less affluent version of bourgeois life, let alone that perfect ideological consensus existed. It is to say that similarities were great enough in essential areas to reinforce bourgeois authority and power, while consolidating the ranks of Americans.

The socioeconomic structure of the nonbourgeois American population helps explain the dynamics of this process. When we speak of nonbourgeois Americans we are still speaking most likely of people either in the middle or toward the upper end of Buffalo's social structure. Only 2.5 percent (77) and 8.8 percent (271) of American household heads respectively could be classified as unskilled and semiskilled. In contrast, 22 percent of American household heads were in the upper echelons of manual work: artisans, machinists, master craftsmen, and foremen. An indeterminable number of these men provided industrial services for commerce, and worked for American dock merchants and ship and boat manufacturers as millwrights, millers, carpenters, joiners, coopers, and boiler and engine makers. Many of the artisans and craftsmen were actually proprietors who employed small numbers of journeymen. Another 22.5 percent of American household heads were in lower white-collar positions (agents, clerks, copyists, salesmen, cashiers, bookkeepers, etc.) or in the catch-all "nonmanual" category that the state census used for such occupations as grocer and engineer. The increasing separation of manual and nonmanual work that accompanied economic development made lower white-collar employment a particularly rich source for the livelihood of the local middle classes.[33]

The lines that separated these nonbourgeois occupations from bourgeois blurred in ways that encouraged both lower white-collar workers and craftsmen to feel themselves a functional segment of the bourgeoisie. Prior to educational credentialing and corporate rationalization of management, office jobs and retail clerkships were frequently obtained through personal patronage. Young men recruited in this way had reason to feel they were undertaking business apprenticeships, and that if their work was acceptable, personal relations guaranteed promotion and perhaps eventually a partnership. Older men who spent all their careers in lower white-collar positions often enjoyed great respect and authority because of their expertise and burden of responsibility. Testimony to the good reputations such men might enjoy was the frequency with which one or two senior clerks and bookkeepers were chosen to serve on ad hoc committees created to do such things as investigate ways of improving the port, or were elected by stockholders or chosen by directors to serve on the boards of savings banks, semipublic municipal corporations, and building and loan associations.[34] Lines were less blurred in the case of the artisans, because they shared personal relations with their bourgeois employers less frequently. But small manufacturers often did come out of the ranks of artisans. By 1861 such former artisans as Sherman S. Jewett, Edward Root, David Bell, George Jones, and Robert Bingham were among the city's leading industrialists.[35] Retail merchants, such as the bookseller Oliver Steele, who had been a bookbinder, were also recruited from the ranks of artisans, depending on their lines of trade. So, too, were leading contractors, such as the partners Robert McFarlane and James Thompson, plumbers and gasfitters, who went from wage earning to employing thirty men within a few years of settling in the city.[36]

Opportunities for entrance into career tracks leading to bourgeois occupations were growing during the period, and this served to facilitate social mobility and to create new linkages extending outward from the bourgeoisie. Clerks began to be recruited on the basis of character or schooling, rather than personal relations, because the need for them was outstripping the scope of intimate social networks. In 1844 the *Commercial Advertiser* spoke of the desirability of such expanded criteria, noting that the public schools contained "many boys, the sons of poor parents, who have been trained of strict virtue [and] close attention to steady business, and who would make excellent clerks."[37] In addition, business colleges were now being established, and were providing credentials that assisted in the social selection of lower white-collar workers. The Buffalo Mercantile College and the Bryant and Stratton Business College, both of which opened in 1854, were the largest of several such institutions that appeared before 1861.[38]

Supplementing economic ties in providing intra-American linkages were both face-to-face social contacts and common social activities, some of which were integrated by class, and others organized separately at various class levels. One of the most significant bases of such contacts was residence. Americans of all classes lived together so frequently that the index of residential dissimilarity for blue-collar and white-collar Americans was only 24.9, a very low figure that illustrates also how very few were neighborhoods like the Hydraulics, where working-class Americans lived with German and Irish workers rather than white-collar Americans.[39] The chief residential area for Americans was west of Main Street and north of the Terrace. While working-class Americans were more likely to live on the far West Side, in the area between Niagara Street and the canal corridor, much of the West Side was integrated by class. The most affluent lived on the major boulevards and others in comfortable, if modest, cottages and two-story homes on the streets and lanes that fed into these thoroughfares. The American West Side had a high level of ethnic institutional completeness. With the exception of the associations, churches, and activities of the Hydraulics or the small, gradually declining American elite enclave east of Main Street, all of the major American social institutions (lodges, churches, fire and militia companies, and voluntary associations) were located there or in the central business district, which was actually a part of the lower West Side.[40]

These institutions and associations offered possibilities for formal contacts, just as coresidence offered opportunities for chance meetings on the streets. While Episcopalian and Presbyterian churches attracted largely bourgeois congregants, and Baptists and Methodists, more non-bourgeois ones, there was some social overlap in the membership of all denominations, especially among Methodists. As elite a congregation as Central Presbyterian could have a highly skilled craftsman, a sailmaker, among its trustees, as it did in 1850. The individual fire companies were organized by class and ethnicity, but the citywide Fireman's Benevolent Association was led by a cross-class American leadership, composed of young artisans, clerks, bookkeepers, small manufacturers, and dock merchants.[41] The BARP, City Temperance Society, and City Dispensary were led by the city's principal American men, but ward committee members of the BARP in American and immigrant wards were American shopkeepers, artisans, teachers, and clerks.[42] The latter were also the sort of men who represented American wards in the common council, for nonbourgeois as frequently as bourgeois men served as aldermen in the wards where they kept workshops and groceries.[43] Similar patterns of contact and cooperation were evident in a wide range of other settings: militia companies, fraternal lodges (especially the particularly democratic Odd Fellows), boards of savings banks and building and loan associations, evangelical efforts such as the Young Men's Christian Union and the City Missionary Society, charities such as the Protestant Orphanage, and in the composition of grand juries.[44]

Neighborhoods, associations, and institutions brought together Americans who differed in the structure of private life. Such differences were less the consequence of different values than of varying degrees of wealth, the situational necessities incident to the practice of various occupations, and differing access to opportunity. However, where such differences existed, principally in household and family structure and property ownership, American patterns were similar enough, compared to Irish or German ones, to reinforce American bonds. Less frequently class cut across ethnic lines, so that social patterns for American blue-collar workers were more similar to those of Irish or German workers.

It is not surprising that home and other property ownership increased with wealth among Americans. In 1855, 58 percent, 43 percent, and 36 percent, respectively, of American merchant, artisan, and lower white-collar heads of households owned real property. That these differences flattened out with age and residential persistence, however, suggests that job security and subsequently ability to save and to sink down roots allowed artisans and nonmanual workers alike to realize the goal of home ownership.[45] Americans also manifested differences in household structure. In part because bourgeois families had the resources to take in relatives and business apprentices, their households were larger and more diversified. The root of such differences also lay in the nature of local apprenticeship. Indentured apprenticeship declined greatly among Americans after the 1836–43 depression. In its place emerged a less formal system of training, without stated obligations and rights, that left the American apprentice more a wage earner than a student of the craft.[46] Thus, few American craftsmen had living in their homes unrelated or related young apprentices; instead most of these nominal apprentices were young men who walked to work from parents' homes in the neighborhood. The fate of American apprenticeship helps to explain why complex households were not the rule among blue-collar Americans.[47] Artisanal families, moreover, may well have seen their own children as sources of income, and male children specifically as likely apprentices to their fathers. American artisanal families had a higher fertility rate (721 children aged 0–4 per 1,000 married women between 15 and 44 years) than was found for American clerks (673), agents (560), and owners (685). Yet as a group Americans had significantly lower fertility than the Irish and Germans, and seem to have shared, within a variable range of practice, norms valuing smaller families.[48]

Only in one significant respect did material circumstances differentiate blue-collar from white-collar American households and create social patterns for the former similar to those of Irish and German households. As a consequence of Buffalo's lack of industrialization, many of its artisans continued to maintain a high degree of occupational independence compared to their counterparts in seaboard industrializing cities who were experiencing proletarianization. For these Buffalo artisans, separation of work and home was not part of daily life, as it was for the city's merchants, professionals, manufacturers, and lower white-collar workers, all of whom left home in the morning, to return perhaps for lunch, but often not until dinner. Many artisans, particularly established, mature ones, worked in shops attached to their homes, as artisans had for centuries, and their daily lives were characterized by interpenetration of work, household, and neighborhood rhythms.[49]

This situation was a significant basis for working-class traditionalism in a world in which bourgeois aspirations and activities were transforming production, making labor a commodity, and destroying tradition along a broad front of daily existence. Yet the absence of industrialization also allowed much of the American artisan class to escape a proletarianization that necessitated the development of a modern working-class politics, and this had important implications for intra-American relations. These artisans retained customary work habits and self-conceptions that reinforced traditional values held in common, across class lines, by Americans and also shared with British and Canadian immigrants. Like its British counterpart, American artisan culture placed high valuation on self-improvement, self-reliance, the dignity and autonomy of the individual, political liberty, material security, and domestic comfort, and it opposed extremes of wealth and poverty and exploitation.[50] All were values that bourgeois and lower white-collar Americans gave evidence of respecting, even as their economic activities were gradually undermining them.

American artisans and lower white-collar workers often acted publicly as if guided by such values, and in doing so demonstrated aspirations to live according to standards of respectability also held by the bourgeois. The quest for independence and improvement of these artisans, clerks, and others, as well as of the property-conscious Germans, figured prominently in the calculations of the merchants and bourgeois men who founded the city's four successful savings banks between 1846 and 1855. These banks created a mortgage market to support home-buying among wage and salary earners eager to take advantage of the city's stock of affordable single-family houses.[51] The desire for self-improvement also was evident in artisan educational and welfare endeavors. Founded in 1833, the Buffalo Apprentices Society had as its motto, "Get wisdom and endeavor to acquire knowledge." The society, which was organized by poor indentured apprentices, acquired a library and sponsored debates and lectures. Through the establishment of a rotating chair, members had opportunities for leadership. The society proved so popular that a few young law and mercantile clerks and merchants' sons were granted requests to join. Yet it did not survive the debasement of the apprentice's status, which came with the collapse of indentured apprenticeship, and expired in the late 1840s.[52]

The Mechanics' Mutual Protection, which was founded in 1843 and lasted a decade, served a number of welfare and self-improvement needs for its membership of established craftsmen. Its antecedents were the ephemeral artisan associations of the 1830s, which were themselves self-consciously modeled throughout the nation on British organizations. The "Protection" had a mutual benefit program for the sick, disabled, and jobless; and it found work for the unemployed, promoted equitable relations with employers, and attempted to shore up the moribund apprenticeship system. But above all, said Oliver Steele, one of its early presidents, its goals were educational: the diffusion of knowledge of the crafts and "self-cultivation." Self-cultivation, said Steele, referring to the improvement of literacy and craft and expansion of knowledge of science and literature, was "the lever which will raise us in our own estimation and the world's." These themes were hardly different than those sounded simultaneously at meetings of the elite Young Men's Association. As the presence of Steele indicates, moreover, a number of upwardly mobile merchants and others were active in such organizations alongside their largely artisanal memberships. Among the officers in 1843, 1844, and 1845 of the Erie County Mechanics Association were not only Steele, but Nelson Randall, owner of the city's most fashionable boot and shoe shop, and Elam R. Jewett and Francis Root, iron manufacturers. These three men had once been craftsmen and retained respect for the historic values of artisan culture. As employers, each could appreciate the association's goal of class harmony. Still, with the initial birth pangs of industrialization in the mid-1850s, the gap between artisan and employer-capitalist would grow, and amiable mutual relations decline.[53]

The goal of self-cultivation led to support for public education. In the 1820s and 1830s, the local workingmen's movement had been a persistent voice for the creation of a free public school system, while bourgeois opinion was divided because some feared the cost would raise taxes.[54] Artisan concern then also encompassed higher education: in 1836 a meeting of artisans resolved to endow a chair of mechanical engineering at the proposed University of Western New York.[55] When at the initiative of much of bourgeois political leadership a public school system was established during the dark days of 1838 and 1839, the artisan's advocate, Oliver Steele, was named its first superintendent. The American artisan and lower white-collar groups, both of which were well represented at the meetings at which the public school system was created, proved even more consistently loyal to it than the bourgeoisie. After 1842 a significant minority of the latter sent their children to new, expensive private schools, though it is also true that even the most affluent neighborhoods had well-attended public schools.[56]

American artisans and lower white-collar workers and their families also participated in moral reform activities derived from evangelical religion. Far from being elite-imposed methods of social control, both revivalism and temperance were genuine cross-class phenomena. But though the fires of the winter revivals burned as brightly at the plebeian Methodist and Baptist as they did at the more elite Presbyterian churches, moral reform did not necessarily have precisely the same functions in the lives of all Americans. It served the differing needs of individuals in various American subgroups. Its latent ethnic functions simultaneously were the integration of Americans into a broadly common way of life, and the development of points of contact and of moral consensus among them.[57]

Temperance, the more continuous and public of the two moral reform activities, provides an example of this dynamic, multiform process. No people were more organized for temperance than American artisans and lower white-collar workers. While the bourgeoisie had two temperance organizations, the Ladies Temperance Union and the male City Temperance Union, between 1843 and 1854 eleven lodges of the nonelite Sons of Temperance and one lodge also of its female affiliate, the Daughters of Temperance, were organized. Seven of the male lodges were founded during 1850–54 alone, years of intense agitation of the liquor issue.[58] The interclass difference in the scale of temperance activity is probably less the result of a significantly variable commitment to abstinence than of the greater role temperance had in providing recreation, as well as moral inspiration, for less affluent men, who had less money for leisure-time activities than bourgeois men. There may be no doubt about the great popularity of the Sons within plebeian ranks. Their conveniently located, well-appointed hall was the meeting place of the Mechanics' Mutual Protection. There the Sons gave massive banquets, such as an 1854 feast for a thousand local members. One of the Sons' goals was the establishment of cross-class "fraternization" for abstinence. The *Christian Advocate* praised the organization for regularly bringing together at banquets men of all degrees of eduation and skill. Bourgeois ministers, professionals, and merchants were invited participants, and some of them were members.[59]

Cross-class temperance activity was also sustained outside formal organizations. Americans of all classes attended outdoor temperance rallies, such as the one in 1850 featuring the noted temperance lecturer John B. Gough, at which 1,159 men and women from Buffalo and outlying areas signed "the pledge" to abstain from consuming and encouraging the use of alcohol. Analysis of a sample of sixty local signers (forty-nine men and eleven women) makes the cross-class nature of temperance clear. Of the forty-nine men, fourteen were merchants, professionals, brokers, and manufacturers; fourteen clerks, teachers, salesmen, and petty public officials; thirteen artisans and contractors; three semiskilled manual workers; and five without occupation. Of the eleven women, their fathers and/or husbands were very largely in the first and second categories.[60]

On the most general level, for all Americans temperance involved the commitment to self-control and moderation in personal habits that was also made at revivals. But in its underlying uses this commitment is likely to have served different functions for Americans in varying social circumstances. To bourgeois women it was also a means for criticizing male power and asserting female virtues beyond the limited domain of the home. For bourgeois men, and to some extent women, too, it had hegemonic functions. Temperance assisted in legitimizing bourgeois-crafted role models, which other classes, it was hoped, would internalize. A commitment to temperance and to temperate personal habits also stood out when noted on the credit report of an aspiring entrepreneur or storekeeper. For the salaried lower white-collar group, a commitment to temperance was an aspect of gathering what Mary Ryan has called "moral capital"—the traits of character that, in the absence of money, had to suffice as the armaments of ambition. For American artisans, temperance was a means of achieving the self-reliance and self-sufficiency they valued, for nothing so sapped the will and undermined character as enslavement to alcohol. An individual, informal commitment to temperance (and even a formal "pledge" through the Sons) did not necessarily mean that the artisan was a teetotaler, let alone that he gave a wide berth, especially during his winter "gay season," to popular amusements, such as music halls and the circus, where liquor might be in evidence. It served instead to shore up the standards by which he might resist self-destructive excess.[61]

Temperance then was a truly integrative reform.[62] It brought together Americans independent of gender, class, age, and occupation. It did not, however, frequently cross ethnic lines, and as a result helped to underline for Americans what was different about them. As much as they were like Americans, British and Canadian immigrants did not often have the same commitment to temperance. The endless toasting at St. George's or St. Andrew's society banquets demonstrates no less. Such extensive toasting was rare at American banquets, where, according to press reports, the glass was not often raised more than seven or eight times, hardly libertine indulgence by contemporary standards.[63] As we shall see, the Germans actively opposed temperance—and indeed led the local antitemperance struggle—because alcohol was vital to their habits of sociability. Irish Catholics, who had their own church-sponsored temperance activity, had an ambivalent relationship to abstinence, whether as a moral ideal or as practical behavior. It is not surprising that only seven foreign-born people were in the sample of those who signed Gough's pledge; six of them were British and Canadian immigrants.[64]

The precise implications of these intra-American linkages in standards, attitudes, and habits were unpredictable. Certainly such linkages did not always have the consequences bourgeois Americans desired. American clerks and artisans formulated the values they shared with the bourgeoisie to suit their needs, so that these became the basis for attempts to improve the treatment they received from American employers. In June, 1851, a large number of merchant clerks presented a well-publicized petition to shopkeepers complaining about the long hours they had to work during the season of navigation, when stores might be open on Sundays and on weekdays to 9 P.M. or even later. The petition respectfully asked "the ladies of Buffalo" to shop only during the day and called upon merchants and shoppers alike to realize clerks needed time for renewal of the body and for "mental improvement." The appeal was difficult for the merchants to deny. It was couched in the rhetoric of their own moral culture, and it was endorsed by local evangelical clergymen on the grounds of equity and Sabbatarian principle. Within a week the proprietors of the fourteen largest dry goods houses, all but two of them Americans, had granted shorter hours.[65] In 1852, after some years of discussion among themselves and with employers, American printers also acted to turn these moral values to their benefit and against their employers. The printers' association, a combination union, guild, and mutual benefit society, passed strong resolutions denouncing local newspapers for making them work on Sundays, which, they stated, should be consecrated to religion, family, and self-cultivation. In 1854, by striking, the printers finally succeeded in forcing the three morning papers to agree not to print a Monday edition, the existence of which had necessitated working on Sundays.[66]

It was the commitment of artisans like the printers to self-improvement, individual dignity, and self-reliance that provided the ideological basis for their class militance. Before 1861, as we shall later see, American iron molders, ship carpenters, building carpenters, and others, at times in concert with British, Canadian, and less often German, artisans, organized unions, engaged in strikes, and in a few instances established cooperative workshops in the hope of achieving a life consistent with these values. Seen in this way, whatever social peace was attained between American artisans and their American employers was often less the product of bourgeois hegemony than the consequence of continuous interclass negotiations. The artisans' aspirations to self-determination and self-cultivation gave them the self-respect they needed to negotiate effectively.[67] Yet to the extent they continued to negotiate within a framework of shared Protestant, individualist assumptions about respectability and social ethics, American artisans were unlikely to create a politics aimed at radically redistributing power and wealth. Hence, their class militance and their accommodation to bourgeois power, which was seen most evidently in their unswerving commitment to a political system that rarely aired their class grievances, were two sides of the same coin. Only when individual strivings for a decent, respectable and secure life were frustrated in a manner they believed violated the moral assumptions of this artisanal culture did they become militant. And then it was not the creation of a new society—a mutualistic, noncompetitive, cooperative commonwealth—they sought, but the ethical fulfillment of the promises of the existing order.

In this, American artisans were very different from many of their German counterparts. The local Germans evolved various types of socialist and radical democratic politics that directly and fundamentally challenged capitalist political economy. Culture and ideology removed such options from the American artisan's labor politics. At the same time, too, the functional and ethnic segmentation of the local labor force combined often with a feeling of civic and cultural superiority to foreigners, by which the American artisan also reinforced his conception of his own social dignity, to impede his cooperation with the more radical German workers. A later chapter will deal with the divided local labor movement. For now it is enough to note that American artisan culture strengthened the linkages that brought Americans together as a group, and helped to shore up what cultural authority the American bourgeoisie achieved. This will become even clearer when the American artisan's occasional challenges to that authority are measured against the much more frequent and insistent challenges presented by the Irish, the Germans, and the Catholic church.

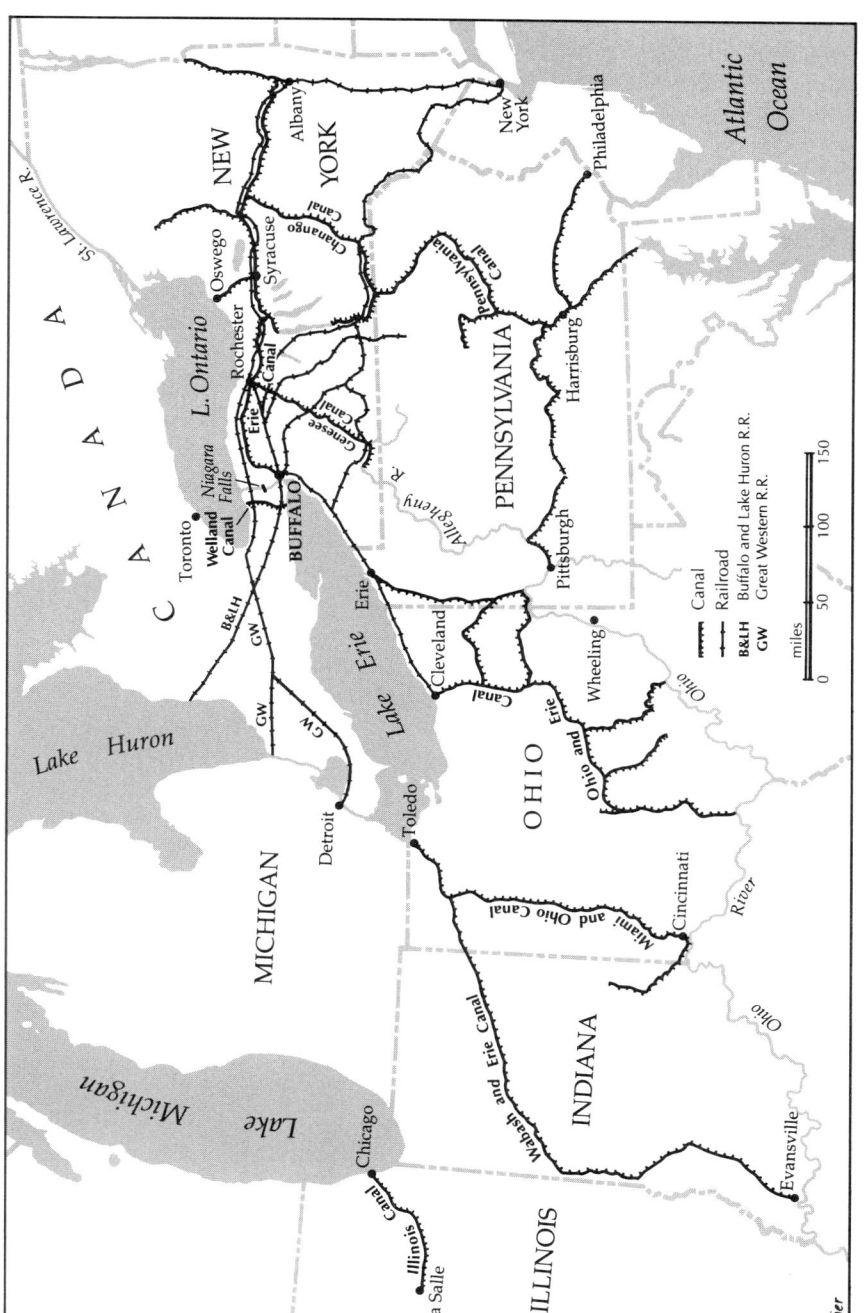

Buffalo: center of antebellum northern transportation routes.

Buffalo in 1936. *Map of the City of Buffalo*, by W. B. Gilbert, City Surveyor (Buffalo, 1836). Courtesy of the Buffalo and Erie County Historical Society.

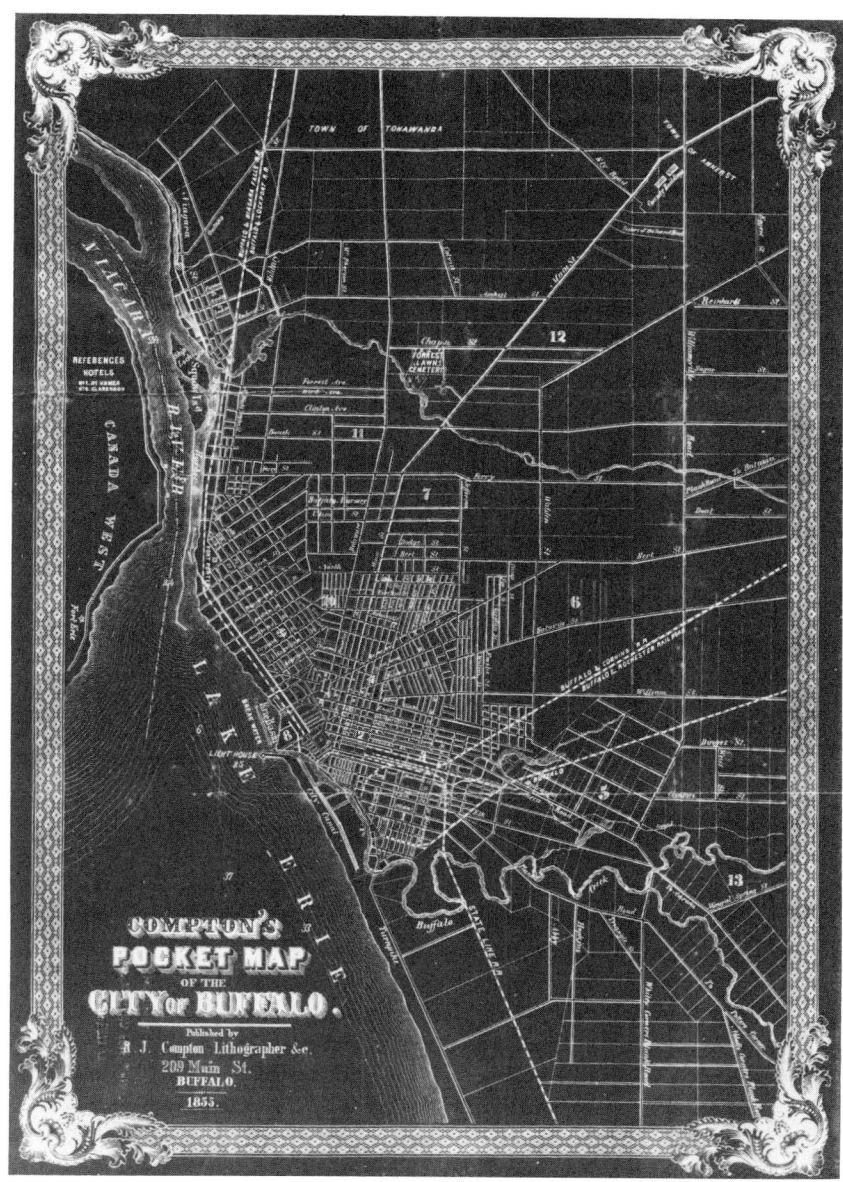

Buffalo in 1855. *Compton's Pocket Map of the City of Buffalo*, by R. J. Compton, Lithographer (Buffalo, 1855). Courtesy of the Buffalo and Erie County Historical Society.

J. W. Hill, *Buffalo*, 1853. C-46096, Public Archives, Canada.

Eduard Hildebrandt, *Street in Buffalo*, 1844. National-Galerie, Staatliche Museen zu Berlin, German Democratic Republic.

Lars Sellstedt, *Buffalo Harbor from the Foot of Porter Avenue*. Courtesy of the Albright-Knox Gallery, Buffalo.

Part Three

The Rise of Ethnocultural Diversity and Pluralism

INTRODUCTION:

Mass Immigration, Ethnicity, and Group Formation

IN the 1840s and 1850s Buffalo developed a diverse, pluralistic population composed of large masses of individuals distinguishable by some combination of shared ethnocultural characteristics and historical circumstances. These distinctive peoples came gradually to have both their own identities and a group life. That they had separate understandings of themselves, varying conceptions of their own self-interest, and unique cultures to defend did not necessarily impede cooperation across group lines. Such cooperation could be seen, for example, in the celebration of the Fourth of July, which was transformed from an entirely American event to a pluralistic civic festival, in which ethnics, representing tne new foreign populations, served on the official planning committee and, as members of ethnic institutions and associations, marched in the official parade. But more commonly, the new pluralism sealed upon American society pervasive patterns of conflict and competition which were especially disturbing elements for native-born Americans.[1]

The source of this new social pluralism was the arrival of the first wave of mass immigration in American national history, which was composed of peasants, small farmers, artisans, and petty traders from Ireland and the German states.[2] The scale of the local demographic transformation is impressive. Bishop John Timon estimated that when Buffalo was incorporated in 1832, its Catholic population was 800. These Irish, German, and Franco-German (Alsatian) Catholics were probably a large majority of the population of foreign residents, since fewer immigrant Protestants had settled in the city.[3] If we add, however, 5 percent to represent, generously, the total of continental, British, and Canadian Protestants, the total percentage of foreigners in a population of 10,000 represents a small degree of ethnic diversity. By 1855 the picture had radically changed. A vast American majority of 85 percent had been overturned, and in its place was a foreign majority almost as large. In that year 18 percent of household heads were born in Ireland, 39 percent in the German states, and 5 percent, the vast majority of them German-speaking Alsatians, in France. Adding the 12 percent of household heads who were British and Canadian, the foreign-born were now some 74 percent. In that year, too, one person in three among household heads was not a citizen; in contrast, in 1846 only one person in six had not been a citizen. The American-born were now a quarter of the population, and a majority in only three of the city's thirteen wards.[4]

This massive population change was not unique. New cities similar to Buffalo in their age, Great Lakes location, and commercial economy also experienced demographic revolutions, though the further west one went, the shorter the period of American numerical predominance before the inception of mass immigration. In Toledo, Cleveland, Detroit, Milwaukee, and Chicago, as in Buffalo, it was the availability of blue-collar employment on the docks, in the building trades, and in industrial shops during years of almost uninterrupted economic expansion that created the preconditions for mass immigrant settlement.[5]

That Buffalo became a leading immigrant-receiving center, however, was greatly determined by its location. The city was the principal transshipment point for much of the passenger as well as commercial traffic that linked together the northern states. Of importance, too, was the international border, which allowed Canadians and European immigrants traveling inland from the ports of Quebec and Montreal to cross over from Ontario to the United States at Buffalo. Knowledgeable local people believed the number of Europeans coming from Ontario increased greatly after the passage in 1846 of federal legislation limiting the number of American-bound immigrant passengers to a fixed percentage of a ship's tonnage, and thus encouraged foreigners to seek to enter the country elsewhere than the large Atlantic ports.[6] Whatever their exact route, immigrants found Buffalo a convenient place to end their journeys. Not only were there both an expanding labor market and cheap land enough in the city for some gardening, stock raising, and wood gathering, but Buffalo was also as convenient an inland city as there was for establishing lines of communication to the Old World and for initiating migrations of family, relatives, and friends. Throughout the 1840s and 1850s Buffalo witnessed a growth of the ticket booking, currency exchange, and remittance services that facilitated chain migration.[7]

All too many journeys, however, came to an *involuntary* halt at Buffalo, largely as a consequence of poverty, disease, and death. It was also a result in some cases of fraud and theft at the docks, particularly by assorted con men and by corrupt transport and hotel agents, called "runners," who were often the immigrants' own countrymen, and who robbed them of their possessions and remaining funds.[8] The number of those stranded at Buffalo was hardly insignificant. During 1855–57, for example, Patrick Short, the local agent of the state Commissioners of Immigration, assisted 11,098 immigrants in need.[9]

The problem of substantial numbers of stranded immigrants reached major proportions in the 1840s and 1850s. Resentment of the obligations it thrust on local people and institutions made American public opinion highly susceptible to outrage before the well-circulated rumors that European governments were emptying their prisons and poorhouses, and sending the inhabitants to America.[10] Such resentments, which obviously fueled nativism, were greatly exacerbated by lethal summer cholera epidemics in 1849, 1852, and 1854. Many Americans blamed them on immigrants, who were indeed likely to contract disease aboard the crowded, filthy boats on which they came to America, and in the slums where they often settled.[11]

So pressing were the human crises that culminated at the docks that it was impossible to avoid for long practical efforts to come to terms with them. The motives involved were both charitable and expedient, for municipal authorities and civic leaders knew that humanitarian assistance put many sick and impoverished immigrants on their way to self-sufficiency and to points west, where they would become someone else's problem. Efforts were launched from a number of directions—sectarian, private and public, at both state and municipal levels. Campaigns to regulate runners and to clear the docks of con men arose simultaneously with the recognition of the need to help their victims and to aid all of the sick and impoverished. Moreover, the common council's regulatory and law enforcement thrusts at the docks and later at train stations were a logical extension of postdepression aspirations to rationalize the use of space at, and bring order to, commercial depots.[12]

The efforts to assist immigrants with charity, medical care, and work expanded in the late 1840s and early 1850s. Prior to the creation of the New York State Commissioners of Immigration in 1847, the local response was largely ad hoc and informal.[13] With appropriations provided by the legislature, and a good deal of allowance for local discretion in their use, however, the Buffalo agent of the commissioners now began to provide emergency material assistance to immigrants in desperate circumstances and to find work for able-bodied adults.[14] Approaches to dealing with the gravely ill, and with broken families and orphans, were also taking shape, thanks largely to a controversial marriage of convenience between public and sectarian efforts. The welfare-minded Timon, who was installed as bishop in 1847, placed caring for the needs of the newly arrived, the most desperate among whom were often Irish and German Catholic peasants, among his highest priorities. He merged his activities with the aim of the commissioners, and under other laws, he capitalized upon the efforts of the state legislature to stimulate local initiatives by making public money available to all institutions, even those with sectarian management, that catered to the material needs of more recent arrivals. Within a few years, the growing list of orphanages, hospitals, and asylums Timon had established were receiving the large majority of the legislature's and the commissioners' local institutional expenditures.[15]

The most affluent and powerful Buffalo citizens, the American bourgeoisie, did not rush to come to the aid of immigrants. In fact, mass immigration posed a sharp moral and practical challenge for them. Wedded ideologically to the idea that economic growth laid the foundations for moral progress, social prosperity, and individual wealth, American employers appreciated the seemingly endless stream of cheap immigrant labor. Yet they resented having to take responsibility for the appalling tragedies that pauperized, sickly, and dependent foreigners placed at their doorstep. This resentment increased alongside their belief that many of the immigrants were responsible for their poverty and were content to live off the charity made available to them. Mass immigration, however, occurred simultaneously with the dawning of the bourgeoisie's sense of obligation to impose its vision of morality, order, and progress on the world. Americans, thus, came soon to feel a moral obligation and a class responsibility to aid immigrants. Moreover, while Americans did frequently voice intolerant rejection of foreigners, enough of them, including such moderate nativists as Millard Fillmore, possessed faith in the absorptive capacities of their society to believe the immigrants would eventually be able to assume all of the rights and obligations of citizenship.

The American bourgeoisie, therefore, proved willing, within the moral and political boundaries defined by its ideology and self-interest, to take on some of the burdens of assisting the immigrants to sink roots into American soil. Much of this assistance was provided on an informal, individual basis. For example, Americans who owned large amounts of East Side property provided land grants to immigrant churches and easy terms to their members, who wished to buy homesteads nearby.[16] But other efforts, such as the Buffalo Association for the Relief of the Poor, the objects of whose aid were overwhelmingly foreigners, were formal and systematic, and involved outright material subsidies to individuals.

The immigrants also had to be brought into the public community—in their relations to government as citizens, taxpayers, consumers of public services, jurors, and when relevant, as lawbreakers, and to the political system, as voters, officeholders, and party officials and party workers. This was especially problematic for Americans. As American politics took form under the pressures of democratization and mass electioneering, politics became an activity into which people were integrated not as individuals, but as members of groups, and principally in northern cities, ethnic ones. Groups were thus encouraged to develop their own civic and political interests and to mobilize to protect and expand them. Immigrants quickly embraced these processes. Their historical and cultural circumstances impelled them toward group identity and group formation. In the course of adapting themselves to American public life they grasped the opportunity to define their own needs and aspirations, and they came to reject American attempts to do this for them. Along with the growing group orientation in civic and political life, which seemed to challenge the heretofore secure status of the independent individual as the moral basis of society, this rejection of American authority loomed especially large in alienating many bourgeois Americans from the new society taking shape around them. Though only dimly perceived by bourgeois Americans at the time, the burden of their historical situation should be clear to us. The world they were attempting to mold in their own image was itself being transformed by processes that eluded their manipulation. However great, therefore, were the social problems created by the presence of the immigrants, the political problem posed by the rise of the immigrants as self-conscious members of active, competitive, and confident groups often seemed a greater problem.

The new ethnic groups were formed in America as a consequence of a complex fusing of Old World social forms, cultures, symbols, and psychologies with New World economic, political and social experiences, challenges, and opportunities. As a linguistic convenience, we must use the words "ethnic group" and "ethnicity" (i.e., ethnic identity and belonging) as if speaking of things that were in themselves complete. Actually, however, particularly in this formative era of mass immigration, both were *emergent*—in the process of becoming.

The importance of this insight becomes clearer if we try to define the ethnic group in preparation for analyzing the Buffalo Germans and Irish. Along with Milton Yinger, we may, for a start, say that the ethnic group is "a segment of a large society whose members are thought, by themselves and/or others, to have a common origin and to share important segments of a common culture and who, in addition, participate in shared activities in which common origin and culture are significant ingredients."[17] From a developmental perspective, however, Yinger's definition, even with its careful combination of subjective and objective components, is still not entirely satisfactory. It provides no sense of the process of a group's creation, of its *ethnicization*. Immigrants cannot be said to possess some primordial consciousness of themselves as members of an ethnic group. Nor can it be said that a feeling of ethnic identity arises suddenly, ex nihilo, upon emigration. Nor do others necessarily see them as members of groups at first. Such external perceptions of immigrants must develop gradually in the context of daily social interaction, while the immigrants' internal understanding of possessing a group identity comes as a result of existential fusing of its Old World cultural inheritance (language, religion, values, beliefs, and expressive symbols) and New World experiences.[18]

New World experiences were framed within several contexts. Perhaps the most important of these, because of its impact on daily life, was the world of work, opportunity, and structured social inequality. The impact of socioeconomic processes upon ethnic group formation was reinforced at Buffalo, because the functional division of labor was also a cultural division of labor, since each of the major ethnic solidarities tended to dominate a sector of the occupational structure. Furthermore, because of this cultural division of labor, class organization, protest, and consciousness bore indelibly the stamp of ethnicity. At Buffalo, therefore, the role of class in ethnic group formation and of ethnicity in class formation must be reciprocally conceived. Yet the particular dynamism of ethnicity, which was the identity within which meaning was attached to so many of the habits and necessities of daily life, combined with the sectoral isolation of each major group in the economy, to leave the working class deeply split along cultural lines, even as workers developed a social consciousness both of class and of their capacity for activism around job-related issues.[19] A second context was participation in government and politics, which exerted, as we have noted, a powerful, formative influence on the ethnic group. Finally, social behavior at work, or in politics, historically has played a considerable role in determining how immigrants have been perceived by others. Accurate observations of social behavior were one basis, though not the only one, for the stereotypes forming the perceptual substructure of interethnic relations. Stereotypes, however, were generally filtered through unreflective ethnocentric or consciously prejudiced lenses.[20]

A process of group formation is also implied in that part of Yinger's definition that pertains to shared activities in which ethnic criteria are significant bases for association. The rise of ethnic association and of duplicative ethnic institutions, and hence of an ethnic subsociety, is a process fed by two overlapping streams of activity. First, there are activities by which individuals seek to perpetuate the foundations of the inherited culture of daily life—marriage, family and household formation, creation of kinship and friendship networks, and neighborhood concentration within boundaries formed by place of origin, common language or dialect, religion, and social class. Second, there are formalistic group activities, which develop simultaneously with the rise of ethnic identification. These include both creation of institutions and voluntary associations (churches, burial societies, sectarian schools, lodges, the press) and group mobilizations for social resources and power (neighborhood political party organization, ad hoc civic lobbies, mass meetings). If family, kinship, friendship, and neighborhood form the private, interpersonal bases for an ethnic social substructure, then communal institutions, associations, and mobilizations form the public bases. The latter train group leadership and discipline members for group service as well as establish the group's public identity and give form and meaning to its public activities.[21] Mobilizations, moreover, are potent bases for deepening ethnic identification, even as they simultaneously function to integrate the group into society. Public life, which has frequently been centered around intergroup conflict and competition, provides ample opportunity for dichotomous, us-against-them thinking.[22]

Not that there is necessarily unanimity within ethnic institutions, associations, and mobilizations. The ethnic group is not a simple, face-to-face community in which there is a general consensus of opinion, however much in its simple segmentary units such as family, household, and kinship networks it contains the possibilities for community.[23] It is instead a large, complex group in which there is a considerable variety of opinion, particularly on the subjects of its own needs and purposes. The internal growth of the ethnic group, in fact, owes a great deal to struggle, which actually has an integrative function because it involves those participating in it more deeply in the group. Such struggle takes place within group institutions and associations and is waged most heatedly within the emergent ethnic leadership that commands them.[24]

With its sociospatial segmentation, the American city was a hothouse environment for the rise of structural pluralism. Buffalo's high indices of ethnic residential concentration lent themselves to a high degree of institutional completeness within ethnic neighborhoods, an absence of social interpenetration among groups, a circumscribing of spontaneous intergroup contacts among individuals, and well-defined perceptions of ethnic territorial boundaries. Territoriality intensified ethnic self-awareness, and to the extent that long-established ethnics chose to continue to reside in the familiar and secure neighborhoods of first settlement, self-awareness reinforced territoriality. Both territoriality and group self-awareness assisted one another in heightening commitment to maintain ethnic associations and institutions.[25] And because voluntary association was so prevalent in America, its use by immigrants actually reinforced ethnic structural pluralism by providing it with both social legitimacy and a high degree of social efficacy.[26]

Not all of Buffalo's groups completely meet the criteria of Yinger's definition. Employing his distinction between "full" and "minimal" ethnicity, in which the former is ethnic identification, an external perception of groupness, a common culture, and structural pluralism, and the latter is a lesser degree of any one or of all of them,[27] the Americans, British, and Canadians may be said variously to display minimal ethnicity. In sharp contrast, the Irish and Germans, to whom we now turn, are clear examples of full ethnicity, though in each case ethnicization had different groundings and lines of direction. The creation of these two new, large ethnic groups was without social precedent in America. Its effects would not only reverberate throughout, but transform, society, which came to integrate them on terms as much their own as those of the Americans who assumed they were society's leaders.

CHAPTER 6

Poverty, Catholicism, and Solidarity: The Formation of Irish Ethnicity

LIFE in Ireland was tightly circumscribed by British colonialism and rural exploitation and poverty. British colonial administration had long sought to suppress Roman Catholicism and the yearnings of the Catholic masses for national self-determination, and to keep the island's inhabitants powerless and ignorant. Moreover, colonial policy had long ago created a class of Protestant, Anglo-Irish landowners, whose privileges and estates were protected at the expense of the native rural population. A system of land tenure, based on the monopolization of the best lands, consigned small farmers to work, as population grew, ever smaller parcels of land, or to join the broadening ranks of a landless rural proletariat composed of laborers and tenants. The growing impoverishment of the masses not only set land-poor Irishmen against the Anglo-Irish landlords, but set Irish rural labor and renters against Irish yeomen smallholders, who also exploited desperate wage earners and cultivators. Class antagonisms were thus added to traditional regional rivalries as sources of division. The catastrophic Potato Famine of 1845–50 revealed the viciousness of these mechanisms of powerlessness, poverty, dependence, and fragmentation. A famine in the key food crop of the rural poor led to the death of perhaps a million and the emigration of a million and a half, and left the countryside a social ruin.[1]

Within these historical constraints, the Irish developed a strong folk culture, which centered around family, kinship, commune, and church. Along with a secular ideology of national liberation, the folk culture served as a basis for a growing sense of Irish peoplehood. National solidarity helped counter internal sources of division, and it provided a basis for early nineteenth-century popular mobilizations for Catholic emancipation and against exploitation by the Anglo-Irish renter class.[2]

Immigration, however, remained a more common strategy than confrontation. Perhaps a million Irish immigrated to the United States between 1815 and 1845, but many of them, especially in the early years, were Protestants whose skills, religion, and individualistic culture helped them gain both acceptance by Americans and socioeconomic mobility. Catholic immigration also increased in those years, but before the famine significantly sized Irish Catholic populations were found only in eastern seaboard cities.[3] There were few Irish Catholics in Buffalo before the late 1840s.[4] Bishop Timon estimated that the city's Irish Catholic population was only 400 in 1832. Fewer than 1 percent of the Irish household heads in 1855 had been in the city before 1830, and only 24 percent (654) had arrived before 1846. Though an Irish parish, St. Patrick's, was established in 1839, its founding was a response not to population growth, but to conflict between the German-speaking majority and the clergy, with whom the Irish sided, at St. Louis Church, the only Catholic parish. Not until St. Mary's of the Lake in 1849 was an Irish parish created in response to population growth.[5]

Famine-era immigration then established the basis for both a sizeable Irish population and Irish ethnicity. Indeed in 1855, fully 56 percent (1,525) of the Irish household heads had arrived in 1850–51 alone.[6] While the prefamine migration was comprised mostly of young, single men and women, the majority of famine emigrants were with their families. Some of these hard-pressed families went to destinations where they could get assistance from already resettled kin and friends. But many had no such chains to link them to destinations and to ease their passage. They were forced to adopt a strategy of serial migration, characterized by brief residence in several locations to earn money to travel in search of better situations. This is suggested by the large number of children of famine-era immigrants born outside both Ireland and Buffalo. Almost half (184 of 384) of the children of Irish household heads in 1855 had been born elsewhere in New York State (37), in the Canadas (29), or at some other American or foreign location (118).[7] The circumstances of these immigrants upon local settlement are suggested by the fact that of those Irish household heads in 1855 who had been in Buffalo for a year, none owned any property—compared to 2 percent among Germans and 17 percent among Americans resident for a year.[8]

Even with the advantage of knowing English, the famine-era Irish had much going against them in America. They had few marketable skills, little education, and no money. Substantial social disorganization—poverty, crime, disease, alcoholism, and family dissolution—accompanied their resettlement in America. Such difficulties were exacerbated by strong rejection by American Protestants of their peasant ways and devout Catholicism, and by the harsh stereotypes that determined popular attitudes whenever the Irish came to mind. These obstacles limited the chances for individual lives and depressed the group's social position. The socioeconomic bases of Irish ethnicity would be quite weak, and the group's constricted range of opportunity would be too narrow to produce a stable, sizeable leadership beyond the ranks of the clergy, who were representives of the only abiding institution the Irish possessed.

Yet to view the 1840s and 1850s as Irish-America's "tragic era" falls short of the mark. The famine-era immigrants had useful social resources in their peasant culture and their religion. Family and kinship ties and a strong female role often survived the famine and served as bases for organizing the domestic economy of the individual household. As the foundation of a stable institution and a coherent morality and worldview, Catholicism proved an essential resource for group formation. So, too, did the group's Old World political and prepolitical experience, its long-established habits of solidarity in the face of external threat, and its emotional nationalism, which was informed by folk memories of oppression and resistance. In America, these Old World forms of identity and organization left a particularly deep impression upon the processes of Irish group formation, as would such New World experiences as political mobilizations in defense of the Catholic church, highly unified and strongly partisan participation in the Democratic party, and intermittent but intense labor struggles.[9]

Irish immigrant life took form amidst the pressures of poverty. In 1855, 57 percent of Irish households resided in lakeshore and canal corridor slums, variously named "the Patch," "the Flats," "the Beach," "the Hook, " and "Sandytown," of the First and Eighth wards. The First Ward, which was 62 percent foreign-born and mostly Irish, had more recently arrived immigrants. Thirty-nine percent of its people were not citizens; in the Eighth Ward, though 80 percent were foreign-born (also mostly Irish), only 13 percent were aliens and thus probably in the country under five years. Another 15 percent of the Irish households of 1855 were to be found in wards Two and Three, further up from the docks and somewhat less congested.[10] These residential patterns reflected both proximity to Irish workplaces and poverty. Along the canal corridor and near the docks one found the cheapest housing. Most of the better-off Irish workers lived in decrepit, small to medium-sized dwellings, which had been subdivided in order to accommodate several families. It was subdivision, rather than the presence of multiunit residences, such as tenements, that accounted for the fact that, while the largely German Sixth and Seventh wards averaged two and five residents per dwelling, respectively, in the Irish First and Eighth, the figures were ten and eighteen, respectively. Though they usually avoided this type of crowding, the poorest Irish often lived in huts no more than twelve feet to a side. These were located on the beach or just off the docks, and constructed of waste boards. Some lived aboard decommissioned canal boats that had been beached. In the densely packed dwellings of these shantytowns, where, said the *Courier* in 1851, one saw "the spectacle of a most squalid poverty hardly credible in this land of plenty," each dwelling constituted a fire hazard to the next. The tidal wave bearing storms that swept the lakes also decimated these neighborhoods.[11] Few of these shacks were owned by their inhabitants. In 1855, after nine years in America, only 31 percent of Irish households owned their dwellings. Only 23 percent of all Irish household heads owned homes in 1855, compared to 56 percent and 54 percent among Americans and Germans. Irish dwellings averaged lower in value, at $1,000, than the dwellings of the other two groups, and 90 percent were made of plank or wood frame.[12]

The Irish nonetheless attempted to fashion familiar living arrangements. As in the old country, they regularly kept pigs, poultry, and dairy cattle in and around their places of residence, as Dr. Burwell found when he attended a birth at a shack on the beach and found himself competing for floor space with the resident swine. In America, too, the animals were a precious asset, though they did nothing to improve the image of the Irish among Americans like Burwell. Irish families regularly supplemented their incomes selling milk in the city, a kind of working-class entrepreneurship through urban agriculture in which the East Side German even more frequently took part. Cows belonging to the Irish could graze freely during the summer in the rich bottomlands south of the central docks and in the wild places along the Niagara, but in the winter, along with the other beasts, they had to be consumed or sold—or admitted to the family circle.[13]

However much culture and tradition shaped it, entrenchment of this way of life was ultimately a consequence of the particular niche in the local economy that Irish men occupied. Their lack of urban job experience and skills combined with the city's tremendous need for unskilled labor to guarantee them a secure foothold only in the secondary labor market. Mattis's sample of 5 percent of all Irish men taken from the 1855 state census establishes that 46 percent could state no regular occupation at all, another 20 percent described themselves as outdoor or general laborers with no fixed working place, and 2 percent said they were steadily employed, unskilled workers at a nameable workplace. Six percent were transport workers—principally teamsters, lake sailors, and canal boatmen—whose skill level was not high. Only 17 percent were skilled or semiskilled, 7 percent lower white-collar workers, and 2 percent owners of retail, wholesale, or industrial establishments.[14] Lack of skills and experience, as well as capital, rather than discrimination, also conspired to impair occupational mobility. Occasionally, it is true, want ads in the local press did specifically express preferences for other than Irish workers, but Germans and even British and Canadian workers were also explicitly excluded at times in such advertisements. There is no evidence of a systematic, customary, or certainly of a legal prohibition against employing Irish workers in better positions. That locally the "NINA" ("No Irish Need Apply") syndrome, which was common along the eastern seaboard, was an individual, nativist idiosyncracy is attested to, under any circumstance, by the fact that such prohibitions exclusively appeared in advertisements for domestic servants. This was a field, however, in which Irish women had a secure foothold, and it was actually, as we shall see, a relatively bright spot in the Irish employment picture.[15]

Unskilled labor was a significantly sized, diverse occupational cohort, but the Irish occupied an especially limiting functional location within it. Many Germans were unskilled laborers, too, more indeed in absolute numbers than the Irish. But the Germans were found largely in building construction, where opportunities for informal, on-the-job apprenticeship were common, because laborers mixed constantly with artisans and craftsmen during the working day. In contrast, Irish unskilled work was a dead end in terms of both skill acquisition and opportunities for mobility. (This helps to explain why analysis of a sample of Irish workers in the 1865 state census found only a modest, 6 percent increase—to 23 percent—in the percentage of Irish semiskilled and skilled workers over the census of 1855.) Irish work was typically little but lifting of heavy objects and digging, work that required toughness of body and spirit rather than experience or skill. Many Irishmen were employed as longshoremen in offloading lake and canal craft, not only of baggage, produce, livestock and finished goods, but also, most critically for the efficiency of the port, grain. Human labor remained essential to the grain business even after the development of the grain elevator, because men were needed to work the mechanical grain-scooping equipment, to shovel grain into elevator bins as they moved on pulleys, and to clear remote corners of ships that motorized equipment could not reach. Irishmen also worked at repairing the sea wall in the outer harbor, digging out slips for warehouses and elevators, mending the banks of the rivers and the canal in the spring, and dredging water courses, basins, and slips. Work they arranged on municipal, state, and federal infrastructure projects was often obtained through Irish interpersonal and political networks within the Democratic party, providing an added incentive for the especially intense quality of Irish partisanship. Irish teamsters, who comprised about half of these workers, were often employed in transporting goods to and from trains and boats and carting off dirt and stones from harbor and municipal projects. This work, too, was obtained through political connections.[16]

There were formidable obstacles to making a living at outdoor, unskilled labor even in a booming port. The work was low-paying, seasonal, and without regular or predictable hours, which further limited earnings. "We discharge daily more or less men depending on daily needs," explained a contractor involved in canal enlargement in 1849. Joseph Dart has left records to illustrate this pattern. He hired a group of six Irishmen in 1846 to do excavating at his port properties. Over the course of approximately seven weeks of work, the two men for whom there are extant pay records averaged 2.4 and 1.9 days a week, at a rate of seventy-five cents a day. In the 1850s Erie Canal laborers could make a dollar a day, when working a full day, but like Dart's laborers, few actually were able to do so. In grain the "scoopers" were paid on a low, piece-rate basis according to the number of bushels offloaded. Even if one had to go from one job to another several times a day, work was plentiful. But labor was hardly in short supply, a fact which explains the very low wage rates, and, a few notable examples aside, the near impossibility of uniting men so desperate for work to struggle against low wage rates.[17] The vast numbers of Irishmen looking for work about the port also explains the callousness of foremen in the face of the constant dangers of longshore work. Grain scoopers were often sucked along with grain as it moved, with tremendous force, through pipes conducting it from elevators to boats (or vice versa), and were asphyxiated in a dense mass of flying grain. In addition, as farm boys, many Irish longshoremen did not know how to swim. When they fell off a gangplank with a heavy load on their backs, drowning was predictable. Yet Irish life, like Irish labor, came cheap, and the attitude toward these accidents may well be summed up by an 1846 incident. When an Irishman fell into the water with a grain sack on his shoulders, reported the *Commercial Advertiser*, "Efforts to save the wheat were successful, but the same exertions were not made to save his life."[18]

Seasonality, underemployment and subemployment forced Irish laborers and their families to adopt various occupational and domestic strategies for supplementing their incomes. Fundamental to the laborers' effort, both in winter and in occasional slack periods during the season of navigation, was a willingness to travel to distant sites to take jobs and to remain away for months if need be. Irish laborers were regularly hired by professional labor recruiters, who worked in cooperation with the Overseers of the Poor, the agent of the Commissioners of Immigration, and tavern and boardinghouse keepers to find men in need of work to lay down railroad track or to dig canals in southern New York State, Pennsylvania, and more distant points, such as Illinois. The public works in Canada also recruited local Irishmen, but to the extent that leaving the country could hinder one's naturalization, many men were wary of going there. The most frequent source of extralocal employment, both in and out of season, was repair and improvement of the Erie Canal itself. Because of the tremendous loss sustained by shippers when the canal was closed during the navigation season, routine maintenance and massive enlargement projects alike were frequently undertaken in winter. Local laborers and teamsters were most often hired to work the Buffalo District, the 117-mile stretch between the city and Montezuma, and were usually near enough to return on Sundays. Near or far, the ease with which recruiters could find laborers demonstrates the chronic joblessness the men experienced. And again, the surplus of labor kept wages down, particularly in winter. Contractors, too, kept wages down further because, they explained, they were obligated to provide travel and room and board for sojourning laborers.[19]

Working Irish women, whose knowledge of English enhanced their prospects in the market for service workers, were able routinely to find jobs in domestic and personal service. They worked as maids, laundresses and domestics in hotels, but most often were employed by affluent American families. The work involved close scrutiny by one's employer, having to be on call twenty-four hours a day, and in the case of the live-in servant, isolation from family and friends. No wonder it was unpopular among those like working-class American girls, whose relative affluence allowed them to try to find something better. But the wages were no worse than those paid women in eastern factories, and were a good deal better where servants were in short supply. Moreover, there were such benefits as a private room, board, and Christmas bonus, and gifts of discarded clothing and other personal items from employers. Under any circumstance, there was little alternative source of employment for women. Without a significant textile and ready-made clothing industry of the type that absorbed female workers in the East, Buffalo could not offer women work outside domestic and personal service.[20] What few industrial opportunities there were for those other than adult men went usually to boys, who worked as helpers and fabricators at petty, low-wage mechanical tasks in small shops.[21]

Irish service work must be seen in the context of the domestic economy of the Old and New World Irish household, in which poverty compelled each member to engage in the struggle to make ends meet. Irish women were found in service both before and after marriage. In 1855 about 19 percent of Irish women were employed outside the home, 86 percent of them as service workers. Almost all of these employed women were young, unmarried girls. Some were solitary emigrants, and many of them hoped to earn money enough to send for family, or at least through periodic remittances to help maintain those in Ireland. Probably the majority, however, were the daughters of local families. Irish girls began leaving their families for service as early as age eleven, and by the years between eighteen and twenty-one, from 46 percent to 66 percent were in service. (In contrast, at age eighteen, 60 percent of American girls were at home.) Though by age twenty-two a majority of Irish girls were married, at ages twenty-eight and twenty-nine nearly one Irish woman in five was still in service and still no doubt continuing to make contributions to the family economy in Ireland or the United States. This pattern of long delayed or no marriage was considerably reinforced by Irish cultural values. The Irish did not look scornfully on an unmarried girl working, or generally on the single woman, and placed a high valuation on celibacy for both sexes.[22]

A contrast to the pattern of single working girls and women is provided by the 6 percent of Irish women in service who were married, some no doubt keeping positions they had prior to being wed, but others taking up work after marriage. Yet the figure vastly underestimates the actual number of married Irish women who worked in service, since many women did service work in their own homes while caring for their own children and keeping house. Laundering on a pick-up-and-delivery basis was a specialty of Irish women. Irish women also took in roomers and boarders, who, related and unrelated, were to be found in 29 percent of Irish households in 1855. Irish women probably also superintended boarding and rooming arrangements at the sixty-odd Irish groceries and at dozens of Irish saloons, where young, single laborers often slept in the basements and in corners. The women cooked, cleaned, and sewed for boarders, and they also served liquor and waited on shoppers. Finally, though it was as much entrepreneurial as service work, Irish housewives peddled and delivered the milk given by their family dairy cows. By 1859 it was estimated that there were as many as forty First Ward family milk businesses, a large percentage of them Irish-owned.[23]

The boarding of relatives and women's contributions to household income were part of a larger pattern of family and kin mutual support that had origins in the peasant villages of Ireland and underwent various transformations, like boarding, while taking root in the city.[24] Support was obtained not only from kin who were boarders, but also from those relatives who lived nearby. In contrast to the Germans, only some 12.5 percent of whom had kin in Buffalo in 1855, approximately 25 percent of the Irish did, a sign of strong immigration chains. Half of these kin lived as boarders in the homes of relatives. The other half resided in the same working-class Irish neighborhoods of the First and Eighth wards. The value of localized kin ties beyond boarding is seen in the godparentage roles kin assumed when they sponsored an infant at baptism. The act of sponsorship contained the promise that should some disaster befall the biological parents, the child would be looked after. For the majority without local kin ties, friends were chosen to act as baptismal sponsors, an eventuality that probably took place less often in Ireland. These fictive kinship ties moved friendship one step beyond its usual obligations to the moral plane of familial mutualism.[25]

Changes in family formation habits also were among the strategies developed for coping with poverty, and they were reinforced by patterns developing simultaneously in Ireland. The famine was a watershed in the history of the Irish peasant family system, marking the acceleration of the trend toward deferred marriage, lower birth rates, and increasing celibacy, which, along with emigration, were means for ending further parcelization of land holdings. The famine Irish in America had their own reasons for adopting these same patterns—the unpredictability of the urban job market for the unskilled male and the inability of male children to make as significant a material contribution as they had on the farm. The Old World situation was not irrelevant, however, for the chains the American Irish established to the Old World linked them to those, many of whom they would bring to America, increasingly adopting the same patterns. This process of change began almost immediately upon resettlement with what appear to be conscious decisions to limit fertility. Calculations based on the 1855 state census reveal lower fertility for the Irish in the fifteen to nineteen (313 children 0–4 per 1,000 married women) and twenty to fourteen (728) age cohorts than for Germans (888; 850) and other immigrants (357; 808), which suggests a break with the higher fertility patterns of prefamine Ireland. The same goal of greater material security was served, too, by a trend toward delayed marriage. Contrasting 1855 and 1875 censuses, Mary Catherine Mattis discovered a consistent increase in the percentage of both sexes remaining single.[26]

No family strategy could be broad enough in the context of poverty and occupational ghettoization to cover all contingencies. Moreover, for those without local kin or friends, these networks were absent. It is not surprising that individual and family disorganization was ever present among the Irish, and that it frequently became the basis of the view of them held by others, especially Americans. In the 1840s the Irish began to supplant native-born Americans in the poorhouse population, and soon their percentage among the inmates was massively out of proportion to their portion in the total population. It continued to rise, straining the facility's already inadequate resources, as the famine Irish arrived in growing numbers, and fell only after their resettlement ended in the late 1850s. Forty percent of the poorhouse population during 1842–48, the Irish constituted an average of 51.2 percent in the 1850s. In 1849, at the height of the famine influx, they reached 63 percent of inmates, 5,863 people.[27] The Irish were by no means the only poor and dependent people in Buffalo. German immigrants produced their share of people needing charitable assistance. During the recession winter of 1854–55, for example, more Germans (9,199) received outdoor relief than Irish (7,841).[28] Aside from the fact, however, that the German percentage of those relieved (46 percent) was equivalent to the percentage of German-speakers in the population, while at 40 percent the Irish percentage was about twice that, the data constitute the exception that proves the rule of comparative Irish degradation. As a population with a large number of skilled workers, it took an economic crisis to put large numbers of Germans on the dole, while the Irish needed assistance in good and bad times alike. In good times, however, they stayed in the poorhouse only in the depths of the winter and generally for shorter periods.[29] In addition, having to seek commitment to the poorhouse represented a much greater breakdown of individual and family independence than did receiving outdoor relief, for the latter was a subsidy to supplement, not a substitute for, income or savings. Under any circumstance, the Buffalo Association for the Relief of the Poor usually also had to provide more outdoor relief to the Irish than to any other people in the city.[30]

The soul-wrenching poverty which necessitated commitment to the poorhouse was not spread evenly among the Irish, but rather concentrated among women. Before the Civil War, women were never more than 45 percent of the total poorhouse population, but among the Irish they were 49 percent (1853–54) and 51.4 percent (1855–59) in the years for which we have inmate data by gender. That so many Irish women should have been in dire circumstances (and probably there were many more who suffered than consented to go to the poorhouse) is related to the relatively large populations of two groups among Irish immigrant women. First, there was the large number of single women. While the sex ratio of the Irish population in 1855 was near parity (99.0), for the ten to twenty-nine age cohort, in which there were many immigrants, it was 83.7. In consequence, it was a statistical probability that women would be overrepresented among the Irish poor—to the extent that especially recent immigrants were likely to encounter difficult circumstances.[31] Second, there was the relatively large number of Irish women who were single parents. Glasco found that 13 percent of Irish households were single-parent, female-headed in contrast to 6 percent among Germans and 10 percent among white, native-born Americans, and that the pattern was strongest for women of childbearing age. Death, desertion, or mutual separation, as well as the temporary but extended absence of husbands working outside the city, all offer explanations. Certainly the crushing burdens of supporting a family on a laborer's occasional wages must have broken the spirit of many a man and led him to desert. As it was, the status in the family of these men was eroded in the act of resettlement. In contrast to their situation in Ireland, they had no skills or land to pass down to their sons, and they were often quite dependent on the money-making activities of wives and daughters.[32] Whatever the explanation, of all the women in Buffalo, Irish women were more likely to enter the poorhouse with relatives, mostly young children, and without men. Indeed the point in the 1840s at which the Irish began to predominate in the poorhouse population, overtaking native-born Americans, marked another turning point in the inmate population's composition. Henceforth, membership in broken families rather than complete, nuclear ones, the customary American pattern at the poorhouse, would typify those admitted with relatives.[33]

The moral breakdown present in desertion was even more evident in other contexts, such as crime, vice, violence, and alcoholism. This was much less a female than male problem. In spite of the many hardships they faced, Irish women were rarely associated with prostitution, even by the nativist press, which never missed an opportunity to heap abuse on the Irish. The impression gathered from the names of arrested prostitutes suggests that they were native-born. Though the city's brothel district was in an Irish neighborhood, Irish women seem to have been rarely involved. Illegitimacy, which would have been as great a departure from Irish peasant morality, appears to have been rare, too, insofar as one may know from parish baptismal records. The Catholic clergy certainly feared for the sexual purity of young Irish girls, particularly those in service in Protestant households where they might be pressured into granting sexual favors. Catholics, lay and clerical alike, also felt that Protestants had much looser sexual morals. But no examples were ever given to substantiate these fears, which were rooted in suspicions about the tempting circumstances of residence in the home of a wealthy infidel. Many girls were probably actually kept out of trouble by the wages service work provided and by the isolation of working in another's home every day but Sunday, when they usually attended mass and visited relatives. The violence and abuse of alcohol involving Irish women, according to reports in the press, usually took place within the family. Some Irish women were beaten by husbands and were partners in their excessive drinking, situations which lead us to inquire into male behavior.[34]

Irish men did experience a much greater tendency toward moral breakdown and a disorganized, self-defeating social existence. This is most strongly suggested by the incidence of their commitment to the county jail, the middle rung of the penal system, between the neighborhood lockup and the state prisons. Here were sent those men found guilty of modest offenses having to do with creating disorder. In the 1840s and 1850s, the percentage of Irish males in the county jail was always much larger than their percentage in the total population, and it rose steadily with the growth of the famine-era migrants: 28 percent (200) in 1846; 40 percent (464) in 1852–53; 38 percent (456) in 1853–54; 43 percent (668) in 1854–55; and 42.5 percent (550) in 1857–58. Jail statistics reveal that the majority of these men were single laborers in their twenties and thirties charged with vagrancy, intoxication, and disorderly conduct, crimes common to the poor.[35] To be sure, such data cannot be interpreted as a representation of crime, and they have to be placed in relevant social, legal, and cultural contexts to be understood. Included in the data are men whose offenses were petty, but who could not pay fines, obviously a problem for any poor people. Moreover, not only were the courts likely to be tough on a people as hated and feared as the Irish, but the values on which the law was based were not those of Irish peasant culture. Behavior which was innocuous in a rural context—drunkenness, fighting, public noisemaking—became offensive and criminal in an urban one. Finally, though we have no way of knowing how many, some of those incarcerated were probably transients, not Buffalo residents.

But all these exceptions noted, violence, excessive drinking, frequently to inebriation, alcoholism, and chronic conflict with the institutions of the law were hardly rare occurrences for the Irish. They were certainly more, too, than artifacts of the process of record keeping. Nor in such behavior is there evidence of prepolitical resistance to American exploitation and demands for cultural conformity, though no doubt a good deal of inchoate anger may have been present in run-ins with the law. The consequences of violence and excessive drinking were most devastating for the Irish themselves, as their own leaders were the first to understand. These behaviors exacerbated the difficulties imposed by poverty, and they alienated the Irish from one another and from other working-class people around them with whom they might have cooperated for their own benefit. Nor may Irish social disorganization and moral breakdown be ascribed completely to the effects of American poverty or the alienation resulting from the immigration and resettlement process, for though both exacerbated them, the roots frequently lay deep within the fabric of Irish peasant culture. This is not to say that the nativist press was innocent of exaggeration and outright prejudice, but even its caricatured portrait of the Irish did not arise in a vacuum.

The Irish drank a great deal, and drinking was deeply integrated, both in Ireland and United States, into the structure of daily life. This could be said of German immigrants, but both in the Old and the New World they largely consumed a much milder brew, lager beer, and they drank in the warm, convivial setting of the beer garden, surrounded often by family, music, and dancing, or in the largely male setting of the corner grocery, a popular neighborhood institution, while playing checkers or cards. Not only did the Irish drink potent distilled spirits, but as important, the cultural and social setting of Irish drinking lent itself to excess and to conflict with the society in which they were seeking to establish themselves.

The moral control of spirits was weak in Ireland. Spirits lacked a sacred function to assist in marking boundaries for its use, and while the church had always denounced inebriation, it did not condemn the moderate use of liquor. Thus, whiskey served exclusively utilitarian functions, which might expand with historical circumstances. In Ireland, whiskey was used as a substitute for food in times of famine and on Catholic feast days, when only one meal was permitted. Folk tradition prescribed it as medicine and tonic, and it was given to children as an inducement to good behavior. In lieu of warm clothing, it offered temporary relief from, not to mention a way of forgetting, the discomforts of the island's cold and damp winter climate. Illegal distillation, which was common in Ireland, provided supplements for peasant incomes, and offered a way of resisting British power by evading imports. Whiskey was at the center of social life from cradle to grave. It was a staple at christenings, weddings, and wakes. Much Irish social drinking, however, was sex segregated, for it took place in a culture characterized by rigid social separation of the sexes. The "shebeen," or rural drinking hut, was perhaps the only male retreat from crowded peasant cottages.

Too, there was an element of male sport and competitiveness, as well as bonding, about the practice of "treating," by which one established a capacity to drink and to spend money.[36]

In America whiskey was socially contextualized in many of the same ways. But it also came to enter the life of young, single men in additional, new ones. The lodging and boarding houses where these men lived and socialized were also often grocery-saloons. Here, too, while waiting around and drinking, many men were recruited daily for work by stevedores and contractors. These employers routinely provided Irish laborers on the canals and railroads with whiskey to keep them contented on the job and preoccupied in the evening at isolated, rural work sites. The cost of whiskey was often deducted from a man's pay.[37]

Irish culture and American circumstances, therefore, both tended to legitimate drinking and to expand the opportunities in which it might take place. As a result, many men went down the road to impoverishment and lack of responsibility to those dependent on them, and ultimately to alcoholism and premature death. Almost as significant in deepening the difficulties with alcohol of the Irish as a group was the deeply felt desire of many Americans to use the law to regulate or to prohibit the use of spirits. These desires were a response to a concrete problem, and hardly exclusively an Irish one, for there were large numbers of intemperate Americans. But in moving the problem of liquor and its control to a legal plane, temperance could transform the Irish tippler, who saw nothing wrong with his behavior, into a lawbreaker and pariah, and indirectly help to form a socially disruptive drinking culture. In so doing, temperance reinforced the solidaristic and alienated bases of Irish male drinking, and worsened the problem it wished to eradicate. Moreover, this complex interaction between the Irish drinker and society assisted in sealing upon the ethnic group its reputation for uncivilized behavior.

Violence, too, was endemic to Irish life on both sides of the Atlantic. Sectarian conflict between Protestant and Catholic, traditional intercounty hostilities between Catholics, (called "faction-fighting") and class conflict between landlords and the government and tenants and laborers were all present in Ireland. Moreover, as in many other societies in which government is an alien and hostile force, violence was frequently resorted to by individuals to resolve interpersonal conflicts. In America some of these Old World hostilities continued, exacerbated by new circumstances and supplemented by new sources of conflict. The historic conflict with Anglo-Saxon Protestants found new soil in which to germinate, but so, too, did conflicts among the Catholic Irish themselves.[38]

Even excluding for now class conflict with American employers, which resulted in such violent confrontations as the Towpath Rebellion, struggles over material resources, both economic and political, account for much of the conflict involving the Irish. Much violence was present in the various workplaces where the Irish labored. Contractors on the public works and railroads often used traditional intercounty hostilities to keep their laborers divided. It was no surprise that Galway Irish, County Mayo men, Corkonians, and "Fardowners" (from Longford) fought with one another at, and tried to drive their adversaries from, construction sites around Buffalo where they were employed, especially when they took part of their pay in whiskey and had little else other than drinking and fighting to do in the evenings and on weekends. One aim of these confrontations, from the laborer's viewpoint, was to monopolize work for his own countymen. Competition on the docks also involved the Irish in violence. Canal boatmen fought for places in line at locks, and dockworkers regularly came to blows and fought too with sailors over whose job it was to offload certain types of cargo. Conflicts on the docks also frequently pitted the Irish in fierce battles with blacks, who at times attempted to work as sailors and longshoremen and were brought into competition with Irish men.[39]

Conflicts between the Irish and American Protestants had a basis in competition for political resources. In Buffalo, as elsewhere, the Irish proved particularly adept at using their knowledge of English and habits of political cooperation and cultural solidarity to win a disproportionate share of political power and patronage for themselves. American resentments not only contributed mightily to the rise of nativism, but when joined by the desire of the Irish to protect their gains, led to frequent clashes at the First and Eighth ward polls. Both groups lived in these wards, but their residences were separated by various physical and symbolic barriers. Election day, however, brought them together with unusual intimacy at the polls. Incidents of electoral violence increased in number and intensity during the 1850s, as nativists went on the offensive and Irish gangs harrassed American voters.[40]

Other social conflicts involving the Irish were largely symbolic in nature, and concerned long-standing sectarian rivalries or assertions of territoriality. Though in nearby Ontario towns the conflict between Orangemen and Irish Catholics frequently erupted into violence, there were too few of the former in Buffalo for this. (Local Protestants and Catholics certainly did, however, take sides verbally on the Canadian confrontations.) Instead, it was between American Protestants and Irish Catholics that sectarian hostilities erupted, and doubtless local Orangemen stood by the side that tradition, culture, and social ties destined them to take. In 1853 an angry crowd of over 200 Irish attacked a group of American Baptists who had come to the docks to get up a revival.[41] A similar encounter took place at suburban White's Corners in 1854 when some Irishmen succeeded in putting a Latin crucifix atop an American Liberty Pole. Three men died in the riot that ensued.[42] Bloody, largely symbolic confrontations also took place between the Irish and Germans, though the two people seldom lived together. A number of men were badly injured in 1854, for example, when some Irishmen attacked a party of Germans who had refused to move off the sidewalk to let them pass. In 1857 a company of Irish volunteer firemen routed a German fire company on the way to a blaze, while a building went up in flames, rather than see the latter arrive first.[43] Such behavior did little to endear the Irish volunteers to American commercial men who worried constantly about the efficiency of those charged with saving their burning warehouses.

The Irish thus displayed much evidence of antisocial behavior, but this is not to suggest that the American image of the Irish was simply based on objective analysis. Stereotypes are distortions, more often derived from fantasy and projection than reality. The ones attached to the Irish were intensely distorted and negative, and thus capable of doing great psychic violence to the immigrants and their American-born children. As such, stereotypes provided impetus for Irish ethnicization, for the group was an essential source of defense and security amidst rejection and hostility.

To begin with, the poor image of the Irish grew out of their difficult daily relations with Americans. No other significantly sized group, not even the German majority, had as many or varied daily contacts with the Irish. As contractors, shippers, elevator owners, and forwarding merchants, as well as employers of domestic help, Americans had regular contact with Irish labor. They had the opportunity to observe at close range the work culture of the transplanted peasants, which they often found wanting. Moreover, Americans lived near enough to the Irish to be able on occasion, through chance encounters on the streets, to observe their individual habits and their domestic relations. Such encounters were not likely to place the Irish in a favorable light, especially when they were being observed by bourgeois people. The disorder and moral breakdown present among the Irish was constantly visible because the nature of Irish life failed to allow for the privatized existence, which, as it was, the American bourgeoisie saw as a basic principle of social respectability. Irish shanty dwellers were forced to use public space as an extension of private space, if only because they greatly lacked the latter, for activities which bourgeois people did in the home—disciplining children, bargaining for services, carrying on domestic arguments. On such occasions, Irish life appeared a horrid spectacle.

Second, literate Americans had access to a vast fund of British stereotypes of the Irish through novels, essays, and excerpts on Irish themes taken from the British press, most notably the much quoted and highly biased London *Times*. Moreover, Irish actors like the acclaimed Tyrone Power were appearing on the American stage to do impersonations of such stock characters as the drunken peasant.[44] Third, Americans' negative attitudes toward the Irish were probably considerably reinforced by those of British and Canadian immigrants, with whom they had cordial relations and relatively frequent social contact. Particularly after the famine, the relations between these groups and the Irish themselves were declining. Irish Catholic and English and Scottish societies, which had had friendly contacts in the early 1840s, cooled because most Irish blamed English government policy for the catastrophe, while the British immigrants denounced the Irish for injecting their parochial, Old World concerns into American life. Representatives of the major British and Irish societies ceased attending each other's annual banquets, and polemical exchanges between local Irish and British correspondents were increasingly found in the press.[45] Fourth, regardless of what any other group felt toward the Irish, American Protestants, especially bourgeois ones, were the only ones with power enough, through control of the English-language press, the courts, commercial credit-reporting, etc., to mobilize prejudices to serve the purposes of discrimination and public hostility, and hence to establish new, broadly ramifying social patterns antithetical to Irish interests.

From the vantage point of the 1840s, however, it would not have been possible to predict intense American anti-Irish feeling. The treatment of the Irish in the daily press was both positive and sympathetic. Though some aspects of Irish conduct were gently satirized in the press, as a group the Irish were seen as a brave, oppressed, and generous people with a tragic past and present. In the early 1840s, the city's leading commercial and professional men signed petitions calling for restoration of Irish self-government. Late in the 1840s a broad cross-section of American leadership contributed money for the relief of the island's starving masses. Both the Whig *Commercial Advertiser* and the Democratic *Courier* spoke favorably of these efforts, and both looked favorably on an anticipated mass uprising of the Irish against British rule in 1848.[46]

But sympathy for the Irish, as they existed in the abstract and faraway, did not withstand the sudden appearance of thousands of impoverished peasants. The 1850s saw a sharp reversal of past perceptions and feelings. The *Commercial Advertiser* turned anti-Irish, as did the *Express*; in both cases the change of views was deeply influenced by growing anti-Catholicism. The *Courier*, the oldest and principal Democratic paper, very occasionally praised the Irish for the generous remittances they sent home to needy relatives, as did the Democratic *Republic*, Buffalo's most outspokenly antinativist American paper. But neither paper sought to defend the Irish specifically. Indeed neither could bring itself to do more than urge justice and tolerance for a vaguely defined "adopted citizenry," which by its labor was increasing the nation's prosperity, and thus benefiting Americans themselves. Both papers at times criticized the Irish, though not as harshly as the nativist press did. The ambivalence of these papers was a product of fear of alienating the many nativist American Democrats on the one hand, and Irish Democrats on the other.[47]

Within a short time, the outlines of the stereotype of the typical Irish man, whom the American press called "Pat," emerged.[48] Pat was ignorant yet cunning. He was feckless, lazy, self-indulgent, and drunken, priest-ridden and superstitious, and prone to violence. He and his kind lived like—and frequently with—pigs. As a laborer, he was a wily strategist. He avoided hard work and stole his employer's goods. He was shiftless; for how else could his frequent joblessness and stays in the poorhouse be accounted for? The *Commercial Advertiser* approved lower wages for the Irish, because, it said, "It is well-known the way the Irish generally work."[49] Pat was a clever knave in his dealings with American power. As a defendant in court, he so confused the proceedings with garbled testimony that the desperate judge dismissed the charges just to be rid of him. On his own ground, however, Pat was the prototypical "Wild Irishman." Frequently drunk and looking for action, he sought amusement in riot and violence, and in the process mocked the manners and morals of respectable Americans and showed contempt for their authority.

Pat, in fact, had no morals; his manners and behavior proved that. Unlike Americans, he did not believe that he should stay home after church on Sunday in order to think about his relation to his maker. He did not appreciate those social superiors who told him he should. As early as 1835, when Alderman Lewis Allen made the mistake of trying to break up Sabbath drinking and fighting on the docks, the assembled Pats took a respite from battling each other to chase the councilman from the scene.[50] Pat's moral sense was blunted by priestcraft and those rituals of the church—confessions, offerings, and indulgences—that made him feel safe from the consequences of his behavior, while leading him to fear and respect no one but his priests. His relation to God was blighted by idolatry (did not Catholics venerate saints?) and by religious pageantry, which the *Christian Advocate* called the church's "emblazoned buffoonery."[51] His understanding of civic obligation was perverted by both the demagogic rhetoric of Irish politicians and the secular teachings of nuns and priests in sectarian schools and in weekly sermons that left Pat putting church interests before the public good. Both priest and politician told Pat and his fellow immigrants to vote Democratic, so on election day, said the *Express* in 1856, out they came "in herds and droves ... like sheep following a leader." They would vote, the paper was sure, "for a horse or an ox if it were on the Democratic ticket." That Pat should come to a bad end was no surprise to Americans. That he should do so surrounded by the symbols and people who had led him astray was appropriate. One may then imagine the reaction of Americans to the execution of twenty-four-year-old Lawrence Fogarty, an immigrant from Limerick, for the murder, while drunk, of an American. Surrounded by priests, crucifix in hand, he mounted the gallows and offered these last words: "I am an Irishman and a Catholic; I have lived and died a Catholic. And its little I thought as a child, I should come to this end."[52] There were many Americans who could find a great deal of explanation in this statement.

Education or prosperity might round out some of the rough corners of Pat's character, but could not fundamentally alter him. As a priest, the Irish man was little more than a crafty power-seeker and none too honest. When in 1856 a national Irish convention met at Buffalo, at the initiation principally of priests, to contemplate emigration to the frontier to break free of urban poverty and nativist hostility, the *Commercial Advertiser*, like the anticlerical German *Demokrat*, could see nothing in it but the priests' desire to speculate in land.[53] Irish politicians, said the *Republic* in 1853, were frequently "demogogues and self-interested wily men," who had no public vision beyond patronage and offices for family and friends, and were trying to freight American politics with such irrelevancies as their hatred of England and "their daydream nationality."[54] When given a public trust, the Irish man proved irresponsible. As a policeman, for example, he was the cop on the beat who fell asleep in an empty lot and had his hat and nightstick removed by pranksters. (Commenting on one such incident, however, the *Commercial Advertiser* said that many of the Irish police were "even worse.")[55] As an entrepreneur, the Irish man cut a poor figure, too. Local credit reporters described Irish shopkeepers as "careless" and "reckless" with money, inattentive to business, "keeping free and easy company," and frequently intemperate. ("Grog shop—with himself as best customer," it was said of one saloonkeeper.)[56] The ethnic leadership that came out of this small class of shopkeepers and others inevitably found little favor among Americans. Liberals such as George Washington Johnson found Irish leadership priest-ridden, and detested its conservatism on abolition and social reform. American conservatives, ever fearful of disorder, were equally unenthusiastic. After observing the major Irish organizations marching in the annual St. Patrick's Day parade in 1857, the *Commercial Advertiser* criticized the intoxication and incompetence of the marchers and went on to question whether the Irish could ever hope to govern themselves in Ireland.[57]

"Bridget," the Irish domestic, was Pat's female counterpart, and Americans could claim even more intimacy with her, because often she lived with them. She had many of Pat's defects, but a number of her own, too. In Hasia Diner's accurate depiction of the stereotype, Bridget "darted from one American kitchen to another, usually shattering the crockery as she went." She was "not very bright or dependable," and she was "a horrendous cook."[58] When she was not breaking household valuables, she was stealing them, and she regularly "toted" food from her mistress's kitchen to her mother's or sister's. She spent money at the market on "lollypops and red ribbons," said the *Commercial Advertiser*, and brought back, at her own slow pace, "inferior provisions." Her friends often came to the kitchen to be fed. Her cavorting at wakes left her too tired to work. Just when she was finally properly trained, she quit—showing no gratitude to her mistress for instruction in manners and for gifts of discarded clothing.[59]

There were surely those Americans, like the Hawleys, who willed money to their faithful Bridget, whose experience was different. But most were deeply discontent with Irish help. Some, like Nancy Spaulding, wife of a prominent lawyer and politician, reached the conclusion after their "girl" quit that they were "fully determined never to hire another,"—even while having to admit to themselves that there was really no other source of English-speaking help, since American women seldom did domestic work.[60] Other Americans, including even Dr. Foote of the *Commercial Advertiser*, refused to give up on Bridget. They urged following the lead of some eastern cities and forming "a society for the encouragement of faithful domestics," a combination employment agency, referral service, mutual benefit society, and recreational organization that would also set standards for the wages and treatment of servants.[61] This was never done, suggesting that either Americans had become resigned to making peace with Bridget on her terms, or they did not wish to be bound to improving her lot.

Like Pat, Bridget, whose views are probably less well-known, had her own opinion of the situation—and of her employer. She was very likely the daughter of immigrants, a mere teenager who had begun life in a one-room peasant cottage. Along with Dr. Foote, she doubtless thought it unfair that her employer was "astonished that she did not at once understand the use of napkins, finger bowls, and dessert knives."[62] Moreover, she awoke at dawn to a day of drudgery. She was isolated from her peers, and might well have felt she was watching her youth recede before her. While she gave much of her income to her family, her employers seemed to have unlimited wealth. Since they often bought in bulk, it was difficult for her to believe that they could possibly miss, let alone need, the bit of food she took home.[63]

As Bridget mastered her circumstances, she changed, and her confusion and incompetence gave way to self-confidence. She took on those of her employer's standards that served her needs. She began simultaneously to see those needs differently, comparing her little room not to her ancestral hut, but to the commodious suite of her mistress's daughter. It was this confidence, which had at its heart a greater valuation of herself and her labor, that led Bridget to quit when aggrieved, or in response to a better opportunity. It was this confidence, too, that led her to come to judge her employers irreverently.[64] Bridget, said Harriet Prescott Spofford, an insightful American chronicler of "the servant question" in a book addressed to the bourgeois mistress, "thinks you are an upstart, for your grandmother was perhaps a shoemaker's wife, and if you were overseas you would be a shoemaker's wife, too." Moreover, said Spofford, Bridget resented being asked "to try to do so much with so little [assistance]" about the house and kitchen, and thus, she "despises your ignorance, and is sure you would starve without her."[65]

Bridget's understanding of her employer's nouveau riche status was not inaccurate, as her employers, in their better moments, would have been the first to admit. But there is a more important meaning to her perceptions. As in the Irish priest's assertion of the superiority, not mere equality, of Catholicism, the Irish parent's rejection of the public schools as inferior to diocesan ones, or the Irish politician's pride in besting Americans in the quest for power and place, Bridget's pride in her competence and toughness and her jaundiced view of her employers represents the emergent, positive side of Irish self-understanding in America. While the impetus to ethnicization was often a self-protective, reflexive turning away from hostility and contempt, it might also be, after time enough to evaluate oneself in the new homeland, something more: the embrace of a newly appreciated self for its endurance and strength, and an appreciation of the resiliency and richness of cultural resources brought from the Old World. Thus, ethnicization could be at once a celebration and a retreat. To understand it only as the latter risks failing to see the extent to which the immigrants might come to take pride in their accomplishments, if only at surviving. Yet to see it only as the former risks failing to see how desperate the social circumstances of those like the Irish could be.

The poverty and lack of entrepreneural experience, skills, capital, and education of the vast majority of the Irish provided weak social bases for the development of ethnic leadership. Such social deficits sharply proscribed the number of individuals with resources and time to play a public role in behalf of the group. Moreover, in limiting both the size of the ethnic market for goods and services and opportunities for passing on artisanal skills, these social deficits made difficult the emergence of a large, self-conscious class of craftsmen, shopkeepers, professionals, and lower white-collar workers, and the accumulation of sufficient capital within the group to generate social mobility and renew the ranks of that class.

There were several consequences of these constricted social patterns for Irish leadership and the class of people out of which it came. First, this essentially petty bourgeois (in the modesty of its means and marginality of its socioeconomic position) class was both small and insular. Mary T. C. McGee, wife of the editor of the first diocesan newspaper, complained after nearly three months in Buffalo that she had yet to make any friends, for there were few of the type of people she hoped to befriend among her fellow Irish.[66] The handful of people she did see were always the same, more a comment on numbers than on her own choices. Second, the weakness of the ethnic market and the small number of craftsmen made two paths of social mobility singularly important in the Irish case. The Catholic church, with its wealth and hierarchical organization, offered opportunities for security, advancement, and prestigious employment. Politics and government provided lucrative, if often ephemeral and petty, opportunity.

The Irish took advantage of both opportunities, and were assisted mightily in doing so by their knowledge of English, cultural assets, such as strong family and kinship networks brought from Ireland, and in church affairs, a precedence of several decades over the Germans in integration into the hierarchy. Though there were probably many more German than Irish Catholics in the western New York diocese, in the early 1850s perhaps as many as two-thirds of the priests were Irish.[67] This frequently irritated German Catholics, just as the prominence of the Irish in politics and government irritated German Democrats—and most Americans. The Germans, however, were especially bitter because, as the largest single group in the local Democracy, they naturally felt their claims to party rewards were greatest. In the midst of a local revolt by both Americans and Germans against Irish control of many of the party's finest positions, "A.L.P.," a German Democrat, complained that forty-six Irishmen, often related through family and making a combined total of $38,000, held city, state, and local offices at Buffalo. Twenty-one of them were in quite lucrative posts, and twenty-five (42 percent) of the city's sixty police were Irish.[68] Third, the narrow base of secular leadership vaulted the clergy to a particularly prominent position and bound the church and the ethnic group yet more tightly together. (Since the clergy's point of reference was as much the church as the group, and the politician's as much as the political party, some elements of the discussion of both will await analysis of Catholicism and immigrant politics.)

The social weakness of the Irish petty bourgeoisie was to a great extent the consequence of its weak material base. In 1855 only 32 percent of Irish household heads had other than unskilled employment: 16.5 percent were skilled; 8.6 percent semiskilled; 2 percent lower white-collar; 2.3 percent professional (mostly priests and lawyers); and 2.7 percent entrepreneurs and owners. The latter were mostly small, and often quite marginal, grocers, saloonkeepers, dry goods and clothing retailers, and funeral directors. There were only two Irish factory owners—Augustine Keogh, who manufactured pianofortes, and William Carland, owner of the city's largest maker of ready-made men's clothing, Gothic Hall, which employed over 200 tailors.[69] The marginality, in size and range, of Irish enterprise suggests the difficulties the Irish faced in providing employment for their own people. The dearth of business had Old and New World roots. In Ireland the poverty of the peasantry and absence of towns curbed the rise of a native entrepreneural tradition, while in America the weakness of the ethnic market was reinforced by a lack of access to commercial credit. Because of both prejudice and a realistic evaluation of the vitality of the Irish market ("Good Irish trade—such as it is," said one credit report), Irish businesses received poor credit evaluations.[70]

The numbers of Irish semiskilled and skilled workers were much larger, though the size of the percentage of skilled, 16.5 percent, is small compared to Americans (22 percent) and Germans (37 percent). Moreover, the range of Irish skilled employment was greatly truncated. Only in ship carpentry (37 percent) and blacksmithing (21 percent) did the Irish exceed their percentage (18 percent) in the population. In most other major trades, they had a much lower percentage.[71] (The figure representing the particularly elite trade of ship carpentry is such an exception as to give us pause. Analysis of a sample of 110 Irish-born ship carpenters suggests, on the basis of both surnames and a comparatively greater residential persistence than that of the Irish population at large, that some indeterminate number of these men may well have been Irish Protestants. But the majority, it seems, were Catholics, as the local press maintained.)[72] No more impressive was the ability of the Irish to retain skills throughout the life-cycle: the possibility of an Irishman being an artisan decreased from 38 percent at ages eighteen to twenty-four to 24 percent at fifty-five or more years. Men of other groups also had difficulties retaining skills as they grew older, but Irish economic status was so tenuous that the net impact of such a loss may well have been greater, and may thus help to explain why, as Katz discovered, the skill ranking of the Irish peaked as early as twenty-five to thirty-four years, but at thirty-five to forty-four for the more highly skilled Germans.[73]

Petty bourgeois and artisanal occupations did not guarantee the Irish a level of affluence equivalent to that attained by other ethnic groups. At every occupational level above unskilled labor, except retail merchant, the extent of Irish property holding was lower than that attained by the Germans and Americans. The value of Irish property was probably less, too. A sample of thirty-eight prominent Irishmen, all but four of whom were unskilled, and all of whom were officers in the four central, secular Irish voluntary societies,* yields an average value per residence of only $1,603. When we exclude William Carland's $15,000 residence, the figure declines to a very low $1,141. Only nine men in the sample were said to own land.[74]

For all this marginality and insecurity, there were some social characteristics conducive to both greater social respectability and leadership within this class. There was the movement out of the slums to the somewhat less congested neighborhoods in the northern sections of the Eighth Ward, where it was said in 1854 that large numbers of "snug little cottages" for day laborers and artisans were being constructed. Other higher-status Irish resided in small numbers in the Second and Third wards. The average residential persistence of the sample of thirty-eight—9.5 years—was much greater than for the ethnic group, and for the eight officers of the Catholic Institute, it was eighteen years, ample time to develop a familiarity with American life, personal roots, and a position of prominence in the few stable Irish institutions and organizations. Moreover, twenty-seven of the thirty-eight were naturalized citizens, and hence voters, allowing them opportunities to compete for political resources.[75] Finally, enough capital had been accumulated by such men to enable them to begin a small Emigrant Savings Bank in 1858 to make loans to Irish families wishing to buy homes.[76] Such modest advances fitted these men to lead the Irish, but

---

* The Sons of Erin, Friendly Sons of St. Patrick, Buffalo Catholic Institute, and the Montgomery Guards and Emmett Guards militia companies.

hardly made them acceptable to higher-status Americans, then or indeed much later. In 1882, when the city celebrated its semicentennial, not one Irish name appeared on the prestigious committee that organized the official festivities, in sharp contrast to the large number of participating Germans.[77]

The secular leadership of the parish priest in Irish communal affairs and in dealings with the world beyond the group was forged in the Old World, where history and culture combined to create firm ties between church, clergy, and peasantry. The destruction of the island's native aristocracy early in the history of British colonialism and the break-up of the Catholic hierarchy in the eighteenth century by the Penal Laws left tremendous authority in the hands of the parish priest. Priests were not found everywhere, however, for the lack of an Irish seminary before 1795 and the rapid growth of population after 1800 produced a shortage of priests, which, together with a dearth of churches, made attendance impossible for as many as half of the island's people. Where priests were present in parish churches, they played a number of roles. At a time when there were few state-supported schools in the countryside, and those that existed were unacceptable because controlled by the established Anglican church, priests provided what little literacy training existed. Moreover, priests monitored both public and private behavior. They sought to purge the peasantry of the folkish religious beliefs that flourished in the context of the repression of the church and the frequent absence of local clergy. In the early nineteenth century, too, with middle-class laymen, they provided rural leadership in the final stages of the struggle for Catholic Emancipation, which culminated successfully in 1829, and in the failed effort to restore the Irish parliament. But the clergy also often sought to suppress popular political movements that might lead to violence and disorder. The clergy acted as intermediary in the effort to substitute negotiation for violence in the relations between landlord and tenant.[78]

These ties were rendered more intimate by both changing patterns in the social recruitment of the clergy and the nature of the clergy's sources of material support. Prior to 1795 the clergy was trained in Europe, and thus was likely to be, given the costs, of a comparatively affluent background. But after an Irish seminary opened, an increasing percentage of priests was recruited from the rural lower classes. Furthermore, because of disestablishment and repression of the hierarchy, the clergy had historically been subsidized not by the church, but by parishioners, according to a system of "voluntary payments" for individual services, such as burials, and "stated obligations," which were dues paid at Easter and Christmas. The poor provided in-kind services, food, or labor. Though state tolerance of Catholicism was written into nineteenth-century law, the Irish continued to uphold this system, because they feared dependence on the colonial regime. As population grew, so did the clergy's income, elevating it to a more respectable style of life, and providing rural boys with more incentives to choose the priesthood as a career.[79]

There were sore points to this relationship. As the clergy's standard of living outstripped that of the poor people it served, priests were charged with greed, arrogance, simony, and exploitation, charges valid enough at times for the newly reconstituted hierarchy to attempt to reform the parish clergy. Some priests were said to be the lackeys of wealthy landlords. The clergy's close scrutiny of manners and morals was as often resented as feared. Yet these sources of friction were little more than an irritant. Shared nationality and religion counted for much more under circumstances of colonial oppression. There was very little secularist anticlericalism in Ireland, and even the rural anti-landlord groups and republican nationalists were opposed more to individual priests than to the priesthood itself. The peasants were sophisticated enough to understand that priests came in many varieties.[80]

Many elements of this pattern of interdependence and mutual support were reestablished and expanded upon in America. The church's civil freedom, the predominance of the Irish in the hierarchy and of the church in Irish life, and the church's comparative affluence because of support by foreign missionary societies and the more stable income of some of the faithful all allowed for a growth of the priesthood at a pace often commensurate with the growth of Catholic population. The numbers of both seminaries and parish churches expanded, as did the number of American-born Irish attending European seminaries. Furthermore, diocesan clergy and those affiliated with religious orders emigrated with the peasantry. In consequence there was no shortage of Irish priests, and as in Ireland, the priest was likely to share the origins of his parishioners. Too, accustomed to support the parish church in the Old World, the Irish continued in this in America. Priests continued to depend on parishioners for most of their income, and the diocese for the balance. Certainly such dependence existed before 1847, when all Catholic parishes in the state were administered from distant New York City. After Timon arrived he placed the building of churches, schools, seminaries, and welfare institutions above provision for the clergy.[81]

Irish priests continued to play a variety of secular roles, both because tradition led parishioners to expect it and because of the weakness of secular leadership. They defended the church in polemics with Protestants and led struggles to maximize its access to public resources, such as monies for schools. With no fewer enemies in America, but freed of the legal restraints that existed in Ireland, the Irish priest developed, as John Higham maintains, a particularly "combative and brutally aggressive" style of public leadership, which infuriated Americans because of its self-confidence and terrified them because of its resourcefulness and single-mindedness. All the while, priests struggled, Jay Dolan has said, to make "practicing believers" out of a people who had not always had churches or priests in Ireland, and to break the hold of the folk religious practices that had filled the subsequent vacuum.[82]

For the moment, however, we will be concerned with the priest's role within the emerging ethnic group, looking first at the priest's efforts to assert the church's hegemonic claim to set and enforce standards of orderly, respectable behavior; and second, at the role of the priest in establishing the parish church, the central institution of the Irish in America.

Just as in Ireland, in Buffalo priests were involved in the effort to civilize what was "wild" in the Irish, and just as in Ireland, their frequent failure when they clashed too sharply with peasant ways reminded them that even Catholic authority had its limits. Clergy and the ordinary masses of the laity often had had different practical understandings of where the spiritual left off and the secular began. In America there were new contexts for priestly frustration. Here a priest's efforts took place under circumstances quite different from the Irish rural parish, where communal bonds and face-to-face relations established within and among generations added group disapproval to clerical sanctions. In the American city the group was comprised of recently resettled people, many of them unknown to one another and hardly more familiar to the parish priest. Then, too, for business and political reasons, Irish secular leadership had self-interested motives for hoping to maintain certain forms of behavior, such as large funerals and loitering about the polls on election day, that clergy deemed dangerous to both the church and the Irish themselves.

Some lines of priestly secular intervention were the same as in Ireland, and hence were a continuation of "a fine old conflict" between priests and their largely lower-class communicants. The church had been condemning what bishops regarded as excesses in Irish burial customs since the 1600s, and its efforts intensified after 1800 as it shed its civil disabilities. Clerics were particularly eager to stamp out boisterous, drunken all-night wakes that preceded funerals. The wake took root quickly in America, where it was joined by new funeral customs, which were just as unacceptable to the clergy. While in Ireland funeral processions had marched to the cemetery, in America, with monies provided by fraternal associations' burial insurance programs, processions were now composed of rented carriages, the number of which quickly became symbols of prestige. These enhanced burial rituals led to the rise of funeral directing, one of the few comparatively lucrative lines of Irish enterprise. They also led to clashes between the laity and clergy. Early in his episcopacy, Timon denounced what he called "disgraceful scenes," drunken, loud, and highly visible carriage processions, that, he claimed, not only cost too much, but "harm our image" in a society in which "such exhibitions are condemned as improper and scandalous." He imposed a four-carriage limit on processions. Soon, too, he denounced "sinful wakes." His priests, however, appear to have been confused about what was now expected of them. Should they attend wakes? Must they refuse a mass to noncomplying families? Must they refuse gravesite prayers when processions had too many carriages? The attitude of the laity seems to have been divided between the desire to obey Timon and the allegiance to folk custom. Secular leadership had an interest in improving the image of the Irish, but may well have felt no need to limit the size of processions at the funerals of "respectable" people. Moreover, funeral directors were loath to cooperate with the bishop in curbing the size of processions and eliminating other expensive extras. By the late 1850s, the bishop was evidently frustrated by his lack of success. He now threatened not simply the denial of mass, but excommunication itself for "bad behavior" at wakes and funerals. He also spelled out exactly what the funeral duties of priests were.[83]

Timon achieved greater cooperation from priests and lay leadership in dealing with excessive drinking. His own efforts were part of a broad campaign within the Irish clergy to counter drunkenness and chronic hard drinking, which exacerbated poverty, caused family tragedy and led to problems with the law. Moreover, the era's leading Irish abstinence advocate, Father Theobold Mathew, formulated a nationalist reason for conquering alcohol. Liquor, he said, was the cause of Ireland's subjugation; national liberation could succeed only after individual emancipation from alcohol had freed the Irish from apathy, powerlessness, and poverty. Furthermore, like Father Mathew himself, many prominent clergy and laymen on both sides of the Atlantic increasingly came to the conclusion that though no theological or moral imperative for abstinence existed, it was a practical route to countering abuse, especially to the extent that for many, moderate tippling led to problem drinking.[84]

Bishop Timon and his Irish clergy adopted various strategies for dealing with the liquor problem. Individual priests, such as Rev. William Whalen, one of the senior clergy at St. Patrick's, used moral suasion, on and off the pulpit. Whalen had become dedicated to the cause after seeing the high incidence of alcoholism among his parish's railroad construction workers, men who received a portion of their pay in liquor.[85] Timon went beyond homilies and informal meetings with individuals to public efforts aimed at changing Irish behavior and reversing American perceptions that the church was apathetic on the liquor problem. The diocesan English-language (hence, Irish) newspaper not only denounced drunkenness, but wrote respectfully of certain temperance schemes, such as tavern licensing, favored by Americans. When it did not favor antialcohol proposals, principally in the case of prohibition, which was deemed impractical, it nonetheless applauded the motives of their advocates, who were largely American evangelicals with whom the church had often openly hostile relations.[86] In 1851 Timon sponsored a visit of the charismatic Father Mathew, whose dignified, popular appearances American Protestants could not help but compare to the successful local crusades (1844 and 1850) of one of their leading temperance lecturers, John B. Gough. Father Mathew administered "the pledge" (of abstinence) to 6,000 men during a week of meetings at St. Patrick's. The bishop himself regularly administered "the pledge" at the cathedral after mass on Sunday.[87]

Timon saw Father Mathew's visit as a way of reaching the average laboring man, through appeals to both Catholicism and ethnic pride. His efforts to curb drinking on St. Patrick's Day, however, were intended to influence the behavior of all classes. Realization of his goal, which was to have "peace, sobriety and friendship prevail," proved very difficult. In Ireland St. Patrick's Day had been exclusively a holy day, but in America it became an ethnic celebration, as much Irish as Catholic, so authority over the day's activities was no longer only in the hands of priests. They tried to regain control. The laboring masses spent the day away from work in parades, dancing, drinking, and speechmaking. These festivities, though loud and boisterous, were generally peaceful, but it was the occasional exception that left the deepest impression on the public mind. Timon continually pleaded for decorum, invoking the honor of the saint and warning against reinforcing nativist stereotypes.[88] But tavern keepers could hardly close their doors on March 17, and active intervention by priests gained little. In 1857 when a priest tried to break up a dance, a riot took place between the majority, which wanted its money's worth of entertainment, and the handful of the cleric's allies. Only the police were able to restore order.[89]

Timon also attempted to influence the celebration of those higher-status Irish who staged the official banquet. The bishop felt that the banquet and the special mass before it should set the tone for the day, particularly by avoiding drunkenness. The higher-status Irish were not consistent, however, in their celebration. From 1842 through 1846 there were two banquets, one of which had been conducted on a "cold water" basis by a Catholic Repeal and Total Abstinence Association. Thereafter, however, this organization disappeared from the records, and the banquet was taken over by the two, newly founded Irish mutual benefit societies—the Friendly Sons of St. Patrick (1846) and the Sons of Erin (1847). Now alcohol replaced water during the long round of toasts. Several priests were always in attendance, perhaps to monitor the proceedings, but it is difficult to believe that at least one or two of them did not raise his glass for the various toasts to the church, the pope, or the hierarchy. One way to limit drinking was to cut the evening short, which Vicar General Rev. Patrick Bede attempted in 1853. He wanted everyone to go home at midnight, but some younger celebrants had other ideas, and got up a dance, probably with a large bowl of punch for refreshment. By 1861 Timon seems to have given up on permanently curbing the use of alcohol. In that one year, however, he did succeed in giving an element of additional solemnity to the banquet by persuading both societies to dedicate the evening to raising money for charity and by presiding himself, probably as an abstainer.[90] Also, soon after, he took the battle against liquor into another realm. He convinced those the *Commercial Advertiser* called "the most prominent and justly respected Irish in the city"—many of the same men belonging to the societies and in attendance at the banquet—to form a "Mutual Benefit Temperance Society."[91]

Timon's efforts to get decorum at the polls were even less successful. Small gangs of drinking men grew accustomed on election day, particularly during the 1850s nativist campaigns, to visit the polls in the First and Eighth wards to intimidate Americans and to counter frauds against Irish voters, and probably also for the sport of it. The bishop's earnest, strictly nonpartisan public pleas came up against more powerful, partisan forces, however, and failed to do more than suggest to Americans that Timon himself neither was behind nor approved of election day violence. Democratic politicians probably did not mind a little muscle at the polls, and were willing to make use of an Irishman's hunger for violent confrontation with real or imagined enemies.[92]

These disagreements should not be allowed to obscure the essential, underlying unities tying clergy and laity together. After all, in disagreement were people with a common commitment to an Irish Catholic culture and identity. The nature of this identity and culture could mean different things to Irish men and women in different objective circumstances and subjective states of mind. But since all of them shared a common commitment to the group and a shared past and present, their disagreements ultimately had the effect of deepening, not lessening, their involvement in Irish ethnicity. Then, too, these struggles between priest and parishioner had such a long history and were such an integral part of daily life, on both sides of the ocean, that they may well have been regarded with that fondness reserved for the predictable events of life.

Certainly the Catholic church was no less the spiritual or social center of Irish communal life for whatever intragroup struggles took place within it. As we shall see in analyzing the rise of local Catholicism, defense of the church was the cause of almost all of the public mobilizations by which the Irish as a group entered the public sphere. Moreover, the church was responsible for giving birth to, or helping to guide, most of the formal organizations of the emerging ethnic group. Indeed, it has been typical in the United States for the Irish to belong to few, if any, organizations not associated in some degree of intimacy with the church.[93] The results were far-reaching in setting the pattern and range of Irish structural separation, which was by far the greatest in the triangular relations of the city's three large social solidarities. In varying numbers German Protestants, for example, had interethnic ties with American coreligionists through participation in revivals, interdenominational meetings and prayer services, and the ecumenical Sunday School Union. As Catholics, the Irish were denied such formal ties with Protestants, while at the same time the de facto ethnic basis of parishes formed territorially resulted in few ties between German and Irish Catholics. One consequence was that knowledge of the organizational and leadership abilities the Irish laity displayed in governing their parish affairs was not routinely available to Americans, who were thus to continue unchallenged in the belief that Pat and Bridget were incompetent and had to have their affairs ordered by all-powerful priests. Religion, as we shall see in analyzing German-American contacts, was not alone in bringing these two peoples together, nor was it alone in keeping the Irish apart. The lack of Irish-owned retail enterprises and of an Irish high-cultural tradition attractive to Americans, also helped. But because Catholicism sent filaments into so many realms of Irish life, it helped provide both whatever stability a poor and ostracized people could attain, and the basis for the high degree of institutional completeness that isolated the Irish.

This relative social isolation was accomplished, directly and indirectly, in several ways. First, along with place-of-origin in Ireland and neighborhood proximity in the city, Catholicism set the basis for Irish endogamy, which, in turn, reinforced group boundaries and strengthened and deepened intragroup networks. Irish parish records, which cannot tell us how many Irish married outside their faith or ethnic group at other churches, do still indicate strict endogamy. In 1855, St. Bridget's parish sacramental records indicate only four (3.8 percent) of a total of 106 marriages were to individuals outside the group. Three were to people with Anglo-American names who were probably Protestants, and thus had to convert to be married by a priest; and one was to a German, who—because there is no notation of conversion—was probably a Catholic by birth.[94]

Second, the Catholic parish cast a wide associational net far beyond attendance at mass and the obligatory twice-a-year confession. The four Irish parishes founded before 1861 each had intense organizational activity which began at the inception of the parish, when priest and laity cooperated in choosing a site for a church and planning its construction and financing. Labor, materials, and decorations were largely provided by parishioners. Management of daily parish affairs remained a cooperative venture. Priests and prominent laymen in cooperation managed parish finances. Small voluntary contributions, pew rents, and payments for oblations provided for the maintenance of priests. Each parish had a number of male and female sodalities and devotional societies and mutual benefit associations. At Timon's urging, too, they organized St. Vincent de Paul societies, which dispensed charity within the parish and assisted in subsidizing the winter activities of the Sisters of Charity.[95]

Probably the most socially integrative parish organization, however, was the parochial school. Both in Ireland and America, the Irish saw state-run education as a front for, at once, Protestant conversion efforts and secular, humanistic culture. Their efforts to create an alternative were as serious as the threat they perceived. In the establishment and maintenance of parochial schools, parishioners' contributions in both time and money were essential, especially because diocesan assistance was quite limited. As in other parish voluntary efforts, women's activities were the key to success. The parish was, in fact, the only institution in which Irish women played a public role. Teas, bake sales, and entertainments for parish schools were their most frequent activities. Still the effort to create parish schools for all Irish children was not fully realized, largely because of the expenses entailed in creating parallel schools for boys and girls. Thus in 1859, in the largely Irish school districts two, three, and four, from 34 percent to 39.5 percent, respectively, of all school-age children were in the public schools. Though these are among the lowest figures in the city and a tribute to Irish sacrifices in behalf of building parish schools, the figures reveal difficult choices. It was young boys who were sent to public schools, largely in the belief that libertine Protestant notions of sexuality and gender equality were so great a threat to the piety and femininity of

Catholic womanhood, and hence to family stability, that female education must be given priority. Sunday religious education, however, was available to both sexes.[96]

Third, beyond the individual parish, the diocese created a number of institutions and associations that involved the Irish. From its inception, the Irish press was the creation of the diocese. In 1852, Timon convinced the Irish nationalist refugee, Thomas D'Arcy McGee, then editing an Irish paper at Boston, to move to Buffalo. The exact nature of "the strong representations and inducements" Timon offered McGee is not known. What is clear is that Timon wanted McGee's the *American Celt and Catholic Citizen* and its successor, the *Sentinel*, edited by the printer and politician Michael Hagan, to provide in English news of diocesan affairs and reminders of religious obligations and to interpret public questions from a nonpartisan, but wholly Catholic viewpoint. In practice both papers were not simply Catholic, but Irish, for neither was concerned with the interests of German Catholics, who had their own paper, *Die Aurora*. Because the diocesan press could not depend on subscriptions from a largely poor, and probably illiterate, potential readership, and Timon's subsidies were apparently small, the Irish clergy took the lead in establishing and maintaining the press.[97] Twenty-eight of thirty-one diocesan priests put their money in a fund to help McGee's paper get started.

The diocese also provided the context, and the bishop the inspiration, for efforts to stimulate Irish intellectual life, to shore up the boundaries of and stimulate pride in Catholic identity, and to enhance the group's reputation. Founded in 1852 by Timon, McGee, and two dozen shopkeepers, artisans, officeholders, and clerks, all but two of whom were Irish, the Buffalo Catholic Institute sought to counter Protestant cultural influences through lectures and the maintenance of a lending library. To challenge bigoted remarks about Irish history and culture in the nativist press, a local auxiliary of the Irish Archaeological Society of the United States was established within the institute. It encouraged the study of homeland literature and history among adult men. For young men in their late teens, the Irish clergy several years later founded a Young Men's Association, which was like the American Young Men's Association, but limited to Catholic themes and concerns.[98]

There were diocesan hospitals, asylums, a school for the deaf, and the citywide St. Vincent de Paul Society that also engaged Irish lay talents. There were very few secularly based Irish charities. The Irish were too poor to support charitable institutions independent of the church, and their outlook toward charity was, under any circumstance, governed by church practice. The Irish contributed what they could, not only at the parish but at the diocesan level, to collections for charity and for welfare institutions. ("They don't even have to be asked," said a priest with pride, in a letter to the *Sentinel*.) A powerful impetus was the fear that dependence on state or Protestant institutions would leave desperate people prey to Protestant conversion schemes and to wretched treatment, governed by prejudice. As we shall see, the local Irish had some justification for these fears.[99]

Fourth, the only secular Irish benefit and fraternal organizations in Buffalo, the Sons of Erin and the Friendly Sons of St. Patrick, both of them founded just prior to the mass immigration of the 1840s, were also deeply affected by Catholic influence. (The only other secular organizations were the two militia companies.)[100] This was the case in spite of the difference in the social bases of the two societies. Established in 1846, the Friendly Sons, which was affiliated with societies of the same name in other cities, had approximately 130 members, most of them over thirty, by 1858. The Sons of Erin, which appeared in 1847 and had 100 members in 1858, was composed of younger and somewhat less affluent men, who were newer to the city, less likely to be able to state an occupation, and less likely to be citizens. Besides supporting some informal charity and supervising funerals of members, both organizations' principal public activity was joint sponsorship of the official St. Patrick's Day celebration. In all these activities, they worked in cooperation with parish priests and diocesan authorities.[101]

Fashioning a group stance toward the opportunities and threats presented by American life was an important activity undertaken by Irish leadership, lay and clerical alike. The Irish shared a long history under British rule of collective mobilization and self-defense and of creating group political norms based on viewing the world in an us-against-them manner.[102] These experiences, perspectives, and habits of action were useful in America, but the Irish found themselves nonetheless in a vastly changed, and in some ways more complex, situation. The ocean separated them from their oppressed homeland, and while they suffered nativist hostility and poverty, they possessed citizens' rights and access to political power. Concerns for their homeland, whose wrongs were now experienced indirectly through the press and letters from abroad, competed with their new disabilities and opportunities for their attention and created potential sources of tension. It would be an important function of Irish leadership, utilizing the forums presented by the ethnic press and ethnic institutions, to forge ideologies that interpreted the group's problems and duties.

The sensibility that Irish leadership brought to confronting this challenge was deeply influenced by traditions, rhetoric, and personal styles from the Old World. Irish history and oral tradition furnished a vast storehouse of historical analogies that could aid in interpreting threats to the group. In 1853, when legislation was introduced in the state senate facilitating the incorporation of Catholic church property, McGee alerted his readers with the headline, "NY PENAL LAWS."[103] The Irish polemical style in Buffalo, moreover, calls to mind traits James Reynolds found in leaders of the Catholic emancipation struggles of 1823-29. Quick temper, verbal cunning, unmerciful handling of opponents, and "tumbling eloquence" that combined "sarcasm, wit, and vituperation," also characterized local Irish leaders.[104] Here is Irish attorney Bernard Hughes, for instance, in a courtroom address characterizing the nativist editor Almon Clapp: "His bigoted writings are like insects who have their birth and education in impure regions from whence they borrow their color and smell."[105] Also characteristic were both an acute sensitivity to slights and what Reynolds calls "a brooding consciousness of oppression." Deepening these was a degree of guilt and despair among those who had survived the famine, only to leave Ireland in a time of its suffering. The result was a lachrymosity, an incessant public exercising of historic wrongs, and an obsessive, growing hatred of England, both of which alienated many non-Irish.[106] In an open letter to the Irish in the *Commercial Advertiser*, "A Scotsman" expressed disgust at this habitual and already highly stylized airing of Old World grievances. "You are in a new country," he said, "yet you must keep up the same old din." Others, especially Americans, he warned, "have had quite enough of it."[107] Indeed, those of a conservative, nativist cast of mind came to see all Irish rhetoric as sodden and self-indulgent, and a substitute for hard work and self-improvement. Through conflation of the Irish style that so alienated them, and the substance of real grievances and profound pain, many Americans were able to feel justified in refusing to listen.

The famine, the failure to regain self-government, and the inability of the island's starving people to rise up in revolution in 1848 made it difficult for local Irishmen to achieve a confident stance toward Ireland's struggle. A despairing tone characterized public dialogue about the island's future. Yet the necessity of responding to the island's crisis forced the local Irish to formulate ethnic attitudes that combined Old and New World concerns. As immigrants seeking to reconcile love of homeland with their American loyalties, the Buffalo Irish gradually came to establish a reciprocal relationship between their commitment to the Irish struggle for national liberation and their American patriotism, and to employ each commitment to reinforce the other. The

United States had fought and won a revolution for national freedom against Britain. Thus, the Irish struggle in the present and the American in the past appeared to be the same, especially when coupled to the view that Britain, arrogant, militaristic, and positioned on the nation's borders, was still a threat to American freedom. Ireland and America had a common enemy, and to this extent the two nations had a common interest. Out of these contentions the Irish forged an ethnopolitical stance which was supported with a rich mixture of Irish and American political imagery. By 1850 St. Patrick's Day toasts routinely expressed Irish political themes in American terms, so that Daniel O'Connell became "Ireland's Washington," and Robert Emmett was juxtaposed with other heroes of 1776.[108] In this way a potentially troublesome dualism was resolved: to be Irish and bear the burdens of Irish history and the Irish struggle made one an American patriot. The precise means for pursuing the Irish cause from an American sanctuary—and particularly the question of how far to introduce Ireland's claims and anti-British feeling into American politics via the Democratic party—remained intensely debated.

Other matters also emerged for consideration. All segments of Irish opinion realized that traditional sources of disunity, such as intra-Irish county rivalries, were a burden to a group with so many social difficulties. All favored unity. But unity to what end? All were for improvement of the degraded socioeconomic position of the Irish. But how, especially in light of the absence of skills and education among the immigrants, was this to be accomplished? All recognized the desirability of naturalization and hence enfranchisement. But how precisely were the Irish to use their power and citizens' rights to improve their social position? All understood they must strive to protect the Catholic church against nativist assaults. But American laws separating church and state made political action in the matter complicated. Moreover, even if protected and secure, what role was the church to play in the group's essentially secular struggles for public power and material improvement? In response to these concerns, two divergent Irish-American ideological constellations—one, clerical and conservative; the other, social democratic and republican—emerged in the 1850s. Sharing common concerns, they had different roots and, on balance, strikingly different answers to these questions.

In its social base, the narrower of the two was the clerical-conservative, which nonetheless gained influence by its association with Bishop Timon, much of the senior and some parish clergy, and a few secular opinion makers, especially the brilliant, controversial Thomas D'Arcy McGee. In the early 1840s, the Ireland-born D'Arcy McGee was a republican revolutionary deeply involved in the national liberation struggle. Along with other members of the Young Ireland movement, by 1848 he had developed an impatience with clerical political hesitation, and wished to stimulate a massed-based peasant insurrection, which would culminate in throwing out the British and reconstructing the nation along liberal, secular and democratic lines. McGee was forced into exile, but remained a republican firebrand in his first years in America. After 1851, however, he veered increasingly toward the opposite pole, espousing an ultramontane conservativism that proved attractive enough to Timon that the bishop sought to draw McGee away from Boston.[109]

Catholic dogma and triumphalism, anti-Protestantism, cultural nationalism, and social conservatism were the framework of McGee's thought during the 1850s. He was both Augustinian and Jansenist in his lack of faith in reason, and in his asceticism and belief in human corruptibility. He now rejected Enlightenment doctrines of secular progress and the liberal, republican political ideas he had fought for in 1848, and in the process broke with former comrades. For him and for all local Catholic polemicists, Irish and German alike, however, the Reformation was the ultimate source of all modern derangements, from rationalism to American abolitionism and European socialism. ("Luther begat Voltaire—Voltaire begat Robespierre—Robespierre begat Fourier—Fourier begat Greeley," he contended in 1852.) It was but a short step to an aggressive anti-Protestantism and a denunciation of the liberal idea of sectarian tolerance and separation of church and state, which McGee saw as nothing more than a cover for Protestant power. Like many evangelical Protestants, McGee believed there could be no real human improvement except through individual regeneration in Christ, but as a Catholic he believed that the individual could find regeneration only in the one true church. Anything that Protestantism touched, it either corrupted or persecuted, so, for him, it was incumbent on Catholics to turn away from all dependence on civic and governmental institutions, especially the public schools, which were variously "infidel" or "godless," depending on the specific offenses with which they were charged.[110]

McGee called upon Irish Catholics to establish their own institutions to protect them from polluting Protestant influences, and this meshed with another aspect of his ethnic ideology. Along with many non-Irish, he felt there was entirely too much emphasis in Irish polemics on past wrongs and present social disabilities, and too little said about what, with self-discipline and unity, the Irish might do for themselves. The blame for this situation lay in the fact that the Irish thoughtlessly absorbed their enemies' ideas and images of them. In America the Irish encountered, he said in 1853, debilitating stereotypes ("a false estimate of their character"). These were founded on "British literature and English ideas" and "stage representation," but also on their own "eccentric conduct." American power and wealth, in contrast, allowed natives to appear "seemingly very superior." The Irish consequently played the parts assigned to them, assuming "the air and action of inferiors" in a "wanton and willing prostitution" of themselves.[111] The antidote was not simply socioeconomic improvement, for that was inaccessible to a people without self-respect. For McGee, what was needed, as a prelude to self-improvement, was inspiration from Irish literature and history, in which role models of dignified and heroic behavior were to be found, and a deepening of Catholic consciousness, for the church was the true source of Irish high culture. McGee's Catholic philo-Celtism is evident in the fact that he was the moving force behind the creation of both the Catholic Institute and the local auxiliary of the Irish Archaeological Society. These same concerns influenced his response to the problems of Ireland, which he claimed now was not ready for independence, and would not be until the Irish rediscovered the wellsprings of their unique national culture.[112]

McGee did have views on material self-improvement. These were influenced by both a hatred for cities as places of impiety and degradation, and a hungering after the presumed virtues of the Catholic, agrarian social order of the Middle Ages. By 1856, three years after he had left Buffalo for the more lucrative journalistic market of New York City, he had become an advocate of "colonizing" Irish slum dwellers on American or Canadian frontiers in villages where life would be centered around farm and church. In that year McGee and his chief clerical ally on colonization, the editor of the Boston *Pilot*, called a national convention, to be held at Buffalo, to discuss the idea. Buffalo was chosen not only for its central location, but also because there was substantial support among senior Irish clergy for colonization. Bishop Timon opened the meeting, and the Buffalo delegation, one of the largest, was composed of his secretary, Rev. Francis O'Farrell, Vicar General Rev. Patrick Bede, and the principal priests of St. Patrick's and St. Bridget's. Only one layman, the prominent wholesale merchant Maurice Vaughan, was on the local delegation. In fact, there was little lay enthusiasm for colonization, in spite of its prestigious advocates. Many disliked the possibility of mass relocation in Canada, as in one formulation of colonization, because it was a part of the British empire, though McGee himself was less and less troubled by this. Moreover, the immigrant masses had to be suspicious of any scheme that would uproot them again, break up the supportive networks they were creating in the cities, and land them in a hostile wilderness. Then, too, the Irish lacked capital for the massive land buying and farm making the scheme required.[113]

The colonization scheme, which yielded no results,[114] suggested a basic weakness of McGee's conservatism—its lack of familiarity with the daily struggles of immigrant workers and their families. McGee did grasp the yearnings of ordinary folk for dignity and self-determination, but his inability to grasp the limits of self-help for a people as poor and downtrodden as the Irish made it difficult for him to conceive practical ideas for improving their lives. Moreover, a deep strain of elitism entered his thought during his stay in Buffalo. His defense of Catholicism did lead him to participate in popular struggles, in which he sought to mobilize the Irish masses on behalf of public funds for diocesan schools or priestly visitation at the poorhouse. Because McGee used appeals to American notions of fair play for all groups, and denounced oppression of the Catholic poor in the language of popular democratic protest, one occasionally could mistake him for a pluralist and a liberal. Beneath the veneer of populist rhetoric, however, was the Catholic triumphalism he shared with much of the clergy. He rejected the idea that Catholicism was simply one deserving sect among many. His outrage at the church's second-class status was caused less by a frustrated sense of fairness than contempt for Protestant hegemony and the political system that made it possible. Thus, while employing the language of American democracy, he increasingly rejected its content. American democracy, he would eventually argue, gave birth to a corrupt, rabble-rousing politics, as the oppression of the church proved. He predicted mass violence against Catholic churches and forced conversion of the masses. At this point in his political evolution, McGee came full circle and turned his back on America to embrace orderly, aristocratic England. As he said in 1853, "Better languish and die under the red flag of England than to live to beget children of perdition under the flag of a proselytizing republic." He now discovered the existence of a structured, neofeudal society, under Protestant, British protection, in Catholic Quebec. In 1857 McGee moved to Montreal, abandoning the United States and Irish-America to the grim fate of godless anarchy he foresaw for pluralist democracy.[115]

Bitterly polemical in style, hyperbolic in language, and irregular enough in personal habits that Timon had to sue him to recover a debt,[116] McGee presents a complex picture of brilliance and instability. Yet his views may well not have been greatly different from those of Bishop Timon, who brought him to Buffalo, or of the men in the senior ranks of the Irish diocesan clergy. For example, just as McGee made his peace with England in his search for order and for security for the church, so it was that, with the Irish church secure by mid-century in its liberties and England free of both the radical anticlerical republicanism that wracked the Continent and the nativism present in the United States, Bishop Timon and his senior priests did, too. They never engaged in that public battering of England that was the staple of Irish political rhetoric. Moreover, though Timon was hardly likely to blurt out criticisms of American democracy when the very existence of the church was threatened by nativists, he nonetheless had certain profound reservations. Early in 1861, for example, he publicly blamed the South for the war that appeared inevitable with the breakup of the Union, while in private correspondence he revealed a belief that the conflict represented God's punishment for persecution of the one, true church.[117] But above all Timon and the clerics around him were cautious in expressing controversial opinions, and this was evident in the pattern set for the next diocesan, English-language paper, the *Sentinel*, and in the choice of Michael Hagan, a more representative ethnic ideologist who was chosen to edit it.

Under Hagan, no doubt to Bishop Timon's relief and perhaps on his orders, the *Sentinel* was more reportorial and less polemical, even in debate with the nativist *Express*, which constantly baited the Irish and the church. But Hagan's paper differed in more than tone. The new editor adopted a course less aggressively sectarian. Hagan did not embrace liberal pluralism, and he was critical of such aspects of what he took to be Protestant culture as the impetus to the social emancipation of women. But he did, perhaps as much out of expediency as belief, call for tolerance among groups and sects. His espousal of Catholic education, and of its claims to public funding, did not proclaim that the church had a monopoly on truth, and argued only that Catholic children were subject to conversion efforts in public schools. Hagan's defense of the church spoke less of the truth of its doctrine than the selflessness of the clergy, which he contrasted with the corruption and self-seeking of many American ministers, politicians, and officeholders.[118]

Hagan's greatest departure from McGee's views, however, was in his social democratic economic and republican political beliefs. Men of Hagan's views appreciated the political liberties available to the Irish in America, and sought to convince those like McGee, who saw nothing but nativism and bigotry, that there was much more to the United States. The country afforded opportunity to oppose bigotry and defend the rights of even the poorest citizens. It was out of such a belief that Hagan found it impossible to espouse colonization. Though he respectfully reported the convention's proceedings and praised the motives of its members, he found its ideas impractical and based on the false notion that there were no secure, employed Irishmen in cities like Buffalo.[119] A meeting of the city's most prominent Irish officeholders, which was convened before the convention and given prominent attention in the *Sentinel*, went even further. Its resolutions affirmed loyalty to the United States, denounced Canada for its allegiance "to the red flag of British tyranny" and rejected it as a site for Irish settlement, expressed gratitude to the many American friends of the Irish while condemning nativism, and finally called for a boycott of the convention. Irish leaders such as Democrats Thomas Merrigan and James Ryan, who organized the anticolonization meeting, believed America afforded practical weapons for a forthright defense of citizens' rights, so it was cowardly to do anything but stay and fight.[120]

Combined with this sober embrace of American democracy was a reformist, prolabor orientation that rejected the excesses of capitalism and sought to use political power to improve the status of wage earners. Its roots in both Irish republican nationalist tradition and American reformism, this social democratic ideology took shape in response to the sufferings of the immigrants, particularly during the 1857–58 depression, and to nativist polemics against the Irish poor, who were charged with being social parasites content to live off charity. Nativism here was seen as both cultural bigotry and class prejudice. Nativists were identified not simply as Protestants, as McGee would have it, but as "the men of white kid gloves and satin vests," who lived off investments and the exploitation of the working classes, and voted Whig. Their wealth was the poor man's tragedy, for as Hagan said, "Create a palace, and you get hundreds of hovels."[121] By contrast, labor was the source of all economic value, and it was unjust and undignified that it be bought and sold in the marketplace. The *Sentinel* denounced banks, corporations, and employers for degrading wages through payments in worthless paper money and orders on stores, and for bribing officials in order to subvert the will of the majority of voters.[122]

Such views crystallized in 1857 and 1858 in two local protest movements, for which the *Sentinel* was the journalistic voice, and for which a number of local Irish politicians expressed support. In the spring of 1857, a "Workingman's Movement," which espoused these views and was comprised very largely of Irish laborers and artisans from the First and Eighth wards, sought to use the ballot box to get action on economic and political grievances.[123] Then during the depression that began that fall, a protest movement arose spontaneously among the Irish unemployed to demand that the city use tax revenues to create jobs and to provide relief for those not able to work. Though usually nonpartisan and temperate in its recommendations, the *Sentinel* gave enthusiastic support to these calls for public action, for which it earned bitter criticism from the nativist press. But Hagan's stature among his readers grew enough for him to be elected alderman in 1858.[124]

Class-based movements did not succeed, however, in becoming a permanent force among the Irish. It was difficult to organize mobile laborers who had no trade. Furthermore, there was no public clerical support for such movements, though it is possible that some informal support existed among the parish clergy, which daily saw the sufferings of the poor. Finally, the political energies of angry Irish workers were continually reabsorbed by the Democratic party. With its historic antimonopoly position and its defense of immigrant traditions, institutions, and religions, particularly Catholicism, the party had great attractions for the Irish, who used it to expand their power and range of employment, and to denounce, in Hagan's phrase, "perfidious Albion." Yet loyalty to the party placed limitations on the development of the ideological system articulated by Hagan. Believing the American Union not merely a cradle of liberty, but a natural bulwark against British power, the Irish approved of the party's bitter hostility to agitation of the slavery question out of fear of disunion. The party went beyond union, however, to embrace a proslavery stance in the 1850s, and Irish Democrats such as Hagan accepted this. No matter how democratic their politics, most Irish possessed intense race prejudice, fear of black economic competition, and resentment that American Whigs and evangelicals had so much sympathy for black slaves and so little for the Irish poor. The refusal of the Catholic hierarchy to condemn slavery in moral and theological terms gave additional legitimacy to this stance. Hagan admitted that slavery might well be a wrong, but slaves, he said, were well treated, and hence their situation could hardly justify jeopardizing the Union.[125] This defensive politics did tie the disparate branches of Irish opinion together. It did little, however, to prepare Irish social democrats or the ordinary folk that they were in a position to influence, to play a progressive role during Reconstruction.

Later in the nineteenth century, when many Irish obtained greater job stability and personal security through factory work and unionization, and when a segment of the American Catholic church developed a social gospel with workerist components, the problems faced by Irish social democrats and republicans in their efforts to fashion an ideological alternative to clerical conservatism would be somewhat relieved. Before the Civil War, however, the oppression of Ireland, nativist hostility, cruel poverty, and an all-encompassing culture of daily life that provided a powerful impetus for ethnicization, all placed profound limits on the ability of the Irish to transcend the political framework of ethnicity.

CHAPTER 7

Buffalo's Germans: Foundations in Diversity

IN their diversity Buffalo's Germans present a sharp contrast to its Irish. While the Irish became a group upon the uniform foundation of a common language, religion, peasant culture, and experience of national oppression, Germans embarked upon ethnicization on a foundation as complex as any ever put down by an American immigrant group. The sources of this intragroup diversity were nationality, region, religion, class, and political ideology. In America, these would overlap and intertwine to create an impressive array of subidentities and subgroups. As an ethnic group, Germans were loosely held together by varying combinations of language, daily culture, and ideology, and by occasional mobilizations in defense of what was common to all of them in their way of life.

Consider national origin. Thirty-nine percent of Buffalo household heads in 1855 were from the German states. But there also resided in the German wards the 5 percent (750) of household heads who were Franco-Germans (Alsatians mostly), 0.8 percent (129) who were Swiss, and 0.1 percent (12) who were Austrian, all of whom spoke a form of German. And there were approximately 125 Bohemians, Dutch, and Polish household heads, who, depending on their exact point of origin, may well have also spoken German.[1] With the exception of the Swiss and the Alsatians, who maintained some degree of public group life while still identifying closely with the larger body of Germans, these peoples have left few tracings, and may or may not have been completely immersed in the population of German-speakers. Origin in what were historically the German states, those once a part of the Holy Roman Empire, was itself complex. Until 1871 there was no unified German nation-state, and the distances between, as well as political and cultural differences among, the kingdoms, dukedoms, and principalities that would become the new German Reich were considerable. Strong regional identities existed among Bavarians, Hessians, Badenese, Prussians, Saxons, Württembergers, Hanoverians, and Mecklenburgers. Within these historic German states were yet more particularistic, provincial, and localistic identities that would assert their influence in America. Throughout the period, for example, many people when registering their marriages listed their place of origin not simply as the Rhineland, or Palatinate, or Bavaria, but rather as "Mainz" or "Franconia."[2]

Crosscutting national, regional, and subregional identities were other sources of differentiation. Though the geographical lines were certainly not unyielding, since the Counter-Reformation Lutheranism and the Reform and Evangelical Reform denominations predominated in the northern German states, while Roman Catholicism was deeply entrenched in the southern and western, Rhenish states. Buffalo's Franco-Germans were nearly uniform in their Catholicism, while its Swiss were both Protestant and Catholic. To add to this confessional diversity, there was a Jewish population of German-speakers, composed of perhaps fifty families, who had few formal social ties, outside the narrow ranks of some liberal circles, with Christian Germans. While churches and synagogues did tend to mix people from contiguous regions, and thus created broader bases of common identity in the New World, historic regional animosities and cultural differences did assert themselves even among coreligionists. The small Jewish population had two synagogues, because of disagreements over liturgy between worshipers from western Germany and Polish, eastern Germany. Among Lutherans, historic suspicions between neighboring Silesians and Pomeranians combined with doctrinal differences to cause fragmentation.[3]

Too, among Germans there was a wider diversity of occupations and a greater range of wealth than among the Irish,[4] so that social class was a potent source of differentiation. Class was also a potential source of conflict because, unlike the Irish, Germans regularly employed their own people. Class, moreover, provided one, though not the only, basis for the deep ideological cleavages that divided Germans in the 1850s. Other sources of ideological conflict were Roman Catholicism, political partisanship, ethnic identity and culture, socialism, Old World revolution, and American slavery.

For all this diversity, it may be thought that language was the principal cultural cement that held Germans together. This is true in a general way, but it must be understood that there was then no one German tongue. The language existed in a number of dialect and literary forms. The immigrants did possess a common literary language, Standard German, which had been the written language of the Protestant Bible since the Lutheran Reformation and, in its spoken form, was often the language of both Protestant and Catholic worship in the Old World. Moreover, independent of religious affiliation, Standard German was certainly known to all those who had studied in the widespread, and sometimes compulsory, primary schools of both the German States and Alsace, where German remained the language of social relations and high culture throughout the period (1648–1870) of the province's incorporation into France. Standard German was also the language of the press wherever German-speakers lived. But while widely disseminated, Standard German was subject to social variation, and in its formality was most often the spoken language in the Old World of urban, higher-status groups. The humbler rural classes, the petty traders, peasants, and artisans who bulked so large in the immigrant population, were likely to speak regional dialects, and these were similar enough to link only those from contiguous states, not the entire group. Southwestern *Oberdeutsch* could with mutual accommodations create a linguistic community among Rhinelanders, Alsatians, and the southern majority of Badenese, Bavarians, and Württembergers. Northern *Plattdeutsch* could, even more easily, bind the smaller groups of Prussians, Mecklenburgers, Saxons, and others from the northern states. But these two broad dialect groups would not have found it easy to converse in daily speech unless they used Standard German. Though English words soon entered German speech in Buffalo, it was too soon to expect the American language to emerge as a *lingua franca* among Germans. Moreover, the emotional commitment of Germans to their language in all its varied forms, and the language-saves-faith formula adopted in America by the two largest German churches, the Lutheran and the Roman Catholic, also impeded the emergence of English in that role. So intraethnic language difficulties remained meaningful in daily life, as Germans themselves recognized. Nothing was more likely to get a laugh from the *Oberdeutsch* majority than the distinctive sound of Prussian speech, often parodied in the Buffalo German press—which was itself written in Standard German. Of even more social significance was the fact that dialect was one of the complex of regional traits, along with religion, locale of birth, and folk tradition and memory, that played a role in America in shaping such social patterns of daily life as the choice of marriage partners, friends, and neighborhoods.[5]

In light of such diversity, which grew more complex over time as the different subgroups of Germans arrived sequentially, it may seem unlikely that ethnicization could occur at all. Indeed, a persistent theme in German-American historiography has been the weakness of group feeling and of the capacity for mobilization among immigrant Germans, whose historians have developed the habit of referring to them ambiguously as an *element* rather than more definitively as a *group*.[6] Still, even as the sources of intragroup diversity and potential conflict grew more complex, by the 1850s a strong sense of German identity and group commitment was becoming evident. And certainly, Americans saw Germans (or "Dutch," a native corruption of "Deutsch") as a group, and made judgments about them as such. This in turn deeply influenced the Germans' emergent ethnic sense of themselves.

The internal bases of German ethnicization were often, depending on the people involved, subtle and abstract. Among the educated or intellectually inclined, there existed the metaphysical notion of a pan-German spirit which could unite all German-speakers. This was evident, for example, in 1841 when the German Young Men's Association was organized. A self-conscious copy in form of the American's Young Men's Association, the German society was founded by nine men whose origins were quite diverse: there were four Alsatians, two Swiss, one Lorrainian, and one (probably two) from the historical German states. They were both Protestant and Catholic. What united these men and sustained the association was a desire to preserve and study the language and literature of Standard German, to learn English, and in their words, "to stimulate the growth of German spirit and self-awareness," about which they appear to have had a common understanding. Though the association grew and the membership remained diverse, they were able to agree enough on the meaning of Germanness to become even more committed to German cultural goals. Eventually they dropped the intention to sponsor English language instruction.[7]

It is not clear how much ordinary folk shared this abstract concept of "German spirit" or were committed to Standard German and its literary products. As we shall see, the radical German artisans of the 1850s drank deeply at the well of German literary culture in their search for inspiration. Moreover, to the extent that language was often conceived as the key to cultural survival across generations, mobilizations for language rights, which took the form of demands for bilingual public education and for publication of municipal government notices in German, were occasional bases for group mobilization. Furthermore, instruction in German was a facet of sectarian school education that made it attractive to large numbers of Catholics, Lutherans, and others whose denominations maintained schools.

But whether or not a conception of Germanness was widely distributed throughout the immigrant population, that conception was itself nourished by a deeper and less reflective, existential commitment to a shared, daily way of life. Larger than, but intimately associated with, language, this way of living encompassed all German subgroups. It was crucial too, because, unlike the Irish, Germans had no central communal institutions to unify, speak for, or sustain them across the many lines that divided them. The group was simply too diverse to create such institutions. In fact, the one institution, the Democratic party, that routinely united large numbers of Germans in common purpose was an American creation. The main components of this way of life were: a commitment to property ownership broad enough to cross class lines; a rich and highly developed popular culture which had roots in northern European folk traditions and symbols; and an extensive pattern of secular, religious and political associations (*Vereine*), which were not mere voluntary societies gotten up for narrow, specialized purposes, but corporate moral communities that exacted obligations for good conduct, fellowship, and participation and were guided by their own codes and aspirations (*Vereinswesen*). Visible aspects of the popular culture were the beer hall and beer garden, which were centers not only for drinking, but for family socializing and recreation and for artistic performance; processions through the streets in costume or uniform accompanied by music; group picnics and excursions; mass communal festivals, such as the midyear St. John's Day and the midwinter pre-Lenten carnival (*Fasching*); and the use of the Sabbath for recreation and physical as well as spiritual renewal. Joined together, the property-holding orientation toward small, tidy homes in orderly neighborhoods, *Vereinswesen*, and the popular culture, with its distinctive forms of sociability, provided similarities in patterns of conduct and purpose among such vastly different subgroups as Jews, Lutherans, Catholics, secularists, "Free Thinkers," and the organized Left.

This ethnic way of life did not lead all of these different German social types to socialize together. Instead, usually separately, each enjoyed the security and fulfillment of what was common to all. But in this way each also came to have a stake in what was common to all, and the defense of this ethnic way of life was, even more than the essentially abstract question of language rights, a basis for collective mobilization. In the 1850s, Germans united to fight nativism, which, in attacking their political rights, threatened their material security and property; and they allied against temperance, prohibition, and Sabbatarianism, which threatened their unique forms of sociability. For German ethnic leadership, it was a short step from recognition of the need for mobilization in defense of ethnic interests to urging Germans to act as a political unit in electoral affairs. Thus, in addition to the desire to share in civic duties, which led to the creation of several

German militia and volunteer fire companies, and in public resources, one of the central bases of German civic and political activity was defense of communal ethnic culture, a situation analogous to the role that defense of the Catholic church played in Irish politics.

Still, such ethnic interests and mobilizations were not able to bind all the wounds within the group, and Germans remained much more deeply divided than the Irish. Some animosities, such as those based on sectarian rivalries, had existed in Europe, and were soon planted firmly in the New World. To these were added conflicts between the leadership of the old settlers ("Grays") and the post-1848 political refugees ("Greens"), Democrats and Republicans, and the advocates of antislavery and antiabolitionism. Yet as was the case with the Irish, there is a paradox in intraethnic conflict: the more members of the emergent group quarreled with one another, the more they became involved in being ethnic and in attempting to determine the destiny of the group. When a new, American forum was found for Old World controversies, the immigrants actually reinforced the weight of tradition, and hence of being German, by arguing with the same parties, in the same mental frameworks, and with the same rhetoric—another "fine, old conflict," in which the parties become so habituated in their roles that they were no longer able to define themselves apart from their adversaries. In a slightly different way, new, American-formed conflicts had the same impact. However bitter the antagonism of Gray and Green, both groups elaborated upon the same symbols and mental references. They interpreted them differently in their efforts to find meanings for Germanness and purposes for Germans in America, but never tried to dispense with them. Both parties, therefore, were in Harold Abramson's phrase "socio-cultural traditionalists,"[8] who even when holding opposite views were bound together by a commitment to a common, historically conditioned identity. The alternative was to become American or to adopt a transnational identity that sought to dispense completely with ethnicity. Very few would take the former course, and for those who did, choice was less the basis for the process than a slow, often barely conscious process of cultural evolution. The latter course was hesitantly adopted by some of the more radical German trade unionists in their quest for allies, but there were too few positive results from such internationalism to make the cultural and psychological sacrifices worthwhile.

Because of the complexity of the task, analysis of the formation of German ethnicity will be spread over two chapters. In this chapter economic and social aspects of the process are analyzed, while in the next, the focus is leadership, ideology and mobilization.

While at a general level the crises created by economic and political modernization account for mid-nineteenth century German emigration, a distinction must be made between the movements of two periods, 1830–44 and 1845–54. Both periods saw mass migration from the area bounded by Westphalia, the Danube, the Rhine, and Saxony, and most concentrated in the French and German Rhineland. The latter years, however, saw migrations, prompted by the devastating combination of economic crises and revolution, that were epic in scale. Between 1830 and 1844 just over 250,000 people from the German states entered the United States; they constituted about a third of the total immigration. From 1845 to 1854 fully 939,000 came to America, 215,000 in 1854 alone, a year when half of all immigrants were German-speakers. Nowhere in Europe, not even Ireland, was the extent of emigration relative to total population then higher.[9]

The numbers are less significant than the different nature of the social groups emigrating in the two periods. The emigrants of the former period were largely moderately prosperous rural, village, and *Heimat* ("hometown") folk of the middling classes—small landholding farmers, petty traders, and independent craftsmen. The farmers were caught in the familiar problems eventuating from the commercialization of agriculture, growing population and increasing intergenerational parcelization of landholdings, and periodic crop failures. Village and *Heimat* craftsmen and shopkeepers were also rendered insecure by those crises. A singular German creation, the *Heimat* was a small incorporated city of no more than 15,000 that served as the residence for a large number of the traditional craftsmen of southern and western Germany. For nearly two centuries life in these tightly regulated islands of social stability, which numbered about 400 in 1800, had been carefully controlled by tradition-bound craft guilds and municipal governments. Together guild and government had controlled entrance into the crafts and access to legal residence, and in so doing regulated marriage, population increase, and economic competition. But such conservatism clashed head-on with the aspiration of nineteenth-century governments to stimulate rapid economic growth through establishing free markets, customs unions, and occupational freedom for journeymen and craftsmen. The rapid expansion of journeymen and the penetration of local markets by cheap manufactured goods imperiled the hometown artisan and the shopkeepers and others traders who depended on him, and stimulated emigration.[10]

The poorer peasants and the village artisans, who were linked economically and socially to the peasantry, were the last groups to adopt emigration as a strategy. Affected negatively by both long-term modernizing trends in agriculture and population growth, the peasantry tried to defend itself through reliance on the easily cultivated potato rather than adopt the more drastic, costly strategy of emigrating. When, as in Ireland, the potato crop began to fail in the mid-1840s, the peasantry and groups linked to it, again largely from the southern and western German states, had little choice but to leave. Village artisans were simultaneously being negatively affected by the rapid expansion of journeymen and by the undermining of cottage industries by manufactured goods. While not as affluent as the farmers and craftsmen, these peasants and artisans were hardly the poorest people in the countryside, for with no indenture system to finance their passage to America, they, like the Irish, had to have been able to sell belongings, use savings, or borrow money to pay their way, options not available to the impoverished.[11]

Socioeconomic reasons do not exhaust the motivations for emigration, for political and religious conflicts are also relevant to the backgrounds of Buffalo's Germans. To be sure, the line between political and socioeconomic crises were often difficult to draw, as were the lines between voluntary and involuntary emigration. Like other large northern cities, by the mid-1850s Buffalo had a few of the middle-class, radical intellectuals who had fled from one German state or another for their roles in organizing the failed 1848 revolutions. But to the narrow ranks of this highly visible group of exiles has to be added a much larger, if indeterminate, number of obscure, radicalized artisans who were not exactly either involuntary exiles or voluntary emigrants. Threatened with proletarianization by the rise of industry and the growing marginalization of the journeyman, many artisans and craftsmen chose to emigrate. Others, however, were politicized and rebelled but were pushed out of their homelands, if not by governmental repression, then by dashed political hopes and the prospect of impoverishment.[12] These obscure men were present in Buffalo in large numbers in the 1850s, and their presence helps account for the brief rise of a German labor movement and the founding of an activist *Turnverein*, a popular organization dedicated to physical fitness and social reform.

Long before the arrival of the '48ers of all classes, in the autumn of 1839, Buffalo had been the site of resettlement of a different group of exiles, who would retain their identity as a community much longer than the '48ers. These were orthodox Protestants, from the provinces of Saxony, Silesia, Brandenburg, and Pomerania, who were called "Old Lutherans" because of their position in the most important Prussian confessional controversy of the day. Out of religious belief and fear of state control of religion, they refused to accept the merger of the Lutheran and Reformed churches decreed by Frederick William III in 1817. They struggled for almost two decades in their homeland, first publicly and then underground, to carry on their traditional religious life. At first opposed to emigration, after years of harrassment perhaps one-third of the 5,000 Old Lutherans concluded that they would seek permission from the authorities to go into exile. A number of false starts prompted by bureaucratic manipulation followed, but eventually they were allowed to emigrate. They left in large groups, led usually by their pastors. Some 550 went to South Australia, and of the remainder who came to America under the leadership of Rev. Johannes A. A. Grabau and his follower, Rev. Carl von Rohr, about 800 believers established themselves in Buffalo. The Old Lutherans were people of humble origin and small means—60 percent were farmers with smallholdings or hired farmhands, while another 35 percent were peasant artisans, mostly shoemakers and carpenters. Beset by the economic woes of the time, material distress predisposed many to emigrate. Living close together for many years in the same Buffalo neighborhoods, they formed the nucleus of two congregations, which were divided partly along doctrinal and partly along regional lines, and soon fell deeply at odds with one another. The local presence of these Lutherans exerted a powerful pull on friends and family in Prussia, and soon migration chains were forged connecting Buffalo and northeastern Germany, which, though not as well represented as a point of origin as the states of the south and east, nonetheless came to have strong local representation. Because official repression of the Old Lutherans ended soon after the emigration of the late 1830s, those who came after the first wave should be thought of as immigrants in search of opportunity.[13]

The settlement of these and other German-speakers in Buffalo over a three-decade period proceeded in quite orderly sequences, according to place of origin and relatedly, religion. Before 1828 there were no more than seventy German-speaking families. Some of them were descendants of Pennsylvania Germans, and hence really German-Americans, while others were recently arrived immigrants. That most were Protestants is attested to by the convening in 1828 of the first local German religious service, which brought together under one roof Lutheran, Reformed, and Evangelical Reformed believers, who soon established St. John's Evangelical Lutheran Church. German Catholic settlement began about the same time. A significantly sized group of Catholics, mostly Alsatians, but including Rhenish Germans and a few Swiss, formed the first Catholic parish, St. Louis, in 1828. For the next decade Alsatian and southern German Catholics continued to form the bulk of the immigrants, though smaller numbers of northern and central German Protestants also arrived and founded churches of their own.[14] The scale of settlement during most of this decade was small.

In August, 1839, for example, a correspondent of a local American newspaper complained that too many Germans were passing through the city without settling, and the loss to Buffalo in labor was tremendous.[15] Within a month, however, hundreds of Old Lutherans arrived. Consequently, even during a catastrophic depression the Fourth Ward, which had most of the city's Germans, saw a 61 percent population increase (3,407 to 5,482) between 1835 and 1840, the largest increase among the five wards.[16]

By 1841 the majority of Alsatians who would be present in 1855 had settled, as had some 15 percent of Badenese and Württembergers and 20 percent of Prussians. The arrival of the majority of the latter and of other subgroups would have to await the massive influx that began after the 1845–46 crop failures. Seventy-five percent or more of the Bavarians, Hessians, Saxons, Badenese, Württembergers, German Jews, and Mecklenburgers resident in 1855 had arrived after 1846, as had 71 percent of Prussians, the majority now from Prussia's Rhenish province rather than Prussia proper.* Because of the disorder accompanying the 1848 political upheavals and the difficulties the disorder of the times caused those wanting to dispose of property, the greatest surge of German immigration, both to America and to Buffalo itself, began in 1851. In 1855 the average length of residence for German men was 7.2 years and for women, 6.9 years; and in that year, only 17.5 percent and 8.5 percent respectively had lived in Buffalo at least a decade or two decades. Unlike the Irish, most German immigrants, largely because of the material resources at their command, had come directly to Buffalo: while 50 percent of Irish children had been born outside Ireland and Erie County, often at some point on their route to eventual settlement in Buffalo, only 4 percent of the Germans' children were born en route.[17]

In 1855 southern and Rhenish Germans were the large majority of the local German population. Of the German-speaking heads of household in 1855 providing a specific German state as a place of origin in the census, 2,174 were from, in order of prominence, Bavaria, Baden, Hesse, and Württemberg, while 898 were from Prussia (including Rhenish Prussia), Mecklenburg, Saxony, and Hanover. Buffalo had more Bavarians than any other American city, and more southern Germans than such equally significant German centers as St. Louis, Chicago, and New York.[18] The significance of such data is considerable, for they suggest the existence of a Roman Catholic majority among local Germans, and the probability of profound Catholic influence in German ethnicization.

---

* There is no way to disaggregate the data to differentiate between the two populations the census recorded as from "Prussia."

As a center for German settlement, Buffalo had a number of attractions. There were obvious ones, such as work for men and women (as domestics) alike and the prosperity of many wage earners, especially skilled ones. There was also the availability of land within the city limits, which, as we have seen in Johannes Züngler's 1835 letter to his fellow Old Lutherans, held out the possibility of small-scale urban agriculture to uprooted peasants too poor to buy farms in the New World.[19] The promise of urban agriculture may help explain the particular attraction of Buffalo to southern Germans, the large majority of whom were peasants and farmers. It helps to explain, too, the pattern of German settlement within the city. Because so much of the city's economy centered around the docks, the only section by 1840 that was comparatively empty of population was the vast East Side, north of Seneca Street. Far from the docks, but walking distance from most industrial sites and the central business district, much of the East Side was a flat, wet meadowland with stands of willow and oak. At its furthest reaches, there were particularly thick forests. The area was suitable for agriculture, wells could easily be dug, and the forests provided cheap fuel and building material, yet residents could work in the more populous parts of the city while living here. Moreover, in the 1840s many found employment lumbering here. Early in their settlement in Buffalo Germans began to buy up vast numbers of small lots, and to use unsettled space for grazing and gathering wood. The land was cheap in direct proportion to its distance from the dockside centers of economic activity. Gradually, as new immigrants came to Buffalo, human settlement pushed its way further toward the distant eastern borders. But farming continued all the while, and Germans continued, according to the census, to be the largest single group of urban farmers right up to the Civil War. Many more Germans dabbled in farming while working as wage earners.[20]

The East Side became the heartland of German Buffalo. Extensive as it was in size, it was less a neighborhood than, as the Germans said, a *Deutschendörfchen* (German village).[21] Eighty percent of the German state immigrants, fully 25,000 people, resided here in 1855, and large majorities of the smaller, related peoples (Franco-Germans, Swiss, Austrians, Dutch, and Norwegians). Probably because of its intensely foreign character, as well as its location, it did not prove attractive to others. Thus, while the Irish and Americans had indices of residential dissimilarity of .49 and .42, respectively, to all other groups, that for German-speakers was a high .60 in 1855, which made Buffalo's one of the most residentially segregated urban, German populations in the nation. Their separation from other working-class immigrants was even greater, as the high index of dissimilarity—71.7 in 1855—between local Irish and Germans suggests.[22]

Until 1853 the German village was one ward, the Fourth, which was by far the most populous, but was kept as a single political entity (and gerrymandered in state legislature elections) to dilute German political power.[23] In 1853, however, the Fourth was finally divided into four wards (Four, Five, Six, and Seven). The new Fourth Ward contained most of the historic nucleus of the German village, a 1.5-mile-square neighborhood on the fringe of the central business district. Accessible to mercantile businesses, professional offices, and Main Street's fashionable shops, it was attractive to Americans, who were 35 percent of its population—a fact that helps to account for the relatively low index of dissimilarity (59.0) between Germans and Americans at a time when the other German wards were overwhelmingly German. Here one found a number of the older and major German congregations and sectarian schools and the clubrooms of secular *Vereine*, such as the Turners and drama and singing societies. The new Fourth and immediately adjacent areas at its northern and eastern fringes became densely packed in the 1850s, especially on such major arteries as Genesee and Broadway, with small stores, groceries, saloons, beer halls and gardens, artisanal and small industrial shops, and breweries. Genesee had a horse-drawn street railroad all the way to Jefferson by 1861.[24] Its lesser, feeder streets, "dirty, unpaved, and crooked," with poor drainage and a high incidence of death and disease during cholera epidemics,[25] were lined with one-and-a-half and two-story, narrow frame cottages. Only on the central streets were there residences housing more than two families—and there were few of these: only seventy-eight on the entire German East Side in 1855, and most of them had no more than three families. Even in the most congested zones, and narrow though the houses were, each often had a deep backyard, with a garden and perhaps a cow. The yards grew more extensive as one journeyed east from the core, until one reached areas such as St. Ann's parish where cows wandered about amidst meadows, marshes, and orchards.[26]

By 1855 the German social structure had taken on clear spatial patterns. The core area of the Fourth Ward and the neighborhoods adjacent to it had a longer-settled, more prosperous German population of skilled and white-collar workers and shopkeepers. Thus, though the Fourth had 14 percent of the German population, its location near the central business district and relative prestige, as well as higher land values, led fully 22.5 percent, 19.5 percent, 31 percent, and 30.5 percent respectively of German nonmanual workers, clerical and sales employees, and shopkeepers to settle here. Most of the Alsatians, perhaps five hundred families in 1855 and disproportionately affluent craftsmen and shopkeepers, lived in or immediately around the Fourth. At the top of the Fourth, along the northern reaches of Main, Michigan, and Ellicott streets, in substantial brick houses lived the most prosperous German retailers and professionals. These men often catered not only to Germans, but to the American carriage trade on the other side of Main Street. The further one traveled beyond the Fourth into the other three, semirural German wards, the more one encountered new immigrants, and hence more Bavarians and other southern and western German manual workers. In the Sixth and Seventh wards there were 70.5 percent of the Badenese and 85.5 percent of the Bavarians, along with nearly two-thirds of the unskilled German heads of household.[27] The outstanding exception to these social-spatial correlates was the Prussian Old Lutherans, who although long established in 1855, had sought out a remote area when they arrived years before. This was the "Fruit Belt" (for its orchards), and became part of the Seventh Ward. They had settled here not only because land was cheap, but because of a desire to isolate themselves from external influences that could threaten their solidarity and doctrinal purity.[28]

While most German neighborhoods were mixed by place of origin, on individual streets Germans often sorted themselves out by Old World identities. In 1855 a quarter to two-thirds of the Mecklenburgers, Württembergers, Hessians, Prussians, and Bavarians, in ascending order, had neighbors on at least one side from the same German state.[29] This created pockets of regional concentration within the *Deutschendörfchen*, often no doubt populated by family, kin, and friends and acquaintances from the Old World. Glasco estimates that some 12 percent of Germans had relatives living in their neighborhoods.[30] Marriage patterns intensified this relationship between residence and point of origin, as did the custom of godparentage. Both Catholic parish records and state census data reveal that Germans seldom married outside their language and religion, and that they married people from their same place of origin. This was true of more than 90 percent of samples of Bavarians, Mecklenburgers and Württembergers, 80 percent or more of Prussians and Hessians, and more than 70 percent of Saxons and Badenese. When these peoples did not choose partners from their own places of origin, they most often were wed to those from neighboring states, who were likely to be of the same religion.[31] The newness of all these supportive and affectional networks cannot be overestimated. All four German wards had high percentages of foreign-born—53, 59, 67, and 66 percent—in 1855. Nor surprisingly the Sixth and Seventh had the city's highest percentages of nonnaturalized residents, 56 and 48 percent.[32]

When Americans spoke of the German town, they seemed impressed not only by its foreign quality ("as little American as the duchy of Hesse-Cassel," we recall the *Commercial Advertiser* stated),[33] but also by the fact, as one of them said, that it seemed "an independent, self-supporting community."[34] This insight was valid when it came to the high level of the town's institutional completeness and its dense, intricately woven social networks. It also had significance for the material bases of those institutions and networks. Compared to the Irish, the Germans had considerably more possibilities for attaining social mobility and prosperity. Their relative assets may be traced to long-term developments in the Old World. While the Irish suffered stultifying underdevelopment under a harsh colonial regime, the German states achieved substantial development after the Thirty Years War. While peasant life was always hard and subject to periodic shortages of food, German peasants generally had diets superior to those of much of the rest of Europe. Enjoying government protection and profiting from the prosperity of the countryside, towns became centers of commerce and craft production. Schooling, sometimes compulsory depending on the state, but available everywhere, widened the range of skills and intensified development.[35] These assets gained from development crossed the ocean with Germans. They soon dominated traditional crafts and attained a foothold in commerce and small manufacturing. Furthermore, while in the Irish wards (One and Eight), one in every fourteen and thirteen people respectively could not read or write in 1855, in wards Four through Seven the comparable figures were one in 658, 167, 34, and 76.[36]

Germans seldom participated in the dock trade. Among representative occupations arising out of waterborne commerce, Germans were only 10 percent of household heads employed as sailors, 5 percent of wholesale merchants, and 8.6 percent of ship carpenters.[37] While Germans distinguished themselves in many entrepreneurial and industrial fields, only two men, the Alsatians George Urban and Michael Mesmer, entered the ranks of grain and flour merchants. Lack of participation was complemented by a lack of interest. Though, as necessary, the German press contained articles on the various government proposals to use tax dollars to subsidize commerce, the *Weltbürger* admitted, in an introduction to one article on harbor improvements in 1845, that "it is perhaps for our readers a matter of minor interest."[38] The paper waited until 1857 to carry its first in-depth analysis of the work of the twelve-year-old Board of Trade,[39] and as the date suggests, interest in the docks was growing alongside the crises of the city's commerce. Throughout the period, as we shall see, the lack of the Germans' involvement in the docks set the stage for their persistent, though gradually declining, reluctance to approve using taxes to aid commerce.

In contrast to the Irish then, Germans were found providing goods and services for internal markets rather than external trade. Within this sector of Buffalo's economy, again in contrast to the Irish, German employment was characterized by its diversity, high level of skills, and degree of self-employment, all of which, like its uninvolvement in interregional trade, furthered the impression of German economic independence. Along with the Irish, the large majority of Germans were manual workers, but there the comparison begins to break down. While approximately 68 percent of Irish men could state no occupation or were unskilled laborers, this could be said of 42 percent of German men, and while only 17 percent of the Irish were skilled or semiskilled, 49 percent of Germans were. Indeed skilled workers, who were 37 percent of those Germans providing occupational data, represented the largest single employment group. Germans constituted large majorities in many of the time-honored, low-mechanized trades: 70 to 80 percent of masons, coopers, and shoemakers; 60 to 70 percent of tailors, butchers, cabinetmakers, and ironworkers, and 50 to 60 percent of carpenters. Germans also dominated the food trades: those with German surnames were eight of fifteen retail bakers, 108 of 163 butchers, and three of eight retail confectioners listed in the 1855 city directory. In the same year, too, German surnames characterized fifty-seven of ninety persons working as brewers and maltsters.[40]

In a city in which manufacturing was generally underdeveloped, the majority of these craftsmen were either independent artisans, who contracted out their services, or journeymen, who worked for older craftsmen and artisans and aspired to become independent. The four East Side wards were filled with little cabinetmaking, brickmaking, harnessmaking, and wood-turning shops, shoe and bootmaking concerns, breweries, etc., employing from four to seven men. There were also many small firms of building contractors.[41] Decentralized employment, often tied to neighborhood of residence and hence to region, religion, and dialect, reinforced the fractured social organization of German ethnicity. But the lack of separation of work and residence for many, and the lack of need to leave the neighborhood in order to find work, also isolated many Germans from the world beyond the ethnic town and involved them more deeply with one another.

In the next five decades many of these German trades fell victim to industrialization, a trend which had already begun among tailors, shoemakers, and cabinetmakers. Nor were most of these trades, as practiced by Germans, often the basis for propelling a man into factory ownership. Whether defined by the number of men employed or the amount of capitalization in plant or equipment, there were few German-owned factories, which suggests less an absence of German prosperity than the presence of the stability-oriented pattern of *Heimat* craft work.[42]

In the 1840s and 1850s these trades were able to offer a great deal to the individual German: self-employment or the hope of attaining it, prestige on terms consistent with Old and New World ideals, and steady work in all but the worst times. Craft employment was apparently within the grasp of many young men, for the German population gave evidence of becoming more skilled as the life cycle progressed. While 37 percent of all employed Germans were skilled in 1855, among Germans in their twenties the figure was 44 percent.[43] Two paths existed into skilled trades for Germans: informal apprenticeship for the unskilled, and formal apprenticeship for young boys. In 1855 there were 1,242 German heads of household who gave their occupations as "laborer." Though they were 59 percent of *all* Buffalo heads of household so employed, they were a minority of the German work force. (There were more Germans employed collectively in just four trades—as carpenters, tailors, cabinetmakers, and coopers.) Most of these laborers were probably new immigrants employed in building construction. This work had distinct advantages over dock work and the other common, outdoor labor done by the Irish. Building went on in all but the worst winter weather, so construction labor did not suffer routine seasonal underemployment. Even more important, construction workers had access through informal, on-the-job apprenticeship to the acquisition of skills. As laborers watched the artisans to whom they brought materials, they could learn elements of a trade. This track into skilled employment helps account for the decrease in unskilled German workers with residential persistence. After fourteen years in the city, there was only a 13 percent chance a German would still be an unskilled worker, compared to a 29 percent chance for an Irish worker.[44]

Another track into skilled employment was formal apprenticeship, which though dying among Americans was firmly entrenched among Germans. One or two boys were routinely found in East Side bakeries, breweries, and small craft shops. In the southern and western German *Heimat*, boys began to leave home to serve their apprenticeships at fourteen, the very same age at which this pattern commences among Germans in Buffalo. By nineteen, some 27.5 percent of German males were apprentices, while another 45 percent still resident in the parental household at nineteen may well have been their fathers' apprentices. By age twenty-three, the first point at which over 50 percent of an age cohort among German men are heads of household, it is likely that these apprentices were now journeymen able to support themselves and a family.[45]

While skilled Germans were integrated into the general local economy—for example, building homes for the large, prosperous American market, there was also a vast, accessible German market for goods and services to be tapped. Largely, though not exclusively, on the basis of serving their own people, for example, Germans were able to account for 9 percent of the city's retail merchants and 14 percent of its clerks. (The figures for the Irish are 4 and 9 percent respectively.)[46]

Germans had crossed the ocean bearing a tradition of petty entrepreneurship, and they were soon found in a number of enterprises. In 1855, for example, they owned eight of twenty-nine dry goods stores, five of thirteen hardware stores, six of sixteen hat and cap shops, and eighteen of twenty-nine shops where boots and shoes were made and sold. The ethnic market itself supported specialty shops selling German books and periodicals, baked goods and foods, toys, notions, and "fancy goods," and exchange banks offering remittance and ticket services that linked Germans to their Old World families. There were also in 1855 four German apothecaries, which provided the vast array of traditional folk remedies.[47] These singular medical traditions led to a demand for German physicians, only five of whom, among sixteen, were recognized by the Erie County Medical Society as practicing a form of medicine able to meet American standards.[48]

The ethnic market for food and drink was particularly important in shaping opportunities in retailing and other fields. The German love for *Lagerbier* gave rise to an ethnic brewing industry, the need for which was intensified because Germans would not drink the more alcoholic, bitter porters, ales, and stouts that Americans brewed. In seeking to provide alternatives, Germans at Buffalo and elsewhere revolutionized American brewing. Aided by easy access to hops grown in central New York and to Great Lakes ice, which enabled storage during aging, German brewing found Buffalo an excellent location. By 1855 Germans operated 75 percent (twelve) of local breweries, and employed 63 percent (fifty-seven) of brewery workers. The number of breweries would double in the next decade. Much of their product, over 50,000 barrels in 1857, was consumed locally, enough daily, said the *Commercial Advertiser* "to float a good-sized canal boat."[49] The sites for drinking were not only eating houses, beer gardens, and saloons, but—probably more typically for the working-class majority—groceries. In 1855 Germans owned 44 percent (109) of the city's groceries, surpassing Americans. Their function as drinking houses helped in the grocery's proliferation. These small establishments were found throughout the East Side, and were often among the first businesses to enter a newly settled area. They usually had a shallow inventory of many types of products, but depended for their survival on the men who came to drink lager in the backroom during the workday at times when they sought relief from routine, and after supper when they came to socialize and play checkers or cards. During the day, men sent apprentices over with a pail to get lager if they themselves were too busy to leave their workbenches. This frequent resort to alcohol during the day typified German drinking in the Old World as well as in America.[50]

The customary consumption of large amounts of beef, pork, and specialty sausages sustained a large number of German retail butchers, who located their shops in public markets and in the neighborhoods. Fully 59 percent (twenty-six) of the city's butcher shops were German-owned in 1855, and they provided opportunities for the prestigious butcher's trade, which was among the oldest in terms of continuous, European guild organization, to thrive in Buffalo.[51]

The residential proximity of Germans and Americans in the new Fourth Ward and in the Main Street corridor facilitated interethnic trade. The most highly reputed German stores were situated in spots that allowed them to tap the American carriage trade on East Seneca and East Swan streets and above the 300 block on Main Street. Just as some American retailers attempted to attract German patrons by featuring German imports or hiring a clerk fluent in German, German retailers made efforts to attract Americans. They advertised in the English-language press and created gimmicks, such as one confectioner's "Franklin Pierce candy."[52] Americans quickly developed a taste for German products. In the 1850s, for example, the virtues of lager ("a mild and amiable poison," said the *Courier*) consumed in genial, outdoor settings proved attractive enough to send large numbers of Americans to Westphal's Gardens and other German-operated drinking places.[53] A few German and German-American attorneys and university-trained doctors also sought American as well as German customers. These medical men often had special skills, such as rehabilitating crippled limbs or creating prosthetic devices, that no local American practitioners possessed. They also attempted to distance themselves from those whom the *Buffalo Medical Journal* called "the rabble of German quacks," with whom, it said, the trained German physician was "unfortunately . . . associated in the minds of the community." In 1856 these physicians formed the German Medical Association, from which they barred practitioners of folk medicine in order to break this association.[54]

By 1861 a number of wealthy men had appeared in these diverse fields of German economic endeavor. In clothing and dry goods there were Stephen Bettinger, Charles Georger, Frank Georger, and Nicholas Ottenot, and there were retail grocers, Jacob Beyer, Philip Becker, Jacob Siebold, Joseph Haberstro, and Henry Hellreigel. In industry there were Jacob Schoellkopf, owner of one of the city's largest tanneries; Jacob Roos and Albert Ziegele, both brewers; and the German-Americans Abram Swartz, who with his brothers and sons manufactured machinery, and Benjamin Timmerman, a furniture manufacturer. There were meatpackers and meat wholesalers Jacob Dold, Christian Klinck, and the German-Americans Franklin, John, and Job Allberger. And there were the grain and flour merchants Urban (also in groceries) and Mesmer, and the hotel owner Philip Dorsheimer. A number were Franco-German Catholics who had come to Buffalo in the 1830s and profited from their well-established roots. Of the immigrants, the majority were from sizeable towns, and were not of peasant origin, and they had emigrated with skills (Ziegele) or money (Bettinger). Both Mesmer and Urban had been fortunate to attain their first employment with affluent Americans who became their patrons. (Mesmer had been a teamster in the employ of Lance Palmer.) Urban, Schoellkopf and Dorsheimer took pride in the speed with which they mastered English.[55] Whatever their backgrounds, at the close of the period these men were poised on the brink of economic, though not social, integration into the bourgeoisie. The 1857–58 depression impeded their plans to open a German Bank of Buffalo with their own capital. After the Civil War, however, now wealthier, they established the German Insurance Company (1867), the German Bank of Buffalo (1871), and the German-American Bank (1882), which collectively had ten million dollars in assets by 1900. That nothing succeeds like success explains why so many of their names were on the roster of the 1881 semicentennial committee.[56]

The aspirations of the majority were more modest. Unlike the Irish, however, the German's solid material foundations allowed them to project goals beyond day-to-day survival. The most important of these was the acquisition of property, most frequently a house, but often the land it was on, too. Noting the avidity with which Germans sought property, the *Courier* in 1847 said, "Their whole energies seem to be directed to procuring a little spot of land which shall become their permanent resting place."[57] It is easy to understand the attachment of uprooted farmers and peasants to having land, but it also must be noted that in the German states most town and village dwellers resided in small, single- or two-family houses, so home ownership was an extension of prior experience.[58] Buffalo's pattern of single-family dwellings facilitated fulfillment of German aspirations, as did the inexpensiveness of East Side land.

Many Germans succeeded in obtaining property. Forty percent of German household heads owned a house or land or both in 1855, compared to 23 percent of the Irish and 43 percent of Americans. With residential persistence, Germans came to surpass Americans. While after only one year's residence 17 percent of American household heads and 2 percent of German household heads owned property, after six years the figures were 42 percent and 51 percent respectively, and the gap widened to 48 and 64 percent for those resident ten to fourteen years, and 55 and 75 for those resident twenty or more years. German aspirations for property crossed class lines: Germans surpassed Americans in every occupation but retail merchant, and they tied among clerk. These aspirations crossed the lines of point of origin: 38 percent of members of the largest north German groups (Prussians, Saxons and Hanoverians) and 38 percent of the largest southern and western ones (Bavarians, Badenese and Württembergers) owned property. By 1855 residents of wards Four through Seven alone owned 49.5 percent of Buffalo's real property. Much of this property was low in worth. With dwellings valued at $1,234 and only 14 percent built of brick, Germans were just about on the same level as the Irish ($1,000; 10 percent). Ward Six consistently had the lowest or second-lowest per capita assessed valuation of real property in the 1850s, while Seven was not much above it in rank.[59] Yet the achievement of Germans in obtaining security on their own terms cannot be overestimated, and the stake in society Germans acquired, across the lines that divided them, provided a basis for the political mobilizations that brought them together as a group and served to integrate them on favorable terms into American society.

Strategies conceived within the domestic economy were the key to achievement of property ownership. These strategies balanced off parents' competing desires for property and for providing male children with a basic education to familiarize them with English, but were often harsh to female children, whose work contributed mightily to the fulfillment of parental goals, but whose dowries do not appear to have had as high a priority.

German immigration was primarily one of families, and secondarily of single men. Unlike the Irish, there were very few single women immigrants. In consequence, the German household was likely to be coterminous with the nuclear family—a wife, husband, and usually two or three children. This was true of 82 percent of German households in contrast to the Irish (72 percent) and Americans (56 percent). In only 9 percent of German households were there boarders and only 6 percent were composed of extended families.[60]

Thus, the German struggle for property was largely dependent on the labors of individual members of the nuclear family. The skilled employment of many German men provided a steady income in good times, and this facilitated planning and saving. But as a matter of course other family members were enlisted. German wives whose labors in the Old World were customarily extremely burdensome, contributed in various ways, but these did not include either industrial employment or domestic service. Few women (eleven) worked in East Side industrial shops, while only 4 percent of German women over twenty-five worked as domestics. German women made their contributions not through wage-earning, but by providing various services that brought money into the home; they marketed garden produce, took in laundry, tended shop or the grocery back room, and cared for boarders and lodgers in their homes.[61]

The lack of wage contributions by adult women highlights the economic contribution of German children, who worked in large numbers from the early teenage years (and sometimes even earlier). German parents, across class lines, commonly removed their children from school sooner than other groups. The low German school retention rate, which was true for both sexes, was frequently lamented by school superintendents. As one said in 1853, "Many of our citizens, principally Germans, who possess a competence or even wealth, take their children from school when they have bones and muscle and intelligence enough to make their services valuable, and devote their days to labor."[62] Several patterns of employment were found among German boys. Boys under fifteen worked as helpers in such East Side industrial establishments as a furniture factory (ten of ninety-three workers) and a tin shop (fifteen of thirty) in 1855, and others may have worked in a similar capacity in First Ward shoe, metal, and leather shops and Second Ward cigar shops, all of which employed boys and were within walking distance from the German town. Another pattern was apprenticeship. At age fifteen some 20 percent of German boys had left home to begin apprenticeships of approximately five years duration. They resided in the homes of German artisans, and gave their wages to their parents. Whatever their work, the majority of boys remained at home through age eighteen, but at nineteen, the majority were living in another's home as boarders or apprentices, or in fewer cases, were married.[63]

The situation was much different for German girls. They left home in large numbers considerably earlier to work as domestics in American homes. Many Americans preferred German servants, in spite of language barriers, to Irish ones. Like the Irish, German girls began to leave home as early as age eleven, during which year some 21 percent entered service. At seventeen a majority were in service, but after reaching a peak at age eighteen (61 percent), the percentage dropped steadily as girls married. The situation was like that of German girls in Europe, but it did show some improvement. In the stern patriarchy that was German rural and *Heimat* domestic culture, girls entered service even earlier. In Bavaria, for example, among the poor and middling classes, they began work as domestics as early as six or seven, while boys stayed home to do farmwork, and waited to begin apprenticeships at fourteen.[64]

Boys had other advantages, too, for while they left day school early, they had opportunities for continuing education in English at public or private night schools. They attended with parental approval, which the 1853 superintendent of schools noted in commending German parents for committing "a less fatal error" than those who failed to encourage their children to pursue any education after leaving day school. German parents also, at least in the superintendent's opinion, seemed to see night school as an alternative to anxiety about the ways boys "employ their evenings."[65] As early as 1837, private evening schools offering Germans English language instruction were being operated by Germans and Americans. Local commercial colleges also offered evening courses in German. Tuition costs, however, made these schools less accessible, so under the leadership of school superintendent Oliver Steele, then serving his second term, the city began free public evening schools in 1849. These schools offered instruction in English and basic literacy to students who were typically, said the 1853 superintendent, "mechanics, apprentices, and others who could not avail themselves of the benefits of the day schools." Approximately 37 percent of these students in that year were German.[66] Girls gave evidence of wishing to attend, but the program was at first limited to male students. Later they were admitted, but only at certain schools, for some principals feared their presence would be distracting. It is not likely, however, that many German girls were able to attend even under these limited circumstances, for attendance in the evenings and in the company of single young men would have clashed with German notions of female propriety. Adult and youth alike, German women continued to live under an unyielding patriarchy, and they had fewer public roles than either American or Irish women.[67]

Sound material foundations and the discipline evident in the domestic economy help considerably to explain the relative absence of moral breakdown and social disorganization among Germans. When compared to the Irish, and indeed to German behavior in Europe, the Buffalo Germans stand out as an especially orderly people committed to living within strict social constraints. Relative to both their own and Irish numbers, Germans consistently had few commitments to the poorhouse. Germans were never represented there in proportion to their total numbers in the population. During 1842–48 and 1849–58, they were respectively 13 percent and 22 percent of commitments. Their highest percentage (29 percent; 1,684 commitments) was in 1854 at the crest of their mass immigration.[68] Indices of family breakdown also suggest German stability. Of all the large groups, they had the smallest percentage (6 percent) of female-headed households—less than half that of the Irish (13 percent), and below that of Americans (10 percent).[69] Moreover, *avowed* illegitimacy was markedly in decline relative to their Old World experience. At the time, socioeconomic pressures in Bavaria were producing high and escalating rates of illegitimacy: 17 percent (1819–34) and 21 percent (1835–49) in a representative Bavarian village. In two Buffalo parishes, St. Mary's and St. Michael's, in both of which Bavarians were the largest group, in 1855 illegitimacy (declared at the time of baptism) was limited respectively to only two births in 116 and four in 219.[70]

Arrest data also establish the German embrace of order. Like the Irish, they were usually arrested for petty offenses typical of the poor and working classes: vagrancy, public drunkenness, and disorderly behavior. But the Germans were seldom in jail. They were usually only between 7 and 16 percent of commitments to the county jail, and averaged annually about 12 percent. Perhaps the data are partly explained by the ability of the more prosperous Germans to pay fines, and hence avoid incarceration. Yet, even if true, the data are consistent with the reports of the Buffalo chief of police on incarcerations in the limited-term lockups of the four city police districts. The third and fourth police districts, where the large majority of Buffalo Germans resided, were among the most orderly. Exclusive of the homeless, who were frequently lodged in neighborhood lockups, during the years 1854–59 the third and fourth averaged ninety-one and 137 commitments respectively per quarter. The American second district averaged 118 and the first, encompassing the waterfront and environs, where there were many transients and Irish, averaged 495.[71]

The benign traditions and social circumstances of German drinking help explain the order in German neighborhoods and the relatively low incidence of arrests. Drunkenness was hardly unknown. How could it be otherwise when drinking was routinely part of all German recreation and was integrated into the work rhythms of both craftsmen and farmers in the Old World, as in the New? Among German immigrants, however, it was not spirits but the less toxic lager that was by far the principal beverage. (In Europe they had distilled a far more powerful potato schnapps, but it never caught on in American cities for want of access to large quantities of potatoes.)[72] Even American temperance reformers were divided on how objectionable lager was. The largest of their national organizations, the American Temperance Union, allowed its locals to formulate their own position on the question.[73] Furthermore, much German drinking took place in the company of the family in the beer hall or garden, and even when it occurred in the all-male preserve of the grocery, it did so governed by centuries-old traditions of proprietorship. In the German states, where liquor licenses were difficult to obtain, proprietorship was prestigious, and carried with it the requirement that an orderly house be kept. That tradition continued in America, even though there was little more than episodic municipal regulation of drinking places. It combined with the orderly personal habits of drinkers to produce decorum. German drinking houses were never a scene of scandal, and no credit reporter ever labeled them "low" or "rowdy," terms used frequently for other local watering holes. Timon and local German priests gave implicit recognition to the fact that German drinking habits were socially innocuous by making no efforts—at least publicly—to prevent German Catholic *Vereine* from taking kegs of lager on excursions or holding social events at beer halls.[74]

While, as in the Old World, temperance had little support in any segment of German opinion, both the secular and religious German press denounced drunkenness. They sought, too, to inspire pride in the tranquility of German drinking places and in the Germans' ability to govern their drinking habits without recourse to abstinence pledges and temperance organizations.[75]

The German press also made an effort to awaken the public conscience to the evil of other forms of disorder. The occasional arrest of some young German thieves or appearance on the streets of begging German children were reason enough for editorials warning parents to discipline their children—or watch them grow "ripe for the gallows." A special object of attention in the press, and among German leaders, was prostitution in German neighborhoods. After a fire destroyed many dockside brothels in 1851, the uprooted prostitutes moved into the Fourth Ward. German editors called for a crusade to eradicate the new brothels. The extent of popular concern may be gauged by the fact that the only example of mob violence by Buffalo Germans during the period was the 1842 attack by some twenty men on a brothel, which was badly damaged in a bombardment of stones.[76]

While opposing disorder and crime, the German press found a perfect foil in the Irish population for its efforts to draw boundaries around ethnic standards of proper behavior. As ideological republicans, the editors of the *Weltbürger* were always in sympathy with the Irish national struggle, but as was the case for many Americans who shared that sympathy, the Irish in the United States were another matter. Gang violence, disorder at the polls, inebriation, and thievery were routinely identified, through jokes and selective news stories, with those whom German editors referred to as Irish "lowlife." The tone was deeply prejudiced, and hardly different from the American press. In effect, Germans were told repeatedly, if they would behave decently, they must not behave like the Irish.[77] This message hardly provided a sound basis for mutual understanding between the city's major immigrant groups.

Solid material foundations assisted Germans in developing a rich ethnic culture and dense network of formal institutions and voluntary associations. In consequence the Germans, like the Irish, had a high degree of institutional completeness. The consequences were more striking among Germans, however, for institutional development took form in the context of three phenomena that set their experience apart from that of the Irish: a very large population, a high degree of residential separation, and a vast array of internal organizational patterns resulting from the existence of many subgroups. In combination these gave substance to the perception that the East Side was a town within the city, "fully equipped," as an American observer said, to be "an independent, self-supporting community." He continued, "Let [the visitor] drop into one of their public houses, and he will find German newspapers on the tables, printed in the German town for German readers. They have their press, their churches, their schools, their theaters, their orators, [and] their commerce."[78] Yet Germans were not nearly as separated socially or culturally from Americans as the Irish. Though the mutual relations, particularly political ones, between Americans and Germans were not always cordial, through high culture, popular recreation, property relations, and Protestantism, Germans developed many more ties with Americans than did the Irish.

The development of both a popular culture and institutions and *Vereine* took place sequentially as the various German-speaking peoples settled in Buffalo. This was not a consequence of the recently arrived immigrants' assertion of nationality or regionalism. However much point of origin was asserted in interpersonal relations, and hence in residential patterns, it had few associative manifestations. Only the Swiss continued to maintain separate organizations, a Wilhelm Tell Society and a Helvetia Men's Choir, based on point of origin. But in all other realms, the Swiss mixed with other German-speakers.[79] The Alsatians and handful of Lorrainians had a Franco-German society in the 1830s, but it soon disbanded.[80] Thus, German *Vereine* and institutions were integrated across regional and national lines, and when they were not, as for example among the exclusively Prussian Old Lutherans, point of origin was an incidental, not a determining, factor.

It was the broader social character and experiential realities of the two waves of immigration on either side of the fateful year 1848 that formed the bases for associational differentiation. Many of the same types of people were present in both waves—craftsmen, farmers, peasants, and petty traders—and this helps to explain how it was that the second wave was often able to fit into or expand upon the German ethnic world the first wave had created. But the congruency of goals and forms was not always precise. Furthermore the second wave often took ethnic life in new directions unknown to the first.

Two sets of needs stimulated the organizational patterns laid down between 1828 and 1848. The first German settlers entered a new city that had few Germans. It was as necessary for them, as it would be for other immigrant groups, to create basic mechanisms integrating them into American urban life. They established three militia companies, six volunteer fire companies, and a loosely structured Democratic party organization. Also, with the publication of the *Weltbürger* in 1837, an ethnic press began to emerge. Composed of secular and religious papers, which appeared and disappeared with astonishing regularity, the ethnic press possessed a dual view of its purposes: providing immigrants with news of their homelands, while explaining and criticizing the new American reality.[81] A second set of needs involved a desire to replicate some of the familiar patterns of daily life of the peasant villages and hometowns from which the settlers had emigrated. From the earliest days of settlement, a popular, ethnic culture of sociability took shape in the German town. The Germans proverbial love for "the good-humored crowd,"[82] was evident in the establishment of summer beer gardens and all-season beer halls.

The continental Sunday was another early feature of the pattern of life. Neither of the largest German religious groups, the Lutherans and Catholics, held that Sunday was a holy day, as opposed to a historically sanctioned, convenient day for prayer. Both believed that physical renewal through rest and recreation was a legitimate purpose for the Sabbath. Germans were guided by these precepts. Depending on the weather, one found them in family groups, often with their *Vereine*, on excursions and picnics, or at the theater, concert, or beer hall. Parades accompanied by band music often proceeded excursions.[83] Customary ways of celebrating Christian holy days also took root in these formative decades. For Germans, Christmas was traditionally less a day than a season, which lasted from Advent through Epiphany and was celebrated with festive parties and balls given by the *Vereine* and the German militia companies. These became justly famous in Buffalo for their music, lager, and conviviality. Just weeks after these ended, another series of balls, often in costume, celebrated the traditional carnival (*Fasching*).[84]

During 1828–48, Germans also laid down the foundations of a number of abiding institutions and *Vereine*. The pre-1848 immigration, as we have noted, was composed mostly of artisans, craftsmen, petty traders, and small farmers from southern and western Germany. Whether as a matter of first-hand experience in Europe or as a much-valued but not directly experienced ideal, for them the corporate moral community, exemplified by the *Heimat*, had profound attractions. It was an organic social unity, in which residents lived in a state of moral equality, deference to legitimate and benign authority, and daily face-to-face relations. Standards of conduct were traditional and uniform. In contrast to the metropolis, there had been little need for the compartmentalization of conduct to accommodate, on the one hand, strangers, and on the other, intimates. This social order had been reinforced by both guilds and tradition-bound political arrangements.[85] Neither the *Heimat* guild nor polity could be replicated in America. But the immigrants could reconstruct some of the formalized social relations that contained the substance, if not the exact form, of the customary moral community. The pursuit of this ideal could not contain all of the energies of the immigrants, let alone accommodate all of their needs, as is evident in the passion of the first editors of the *Weltbürger* for political and civic integration. But it did inform the thrust of many organizational activities during these formative decades.

This becomes evident when we analyze the secular *Vereine*, which appear to have been not single-focus organizations but particularistic embodiments of an ethical way of life. In Europe Germans had developed a number of musical traditions, and these had been the basis for different types of recreation. German immigrants found America to be "a land without music," or simply of bad music, and they sought to correct the situation.[86] The first "German Singing Society" was founded in 1844, and would eventually become known as the "Leidertafel." At its founding the organization, which never had more than forty members, chose a committee to write a constitution. In sharp contrast, say, to the founding of the Americans' New England Society, in which a very general purpose (a yearly banquet) and criteria for membership (New England birth or ancestry) were perfunctorily written down,[87] this constitution was a comprehensive document. It presented its general purpose in a high-minded fashion ("the encouragement of music, especially men's and mixed chorus singing as well as promoting good fellowship and the love of art and beauty"), and established the election of choirmasters, made good character as well as musical ability (to be decided by members who interviewed each applicant) the criteria for joining, and demanded regular participation in rehearsals and performances.[88] Grand purposes informed by a spirit of common endeavor also underlay the Young Men's Association, which was founded in 1841 not only for instrumental reasons of study and individual cultivation, but "to cause the growth of the German spirit." The association, which had 122 members in 1845, and about 200 in 1857, also demanded participation in business meetings and at a certain number of public events.[89]

This quest for reconstruction of the familiar face-to-face community of moral equals reached a high point in the establishment of religious institutions and the welfare, recreational, and spiritual *Vereine*, schools, and seminaries within them. Individual churches were frequently organized at the initiative of a preexisting community of believers. Moreover, congregational endeavor was guided by a vision of organic unity and moral equality within a consensual community of like-minded people, who agreed to pay dues and participate, in ways varying from denomination to denomination, in governance, while ceding ultimate authority to ministers or episcopal hierarchies.

Beyond restoration of familiar social relations and institutionalization of a communalistic ideal, religious institutions played a significant role in forming the German ethnic group out of its constituent parts. Not only did they bring more people together than any other immigrant institution, but more important, they mixed under one roof and denominational label German-speaking people of diverse national and regional origins. They were in effect German melting pots, and as such they began the process of creating new German ethnic feeling. There were two significant religious melting pots: one northern and Protestant, and the other Alsatian, southern and western German, and Catholic. This situation did little to break down dialect barriers, and it assisted in bringing deeply rooted denominational rivalries rapidly to the surface, hence creating stumbling blocks in the process of ethnicization. Yet the religious, intraethnic melting pots stimulated a widening of individual visions in ways which were consistent with a German ethnic identity, if not with group unity. The central ingredients for a larger integration, as those aspiring to lead the group into the American civic and political mainstream realized, would have to come from another direction.

By 1848 every sector of German Christianity had come to life in Buffalo, and the small group of largely German-speaking Jews had organized a synagogue.⁹⁰ While adding little that was new to the representation of denominations, however, the 1848–54 mass immigrations did have important demographic consequences for religion among Buffalo Germans. In the 1840s, following the large in-migration of the Old Lutherans, a rough parity existed between German Catholics and Protestants. But, as the rapid expansion of East Side parishes soon made evident, it was the mass emigration out of the heartlands of German Catholicism that now gave local German population growth its dynamism. The implications for ethnicization, politics, and American-German relations would be profound. For now, however, we will sketch the rise of the many institutional forms of German Christianity. It was largely because of the proliferation of German churches—and drinking establishments—that in 1857 a correspondent for the Troy Times called Buffalo a city of "churches and breweries."⁹¹ One way to categorize this seemingly endless stream of religious identities and institutions is the tripartite division of Roman Catholics and of Protestant denominations, which were established either by lay immigrant initiative or by American evangelicals for Germans.⁹²

Old World traditions mingled with New World contingencies to shape the life of the six antebellum German Catholic parishes—St. Louis (1829), St. Mary's (1843), St. Francis Xavier (1849), St. Boniface (1849), St. Michael's (1851), and St. Ann's (1858)—which possessed a total of some 10,000 adult congregants by 1860, perhaps 60 percent of Buffalo's German-speaking Christians. Alsatian, Rhenish, and Bavarian Catholicism had been shaped in a region of Europe characterized by strong religious competition between Catholics and Protestants and hence by a singular devoutness in all faiths. Yet largely because of the historical preoccupation of the hierarchy with ecclesiastical politics, only the lower ranks of the priesthood, men of little learning and humble origin, were involved in daily religious life. The result was a Catholicism that made up in the richness of its devotional traditions and Sunday processions for what it lacked both in doctrinal sophistication, and with church attendance in decline and the sole formal requirement of faith an Easter confession, in personal piety.⁹³

The expectation of local autonomy in religious matters was joined in America to a desire for linguistic and ethnic autonomy at the level of the parish. This came about in a number of ways. First, Germans suspected Irish priests and bishops, who then controlled the American church, of wishing to appropriate German resources. Moreover, they found Irish rites and dogma cold and spare. Germans, therefore, desired to be free of control by Irish bishops, and this set the outer boundaries of the desire for parish autonomy.⁹⁴ The inner territory was established at the time of the organization of parishes when immigrants bearing Old World religious customs and seeking a new source of stability in their lives moved to create a congregational order. All of Buffalo's parishes were begun on the initiative of laymen working with individual priests. Laymen were involved in the actual construction of churches. They donated building materials and labor in the evening or on Sundays, and usually received advice from a priest with architectural knowledge. Residential patterns helped to solidify a possessive feeling toward the parish, for each parish was, in effect, a national parish comprised only of Germans. Germans saw no reason, moreover, to use any language but their own, which they regarded as the key to preserving faith and culture.[95] Finally, Germans brought traditions of lay management of daily parish affairs from Europe. These traditions were especially strong among Alsatians, who until about 1850 probably constituted a majority of the wealthiest and most prestigious parish, St. Louis. After 1801 lay management of Catholic parishes was guaranteed by law in France, but its informal, local history went back further in time. Based on traditions brought from France, St. Louis Church's Alsatian Catholics initiated a struggle for control of parish resources that would also be informed by interethnic hostilities and eventually by American republican ideas about separation of church and state. This struggle went on for years, and in the meanwhile assisted in forming a context for the pattern of parish development. St. Michael's and very likely St. Boniface, too, were founded by Germans who had seceded from St. Louis believing the Alsatians were wrong to defy the hierarchy.[96]

Practical circumstances forced Irish bishops to cede a degree of parish autonomy to Germans, a fact the well-publicized St. Louis struggle masked. For the first two decades of Catholic life in Buffalo, the local faithful were within a diocese encompassing all of New York State and were ruled from New York City, with great difficulty because of inefficient communications. Bishops had little choice but to recognize a degree of independence at the parish level everywhere at a distance from the metropolis. Moreover, Irish bishops had to acknowledge, as Timon would, their lack of knowledge of German religious customs and very often of the German language. They also understood that both custom and linguistic continuity were central to preserving faith. Thus, Germans had to be allowed to have German priests. Since there were so few diocesan priests who spoke German, bishops came to depend on priests from German religious orders to staff parishes. (St. Louis, a diocesan parish, was an exception; it was governed directly by its diocesan bishop, the immediate context for its conflict with the hierarchy.) The largest and throughout the period poorest parish, St. Mary's, set the mold in 1843 when Bishop John Hughes invited the

Redemptorists, an order with a history of serving the Bavarian poor, to take over the parish. Timon, who found only five German-speaking diocesan priests in western New York when he arrived in 1847, invited the Jesuits to take control of St. Francis Xavier, St. Michael's and St. Ann's after laymen had expressed a desire for creation of these parishes.[97] Some 75 percent of the city's German Catholics ultimately were attended by priests like the Redemptorists over whom Timon had, in the words of Papal Nuncio Gaetano Bedini in 1853, "no control."[98] The bishop's rule was at best indirect, and he made it more so when, to shield himself from ethnic hostility, he created the office of vicar general to the Germans, staffed by a German priest, shortly after coming to Buffalo. In 1850, furthermore, he decided to subsidize a German Catholic newspaper, *Die Aurora*, which communicated the bishop's wishes, while it defended the church against its enemies and served as an exponent of German Catholic culture and life.[99]

Like the Irish parishes, each of these six parishes was a world in itself, with an internal social organization that encouraged participation by both sexes and people of all ages. Daily administrative affairs were under the management of parish priests and elected trustees, who were prestigious, residentially persistent, and prosperous craftsmen and shopkeepers. There were devotional sodalities for married and unmarried people of both sexes; confraternities for developing religious habits in younger children and older boys; a society for care of departed souls; and a men's mutual benefit society. These men's societies cooperated across parish lines to establish a diocesan German cemetery in 1859.[100]

All the parishes but comparatively small St. Francis Xavier maintained schools, in which instruction was provided by German nuns brought to America to teach. They resided in convents next to the schools. Parish schools were objects for frequent fund-raising, especially because efforts were made to provide tuition for the poor. Still, particularly in poor parishes, boys often attended public schools, while, for the same reasons that motivated the Irish, girls were singled out, when a choice had to be made, for a Catholic education. In 1859, in the twelfth school district, the neighborhood around St. Mary's, some 41 percent of school-age children, mostly boys, were in public school.[101]

The varieties of Lutheranism and Calvinism accounted for perhaps a third of local German Christians. Lutheran and Reformed congregations, like Catholic parishes, began with lay initiatives, when adult men met and forged a charter. Moreover, like the Catholics, these Protestants conceived of religion as a means to preserve German culture and identity and to forge a moral community. They created small social universes comprised of day schools, Sunday schools, benefit

Vereine, and in some cases, cemeteries, orphanages, and seminaries. Yet such similarities mask an essential difference between these congregations and Catholic parishes: diversity. These Protestant churches were far removed not only from the vast international, bureaucratic, and hierarchical world of Catholicism, but also from each other. Furthermore, they were not static in theology or denominational identification during the period, and this makes it difficult to characterize them.

There were six Lutheran and Evangelical Lutheran churches in the 1850s. Holy Trinity Lutheran Church (1839) and St. Andrew's (1858) were created by Old Lutheran immigrants and were affiliated with the Buffalo Synod, which was established in 1845 by Rev. Johannes A. A. Grabau, the most powerful cleric among the refugees. Three Lutheran churches became affiliates of the rival Missouri Synod: First Trinity Evangelical Lutheran, which was founded in 1839 by Silesians and Pomeranians following a doctrinal conflict among Old Lutherans, St. Paul's Evangelical Lutheran (1843), and St. Andrew's Evangelical Lutheran (1858). While each of these churches was associated with recent immigrations and committed to the German language, St. John's Evangelical Lutheran (1832), which had been founded by the city's pioneer German-speakers, was affiliated with the New York Synod, comprised mostly of eastern Lutheran congregations established by eighteenth-century immigrants. Like other churches of this synod, St. John's had begun by 1860 to conduct much of its worship in English.[102]

Lutherans shared a theological lineage traceable to Martin Luther's *Augsburg Confession* and an emphasis on personal piety and individual vocations that created social and political conservatism. But their historic quest for doctrinal purity led to a disputatious style of theological debate and a conflict-ridden history of fragmentation. Differences among Old Lutherans, Missouri Synod Lutherans, and Evangelical Lutherans were large and widening significantly. Old Lutherans and adherents of the Missouri Synod were committed to a strict confessionalism based on liturgical purity and adherence to the New Testament and the texts of Luther, his peers, and his spiritual descendants. Evangelical Lutherans were more strictly bibliocentric, and their worship, in contrast to the austerity of these synods, was characterized by a warm emotionalism, the evocation of the individual religious experience, and zealous preaching. With the exception of St. John's, the Evangelical Lutheran churches rejected constraining synodical ties, and joined the loosely conceived Evangelical Association of North America. Their congregationalism within a decentralized polity made them more like the Missouri Synod churches than those of the Buffalo Synod. After coming to America Grabau evolved hierarchical views of the ministry that led him to be called "the Lutheran Pope," and paved the way for conflict in his congregation and synod.[103]

Zion Evangelical Reformed (1845), St. John's United Evangelical (1850), St. Stephen's United Evangelical (1853), and several smaller congregations identified with Calvinism and Reform. United Evangelical churches were products of the merger of Lutheran and Reformed churches then taking place at the pleasure of German state governments. This was the same merger Old Lutherans rejected, largely because it left the more rigorous, demanding Lutheranism in a weaker position. Conflicts associated with the attempt to merge these faiths were present in the city. St. Stephen's was formed after a schism at St. Paul's Evangelical Lutheran that led many of those inclined toward Calvinism to leave. These three congregations were rationalistic in doctrinal matters, rejected the supernatural, and demanded simplicity of worship. They also left room for the formulation of personal religious views. They were wholly congregational in governance, rejecting synodical affiliation, but they did cooperate in such practical matters as charity and establishing cemeteries and Sunday schools. Unlike Catholics and Lutherans, who maintained parochial schools in the belief that the public ones were godless and inspired assimilation, these churches embraced public schools. They were, however, committed to German as the language of faith and of the home.[104]

Perhaps 10 percent of East Side Christians worshipped at churches organized by German ministers who were missionizing for American denominations, which supplied resources and moral support to their German adherents. In 1846 and 1852, German Methodist missionaries established churches. The Baptists founded two, in 1848 and 1859. The largest of these American-affiliated congregations was St. Peter's German Evangelical (1832), which was assisted by Presbyterians. Its minister, the Swiss Rev. Joseph Gumbell, was himself a member of the American First Presbyterian Church. Gumbell brought together Protestants from Württemberg in forming the congregation. In the late 1840s, Presbyterians also helped establish a breakaway Old Catholic congregation, which, under a former priest, Rev. L. Guistiniani, attempted to return to the simplicity of the early church by rejecting the Catholic ecclesiastical order. Finally, the city's Unitarians helped form a small German Free Christian Church in 1850. These congregations shared elements of the worldview and doctrine of the larger German Protestant churches, but departed in their secular and social views. They embraced Americanization; both the Baptists and St. Peter's integrated English into their worship. With the exception of St. Peter's, which maintained a day school, they encouraged public school attendance. Moreover, their pietism occasionally extended into realms normally uncharted by German churches—temperance, Sabbatarianism, opposition to the theater, etc., all at variance with German popular culture. Baptist Rev. Alexander von Puttkamer, a temperance enthusiast, was one of the handful of Germans signing Gough's pledge in 1850.[105]

The small social world that was the German church maintained guarded frontiers against traditional rivals and antagonists. While this hardly made for cordial relations, American life and attitudes forged in Europe nonetheless brought people together in complex ways. Lutherans fought one another in the religious press, but united in denouncing their historic foes, the Catholics. Grabau warned of papal conspiracies to destroy the American republic. Yet Grabau's condemnation of secret societies like the Masons and Odd Fellows could easily have come from Bishop Timon, and both men and their followers united—at arm's length—in opposing the monopolistic position of the public schools. Catholics condemned Lutherans and other Protestants as apostates, but joined in taking anti-Semitic swipes at German Jews. German Baptists distrusted Lutherans, whom they blamed for the problems their faith had taking root in Germany. Gumbell accused the Buffalo Synod Lutherans of intolerance, while Grabau continued to condemn Calvinism, as he had in Prussia when he opposed the unification of the Lutheran and Reformed churches. Yet Baptists, Lutherans, and Gumbell's independent congregation all sought to evangelize Catholics in order to free them from the hold of the pope.[106]

The general configuration of the German social order was further complicated after 1848 by the arrival of radicalized artisans and middle-class intellectuals. Exact numbers are not known, but their influence far surpassed their numbers. They created a radical social substructure guided by pan-German cultural and political nationalism and radical democratic and socialist politics, as well as anticlericalism, anti-Catholicism, and "free thought" (both atheism and agnosticism). The social universe created by the '48ers, or "Greens" as they were called, nonetheless did have something in common with that established by the "Grays" in the previous two decades. The '48ers, too, displayed the same ethical longing for the purposeful, morally constituted community that the Grays had demonstrated in creating their *Vereine* and churches, and the world they made was also suffused with Christian and German popular cultural folk symbolism and sensibility as well as with their own political commitments.

Even before they arrived, their ideals and courage had begun to influence the Grays. Prior to the revolutions, for example, there was only one German fraternal lodge, the Walhalla Odd Fellows Lodge

(1847). In 1848, however, the first of three lodges of the Harugari was created. Distinctively culturally nationalistic, the order was named for a German pagan priest who had defied the Romans. Members had a duty to preserve the German language, and the lodge took part in the struggle against nativism. In 1849 the first of two German Masonic lodges was founded; the Masons were associated with deism and rationalism, and were opposed to religious and political tyranny.[107] Furthermore, it was such pillars of the Gray establishment as Dr. Frederick Dellenbaugh, Jacob Schoellkopf, Dr. Joseph Hauenstein, Charles and Frank Georger, Philip Dorsheimer and Dr. Francis Brunck who, in 1851, organized the local pledge of the German National Loan, a fund for continuation of the political work of the failed revolutions. In the same year and in 1852, they and the local American elite organized the official visit of the revolutionary hero Gottfried Kinkel and the massive, 25,000-person reception Buffalo gave Louis Kossuth.[108] And finally, it was the German Young Men's Association which, again in 1851, organized St. John's Day, the outdoor celebration of the coming of summer that resurrected a traditional German folk festival. A popular feature of the local scene for many years, St. John's Day was a celebration of German culture, complete with choral singing, processions, picnics, band music, drama, and gymnastic exercises. The first festival, which drew 3,000 people, also gave evidence of a quickening of political idealism as well as the cross-fertilization of pan-German cultural feeling and American political symbolism. A tableau vivant, evoking representations of peace and justice, before a backdrop on which was painted both a portrait of Washington and the gravesite of the 1848 Viennese martyrs, was staged.[109] St. John's Day set a precedent for two other celebrations of German culture: the 1859 *Schillerfest*, celebrating the writer's centenary, and the 1860 *Sängerbundfest*, which brought together in competition German singing societies from throughout North America. The gathering force of pan-German cultural feeling influenced the development of a feeling of ethnic identity, and hence gave impetus to ethnicization.

However much they might accept the Greens' German culturalism, few Grays were able to agree completely with '48er "free thought" or political ideology in any of its several varieties. Thus, the Greens were not easily integrated into the institutions and *Vereine* of the Grays. They created their own intricate associational and institutional network, which, to the extent it was consciously informed by ideology, was different in its stated purposes from that created in response to practical needs by the Grays. Prior to the 1848 revolutions, there had been little German activity in the weak local labor movement. Then in 1849 the German-American Workingmen's Union (GAWU) was formed. Its purpose was to encourage political activism and mutual assistance through support for workers' cooperatives and a benefit fund for the sick. In addition, as "American" in its title sought to imply, it made gestures of solidarity toward American workers. Many of the members of the GAWU were tailors, shoemakers, and furniture carpenters, all of whom founded craft unions in 1850. The GAWU itself assisted each of these unions in creating cooperative workshops. At the same time that many of these craftsmen were involved in unions and cooperatives, they were affiliated with the Workingmen's League, a utopian communist movement organized by the refugee radical Wilhelm Weitling and headquartered in New York City.[110]

A number of these same radical workers, especially the younger ones, also would join the *Turnverein*, which was created by twenty-one GAWU members in 1853, when that organization was in decline. By 1855 the *Turnverein* had 160 members; the majority were recently immigrated skilled tradesmen, but there was a significant minority of clerks and shopkeepers. The Turners traced their program, a mixture of radical politics, physical exercise, and mental culture, to a movement founded in Prussia in 1811 to instill patriotism and self-confidence in the politically weak middle classes. Banned from 1819 to 1848, the Turners enjoyed a long underground existence, but after the failure of the 1848 revolutions, in which they participated, many emigrated.[111] They became one of the most politically and socially active elements among '48ers. They continued their exercise and cultural activities, but soon developed a politics appropriate to their American homes. They stood against nativism, slavery, temperance, Sabbatarianism, and religious bigotry. They supported public education against its sectarian critics, and advocated a loosening of the social strictures on women. They were not all socialists, and they were distinct from the German labor movement, with which nonetheless they were in sympathy. In general, their views were most compatible with middle-class radical democracy.[112] They had significant tensions in their own ranks, and in 1856 split over whether active support was due the new, free soil Republican party, and whether to build a new headquarters. The mostly younger, intensely antislavery and expansion-minded men became the "Turner Forwards," while an older, smaller group, usually moderately antislavery but strongly Democratic and more modest in its associational goals, became the "Men's Social *Turnverein*."[113]

However radical, '48er associations and institutions appropriated the forms and feelings of German folk traditions and popular and high cultures. The Turners and others were an important local source for the vitalization of pan-German public culture. The GAWU and the Turners each organized drama and singing societies. Weitling's organization denounced the activities of existing German *Vereine* as escapist and trivial, and sought to create its own cultural associations dedicated to using German history and Christian moral tradition to create a heroic proletarian art. Dressed in customary white pants and brown blazers, Turners staged processions and marching drills. Their shooting contests and gymnastic demonstrations were regular features of St. John's Day, which they annually helped to plan, just as they took part in staging the 1859 and 1860 festivals. They gave many Sunday exhibitions, at which they unabashedly served beer. This underlying pattern of cultural similarities and earnest ethical concern the Turners shared with other sectors of the German population partly served to counterbalance the divisions precipitated by their radical activism.[114]

Two questions now suggest themselves. How many Germans were actually involved in these varied ethnic subcultures? How mutually exclusive was each relative to the others? Because complete membership data are not available, these questions cannot be answered precisely. But even if data were available, important issues in their interpretation would still have to be resolved. There are degrees of affiliation and adherence to the ethos and goals of an organization. It is one thing to belong, and another to attend, even when one accepts the obligation to participate and one's own values insist on it. Germans might have loved "the good-natured crowd," but leaving the house or corner grocery on a winter weeknight to attend a lecture did not always appeal even to the most earnest Turner Forward. When in 1860 the leaders of that organization criticized the public for just such apathy, the editor of the *Weltbürger* acknowledged that they were not the first organization to make "this sad discovery."[115] Furthermore, the impact of an organization cannot be said to lie only in the size of its membership, or within its own formal borders. The Forwards, for example, probably never numbered over 150 before 1861, but their outspoken militance on slavery helped transform German political debate, and hence influenced partisan alignments. Questions about the extent of authority within the emergent ethnic group must, therefore, be substituted for the narrower question of "How many?"

The question of the exclusiveness of social substructures, a meaningful index of authority and the ability of substructural ways of life to provide fulfillment, is similarly complex. In its revelation of the capacity of individuals to hold different, seemingly contradictory ideas, behavior often seems fraught with paradox. The beginnings of local German socialism may have been a speech given in May, 1849, by a Dr. Ciolina, who, echoing Marx, called upon "proletarians of all lands to unite!" and abolish capitalism. Dr. Ciolina was also a member of the most socially prestigious singing society that same year.[116] Similarly, a few Alsatian Catholics of St. Louis Church, including at least three who had served as parish trustees in the 1850s, were Odd Fellows and Masons, in spite of the church's hostility to secret societies, particularly the deistic Masons.[117]

Some generalizations on exclusiveness may nonetheless be ventured. The world of the radical Germans of the 1850s was perhaps the most exclusive. Because it possessed its own ideologically conditioned *Vereine*, it had no need to partake of the secular, nonpolitical *Vereine*. Few of the radicals' names turn up among local church members. A few Turners do appear to have been members of the most ecumenical of the secular *Vereine*, the German Young Men's Society, but the Turners, as we have noted, were by no means hostile to all aspects of a conventionally respectable bourgeois life style. For their part activists in the secular *Vereine* appear to have been less likely to have made church a central activity. Perhaps some belonged to no church at all (for none is mentioned in some of their autobiographical profiles), while at least one prominent *Vereine* activist's "church," to which he left a substantial fortune, was the Free Thinker's Society.[118] Affiliational links between religious and other substructures do present considerable variety. The orthodox Lutherans, especially of the Buffalo Synod, were exclusively engaged by their own institutions and networks, as were most Catholics. However, Alsatian Catholics, some of them quite active in their parishes, and more liberal Protestants, do appear regularly in the annals of secular fraternals, singing societies, etc.[119] Such patterns are explained by residential persistence and social class at least as much as by denomination and nationality or region of origin. This is likely to the extent that voluntary associational activism, outside of church, has often been correlated with higher-status individuals, who have the time and money to pursue, and the sophistication to understand, the benefits of affiliation. Whatever the precise connections, one thing seems certain: local Germans were integrated into their own group in dozens of complex, crosscutting ways. Yet for all this substructural pluralism, they shared a great many cultural forms and a sensibility shaped by customary moral and social traditions.

The German's high degree of institutional completeness reinforced and was reinforced by an insignificant degree of assimilation into American institutions. It is true that a few prominent, long-resident Germans and German-Americans had begun to take steps toward assimilation. Soon after immigrating, Georg Urban became "George." Dr. Dellenbach anglicized his name to "Dellenbaugh." Dr. Ernest Kreh to "Gray," and Abram Swartzenbaugh to the slightly less distinctive "Swartz." Philip Dorsheimer's daughter and George Urban's son married Americans, and both men had many American friends. Franklin Allberger was an Episcopalian; the insurance agent and notary Jacob Krettner, a Presbyterian. Yet these were hardly common occurrences. In the 1855 city directory there were only five German names among the 210 officers of non-German associations. Even the few men with such assimilative characteristics identified themselves as German, and usually lived on the East Side.[120]

Germans and Americans frequently did come in contact with one another, across language, class, and religious lines, in ways that worked to bring about close, sympathetic relations. The Germans' strong material foundations, religious diversity, popular culture, and artistic activity all formed contexts for positive, daily encounters. These, in turn, provided concrete experiences that refuted negative stereotypes, which, in another part of consciousness, both groups held toward each other.

These stereotypes are easily sketched. There were Americans who found Germans imperfect material out of which to mold citizens of a democratic, capitalist society. Alternately coddled and abused by authoritarian Old World governments, the argument ran, the average German immigrant man was sluggish, unprogressive and had a slavish personality. He lacked initiative in all activities, public and private, said the *Commercial Advertiser*, and he viewed himself "as a child or protege of the government, and not as one of its supporters or constituent parts."[121] The proof, for those who sought it, was gathered from various realms. For credit reporters, it was the shabby neighborhood grocery, with its shallow inventory and backroom lager shop, where perhaps the owner spent too much of his time chatting and drinking.[122] For American exponents of "true womanhood," it was the way German men allowed their women to become "beasts of burden," as the editor of the *Commercial Advertiser* said after seeing a German woman walking with a pail of manure balanced on her head.[123] For temperance advocates, the German was guilty of perpetual overindulgence, which caused his inattention to serious matters. Said one credit reporter of a shopkeeper, his habits are "not good," for he is "generally pretty full of beer."[124] In 1856 the *Commercial Advertiser* printed the perhaps apocryphal story of a German cop whose weakness for lager led him to fall asleep his first night on the job, only to have his badge and club stolen. (Six months later the paper would print the same story about a new Irish policeman.)[125] For Americanizers, there was the Germans' loyalty to their native tongue and their tendency toward apathy in civic life.[126] For employers, there was the radicalism of the German working class, which, the *Commercial Advertiser* complained, was "imbued with communistic ideas."[127] And for evangelical Protestants, there was German opposition to Sabbatarianism and temperance, and the '48ers' atheism and anticlericalism. The evangelicals also shuddered with horror at the medievalism reflected in German Catholic religious processions.[128] For Germans most of these demeaning images were summed up in the hated American epithet, "Kraut!" which was flung at them publicly as early as 1838.[129]

The Germans themselves routinely labelled Americans "hypocrite," "Puritan," "rowdy," and *Mucker* (grumbler). Germans found at the heart of many an American's character an instability that manifested itself in wild recreation, cultural extremism, or foolish risk-taking, and was exacerbated by materialism, religious fanaticism, and lack of introspection. For Germans this was clear, for example, in the related cycles of financial panics and religious revivals. American speculation superheated the economy, devaluing currency, raising prices of essential commodities, and hence imperiling the security of ordinary folk. Then the speculative bubble burst, and Americans developed what the *Weltbürger* called "a moral hangover." Plagued by guilt and fear, those who yesterday were indifferent to religion, today became orthodox believers at emotional revivals that hardly encouraged sober, judicious thinking.[130] Yet it was at revivals Americans committed themselves to improving the world—by interfering with the lives of others. No one was more the object of German contempt than the American *Weltverbesseren* (do-gooder), who, led by fanatical preachers and unsexed women, told orderly Germans how to behave on Sunday and what to drink. What especially galled Germans was that *American* "rowdies, under the influence of brandy and whiskey," routinely exhibited "scandalous and crude behavior" at German cultural events and beer halls.[131] The American passion for moral improvement was as frequently the object of satire as anger. When in 1847 the Whig mayor proposed a pound for loose pigs, the *Weltbürger* said acidly, "The swine will be taught virtue in the pound; it is said that the Whigs would like to create pounds for the human population."[132] Yet Americans spoiled their own rowdy children, and American men, unlike their German counterparts, abdicated their responsibility to establish social morality to their meddling, aggressive wives.[133] In all this behavior Germans found a strong element of self-deception. What else could allow Americans to evade insight into their own greedy motives, to remain unwilling to learn from the rest of the world, and to refuse to see the failings of such institutions of their creation as banks? No wonder Germans questioned the moral seriousness of American religion. As the bookseller Conrad Baer wrote in an Old Lutheran journal, Americans had falsely wedded the gospel to self-serving materialism: "To make money remains the highest principle and drive which the American people in general mean by doing good, and 'go help yourself' is said so often that it is truly a prayer in their catechism."[134] The *Weltbürger* put the matter even more sharply. "As everyone knows," it said in an 1855 editorial entitled "Crime," the typical small-town American banker, though active in church and known for piety, "should probably be in jail."[135]

These stereotypes are composites of many opinions; no one individual probably believed all of them at once, and many might well have experienced a divided consciousness when thinking about the ethnic other. Moreover, the American view of the Germans never had the unrelentingly harsh specificity that was given to fashioning Pat and Bridget. Under any circumstance, in daily life Germans and Americans encountered one another in a variety of situations, which created the bases of a rather good-willed mutual accommodation that was virtually absent in the relations between Americans and the Irish.

The singular economic integration of the Germans—providing goods and services to the local market—led to a number of positive interactions. For American consumers, especially the affluent carriage trade, many of the good things of life were associated with German craftsmen and shopkeepers. The artisans and craftsmen who built their solid, beautifully decorated homes were often German. Germans were also well-represented among those selling food, drink, clothing, leather goods, and such luxuries as watches, jewelry, and imported china.[136]

The humbler East Side laborer, artisan, or grocer could win American respect by his passion for owning a home of his own, by keeping his neighborhood free of vice and crime, and by possessing the rational calculation, industriousness, and steadiness that made these goals realizable. Many leading Americans, dating back to Joseph Ellicott, respected these German values and goals. When mapping out western New York for the Holland Land Company, Ellicott expressed the desire for German settlement. "As these people generally have money, we shall profit by them as well as by their industry."[137] Such wealthy, later-day landowners as James Wadsworth, Jabez Goodell, George Hays, P. A. Barker, and S. V. R. Watson made large profits parceling out their extensive East Side tracts to Germans.[138] This passion for property had other social benefits for Germans in their relations with Americans. It encouraged American attorneys to compete to represent Germans in real-estate transactions, and hence to employ German clerks to seek out ethnic business. It encouraged American fire insurance companies, such as Aetna, to strive to write German business, and to employ German agents like Krettner.[139] It provided one incentive for capitalists to organize savings banks and building and loan societies.

From their inception, the Americans who began these banks recognized the importance of the local German mortgage market, and understood that Germans possessed substantial capital. They attempted to sell bank stock to affluent Germans. They printed their prospectuses in German and circulated them on the East Side, and, like the big commercial banks, appointed German stockholders as directors, which also probably increased German trust in the banks. Germans constituted 20 percent of the first board (1846) of the largest savings bank, Buffalo Savings Bank, and 28 percent of the first board of the commercial Manufacturers and Traders Trust.[140] Property even helped redeem the lowly German grocer. Fear of the loss of property, credit reporters said, usually kept German shopkeepers from the faddish expansions of inventory and risky relocations that depleted private assets and ended in bankruptcy. Thus, for every comment about the lack of dynamism of German retailers, there were also the credit reporter's highest encomiums: "safe," "steady," and "prudent." The reporters also knew, of course, that if a German got into business difficulty, he was likely to have property to sell to pay his debts.[141]

Buffalo schoolmen recognized that Germans acquired property frequently by sacrificing children's education. But Germans redeemed themselves through both night school attendance and the efficient use they made of the public day schools when they attended. "Though there is much that is peculiar in the 'Dutch,' both in manner and dress," said a local teacher, "they are so regular in their attendance, so orderly in their conduct, and so quick in apprehending all that we teach them that by far the largest portion of all that is noble and useful in man will be found in our German element." The discipline and attentiveness of the young German was especially evident in the way many took to English. After touring the largely German School #13, the *Courier*'s editor stated, "We have been shown quite creditable compositions written by youngsters who have been but a few months in this country." Night school teachers and principals reported the same high performance in English, and predicted success for these students in adult pursuits. Evidence confirming these predictions seemed to appear in 1859 when the German schools, #13 and #15, alone sent seventeen of the forty students promoted to the recently established city high school. German educational success was complemented by the realization of many teachers and principals that important innovations in American education, such as vocal instruction and classroom singing, were German in origin.[142]

Lodge and church ties also produced positive interactions. German Masons, Odd Fellows, and the small lodge of temperance-oriented Druids took part in fraternal exercises with American counterparts.

American Masons publicly expressed gratitude to Germans for helping to revive the order from the depths to which anti-Masonic politics had brought it.[143] To aid struggling German Protestant congregations, Watson, Goodell, Hays, and Barker gave German churches gifts of lots, at the same time hoping to sell East Side land to congregants who would want to settle nearby. American ministers and prominent laymen also attended cornerstone layings at German Methodist, Baptist, United Evangelical, and Evangelical churches, and the same ministers would occasionally preach at them. These churches participated in such formal ecumenical endeavors as the Protestant Sunday School Association, and informal ones as the intense revivals of 1857–58.[144]

American Protestants saw other Germans, both Catholic and Protestant, as ripe for missionizing. The suspicion that there were many unchurched German Protestants led the American Tract Society to hire a German colporteur, the local YMCU to distribute German Bibles and establish neighborhood prayer meetings on the East Side, and Methodists, Baptists, and others to maintain by 1859 over a dozen German missions.[145] The belief that many German Catholics were too independent to accept the dictates of the church led to similar efforts. Nothing spurred Americans on more than the long struggle of the St. Louis trustees against various bishops. This struggle also caused American Protestants eventually to enlist on the side of the trustees, offering moral support and political assistance. Conscious of the power of American opinion, the trustees themselves established a "Press Committee," which filtered information to American newspapers.[146]

The struggle proved to many Americans that, in the words of the *Commercial Advertiser*, Germans were "imbued with the spirit of freedom of conscience, and yield no blind submission to priestcraft." In so doing, it helped convince them that Germans were better material for citizenship than the Irish, who were regarded as lacking independence because priest-ridden.[147] But efforts to convert German Catholics yielded little. With the exception of the Presbyterian-subsidized congregation of Old Catholics, which lasted only a few years, there is no evidence that German Catholics left the church because of missionary efforts.

In high culture, artistic performance, and popular recreation Germans developed activities in the 1850s that excited many Americans. Under the cultural domination of Americans, the city had known no civic festivals with broad public participation beyond the Fourth of July and the occasional memorials to departed statesmen. There had been little in the way of musical life or, beyond an occasional touring company, serious theater. The Germans changed this, and Americans seem to have agreed for the better, by creating opportunities for the enjoyment of art and for popular recreation. They reached out deliberately for American patronage and participation. They were not only proud to display the fruits of their *Kultur*, but eager to manage American impressions and gain American approval.

German popular events, such as the annual St. John's Day, the 1854 and 1858 *Turnerfesten*, and the 1860 Grand Lager Beer *Fest*, were all accessible to Americans, who were exposed through them to German forms of recreation. Established in 1851 by the German Young Men's Association, St. John's Day soon became a true people's festival, with thousands of active participants from German *Vereine*, bands, choral and drama groups, the Turners, and passive participants drawn from the city-at-large. As the years passed, the program grew fuller and more varied, and came to consume the entire day. There was no hiding the sense of anticipation in the American press as the annual festival neared. Particularly eager was the nativist *Commercial Advertiser*. Said its editor on the eve of the 1854 celebration, "These reunions of our German fellow-citizens are always pleasant entertainments, and a happy time can be passed by visitors as well as by those more directly involved. ... A German festival is always full of life, spirit, and fun; and men, women, and children enter into the amusements with a zest truly refreshing to behold."[148]

The sources of Americans' rave reviews of St. John's Day were varied. The exotic, multiform program was attractive, offering everything from choral singing and ballroom dancing to foot races and games, such as *Sackhüpfen* and *Würstschnappen*, that all could play. The Turners' precise and graceful gymnastics were especially popular. They are, said the *Commercial Advertiser* in 1858, "so foreign to our native sports that their observance is a novelty not lightly to be missed." But the German program committee consciously incorporated familiar American activities, too; horse-racing and fireworks were added in the 1850s.[149]

The attraction went deeper, however, than the program. As an American complained in 1856, Buffalo was so singularly lacking in public parks and private American pleasure grounds, that Forest Lawn Cemetery was thronged with picnickers on summer weekends. Its managers were forced to sell tickets to regulate use of the consecrated grounds.[150] But because of St. John's Day, Americans learned of Westphal's Gardens, a private park and beer garden in the bucolic reaches of upper Delaware Avenue where the annual *Fest* was held. Westphal's, Americans discovered, was not as some had expected, "a sort of territory devoted to the foreign population and teutonically tabooed." Americans were made to feel welcome and invited to return any time they wished.[151] Beyond Westphal's lovely natural setting, there was the fact that Americans, who were not accustomed to public familial socializing outside the home, were able, as were Germans, to bring their families there. "Unlike Americans," said the *Commercial Advertiser* approvingly, "but just like sensible people, [German men] take their wives and children with them on these occasions, and make it a day of pleasure for all." What allowed respectable American men to come in full certainty that their wives and children would witness nothing untoward was "the perfect order" prevailing at the *Fest*, which was always free of riot and aggressive drunkenness. The German organizers were privately concerned that the increased attendance of Americans, which they coveted because they were eager to impress the city's elite, would result in rowdiness—by Americans, whom they believed to be prone to irresponsible drunken behavior. That it did not was probably due to the deliberateness with which the local *Vereine* patrolled the grounds during the *Fest*.[152]

The consequences of this American embrace of German popular culture went beyond the acquisition of a high regard for things German to an enhanced appreciation of the German character. "These festivals," said the *Commercial Advertiser*, "display the German character in a favorable light." The Germans, said the paper, could do what Americans could not: "enjoy themselves in a simple hearty manner."[153] One reason, Americans came to feel, was that lager allowed them to drink without the frightening social and physical effects of liquor. In the context of American preoccupation with moral and social control and with the threat many of them believed alcohol posed, this insight offered the basis for a middle position between complete abstinence and destructive overindulgence. Unlike "maddening, corroding ... brandy, liver-eating gin, and stomach destroying rum," the paper said, lager is "more a kindly sedative than a stimulus." Bourgeois men, frequently fatigued from incessant labors at their desks, could easily "bear a little muddling without injury."[154] On the basis of such observations, tested annually at the *Fest*, and analysis of arrest data, by 1860 the paper had come to favor selective enforcement of the liquor laws. In the Irish First Ward, it said, drinking and disorder were "synonymous," and stern police measures were needed. But in German wards, "where a riot of any kind is a rare occurrence," the laws might safely "be cancelled to national custom and habits which have become a birthright."[155] Even the *Christian Advocate* had begun to write of lager in an anthropological and historical, rather than a moral, way.[156]

Presented with these models of rational recreation and self-control amidst pleasure, Americans began to copy them in their own lives and communal activities. By 1855, many were spending July Fourth at Westphal's. Influenced by the Turners perhaps, they also developed a taste for German exercise, and attended several downtown gymnasiums Germans were operating for American clients. As the *Courier* said, "The exercises are strength-giving, invigorating and Doctor-cheating, especially for accountants, bookkeepers and the whole sedentary tribe."[157]

The quality of American life was also enhanced by opportunities to consume German high culture. In the 1850s the German Young Men's Association gave performances in English of Goethe, Schiller, and Shakespeare to benefit local charities. German musical performances were regularly put on by touring orchestras and chorales, by local professionals, such as the private orchestra of conductor Gustav Poppenberg, and by local amateur groups, such as the *Leidertafel*. Poppenberg together with *Leidertafel* director Karl Adam orchestrated a number of memorable productions of sacred and secular music. The two men courted American patronage, advertising in the American press, and for especially important performances, renting elegant St. James Hall. That many of these performances were held on Sunday and that beer was sold in the lobby did little to curb American attendance, though evangelical opinion was certainly not pleased.[158] Also seeking American patronage were the organizers of the two great local festivals of the arts—the *Schillerfest* and the *Sängerbundfest*. They not only advertised and arranged the schedule of the most spectacular events to accommodate businessmen, but added some of the elements (massive processions, tableaux vivants, and food specialties) that made St. John's Day popular.[159] The singing festival was capped by a "monster concert," which had to be held at the railroad station to accommodate a sixty-five-piece orchestra, a choir of 600, and 10,000 spectators. Among others, the concert was attended by "the elite of Buffalo," who were afterward invited by the organizers to attend a banquet of German delicacies at St. James Hall.[160] Such activities as the *Festen* not only brought both peoples together in an amiable setting (and it seems not only elites, if the 10,000 figure is correct), but broadened American cultural horizons. It is no wonder that Americans in Buffalo named their first society to encourage classical music the "Mendelssohn Association."[161]

None of these positive interactions, not even performances in the universal language of music, could be completely successful if there were a total lack of spoken and written interethnic communication. Early in the period there was little evidence that communication would be easy. Few new German immigrants knew English, and perhaps even fewer Americans knew German. As employers, Americans routinely butchered German names on payroll sheets, and in despair Anglicized them.[162] Public officials had their difficulties, too. The Common Council clerk in 1839 grew so distracted trying to decipher old-style German handwriting on a petition that, after crossing out several futile renderings of the first names, he wrote, "Sundry Germans." The problem became so acute that resolutions were introduced in the council to the effect that "great care be taken in giving correct spelling of all names, especially German names."[163]

Leaving aside for the moment the controversial question of legislated bilingualism in government affairs, we find that linguistic accommodations were being made by individuals among both peoples. Some Germans might sneer that English was a language merely of business, not of culture, but for instrumental and material reasons they were striving to learn it. Young men attended night schools and private business colleges where they learned English to get better-paying employment. Those who did not have such an opportunity no doubt learned a great deal through ordinary commercial and property transactions, in which English was often used because no German word would do precisely. By the late 1850s German advertisements and store signs were regularly employing "lunch," "hotel," "lumberyard," "lawyer," "tax," "Yankee notions," and many other words, and such hybrids as "die lotten" (lots), "jobbing-priesen" (job printing), and "Hurrah für die Bargains!" What the *Commercial Advertiser* called "Dutch-English spelling" was a common fixture of such East Side signs as "groceryes," "blacksmit," "yest" (yeast), and a much chuckled-over doctor's sign, "Ichcoures mitsymperti." ("I cure with sympathy.")[164] Formally cultured Germans, such as Karl Adam, gave evidence of greater fluency. Adam began in 1853 to give introductory "music appreciation" lectures in English before concerts.[165]

Americans did not feel the need to go quite as far by mastering German. For many, including those, such as the *Courier*'s editor, who were sympathetically inclined toward immigrants, German affairs were an impenetrable mystery because of language, and they had to depend on often inaccurate sources to find out about East Side events. Others made a stab at dealing with German with ludicrous results, as when one editor translated *Weltbürger* (cosmopolitan) as "world mountaineer," unmindful of the difference between "burg" and "berg." Another called the "Schweizerbund" (Swiss Association), the "Schweizerhund" (Swiss dog). Yet notices for German lessons for Americans frequently appeared in the press. Businessmen, professionals, and shopkeepers understood that bilingualism was of benefit to them. George Washington Johnson, who had learned German as a student, testified to this, for he extended his legal practice, as did several other lawyers, not simply by hiring German clerks, but by translating German documents for other attorneys and taking on German-speaking clients.[166]

After a program was initiated in 1862, German also became a popular elective at the Buffalo high school, where, in addition to the standard literary exposure, more than one American must have acquired a facility for the language useful in daily life.[167]

The benefits to society and to the Germans that these mutual contacts and accommodations created can be easily exaggerated. On the level of individual interactions, Americans were displaying a willingness to embrace cultural pluralism. Indeed, in a pattern that would become familiar in American life, cultural diversity had already become a consumer item for those Americans sufficiently affluent and motivated to pursue recreation and mental stimulation beyond their own workaday world. But American acceptance of social pluralism, which comprehends integrating culturally diverse groups into existing public institutions, such as public schools or government, was another matter. Even in the short run, these positive, individual interactions were not sure enough to ward off the sociopolitical crisis of the mid-1850s over the civic role of immigrants. In fact, at the time these positive contacts and interactions were gathering force, that crisis reached its height in nativist assaults on the citizenship rights of all foreigners, including those who conducted Beethoven or who led twenty-one affable young men in forming a human pyramid. Meanwhile, as we shall now see, the Germans themselves were faced with the challenge of finding ways to integrate themselves as a group into their new homeland. Though the precise extent and nature of that integration would be a matter for debate, this felt need for integration would persistently run up against the problems of both the ambivalence Americans displayed toward Germans and the Germans' own diversity and disunity.

CHAPTER 8

Buffalo's Germans: Leadership, Ideology, and the Struggle for Unity

Each day, as a consequence of formal and informal interactions among Germans, older and parochial identities slowly were being eroded and replaced by new, more inclusive ethnic ones. This integrative process lent itself to group formation, but there was still too much that divided Germans for them to be spoken of as a *group*, in the strict sense of the term. They were rather a large body of people sharing some significant social and cultural characteristics. It remained the task of those who were impatient with this gradual, natural process of social evolution and who wished to exert ethnic group leadership, as opposed to leadership over one of the East Side's several substructural parts, to bring these parts together around ethnic symbols and interests and by doing so speed ethnicization.

Germans were well endowed with social attributes that made for effective leadership—literacy, craft and business skills, a sound material base, demonstrated organizational ability, and among some of them, the political experience available in the hometowns and to the '48ers. What they did not possess was the sense of common identity and destiny associated with feelings, which the Irish had, of shared peoplehood. Unlike the Irish, moreover, they lacked the sacralized dimension of peoplehood that came with sharing a common faith. They were deeply divided along religious lines. Far from being unifying forces, their clergymen were often agents of intense particularism, especially among the strongly sectarian Lutherans and Catholics. What Germans did possess was an understanding that they spoke a similar enough language, shared some habits and rituals key to the psychological fulfillment of daily life, and valued the ownership of homes in orderly neighborhoods. How these commonalities might be fused together to create ethnic consciousness, identity, and purpose was the major problem facing those aspiring to lead these immigrants.[1]

Before 1848 such leadership would come from shopkeepers, professionals, and craftsmen. Though deeply German in their self-concept and daily culture, these men also had some economic and political ties with Americans. Their approach to ethnicization was, in part, conditioned by this bifurcated experience, for they saw the massive challenge of civic and political integration into American institutions as the key to accomplishing ethnicization. The issue of the place of the German language in public life in America seemed especially significant to them as a basis for stimulating ethnic feeling and mobilization. While the Grays were bent on inclusion, the various factions of Greens tried to mobilize Germans around a program of reform of American institutions and structural social change based on the eradication of slavery and modification or destruction of capitalism.

Neither orientation, however, could overcome existing divisions. Indeed, in ways not always predictable, they exacerbated them. In the final analysis, opposition to American nativism and assaults on the prerogatives of East Side popular culture, combined with a growing, European-conditioned German nationalism and the defense of small property interests to accomplish the ethnic unity and mobilization that eluded the more purposeful efforts of Grays and Greens alike. In this sense, German ethnicization was to a significant degree a democratic movement from below as much as a top-down imposition of ethnic leadership. Here the concern is ethnic ideology and leadership, and the struggle of the latter to use the former in the service of ethnicization. To be analyzed are both the search by various elements of ethnic leadership to find irreducible, common material and cultural denominators to act as a glue for unifying the group and the ways in which this search was influenced by and influenced the masses of ordinary folk. Ethnic political behavior, as it manifested itself in elections, party activities, and most group civic mobilizations, and as it effected ethnicization, will be analyzed in the final chapters.

The appearance of the city's first German-language newspaper, the Buffalo *Weltbürger*, on December 2, 1837, marked the initial effort by men aspiring to ethnic leadership to mold Buffalo Germans into a self-conscious community of purpose. Early on, the paper defined its purpose as the "instruction of Germans in American politics and constitutional rights." On the basis of this broad goal, it would go on to develop an ideology that established a strong, reciprocal relationship between ethnicization and group political and civic activism. In effect, through learning to act as a group in American public life, Germans would learn simultaneously to think of themselves as German.

The men who guided the paper represented a broad spectrum of the diverse German social types involved in public affairs. Under its first publisher, Georg Zahm, a Catholic printer and bookstore owner from the Palatinate, and editor, Stephen Mollitor, a professional journalist, the *Weltbürger* began a decade of virtual monopoly of local German journalism. Millitor soon left for an editorship in Cincinnati, and Zahm would die in 1844.[2] In 1845 the paper came under the control of Dr. Francis Brunck, who, sometimes alone, sometimes with partners, edited it until 1875. (In 1853 it merged with the *Demokrat* to become the *Demokrat und Weltbürger*.) Unlike Georg Zahm, who was an artisan of obscure origins, Brunck had been born in Winterturn, Rhenish Prussia, the son of an affluent Protestant squire, and had the benefit of an excellent education at the universities of Würzburg, Munich, and Heidelberg. After a month's imprisonment for his involvement in the failed 1830 revolutions, he was forced to emigrate. He came to America with a medical diploma, and following settlement in Buffalo in 1839 practiced medicine before taking up editorial work. Brunck wrote for a readership of artisans, craftsmen, and laborers from outside their own experience, but his keen intelligence, precise prose, and compassion made up for what he lacked in direct experience. He was an elemental force in German affairs until his death in 1887.[3]

In the belief that partisanship was in conflict with the goal of "instruction," the paper began its life espousing nonpartisanship. But the rise of the paper coincided with the start of the economic depression, which hit the local working classes very hard. They were dependent, directly or indirectly, on Rathbun's empire, and fell victim not only to its collapse, but to the banking practices on which it had rested. Many Germans were left holding worthless bank notes. The paper was soon taking a position on banks consistent with Democratic party ideology. Furthermore, Whig politicians had begun making anti-immigrant remarks and espousing various proposals for curbing immigrant political rights. Thus, along with the mass of German voters, the *Weltbürger* quickly came to see the Whigs as the political front of a privileged, nativist elite, and to ally actively with the Democrats, who defended immigrant cultures and citizens' rights and put forward a populistic antibank, antitariff, and antimonopoly platform. Georg Zahm was soon campaigning for the Democrats, who were fast awakening to the growth of the local German vote, and saw Zahm, the first local German asked to do partisan electoral work, as a valued asset. Along with Dr. Ernest Gray, Philip Dorsheimer, and others, he organized the city's first German Democratic rally during the 1838 municipal campaign. Jacob Zahm, a brother, was a founding officer of the first German partisan organization, the German Democratic Association, founded in April, 1840. On the strength of this activism, the *Weltbürger* was soon discussing German claims to nominations and patronage.[4] The paper's partisanship led to the creation of a number of German Whig sheets. The first, *Die Freimüthige*, was begun in 1843 by Millard Fillmore and his political allies with the missionary purpose, as Fillmore said, of providing foreigners with "a proper" introduction to American life. Until the emergence of the *Telegraph* in the 1850s, most of these German Whig papers were ephemeral and had a small readership. They spent a great deal of time on the defensive, fending off the editorial thrusts of the *Weltbürger*. In doing so the German Whig press probably reinforced the *Weltbürger*'s authority on the East Side.[5]

Zahm and Mollitor realized that "to mold Germans into useful American citizens," another formulation of their purpose, they had to first mold them into a German group able to act for itself. In the new age of mass politics, individuals, especially at the municipal level in the North, were increasingly admitted into the political structure, and allowed to gain influence, power, and resources, as members of ethnic groups that were presumed to be unified under their own leadership. In such a politics, national, regional, religious, and linguistic divisions among the immigrants were a liability. Whether under the Catholic Zahm or the Protestant Brunck, the paper made it a policy to do nothing to aggravate the most potent of these divisions—religion. It urged a separation of church and state, and mildly criticized clergymen such as Rev. John Lord and Catholic Bishop John Hughes for mixing politics and faith. But it refused to become involved in the bitter struggle between St. Louis Church and the hierarchy, just as it declined to become involved in intersectarian controversies. It wanted readers from all confessions, for that was the only path to ethnic unity.[6]

Added to intragroup divisions was another weakness the paper believed that Germans possessed—political and civic apathy, a theme it repeated frequently. In 1838 it said that Germans in America were often rightly charged with being "negligent and phlegmatic in their public and private affairs," and that this was an important reason "why they ordinarily put up with conditions which native-born citizens refuse to endure."[7] Later the paper would adopt a less critical tone. It said simply that the Germans were "patient"—to the point that "they bestir themselves ultimately only if an evil becomes so bad that it steps out of its usual boundaries."[8] As we have seen, Americans also came to see this public lethargy as typically German, a symptom, as one of them said, of a "lymphatic quality" in the German character.[9] To be sure, among German leadership and native-born Americanizers alike there was in these judgments a good deal of prejudice, which was fueled by impatience with people who did not act as one wished. The immigrant masses were not indifferent to their public obligations or welfare, but they had their own distinctive priorities. Thus, for example, while they did not show a great deal of interest in the workings of the dock trade (for that matter, neither did the *Weltbürger*), they could be mobilized to go to the polls to decide whether their taxes should be used to subsidize infrastructural improvements desired by the dock merchants. Yet, as we shall see in later chapters, these negative judgments were not completely off the mark.[10] Brunck and others were correct that Germans were slow in organizing to protect their interests and narrow in defining those interests. Their European experience had not prepared them to participate in a democratic system or to think in terms of group interests, let alone of a broader common good.[11] In addition, the foreignness of their language, as the *Weltbürger*'s editors understood, also inhibited civic and political involvement.

The *Weltbürger* set out to instill feelings of group destiny, combat apathy, and prepare Germans for civic and political participation with a multifaceted program. First, it urged new German immigrants to learn the laws governing naturalization. It regularly goaded those who had been in the country for the requisite two years to file declarations of intention to become citizens. For alien and new citizen alike, the paper recommended gaining familiarity with the Constitution and the political process, as well as with the patriotic symbols and rituals of the new land.[12] In 1838 the paper warned that whoever failed to observe the Fourth of July "with joy and enthusiasm is no friend of freedom," and could not be a good citizen.[13] Similar browbeating accompanied admonitions to learn about contemporary political issues. "You cannot complain about the results if you do not take part in the process," it warned in 1846 before a liquor licensing referendum.[14] And more frequently than any other admonition was the plea to vote. In the 1840s local Democratic victories were by slim enough margins, when they occurred at all, that Germans came to believe they could make the difference to their party and, in turn, profit themselves.[15]

All this advice would have little ethnic meaning to Germans unless they possessed a consciousness of themselves as a people with a common identity, interests, and destiny. To create this consciousness, and doubtless, too, out of a sense of outrage, the paper regularly printed anti-German and anti-immigrant statements, which usually had the added benefit of emanating from national Whig leaders or their local ideological comrades. (Dr. Lord was always accommodating.) Insults at the local polls, such as the familiar refrain "Kraut!," were exposed.

These statements and incidents furnished the basis for emotional pleas for unity and activism.¹⁶

Within a few months of the paper's first issue, an occasion arose in which the Germans were able to use one of their cultural assets—a martial spirit—to fulfill a civic obligation. American aid to rebellious Canadian republicans led, on December 19, 1837, to a British attack on an American boat delivering supplies to rebels camped on an island in the Niagara. For a time war was expected, and tensions remained high for many months.¹⁷ Among the local militia companies established to deal with a British invasion were the German Steuben Guard and Lafayette Guard. Although there was no fighting, the two German companies distinguished themselves for their snappy drill. Also, they hosted a military ball, which was intended, the planners said, to bring German and American militiamen together in a carefree setting to "break down barriers." It is not clear if Zahm was correct in saying that the rise of the German militia had "opened a new era for our local Germans" by demonstrating "their patriotic zeal" and "eagerness to take part in local affairs." But it does seem clear that even at this early date the Germans were proving themselves skilled at ethnic impression-management, a game at which they vastly outpaced the Irish. The ball was the height of the 1837–38 winter social season. The coming years would find German militia companies not only playing a highly visible role in local militia affairs, but staging more of these popular festivities.¹⁸

Routine civic and political participation, however, raised more complicated issues. In their militia companies Germans could speak their language without being penalized for it. But in the courts, public schools, tax assessor's office, or police station, speaking a foreign tongue was a disadvantage. The *Weltbürger* inevitably had to raise the problem of the status of German in the public sphere, for the problem of language was key to taking advantage of private opportunities and to paving the way for group civic and political integration. Moreover, even in its several varieties German was one of the few common denominators possessed by all members of the emergent group. Thus, as a focus for establishing ethnic political interests, the issue of language was an excellent foundation on which to build group consciousness.

The fate of German, however, did not necessarily have the same meanings to all who reflected on it—even when allied in public debate. The Americanizers at the *Weltbürger* looked forward to full German participation in American life. For them the fate of German could not simply be a sentimental matter founded upon nostalgia for the ancestral village. Indeed during the paper's first decade the thrust of its editorials was that only those European habits, values, and ideals not interfering with one's ability to function effectively in American public life should be retained. This formulation obviously left a great deal to interpretation and could be as restrictive or broad as suited individuals. Moreover, the paper's precise position on the long-term future of German was never spelled out.[19] Still it is not likely that the *Weltbürger*'s ideology, with its insistence on full participation in the public life of the new society as the goal around which the desire for cultural retention must be shaped, was fully congruent with the attitudes of the ordinary new immigrant. These people, too, looked forward into their New World futures when the subject was material opportunities. Yet by all accounts they were slower to grasp the benefits of civic and political participation, and felt little concern about ethnic group formation. Because German-speakers were too fragmented for ethnic identification, and there was at the time no one German nation with which to identify, their own identities were defined by varying combinations of region, locality, dialect, religion, and class. For them, language, like religion, was a means of preserving these identities, and for keeping alive as many familiar Old World habits and values as were practical and necessary to preserve intergenerational continuity. It might have been in their self-interest, therefore, to put aside differences and unite on the question of the fate of German. But even with the awareness some had of a pan-German history and literature, language lacked powerful enough cultural symbolism to stimulate an overarching ethnic unity.[20] This was a lesson that the paper and its ideological allies would soon learn.

The first of the issues involving language that the paper raised was the problem of the language of municipal government communication. It caused no dissent among its readers. The paper knew that Germans were having trouble dealing with officials because they could not communicate with them. The clerk of the Common Council could not read their petitions, nor the courts take their testimony. Too few had enough knowledge of English to serve on a grand jury. Butchers and bakers often could not read the ordinances closely regulating their trades, and property owners had problems making sense of the rolls produced by the tax assessor. No translation of Common Council proceedings was available. In March, 1839, the paper suggested that all council documents be printed in both English and German. There was little precedent anywhere in the nation for such official quasi-bilingualism, and American opinion was reluctant to accept it. In response to a German petition that July, however, the council did allow selected German papers to translate and reprint all council transactions. Those papers chosen would be paid by the council.[21]

The decision to establish this procedure carried important consequences for local German journalism. In effect, the council could now create an official German paper. As the city's only German paper, the *Weltbürger* profited immediately. Moreover, if German papers with the right political affiliations did not exist, they would have to be invented. This was the case at first with the German Whig press. It lacked a mass base, and was kept alive, between election campaigns, by patronage in the form of municipal printing contracts, awarded by Whig councils, as well as by outright cash grants, advertisements, and loans underwritten by individual Whigs.[22] The scope of this public subsidy widened in the future, as more levels of government came to adopt a translation-and-reprinting policy. The water commissioner and city health officers eventually decided to use this method of communicating with Germans, as did locally based federal agencies. Local postal officials for awhile paid German papers with the right partisan ties to publish the often massive lists of unclaimed letters, most of them for new immigrants.[23] Broadening the scope of these language services would eventually become a partisan matter for the *Weltbürger*. The paper sought, mostly successfully, promises from candidates to hire German clerks, which also widened the scope of German employment opportunity. Eventually, German clerks were found at the post office and at the assessor's office, and there would be two German health inspectors, all appointed in the name of easing communication between government and the immigrants.[24] Official translators were also brought into law courts on a routine basis after the mid-1840s.[25] Almost as if to give symbolic legitimacy to this semiformal bilingual policy, the prestigious committee controlling the city's official July Fourth celebration eventually allowed a reading of the Declaration of Independence in German.[26]

Much more controversial for Germans and Americans, too, was the second language issue—the problem of the language of instruction in public schools. The paper did not begin its efforts to get Germans to enroll their children in the new public school system with the intention of raising the problem of bilingual education. At first Zahm and Mollitor had seen the schools primarily as a new, important sphere in which to participate. They must have known, however, that the language issue would greatly influence German receptivity to public schools. In fact, language became a major source of controversy among Germans and between many of them and Americans. For German secularists and liberal Protestants, who were not drawn to set up their own private or sectarian schools, and for conservative religionists too poor, individually or collectively, to support sectarian schools, the issue became a major test of American willingness to support a pluralistic, democratic culture. For Germans supporting parochial schools, it offered a basis for attracting those wanting German in their children's schools and for criticizing the competition, the public schools. For Americans, it was a question of how far they would be willing to bend public institutions, which they believed should be molded in the image of the only legitimate American culture—their own. It was also for them a question of whether the immigrants' children would be Germans or Americans.

When the public school system was created in 1838-39, the establishment and administration of individual schools were tied directly to the aspirations of neighborhood residents. Thus, the schools were especially attractive to those seeking opportunities for civic activism. Residents had to petition the council in sufficient numbers to demonstrate that they could maintain enrollments to warrant a school. At the meeting at which they got up their petition, they were also to elect a clerk and an administrator for their district school. Moreover, there was no board of education in Buffalo until 1916. Instead, the Common Council, composed of elected ward officials, served as a board, making the schools directly responsible to officials chosen at the most localized political level.[27]

The organization of the new public school system must have appeared to Zahm and Mollitor to present an excellent opportunity for mobilizing Germans as a group. Throughout 1838 and the first months of 1839 the *Weltbürger* encouraged all Germans, especially those in the largely German twelfth school district, to begin to organize schools. The editors were discouraged when five months passed between the twelfth district's first and second school organization meetings. Not until May, 1839, did the petition campaign progress to the point that the council authorized purchase of a lot for the neighborhood school.[28] In the meantime, the paper regularly criticized German parents for their seeming indifference to their children's future and to "things of the spirit."[29] During the same period, Zahm and several other men organized the first German Democratic rally with the thought of promoting the need for a German councilman.[30] In April, 1839, Dr. Frederick Dellenbaugh, a Swiss Lutheran, was elected to one of two seats from the increasingly German Fourth Ward. The paper urged Dellenbaugh's election on the ground that only a German could work effectively for the two most pressing German issues: printing council business in German and obtaining a school for the twelfth district.[31]

The *Weltbürger*'s criticism of Germans for apathy in the school organization process was not completely fair. During 1837-39 Buffalo Germans were concerned with schooling, but not primarily with the public schools. Sectarian education was expanding rapidly. By 1838 a

Catholic school had been established at St. Louis Church, and German Evangelicals had founded their school. The Old Lutherans, then settling in the city in large numbers, brought a strong commitment to sectarian education and hostility to state power over schools.[32] Equally vigorous were the efforts made to create a private, nonsectarian, German-language day school, which opened in 1838. It had the backing of a number of prominent German men, who contributed generously to finance its opening.[33]

Both types of nonpublic schools were reflections of what was perceived to be lacking in public schools. In both cases language was crucial to filling the vacuum. In the case of those advocating sectarian schools, what was missing was religion, and they espoused the idea that language-saves-faith. In the case of the private, nonsectarian school, it was German culture, as it was conveyed through the German language, that was missing. But while the inception of sectarian schools had begun prior to the organization of the public schools, and had European as well as American roots, nonsectarian private efforts had begun *after* the cultural character of the public schools had become clear, and were probably a direct response to the presumed deficits of those schools. Among the backers of this day school were such men as baker Conrad Hellreigel and grocer Wilhelm Rinck, both of whom in the coming years would have important commercial and political relations with Americans.[34] Even men like them, who were comfortable in their dealings with Americans, desired their children to have familiarity with the language of their fathers as well as a knowledge of English. The reasons are not difficult to discern. While concerned about and skilled at taking advantage of American opportunities, they saw in German a language of culture and tradition that could bind the generations together. German would assist immigrants to ward off the instabilities inherent in immigration and resettlement in a new land characterized by social fluidity and custom-smashing change.[35] It was understandable that the founders of the German day school put dialect differences aside and united around the teaching of Standard German. Though the language issue had not been firmly decided, they were unsure that the public schools would provide German, and hence they were willing to create their own educational alternatives.

The *Weltbürger* had helped to unleash popular interest in education, but the editors, who had their eyes on American opportunities rather than on cultural retention, had not anticipated the various directions that interest might take. By late 1838, however, the paper acknowledged that the language issue was being widely discussed, and it opened its columns to those with opinions in the matter. Other than a bland statement that some combination of German and English should be taught, the editors offered no opinion of their own. Correspondents, however, urged not bilingual education as it would be conceived in the twentieth century, but rather extensive instruction in German in the primary grades, in which, nonetheless, basic subjects would be taught in English, the language identified with new opportunities.[36] Sensitive to these desires, the *Weltbürger* was unable to promise that German would be offered when the largely German twelfth district school opened in September, 1839. It stated instead that the matter would "soon be decided," and urged Germans to enroll their children. It held out the somewhat deceptive hope that if enough Germans attended public schools, some sort of language instruction would be instituted.[37] But no evidence exists that the council, in spite of Dellenbaugh's presence, took up the question. Nor does it seem Dellenbaugh ever presented it. Furthermore, Americans did not join the debate. They probably unquestioningly assumed that public schools should reflect the Anglo-American culture they saw as *the* American culture, and that to learn that culture was to learn to be an American. The disappearance of the issue from the *Weltbürger* probably reflects defeat of the aspirations of those Germans who wanted their language taught in the public schools.

While German did not gain a foothold in the public schools, the debate helped to stimulate further a competitive market for German enrollments. The public schools were soon found lagging. Reluctant to assert themselves as a group and still without significant enough power citywide to force their desires, Germans wanting the language chose to patronize schools that suited their needs. By 1840 populous German districts were far behind American, British, and Canadian ones in public school enrollments. (There were as yet no largely Irish districts.) In 1845, there were 515 children in the increasingly German thirteenth and fifteenth districts enrolled in nonsectarian private schools alone; they represented 43 percent of the school population of the two districts.[38] When this figure is added to the percentage of pupils in sectarian schools, it is obvious most German children were being kept out of public schools. Indeed the public schools may well have been a last resort for Germans—limited to the approximately 33 to 40 percent of all German families who were unchurched or too poor to pay tuition at, or residentially isolated from, nonpublic schools. While school superintendents in the 1840s acknowledged these patterns, they did not seem anxious about them. Their main concern was financial security for the new school system, and they were pleased that a large enough group of English-speaking public school pupils now existed to ensure fiscal health for public education. There appeared no compelling institutional need to accommodate German-language aspirations to tempt Germans into public schools.[39]

In the next years the issue of language and education would become linked as much to the problem of German sectarian rivalries and animosities as to the increasing appearance among Americans of a hardened vocal opposition to bilingual schooling. As the Catholic population grew in the 1840s Bishop Timon was under great pressure to create parochial schools in every local parish in spite of the great expense. In this context, there was growing resentment among Catholic parents and clergy that Catholics had to pay taxes to support public schools at the same time that they were bound to support diocesan schools through tuition payments and voluntary offerings. Catholics were eventually joined by perhaps their most unrelenting sectarian enemies, the Old Lutherans. They, too, were committed to the idea that language-saves-faith, and they, too, pledged to maintain sectarian, German-language schools. But they were also too poor to support such schools comfortably. But Americans in Buffalo and elsewhere were increasingly just as outspoken in opposing the use of tax monies to maintain sectarian schools as they were in opposing bilingual education.[40]

By fall, 1850, the issue of private and sectarian versus public schools was again being debated, and the matter of language was again involved, though now in ways that, given the usual internal politics of the German immigrant group, were not wholly predictable. In September the lay trustees of two German Catholic churches, St. Mary's and St. John's, petitioned the council to ask that their parochial schools be adopted as public schools to make them eligible for public funds. The grounds were not the usual complaints about double taxation, though these were certainly implied. Instead the trustees stated that, as matters now stood, only in parochial schools could the immigrants' children obtain knowledge of the parental language and literary culture.[41] Thus, each parent's choice of sectarian schooling had not really been a choice at all, but a necessity born of the unwillingness of public schools to offer what these parents considered a vital element in the education of ethnic youth. Critics were quick to claim that this new defense of sectarian schools was disingenuous.[42] Even if so, it was a deft strategy. In moving the question of the public schools' monopoly on tax revenues from a sectarian one (of Catholic needs) to an ethnic one (of language), the Catholics attempted to assert ethnic leadership and to rally all the immigrants, regardless of confession, around the powerful symbol of the mother tongue. Perhaps, too, they hoped for sympathy from the substantial number of non-Germans who also had an interest in the welfare of Buffalo's thirty private and parochial schools.[43]

This strategy was only partially successful. The Buffalo Synod Lutherans cooperated to the extent that they accelerated their own public questioning of the monopoly position enjoyed by the public schools.[44] But other German-speaking Protestants, probably those with a commitment to American-style public education and perhaps a dislike of Catholics, moved to check the Catholics' efforts. These German Protestants flooded the council with petitions against the Catholic trustees' claim. The council's committee on schools was quick to note this when rejecting the petition's requests on the usual grounds of separation of church and state and opposition to public subsidizing of bilingualism and hence of multiculturalism.[45] But the council, which was then composed wholly of Americans and evenly divided between Democrats and Whigs, was doubtless aware of the growth of immigrant, and especially Catholic, political power. Though refusing the Catholic schools public money, it did not choose to take a position on the committee's suggestion that a system of district option, which was being tried elsewhere in the nation, be employed. If enough parents petitioned for German, under district option someone would be hired to teach it. The council thus seemed to imply a desire to resolve the language issue on terms favorable to German.[46]

The Catholic petition had helped to revivify the language issue after almost ten years of dormancy, and an initiative now developed in the wake of the council proceedings to petition for German instruction. Catholics and Old Lutherans played no role here, offering to those who sought it evidence that their interest was less in language than in shoring up sectarian schools.[47] (This view was further confirmed by the prominent role of the two denominations in mobilizing voters against the public school law in a statewide referendum that fall. Though the law was massively upheld in Buffalo and in the state, the most determined opposition in the city came from those precincts heavily populated by recently arrived Irish and Germans.)[48] It was claimed that German priests were actively opposing the language campaign. Perhaps they feared public schools would become more attractive to German Catholics if their language were added to the curriculum. Instead support came from large sections of the more liberal German Lutheran synods and from other Protestant denominations.[49] Also joining the campaign were the two principal German papers, the *Weltbürger* and the new *Demokrat*. These were also the same forces among Germans taking a strongly pro–public school law stance in the referendum, a situation that widened the denominational breach among German-speakers.[50] Evidence of the intensification of such divisiveness was apparent in the *Weltbürger*'s response to the results of the referendum in the heavily German—and very likely, Bavarian Catholic—eastern precinct of the old Fourth Ward. The paper, which had begun its existence in 1837 hoping to unify all the diverse elements among Germans, now denounced what it called "the Jesuitical foundation" of the vote.[51]

But by the close of the petition campaign the *Weltbürger* had its own ambivalence. It now voiced the same fears about the consequences of public subsidy of German language maintenance that many Americans had. If German were taught in the public schools, would not this give legitimacy to similar claims by other groups, should they care to assert them? Where would the process of linguistic accommodation end? Were not general taxes, such as those that supported public schools, collected for the general good, not that of a particular group? Yet the paper also stated that cultural democracy was best served by some system of district option. And the paper was distinctly uncomfortable with the notion that English enjoyed a de facto privileged position in the schools. This ambivalence constituted a new element in German cultural politics. The paper was now showing anxiety not only for the fate of German in America, but also for the state of a particularly troubled social pluralism.[52] This pressing, dual concern was apparently shared by others. A 160-signature petition, signed only by Germans and opposed to the teaching of their language on the same ground which now troubled the *Weltbürger*, was soon delivered to the council.[53]

Such signs of faltering German purpose, when combined with perceptions of deepening intraethnic sectarian divisions, were not lost upon the council. In January, 1851, the council voted to postpone indefinitely a minority proposal from within the schools committee to grant the request of a 300-signature German petition for instruction in their language in four district schools.[54] The vote was nine to one, with four of the five Democrats, including the sole German councilman, voting with the majority. The council had responded to arguments from a committee on schools majority report, which voiced fears about setting precedents that would escalate demands for language rights, and which urged Germans to teach their "excellent" language at home and encourage their children to learn English at school for the sake of citizenship and commercial success.[55]

The question of German was not brought up again for sustained public debate in the 1850s, though an occasional petition in support of German instruction in public schools reached the council.[56] The pervasiveness of American nativism placed proponents of public subsidies for cultural pluralism on the defensive for much of the decade. Too, in spite of increased Democratic, and hence German, political power, the sectarian divisions among Germans weakened their ability, and indeed sapped their willingness, to make language a public issue. The *Weltbürger*'s ambitious program for building an ethnic group through mobilizations centered around the public schools had foundered on the rock of entrenched, particularistic interests and animosities.

At the time the abiding problem of language and schooling was being debated in 1850, the social character of the East Side and of both ethnic leadership and ideology was undergoing profound changes. These changes not only influenced German responses to the 1850 debate, but, more important, set the stage for the central, intragroup ideological struggles of the 1850s. The infusion of new issues and ideologies by the various groups of '48ers and by some radicalized, long-established residents would disturb existing patterns of memberships and loyalties among the immigrants. Anticlericalism, antislavery, and anticapitalism would cause potential for fragmentation along new lines at the very time that American nativism and attacks on German popular culture by American Sabbatarians and temperance advocates seemed to demand ethnic unity.

As we have already noted, even before the arrival of the bulk of '48ers and the other immigrants of the great influx of 1851–54, there were local signs of the influence of European republican struggles and pan-German cultural and political nationalism. Collections were taken up, rallies staged, and issues debated and their relevance to America's Germans pondered. Dr. Brunck led the *Weltbürger* into full editorial involvement with the revolutionary and nationalist thrusts of the times. Brunck built upon and transformed the paper's ideological orientation. On the one hand, in calls for Germans to destroy the feudal nobility, he tied their struggle to that of the American revolutionaries in a way similar to the parallels between Old and New World events continually drawn by the Irish nationalists. Germans were afforded the opportunity to become more patriotic Americans and better citizens through support of the European struggles.[57]

On the other hand, while Brunck continued to believe that it was "the duty of each immigrant to familiarize himself as soon as possible with the laws and arrangements of the new homeland" and become "a worthy citizen of our free states," as he said in 1851, he was willing increasingly to embrace a second mission for German immigrants. In its first decade the paper had asked Germans to surrender all the elements of Old World habits and beliefs that interfered with citizenship. Under the influence of German nationalism, however, Brunck now called on them "to foster the German character and German customs

[and] the flowering of German art and literature on this side of the ocean."[58] The German Young Men's Association had begun life with a similar goal, but had intended this orientation solely for intragroup life. Brunck now went further. German culture was to be made "the common property of the new homeland," which had much to learn from the fatherland.[59] Thus, though Brunck was careful to tie together European concerns and American citizenship and ideals, he argued that Germans had a duty to live a German life in America and to spread German culture, while simultaneously participating in American civic and political institutions. This dualistic interpretation of what Germans should aspire to in America was a new element in the paper's ethnic ideology, and it would serve to reinforce German confidence and steadfastness in the struggles with nativists and cultural conformists in the 1850s.

That, however, was not the end of the modifications in the *Weltbürger*'s ideological position. For years the paper had been struggling to avoid heightening sectarian conflict in order to combat ethnic fragmentation, and to hold the loyalty of readers of all confessions, including most particularly Catholics, whose church was a powerful, international institution with activity enough in public affairs to be an easy target. The paper had respectfully advised the hierarchy to improve its public image and embrace the separation of church and state. The Catholic church's role in opposing the European revolutions, as an integral component of what the revolutionaries referred to darkly as "the Reaction," largely accounts for the change in this nonsectarian orientation. The change took place gradually. In June, 1851, for the first time, Brunck gave editorial support to the St. Louis laymen in a moderately worded statement, which was still conciliatory toward the clergy. By May, 1853, the paper had become outspokenly anticlerical. It now charged that members of the hierarchy had "tied their fate to despotism," and would fall with it when revolution finally succeeded. This outspoken stance toward the Catholic hierarchy also coincided with the merger of the paper that year with the city's other Democratic, German paper, the *Demokrat*.[60] Though still the leading figure at the paper by virtue of the force of his personality and a greater share of the paper's assets, Brunck would share some editorial duties until 1859 with the '48er exile Dr. Karl De Haas, who was strongly anticlerical.[61]

The paper's opposition to the Catholic clergy deepened in the 1850s, as Brunck came to the conclusion that "the Reaction," now allied with an equally antirepublican, American nativist plutocracy, was at work in America. This belief led the *Weltbürger* finally to ally with the St. Louis parish laity. In the late 1850s the paper's position changed somewhat. As the bitter memories of 1848 faded, it would argue instead that the Jesuits and American nativists were two fanaticisms that fed off one another, and each in its distinct way was a threat to liberty. Still, it was testimony to the intensity of the experience of 1848 that, however strong the paper's invective against nativists, its most venomous remarks remained reserved for the Catholic clergy. American nativists, it appears, at least had the virtue of being antipapist. For its part the German Whig press was even more anti-Catholic, a position consistent with that of the nativist-inclined American Whigs who subsidized it.[62]

Such transformations in the *Weltbürger*'s stance suggest how much the pressure of events, foreign and domestic, in the late 1840s and the 1850s was influencing the consciousness of thoughtful Grays. Nonetheless, as an exemplar of pre-1848, Gray leadership, the paper was subject to a great deal of ideological abuse from Green exiles. However much ideologically divided among themselves, the local '48ers agreed that Gray leadership was inadequate in ideology, feckless in political execution, and devoid of culture. Some of these charges they backed with arguable contentions, but style of discourse seems in the final analysis to have been more significant in dividing the two segments of immigrant leadership.[63]

To be sure, there were ideological differences between Grays and Greens. Among the activist proletarian '48ers, many espoused some sort of socialism, and both they and the radical democrats, no matter how much Christian imagery and folk culture informed their vision, embraced anticlericalism, and often also atheism or agnosticism. The *Weltbürger* rejected both radical reorganization of society and secular humanism. The principles of socialism might be noble, the paper contended, but they required that people become angels; and anyway, they were of doubtful relevance to America, where individual rights were enshrined in law and culture and a frugal and ambitious man could do well for himself. In America national trade unions would suffice as a countervailing force to monopoly and plutocracy.[64] As far as opposition to religion, as opposed to the clergy, the paper was equally pragmatic. When a journal, the *Morgenröthe*, which was edited by the head of the largely '48er Free Thinker's Society and dedicated to the proposition that "there is no God; no godly power; no providence," began publication in Buffalo, the *Weltbürger* submitted that the enterprise was doomed. The paper stated that "the circle of true atheists is very, very small," because most thoughtful people choose to hedge their bets, keeping their hearts and minds open to the possibility of the existence of a supreme being.[65]

The paper's strategy of discourse here, its pragmatism and refusal to think out in print complex questions involving abstractions beyond the understanding or the concern of the average reader, was very much at odds with the intellectual seriousness, unyielding commitment to principle, and powerful, didactic, and direct language that characterized the style of the '48ers. To the Greens, Gray leadership suffered from laziness, both in thought and in practical political activity, and it shied away from public struggle. Moreover, Greens found Grays excessively enamored of America, and accused them of adopting the same materialistic, opportunistic, and temporizing frame of mind that characterized Americans. Forty-eighters, after all, were exiles as much as they were immigrants. Greens had come to America less by choice than because they were forced directly or indirectly by political circumstances from their homelands. They were idealists who refused to submerge their struggle-oriented critical faculties out of a feeling of gratitude to America for having taken them in. From their first years of exile, they harshly criticized the cultural banality, passion for money-making, arrogance, and hypocrisy of Americans. They found basic flaws in the very structure of American society that demeaned and menaced the entire American experiment. America, for the '48er, was not always that different from Europe. Its oppressions and injustices were simply more masked behind a facade of egalitarian rhetoric and republican legality that produced the illusion of freedom.[66]

Grays had made criticisms of American laws, courts, and banks for many years, and they, too, were appalled by the gap between American rhetoric and reality. Yet, to them, the '48ers vision of America as a nation not unlike the feudalistic kingdoms of Europe was incorrect and fatuous. It revealed an inability or refusal to make important distinctions, and an unwillingness to transcend their own experience and to learn from new circumstances. Acknowledging America's defects, Grays nonetheless embraced the spirit of its laws and looked to the improvement in its institutions. American slavery had no defenders among Grays, but nonetheless many had come to feel it was not nearly as harsh as either feudalism or industrialism in Europe. The new exile must not forget, said Brunck in an 1851 editorial, that he has "lived so long in police states, with all their wrongs, that he sees the entire world that way." Hence, for his eyes "the full look at the sun of freedom is still somewhat intolerable." He must also acknowledge that American freedom of the press made the '48ers' incessant criticism possible in the first place. Grays, however, Brunck maintained, must be patient with these newcomers in spite of their occasional "crazy ideas." They must cease calling them "vagabonds" and "boasters," remember their sacrifices in a good cause, and give them time to adjust to a new land.[67]

Such advice was probably often difficult to follow. Not too many months before this call for compassion, Brunck had launched a blistering attack on the man, De Haas, who would become his partner. (He would continue such attacks on '48er spokesmen even after his plea for tolerance.) The two men had been engaged in a typical Gray-Green verbal struggle. Many of the higher-status, intellectual '48ers saw the ethnic world Grays had created in Buffalo as stolid, self-satisfied and unsophisticated—little more than, as the '48er Karl Heinzen had characterized German Buffalo, "beer, dance, and business"—to which he might have added "church." In this case De Haas had editorialized that Buffalo lacked German high culture, in the form of a professional theater, because Grays were "lower and middle class in origin," rather than of the enlightened "educated and cultured strata." Brunck was furious. De Haas was accused of arrogance and elitism. "Buffalo, open your ears," Brunck said sarcastically, "and awake from your dumb, animal-like condition. A new oracle is among you!" Culture of the type De Haas desired, Brunck contended, was paid for with the blood of the poor in Europe and was a luxury in hardworking democratic nations. For Brunck, De Haas, an educated radical of a privileged background, bore the worst of the elitist values of the culture he had fought to transform.[68]

The number of bourgeois radicals like De Haas, who in Buffalo were clerks, shopkeepers, teachers, journalists, and doctors, was not large. But they made up in political energy, ideological coherence, uncompromising language, and penchant for controversy what they lacked in numbers. A romantic aura attached to some because of heroic behavior in the past. Though they made a strong defense of free labor, their politics, as De Haas's remarks suggest, were not always proletarian, although for a time in 1850, the *Demokrat*, too, voiced socialist principles. Instead their fundamental concerns were German national unification in a republican state, pan-German cultural nationalism, civil liberties, and anticlericalism. They were more often for free and open markets and the reconciliation of classes than socialism. They espoused trade unions to protect workers from monopoly, and advocated that the trans-Mississippi West be preserved as a haven for free white labor. Civil libertarianism and anticlericalism predisposed them to a strong defense of the Continental Sunday and German drinking habits. Their dislike of the clergy, especially the Catholic clergy, was less a product of hatred for religion per se, though there were few believers among them, than opposition to the secular activities of clergymen. While they may have condescendingly felt pity for the individual believer as a victim of fear and superstition, they gave little evidence of hostility of the type that American nativists displayed toward the individual Catholics for their piety and obedience. Bourgeois '48ers were likely to be active members of the secular *Vereine* that most supported German high culture: the Young Men's Association and singing and drama groups, and the more political organization of local Turners, known as the Forwards, which also had working-class members and thus served as a point of contact between both groups of radicals. Such affiliations were an expression of cultural nationalism. But though cultural nationalists, they were not content to set themselves off in a cultural ghetto. Their enthusiasm for German high culture was also an embrace of the universal values in its art and literature. They saw German art in a missionary light, as a means for awakening German immigrants and Americans alike from moral and cultural lethargy.[69]

Thus, in their singular way, they were internationalists and cosmopolitans. This orientation would ultimately produce, as hopes faded for a resurgence of revolution in Europe and interest grew in American politics, a willingness to cooperate politically with progressive Americans. The immediate impetus was the intensification of the struggle over slavery; and their free-soilism, hostility to the Catholic clergy, and liberal nationalism led to their part in the founding of the Republican party. Viewing the American crisis over slavery through their particular lenses, they saw slave owners as an antirepublican, landed aristocracy not unlike the feudal class they had fought in Europe. They found the union of the slaveholding South and the adherents of the Catholic church in the Democratic party proof of the mortal danger facing the American republic. It was this conviction that led in 1859 to De Haas's break with Brunck, who remained a Democrat in the belief that nativism and monopoly were greater evils than slavery. De Haas would edit a Republican paper. Thus, by the late 1850s, their European-forged political values and outlook had been transformed in ways consistent with American radicalism. Simultaneously, as antislavery ideology gathered force inside the Republican party, they came to respect the possibilities of American democracy.[70]

The most important figure among Buffalo's bourgeois exiles was Dr. Edward Storck. Born in 1831 to an affluent Baden family, he had an excellent education. While a university student, he was involved in the 1848 revolutions, after which he sought exile in America. He came to Buffalo shortly after arriving in the country, and worked for a time as a bookkeeper at a brewery. But he took quickly to English, Americanized his first name, and soon was supporting himself by teaching French and German to Americans. Perhaps because he came to America at such an early age, Storck was as much at home in the American as the German ethnic world. He took his medical degree at the University of Michigan in 1853 and established an excellent practice among both Germans and Americans. In 1854 he married an American woman. He was deeply involved in the cultural *Vereine*, and used them to bring Germans and Americans together. He was, for example, one of the organizers of the 1860 *Sängerbundfest*, which was noteworthy for courting American attendance. Originally a Democrat, Storck became a Republican soon after the party was organized, out of antislavery convictions. He fought against the nativist tendencies in the new party, and along with then better-known men, such as Buffalo's William Dorsheimer and the famed Wisconsin '48er Carl Schurz, established an important German presence in the party, which was particularly evident at the 1860 convention, to which he was a delegate. Storck served in the Union army as a doctor, and also raised troops. He eventually emerged as the city's most prominent German Republican, and before his death in 1897 served in a number of elected and appointed positions. His political influence made him a key actor in the post-1865 struggle for German language rights in the public schools. Storck's Germanness, cosmopolitanism, intellectual cultivation, and political commitment are the positive marks of the bourgeois '48er tradition.[71]

Though considerably larger in number, the plebeian '48ers were less well known. In the Old World they were largely "the little men," political descendants of the sansculottes of 1789, who as poor but self-employed artisans, craftsmen, petty traders, and farmers with small property holdings, lived between the bourgeoisie and the *lumpen* poor. In Europe they had looked both ways in identifying themselves: as poor people, they sympathized with the impoverished, unskilled laborer and factory hand, but as smallholders and owners of their own tools, they, along with the affluent, feared upheaval from below. While most of the activists among them were socialists of one of several varieties in 1848, the majority of the "little men" were less definite in their beliefs. Above all else, they had been opponents primarily of the unequal distribution of wealth and power who nonetheless thought class cooperation possible. Of those who came to America, the large majority were journeymen, who had been radicalized in Europe by fears of being reduced to wage earners. They had been ideologically at odds with the bourgeois '48ers, because the latter's passion for national unification and free trade among German states threatened to destroy protected local markets and localized guild privileges. But they also desired reforms in the guild system to make entrance into the ranks of masters easier, and this put them at odds with master craftsmen. What united the three groups—bourgeois liberals, plebeian radicals, and communists—was hatred of princes, reactionary clergy, and other self-selected privileged groups, passion for civil liberties, and opposition to great disparities of wealth and power.[72]

These radicalized workers found that life in America did not free them from some of the insecurities they had known in Europe. While industrialization had not progressed as rapidly in much of America, the independence of skilled workingmen was being subverted by small-scale manufacturing in such heavily immigrant, German fields as shoemaking, furniture-making and tailoring. They also found that under the leadership of Grays there had been little organization of German labor.[73]

Along with the few radicalized workers of earlier migrations and a few bourgeois socialists like Dr. Ciolina and briefly De Haas, the most radical of these '48ers developed an ethnic labor politics. Its ideological and tactical bases shifted frequently in the 1850s as they searched for a means of arresting the decline of skilled workers' standard of living and independence. For a brief period in the late 1840s and early 1850s this politics would provide one, the more radical, of the two centers of the local German labor movement. The other was provided by the German trade unions, which drew their support from old and new immigrants in beleaguered crafts. The boundaries of the two centers, however, were highly permeable for a time, both because of the radicalization of German political attitudes in America that accompanied 1848 and the need many felt to respond politically to the first of a long, traumatic series of pressures local industrialization would exert on skilled workers. But ultimately, though the trade unions at first depended on radical energies, they were too practical in their basic material goals to tie themselves closely to radical ideology.[74]

For their part, the radicals did not seek merely to influence the German trade unions. Indeed, conceived in internationalism, the radical workers' movement hoped to break the bonds of the ethnic group, while remaining deeply rooted within it. It did not succeed in either goal. The radicals purposefully approached the non-German working classes, staging multiethnic rallies and organizing the practical lobbying activities of the German-American Workingmen's Union.[75] But such efforts soon declined before the force of specifically ethnic concerns and activities. First, the GAWU would dedicate much energy to the singularly ethnic purposes of creating German singing and drama societies, which represented the workers' dedication to German culture, even as they upheld internationalism.[76] Second, the GAWU became deeply involved with the struggles of the wholly German craft unions as well as with their cooperative workshops.[77] Third, and related, the GAWU was submerged for a time in Weitling's Workingmen's League, which was also—in leadership, membership, and cultural activities—

wholly German.[78] Among German-speakers, the position of the radical workers' movement, for all its intense ethnicity, would remain marginal. It failed to organize workers outside a few threatened trades (shoemaking, tailoring, and furniture-making), and even in these trades workers were organized but briefly.[79] Also, while Gray leadership was enthusiastic about the GAWU's mainstream political activism, especially when it appeared likely to benefit the Democratic party, the rhetorical excesses of the more radical socialists, especially Weitling, proved deeply troubling to Gray moderates such as Dr. Brunck. The *Weltbürger* not only rejected Weitling's social vision, believing socialism a utopian delusion, but accused him of personal dishonesty in the management of the movement's funds—a not auspicious beginning, it was said, for the moral transformation of society. Radical democratic papers, such as the *Demokrat*, might briefly follow Weitling's line, but eventually they, too, were frightened by Weitling's vision of a final, violent spasm of revolution.[80] From the right of the ideological spectrum, where the great mass of Lutheran and Catholic believers were probably situated, there was a formidable ideological response to the challenge of radical ideas, Weitling's and other's, too. Seen from this vantage point, therefore, the radicals' outstanding achievement within the ethnic group—the creation of a working-class associational network—was a product not only of their own political vitality, but of their inability to appropriate the ethnic *Vereine* and institutions created by the Grays during 1828–48.

Nowhere was it clearer how sharply the '48ers, in spite of their aspirations to universalism, reinforced the major fault lines of the immigrant group in the early 1850s than in the conservative religious communities. While the Buffalo Synod was founded in 1845, it was not until 1852 that its spiritual leader, Rev. Johannes Grabau, felt the need to establish the synodical *Kirchliches Informatorium*, to act as a voice in his struggles with his enemies. Those enemies were now legion. Some of them—Americanization, the Missouri Synod, and the Catholic church—were long-standing antagonists. But while it was true that Grabau's doctrinal war with the Missourians was intensifying, and that he was alarmed by the growth of American Catholicism, it was nonetheless the rapid rise of the forces of radical, secular humanism and anticlericalism among Germans that was on his mind in the early issues of the synod's publication. The paper's credo, "The Great Errors of the Time," revealed the profound mental gulf separating the large body of orthodox Lutherans from the radical '48ers of every stripe. Grabau's list of "great errors" was an indictment of the belief that human affairs could be controlled, let alone improved, by reason and that humanity was anything but depraved. There could be neither freedom nor morality without God. To the extent there was a social ethic in Old Lutheran confessionalism, it was pietistic. It called for individual moral regeneration through prayer and charity. Furthermore, challenging the state was, in spite of their own history, anathema to these Lutherans, who usually maintained that state coercion was necessitated by the utter corruption of the individual.[81] The Old Lutherans had implicitly departed from this belief in their long, reluctant struggle for communal freedom with Prussian officialdom and much more modestly, in their 1850 dissent against the monopoly of the public schools on tax monies. But their deeply troubled history after going into exile was shaped by Grabau's unceasing effort to reassert authoritarian and orthodox tenets in the governance of their intracommunal affairs.[82] In such a historical and theological context, it was unthinkable for Grabau to approve of class war against the state or employers in the name of a better world, even though he himself, from his theological position, had growing doubts about the correctness of the American social order.

This same struggle was fought even more intensely by the Catholic church, whose identification with "the Reaction" made it a certain target of '48er abuse. Moreover, the long, bitter conflict between the hierarchy and the laity at St. Louis parish created acute anxieties among the clergy, which alternately blamed the laymen's resistance on stubbornness and misunderstanding and on the influence of secular humanism on the trustees, a few of whom were Masons and Odd Fellows.[83]

In response to their probably correct perception that anti-Catholicism was spreading throughout the East Side, in 1850 Bishop Timon organized a counterattack. He decided to subsidize a German-language weekly. *Die Aurora* began publication under the direction of the printer Charles Wieckmann, whom, doubtless, Timon had carefully screened.[84] The bishop and German clergy shared the Old Lutherans' dislike of the secular order, and the paper reflected this in its denunciations of the Enlightenment and all its work. But the paper did show a practical willingness to seek ways of accommodating the church to American life, and this placed it in contrast to McGee's Catholic weekly, which was produced during the German paper's first years. In providing German Catholics with ideological weapons against secularists, republicans, nationalists, and socialists, *Die Aurora* not only denounced their beliefs from a religious perspective and upheld the legitimacy of existing political and social arrangements, but took on those who claimed the church was the enemy of tolerance and progress. Catholicism was said to be compatible with science, technology, and economic development, and hence with American life. Moreover, though itself nonpartisan, *Die Aurora* encouraged civic and political participation, and hoped that the votes of laymen could be used in influencing struggles for communal liberties, such as the efforts of diocesan schools and welfare institutions to obtain public monies.[85] Bishop Timon also encouraged Catholic laymen to organize their own efforts to bolster the church's authority and the confidence of the faithful. In the belief that it was penetration of the Catholic immigrants' mental world by '48er ideas that had sharpened the dissent of the rebellious St. Louis laity, the heads of the male mutual benefit societies of the other German parishes in 1854 created a unifying superstructure for their organizations and dedicated it to finding ways to vitalize the relation of the laity to the church. Within a year, the new society had become the basis for a national organization, the Catholic *Central-Verein*.[86]

Thus, the early 1850s found the various substructures of the East Side German town both deeply at odds with one another and immersed in working out the meanings of being German in America. In intensifying the involvement of many of the immigrants in being German, the ideological combat of the time certainly increased the ethnic identification of East Side residents. But it hardly brought about ethnic unity, the capacity to work together as a group. Beyond that moment of fragmentation, however, lay the great and unifying communal struggles—against nativism, temperance, Sabbatarianism, and high taxes—of the mid-1850s. These would revivify the *Weltbürger*'s original understandings of the ways in which mobilizations in defense of group interests could be used not only for the betterment of German immigrants, but also for the achievement of a unity that greatly enhanced ethnicization. But just beyond these communal struggles lay the divisive conflict over slavery and the fate of the Union, which would deeply preoccupy Germans in the late 1850s. Out of the dialectic of unity and division by 1861, a new, internal order would begin to emerge among local Germans.

CHAPTER 9

Class and Ethnicity in the Rise of Labor

In response to dislocations in the processes of work during the early stages of industrialization, local blue-collar workers, most of them newly settled immigrants, came to possess and to act upon a new self-understanding. They increasingly saw themselves as members of a distinctive, wage-earning class which was losing control of the means of its subsistence. They concluded that they had to assert their claims to the fruits of their labor, not only through the vote, but at the workplace, and that they must do so in solidarity with others suffering the same grievances. They also began to conceive of alternatives to the emerging system of industrial capitalism. Yet the rise of this new self-understanding, and the oppositional and alternative ideologies to which it gave rise, did not lead to any but episodic and tentative steps toward working-class unity. The Buffalo working class remained elaborately segmented. This chapter will analyze the sources and the effects of this segmentation upon working-class organization, ideology, and behavior.

There were a number of sources of segmentation.[1] Rudimentary as the city's economy appears by twentieth-century standards, it nonetheless had considerable functional and technological complexity. Three broad, interlocking sectors—commerce, traditional crafts, and industrial shops—employed workers in some 338 different occupations during the late 1850s. These workers represented a wide range of skills. Some 50 percent of the 15,392 household heads in 1855 were unskilled, or they had no occupation, which probably meant that they were unskilled, outdoor laborers then unemployed. The large number of unskilled laborers suggests an important source of the weakness of Buffalo's workers. The unskilled were often too transient to be organized, and too easily replaced to risk going out on strike. Moreover, the unskilled were divided by both function and access to opportunity. Building laborers had greater opportunities for lasting employment and the acquisition of skills than did other types of laborers.[2] Another 30 percent (4,599) and 5.5 percent (847) of household heads in 1855 were, respectively, skilled artisans and craftsmen, and semiskilled workers.[3] Skilled workers practiced a large number of traditional trades from baking and butchering to tailoring and blacksmithing as well as such relatively new trades as lathe operating, toolmaking, and diemaking. Semiskilled workers often had a subordinate, ancillary position to skilled tradesmen. There were leather workers who spent their days cleaning, trimming, cutting, and dressing hides that then received skilled applications by curriers; millwrights who set up machinery in metal shops, but neither designed that machinery nor fabricated objects with it; and pourers and smelters in iron foundries who reduced and refined pig iron, but did not mold it.

Even more dynamic processes of differentiation were being created by the city's first tentative steps toward industrialization, which were evident in the three or four years before the 1857–58 depression, and thereafter as the depression waned. In the 1850s most local capitalists continued to follow the highly lucrative path of least resistance—shipping via the lakes and Erie Canal. But an increasing number of individuals, often by way of linkages with commerce, were putting money into industry, especially in shipbuilding (2,000 workers in 1855), metal and machinery (1,600), tanning (500) and furniture-making (600). These were, in order of appearance, the city's most highly capitalized industries.[4] A very few large establishments, such as William Carland's Gothic Hall clothing firm which employed some 300 tailors at its height in the mid-1850s, existed in other fields.[5] The significance of these pioneering ventures took on new meaning during the 1857–58 depression. A number of progressive entrepreneurs and the *Commercial Advertiser* came to the conclusion that Buffalo "needed a permanent business, separated from lake commerce and independent of its fluctuations to hold it steady in a future crisis" and provide year-round, indoor employment for all its wage earners, many of whom were suffering seasonal underemployment. The program that emerged in 1857–61, which became the basis for the Buffalo Association for the Encouragement of Manufactures (1860), advanced a number of ideas to promote industrial development. It called for efforts to attract industrial capital; new banking facilities to accommodate the needs of industry; railroad connections to the western Pennsylvania coalfields; a fleet of large steamships to bring iron ore and copper from the newly-opened Lake Superior country; and the opening of blast furnaces so that Buffalo could produce its own metals. By 1861 all parts of this development program and a number of projects to restructure and revitalize commerce were in the works.[6]

Though recovery was slow, the foundations of long-term industrial development were finally being set down firmly. In spite of the large number of business failures during 1857–58, by mid-1860 the number of factory workers had increased 43 percent over 1850 (3,884 to 5,563), while the number of firms with fifty or more workers had grown from 16 to 23.[7] There was now significant production in such new fields as the manufacture of steam tugboat engines and of oil rigging equipment, and in such already established fields as meatpacking. Even more significant developments took place in iron production. By the end of 1861, two blast furnaces had opened. The prospect of cheap, locally produced metal inspired the expansion of a number of metalworking shops and the creation of a few new, large businesses, such as the Buffalo Scale Works.[8] Still it is easy to overestimate the scope and scale of the industrialization of the 1850s and early 1860s. Productive capacity was still underutilized in basic industries, such as iron milling and metalwork. Moreover, in spite of an increase in the absolute numbers (1,636 to 2,174) of workers employed in shops with fifty or more workers, there was actually a somewhat smaller percentage (39 percent) of industrial workers in such shops in 1860 than there had been in 1850 (42 percent).[9] Yet, halting though it was, the trend toward industrialism which had barely been detectable in 1850 was apparent to many by 1860. It was evident for the *Weltbürger* in the growing numbers of Germans working in industrial shops, and for the *Christian Advocate* and the *Commercial Advertiser* in the routinized comings and goings of what the papers called the "tin-pail brigade"—wage earners, who made their way to and from factories at the lower end of town, lunch pails in hand. It was hardly coincidental that 1860 saw the sudden end of the indifferent public attitude toward time that had characterized the commercial economy of the past, which had been geared largely to the seasons and to daylight and had knowingly put up with inaccurate church clocks. In that year new and precise clocks were installed at public markets and fire stations.[10]

One effect of the industrialization of the 1850s was to increase differentiation among industrial workers. In effect the city now had four coexisting industrial systems. These provided quite different work experiences, even for those employed in the same jobs and practicing the same trades. The first system was traditional artisanal or craft production, in which skilled workers shaped an entire product by hand, utilizing tools they owned and skills they had learned as apprentices.

Theirs was a life of unremitting toil, and they knew a day-to-day insecurity that factory workers would not know. But they controlled the pace and conditions of their work, and they owned the product they created and controlled their remuneration through their ability to set prices. Though this time-honored industrial system continued in fields such as building carpentry and the various food trades, it was affected by the increasing scale of urban activities and by new technologies. As the size of urban building projects grew, no one carpenter or mason, together with a few journeymen and apprentices, could undertake the choicest commercial or residential jobs. Hence, contracting arose to bring workers together for large construction projects. While smaller ones were done much as before, and even larger ones involved the application of traditional skills by artisans owning their own tools, contracting meant a loss of control over remuneration and definition of tasks on the job. Yet even where innovations such as contracting had not entered the local skilled worker's life, industrial competition might still affect him—and for the worse. He fell under intense pressure to simplify methods, compromise aesthetic and technical standards, and lower prices in order to deal with the challenge of mass-produced factory goods. The result, however, was less likely to be maintenance of a competitive edge than pauperization for the independent artisans waging this struggle.[11]

The other three industrial systems represented significantly greater challenges to customary production methods. These were pioneered at Buffalo, as elsewhere, by entrepreneurs with two distinct socioeconomic backgrounds. There were the countless master craftsmen and ambitious journeymen such as Thompson Hersee and his partners, Benjamin and Joseph Timmerman, who manufactured cabinets, and S. Swartz and his brothers, who produced engines and boilers. They used savings or loans and knowledge of their own trades to create streamlined production methods that greatly increased output. In doing so, they subverted their trades, as customarily practiced, from within. Also, there were merchants, such as the hardware merchant family, the Pratts, who sought to dominate not only distribution and sale of what they merchandised, but also its production. There were also those such as the Wilkesons, who went into a field of production, in their case iron smelting, in which they had no prior involvement.[12] In the second industrial system, skilled tasks once performed completely by one worker were being portioned out among a number of wage earners in order to increase production and control workers. This system often introduced piece-rates as a method for determining remuneration. It was compatible, as in Buffalo's medium-sized shoe shops, with "putting-out"—i.e., subcontracting various elements of production to households and shops outside a central workplace, where the item might be completed. In the third industrial system, simple, hand- or foot-powered machines were introduced. At the time, for example, this technology was found in industries in which leather was used in making shoes or saddles or harnesses, and in garment-making. Sewing machines, introduced in the 1850s into shoemaking and the ready-to-wear clothing industry, were driven by a foot pedal.[13] In the fourth, complex machinery powered by external sources was introduced. Such technology was employed in Buffalo in a few fields. Paint factories, iron mills, flour mills, and the planing mills serving shipbuilders used steam-powered machinery, as did the large tanneries manufacturing patent leather. The larger furniture factories and breweries also probably used steam-powered machinery by 1860.[14]

For skilled workers who had not worked for wages before, participation in these three industrial systems constituted an especially sharp departure from the past. They no longer owned their tools or the products of their labor. Though at this time skills were only infrequently obliterated by new production processes, they were certainly being diluted, and skilled jobs were being restructured so that workers had less control over production. They were also becoming dependent on wages, and had no other means to support themselves. Finally, few could hope to own shops or factories, because the capitalization required was increasingly beyond their capacities to save, let alone borrow.[15] Yet the small shop with simple technology, not the large factory, continued to predominate at Buffalo. Dependent as many artisans and craftsmen, not to mention those with less or nothing in the way of skills, were becoming on the wage, few workers were being reduced to machine tenders. Even in the city's largest workplaces, such as the Jewett and Root Stove Works, which had 250 workers in the mid-1850s, people of different ranks of skill—from master iron molders and journeymen, through semiskilled pourers and furnacemen, to child helpers—worked together in small groups. These groups utilized, with some new variations, traditional production methods of iron molding.[16]

This diversity of productive systems helped to segment a work force that simultaneously was deriving its social complexity from ethnicity, gender, and age. The material and social foundations of the working class were closely related to the extent that women and children entered industry as a result of these new production methods and technologies. Largely because of the absence of cheap power, Buffalo lacked the extensive, highly mechanized textile, shoe, and garment factories that employed so many women and children in eastern seaboard cities. Still, even the more rudimentary new technologies and participation in increasingly competitive markets that characterized the city's emergent industrial economy did create a somewhat enhanced demand for low-wage, low-skill labor. In part this vacuum was filled by women and children, neither of whom had the skills, permanence in the labor market, or social power to compete for better-paying positions that carried opportunities for acquiring skills. The number of women in industry was not large, but it was growing—from ninety-four (1855) to 346 (1860), when women were 6 percent of local industrial workers. These were mostly young, unmarried, needy women, for whom employers showed a preference in the belief they were unlikely suddenly to quit. They were employed doing needlework in Buffalo's one shoe factory, Forbush and Brown, and in several small, ready-to-wear clothing shops. Probably just as many married women, whose domestic responsibilities and cultural values made it impossible for them to work outside the home, did needlework at home on a putting-out basis, but were not officially counted among wage earners.[17] Few girls fifteen or younger worked in industry, probably because better opportunities existed for them in domestic and personal service. In 1855, there were 128 girls employed in industry. They did low-skill, repetitive work in gold-leafing and -foiling, type-founding, and syrup-making.[18] Boys, however, were employed in industry in much larger numbers: 397 in 1855. They constituted fully 19 percent of the work force of 2,117 in the many and varied settings in which they worked.

Because of service as apprentices, boys had always done industrial work in larger numbers than women and girls. But as a system for teaching boys skills and integrating them into the ranks of skilled workers, apprenticeship among Americans had been in decay since the 1830s. Increasingly boys in industry were not apprentices but manual workers. In America, where craft traditions were shallow, guilds nonexistent, and unions often too weak to enforce craft discipline, there was little to stop a young man without proper training from practicing a trade. Nor was there much to stop capitalists wishing to break down skilled work into low-paying, mechanical tasks, and craftsmen and artisans facing stiff competition from factory-made goods from transforming apprenticeship into wage labor. Under these circumstances, boys were offered little instruction and were used in limited, routine operations making type, shingles, mirror and glass frames, rope and leather, in all of which low skill, task differentiation, and simple machinery predominated. Other boys were helpers to iron molders under conditions that ranged from traditional apprenticeship to ordinary wage labor. In contrast to the vagaries of apprenticeship among Americans, on the German East Side customary apprenticeship remained firmly entrenched in the brewing, food, leather, and building trades among immigrants who retained Old World notions of craft training and discipline.[19]

Combined with the different experiences of work available, the diverse social character of the industrial work force fractured and weakened the wage-earning population. So, too, did high, though variable, rates of residential impersistence, for voluntary departure was a common, individual alternative to class organization and class struggle.[20] Yet for all this structural weakness and fragmentation, a significant degree of reintegration of the working population took place through ethnicity. Facilitating this was the fact that ethnicity overlapped with the functional segmentation and hence, with industry, occupation, skill levels, and systems of production. We have already observed the extent to which the Irish worked as unskilled, outdoor laborers on the docks, railroads, and canals, Germans were dominant in building labor, the building trades, and many traditional service crafts, and Americans were skilled mechanics, such as machinists, who were frequently employed serving dockside commercial interests, and, on the West Side, in the traditional mechanical and building crafts. A few significant, multiethnic exceptions did exist—notably sailors, ship carpenters, and factory-based iron molders. But even in the increasingly important field of iron molding, one ethnic group often predominated at a workplace. In Buffalo, therefore, much of the working population led its life on the job just as it did off it, alongside people of the same birthplace, language, faith, and general cultural background. As a consequence, the experience of class was lived within ethnic boundaries among workers who, at this point in history, lacked a shared experience of participation in a stable, customary way of life within a culturally homogeneous American working class. Thus, in Buffalo, class (defined as the continuous and broadly ramifying process of socioeconomic integration and differentiation and of identification of group interests, grievances, and aspirations) interacted continuously with the equally significant sociocultural process of ethnic group formation. We have already seen as much in analyzing how deeply the formation of an urban, ethnic way of life for the Irish and Germans was affected by the various material bases of the individual household economy.

In light of the intimate associations between class and ethnicity, we are able to speak of *a* working class in Buffalo only in the most general, objective sense of the existence of an increasing number of people working for wages. It is more accurate to speak of working *classes* that were visible daily in three distinct ethnic varieties—Anglo-American, Irish, and German. Though the local press did not think of class in a modern, sociological sense, but was more concerned with the distinction between producers and nonproducers, or, as the *Weltbürger* said, between those who did or did not earn "their daily bread by their own activity," local newspapers acknowledged this crucial link between people as workers and people as ethnics. Editors identified bodies of workers as frequently by ethnicity as by such social characteristics as occupation or skill. In its efforts to generalize about the character of the work force, moreover, the press spoke, as did the *Courier*, of "the several laboring classes of the city," by which it meant *ethnic* classes.[21]

For our purposes, the most significant illustration of this relationship between class and ethnicity is found in the development of working-class struggle. Though conditioned by the variable experiences of skill, job, sector, wage, gender, age, and productive system, Buffalo workers shared many pressing grievances. Because mechanization on a large scale was limited in most fields to the last years of the period, work process issues, such as deskilling and task differentiation, though by no means unknown, were less often a source of class struggle than questions of compensation. Much conspired to keep local workers' wages low. First, superimposed on the seasonal cycle of the local economy, which brought wintertime hardships to many wage earners, was the business cycle, which caused more long-term difficulties. During troughs in the cycle (1837–43, 1854, and 1857–58), workers suffered not only unemployment, but wage cutbacks and speedups. These led to defensive struggles to maintain the existing wage scale and pace of production. During periods of recovery and growth, workers suffered the stickiness of wages which had been depressed during the previous trough in the cycle, relative to the much more volatile price scale. The increase in rents and the cost of food was a universal complaint in the prosperous five years before the 1857–58 depression. Employers' reluctance to raise wages in good times was a product not only of greed, but of both the acceleration of threatening competition and their own pessimistic market calculations.[22]

These same fears led to various efforts by employers to repossess wages, the second source of low wages. Buffalo workers were at times paid in uncurrent specie. This was facilitated by the fact that because of low capitalization and the seasonal inelasticity of the local economy Buffalo banks, as a body, periodically were not able to fill local currency needs. Local workers, however, proceeded on the premise that employers who truly wanted to could find ways to pay them in currency that had value. Even more common, and indeed the leading source of local class struggle during the period, was payment in "orders"—the so-called storepay system. In the late 1840s for example, workers were paid as much as 25 to 50 percent of wages in scrip or signed notes redeemable in the groceries of specific merchants. This system, which was adopted by many employers because of cash shortages, was not inherently corrupt, and reputable employers, such as the Wilkesons and the municipality itself, used it. Even at its best, workers disliked the way it removed use of their earnings from their control. But the system was easily corrupted, and many workers experienced only its abuses: inflated prices and inferior goods sold by shopkeepers who made excessive profits and kicked back money to employers. On at least one occasion, too, workers discovered that an employer owned the stores at which their scrip was redeemable.[23]

Struggle against these and less common forms of exploitation was conditioned not only by situational and structural factors specific to the local economy and to particular industries and jobs, but also by ethnic identity and culture among Anglo-American, German, and Irish workers. Each of the three great solidarities developed distinctive approaches to a class politics. Ethnic identification lent itself to the development of habits of solidarity among ethnic workers. Ethnic culture provided an essential basis for the organization, forms, and ethos of craft traditions and protest. This is not to say that the three approaches completely lacked common ground. It was a commonly understood, naturalistic symbolism that enabled German and other butchers to agree to present themselves in white frocks and scarlet sashes in the annual Fourth of July parade. But in this case, as in others, the ethnic vessel in which the symbolism was contained was itself distinctive enough that, as a practical matter, the German butchers would organize only themselves to defend their interests as craftsmen. Numbers mattered, too; it was relevant that fully two-thirds of the butchers were German, and the other third were scattered among several groups and less easily organized by those wanting to unify butchers.[24] It need also be said that there is no evidence that German butchers consciously barred other ethnics in the trade from their ranks. Indeed, butchers and others, too, at times sought to overcome the exclusivism to which ethnicity consigned their class organization.

What is more to the point is that ethnic identity and culture provided a familiar and psychologically compelling basis for the organization of the German majority of butchers, and simultaneously, though not intentionally, led to the practical exclusion or marginalization of others who were not members of the majority group in the trade. The remaining minority of workers in a field might have their own organization, as was true of American shoemakers, whose trade in Buffalo became overwhelmingly German. But such organizations were destined by numbers alone to impotence. Even more compelling evidence of the common class elements contained within these separate and distinct ethnic vessels was that in their singular, uncoordinated struggles, workers from all three solidarities put forth common assumptions about class justice. They espoused a producer theory of value, by which wealth should rightly belong to those who produced the world's goods. Furthermore, each appropriated elements of the American republican tradition in shaping an ideology to justify struggle and to establish the moral basis of a more just and equitable social order. For example, independent of ethnicity, local workers held antimonopoly attitudes, which denounced excessive concentrations of wealth and power for undermining democracy and subverting the dignity and life chances of working people. Workingmen of all backgrounds, too, believed that the franchise gave them dignity and equality that the emerging industrial capitalist system must not be allowed to destroy. They espoused the use of the vote as a principled means for obtaining class justice in a system that, most continued to believe, made justice possible, if not always easily obtainable.

But while the predominant thrust of class struggle was contained within ethnic boundaries, there did emerge, fitfully and hesitantly, another tendency of working-class protest that was multiethnic and internationalist. It did not seek to end the hold of ethnic identification and culture on workers, but rather to find ways of mobilizing ethnicity in the service of class. It was multilingual, and it found ways to grant both symbolic and practical recognition to the individual groups it sought to bring together. This multiethnic tendency asserted itself episodically but with surprising vigor, even during the climax of political nativism in the 1850s. Yet the effort to unite the working classes politically against the order system was considerably less successful. Labor militants failed to break the partisan hold of established political parties, which continued to integrate workers into politics as members of ethnic groups not of a united working class. Consequently they failed to shape political debate or gain access, as a class seeking its own goals, to the power of the state.

We will now analyze these various ethnic and multiethnic tendencies in the development of local class struggle.

The Americans

A distinctive class politics linked American workers. In the 1840s and 1850s this politics bore the imprint of the experience of the earlier Jacksonian workingmen's movement, which had had its own ideological analogues in the Chartist movement and craft union organizations, in Britain and its white Protestant colonies. (In consequence, Buffalo's Anglo-Canadian workers, who were as overwhelmingly likely to be skilled as their American counterparts, had access to the same fund of ideas, just as they did to the religion, neighborhoods, and institutions of the Americans.)[25] With the inception of industrialization in Buffalo and the increasing erosion of opportunities for self-employment, this politics, which was so closely identified with the self-concept and welfare of the skilled worker, underwent a severe testing. Yet, while American artisans and craftsmen would change their tactics and their forms of organization to meet these challenges, there is little evidence that they fundamentally changed their distinctive view of themselves. They continued to see themselves as independent men of craft whose skills were socially indispensable, even as forces unleashed by the growth of industrial capitalism were destroying their independence and their crafts.

American class politics was founded upon two interrelated beliefs: the dignity of craft and the inalienable rights of Americans. The legitimacy of these beliefs was, in turn, established through Protestantism, American republican tradition, and the producer's ethic. The conception of the good society founded on these beliefs was one in which equality of opportunity, unfettered by monopolies and plutocrats, furnished the mechanism for continuing self-improvement and material reward in direct proportion to one's skill and effort.[26]

American republican tradition and Protestantism provided American skilled workers with both a feeling that the state belonged as much to them as to wealthy men and a conception and enumeration of rights, which inhered in American citizenship and in membership in the human family. Fused together in this way, Protestantism and republicanism asserted that American "freemen," as a local convention of artisans resolved in 1839, possessed the right "to time to develop their God-given capacities." In other words, they had rights not only to cultivate, use, and profit from their talents and skills, but to determine, insofar as it was practical, the nature and extent of that cultivation, use, and profit. Because it left wage earners dependent and usurped their individual processes of cultivation, the convention called the payment of wages in debased currency or in storepay the "enemy of God, freedom, and human happiness," and hence of both the secular and spiritual orders.[27] American artisans felt secure enough in the promise of both orders that when faced with injustice, they could state, as the printers did in 1847 in resolving to fight wage cuts at the *Morning Express*, "to ask for nothing but what is right and submit to nothing that is wrong."[28] For such men the willingness to engage in the unremitting struggle for liberty was the measure of American dignity and manhood.[29] Yet they also lived with the perception that their dignity and manhood were being usurped by a new economy that gave free reign to the scheming, manipulative, selfish side of the human personality ("our animal inclination"), and which installed the rule of avarice ("the Archbishop of differences between men").[30] Thus, the resolve of the 1839 tradesmen's convention "to retrieve their lost rights"[31] expressed a sense of longing for the past and a growing desperation about the difficulties they faced in supporting themselves and living up to their ideal conception of themselves.

The producer's ethic was the basis for belief in the importance to civilization of the skilled worker, and as such, it reinforced his claims to dignity. It was not simply overcompensation for the erosion of that position that led them to compare their crafts favorably with bourgeois occupations, but a belief that labor was the source of all wealth and hence of civilization itself. This belief set the tone for much of their rhetoric of self-defense and struggle. Craft, said Oliver Steele in his presidential address before the Erie County Mechanic's Association in 1842, had "mental and moral superiority" over wealth, even when the latter was earned by honest effort.[32] Too often, however, tradesmen felt, wealth was not the product of honest effort, especially when it was in the possession of those like lawyers and bankers, who appeared to live parasitically off the toil of others. Too often, furthermore, professionals and businessmen held condescending views toward those who worked with their hands. In a letter to the *Commercial Advertiser* in 1844, "Eneas" denounced all those, especially lawyers, who believed "that the tools of the artisan were a disgrace to learning and not needed for the happiness and improvement of man." The skilled trades, said "Eneas," are "directed by those of enlightened minds and liberal views who may be imitated by those of the legal profession to their advantage."[33]

The moral superiority of the skilled worker over the idle and active wealthy alike and over "political demagogues," who tried to make a living off politics and were another constant target of the tradesmen's abuse, was reinforced by a rich iconography and rhetoric useful in asserting claims to social respect. A visual representation of the moral bases of those claims was presented in every Fourth of July and commemorative procession. At the time of the 1832 centenary of Washington's birthday, sailors, steam engineers, butchers, carpenters, printers, and men of other crafts all marched alongside floats with banners proclaiming the nobility of craft heroes and extolling the role of various crafts in the progress of civilization.[34] The printers usually placed a working press on a large cart, and their banners spoke of their contribution, via the book and newspaper, to human enlightenment. The printers also had strong claims to an important symbol of American patriotism as well as craft—Benjamin Franklin, whose birthday they celebrated at an annual banquet. Franklin served quite effectively to anchor the contributions of their trade. He epitomized the long line of artisan-intellectuals who had facilitated the growth of human freedom. Printing, said H. H. Whitcomb, a local journeyman printer in an 1852 Franklin Day address, had ever been the greatest tool in turning back "the oppression of social distinctions." Franklin, too, had other symbolic uses for printers and all skilled workers. As Steele said in 1842, Franklin, "the poor printer" without formal education, was an inspiring example of the triumph of self-cultivation.[35]

Self-improvement was a central tenet of the American skilled workingman's ideology. The self-improvement he contemplated was no mere striving for wealth. While it was certainly compatible with the bourgeois conviction that men who tried could be successful in America and had an obligation to strive to become so, these Americans were not consumed by a desire to get rich or become capitalist entrepreneurs. Nor did they adopt bourgeois behavior in pursuit of their goals. The American tradesmen's conception of self-improvement, while encouraging material comfort, was rooted in traditional, easygoing notions of work. They rejected bourgeois ideas of work discipline, and hence were not at home in the new era of increasingly regimented work processes. This much was clear in the "Timebook" of the dockside mill-builder Danforth Franklin, whose thirty-one American carpenters and millwrights regularly stretched out their weekends by celebrating "St. Monday."[36] Moreover, the American tradesmen's ideology looked with disfavor at the quest for riches, and was thus in a state of tension with the spirit of modern capitalism. It urged the acquisition of craft and the cultivation of craft excellence over, in the words of the 1839 convention's resolutions, "the inclination to acquire riches," which was bound to cultivate "avarice" and "the animal inclination" to place one's wants over another's.[37] Such views powerfully reinforced the antimonopoly politics of the American skilled worker.

Yet this quest for self-improvement through craft led quite easily to the disruption of its own moral universe. The traditional-minded man, rooted in the habits of the simple economy of the past, would probably not have sought to earn more than he needed. But for the more ambitious, development of skills and excellent workmanship led, through innovations in the creative process, patents, and general competitive ability in an expanding economy, to the acquisition of a surplus, which it was tempting to use as capital. One was soon employing others. To be sure, master craftsmen and artisans had always employed journeymen and apprentices. The point, however, had been that these men and boys were to be put on the road to self-employment and independence. Now, under the intense competitive conditions of the time, self-employment was being undermined, and employing others in an industrial setting increasingly meant paying wages to hired hands, who were unlikely to ever be employers themselves. A small but growing number of talented and competitive American tradesmen did become employers in the 1840s and 1850s. There were those like Danforth Franklin, once a journeyman, who became successful contractors, the most common entrepreneurial path for craftsmen and artisans. A smaller number, from the iron molders Francis Root and Sherman Jewett, who became major industrialists, to the artisan Hunting Chamberlain, who opened a modest-sized but prosperous wagonmaking shop, went on to establish factories.[38]

If there was a moral contradiction at the heart of such upward mobility for those who experienced it while continuing to think of themselves as workers, it did not always dawn on them or even on the people they employed. As a new development, industrial capitalism still seemed an aberration. The customary social relations of production might still be restored through reform and public education. Moreover, even an employer in ruthlessly competitive markets could exercise the moral choice not to let "the animal inclination" govern relations with wage earners. Out of such assumptions came other tenets of the distinctive ideology of American tradesmen. They rejected the ideas that class conflict was inherent in modern economic arrangements and that the logic of the market, rather than traditional morality, must govern those arrangements. "We do not appeal to the poor against the rich," said the 1839 convention's resolution condemning storepay, "but to truth and right against error and vice in the name of Christian morality and humaneness."[39] "Principles of reciprocal justice," said an 1847 meeting of American newspaper compositors and printers, who were protesting low wages, should govern the relations between labor and employers.[40] When such relations broke down, American craftsmen and artisans eschewed "coercive means" and "violent measures" and sought "peaceable redress" through what was variously described as "quiet and firm means," "fair and reasonable means," etc.[41] That principles of "reciprocal justice" did still obtain sufficiently at some industrial shops to reinforce belief in the efficacy of this ideology was apparent in 1854 when American molders at Jewett and Root assembled to present a watch as a retirement gift to a foreman, who, the men believed, had discharged his duties in an "able and gentlemanly manner." Such foremen continued to be role models for ordinary wage earners. This was clear in the address given at the ceremony by Alonzo Brooks, a molder. "Foreman!" said Brooks, "what sacred memories cluster around that name. It awakens feelings which inspire the molders with that ambition which leads men to honors in life."[42]

For much of the antebellum period there was a close relationship between these beliefs and the forms and goals of American skilled workers' organizations. With the exception of brief experiences of union organization and striking in the inflation-ridden mid-1830s and in the 1850s, unions and militance were far from representative of the preferred forms of working-class activity. Though there were a few trade unions among such highly skilled Americans as printers, more common were the various multifaceted organizations that sought to combine all skilled workers under one broad umbrella in order to break down the fragmenting lines of craft specialization and to pursue a wide range of mutual interests. The Erie County Mechanic's Association, the Mechanics' Mutual Protection, the Mechanics and Apprentices Association, the Mechanics' Mutual Association, the Mechanics' Institute, and, as a sort of junior auxiliary, the Buffalo Apprentices Society were the leading organizations of this type. In the case of all but the Apprentices Society, these organizations did not restrict their membership to skilled workers. They admitted employers, managers, and occasionally the unskilled. The Erie County Mechanic's Association, founded in 1841 and probably the largest of them, had upwardly mobile craftsmen, such as Jewett and Root, who were then becoming major manufacturers, among its officers and ordinary members.[43] Steele, the printer-turned-bookseller and school administrator, was its first president. Of course, a certain but not easily defined point was reached at which such men found it difficult to continue to participate. After the mid-1840s, the affluent Steele frequented bourgeois social circles, to which he was linked through marriage, and became involved in the conservative, probusiness mainstream of the Democratic party. Moreover, he had embarked on the ideological path that would lead him by 1860 to espouse a belief in the God-given stewardship of wealth.[44]

Other wealthy or simply upwardly mobile men, however, continued to be present in the organizations of skilled Americans even as men like Steele dropped out. Along with the tanners, printers, and tailors who made up the officers of the Mechanics' Mutual Protection in 1854 was George J. Webb, the powerful foreman of all printing operations at the *Commercial Advertiser*. That he was part of management, it must also be noted, did not stop the printers from electing Webb president of their union during the 1850s. Nor did the fact that he was the Buffalo receiver of the Great Western Railroad stop local printers from choosing H. H. Whitcomb, a local printers' union activist, delegate to their union's national convention, where he was elected secretary.[45] Furthermore, men of Jewett's and Root's class continued to be involved in these associations in a variety of ways even after ceasing regular activity. After the Erie County Mechanic's Association fell into decline because of partisan divisions, discussions began early in 1856 toward reviving the organization. "Some of our leading manufacturers," said the *Courier* approvingly in 1856, "are ready to take hold of the matter."[46]

Consistent with the centrality of self-improvement in the ideology of American craftsmen was the emphasis of these associations, and of the few American trade unions, such as the printers and journeymen cordwainers organizations, on promoting both craft and public education for their intellectual value. While breaking down the barriers that separated lines of trade was its central larger goal, the Erie County Mechanic's Association had as its principal activity holding exhibitions displaying craft techniques and newly invented machinery, diffusing information about various trades, and sponsoring debates and public lectures. It hoped, too, eventually to open a lending library for members.[47] The self-improvement ethic was apparent, too, in upholding some standards of respectable personal behavior shared in common with the evangelically inclined elements of the American bourgeoisie. The Mechanics' Mutual Protection, the goals of which the *Courier* said in 1844 were much "like the Odd Fellows," met socially every Tuesday at the Sons of Temperance Hall, at which no liquor or beer could be served. For their part, like fellow printers elsewhere in the nation, American printers made the quest for a work-free Sabbath, which the existence of Sunday newspaper editions blocked, a major goal in the 1840s and 1850s, because, they said, they needed a day of rest for spiritual and intellectual as well as physical renewal.[48]

The political programs of these associations and unions were those of men who wished the chance to be their own bosses and develop their own capabilities unfettered by forces that would reduce them permanently to wage earners. Their standard complaints centered around whatever curbed the independent tradesman's ability to remain competitive and self-sustaining and the journeyman's hopes to be self-employed. Because the inroads of wage earning were already deep, practical measures were urged to reform, as opposed to do away with, the wage system. American artisans and craftsmen spoke in favor of laws to strengthen the state's 1831 mechanics' lien law and to abolish the order system, which independent tradesmen also strongly favored because as subcontractors on larger projects, they were often paid in orders. Senior artisans and craftsmen and journeymen, too, united and joined with merchants to send a delegation to Albany to lobby for the passage of a bill curbing the competition of goods made in the state's prisons. Other goals uniting senior and junior tradesmen were tuition-free public schools financed by real-estate taxes, the reduction of public lands prices so that the average urban family might obtain a farmstead, and the exemption of houses valued at under $1,000 from public auction because of debt.[49]

Internal tensions wracked these associations and unions in the 1840s and weakened them at the time they were faced with emergent industrial capitalism. Masters, journeymen, and apprentices might occasionally cooperate, but their interests were hardly entirely congruent. In many trades, senior tradesmen complained that journeymen were willing to work for too little and to turn out inferior goods, while journeymen complained, as apprenticeship fell to ruin, that apprentices were not serving long enough terms. These tensions were greatest in trades in which factories were appearing, but they appeared, too, in trades in which factory production was weak, but wage earning, as a seemingly permanent condition, was taking hold. In 1847 Buffalo's journeymen cordwainers, hard-pressed by competition from factory-made shoes, agreed at their monthly meeting that apprentices should serve until twenty-one years of age, a relatively late point for the termination of apprenticeship. Similar conclusions were reached by journeymen printers in 1861. They complained that "runaway apprentices" were depressing the wage scale. But journeymen also joined with apprentices to claim that some master shoemakers were bent on transforming them into mere wage-earning shop hands.[50]

Equally pressing were partisan tensions within these American workers' organizations. These could be expected to the extent that Americans were the only sizeable solidarity whose members regularly split their votes between major parties. Such tensions did not always mean divisive conflict. At the 1839 tradesmen's convention, Democrats voiced suspicions about the dominance of Whigs in the meeting's leadership positions. But these Whigs were able to frame resolutions on banking and currency reform so broad in their class appeal that they were acceptable to Democrats.[51] Yet this type of understanding was the exception, as the experience of both the Mechanics' Mutual Protection and the Erie County Mechanic's Association suggests. The failure of the latter in the mid-1840s was due to the fact that Whigs and Democrats alike sought, said one member, to make "illegitimate combination" between the association and their respective parties, both of which had held out "inducements" to individuals who could effect a practical merger. The Protection split apart in 1854 when some members decided to renounce the current leadership for partisanship and begin a new organization, which swore to "confine its usefulness [to] the benefit of the mechanics rather than be used as a machine for political demagogues."[52]

The greatest problem, however, with these American organizations was that they were being rendered anachronistic by transformation of production. This process, combined with the effects of the 1857–58 depression, prompted the beginnings of a search for mechanisms for negotiating for power within the wage system. In consequence, unionization and militance increased among American tradesmen, and older organizational forms fell into decline.

American artisans and craftsmen responded to their declining fortunes during the 1850s in two ways. First, unions appeared among Americans in trades in which there had been little or no organization in the past—building carpenters and joiners, engineers, machinists, and blacksmiths, for example.[53] Second, efforts were made to create more militant organizations in the very few trades, particularly printing, where there had been some union activity. Among newspaper printers, unionism was hardly new, largely because the roles of publisher and printer had increasingly been separated throughout the first half of the century. So when twenty-seven printers working for local papers created a new union in 1852, after several years in which an older one had been allowed to lapse, little seemed innovative about their activity. Indeed the principles they announced were firmly within the American tradition of labor politics. They renounced violence and confrontation in favor of cooperation with capital. Moreover, they elected (and re-elected a year later) foreman George J. Webb their president, and proclaimed their primary goal the end to all Sabbath work. In spite of this moderation, and in spite of the fact that by 1861 the union had succeeded in organizing only a third of the newspaper printers (mostly young, journeymen compositors), the new union did show greater militance on wages than any previous printers' organization. Wages were sluggish in the prosperous early and middle years of the decade, because of intense competition among a growing number of local newspapers for shares of readership and the job printing market. Then wages fell in the depression. During the tentative recovery in the spring of 1859 the union struck the *Commercial Advertiser*, *Express*, and *Republic*, and won an increase in wages of five cents for every 1,000 ems of type set.[54]

In spite of the printers' militant example, one is struck by the extent to which in the 1850s militance and class organization were absent among American tradesmen, especially in comparison with the immigrant Irish and Germans. Nor did Americans seek cooperative alternatives to the wage system, as German craftsmen did during the decade in a search for self-determination. To the extent American workers did seek cooperative alternatives it was not as producers, through creating cooperative workshops, but as consumers, through establishing a communally run store. In 1859, as the recovery gathered strength and prices rose, a large group of American, with some British immigrant, workers, founded a cooperative grocery store, and attempted unsuccessfully to interest workers in shopping there.[55] It is difficult to escape the conclusion that, while most American craftsmen and artisans certainly did not understand themselves as men-on-the-make, nonetheless habits of solidarity and class consciousness came reluctantly to those who were still an elite and privileged section of the local working classes. For all the hated changes in the practice of the skilled trades, American tradesmen were highly skilled, relatively prosperous, possessed of citizens' rights, American in an immigrant city, and able not infrequently to share neighborhoods, churches, and voluntary associations with the American bourgeoisie. Moreover, an ideology placing emphasis on individual development could cunningly become the vehicle for encouraging individual mobility, even when the economic context of that mobility was the not especially admired emergent industrial capitalist system. Too, Americans at all class levels possessed weak ethnic identification to reinforce habits of solidarity. It is not surprising then that their antebellum labor history in Buffalo sharply contrasts with those of the Irish and the Germans.

The Irish

The Buffalo Irish established a distinctive style of working-class protest based on the interaction of cultural traditions and habits of solidarity fashioned in the Old World and the chronic poverty and joblessness they knew as unskilled workers in America. This style was evident during the period in two types of struggle. The first was the dozens of spontaneous strikes—often brief and usually unsuccessful—among unorganized, unskilled workers at construction sites on the public works or railroads in and around Buffalo. The most dramatic of these by far was the "Towpath Rebellion" of January, 1849, in which the local militia was called out to suppress a strike by some 600 laborers, almost all of them Irish, against contractors engaged to widen a section of the Erie Canal.[56] The second was the "Work or Bread" demonstrations during the depression spring of 1858 when Irish laborers from the First and Eighth wards staged outdoor rallies and marched to the mayor's office to demand that the city create jobs for them or provide them with food.[57]

The causes of both strikes and demonstrations lay in the conditions of employment of unskilled, outdoor laborers. Laborers were frequently lured to work sites by contractors' promises of high wages, only to find they were to be paid at lesser rates and/or, in some percentage, in storepay. Also, they sometimes found they were paid irregularly and partially, with the balance promised at a later date. Frequently the terms of employment were more demanding than they had been led to believe. Whatever the case, the laborers struck for what they had been promised or thought they deserved. Strikebreakers, easily recruited from the ranks of the large population of unskilled immigrant workers, were sometimes hired to replace these men, and became the objects of violence. In contrast to the strikes, the 1858 "Work or Bread" protests represent another aspect of the outdoor laborers' plight. They were a product of the suffering of the poor and unskilled who were the first fired in periods of depression and, because in the best of times low paid and chronically underemployed, the least likely to have sufficient savings to weather an extended period of unemployment.[58]

Various influences on the forms, practice, and ideology of Irish protest were found in ethnic and American cultures and in the exigencies of daily life in the lowest reaches of the contemporary northern economy. The volatility of the market for outdoor, unskilled labor, combined with its lack of continuity in one job over time, constant underemployment, and frequent travel, often at considerable distance from home, to find work, made union organization all but impossible. Thus, laborers' strikes were more or less spontaneous outbursts of anger, which were largely shaped by the requirements of the moment. The superfluity of unskilled labor made it quite easy for employers to fire agitators and strikers and replace them with strikebreakers without much inconvenience. Scabs could be found among the Irish themselves, but they were usually few in number. Only several dozen Irishmen could be found to attempt to break the strike on the towpath in 1849, and most likely they were men desperate enough at the height of the winter to take any job, no matter what the risk. Scabs were sometimes not told the circumstances of their employment. Contractors, however, often proved adept at manipulating traditional faction feuds among the Irish to set strikers and strikebreakers against each other.[59]

Strikebreaking usually led to violence, which was one of the other characteristics of Irish class politics. Violence, as we have noted, had a long political history among the Irish, who had frequently resorted to force as a means of protest and intimidation against English landlords and colonial officials. The Irish understood not only how violence in contexts of their own choosing was an equalizer against a powerful enemy, but also how potent and strategic was the *threat* of violence, which gave one some of the same benefits at much reduced cost. The Irish Catholic *Sentinel* showed some of this strategic skill. It was especially deft in 1858 at combining denunciations of unemployed workers who threatened violence with dire predictions of the inevitability of violence unless the suffering of the unemployed was eased.[60] But violence, too, was endemic to Irish slum life, where it was frequently a characteristic of interpersonal relations. Thus, violence was often also an unthinking reflex among the Irish. Whatever its precise roots, its use and the threat to use it stood in sharp contrast to the American tradesmen's rejection of threats and violence as immoral and beneath their dignity as well as an intrusion upon the legitimate rights of employers to conduct their enterprises free of intimidation.

Another characteristic of Irish class politics which separated it from that of Americans was the extent to which the Irish, when engaged in struggle, frequently called upon the resources of the ethnic group beyond the body of aggrieved workers and beyond the ethnic working class itself. Explanations for this solidaristic behavior are not difficult to find. Americans' strikes and protests had to be conducted against coethnics, and thus their base of intracommunal support was foreshortened at the start. In contrast, there were few Irish employers. Irish strikes were always against American public works contractors, and to that extent, in pitting the affluent descendants of British Protestant immigrants against impoverished Irish Catholics, must have been laden for the latter with a particularly emotional symbolism. One must also consider the comparatively flattened social structure of the Buffalo Irish, who had only a relatively small percentage of people in the ranks of skilled, professional, or entrepreneurial employment. Such occupational homogeneity implies a high degree of common class experience. Whether through personal experience or the experience of family or friends, this lent itself to the capacity to empathize with striking laborers.

The Irish were not completely incorrect to adopt a belligerent attitude toward their American employers and, during strikes, toward Americans in general. When on strike, they frequently found themselves isolated. American opinion, including that of their partisan allies, American Democrats, was frequently hostile. Their reputation for violence put Americans on guard in any public conflict in which the Irish were involved. To be sure, American editors and authorities were not always completely confident that German strikers would behave much better, but they were not predisposed to expect violence from the Germans as a people as they were from the Irish. Moreover, in contrast to the Germans, the Irish often realized American fears, especially when confronted by strikebreakers. The Democratic *Courier* did not seek to explain, let alone justify, such behavior on the part of Irish strikers, though the paper frequently found ways to flatter the Irish. It was noticeably cold to the strikers during the briefly violent Towpath Rebellion, and it branded as "outrages" incidents of violence against strikebreakers during another, smaller-scale strike of canal laborers in March, 1850. The usually Democratic and always pro-craft union *Republic* often defended the tactics of formally organized workers, but found it difficult to justify the actions of shifting bands of unskilled, outdoor immigrant workers, whose protests seemed, as in 1858, to be a menace to public order. Not surprisingly, the conservative, nativist papers, the *Express* and *Commercial Advertiser*, were even harsher in their judgments. Yet in 1858 they had in common with the *Republic* the belief that the unemployed should either accept jobs at any wage, even below subsistence, or migrate to rural areas in search of farm work. All three papers denounced the notion that the municipality should use tax dollars to relieve the unemployed.[61]

Though mass violence took place periodically in various social contexts, only once during the period did the Americans who controlled the city government feel fearful enough to call out the militia—during the Towpath Rebellion. This official response was arguably not necessary, for though there was some bloodshed, no serious injuries or destruction of property occurred. By the depression spring of 1858, local officials were not prepared to wait until even a mild blow was struck before mobilizing the police power to deal with the Irish unemployed. With the *Sentinel* warning that violence would be inevitable if suffering were not immediately relieved in dockside neighborhoods, and with the Work or Bread demonstrations growing in size (to over 600 men) daily, Democratic Mayor Timothy Lockwood deputized seventy special constables to guard municipal offices and to protect him when he was called upon by the leaders of the demonstrations.[62] (The only local American Democratic officeholder of any stature who consistently showed sympathy for strikers, whatever their background, was frequent candidate, sometime officeholder, Isaac Vanderpoel. With his law partners, he defended, free of charge, German strikers brought to court in 1850 on allegations of assault and trespassing while on the picket line.)[63]

The Irish combated their isolation by marshalling the resources of their own communities. Ordinary folk helped on the picket line. For example, during the Towpath Rebellion large numbers of Buffalo Irish, and some Germans and Americans, came out to supplement the strikers. Armed with pitchforks and, it was said, an old rifle or two, they lined up for a mile along the towpath to help intimidate both the strikebreakers and contractors. Higher-status Irish took the lead in organizing a rally in support of the towpath strikers in the heart of the central business district.[64] Some of the vast resources of the Catholic church were utilized, too, though not in obtrusive ways. Whatever their private thoughts, Timon and his priests did not speak out publicly on the occasion of strikes and worker protests. But the diocesan *Sentinel*, which received both guidance and some degree of subsidy from the bishop, was outspoken in its sympathy for the poor and support for the Work or Bread demonstrations. Furthermore, under its editor Michael Hagan, in 1858 the *Sentinel* put forward practical proposals urging Mayor Lockwood and his council to seek out state and federal money to begin needed public works projects that would put the unemployed to work.[65]

That Hagan himself was at that moment a member of the city council highlights another aspect of ethnic community involvement—the role of politicians in Irish workers' struggles. Both officeholders and party operatives lent assistance, ranging from moral support to active intervention. These acts of solidarity were the result of personal relations between the working-class majority and the small strata of higher-status Irish. Moreover, while Irish politicians could not determine the terms of employment on public works projects, they did frequently use political influence to find such work for their countrymen. They were well aware of the conditions general laborers faced in taking such work. They were prominent among the higher-status Irish organizing the 1849 rally in support of the towpath strikers.[66]

The politicians' support, however, went beyond reactive concern to proactive organization of the Irish working class under the banner of the proletarian-oriented, social democratic variant of Irish ethnic ideology. In September, 1857, two events propelled Irish politicians into an active role. The first was the recent panic and the prospect of a winter of suffering for the Irish unemployed. The second was conflict in the local Democratic party that pitted the Irish against the reigning American wing in a quarrel over nominations and patronage. The two events merged in the minds of Irish ethnic leadership, because together they constituted a threat to the group's tenuous material bases. Irish politicians responded with the inventiveness for which they became famous. Under the leadership of Buffalo's one Irish municipal court judge, John Murray, its two Irish aldermen (Hagan and Thomas Merrigan) and perhaps a dozen shopkeepers, saloonkeepers, and lawyers, who were the principal Irish ward politicians, a Mutual Protection and Equal Rights Association was formed. Affiliated with it, and formed at the same time, were neighborhood workingmen's clubs in the First and Eighth wards, which were greeted with considerable popular enthusiasm. The political purposes of the association and the clubs combined traditional Democratic ideas (antimonopoly and distrust of banks) with calls for greater efforts to naturalize Irish immigrants, in the hope of increasing Irish voting and bolstering the group's position in the local Democratic party.[67]

The rapidly deteriorating economic situation overtook the new association's broad, reformist goals and gradualist outlook, and heightened anger with the American wing of the Democracy, which, though in control of the municipality, was resistant to using the city's resources to aid the poor. During the winter of 1857–58 many of the Irish poor lived off diocesan and parish charities or at the hated poorhouse, as their usual hand-to-mouth existence collapsed. The spring brought no relief, and in fact large numbers of once steadily employed laborers now found their savings were exhausted. The efforts of employers and the press to get these laborers to work at less than subsistence wages failed. It was not only the men's conception of their worth that accounts for this, but also community pressure. Those who did consent to work at reduced wage rates of about seventy-five cents a day were abused in the streets by other Irish working people.[68] The newly installed city administration of Mayor Lockwood offered little more than the customary depression era prescription of retrenchment, fiscal reform, and lower taxes, and the press denounced proposals for direct relief. All segments of elite opinion, however, were willing to heed the *Sentinel*'s call to seek out state and federal funds for local projects. At Councilman Hagan's urging, the council passed a resolution urging Congress and the legislature to begin various already mandated projects and the semipublic, locally based Turnpike Company to finish a bridge.[69]

When in June, 1858, the very largely Irish Work or Bread demonstrations erupted, with almost a thousand participants, they were led by men who were identified as lesser Democratic ward heelers, considerably more obscure than Merrigan, Murray, and Hagan.[70] While it is impossible to prove that there was any overlap in the constituency and ward leadership of the demonstrations and the previous fall's neighborhood workingmen's clubs, the principal energies of the grass roots protests came from the same dockside, Irish proletarian neighborhoods that had greeted the politician's efforts with enthusiasm. As divisions among Democrats were healed and prosperity returned, these energies declined.

Thus far the differences between Irish and American class politics have been emphasized, but there were similarities between the two in both ideology and workers' self-conception. The views expressed on the Irish side have to be derived from the statements of the politicians who created the Irish political and labor association in 1857, and thus represent articulations of the group's elite. But it is doubtful they could have organized ordinary folk with notions vastly outside their frames of reference, so the association's principles are hardly irrelevant. Unlike the American, the Irish worker could not place any emphasis on the moral stature and aesthetic value of his craft. But he did respond to those who appealed to his sense of the dignity and worth of his labor and to his longings for personal and family improvement. The organizing resolutions of the Eighth Ward Workingman's Club espoused the producer ethic, proclaiming workers to be "the bone and sinews of community." Since both social progress and welfare depended on them, said the resolutions, society must carefully protect them against exploitation. The American equal rights tradition and belief in the duty of citizens to struggle for justice were also accessible to the Irish laborer, even though he was a newcomer. Thus, the Eighth Ward resolutions stated, "The remedy for abuses is in the hand of working men; they do the work, pay the taxes and deposit votes; and it is their duty to establish Equal Rights as laid down by the Constitution of this Country." Finally, the clubs in both Irish wards articulated the belief that "mental improvement" was a means, along with class organization and political activism, "to elevate, merit, and dignify labor." To this end, too, the bylaws of the First Ward club barred drunkards and abusive or profane language from its meetings.[71] The Irish laborer may well have had more in common in terms of personal values and self-conception with the American skilled worker than perhaps either was aware. But so much divided them, including the nativist bigotry of many Americans, it was difficult for either group of workers to discover this.

The Germans

During the Towpath Rebellion, Lieutenant Solomon Scheu, a German officer commanding militia soldiers guarding strikebreakers, was arrested for expressing sympathy for the Irish strikers. Meanwhile, alone among the city's major dailies, the *Weltbürger* criticized the use of the militia to protect private contractors, and it denounced inadequate wage rates and storepay, which had brought on the strike.[72] These incidents suggest one of the central characteristics of German class politics—a class consciousness broad enough to lay foundations of solidarity even with a people, the Irish, with whom Germans had little daily contact, and toward whom not a few Germans had cultural prejudice. In this broadness of vision and political sophistication, both best expressed in internationalism,[73] the Germans came closest to possessing the beliefs often attributed to a proletariat that conceives of itself as possessed of unique interests and acts upon this self-understanding. Yet this internationalism lay almost entirely on the level of ideology and rhetoric. In actuality, the active, multitendencied German labor movement that emerged at Buffalo in the late 1840s and early 1850s was just as self-enclosed as its American and Irish counterparts.

The reason for this tension lay in attitudes rooted in Old World experiences of exploitation and oppression and in the German's distinctive ethnic culture. So intimately tied to the comfortable, sustaining trappings of Old World culture were Buffalo's German workers and their more bourgeois, coethnic, radical allies, that their ideological internationalism was inevitably deflected by the distinctive ways in which they organized themselves, the symbols inspiring and guiding their actions, and the habits and behaviors of daily life outside work.

The predisposition of German workers to class consciousness and certain individual characteristics of that class consciousness had European roots. Unlike the Irish in their island homeland, where class oppression and exploitation were colonial in nature and where capitalist modernization was severely retarded, Old World Germans had experienced some of the dislocations of a modernizing economy prior to immigration, and had found them poison to such revered aspects of traditional life as guilds and peasant family plots. The experience had left them with an acute sense of the ability of emergent capitalism to dispossess and to exploit, and with an intense distrust of modernizing social elites, which they joined to their equally intense hatred of the precapitalist nobility that monopolized political power. This frame of mind contrasted with the Irish perception of injustice. The Irish saw injustice toward them in terms dictated by prior, colonial oppression, so that grievances became for them *national* grievances. When combined with Old World habits of solidarity, these perceptions led the Irish to their marked cross-class, intraethnic solidarity during strikes and demonstrations. A distinctly heterogeneous people with a history of class rather than national oppression, Germans lacked a common national framework for interpreting injustice. Hence, class was the salient ideological feature of their workers' movement. Appeals expressed in the language of class struggle were far more likely to unify German workers than appeals to nationality.

Though Germans were almost as likely to be skilled workers as Americans, the intense German consciousness of class also contrasted markedly with the American worker's view of both his problems and his opportunities. The American valued craft for its own sake as well as because it was a means to material improvement. He continued to believe that American society was open to men of humble beginnings who possessed talent and ambition, and he continued to have pride in the possession of political rights in a state which he regarded not as his enemy, but his by birthright and law. The German peasant and tradesman, in contrast, had experienced a severe narrowing of material options in Europe, and in the larger, most significant spheres of political action, powerlessness and, in 1848, defeat. Such experiences created a brooding sense of social injustice and a sharp eye for unfairness that, in turn, produced an acute sensitivity to the ways capitalism compromised American democracy. German workers' skepticism about the American political system sharply contrasted with the political faith of American workers.

The resulting differences in ideology between German and American workers became evident on several levels. Like Americans, Germans espoused a producer theory of value. That workers were the source of all wealth, the *Weltbürger* said, is "something so clear, no declaration is needed to understand it."[74] But in contrast to Americans, they did not hold to the belief that labor was necessarily valuable in itself, and they expressed none of the sentimental views of work that American worker-spokesmen did on public occasions. For Germans, culture alone was the key to self-cultivation, and work was an instrument toward material improvement and security, especially through property acquisition. Germans expressed little confidence that the American system was geared to making such improvement easily accessible to the average worker. As early as 1839, Germans complained that the country was run by its own aristocracy, which, though not hereditary, was no less greedy than its European counterparts. Frustrated in their efforts to raise the price of firewood, a spokesman for the all-German Sawyers Association in that year castigated those he called American "*lumpen*" barons"—building contractors—and other employers and crooked bankers. These Americans, he said, were living by currency and wage manipulations that cheated workers like the sawyers out of their just rewards.[75] The native aristocracy was often compared to the hated German nobility, a compelling analytical device to spur German workers on to militant stands against employers. "Have you freed yourselves from Germany," said a striking German iron molder in 1860 criticizing his coethnics for allowing themselves to be used as strikebreakers, ". . . in order to trade one system of tyranny and oppression for another?"[76] The charges against the American *lumpen* aristocracy, all made in characteristically bitter, direct language, were of unrelenting greed and subversion of the spirit of the Constitution and the laws. Out of this antimonopoly creed came an understanding of the tenuousness of bourgeois liberties, a constant theme in rhetoric of German defenders of the working classes. In 1849 the *Weltbürger* found, in the use of the militia to protect private contractors, evidence that American freedom and equality before the law "are truly in many instances an empty shell."[77] Letting his punctuation speak for him, the German molder previously quoted made the same point in speaking of America as "this free (?) land."[78]

This view of America was softened in several ways that made its implications for the German worker's future in his new home somewhat less bleak. Though pessimism about America existed in immigrant consciousness long before the arrival of the radicalized artisans and intellectuals of 1848, it was they, more than the earlier arrivals, who were particularly adamant and persistent in a gloomy view of the new homeland. So intensely critical was the rhetoric emanating from the pens of many European radicals and '48er intellectuals, that it pushed, as we have seen, the more established Grays toward both a thoughtful, though hardly gushing, defense of America's treatment of workers and more generally an espousal of American exceptionalism. The ideological consequences for the working classes were important. First, though recognizing the limits of bourgeois liberties, and hence skeptical of the more exaggerated claims about the superiority of American institutions, Grays came to see these liberties as tools for creating the conditions of class justice. Not only did they empower the workingman, said the *Weltbürger* in 1850, but they provided "education for the spirit and heart," which produced a democratic cultural climate for politics and opened Americans to the possibilities of freedom and justice for workers. Brunck did not underestimate the power of the *lumpen* barons. But he contended that in sharp contrast to Europe with its idle nobility, the United States had a very large percentage of its people who were members of the productive classes. They had the numbers as well as the legal and political tools to wage the battle for justice. The Grays also argued that American prosperity made it possible for the poor and working classes "not to be at peace with their fate"—i.e., not reconciled to poverty. While acknowledging the extent and political significance of inequalities of wealth and income, Brunck still believed the country so rich that "every worthy individual here can work his way out of poverty." "Character, perseverance, and diligence," said the *Weltbürger*, had transformed many Germans from penniless greenhorns to secure homeowners. "One sees here new streets, which in the last four or five years have filled up with homes whose owners are workers in the strongest, strictest sense of the word."[79]

While Brunck sounds here to be parroting the conventional American mobility ideology, the resemblance is more apparent than real. The *Weltbürger* never suggested that individual mobility was anything more than a means to individual security. It was not a solution to social injustice, which required instead a class response using the appropriate political mechanisms. "There are constitutional remedies here which the working classes can effectively use," the paper said. "The people govern themselves here and if they bring together their power, all ... wrongs collapse like a house of cards."[80]

This recognition of the need for the unity of labor was shared by many who claimed to speak for the German working class, and united opinion leaders among Grays and Greens alike, whatever their views of the character of American society. "Only through combination," said that angry molder in 1860, "can workers extricate themselves from the situation of moral and physical bondage under which unfortunately the producing classes of the country remain." "Unity makes strength," said a German shoemaker later that year when applauding the rise of several new unions, "and it is the only way the worker can help himself to obtain a sustaining wage." The *Weltbürger* in 1850 advocated comprehensive, universal organization, beginning with each trade in each locality and working outward to a national confederation of all producers.[81]

Such comprehensive organization eluded the working classes, but Germans went further than anyone else in making organization a principle of action. In 1849 they organized the German-American Workingmen's Union (GAWU) to bind together all the German trade unions, thus allowing them to break out of the narrow confines of craft. Though there is no indication that American unions were asked to affiliate with the GAWU, American workers and their organizations were enthusiastically invited to participate in rallies and lobbying efforts, especially those seeking remedies to the order system.[82] Such internationalism was seen, too, in the public expressions of sympathy for the towpath strikers.[83] For some Germans, the quest for solidarity even crossed gender lines. No other male workers extended their organizations to women workers as did German tailors in 1860. They pragmatically, but no less warmly, invited the German seamstresses, whose presence in the trade was growing as employers sought low-wage labor, to join them.[84]

This abiding interest in solidarity, however, should not lure us into thinking that German workers possessed the heroic proletarian consciousness that Marx projected. As the German passion for property-owning suggests, German workers were as interested in getting a stake in society as they were in changing it. Their radicalism was descended from the Old World mentality both of the sansculottes of 1789 and of the plebeian radicals of the first decades of the early nineteenth century, and not a prefiguring of Marxian class consciousness. It was a radicalism that voiced the resentments not only of artisans, craftsmen, and more affluent peasants, but also of small shopkeepers, petty traders, and lower white-collar workers against anything that rendered their small property holdings and precarious social position less secure. In Buffalo this property orientation expressed itself politically in German cottage owners' mobilizations against the growing tax burden resulting from costly infrastructure schemes that seemed either to be unneeded or to benefit only commercial interests. In their refusal to challenge the premodern, inegalitarian organization of the traditional trades, German workers also showed reluctance to part company with the plebeian mentality from which their class ideology sprang. The legal basis, social functions, and organic connections to the life of the German *Heimat* of the craftsmen's guilds and journeymen's brotherhoods, could not be reconstituted in America. But some trappings, doubtless endowed with many traditional meanings, could, for apprenticeship was deeply entrenched on the East Side. No German immigrant workers' organization attacked the prerogatives of the city's masters. If there were calls for reform of the system of traditional training, they never entered public discussion. While there were injustices in that system, it nonetheless was viewed as essential to the eventual independence of skilled tradesmen. Moreover, through regulation of admission to the crafts, it offered some security against low wages and unemployment.[85]

The German workers' movement established three distinct presences in the late 1840s and early 1850s: trade unionism, political reformism, and communism. In both tactics and ideas, the three overlapped at times, and were able to provide mutual reinforcement. It was in the interest of the various trade unions to unite to seek political reforms that aided workers. Also, though for different reasons, both Weitling's Communist movement and the more conservative trade unions saw cooperative workplaces as beneficial to workers. Moreover, all three types of activity were deeply immersed in German ethnic culture, which functioned to anchor them in the neighborhoods of the East Side, while simultaneously differentiating them sharply from the various non-German workers' movements.[86]

German trade unionism was at least as old in Buffalo as the 1839 Sawyers Association. But prior to 1849–50 German unions had little more than an episodic existence. It remained for the new, politicized immigrants to create organizations with greater staying power, if little more success against employers. German trade unionism developed in crafts in which the independence of local skilled workers was being undermined by the spread of factory production. Thus, it arose almost exclusively among those producing for markets beyond the East Side, where much production was for local consumption, and it pitted German workers against non-German employers. The German unions were generally interested in bread-and-butter questions, not in long-term social transformation, and they were defensive in their actions, which sought to ward off employer impositions.[87]

The pattern of union organization varied only slightly among tailors (1849), cabinetmakers (1850), and shoemakers (1850), but diverged sharply in the case of the iron molders (1860). (On the other hand, the butchers' union, founded in 1858, functioned more as a political lobby, reflecting the extent to which, in their dual capacity as workers and petty entrepreneurs, most butchers were preoccupied with the problem of city licensing laws.)[88] In the cases of the tailors, cabinetmakers, and shoemakers, among whom Germans were approximately 68, 66, and 77 percent of the trade in 1855, a combination of capitalist entrepreneurship and technological change was causing the decline of their standard of living and beginning to undermine traditional artisanal independence. By 1850 cabinetmaking as traditionally practiced was in decline because the stocking lathe was mechanizing woodturning. Factory-made, ready-to-wear clothing was undercutting the position of tailors, which would continue to decline with the introduction of the sewing machine. Cutters, sewers, and finishers were being brought together into both shoe factories and simple artisan shops by capitalists with the money or credit to buy large quantities of leather and invest in sewing machines. The precipitant for union organization in each trade was low wages and/or the imposition of storepay, which not only attacked workers' living standards, but probably, too, crystallized for them the precise measure of their dependent status as wage earners.[89]

But in only one case, the journeymen tailors, did a confrontation with employers follow on the heels of union organization. In June, 1850, William Carland claimed that because of debts he lacked the specie to pay his overwhelmingly German tailors at Gothic Hall in cash, and sought to impose storepay. The recently unionized tailors (about two hundred men) struck. To underline their grievances, they staged a characteristically German procession, which borrowed the symbols and behavior of such traditional Old World public protests as the *charivari*, and was accompanied by a band. At the climax of their procession, an effigy of Carland was pilloried and then, after a mock trial, hung—protest behavior in which no other local workers but Germans ever engaged. They were soon joined by other German union tailors, who were also on strike against some large employers for better wages or payment in specie. The latter were willing to help picket Gothic Hall because, as the city's largest clothing factory, it was a convenient symbol of the derangements in the trade, and it helped set wage standards. Confident that he could always fall back on the desperation for work of the needy immigrant Germans he usually employed, Carland moved to break the strike. He refused to negotiate, and took the strike leaders to court where he won sizeable damages from them on charges of trespass and intimidation. Carland's tailors drifted back to work. The concurrent tailors' strikes soon ended in failure, too. Their cause lost, the tailors responded by attempting to leave the wage system. They formed a cooperative workshop. Eighty or ninety men were at work in this shop when it opened in the fall of 1850.[90] German cabinetmakers and shoemakers also formed unions in 1850, and they had the same grievances—inadequate wages and storepay—that had led to the tailors' protests. Perhaps fearing the same consequences that befell the tailors, they did not strike, and went immediately about creating cooperatives.[91]

But the cooperative workplace did not prove a challenge to capitalism. The cooperatives could not offer the low prices and wide selection found in stores tied to capitalist producers. Furthermore, many tradesmen were willing to give no more than moral support to these ventures. They feared that leaving the wage system, with all its indignities, involved too much risk. Thus, in contrast to the significant number at the tailors' cooperative, only ten cabinetmakers showed up for work during their cooperative's first weeks. The shoemakers' and cabinetmakers' cooperatives collapsed within a few years, while the tailors' limped along for seven years and had to undergo several reorganizations, only to fold for want of customers and workers on the eve of the depression.[92] Simultaneously the trade unions themselves went into decline, so that by 1855 only the tailors could boast of a sizeable membership.[93] Meanwhile, employers like Carland grew stronger and more in command of their labor during the prosperous period in the 1850s. In 1854 Carland hired 300 additional tailors in a major expansion of his operations. He and the lesser clothing manufacturers were able to keep wages down to the extent that in 1860 they were one to two dollars a week less than elsewhere in the nation at a time of escalating prices for basic necessities.[94] But for these reasons, German unionism would once again develop. After inconclusive strikes in 1860, which exacted wage gains in some shops but not in others, the tailors' union went on an organizing drive to prepare for the next round of confrontations, and added 100 tailors and seamstresses to its rolls. German shoemakers also reorganized, while bricklayers and masons organized for the first time, called a strike for two dollars a day and won concessions from the large majority of employers.[95]

The German iron molders' situation was different. The rise of their union in 1860 was stimulated not by wage issues, though wages were depressed, but by a work-process question, the use of helpers, which reflected industrialization of that sector of the trade in which most Germans worked. Some 60 percent of the city's molders, Germans were concentrated in the largest iron shops, such as the Jewett and Root Stove Works and the Braley and Pitts Agricultural Works. In shops like these, work was divided among semiindependent crews composed of craftsmen, semiskilled assistants, and boy helpers. The crews were responsible for pouring metal into precut molds and then, as the metal hardened, crafting finished objects, such as stoves. Molders hired their own helpers, the presence of whom made for speedier production in an industry where wages were pegged to piece-rates.[96]

The question of helpers posed the same sort of problem for German molders as the degeneration of apprenticeship did for American craftsmen. Molders feared that the increasing number of helpers as the industry expanded threatened to flood the market with young men with sufficient training as molders to depress the wage scale. Efforts of molders elsewhere in the nation in 1859 and 1860 to win strikes on this issue were defeated, because unemployed molders were recruited from other localities to break strikes. It was for this reason that the national Journeymen Iron Molders Union had sent its Philadelphia-based president, Isaac J. O'Neall, to Buffalo and other cities in April, 1860, to organize molders into one strong, national union. Local Germans heeded his calls for craft solidarity. His appearance was the precipitant for the establishment, out of a small local founded three months before, of a greatly enlarged molders' organization, which immediately took up the issue of helpers.[97]

Local factory owners were opposed to accepting union work rules on helpers, which they claimed would curb productivity. Moreover, because it was the molders who hired helpers, employers argued that the problem was the molders' and not their own. The pro-labor *Weltbürger* not only accepted this argument, but accused the molders of seeking to block a route into the trade that many of them had once trod.[98] After some months of heated discussion with several large employers, in 1860 the molders struck. But there was division in their own ranks, as the minority of nonunion American and other non-German molders continued to work. Moreover, unemployment was still high, so strikebreakers were easily recruited, especially among Germans, some of whom had been out of work for two years. Union molders themselves could not afford to stay out of work long, and the union had no strike funds to assist them. From one perspective, the entire situation symbolized the decline of patriarchal craft organization Germans had long valued. But the strikers knew of no other mental framework from which to articulate their protest against the growing presence of scabs from their neighborhoods at the factory gates each morning than the traditions of their own craft-based work culture. Writing in the *Weltbürger*, a striker begged German fathers to keep their sons from scabbing: "In God's name do not let your sons interfere with the means by which German family men are fighting for their livelihood." But this appeal, and others like it, failed, and the strike was lost.[99]

The GAWU was at its inception both an extension of the German tailors, furniture makers, and shoemakers trade unions, and a recognition that by themselves the unions were inadequate to serve the interests that workers shared across craft, and ultimately even ethnic, lines. While the GAWU supported the unions and raised money to get their cooperatives going, its chief purpose was lobbying. Its German members were no doubt Democrats, but the association itself was nonpartisan. It polled local candidates on such questions as the order system before making endorsements. Its first priority was the end of the municipality's use of storepay, and to this end it exerted pressure on council candidates. It sought, too, more security for small property. It protested street, sidewalk, and other improvement projects on the East Side that were deemed unnecessary, and it lobbied alongside Americans for legislation to secure homes against repossession by creditors. Candidates responded seriously to the GAWU's queries, and most area legislators of both parties were able to back some aspects of its legislative program. At its 1851 first anniversary celebration, which was attended by the council, and most local officeholders, Mayor H. K. Smith gave the GAWU credit for being "the driving impulse" for new state laws: one protecting homes against forced sale for debt, and another strengthening workers' protection against public contractors who failed to pay wages.[100]

Another set of GAWU goals involved what officers called "mental and moral improvement." From the start, it had a singing society and an amateur drama group. With the decline in membership in the three unions that had established it, the GAWU's political work declined and its cultural activities increased. After a September, 1851, reorganization necessitated by declining dues, cultural efforts became dominant. As a result, the organization cut itself off from opportunities to ally with American workers, and became more deeply embedded in the ethnic group. After 1853, the GAWU disappears from the sources. Through mergers, however, its singing society and drama group were integrated into the larger and more prestigious *Liederkranzen* and the semiprofessional Thalia Theater Company.[101] In 1853, the GAWU's remaining members—twenty-one young artisans, shopkeepers, clerks, and grocers—founded the city's first *Turnverein*, which appears to have been the final legacy of the GAWU.[102]

The German trade unions, the GAWU, and the Turners looked no further than the reform of capitalism through increased worker bargaining power, through lobbying, political pressure, and unionization. In contrast, Wilhelm Weitling's Workingmen's League was dedicated to the creation of a new, communistic, order. Yet Weitling's movement also accommodated the desire of workers for improvement in their present circumstances. Moreover, it, too, was deeply immersed in German ethnic culture. As a consequence, and because Weitling's movement gave expression to many of the same class anxieties, resentments, and aspirations as the German trade unions and the GAWU, many individuals were involved in all three at once.

Because of the activities of men like Dr. Ciolina, socialism had been under public discussion for at least a year when the New York–based Workingmen's League made its local debut in the spring of 1850.[103] What the exiled revolutionary Weitling brought to the strivings of the few German socialists was an organization, complete with a well-edited journal (*Die Republik der Arbeiter*), a stirring message of millenialist expectancy, a passion for justice and a comprehensive program of both short-term, practical and long-term, revolutionary goals. The program, which combined the goal of socialism with some American reform ideas about banks and tariffs, called for establishing cooperative stores, warehouses, and workshops, as well as savings banks and farms. These were intended not only to create immediate alternatives to the oppressive wage system, but to plant the seeds of communism within capitalist society. Though anticlerical, it courted religious believers by rejecting atheism. Its membership was open to small shopkeepers, clerks, and professionals, excluding only capitalists. Though it saw strikes as defensive actions, dissipating the energies of the working class, it recognized them as necessary, legitimate, if short-term, responses to injustice. *Die Republik der Arbeiter* paid a nod to issues in American politics by opposing slavery, racism, Sabbatarianism, and temperance, while calling for land reform and women's rights. But these concerns were not a prominent part of the league's project. The league was German in its cultural work, sponsoring with variable energy singing, drama, and children's and women's *Vereine*, whose activities all forwarded the messages of German radical culture.[104]

This eclectic approach and Weitling's own powerful German rhetoric appealed to recently immigrated, socially insecure men in traditional trades then in the throes of the early stages of industrialization. These were men who possessed an anticapitalist, but distinctly preindustrial, outlook that harked back to the order of German towns and villages. By the early 1850s they were reaching America in significant numbers. The league took Buffalo and other cities by storm. The membership of the GAWU voted to accept Weitling's principles in their entirety. By November, 1850, the league could claim some 606 members from the GAWU (260), the tailors' union (108), the cabinetmakers' union (188), and the shoemakers' union (50). There were also an unspecified number of smiths and wheelwrights. Buffalo sent a delegation of several hundred men to the league's first convention in distant New York City that fall, and by January, 1851, there were 1,155 Buffalo Germans subscribing to Weitling's journal. The league's first local head was Conrad Jüngerich, the tailors' union militant who was one of the leaders of the strikes against Carland and other garment producers. Too late organized in Buffalo to be active in the tailors' strikes, the league nonetheless joined the GAWU in backing the creation of craft union cooperatives in that and in other trades.[105]

That Weitling, unlike Karl Marx, had little notion of precisely how his new society was to be realized through the processes of history was only one reason for the league's failure in Buffalo and elsewhere after 1851. The weaknesses of Weitling's ideology and his bitter rhetoric, which courted violence and denounced established German ethnic leadership, led, as we have noted, to harsh criticism from local social democrats, reformers, and religious conservatives. At the same time the league suffered a devastating defeat in New York City, as the Proletarian League, which professed the scientific socialism of Marx, increasingly made inroads into its membership. It was weakened from within by poor management and Weitling's own highly authoritarian style of leadership. It suffered locally, too, from the decline of the GAWU and the German trade unions. By 1854 it was defunct in Buffalo, as elsewhere.[106]

For all of these many failures, German workers had nonetheless developed organizational skills and energies, ideological and rhetorical sophistication, and aptitude for rooting a New World politics in the fertile soil of their own ethnic culture that would soon be of use to many of them in the battles against nativism and slavery. Furthermore, these same abilities and habits of solidarity would inform the vastly expanded local German trade union movement and the internationalist, but heavily German, socialist movement of the late nineteenth century.[107]

Multiethnic Working-Class Politics

Multiethnic working-class activities took three forms: political efforts, strikes and union organization, and the creation of cooperative institutions, principally stores. The last was the weakest of the three, because it involved marshalling resources and capital workers lacked. Political work was frustrated by the nature of the party system and the partisan habits of the working class itself. Workers firmly attached themselves to different parties. Moreover, the two major parties needed to create cross-class coalitions to win elections, so it was difficult to persuade them to take up issues, such as the order system, that would alienate employers. Workerist third parties could not break the hold of workers' established loyalties. But struggles at the point of production enjoyed considerably more success, though the number of cases is limited.

The first stirrings of multiethnic activity were hindered by the scarcity of work during the long depression of the late 1830s and early 1840s. A meeting late in 1841 attended by Irish, German, and American workers passed resolutions against the depressed wage scale and a long list of abuses, especially storepay. But alongside such unified efforts were nativist actions by the then dominant American sector of the labor force to suppress immigrant competition. In early 1844 when the recovery was beginning to gather force, American gangs attacked Germans who had come to Black Rock to seek work. Two months later, American draymen unsuccessfully lobbied the Common Council in an effort to block the growth at the docks of the number of immigrant Irish carters.[108] With prosperity came less anxiety about the scarcity of work and more concern over inflation and such abuses as storepay, which were shared burdens and lent themselves to efforts to forge a common front. Moreover, the German working-class movement, with its occasional internationalism, had just begun to take form, and it lent energy to multiethnic labor activism. Thus, during the years 1847 and 1850, under the separate but unifying efforts of Germans and Americans, the outlines of a multiethnic class tendency in electoral and pressure group politics began to take shape.

The initial multiethnic thrust against the order system was set in motion by an association of American journeymen cordwainers, which sponsored a large rally in May 1847. This rally turned out to be the first in a series that summer of increasingly well-attended, multiethnic gatherings at which the order system was denounced and resolutions passed making future voting decisions dependent on the willingness of candidates to work against storepay. After this American effort declined, in 1850 it was the GAWU, in the midst of that year's demonstrations and strikes by German trade unions against storepay, that organized two widely attended rallies against the same abuse. Here, too, it was resolved to create a central organization of workers of all groups to exert moral, political, and economic pressure against orders.[109]

Just as significant as the goals of these rallies was their organization, a subtle blending of internationalism and broad, unifying Americanism in sharp contrast to the ways the three ethnic class tendencies organized themselves. Both sets of rallies were held not, as was usual in ethnic class protest, in neighborhood halls or taverns, but rather in central locations, such as the Liberty Pole or the Court House Park. These were sites endowed with an inspiring American symbolism that allowed the proceedings to be linked with the hopes men placed in popular republican traditions and institutions of government. Moreover, while both sets of rallies used English as the language of the day, the organizers took pains to have extensive remarks made in German by well-known local men. At an 1847 rally, Dr. Brunck addressed the entire rally in English and then spoke to German workers in their own tongue, while in 1850, Conrad Jüngerich and Andreas Kraffert, leaders of the striking German tailors, addressed Germans. Both sets of rallies prominently featured men from the three large ethnic groups on the podium as officers and members of resolutions committees. Patrick Smith, the Irish councilman, was president of rallies in both years. The largest of the two 1850 rallies went furthest in providing balance among officials and symbolically paying respect to ethnic participation, while maintaining an umbrella of Americanism. It had two vice presidents and two secretaries—in each case, an American and a German—to ensure absolute fairness in language matters. The German vice president and secretary worked together to translate the resolutions into their language, after which the latter read them to the assembled German workers.[110] The effect of such pains must certainly have been greater attendance. There seems no other way in a city with so large a German population for rallies to have been sizeable enough to be called "one of the largest public meetings ever convened in our city" (1847), or to have had as many as 800 workers in attendance (1850).[111]

But the order system proved intractable. Given the hold of ethnic culture and identity on workers and the functional segmentation of the work force, workers soon returned to the familiar ethnic organization of class politics. The journeymen cordwainers decided to organize a local club of the American Labor Union, an ephemeral, national American organization that supported cash wages. The cordwainers and other American tradesmen moved shortly thereafter to create a local Mechanics and Laboring Men's party, which unsuccessfully ran candidates for the city's two state assembly seats and, the following spring, for mayor, before finding its way into the Free Soil party. In the process of politicization, the goal of ending the order system was lost. By the 1849 mayoral election, not a word about this enduring injustice remained in the new party's platform, which dealt instead with public lands, public schools, and mechanics' lien laws. Moreover, though the new local and national parties briefly attracted the support of such prominent ethnic leaders as the Alsatian dry-goods merchant Joseph Haberstro and the Irish ward politician Patrick Coffee, the average Democratic Irish and German workingman refused to change parties.¹¹² In a similar series of developments, after failing in their efforts to keep up the momentum of the multiethnic anti-storepay campaign, the leaders of the GAWU found their way back to ethnic class protest (trade unionism and cooperative workshops) and to ethnic cultural activities.¹¹³ For the remainder of the decade, therefore, little in the way of citywide, multiethnic organization of the working classes took place. Not until 1859, when there was a rapid rise in prices, was there another such activity: an unsuccessful effort was made by Americans to organize a multiethnic cooperative store.

It may be tempting to attribute the decline of multiethnic mobilizations in the 1850s to tensions prompted by American nativism. Such a view, however, runs headlong into the remarkable degree of interethnic class solidarity achieved in strikes and activities in various individual trades during the decade. To be sure, the number of trades was not large. But the instances are all the more noteworthy because the most successful saw the unification of Irish Catholics and American Protestants, the two people between whom nativism drove the sharpest wedge.

Tracings of multiethnic organization may be found in a number of trades, but the efforts were brief and episodic. In various combinations and proportions, Irish, German, Anglo-Canadian, and American painters (1850), plasterers (1853), bricklayers (1853), whitewashers and paperhangers (1861), and masons and bricklayers (1861) attempted to organize trade unions. Most efforts failed quickly. These trades achieved no permanent organization until after the Civil War.¹¹⁴

The ship carpenters and lake sailors, however, had quite different experiences. (Lake sailors considered themselves, in contrast to steamboaters, skilled workers, because they depended on traditional technology for navigation and locomotion, and had to combine knowledge of sails, weather, and wind in their work.)¹¹⁵ During the 1850s, the solidarity of these workers was apparent in their strike behavior rather than in formal organization, for only the ship carpenters were unionized, and they not until 1860. In bitterly contested strikes in 1855 and 1860, the sailors demonstrated impressive solidarity. They routinely turned out 300 to 400 striking sailors (a large percentage of the sailors likely to be in the port at any given time during the navigation season) for rallies, demonstrations, and processions.¹¹⁶ Both with and without ship caulkers, and on two occasions in tandem with the sailors, ship carpenters staged disciplined strikes, and relative to the rest of Buffalo labor, struck quite frequently (1855, 1858, 1860, and in both February and March of 1861). They showed an intense solidarity, and maintained a mutualistic ethic. Like the sailors, there was little wavering in their ranks during strikes, but they were also able to surmount a challenge that the sailors never faced—deliberate efforts to divide them. In March, 1861, ship carpenters at a large dry dock succeeded in wresting a wage increase, but only with a last-minute proviso that the higher wage would be paid to more efficient workers. The balance of the work force were immediately fired. Resolving to stick by their fired workmates, and believing that their own workload would be increased, the remaining carpenters refused to return to work and exacted the rehiring of the others.[117] In the case of both trades, solidarity was the key to the success they had in achieving strike goals, which were invariably either higher wages or an end to, or reduction in the percentage of, storepay. The sailors were also helped by acute shortages of mariners at the port in the early 1860s.[118] Perhaps above all else, both occupations were essential to the health of the dock trade, a fact sailors and ship carpenters chose to highlight at times by striking within a few days of the opening of navigation.

In accounting for the solidarity of these workers, one finds a singular blending of cultural and social homogeneity and ethnic diversity. Great Lakes sailors typically were of two types: the majority were nonresident workers, who came from ocean to inland ports for the Great Lakes shipping season and returned east in the winter to ship out again on the seas; and a smaller group of men were resident at Buffalo or other inland ports. Many of the latter had once been ocean sailors, but having taken on families, they found lake sailing a way of maintaining their occupations without having to suffer prolonged absences. While the 226 Buffalo household heads employed as sailors in 1855 came from a wide variety of national backgrounds, approximately 80 percent were English-speaking (Americans, British, Canadians, and Irish Catholics), with only a small minority of Germans, French Canadians, and Scandinavians. Possessing a *lingua franca* and a common pattern of past or present itinerancy, most sailors also shared a unique work culture embedded in a social isolation that intensified their relations with one another. While lake sailors did not experience the prolonged, forced communality of months or even years at sea, they did spend long periods of time at work on ship together, typically in groups of twelve under two mates, who were responsible to a skipper. Except for the minority with homes and families, in port they continued to live together, either aboard ship, or for more extended periods, in one of the dockside sailors' boardinghouses. They seem rarely to have ventured beyond the docks, where services existed to cater to their needs.[119]

Reinforcing these intense social ties was pride of craft, which they often demonstrated in their contempt for watermen requiring fewer skills and in their strike behavior. Pride of craft was rooted not only in skills, but in a distinctive array of symbols, popular ideology, and sense of craft history. During strikes, the sailors' dockside processions took place to the tune of their craft anthem, the "Sailor's Hornpipe." They carried banners with slogans rich in popular republican traditions and craft history: "Free Trade and Sailors' Rights" (a motto of the War of 1812), "Union and Combination in a Noble Cause," and "Our Rights We Want and Will Maintain." Their concept of popular rights stood the sailors squarely within the emergent multiethnic tradition by providing an umbrella of American beliefs broad enough to bring men of diverse backgrounds together.[120]

The sailors' solidarity was reinforced by the largely negative way the world beyond the docks regarded them. For residentially stable, bourgeois people, sailors were alternately objects of pity and philanthropy and fear and contempt. To the popular images of the aged or sickly mariner, without friend or family, and the drunken sailor idling away the Sabbath in a dockside saloon, evangelical Christians responded with charitable collections, dockside missions, and marine hospitals. One of the few causes bourgeois men embraced enthusiastically was sponsorship of excursions for disabled seamen. Striking sailors, on the other hand, strained this occasional paternalism. The sailors' extralocal origins and work and spatial isolation within the city created xenophobic prejudice, which was quickly verbalized when sailors with grievances disrupted commerce. "Hangers-on," "strangers," and "motley, villainous looking set of vagabonds" are but a few epithets the *Commercial Advertiser* and the *Courier* threw the way of striking sailors. No group of striking skilled workers so quickly prompted the mobilizing of special contingents of police. In both 1855 and 1860 the police were ordered to go to the docks at the smallest suspicions of rowdiness. In 1855 they were led by Democratic mayor Elijah Cook himself.[121]

The sailors were not wholly without friends. Their alliances were an informal extension of their own work culture and life style. Many proprietors of sailors' boardinghouses were formerly seamen themselves. In addition to providing cheap lodging, these men routinely gave sailors information about available work and extended them personal loans and credit on the costs of lodging and board. During strikes, they provided sailors with moral and material support. In 1855 the agreement of seventeen boardinghouse keepers to extend credit to sailors until they achieved their demand of a dollar a day gave mariners the edge they needed to force their employers into an agreement.[122]

The multiethnic solidarity achieved by ship carpenters had some similar roots, but there were important differences. The majority possessed a *lingua franca* in English: a sample of 110 drawn from the state census of 1855, which records 151 household heads employed in this trade, suggests that nine in ten were English-speaking (26 percent American; 30 percent British and Canadian, and 33 percent Irish Catholic). In contrast to sailors, ship carpenters were a widely respected part of the local working population. They came closest to being an aristocracy of labor in an industry which the *Commercial Advertiser* called "one of the glories of Buffalo."[123]

The ship carpenters' residential persistence, working-class respectability, and modest affluence, which gave them a singular social profile, were founded on a solid industrial base. Up to 1857 local shipyards expanded rapidly because of the increased demand for new vessels, growth of ships needing repair, and availability of vast stores of cheap upstate and Canadian timber. Work was plentiful and wages high. Moreover, although days were lost to bad weather in winter, this was also the season when a great deal of repair work was done. In 1853, *Hunt's Merchants' Magazine* reported that local ship carpenters "received good wages throughout the year." Certainly their wages were higher than those of the house and building carpenters, a fact that probably doomed the brief effort ship carpenters made to unite with the latter in the 1850s. In 1861, for example, when ship carpenters' wages were $1.75 a day, considerably below the $2.50 they had been making in the good times of 1856, the house and building carpenters received $1.50 a day and the furniture makers only $1.25. Canal boat builders, whose work required less skill because of the simplicity and uniformity of the design they employed, also made $1.25.[124]

Stability of residence and a decent living standard followed from these conditions. While 74 percent of the sample were foreign-born, 43 percent were naturalized and hence had been resident in the country at least five years. Fifty-five percent had been in Erie County itself more than five years. The immigrant ship carpenters were slightly more persistent than the foreign-born population generally. (Of the Irish and German household heads, 52.9 and 49.2 percent had been in the country more than five years.) In total, between Americans and naturalized foreigners, fully 69 percent of the ship carpenters were citizens.[125]

Most lived in a respectable domesticity in the prosperous 1850s. Most had recently begun families, as a *Commercial Advertiser* reporter said in 1857 in a highly complimentary essay. "Mike," an Irish Catholic carpenter whom the reporter took to be representative of the group, "has a bouncing wife, two years married, and two children." Seventy-six percent lived in the First and Eighth wards, beyond dockside slums, in ethnically mixed neighborhoods lined with frame cottages. Their homes were modest, averaging only $867 in value, and only a third owned the land on which they lived. The neighborhoods themselves were crowded and could not escape the noise, pollution, and congestion that came with the industrial and commercial functions around them. But ship carpenters and their wives made the most of homes that had to be close to work. They decorated their cottages in keeping with income and taste. The value of their personal property averaged a not inconsiderable $5,000. "Their homes," said the reporter, "are in general quiet and clean, their tables well-spread with the most solid of viands, [and] mahogany and haircloth are not wanting in their rooms."[126]

There was little conspicuous consumption among them, however, and most were said to give a high priority to saving. Shipyards commonly gave men the option of putting some percentage of their weekly pay "on-call," a savings plan by which wages were left to accumulate, while employers earned interest which they pledged to use for financing the expansion of operations. In 1856, a year of full employment and relatively high wages at the shipyards, these wages were "hardly ever called for until the hand leaves the yard." Times grew difficult in 1857 and 1858, and many of these accounts were closed. By such means, the ship carpenters were able to avoid charity, something in which, it was said, they took considerable pride. Furthermore, their employability when times improved gave shopkeepers confidence to extend them credit during depressions.[127]

The ship carpenters were not, however, blue-collar copies of the uptown merchants. They lived by their own code. There was little intemperance among them, and few days were lost at the shipyards to drunkenness. But they were, it was said, "fun-loving men." They sponsored their own autumn dance, and liked the circus and variety hall, as well as an occasional glass of whiskey. While not given to settling their occasional quarrels with violence, when they fought, it was "in a square, stand-up manner with two fists. They know nothing of knives or slung shot." They went to church, but were neither pious nor preoccupied with doctrine. The Irish ship carpenters, who were described as "second growth Irish," or "Yankee Irish," because of the relatively extensive time they had spent in the country, were especially attractive to the anti-Catholic *Commercial Advertiser* for what its reporter made of their religious behavior. "Their wives are good Catholics, and they allow the women to regulate their religion." But "Mike" and others were likely to "sleep through mass and [be] more familiar with the *Jolly Sangster* than their prayer book."[128] Such claims may well have been as much a projection of bourgeois hopes as they were pictures of the ship carpenters' lives. Yet there is an important truth in them— these men occupied a recognizable, perhaps quite unique, place within the local working classes that contributed to their self-understanding and to the heightened solidarity evident, for example, in large funeral processions they mounted for brother artisans. No tradesmen in the city quite as regularly or as massively turned out publicly to honor their dead. In October, 1860, they got up a 130-man funeral march for one of their own.[129]

But life-style could account for only a part of the solidarity the men achieved. They knew the value of their work to the health of the lake trade, and they knew the value of their individual labors. Their work was, as the *Commercial Advertiser* said, "very severe." They labored outdoors in as harsh winter conditions as existed in America. They often were pressed to meet deadlines for the completion of large projects. Yet, if severe, these same conditions impressed them with their toughness and capacity to perform considerable feats of craft when they worked together. Moreover, though they were wage earners rather than independent artisans and craftsmen, they retained a considerable measure of control over production. Their labors were accomplished according to traditional rhythms and cooperative divisions of work, without the intervention of the time-motion calculations and machinery that were usurping craft. Too, traditional apprentice training prevailed in the shipyards. Men took on their own apprentices and trained them in cooperative arrangements with employers.[130] Not surprisingly, ship carpenters acted more forcefully—and successfully—than any other segment of local labor in 1858–61 to reverse the wage cuts and impositions of storepay they had accepted from hard-pressed employers during the depression. Their militant, solidaristic approach to class struggle was seen in multiethnic cooperation, disciplined strike behavior, and a strategic alliance with the ship caulkers in 1860 to form a union in order to give credibility to the threat to close down the shipyards when they were engaged in prolonged bargaining.[131]

The achievement of the sailors and ship carpenters arose out of singular circumstances within each trade and out of the uniqueness of the culture, during and after work, and social organization of the workers themselves. Based on economic and social processes not found in other occupations or trades, that achievement was destined to be unique. As a consequence, ethnicity continued to reign supreme as both the basis of class politics and the vessel containing the daily experience of class for Buffalo's blue-collar majority.

CHAPTER 10

The Catholic Church and the Emergence of a New Interconfessional Order

On an October evening in 1847, John Timon made his impressive first appearance in Buffalo. A procession of a thousand torch-bearing Irish and Germans marched to the railroad station, where the assembled parade and a decorated coach greeted Timon and three Catholic bishops there to install him as head of the newly created Diocese of Buffalo. To the beat of a bass drum the procession and coach traveled two miles up Main Street to St. Louis Church, where the next day the ceremonies would take place. The parade route was lined with Catholics and Protestants, and the installation was attended by Buffalo's elite. Yet, in spite of the unaccustomed mix of crowds in a highly symbolic and emotionally charged circumstance, nothing untoward took place.[1]

A complex mixture of emotions formed the basis for the reception the two great religious groups accorded the bishop, who not only had never visited the city before, but knew none of its residents. The bishop's own Catholic believers were anxiously expectant. They understood the positive potential of the church when it was led by an active, resident bishop. The church furnished continuity between the Old World and the immigrant and American-born generations. Thus, it provided cultural coherence and moral stability for uprooted peoples; especially under the leadership of a sympathetic bishop, who through his appointment of priests, generosity with institutional resources, and tolerance for religious folkways could support immigrant aspirations for strong, stable, ethnic parishes. Yet Catholics were aware that the church had its own institutional needs and goals, and that these were not always congruent with the aspirations of its parishes. The new diocese was not only created to serve their needs, but also to provide a better means for managing the church's own interests than had existed when there was one large Diocese of New York. Now there were to be two upstate dioceses (the other centered at Albany), in large part for administrative convenience.[2] While the church and parishioners did not always have the same goals, the laity hardly spoke with one voice. Catholics were divided by national origin, language, religious customs, and social class, and this did not make ruling them any easier. Timon soon had to ponder such divisions. Shortly after his installation, the rebellious trustees of Buffalo's oldest and wealthiest parish, St. Louis, told him he would not be welcome to make their church his cathedral or their parsonage his residence. The bishop retreated to the more congenial, but humbler St. Patrick's.[3]

For their part, local Protestants, and most especially Americans, had many fears about the social and spiritual roles the new diocesan structure might play. In the city's early years, Protestant-Catholic relations were genial enough that in the absence of a local priest the few local Catholics had been invited to attend Protestant churches for ecumenical worship. Itinerant priests were invited to use Protestant churches to say mass to their flock for want of Catholic structures. But Protestant fears had grown alongside the increase in Catholic population. Now, as Catholics threatened to become a local majority, creation of the diocese proved the Catholic church was a permanent fixture on the local scene.

The mental framework through which American Protestants contemplated the rise of local Catholicism hardly ensured sectarian peace. Folkish anti-Catholic prejudice was brought to America by the first English settlers. Later Americans developed substantial ideological reservations about the church. Roman Catholic doctrines, rituals, internal organization, and the institutional behavior of priests and members of the hierarchy, seemed to be antithetical to the Enlightenment values and republican ideology that underlay American political institutions. Indeed, not only did Catholicism appear incompatible with a progressive, republican society, but it was doubted that the church could ever assist in preparing its overwhelmingly immigrant flock to assimilate American ways.

The republican critique of the Catholic church is easily summarized. The church had long demonstrated its corrupt, antirepublican, and unprogressive nature. It was always hostile to science and technology, which were liberating humanity from want. (Witness the fate of Galileo.) It was historically the ally of every despot and tyrant prince, as it had most recently demonstrated in the 1848 revolutions. Even Catholic claims that colonial Maryland, with its Catholic roots, had been a haven of religious tolerance were elaborately refuted by the *Com-*

mercial Advertiser. By maintaining a doctrine that interposed a priesthood between man and God, furthermore, and by allowing the Bible to be monopolized by the clergy, the church suppressed the liberty of individual judgment and conscience on which republican government depended. It treated men and women, said the *Commercial Advertiser*, as children, "who must put their trust in the assurance of parents and teachers" at a time in which "in accordance with the spirit of the age, a more reasoning faith founded on the convictions of the individual mind is required of other faiths."[4]

The church, it was contended, retained its hold on the faithful through artful manipulation and psychological terror. Its rituals, said the *Christian Advocate*, were "mummery" and "emblazoned buffoonery." Its piety, as demonstrated in the veneration of saints who led bizarre, self-denying lives, was "deplorable." Its canon law was a "humbug." "Selling" indulgences and sacraments encouraged false piety and false hopes for salvation, while impoverishing the faithful and corrupting the clergy. Excommunication was a relic of "medieval tyranny and priestly despotism."[5]

Behind this tyranny was a global sectarian machinery emanating from the Vatican. It encompassed secret organizations, such as the much feared Jesuits, foreign missionary societies, and diocesan schools, colleges, hospitals, orphanages, and newspapers. Their larger purpose was subversion. America now loomed larger in the papal strategy because since 1848 the security of the European church could not be assured. This machine was oiled by contributions from those held in terror over the disposition of their souls. The advance agents of this vast conspiracy were diocesan bishops and the parish clergy, morally corrupt, but masterful at intimidation, propaganda, and argumentation. The clergy proved that its mission was not moral or spiritual welfare by its indifference to temperance, the sanctity of the Sabbath, and poverty. Indeed it caused poverty by exacting contributions for its own maintenance and for the construction of grandiose churches. Meanwhile, through taxes, Protestants paid to maintain a poorhouse, in which Catholics were the majority of inmates. A priest's real purpose was spreading the power of the pope, and this led naturally to subverting American institutions. The clergy interfered in elections by choosing its favorites and mobilizing believers into a voting bloc. Moreover, it weakened public institutions, especially the public schools, by its persistent ideological assaults, and by creating sectarian counterinstitutions and then demanding public monies for them. If these demands were met, the result would be an unwanted religious and cultural pluralism and a breach of the constitutional doctrine of separation of church and state. There might eventually be papal domination of America. Republics, after all, were fragile; they depended on the autonomous individual conscience and on popular trust and good will. They could not long survive the onslaught of conspiracies mounted by dedicated, disloyal, and scheming fanatics. "Week by week," said the *Commercial Advertiser*, "we chronicle some new triumph of that church, which now holds lands and wealth enough in our city to make us wonder where the end shall be."[6] It would be Timon's task to allay these fears. If he failed, neither he nor the church would know any peace.

This view of the Catholic church was held by many Americans in the late 1840s and throughout the 1850s. Temperance advocates, evangelically oriented ministers, officeholders, and politicians, both ideological liberals and conservatives, and to one extent or another all American newspapers demonstrated belief in these ideas. American fears were often deepened by injudicious, aggressive rhetoric by Catholic editors, especially D'Arcy McGee, priests and bishops, and politicians. They routinely labeled Protestant denominations mere "sects" and called them "schismatic." They assaulted Protestant beliefs, predicted Protestantism would disappear before the force of Catholic truth, criticized the state of creedal freedom in America, and demanded tax support of Catholic institutions.[7] Yet, Catholic rhetoric aside, many negative American perceptions were based on incorrect assumptions about how the church functioned and what its priorities were. For, as we shall see, in reality the church was far more diverse and fragmented in its internal structure of authority, pragmatic in its approach to American life, and problem-ridden and divided against itself than Americans could ever have imagined.

If the emotionalism and exaggeration of Americans made the task of coming to terms with Catholicism more difficult, so, too, did their gathering recognition that the church had some positive things to offer.[8] While this recognition clashed confusingly with anti-Catholicism, it left an opening for Timon in his efforts to provide security for the church in western New York. In this chapter, it will become clear that at the time anti-Catholicism was at the center of American political life, American Protestants, especially affluent and powerful ones, were simultaneously coming to the practical conclusion that the church and its clergy might prove allies in the struggle for social control over the immigrant masses. They saw the value of Catholic welfare work, which relieved so much suffering among sick and impoverished newcomers, and of the efforts of Father Mathew and parish priests to defeat the terrible scourge of alcohol among the Irish. From such a perspective, in their self-denying devotion to the spiritual and material needs of the faithful and their hardworking, ethically ordered lives, priests and nuns might be seen not only as socially useful, but as proper role models for immigrants. That the church could exact the sort of selfless, disciplined behavior evident among those Sisters of Charity who opened a hospital at Buffalo in 1848 and saw the city through the next year's cholera epidemic suggested that by the power of example and doctrine it could do so from lay adherents.

American Protestants also came to see the Catholic church playing a significant role in high culture like that played by Germans in enhancing the quality of daily life through such popular innovations as beer gardens and St. John's Day. Through the elite academies opened by European teaching orders, the beauty of its churches, and the musical presentations and lectures Timon and others offered at Catholic churches, the church fostered in many bourgeois Protestants the feeling that Buffalo was something more than a mere utilitarian transshipment point, an arena for endless battles for wealth and power, and an inchoate agglomeration of shabby, disease-ridden ethnic neighborhoods besieged by social problems. Through the church the city instead seemed to have roots in an ancient cultural tradition and a continuous past, not merely in the opening of the canal. This feeling enabled bourgeois Americans to transcend their habitual immersion in functional, practical values and activities, which, as the *Commercial Advertiser* often admitted, left them too busy to take interest in enhancing the quality of life.[9]

Thus, the institution whose dogma, governance, and presumed political activities Americans routinely reviled was assisting them to care for and discipline the poor and to anchor themselves in time and space and pay heed to aesthetic values. No American institution had such complex potential. But from an American perspective that potential could be used for good or ill. Much depended on the character of the diocesan bishop and the clergy under his authority. So Americans watched the new bishop and waited for him to play his hand. However dimly many of them perceived the Catholic church that October night in 1847, they probably sensed that the new bishop would touch their lives as well as those of Catholics.

In the first years of the century the church had little presence in Buffalo other than the occasional appearance of a priest to administer to the spiritual needs of the few white, Catholic residents.[10] This situation was transformed by the settlement of the first wave of German-speakers in the late 1820s. When he visited Buffalo in 1829, New York diocesan Bishop Jean DuBois found about 800 recently arrived Swiss and Alsatian Catholics.[11] DuBois and the most prominent Catholic layman in Buffalo, Stephen Louis Le Couteulx de Caumont, the wealthy scion of a French noble family who had accumulated local property holdings while engaged in business, agreed that a resident priest must be established. Le Couteulx was to become the leading benefactor of antebellum Catholicism in Buffalo.[12] Beginning in 1829 with the gift of the deed for the large lot on which St. Louis Church and its adjacent cemetery would be located, he gave the diocese one parcel of property after another. Thanks to the labor of parishioners and to $3,000 in contributions brought from Europe by the Alsatian Rev. Nicolas Mertz, the first parish priest, a crude, wooden church was erected. By 1831, when the first mass was said at St. Louis Church, the composition of the parish—which is to say, of the city's Catholic population—had changed. Many of the Swiss had gone west. They were replaced by more Alsatians and by Germans and Irish, who were perhaps 45, 30, and 20 percent, respectively, of the local Catholic population. The rest were French and Quebecers.[13]

The Catholic population doubled by 1843, and a new, much larger church was constructed on the same site. Yet there was but one priest, and he also had missionary duties throughout the region. The shortage of priests, especially German-speaking ones, was one of several problems worrying DuBois's successor, Rev. John Hughes, the fiery Irishman who became bishop in 1838. The Buffalo area was the most distant from New York City of the locations in Hughes's diocese, and his efforts to have the church's many interests there represented and protected by a few overworked priests were unsuccessful. Moreover, there were too few churches in western New York, and most were small and debt-ridden. Their poverty made it impossible for the parishes to take on the added burden of providing alternatives to the public schools, which Hughes saw as Protestant devices for alienating Catholic immigrant children from their parents' faith. But Hughes could do little more than identify these problems and hope that local people would find ways to solve them. Timon would inherit these problems, now grown more complex with the passage of time and the arrival of large numbers of poor immigrants.[14]

Hughes's efforts to deal with the distant western region of the diocese were rendered more difficult, as would be Timon's, by the situation at St. Louis parish. Hughes hoped to have the laity there control its affairs in obedience to his wishes and to the few priests he sent, but the St. Louis laity had its own view of its prerogatives and of Hughes's and eventually Timon's proper role in governing the parish. As a result, two decades of conflict ensued over which party would have the greater power—the bishop, acting as a representative of the pope and through his priests, or the parish's lay trustees, acting according to custom and eventually, by virtue of legal incorporation, American law. Both Hughes and Timon fought several such battles in their diocese, but the St. Louis struggle was one of the most bitter and prolonged in the history of the American church. Before it ended in 1855, St. Louis Church would be placed under interdict, the trustees excommunicated, American Protestant nativists recruited as allies by the trustees against the church, and the Vatican forced to intervene.[15]

The root of the conflict was the fact that the Franco-German majority at St. Louis parish had come to America in possession of a centuries-old tradition of lay management of parish temporal affairs. This included responsibility for ornamentation and maintenance of parish churches and cemeteries, payment of parish employees, and sometimes, too, collection and distribution of parish charities. (German Rhinelanders, who for many years were the parish's second-largest group, had known a similar system in their homelands, and this reinforced the parish's belief in the appropriateness of lay management.) Bishops regularly complained in Europe, as they would in America, that parish trustees acting without the strictest clerical oversight squandered funds. Both in Europe and America, however, episcopal authorities had little choice but to accept lay management because parish priests were usually overworked and bishops resident in distant cities. Moreover, in an effort to renew parish life, the Counter-Reformation Council of Trent had approved of such lay responsibilities within carefully defined boundaries. Thus, lay management became a venerable prerogative in Alsace, agreed to out of practical necessity by episcopal officials, and legitimized by canon law and custom.[16] It would take form in such French North American communities as Quebec, Detroit, and Louisiana. Then it would begin its own, local processes of growth and change, adding, for example, in place of episcopal nomination of trustees, as in Europe, parish elections. Bishop DuBois himself approved of such elections for St. Louis Church.[17] Moreover, American trustees could take advantage of state incorporation laws. St. Louis trustees incorporated in 1838 out of fear that changes in episcopal practice mandated by the American hierarchy at its recent Baltimore Councils, and likely to be institutionalized by the newly installed Bishop Hughes, would curb lay prerogatives.[18] That the majority of the American hierarchy in the mid-nineteenth century was Irish and Irish-American also boded ill for trustees. No such trustee system had existed in Ireland, and these bishops were prone to see unfamiliar assertions of trustee power as disobedience. This was, in fact, how Hughes interpreted the matter. He acted immediately upon becoming bishop to rein in the trustees. He promulgated an antitrustee *Pastoral Letter* and disciplined New York City trustees, before turning his attention to Buffalo in 1843. A compromise was reached only after Hughes briefly withdrew St. Louis's priest. But soon the trustees were interpreting the agreement in line with their own position. Relations were strained when Timon arrived in 1847.[19]

Meanwhile in combination with ethnic and language competition, differing religious customs, the growth of Catholic population, and the physical expansion of the city, the issue of lay prerogatives gave form to the prediocesan church. During St. Louis parish's first years, its various ethnic constituencies, increasingly packed into the crowded church, lived in uneasy peace. When the priest delivered a homily in English, the Germans hissed, and when in German, the Irish minority returned the insult. After Hughes encouraged priests to stand up to the trustees, ethnic hostilities increased. Aware that the authority of their Irish bishop lay behind such assertions of priestly power, the Irish broke with the trustees. Gradually the political issue of trusteeism accreted an emotional, ethnic dimension. Soon the Irish were complaining of harrassment, and left St. Louis parish, which, as it was, lay too far from their dockside neighborhoods for convenience. With Hughes's support, in 1841, they founded their own church. The last Irish at St. Louis probably stayed on no later than 1844 when the conflict reached a crisis. Most of the small minority of French-speaking Catholics left, too, because their refusal to support the trustees' disobedience brought to a head historic animosities between the French and Alsatians. The French soon established their own parish, St. Peter's.[20]

By 1847 St. Louis parish had become entirely German-speaking. But this did not ensure internal harmony. Even with a new building, the church could not accommodate the rapid increase of the German population, which was settling ever further away from St. Louis Church. Moreover, the impoverished, new immigrants complained that the more affluent, long-settled artisans, shopkeepers, and craftsmen at St. Louis looked down on them. Perhaps, too, they disliked the trustees' warfare with the bishop. In 1843 many newcomers left to establish, with the aid of Redemptorist Fathers, their own East Side parish, St. Mary's, which was a bastion of loyalty to the bishops during the conflict. Thus, not only was the dissident St. Louis Church the oldest parish in 1847, but possessing the finest church, the largest school, its own cemetery, and the most affluent parishioners, it was the wealthiest—a formidable opponent for any bishop.[21]

This was the situation Timon faced when he arrived. It joined a host of institutional problems Hughes had identified, but left untouched. Added to them were the equally pressing human needs of the new immigrants. None of these human and institutional needs menaced the existence of the church, however much they strained its resources. Soon Timon would have to contend with forces that actually did pose an ideological and even physical threat to the church: American nativists and the deeply anticlerical '48er refugees. And all of these challenges were spread throughout a diocese that encompassed almost the entire state west of Syracuse, a socially and economically variegated region of cities, farms, and towns, and of wealth and poverty. As Timon later remarked looking back on the conditions he faced in 1847, "A bishop perhaps never began under circumstances more discouraging."[22]

Timon had a familiarity with American life so extensive that he was rather unique among contemporary bishops, most of whom were European. He was born in 1797 in a log cabin on the Pennsylvania frontier to very recently immigrated Irish parents. His father was a dry-goods storekeeper, and during Timon's youth the family lived well enough to afford him an excellent education at a Maryland Catholic academy. While residing in St. Louis and working for his father, he fell into a friendship with a priest of the order of St. Vincent de Paul, a French order especially known for its work among the poor. Timon was influenced to enter the priesthood. After seminary training, he was an itinerant missionary among Native Americans and frontier farmers, most of whom were Protestants, in Missouri and Arkansas. He lived with considerable privation, and experienced hostility. But he learned to get along with Protestants, while explaining and defending the church, and found that familiarity bred tolerance, though very few conversions. He also developed an evangelical fervor to his preaching as a result of his efforts to communicate with frontier Baptists and Methodists.[23]

Timon excelled so in his work that in 1835 Vincentian authorities named him to head the order's American missions. In the years before he went to Buffalo, he distinguished himself at establishing seminaries, disciplining priests, and raising money in Europe for his order's American projects. A record such as this in the American church was sure to catch the eye of the Vatican, which sought men exactly like Timon (American-born, yet trustworthy by all institutional criteria, skilled managers, and effective spokesmen for the church) to run its affairs in the United States. It was inevitable that Timon would be made a bishop, and he received seven offers of a diocese between 1839 and 1847. Each he refused, because he feared the combination of massive responsibility and a sedentary existence. Yet with each refusal, the probability of eventually having to accept increased. Timon was anxious by 1847 not to appear prideful, and concerned, too, he later said, that the appointment he would have to accept might be in a diocese with slavery, which he disliked after years of exposure to its cruelties. He was cornered; he went to Buffalo.[24]

When he arrived, his personal situation was hardly enviable. He had no local contacts and was representative of a church that was—and remained—isolated in local Christianity. He was never asked to participate in any ecumenical projects, such as the Sunday School Union or the Christian Union. He lacked a library of basic Catholic texts from which to derive his pastoral letters and synodical decrees. Because of his years on the frontier, he knew few members of the northern hierarchy. He did, however, profit from the confidence of Hughes, who shared with him the lessons he had derived from his own, often bitter, experience with the St. Louis trustees, and from the friendship and advice of Baltimore Archbishop Francis Kenrick.[25]

Timon, moreover, had come into a situation in which he was governing a body of Catholics who were increasingly German. The diocese contained some 30,000 German Catholics by 1850. (For this reason some powerful clerics at the Vatican had in 1846 counseled that a German should be named bishop.)[26] Timon's ability to speak German was hardly confident, and after his initial, faltering attempts to preach in German, he stopped trying. Nor did he know anything of German religious customs, something that he discovered in preparing the diocese for Easter in 1848. Among the matters on which he sought Kenrick's advice were German grammar and usage and German religious traditions.[27]

The problem of his relations with German Catholics was complicated by the struggle with the lay trustees. Timon soon experienced his own baptism of fire in dealing with them. Fearing that Timon would pick up where Hughes had left off, and sharing the widespread belief among German Catholics that Irish bishops wished to take their resources and give them to the poorer Irish, the St. Louis trustees adopted an antagonistic stance. Not only did they deny Timon permanent use of their church and parsonage, but they answered his veto of their request to enlarge their church by beginning the work while he was out of town. Also, they refused his suggestion that Sisters of Charity teach at their parish school. Finally, the trustees told the parish gravedigger not to accept burials ordered by the bishop.[28]

Both his own personality and his concern for the public image of the church led Timon to hate public controversy. He opted for a type of indirect rule in dealing with Germans. One of his first acts as bishop was the appointment of St. Louis's pastor, Rev. Francis Guth, as vicar general to the Germans. (There would be one for the Irish, too.) Guth was employed to translate the bishop's words and deeds into terms understandable to Germans.[29] Furthermore, following Hughes's lead in giving permission to the Redemptorists to organize St. Mary's, Timon asked German Jesuits to create three of the four new parishes of the late 1840s and the 1850s, and thus solved with one stroke his shortage of priests and his difficulties in dealing with Germans. In all, four of the five German parishes in Buffalo in 1860 were out of Timon's direct control and in the hands of religious orders.[30] Finally, in 1850 the bishop established the *Aurora* as the diocesan German-language voice.[31]

This policy of indirect rule did not have all of the desired consequences. Whatever Guth's ethnicity, St. Louis parishioners saw him as the Irish bishop's man, and made life so difficult that he was forced to leave the parish in 1850.[32] Forces beyond Timon's control also contributed to his inability to reach an accommodation with Germans. St. Louis parishioners and other German Catholics were influenced by the anticlericalism of the 1848 revolutions and later by the rise of American anti-Catholic nativism. Few were led to open apostasy, but new legitimacy was given to the struggle against meddling by priests in what the St. Louis laity regarded as its prerogatives. The St. Louis trustees increasingly marshalled republican ideas and rhetoric to defend customary prerogatives. Through their self-described "press bureau," which in democratic fashion appealed to public opinion over the traditional authority of the church, they did an effective job of employing ideas of civil rights and separation of church and state before American and both non-Catholic and, it appears, Catholic German audiences. Few Catholic Germans outside the parish rose in defense of Timon. The *Weltbürger* grew more partisan in behalf of the laymen. American opinion, too, swung increasingly into active hostility to the church on the issue. This support provided the laymen with confidence. At the same time, organizing and explaining their resistance in the court of public opinion was a significant Americanizing experience that further emboldened them.[33]

Timon brought important assets to his job. There was his forceful personality—zealous, impulsive and good-natured, yet skillful at making a dignified public appearance.[34] American papers seemed to agree with Mary McGee, who called him "the model bishop," for his "affability, humanity, and charity." The *Republic* said that Timon was "a venerable ecclesiastic, pleasing in his manners, and filling well our notions of what his office requires." Even the evangelical *Christian Advocate* said that he was "highly educated and a man of enlarged and liberal views." His public lectures, said the *Courier*, "are distinguished for their deep thought and acute logic," and were increasingly "well-attended by people of other persuasions, as well as his own." In fact, Timon was often asked to lecture in liberal Protestant churches, and a traveling correspondent of the Philadelphia *North American*, passing through in 1850, stated that he was able to "mingle freely in society with all orders and creeds," and that "by his courteous manners and intelligent conversation, he is everywhere a welcome guest." The *Weltbürger*, too, acknowledged that while the church was corrupt, Timon himself was "decent and dedicated."[35]

Timon was a complex man, however, and seemed frequently at war with himself. His zealousness was tinged with impatience and other emotions he frequently could not control. He was easily moved to anger, sarcasm, or tears. Few Americans or lay Catholics saw this side of him, for it was reserved for his priests, and ultimately it poisoned his relations with them. Moreover, when joined to the crushing load of responsibility he had at Buffalo, his love of action led to an inability to allocate authority and rendered him unable to administer diocesan affairs efficiently.[36] And here, too, his priests suffered most in consequence.

The positive impression Timon made on American Protestants and his skillful efforts to manage their impressions of the church had deeper roots than the cautions he exercised in daily intercourse with them. Timon was American-born, and, as a missionary, had spent more time during his adult life among American Protestants than among his co-religionists. He understood the ideas that moved Americans and the aspirations and fears that governed American public life. In consequence, he could proceed with considerable skill in fashioning his public role, especially in controversial matters. He was a patriot who spoke the emotional language of American nationalism. Just as important, after his own fashion, Timon subscribed to important elements of the national civic ideology, which, he believed, was compatible with the spirit and dogma of Catholicism. Like other bishops of the day, Timon argued that the Catholic church was dedicated to the same ideas of freedom and liberty of conscience that were enshrined in the American Constitution, and he illustrated the point by recalling the prominent role of Maryland Catholics in the Revolution. Yet he believed nonetheless that the Catholic nations of Old Europe were freer than Protestant countries. In principle he supported the separation of church and state, which served to protect Catholics against the intolerance of the Protestant majority. But when Timon used words like "liberty" and "freedom" in asserting the church's claims, his understandings were not always the same as those of Protestants. Timon had in mind formulations that defended creedal freedom against demands for conformity and cultural homogenization. Moreover, though he would hardly have said so in public, he was doubtful of the prospects for any government based on universal manhood suffrage. He believed, he said during the secession crisis, the rapid expansion of the electorate made not only nativism and social disorder, but Civil War, inevitable.

Nor was consistency always his strong point. His advocacy of the separation of church and state ran up against his attempts to gain public funding for Catholic schools and welfare institutions. Indeed he believed that as "the Mother church" of Christianity, Catholicism should not be treated as just another sect, but given special consideration in matters like school appropriations.[37]

Yet counterexamples to the appraisal of Timon as a man of enlightened American republican views miss an important point that eluded his most thoughtful American contemporaries in the heat of the public controversies. Far from acting in public life in line with the dictates of a vast international and conspiratorial machine emanating from Rome, as many American Protestants believed, Timon proceeded largely from an intuitive understanding of the possibilities and limitations American society presented him as a Catholic bishop. In governing his diocese, he was guided not by foreign, European assumptions steeped in medievalism and intrigue, but by a frequently unrationalized mixture of Catholic piety and loyalty to the institution of the church and homegrown pragmatism, American civic ideology, and bourgeois gentility. The Vatican usually declined to offer him instruction on how to do his job.[38] Indeed, from the start he spent much more time explaining to European church officials why his diocese was important (Niagara Falls tourism; the international border; the linchpin of northern commerce, etc.) and why he needed financial assistance, than he did in acting upon advice from abroad.[39] He was eager to assert the grandeur of his church and angered at its marginal position in his country. Timon needed no one to explain to him how he should proceed in confronting the challenges he faced.

Timon's inbred, native sense of the limits and possibilities inherent in his situation is especially clear in two contexts: his response to the American political process and his role in ending the intense conflict at St. Louis Church. Though charged on occasion with partisan behavior, Timon actually studiously avoided personal involvement in politics in fear of giving the church's enemies the ammunition they needed to destroy it. He understood that the campaigns of most concern to devout Catholics—for example, defeat at the polls in 1849 of a poorhouse superintendent, Lester Brace, who refused to allow priests to enter the premises and was almost defeated for reelection as a result—did not require his intervention because Catholic interests were already clear.[40] Moreover, by 1847 party positions were such that Catholics knew that they stood a far better chance of having the church's interests protected by Democrats. But Timon went further than passive noninterference in elections in shielding the church from charges of partisanship. He constantly enjoined Catholics against participation in partisan strife. His 1860 election-eve instructions to Catholics on how to behave at the polls ("There must not be any scandal, any uproar, any violence") could have served as his rule for guiding behavior at all elections and public events.[41] He publicly disavowed efforts to use his name to endorse candidates.[42] He warned priests against electoral involvement, and his reputation among them for punishing the disobedient was strong enough to give them pause. Still he could not monitor all their activities, and in the 1856 presidential contest, some Buffalo priests were active against the nativist American party. When reports of this reached Timon, he publicly promised to discipline the offenders.[43]

The nonpartisan policy also affected the diocesan press, but unevenly and only gradually. After his experience with the outspoken D'Arcy McGee, Timon recognized the dangers in having so partisan a paper representing the diocese as the *American Celt*. In 1853, he guided the new *Sentinel* into a nonpartisan stance, characterized by little reporting of party activities, no endorsements, and generally conciliatory rhetoric. For full-time editor, he chose Michael Hagan, who had the virtue of being both a canny politician and American-born. The nonpartisan policy was prompted as much by fear of nativist reactions as respect for the principle of separation of church and state. The *Sentinel*'s contemporary, the *Aurora*, was considerably more outspoken on political issues, but it was written in German and was thus inaccessible to Americans searching for weapons in their struggle against the church. The *Sentinel*'s policy was somewhat relaxed in the mid-1850s when nativism embittered local campaigns.[44]

Timon used a similarly cautious and defensive, yet flexible approach in his attempts to end the St. Louis affair. For some years, however, he was hindered in his freedom of action by forces in Europe and in America that were beyond his control. Moreover, the highly centralized structure of institutional Catholicism, which lacked intermediary bodies to resolve conflict, continued to work to polarize this, like other, disputes within the church.[45] In dealing with the parish, Timon consequently was forced into behavior, such as excommunication, he himself regretted.

While Hughes believed, as he said in 1848, that the rebellion would collapse as the trustees aged and mellowed, Timon discovered that the opposite was taking place. Buoyed by the republican resurgence of the late 1840s and early 1850s, trustees and parishioners grew confident in their resistance to the hierarchy. They defied Timon on a number of questions and, against his wishes, began an expensive addition to the church. In response, Timon attempted to impose a new trustee board composed of unelected men he had chosen, but the effort was so unpopular that when it was announced after mass one Sunday a near riot ensued and the priest fled for his life. By 1852 Timon felt it necessary to withdraw the priest permanently and place the church under interdict. Trustees and parishioners responded with a 414-signature petition, representing the large majority of the parish's male adults, which decried the repression of their spiritual life. At the same time the parish's chief spokesman before the church fathers, Louis Le Couteulx's son William, wrote articulate letters to Rome, and traveled there, too. He argued convincingly that this attempt to discipline the parish damaged the church in the eyes of American Protestants and aided the church's enemies. William Le Couteulx seems to have been better connected in Rome than Timon himself. The bishop was frustrated by his adversary's success in arguing the parish's case abroad. Against the better judgment of a number of American bishops, in 1853 the Vatican dispatched Italian Archbishop Gaetano Bedini to Buffalo to adjudicate the case.[46]

Timon probably grasped that while Bedini would decide the matter in his favor, the archbishop, who had been active in mounting the bloody defeat of the 1848 republican uprising at Bologna, and who personified the much feared extranational power of the church, would be unpopular with Americans and German exiles. Indeed Bedini's presence in Cincinnati, with its large '48er population, inspired riots, and threats were made on his life.[47] This did not happen at Buffalo, though the *Weltbürger* featured the charges against him, and Americans were hardly pleased by his presence. But the consequences of Bedini's visit presented Timon with increased difficulties. When Bedini did rule against the parish, which continued its resistance anyway, Timon believed he was left with little choice but to excommunicate the still disobedient trustees. This action in June, 1854, proved unpopular with a wide spectrum of local opinion.[48] Excommunication was roundly and passionately condemned. The *Christian Advocate* denounced the bishop's order of excommunication as "horrid—filled with curses and anathema and banning," and agreed with the Buffalo *Democracy* that a grand jury should indict the bishop for libel and provocation of social ostracism. The *Commercial Advertiser* spoke of the order as "the insane malediction of a churlish priest." The Democratic *Courier*, the American paper least prone to question the church's activities, had encouraged the trustees, when excommunication was imminent, to refuse "to fall in with these Italian notions of ecclesiastical absolutism."[49] Even more ominous from Timon's point of view was the parish's entrance into an alliance with American nativists. The trustees retained the legal and political services of the brilliant anti-Catholic attorney, state Senator James O. Putnam, who decided that the only means of assisting them lay in legislation. Hughes had unsuccessfully sought legislative relief from trustee claims in 1853. Now in 1855, with Putnam himself taking charge and gathering up votes from nativist colleagues and those eager to appease the growing prejudices of constituents, a law was passed making legal ownership and inheritance of church property by members of any episcopal hierarchy impossible.[50]

In this climate of polarization and growing danger to the church, Timon revealed his skill in diffusing controversy. He had always spurned harsh rhetoric and public emotion in the St. Louis conflict, and now characteristically he opted to remove the matter completely from the public arena of legalities and rights, and to seek conciliation through the church's spiritual resources. Timon detected evidence of a spiritual crisis among St. Louis parishioners. Since 1852, there had been complaints that they were "deprived of religious succor," and that they were made to bear "spiritual deprivations" and "the greatest spiritual privations"; and they described themselves as undergoing "spiritual suffering." The exact nature of this suffering is unclear, for while their priests had been removed, there is no evidence that rank-and-file St. Louis loyalists were denied sacraments when they presented themselves at other churches. The situation of the trustees, prior to their June, 1854, excommunication, may well have been more proscribed, but this, too, is unclear. We cannot know how common was the situation implied by the marriage of a trustee's son and the daughter of a protrustee parishioner: the ceremony was performed by a Protestant minister for want of an obliging priest. Perhaps most influential was the intense anxiety bred of the *possibility*—and for the trustees the certainty—of being denied the sacraments, especially the last rites, which may well have been on the minds of the approximately one-quarter of the parish over 50.[51]

In September, 1854, Timon made his move. He allowed the temporary lifting of both the interdict and excommunication, and invited the eminent German Jesuit Father F. X. Weninger to give one of his widely reputed "missions" (i.e., revivals) at St. Louis Church. Doubtless after prior agreement with Timon, Weninger offered simultaneously to mediate the conflict. In so doing, both Timon and Weninger sought the means, hitherto lacking, for removing the struggle from the laity versus hierarchy mold in which the structure of the church had cast it. The trustees, seeing the web being spun to trap them, refused to attend the mission and to accept mediation. Probably in consequence of their decision, the mission was only modestly attended, and the large majority of the parish's male voters unanimously rejected the offer of mediation. The next year, however, not long after the passage of the Putnam law, Timon made another effort, lifting the interdict and excommunication to allow Weninger the same opportunities. The event was a huge success. Perhaps having risked so much in allying with the church's enemies, the parishioners' spiritual anxieties had reached intolerable proportions. Three of the trustees, Timon said with obvious satisfaction, had been "converted" on the spot. Whether this conversion was political or spiritual is unclear, but it is clear that Weninger's second offer of mediation was quickly embraced. After an agreement was drafted that allowed the parish to remain incorporated and enjoy a greater degree of self-government than other diocesan parishes, but gave Timon the right to examine its books and consult on all major expenditures, the church was reopened and its priest restored. In the future, the agreement would be subject to differing interpretations and debate, but conflict would never again break out of the boundaries of the Catholic church.[52]

In a hostile environment that he read with skill, Timon succeeded where both the Irishman Hughes and the Italian Bedini had failed, preserving the authority and unity of the church and setting back the efforts of its enemies. None were more disappointed than the city's Protestant politicians and opinion leaders. In encouraging the parish, they had looked to the controversy to check Timon's power and, if the parishioners were to leave the church altogether, to provide a local vindication of the Reformation. They apparently had not reckoned on the depths of Catholic belief nor on the complex ambivalences that accompanied Americanization. Nor had they foreseen what a formidable opponent the bishop was.

Within a year of arrival, Timon established priorities for the institutional development of the diocese. These were: repair or complete replacement of churches, where they existed; the building of new churches; more and better Catholic schools; a seminary with dormitories; subsidies for priests in particularly poor parishes; and a cathedral in a prominent location where it could serve as a symbol of the grandeur of the church. This list would soon be supplemented by another, which represented the welfare needs of the growing numbers of new immigrants, as Timon, the Vincentian with an acute sensitivity to the problems of the poor and needy, came to understand them.[53] From the start, however, the bishop experienced immense frustration in raising the monies needed for all these ambitious projects. The search for financial resources, both from external and internal diocesan sources, became an all-consuming preoccupation. It would take him away from the diocese for months on end, involve him reluctantly in public controversies that did not always place the church in a favorable light, and alienate him from his priests. Yet such results of these efforts as St. Joseph's Cathedral and Sisters of Charity Hospital markedly enhanced the church's standing with Protestants and served recognized community needs.

Early in his episcopacy, Timon maintained that the financial problems he encountered arose from the fact that because Buffalo in particular was being settled only by impoverished immigrants who became stranded on the way west, his was America's poorest diocese.[54] It is doubtful the statement was true. There seems little reason to believe Buffalo poorer than any other place populated exclusively by immigrants, a characteristic of most northern dioceses. Moreover, immigrants became stranded at many points in their journeys to the interior. Buffalo's problem was not unique in this respect, nor surely were all of its immigrants involuntary settlers. The bishop, whose passionate nature often led him to exaggerate, probably hoped to attract sympathy from potential contributors, especially in distant Europe. He also sought to impress upon them the gap between Buffalo's importance as a city and the poor representation the church made of itself there.

But Timon did have trouble raising money within the diocese, and this requires explanation. To some extent rivalries between its two major cities were to blame. Leading Rochester Catholics believed that their city should have been the seat of the diocese, and were loath to contribute to building a cathedral in Buffalo. Many diocesan Catholics outside Buffalo also felt they would not benefit from diocesan welfare institutions located there. Probably just as important, too, were the traditions of giving that immigrant Catholics brought to America. These and poverty set limits on their contributions to the church. While in Ireland there was no such thing as pew rent, the Irish were nonetheless accustomed to giving money for parish and diocesan causes out of pocket. In America, though the poor could attend early masses when pews were open to all, their churches collected pew rents for support of the parish, and they gave generously to diocesan projects beyond their own parish. But many were so poor that the bishop could hardly count on the Irish to sustain the diocese. In Europe and America Germans limited their contributions largely to the parishes, a pattern reinforced in a diocese such as Buffalo by their distrust of Irish bishops.[55]

Timon was more than once embarrassed by the lack of popular financial support within the diocese. He was many months late, for example, in announcing the results of the 1849 annual collection for the pope, and when he did, it amounted to only $288 for the entire seventeen counties of the diocese. In Buffalo itself, the 1852 Christmas collection for the cathedral construction fund yielded large contributions only by some Protestant politicians and businessmen, though a few Irish families gave five or ten dollars. In contrast the thousands of parishioners of the largest parish, St. Mary's, gave $49.31. More than once Timon had to repeat calls for funds, demand his priests redouble their efforts, and personally organize charitable teas and fares.[56]

But Timon went further. He sought control of parish resources for diocesan purposes. Doubtless there was a grain of truth in the charge that his willingness to challenge lay trustees, at St. Louis Church and at Rochester, where he encountered a similar, less bitter problem in a German parish, was more than a matter of discipline, though it was largely that. Timon very probably did wish to use such parish resources as cemeteries, where he could bury the diocesan poor at low cost, and he knew, too, that he could control parish expenses better than trustees, who wanted their own debt-producing, highly ornamented, spacious churches.[57] The clergy probably applauded efforts to put trustees in their place, but Timon's other ways of gaining access to parish resources stirred profound resentment among them, and finally in 1864 prompted a rebellion by a number of diocesan priests. They charged in an angry broadside, which was circulated throughout the diocese, that annual Christmas and Easter collections for the support of the clergy never reached them because Timon used the money for his own purposes. They maintained, too, that Timon interfered with the writing of the wills of dying parishioners and had them divert their assets to him rather than, as they were said to originally intend, to their parishes. Whatever the truth of these claims, there is no doubt Timon drastically curbed the income of diocesan clergy. He forced priests to accept low living standards and tried to gain control over their private sources of income. He disciplined them severely when he discovered they had saved money, even for such purposes as assisting family. At diocesan synods he made collections from among them. He expected them to live, as he did, a life of self-denial.[58]

That all such efforts to raise money within the diocese yielded little besides frustration and bitterness is evident in the energy the bishop had to expend seeking resources beyond it. One obvious alternative was public money derived from taxes. Along with other members of the northern hierarchy, Timon and his principal advisor in the first years, head Vicar General Rev. Bernard O'Reilly, believed that such Catholic institutions as schools, hospitals, and orphanages should receive public funds because their activities contributed to the common good. Also, it was argued that Catholics paid taxes for the support of public institutions which, for creedal reasons, they did not use. In effect, since they had to support their own sectarian institutions, they were twice taxed. It was only fair that their public taxes be returned to the Catholic institutions they did use.[59]

This view challenged American conceptions of the boundaries of church and state, sectarian and nonsectarian, and public and private. Most American Protestants did not feel the public good was served by encouraging sectarianism, because they feared the explosive potential of the sectarian differences. And, of course, *Catholic* sectarianism was even more greatly feared, for behind every Catholic demand, Americans perceived the long arm of the pope. They worried, too, about establishing a precedent that implied the political accommodation of the self-defined needs of every religious, racial, and ethnic group. It was evident to them that a multiethnic, multiconfessional society would never attain cohesion without public institutions maintained by the money, self-interest, and ethical commitment of everyone. As was also clear in the conflict over German language instruction, public schools bulked especially large in the American view. The public schools were to pass on a common culture and language to the young, and thus provide the foundations of individual integration into society, and hence of social order—on terms Protestants approved. It was this very purpose that made the public schools the most contentious of issues, for Catholic parents feared that the acculturation planned for their children involved a shedding not only of their religion and in the case of the Germans, their language, but of such deeply engrained, conservative ethnic ways as female sexual purity and domesticity.[60] Protestants did not inspire confidence when debating these matters. Semi-consciously they defined American culture as *their* culture and used the words "Protestant," "American," and "public" interchangeably. For example, the *Christian Advocate*, in responding to Catholic complaints that priests were barred from the Erie County Poor House, began its reply, "Our Protestant institutions never oppressed a Catholic." When asked to explain themselves, Americans said that it was right that those whose ancestors had founded the nation, and who were here when the immigrants arrived, should dictate its standards, which were, after all, superior ones in their republican virtue. Nor, finally, did Protestants find the argument for distributional justice impressive, since double taxation resulted from free choice in supporting sectarian over public institutions.[61]

The response of Timon and such advisors as O'Reilly was not always consistent. When Americans argued that only the nonsectarian public schools should receive tax monies, and that Sunday schools and home instruction should provide religious education, the bishop joined his usual evangelical adversaries Rev. John Lord and Rev. John Robie, themselves a minority among Americans in criticizing the public schools, in calling the public schools "godless."[62] When Protestants replied that while religion was not taught in the public schools, nonetheless a nonsectarian Christian morality was taught through common readings of the Bible and of didactic moral tales, Timon and diocesan spokesmen replied that here was proof the public schools were a cover for Protestant proselytizing. Catholics succeeded, to the horror of those like Dr. Foote who believed it the source of republican liberty, in getting the Protestant Bible out of the classroom in New York State in 1853. From time to time they successfully challenged textbooks they deemed sectarian, as did Timon in 1863 in the case of a moral philosophy reader used at the high school.[63] But in spite of petitions to the city council from Buffalo parishes and of Timon's public appeals to distributional justice and creedal liberty, no aid was forthcoming for Catholic schools. The polemical exchanges over the school question, however, did polarize public opinion along confessional lines in the 1850s and probably contributed to making local converts to nativism.[64] Timon probably came to wonder whether raising the issue was worthwhile. Yet it would have been impossible for him not to, for with far fewer resources, Catholics had as much invested in the education of their children as their Protestant counterparts.

The growth in New York State of Catholic political power, however, soon led to a modest reformulation of the customary, Protestant-defined, civil boundaries in the somewhat less controversial area of welfare institutions. Beginning in the late 1840s, the state legislature made funds available to Catholic hospitals and orphanages upon application by a diocese. Hospitals serving the immigrant poor, it was now successfully argued, should receive money if they opened their doors to all religions, and did not proselytize. Orphanages, too, should receive public monies because they operated schools in localities where there were no convenient or existing public, custodial alternatives. The legislature made these funds available in three ways. First, the state commissioner of immigration returned money to hospitals and orphanages for each impoverished immigrant they served. Second, the poor relief law was amended so that county superintendents of the poor had to recompense these same institutions for services such as schooling and medical care provided those children under twelve who could not be assisted at the poorhouse. Third, substantial grants for capital development were made to sectarian institutions where there were no convenient public ones.[65]

Timon used these sources of funding, and while this involved him and O'Reilly in public controversy, public monies did lighten the load of diocesan responsibilities. Through sympathetic politicians of both parties, Timon obtained capital development funds from the legislature. In 1849, for example, O'Reilly and Timon enlisted the powerful influence of Thurlow Weed, chief operative of William Henry Seward's wing of the state Whig party. The Seward Whigs courted immigrant votes, in contrast to the nativist elements of their party. They united with Democrats in 1849 to vote a $9,000 appropriation to construct and equip a local hospital, which was run on a strictly nonsectarian basis by the Sisters of Charity and was for a decade Buffalo's only hospital.[66] In 1865 Timon began lobbying to obtain appropriations for the construction of adequate facilities for the diocesan school for the deaf, a pioneering venture.[67] Per capita payments made locally by immigration officials also became important to diocesan welfare institutions. Between 1851 and 1860, for example, the state commissioners of immigration paid annually about $3,712 in per capita payments to Sisters Hospital for services provided to indigent, sick foreigners. By 1860 diocesan welfare institutions were receiving 86 percent of the approximately $10,000 given annually to Buffalo facilities in these per capita payments.[68]

Timon's successes in getting public funds angered such Americans as Dr. Lord, who had acute fears of the church and were envious of its triumphs. It would take years for people like Lord to accept the principles embodied in laws written in the distant state capital. For them, these laws represented the unwelcome imposition of pluralism upon the local social order. Early in 1850, when he wrote a series of highly polemical public letters denouncing recent appropriations for the hospital and a Catholic petition drive for more money, Lord was very much aware of the growth of the church's civic activism. Not only did he know about the $9,000 grant, but he lived with the bitter fact that the Protestant orphanage, of which his wife was a founder and trustee, had received only $3,000 in its own recent application for capital development funds.[69] Catholics, Lord charged, were becoming "the almoners of Protestant charities," and exacting conversions from needy Americans in exchange for medical care, food, and shelter. He argued, too, that only the will of the hospital's board of trustees, which he correctly pointed out was composed (and would be until 1855, when the Sisters took complete control) of Catholic laymen handpicked by the bishop, kept a semipublic hospital from being transformed into a "nunnery."[70] Lord's charges that proselytizing occurred at the hospital were refuted by O'Reilly, then nominally in control of the diocese while Timon was in Europe.[71] Still, the American outcry after Lord's letters led the legislature in 1850 to vote to put off for three years further aid to the hospital, so that other local institutions could catch up in the extent of their subsidies.[72] Furthermore, Lord's warnings helped to mobilize the forces of nativism by focusing Protestant fears, which were usually nebulous or exaggerated projections, on real targets and issues. Timon understood this, yet cringed at the prospect of public debate. He preferred to let the hospital's record of service, especially in the summer, 1849, epidemic, speak for itself. He was privately sharply critical of O'Reilly's audacity in responding publicly to the city's senior evangelical minister.[73]

Because of Timon's problems raising money within the diocese and the political costs he paid for success in obtaining public funds, he was fortunate to have access to private sources of money outside not only the diocese and government, but the United States. He had distinguished himself when he headed the Vincentians for his skill in tapping such resources. He spoke disdainfully of his ability "to beg" for a good cause,[74] but, as bishop, he proved a master at the task. He traveled frequently in search of money, and was sometimes away from the diocese for months at a time. Some fund-raising was done among wealthy Catholics in New Orleans and in Mexico, whose languages and cultures he was familiar with from his earlier career in the church. He went to both places in 1852 and again in 1853 when he feared work on the cathedral would end for want of funds.[75]

Wealthy individuals and Catholic religious institutions in Europe proved even more useful. He kept in constant contact with both through the mails or frequent trips. Rev. Francis Guth also traveled to Europe in behalf of the diocese. A month before his arrival in Buffalo, Timon had already begun corresponding with the three principal European missionary societies that aided American dioceses: the Society for the Propagation of the Faith at Lyons, the *Ludwigsmissionsverein* at Munich, and the Leopoldine Society at Vienna. The first and third were interested in both French and German-speaking immigrants, while the second, only in Germans.[76] To all three, Timon wrote plaintive letters offering a highly selective, despairing view of the diocese and its needs. To the authorities at Lyons, he greatly exaggerated the number of French immigrants in the diocese, while to all three, he overstated not only its poverty, but the extent to which he was dependent on wealthy local Protestants for money. At other times, however, he said these Protestants felt only "the blackest prejudice" for Catholics, and would give only "bread and old clothing," and then in exchange for immediate conversion.[77]

In fact, what impresses the latter-day observer is how halfhearted Protestant efforts to evangelize Catholics were, and how few successes they scored, even in the early 1850s when Protestants were most active. These efforts were limited to Germans. Only an occasional street preacher seemed to want to convert the Irish, or perhaps believed it possible. Protestants did not go beyond employing an American Tract

Society agent to pass out Bibles, or sponsoring briefly a small Old Catholic congregation, which rejected the authority of the church. By 1856, the *Christian Advocate*, which endorsed conversion, was reduced to advising Protestants to talk to servant girls and dispel "the false notions of Protestantism among them."[78] Whether Protestant rhetoric and a few seemingly menacing situations, which soon to be analyzed, were enough in light of these failures to convince Timon of a threat, we cannot really know. Perhaps, however, it was his inability to sustain such fears of mass conversion that occasionally led Timon to use a different argument in appealing to the missionary societies. For he would also at times say that Protestantism had "run its course" and was in imminent danger of collapsing because of mass defections—if only he could build a large seminary to train more priests to offer religious instruction to all those Protestants who requested it. While these claims probably warmed the hearts of European church authorities, they had little substance. Timon never mentioned the names of any converts in his confidential correspondence with the missionary societies.[79]

But Timon was an effective salesman. In his first two trips to Europe, in 1848 and 1849, he raised $8,000 from the three societies, the pope, and Prince Metternich, while other sources gave him vestments, sacred vessels, relics, and paintings. During his tenure of office (1847–67), he received $110,214 from Lyons, where his contacts reached back to his Vincentian days. He also obtained $10,920 and $6,800 from Munich and Vienna, where he was less well known, but where the fears he raised that anticlerical '48ers were exploiting the St. Louis Church conflict to hurt the church brought increased contributions in the mid-1850s.[80]

Yet here, too, success carried a cost. Protestants who thought the matter through, such as the editor of the *Commercial Advertiser*, knew that the local Catholic population could hardly support all of the building Timon accomplished. They wondered who or what was behind the local and national growth of the church. They knew Timon frequently went to Europe, because his movements were reported in the press. It did not take much imagining to project the financial power of the Vatican and the missionary societies, with their distinctly unrepublican connections in the European aristocracy, onto the local scene. Indeed, the missionary societies were already the bêtes noires of nativist conspiracy theorists.[81]

Timon's clergy was not much more sympathetic to his fund-raising efforts abroad. They accused him of being away too frequently, of not fairly dividing funds he gathered, of "begging," and of dishonest representations of the diocese. "You know the streets of Paris better than you know those of Buffalo ... and the names of the doors of Dublin are more familiar to you than your own breviary," said the bitter, anti-Timon manifesto published by dissident priests in 1864. "You have begged all over Europe, telling lies of the poverty of your wretched diocese and poor people."[82]

Actually Timon did go a long way toward fulfilling the priorities he set, though sufficient funds were never found to equal his ambitions, and he had to balance off one set of pressing needs against another. One of Timon's goals was to strengthen the parishes by increasing the number, and improving the quality, of priests, churches, and diocesan schools, the vital institutional network through which the average believer came to experience the church. Because of his own years on the frontier and what he could glean from European-born priests such as Guth and O'Reilly, Timon probably came to this field of activity conscious of the contingent nature of that religious experience. In Europe, because of shifting combinations of indifference by the hierarchy, regional shortages of priests, and government oppression, many Irish and German Catholics who were intense believers frequently knew their religion more through folk culture than through practice of the faith. They had attended church rarely, and were ignorant of the formal doctrines of the faith. American Bishops and European missionary society officials feared that such people would lapse into indifference, or were ripe for conversion. The activities of anticlerical '48ers, American nativists, and Protestant evangelicals fed their fears.[83]

When Timon came to the diocese there were only eighteen priests. There were only ten priests who could speak German. Most of them were in Buffalo and had to travel extensively around the region. Of the eighteen, a number were elderly and infirm, and would die within a few years of Timon's arrival. A few others, mostly isolated in rural parishes, were intemperate or, in Timon's words, living lives of "scandal," and had to be dismissed. As a consequence, Timon had to build the clergy from the ground up.[84]

Shortly after arriving, Timon began a seminary. For a decade little more than rented lodgings and basement classrooms, it was supervised by him and one or two diocesan priests. In 1854 there were only ten seminarians, and it had become clear to Timon that he could not hope to train enough priests to fill rapidly increasing diocesan needs. He began to negotiate with Catholic seminaries in Rome, Genoa, and Dublin for fellowships for his brightest candidates. When negotiations failed, he assumed these educational costs out of diocesan funds. The candidates who went abroad, usually young Irish-Americans, began in 1851 to take over important Irish parishes.[85] Timon met the problem of the need for German priests largely by inviting German Jesuits into the diocese to organize new parishes, which, in turn, were not under his direct control, but under that of Jesuit authorities. Timon also conducted a correspondence with other bishops in the rarely realized expectation that they had more German-speaking priests than they needed.[86] Finally he simultaneously expanded the clergy and relieved some of the pressures on priests by inviting various American and European orders, male and female, to staff diocesan schools and welfare institutions. By all these means, within three years the total number of clergy had been expanded to fifty-eight, which does not include the dozens of nuns who were now working in the diocese. Some 41 percent (twenty-three) of these priests were German.[87]

In nineteenth-century America, bishops usually ruled with an iron hand, because they feared that the fluidity of American life, American criticism of the hierarchy, and the absence of state power behind hierarchical authority all made priestly insubordination likely. In the Buffalo diocese this stern rule was exacerbated both by the rapid expansion of the priesthood, which brought suddenly a rush of young, inexperienced men into demanding roles, and by Timon's self-denying life-style and difficult personality, which was alternately paternal and arbitrarily authoritarian.[88] The result was years of bitter relations that culminated in the open revolt of 1864.

As a Vincentian official, Timon was reputed to be a tough manager of men, and as bishop he continued to earn the label.[89] It was not simply that he insisted on a spartan standard of living, or that he used parish revenues for diocesan purposes. He ruled arbitrarily, and showed little sympathy for priests when they came to him with troubles. Their jobs were demanding. Parishes continued to be understaffed, and priests overworked. In addition to saying mass and providing the sacraments, they were responsible for the frequent missions and jubilees Timon decreed to revitalize the faith. Moreover, they had to obtain compliance with his often unpopular pronouncements against aspects of Irish ethnic culture—boisterous wakes, lavish funeral processions, excessive drinking, loitering at the polls, and membership in secret nationalist societies. (The latter decree affected the German Masons and Odd Fellows, too.) A number of priests drank too much, and at least one belonged to a secret Irish nationalist order.[90] Irish, German, and French priests alike frequently disliked the funeral rules. They shared the burial customs of the laity, and the income they raised from funerals would be lost if they insisted on rules that colleagues in a neighboring parish might well ignore. Moreover, they had reason not to want to alienate funeral directors who were, especially among the Irish, usually among a parish's affluent men. Many priests, too, found it morally reprehensible to have to enforce an 1860 decree making it more difficult to bury the poor without cost. Free burial of the needy remained a principle Timon embraced, but he found it difficult to maintain Irish cemeteries, because so many families claimed inability to pay burial costs.[91]

Timon's authoritarian rule exacerbated these tensions, which were hardly unique to his diocese. He frequently made unannounced visits to parishes to check up on priests. The practice resulted from a suspicious nature and a difficulty delegating authority to his vicar generals. He punished improper behavior, recalcitrance, and insubordination sternly by assigning priests to remote parishes, a practice that inspired fear, and perhaps respect when applied consistently, but rarely love. And he showed little sympathy for them. He responded to complaints with cryptic biblical quotes and the refrain, "Priests suffer." When one priest said that his life had been threatened in the execution of his duties, Timon replied, according to his biographer, "Then you will die in a good cause."[92]

These struggles were hidden from public view. American Protestants had no way of knowing that the unswerving, fanatic unity and devotion they believed characterized the Catholic clergy could hardly be formed under the circumstances present in the diocese. They continued to believe that the priesthood marched to the beat of one, and only one, drummer, because a combination of folklore and ideology and isolation from Catholics led them in that direction. Moreover, the hardworking, self-denying moral discipline that Timon exacted from most of the diocesan clergy (and indirectly, by example and suggestion, from nuns and priests of religious orders in the diocese) seemed to establish the case for belief in total hierarchical control and complete clerical obedience. Yet if the social and political consequences of Catholic discipline were feared by Americans, the moral behavior of the clergy was also, somewhat paradoxically, respected. While nativists expressed disapproval of the appropriations of public funds for Sisters Hospital, they respected the Sisters of Charity for their devotion to the sick and dying, which the *Commercial Advertiser*'s Dr. Foote called "something beautiful and touching." Foote attributed this behavior to nothing less than the moral authority of both the institutional church and Catholic dogma. "How poor and insignificant must appear the fleeting strifes, competitions and honors of this world to those animated by the firm belief of the certainty of enjoying eternal bliss," said Dr. Foote, conscious, he continued, of the fact that Protestantism could make no such guarantees.[93]

It was a short step to believing that the Catholic clergy might become models not only of compassionate charity, but of self-sacrifice, discipline, and accepting, otherworldly piety. The clergy elsewhere and in general might have been regarded, stereotypically, as venal, corrupt, and depraved, but views of the local scene, populated by living, working clergy, were different. Even at the height of organized nativism there were few editorials in the three principal anti-Catholic papers, the *Commercial Advertiser*, *Christian Advocate*, and *Express*, that questioned the personal habits of individual members of the city's Catholic clergy, as opposed to its presumed political activities or passion for building ostentatious churches. Nor did these papers make allusion, through a local, individual example, to the gossip and folklore about the supposedly depraved, unchaste lives of priests and nuns. That Catholicism exacted such disciplined moral behavior in behalf of order and benevolence as local priests and nuns exhibited suggested that religion might also do so from lay adherents and that priests, from Father Mathew to the average parish pastor, could be the medium of that benign influence. Such secular influence was criticized when it came to electoral politics. But when the matter was inculcating the moral character that kept people sober, orderly in their homes and on the streets, and out of the poorhouse, it was deemed laudable, and where it was to be found, as in the church's temperance activity, it was praised.[94]

The positive influence of the church on social discipline was examined in another of Foote's editorials, "Matins," published in 1858, and immediately reprinted in the *Christian Advocate*. He reflected on the bells of St. Louis Church sounding before dawn to summon Catholics to mass, and he conjured up the vision of "the vast, cold church and its kneeling worshippers." He marveled that the Catholic immigrant worker in the city's new factories, "the man whom we see going to his work before the steam whistle sounds seven o'clock" had already been at mass. Such rigorous piety and discipline "must have a wide influence in shaping the character of our foreign population." With such thoughts in mind, both papers would begin to express pleasure when Catholic churches were filled at Lent, and to laud, as did Rev. John Robie, "the good work" done by Vincentian fathers in staging a well-attended mission. Protestants had begun to grasp the extent to which their historical adversary could be of use in building order, capitalism, and democracy.[95]

Partly in consequence of the shortage of priests, and partly the lack of structures, when Timon arrived local Catholic churches were very crowded. In 1848, he claimed, 6,000 regularly sought Sunday communion where only 1,000 could be accommodated. Several years later, he worried that there was such a crowd at the communion rail where he was celebrating mass that someone might be hurt. In consequence of this crowding, the physical expansion of the city, and the secession of opponents of the St. Louis trustees, Timon found it necessary to build five churches between 1848 and 1853. Timon would have preferred, he wrote church officials in Lyons in an appeal for funds, to build brick and stone churches in order to prevent degrading comparisons with Protestants, but he was not able to do so in the case of the five new structures. Between what little he was able to give the parishes and the small sums parishes generated from within, most of the churches were unimposing wooden structures.[96]

Timon had similarly modest success in building a Catholic school system. Though he complained bitterly against the variously "Godless" or "Protestant" public schools, he could not make attendance at parochial schools a religious obligation. The diocesan schools could not accommodate the majority of Catholic children in Buffalo. Adding to his frustration was the poor impression the Catholic schools made. The public schools were not actually the "magnificent" buildings Timon described in a letter to *Ludwigsmissionsverein* in 1848, but neither did they meet in the small basement rooms of humble churches, as did some parish schools.[97] Many Catholic parents were as frustrated by the situation as their bishop. The largest vote in the city for repeal of the state's antisectarian public school law in an 1850 referendum came from those sections of wards One and Four populated by new Catholic, Irish, and German immigrants.[98] Catholic parents faced a choice between inadequate, poorly equipped parish schools, where they wanted to send their children, and up-to-date, well-appointed public schools, of which they did not approve.

What Timon did accomplish at Buffalo was the creation of schools in every parish (and even a few winter night schools to compete with the public ones), replacement of lay teachers with nuns and priests from venerable teaching orders, and establishment of a small high school. He was aided in achieving acceptance of these schools among Germans by their desire for German as well as English language instruction. Faced with the necessity of choosing which groups of children should attend the frequently overcrowded parish schools, the bishop and Irish and German parents agreed that the first priority should be a Catholic education for girls. In light of the low opinion immigrant men had of American women—as spoiled, selfish, forward and outspoken—and of the widespread belief in the crucial role women must play in creating the ideal Catholic home, the choice was not surprising. By 1859 there were approximately 2,400 girls and 1,200 boys in all of the diocesan schools.[99] Outside this parish-based school system, various orders the bishop invited to the city operated four academies and day schools. All of them charged high tuition. Thus, they were accessible only to bourgeois Protestants, who, guaranteed a classical education by "cultured" (i.e., European) teachers from venerable religious orders and promised no religious teaching or proselytizing, sent mostly daughters to them. With the children of eminent men such as Fillmore enrolled in them, these schools contributed to the local prestige of Catholicism, though it is possible that they suffered declining enrollments during the years of most intense nativism. Moreover, an alternative for girls was created with the opening of the elite Buffalo Seminary. These private Catholic schools certainly did not contribute to the education of the Catholic poor.[100]

The modesty of parish churches and schools intensified Timon's desire for a majestic cathedral in a prominent spot visible to lake, canal, and rail travelers and to elite Protestants, from their homes and offices. Compensatory striving in reaction to the church's isolation and poverty was not the only source of this goal. There was a practical need for more facilities, especially for the Irish, who were unable to keep up with the pace set by Germans in creating parishes. It was, moreover, the more affluent, residentially stable Irish, residing on the fringes of the central business district, who were most in need of a new parish. They were staunch Catholics and generous with their money when the church required contributions. Both from a locational and social perspective, a new downtown cathedral parish would have functional value.[101]

Timon placed himself at the center of the planning and construction of St. Joseph's Cathedral, and thus experienced all of the difficulties the project encountered. He conceived of the idea not long after arriving, when he was denied regular use of St. Louis Church. Shortly after, he began fund-raising. With $2,000 in gold from the pope, he employed an architect to whom he presented general plans for a cathedral and parsonage derived from his own study of Gothic cathedrals. Not until 1851 was enough money raised to break ground.[102] Meanwhile he wanted to buy land in a prominent location. Fearing that American Protestants would attempt to interfere, during a period of two years he quietly acquired through third parties some lots situated in the heart of the commercial district, not far from the oldest, most prestigious Episcopal and Presbyterian churches.[103]

There were Americans who were displeased with the location, but they discovered Timon's activities too late to block them. They disliked the scale of the project, too. The *Express* and *Christian Advocate* probably voiced a common sentiment in contending throughout the 1850s that God and humanity would be better served by less ostentatious churches and more efforts to relieve the growing numbers of Catholic poor. The *Commercial Advertiser* agreed; and it articulated a concern that was probably also widespread among Protestants: in light of the marginal circumstances of so many local Catholics, what, presumably sinister, forces were paying the Cathedral's many bills?[104] Yet such criticisms did not exhaust the Protestant response to the cathedral, to which many bourgeois Protestants were ultimately drawn. To some extent they supported the project with well-publicized cash contributions because it won them favor with Catholic consumers and voters. Too, it was recognized as the *Courier* said, that the Cathedral would stimulate tourism by diverting travelers into Buffalo for sightseeing.[105]

But the sources of the cathedral's attractions were deeper. They lay in a hunger among many businessmen and professionals for aesthetic improvement of the core neighborhoods where many of them lived and worked, and in a provincial bourgeoisie's spiritual strivings for high culture and identification with a continuous cultural tradition rich in historical associations. Some of these impulses were then leading growing numbers of affluent Protestants to travel to the centers of their civilization in Britain and especially in continental Europe, and to seek out during their travels Catholic churches and the Vatican itself as attractions. This is what Fillmore, a contributor to the cathedral fund, did in 1856, the year in which he had an audience with the pope at Rome and was the nativist, American party candidate for president.[106]

Prior to the opening of the cathedral there were very few distinctive buildings in the commercial district that gave dignity to the scene observed daily by merchants, lawyers, and others. Public space in the business district was undeveloped—used, abused, and left to the ravages of neglect. Few parks or planted squares provided opportunity for quiet repose. Even the charming area a bit further uptown, "The Churches," which was formed by the conjunction of several diagonal streets and contained mansions and several elite Protestant congregations, was invaded by street vendors in the 1850s. Efforts to beautify the city's core with a new park early in the decade produced a major confrontation between low-tax Germans and Americans and a well-meaning city council.[107] When completed in 1855, St. Joseph's, along with the gardens around it, lent eye-catching beauty and culture to this uninspiring landscape, just as Timon hoped it would. Considerably more ornate and larger than its only architectural rival, nearby St. Paul's Episcopal Church, it was pronounced "a model of design and workmanship" by the *Republic*. Even the *Commercial Advertiser* admitted that the cathedral's artwork, much of which Timon brought from Europe, was "beautiful."[108] The events and ceremonies at the cathedral added to its attractions. Protestants were impressed by the rich pageantry of the June inaugural events (which many of them, along with ninety-five priests and eighteen bishops, attended), and, said the *Commercial Advertiser*, by the "very imposing" ceremonies attending the consecration of the bells in 1857. Protestants also regularly attended lectures there given by Timon and other priests, even when the subject was religion. Larger numbers still were present at benefit concerts for Catholic charities, such as the 1857 and 1859 performances of Handel's *Messiah*.[109] Thus, the cathedral created a cultured counterworld, within the heart of the modernizing city, yet somehow magically removed from its utilitarian commercial environment. It offered to non-Catholics as well as to Timon's own flock the possibility of both transcendence of the workaday world and therapeutic repose.[110]

Practical matters and pressing human needs continued to work on Timon's conscience. Protestants pointed out that any church whose adherents were as impoverished as Timon's flock needed to put its energies and resources to work in directions other than creating spectacles and imposing structures. In fact, the complex welfare needs of Irish and German immigrants were constantly on Timon's mind, and his various responses made him a pioneer in the rise of American Catholic charity.[111] Furthermore, because the American Protestant response to poverty and other local welfare needs was, besides the poorhouse, largely nonexistent before 1847 and inadequate after it, Timon simultaneously, almost single-handedly, created the institutional foundations of much of local charity.

As we have seen, the American bourgeoisie was usually incapable, or at best painfully slow, to organize private responses to the social problems around it, especially when immigrants were the sufferers. The Buffalo Association for the Relief of the Poor (1853) was deviled by the effort to separate the worthy from the unworthy poor and by a lack of support from affluent people. During the 1857–58 depression there was public confusion about whether the association still existed.[112] The other private Protestant charities, the various church societies, and the orphanage, women's industrial school, and public dispensary catered largely or exclusively to American Protestants, Buffalo's least needy group, and were also frequently underfunded. The inadequacy of Protestant responses to the needs of the immigrant poor resulted from forces deeper than the vast social distance between native and foreigner. Bourgeois ideology located the cause of poverty in the individual by identifying poverty and its attendant ills with improvidence and refusal to save during good times when there was work, and by unwillingness, in bad times, to take low-wage work or to move in search of jobs.[113] American Protestant culture deeply reinforced this orientation toward seeing the individual as the root of social problems. Their religion taught Americans, the *Commercial Advertiser* said in 1858, that they must "work out [their] own salvation with fear and trembling," without the aid of an apostolic church.[114] It also led them to see individual success in the world as a sign of grace and failure of sinfulness. It is not surprising that Protestants gave a great deal more thought and effort to reform of the individual character than to charity and institutionalized public welfare. The former led people to stand on their own feet, while the latter created dependence and sapped initiative.

American Protestants saw the public schools and the institutional church as necessary for proper socialization of the young and maintenance of morality in the adult. (It was not surprising that the most successful Protestant charity was called a "school.") In addition, Sabbath and temperance laws, some thought, stimulated individual self-control and discipline. But bourgeois Americans never fully trusted the argument that laws or social institutions could go beyond frightening or punishing to somehow inculcate in people core values their characters lacked. One internalized these values (self-help, self-control, sacrifice for family, obedience to legitimate authority, and deferral of gratification), upon which individual independence, social order, and republican government were thought to depend, instead by modeling one's character after those of parents, ministers, teachers, and public men and women, and by constantly struggling with oneself. Where cultures were deficient, as it was assumed was the case among the Irish, neither proper role models nor belief in self-improvement could exist. This lack of confidence in social engineering and contempt for the group and individual wanting in character explain the faulty efforts at charity organization and the occasional ridicule of the poor who were observed begging, taking food at a soup kitchen, or protesting for "work or bread." These attitudes also explain the unflagging commitment to the formula semiconsciously developed for dealing with the poor, even in the face of continual evidence of the inadequacy of its prescriptions. That formula was: the poorhouse for the lazy, intemperate, and socially unrespectable foreign poor: the workhouse for the criminal poor; and private, outdoor relief for the respectable deserving poor such as widowed, orphaned, or disabled Americans. The formula attached highly culture-bound moral categories to the victims of impersonal social processes. When applied, the formula did nothing to eliminate poverty, little to explain it, and not a great deal to mitigate its effects.[115]

As a Catholic, Timon was not freighted with these ideological burdens when thinking about poverty. For him, too, liberty and social order might depend on the individual, but in a superficial way. Only the apostolic church could provide the means of fitting the individual for society, and there could be no hope for either society or the individual except through the church. Moreover, especially in Ireland where a strong current of antimaterialism and otherworldliness characterized preaching, the church did not contend that poverty or wealth was a key to understanding the state of the soul. The individual had no obligation to strive to be successful, and poverty was not a moral failure, but a misfortune. Out of Christian love, one sought to lessen its effects, but it could never be eradicated.[116] Timon's anxieties about Protestant intentions toward the poor also impelled him to lessen the consequences of poverty. Like many northern Protestant-controlled welfare institutions, the Erie County Poor House and the Buffalo Protestant Orphanage had bad reputations among Catholics. The quality of care, especially at the former, was one problem, but just as significant to Timon's mind was the refusal of both institutions to admit priests to cater to Catholic spiritual needs. Protestant ministers were allowed to visit. Furthermore, the orphanage, to which local courts occasionally assigned the homeless, placed children in foster care if they could not be returned to a parent or guardian, and it was thus legally possible for a Catholic child to be sent to live with Protestants.[117] Thus, Timon might argue that Protestant charities were not merely grudging, but exacted conversion as the price of assistance. No proof was ever offered that such a quid pro quo scheme was randomly applied, let alone institutionalized. Few Catholic children ended up in the orphanage, and brief stays in the bedlam that was the poorhouse hardly seem conducive to the conversion of anyone. But living in a time of sectarian hostilities, it is not difficult to understand how Timon came to—and was able to play upon—such fears.

Immediately after arriving in Buffalo, Timon began his welfare activities by encouraging the establishment of parish St. Vincent de Paul societies.[118] Next, he created welfare and custodial institutions. He was involved in this institution-building activity at every stage. He acquired lands, often donations of the Le Couteulx family,[119] rented or planned construction of buildings, arranged for women's religious orders to come to manage facilities, sought donations from the European missionary societies and arranged for local collections, and drew up incorporation papers, which he often personally presented to legislators at Albany.

Just as impressive is the range of needs Timon addressed. He began in 1848 with the establishment of Sisters of Charity Hospital, which was located at first in a rented building near St. Louis Church, but within three years had newly constructed quarters. In 1849 Timon turned to the needs of orphans, establishing St. Vincent's Female Orphan Asylum under the care of the Sisters of Charity. Two years later St. Joseph's Male Orphan Society was established under the care of Sisters of St. Joseph; it was shortly thereafter merged with a trade school, St. John's Protectory, which Timon also established. Largely because of cholera epidemics, both the boys' and girls' orphanages had some 100 residents by the late 1850s. During the next decade, institutions were created for pregnant married women, widows with small children, prostitutes and unwed mothers, the deaf, the insane, and the aged and infirm. Like the German Jesuit parishes, most of these new institutions were not under Timon's direct control, but that of the various orders of nuns. They served diocesan needs and cooperated with diocesan officials. But those who managed them answered ultimately to other authorities. Timon did not possess the deeds to the various institutional properties either.[120] In addition, after 1848, the year of their arrival, the Sisters of Charity ran a winter soup kitchen with food supplied by parish St. Vincent de Paul societies. During hard times and in winter, the heated, clean charity kitchens were dispensing bread and soup to as many as 1,000 Protestants and Catholics a day. For many of the unemployed during 1857–59, these kitchens were the only thing separating them from starvation.[121]

The parishes also formally committed themselves to aid diocesan activities in behalf of orphans, widows, and others. But whether because of the poverty of many Catholics or their lack of traditions of giving, parish funds could provide only a fraction of the money required. Even the boys' orphanage, which enjoyed great popular support, had 42 percent of its expenses, from May, 1855, to January, 1857, paid with public funds. Dependence on public monies increased in the 1850s in the case of the diocesan hospital. As the number of patients and range of services increased, costs escalated beyond the capacity of the diocese to maintain a significant share of costs. During 1848–56 public monies accounted for 71 percent of the hospital's income, while diocesan sources were 19 percent and patient fees 10 percent.[122] Not surprisingly nativists raised objections to the growing public subsidy of these projects. During the 1850s criticism was routinely voiced by the *Commercial Advertiser*. But more significant is the lack of enthusiasm the general American Protestant public and wide segments of bourgeois leadership showed for attacks on the hospital, orphanages, and other institutions. Even Dr. Foote's editorial criticisms were not attacks on specific institutions, which he and others learned to respect for the useful work they did, but instead charged that the church was commanding too great a share of public funds.[123] In countless ways it had become evident that these facilities, and especially the hospital, because it catered to everyone and was the only such institution for over a decade, were becoming necessities.

The hospital had many claims on the Protestant public. It stuck by its original declaration of nonsectarian principles with, said the *Buffalo Medical Journal*, the organ of the American Protestant Buffalo Medical Society, "a fastidiousness which some may think is carried to an undue degree."[124] No Catholic proselytizing was ever proven—nor indeed even alleged after Lord's charges in 1850, and ministers of all faiths, including eventually Lord himself, came routinely to visit patients. Protestant ministers assisted in the process of referring the sick to the hospital. Americans regularly formed a significant part of the patients cared for, constituting 30 percent as early as 1849. Moreover, the sisters constantly expanded the range of their services and hence of the people they served. They established an outpatient clinic that offered free medicine and treatment every morning, and opened a wing for patients with contagious diseases. All the while, the sisters gained a reputation for selfless service. The hospital was always open to deal with the needs of sufferers. Their bravery during the 1849 cholera epidemic earned them high praise. Finally the hospital opened its doors to all local doctors and medical students, and both gained important clinical and surgical experience there. It soon became one of the premier teaching facilities in the country, and it pioneered in offering students clinical rather than simply lecture instruction.[125]

Support was forthcoming from the medical faculty at the University of Buffalo as well as from the Buffalo Medical Society, whose journal became accustomed to calling the facility a "public" hospital and passionately defended it against Lord's charges by citing its nonsectarianism and charging that Lord was motivated solely by "prejudice" and "denominational feeling." The journal also praised the hospital's cleanliness and low mortality rate that were a sharp contrast to the poorhouse clinic. Thus the overwhelmingly Protestant medical establishment, members of which were pillars of bourgeois society, fell into an unlikely alliance with the Catholic church.[126] Some strange configurations of interests and loyalties resulted. Among the physicians on the hospital's first medical board and for years on its staff was Dr. Josiah Trowbridge, a prominent anti-Catholic.[127] Others besides doctors found that the need to use the hospital posed a contradiction for them. Judge Nathan K. Hall was Fillmore's friend and adviser, and followed the former president into the American party in 1856. But when he reached the conclusion that his ailing son could not be treated at home, he was quite willing to send him to the sisters' hospital.[128]

Yet even Protestant friends of the hospital were not entirely convinced. The *Commercial Advertiser* and *Christian Advocate* agreed the hospital was useful and nonsectarian, and eventually were able to suggest donations to charitably inclined Protestants. But both papers also felt, along with Trowbridge and other eminent American Protestant doctors on the staff, that there was a need for another hospital that was "public" to the extent that it was identified with no one confession, yet controlled by bourgeois Americans.[129] There was perhaps less ideology and prejudice in this than pride, a dislike of having to admit dependence on the Catholic church. As Lord himself said plaintively in his attack on the hospital, "If we are so dependent on the Romanists, it is time we bestirred ourselves."[130] The result was a salutary competition that profited the public greatly. After two failed efforts, due to lack of interest and financial support, to establish *their* hospital, in 1858 American civic leaders opened the doors of Buffalo General Hospital. Protestants simultaneously were increasing support for their own orphanage, which continually had been bested by Catholic institutions in the competition for public monies.[131]

Coexistence did not necessarily breed either cooperation or even good-natured rivalry between these various types of public facilities. During the Civil War, Timon rejected pleas that he not, on the basis of the sisters' donated labor, underbid Buffalo General Hospital to obtain Navy contracts for the care of servicemen.[132] Nor did peaceful institutional coexistence necessarily spill over into other areas of civic welfare activity, let alone impede the rise of political nativism. As we shall see in analyzing immigrant civic mobilizations, Catholics had to wage campaigns for equality at the poorhouse, on which they continued to depend because the diocese could not provide adequate relief for any but a minority of the faithful. Also, schemes to use ostensibly public institutions controlled by Protestants to wrest delinquent Catholic youth out of their homes and neighborhoods in the name of order and education could still be hatched in the late 1850s, and had to be contested by Timon and his allies.

Yet there can be no doubt that during the 1850s there emerged a new, more tolerant and interdependent, interconfessional order, which profited everyone, while forcing significant mutual accommodations between American Protestants and foreign Catholics. Tailoring his own actions and the character of the diocese itself to suit the American environment, Timon was successful in demonstrating the usefulness of the church to a society that was hardly predisposed to be hospitable to it. For their part, in ways they understood and in others they could not completely fathom, American Protestants were touched by the Catholic presence and well served by it.

Beyond the time and place of these contending parties, however, lay a process with important implications for the future. The boundaries of the American mainstream were being reshaped and broadened. Like those immigrants favoring German-language instruction in the public schools, Timon discovered that American Protestants assumed that children must learn a common culture and common language in schools run by the state, and that while other sectarian or minority culture schools might exist, they could not be considered legitimate guardians of the public culture. Yet in other realms of public life, through the interaction of the Catholic church and American society, "public" was now being stretched to mean whichever institution might provide, as did Sisters of Charity Hospital, the best social goods and services in the civic marketplace. To reach these new boundaries, both the Catholic church and American guardians of republican society had to modify their expectations, beliefs, and behavior. In these not always equal but nonetheless mutual accommodations lay the genius of the merging system of American social pluralism. Politics, to which we now turn, was rapidly being shaped around just such modifications, to the extent that it would become the principal mechanism for expressing that genius.

Part Four

The Politics of Pluralism

INTRODUCTION:

Politics, Pluralism, and Social Integration

By the first mass immigration the American political system and the political culture endowing it with emotional and intellectual meanings were well formed. Immigration would add significant pluralistic purposes and forms, but the institutional framework of politics was the product of a complex fusing of ideology, tradition, and experience during colonial and early national history.

During the national liberation struggle that culminated in the Revolution, and subsequently the years of constitution making, Americans brought together diverse elements in shaping their politics. From Protestantism came trust in the individual moral conscience and faith in the efficacy of voluntary effort in the public sphere. From English common-law principles, Enlightenment political theories, and abiding Renaissance traditions of civic humanism came republican beliefs that government must be restrained by law and an active citizenry or it would serve no ends but its own; and that the basic aim of government must be protection of the citizen's liberty and civic equality against special interests wishing to use the state to destroy the rule of law and the bases of individual self-sufficiency.[1]

Because of elite fears of majoritarian tyranny and widespread commitment to certain nonhereditary deference relations, the political synthesis of the late eighteenth century did not implement democracy, even as new state and federal constitutions institutionalized representative government. In combination with the defeat of monarchy and colonialism, however, the tremendous scale of geographical mobility after the opening of the West, the growth of property-holding and taxpaying, the rise of commercialized agriculture and interregional markets, and the Second Great Awakening all paved the way for expansion of political rights. Deference relations declined as people came to doubt that they were obligated to vote for their "social betters." A powerful process of reform was unleashed that cemented new relationships between citizens and government and gave root to a new culture of politics. The suffrage qualification was democratized in state after state to include all native and naturalized white male adults. Paper ballots replaced oral voting. Presidential electors were chosen by popular rather than legislative balloting. Local and state judges and administrators were elected, which swelled the number and frequency of elections. Nominating conventions replaced closed caucuses in selecting candidates, and the list of elected public officials grew at the expense of appointees.[2]

No more important innovation now developed than the rise of the modern political party. The expansion of the electorate and the increasing frequency of elections routinely required mass organization of voters. In turn, loose aggregations of factions were in the 1830s and 1840s transformed into two mass parties, Whigs and Democrats. The two parties moved to establish their partisan machinery at the various levels of the federalized political system, to monopolize the flow of political information through a subsidized press, and to enforce party discipline. Nominating conventions might be open, but those controlling agendas and procedures had special advantages. Ballots might be secret, but the form of the ballot, a colored ticket distributed by the parties at the polls and handed by voters to partisan election officials rather than placed directly in ballot boxes, allowed close scrutiny of voters. This method of voting also allowed for penalizing dissident candidates by erasing their names from ballots and replacing them with more pliable politicians. Patronage, which previously had been tied to family and personal relations, as well as government contracts for printing and infrastructural improvement and outright cash grants, emerged as partisan methods of rewarding party loyalty. The number of appointed positions and of government jobs and contracts was simultaneously growing, especially in cities, to accommodate the needs of growing populations and the growth of commerce.[3]

Political leadership changed in tandem with the rise of mass politics. When party identification was weak, socially prestigious, affluent professionals and entrepreneurs had organized local electoral activity. Elites and plebeian and working classes had been linked through a mutualistic ethic of noblesse oblige, by which employment and various types of informal patronage were exchanged for deference. But deference relations collapsed with the expansion of the economy, electorate, and the nation's borders. Moreover, immigrants brought their own systems of authority and generated their own leaders. Then, too, the populist style required of an active candidate was distasteful to many men who claimed respectability. For them, politics now seemed a nasty business of flattering the masses and putting partisan interest above the common good, both of which contradicted the sober style of the post-1843 businessman. His absorption in business, concern for the ethics of his actions, and image of himself as building a decent, progressive civilization left neither the time nor the inclination for campaigning, let alone for flamboyant acts of charity and personal patronage. While gaining popularity with the masses, elite men "lost class" with their fellows by connecting themselves too closely with party activities. Of course, as taxpayers and those profiting from a good investment climate, such men and their retainers among lawyers and others needed politics too much to absent themselves completely. They funded party activities, accepted honorific party posts and ad hoc advisory positions in government, ran for such prestigious offices as judge and mayor, and maintained communications with party leaders, especially at the state and national levels, where important economic legislation originated. Furthermore, when corruption was perceived to be raising the costs of government to unacceptable heights, elite men reentered politics as reformers. But they seldom involved themselves in the day-to-day running of local party affairs or in getting out the vote through ingratiating acts of patronage and backslapping fraternity. These tasks now fell to men, often neighborhood retailers, saloon keepers, and contractors, who were less socially prestigious, though often no less affluent (for politics was still expensive).[4]

Open access to power imposed the obligation to compete for it. In turn, a unique political culture emerged to establish the rules and values attached to electoral processes. The dominant standards of this culture were an informed citizenry, high levels of formal participation, and a constant flow of information between citizens, parties, and government. Realization of these standards depended on both the positive psychological disposition toward government and politics possessed by an empowered citizenry and the extrapolitical experience of voters, especially in voluntary associations and ad hoc citizens mobilizations. The civic activities of hard-pressed taxpayers protesting rising rates, grieving trade unionists lobbying for laws in their behalf, and members of churches or ethnic associations seeking charters from government all provided training and inspiration for political involvement. Thus, partisan-political and governmental-civic integration reinforced one another. Experiences in more private realms were also tapped by the political culture. The strictly internal activities of voluntary associations in organizing their own affairs assisted in preparing people for politics. In a sense then the struggles among Old Lutheran congregants or St. Louis Church parishioners were breeding grounds for democratic citizenship, all the more so when the issues were ones of republican self-government against the claims of traditional authority. Early experiences within the family that made for a trustful disposition were also significant. Like the family's domestic system of authority, the political system was based on representation and characterized by unequal power relations, and it, too, depended on a balancing of involvement and quiescence. The routine work of government and of party machinery could not be accomplished under conditions of constant scrutiny by the general citizenry.[5]

The shortcomings of the politics of the second-party system are easy to discern. The new political culture sought to integrate diverse, competing groups through the common rules of the electoral game, but not to lay down ideas about the collective ends of politics. It would find itself vulnerable before the assault upon traditions of government activism that accompanied the rise of a capitalist ideology that sought to substitute notions of spontaneous order through market forces and interest group competition for ideas of commonwealth. Furthermore, a politics based on the frequent, opportunistic fashioning of electoral coalitions of diverse groups soon displayed a propensity to deflect rather than resolve problems and to substitute party-managed propaganda and symbols for information, discourse, and statecraft. In flattering the average white, male voter, frequently with recourse to bigotry, political rhetoric reinforced already rigid gender and race boundaries and further burdened already weak social groups. The corruption accompanying the pursuit of party and individual advantage was hardly the best civic education for immigrants, let alone productive of cheap, efficient government.[6] Perhaps, as Amy Bridges says, this politics created an unintended political community that no one but the politicians who directly profited from it could wholeheartedly endorse.[7] Yet the new, American forms of politics proved, in the passions of mass campaigns and high voter turnouts,[8] able to involve the vastly different types of citizens of an increasingly pluralistic society in public affairs. Even the disfranchised northern free blacks and voteless women created, through moral suasion, campaigns aimed at voters, and memorializing legislatures, a nonelectoral political life that closely mirrored the broader expectations of the culture of the second-party system.[9] In such a political context it is easy to imagine the greenest immigrants coming to feel that quick access to the collective life of their new homeland was gained by becoming citizens and voters.

Beyond the efficient integration of politics lay the integration of society through politics—the social contribution of the second-party system. The social functions of politics manifested themselves most significantly in shaping class struggle and in ethnic group formation and interethnic relations. American history has hardly been unique in witnessing a capitalist social revolution that generated profound social conflicts. What is unique is that a democratic political system and culture, born of a revolution with which ordinary folk proudly identified, preceded the advancement of capitalism and formed essential parts of the context in which those social conflicts were resolved.[10] The decentralized federal state in nineteenth-century America, was, as Alan Dawley says, contested terrain, not as in Europe "a fortress of central power entrenched behind earthworks of secret police, tax collectors and provincial administrators [and] engaged in war against its subjects."[11] While the expansion of capitalism centralized power in fewer hands, and increasingly undermined the bases of working people's self-sufficiency, they did not feel disfranchised, and they basked in the dignity the franchise imparted to them. They held to the belief that government could and should be made to serve their interests, as Buffalo workers demonstrated in their effort to take the order system into politics. There would be large numbers of strikes and work-related protests, many of them violent, in American history. But the ballot and the parties, which mediated between groups and channeled conflicts into nonviolent, routine processes, offered a political alternative. That alternative was narrowed sufficiently that class issues infrequently became sources of partisan contention, as we have noted in the case of Buffalo.[12] Economic elites, however, were forced as a practical matter to accept the democratic rules of politics. Wealth, of course, gave them ample opportunity to protect their considerable interests, corrupt government, and subvert the democratic aspirations of ordinary folk. But not infrequently they needed no prodding to accept democracy, for they had their own formulations of democratic values, increasingly oriented toward bolstering entrepreneurial capitalism. Moreover, democracy legitimized their wealth by seemingly proving that it was earned, not inherited through an aristocratic lineage and hereditary landed estate.[13] The frequent presence of worker and employer, as partisans of democracy, in the same political party gave the parties a socially distinct, autonomous identity, and thus created a social universe that was itself a counterpart to class.[14]

The impact of the new politics on ethnic group integration was equally profound. More than any other realm of local social life, politics brought native and foreigner together in common activities, institutions, and aspirations. Yet simultaneously, while assisting the foreigner's movement into society, politics also hastened ethnic group formation. The paradox is more apparent than real. The ethnic group, through the medium of the political party, entered the political system. The immigrant himself entered, not as an individual, but as a member of the ethnic group, which was consequently strengthened not only by his enhanced loyalty, but by having political interests and resources to protect and expand.[15] Thus, the processes of pluralism in politics and of ethnicization were mutually reinforcing, as we have noted in analyzing German group formation. Those aspiring to lead German immigrants perceived early that political activity in pursuit of ethnic goals could develop group feeling and consolidate their own leadership.

That immigrants were easily fit into the new political system, which is attested to in the 1850s by high voter turnout rates at Buffalo and other immigrant-receiving centers,[16] resulted from two related developments: the lack of rigor and exclusivity in the method by which foreigners became naturalized citizens and voters; and the efficiency with which the emergent ethnic group could be brought into the polity by politicians seeking convenient ways to organize a mass electorate.

Americans embarked upon their national history with a split vision of the absorptive capacity of their society and the benefits of a culturally diverse population. The benign workings of the first melting pot of the colonial period led some to an optimistic vision of themselves as, in John Higham's words, "a truly cosmopolitan people," fortunate to possess "a universalistic and eclectic sense of national identity."[17] But others, frightened by the prospect of being inundated with foreign-speaking immigrants of different values and habits, were less sure. Both groups agreed that some method of social homogenization was required if the nation were to attain cultural coherence and political viability. A consensus emerged that the issue was not whether the new immigrant should be allowed to become naturalized and a voter. Instead the relevant matters were understood to be first, how much time sufficed for a new arrival to become sufficiently versed in the values of his new society to play a role in its governance, and second, what constituted the standard by which his preparation was to be measured.[18]

The process of naturalization and federal citizenship, with voting rights, decided by Congress in 1802 was ingenious in its simplicity, demanding in its terms, and educative in its purposes; and it was uniquely liberal. It tied naturalization and voting together, and made achieving the latter, which was available only through birth and property in Europe, contingent on naturalization alone.[19] Naturalization itself was to be dependent on "belief, will, consent and choice,"[20] prefiguring the activism demanded of members of the polity by the civic culture. After two years' residence in America, those over eighteen at the time of arrival had to make a public declaration of intent to become a citizen. Three years later, one completed the process at a local court. There it was necessary to demonstrate good character and desire to remain in the country, and after showing an understanding of its principles, to swear allegiance to the Constitution and renounce allegiance to any foreign sovereign or state.[21] Incentives to undertake the process were substantial. Following the initial declaration of intent, immigrants could, in New York State, own and sell real property with the protection of the laws, which must have seemed significant to Buffalo's property-conscious Germans.[22] Because most immigrants took more than five years to acquire substantial property, even more significant was that voting in federal elections (and by state law, in local and state elections) became possible after naturalization. In its 1846 constitution New York State, which continually lowered court fees to make naturalization more appealing, adopted undemanding residence requirements for naturalized citizens wishing to become voters. Immigrants had to be naturalized only ten days to vote, provided that they had been a state resident for one year, a county resident for four months, and an election district resident for thirty days. No oath was required to attest to length of residence, and until 1859 there were no state registration laws, so that under guidance of politicians many probably came to cast their ballots before the laws allowed. Party operatives and their partisan allies among judges were the ones who taught immigrants what the process required, helped them meet their fees, and get them into court in time to cast a vote in the next round of elections.[23]

Under the law, immigrants became naturalized not as members of groups but as individuals, and they became familiar with an American legal system in which, as bearer of rights, taxpayer, defendant, or plaintiff, the individual and not the organic community was the basic unit of integration. Yet it was as members of groups that they entered American politics. The reasons for this involve the conjunction of electoral federalism, which created various levels of territorially rooted constituencies, and the need to organize efficiently a mass electorate. The political parties organized voters where they lived, in their electoral districts. In northern cities voters lived in identifiable, self-constituted groups, in extensive, territorially based ethnic neighborhoods, which had their own leadership and internal systems of political communication in communal institutions, the ethnic press, the neighborhood tavern, and family, kinship, and region-of-origin networks.[24] For politicians, the situation was ideal. Not only did it facilitate getting out the vote, but it allowed for a relatively light-handed, indirect rule over ethnic voters, who might have grown resentful of outside political control of their own neighborhoods. In fact, ethnic control of ethnic politics was more a matter of symbol than substance. The political parties purposefully managed the process by which groups bargained on behalf of individuals for patronage and public resources. Moreover, they guided the process of group empowerment by determining where, when, and how ethnic leadership was brought into decision-making positions in both party and government. In the process, the parties also educated this leadership to deal effectively with the world beyond the group. Thus, while politics continually impeded the consolidation of an independent working-class movement by luring its leadership into party and government, it proved a training school, with a curriculum constantly improvised by American party leaders, for the leaders of the ethnic groups that were the basic units of partisan activity.[25]

Nonetheless electoral federalism did vitalize ethnicity, and was in turn vitalized by it. Even as the nationalizing forces of capitalism were stimulating the centralization of power and influence, local government, though increasingly linked economically and politically to these new, national centers, remained a bastion of democratic participation. Localities enjoyed more autonomy than they would possess in the next century in matters such as schooling and law enforcement. A significant amount of decision making over issues of this type actually remained rooted in wards, precincts, and school districts.[26] In one form, therefore, the ethnic group, already forming as the result of shared origins and experiences of uprooting and resettlement, emerged as a mobilization of coresident citizenry joined together in political parties, voluntary associations, and ad hoc groups to obtain an equitable distribution of public resources. Thus, the territorially based, urban ethnic group became one of the most political of social entities, for it constantly brought foreigners into an active relationship with the polity.

As Ira Katznelson has noted, where urban politics was established on a foundation of territorially based ethnic groups, there were profound effects on the agenda of politics and the resolution of social conflict. As work became separated from residence, and residence began to be located in neighborhoods with an ethnic character, conflicts associated with work and economic inequality and those associated with religion and culture might be played out in separate settings, each with its own groundings. "Each kind of conflict," Katznelson says, "has had its own separate vocabulary and set of institutions: work, class, and trade unions; community, ethnicity, local parties, churches, and voluntary associations."[27] Electoral coalitions could be fashioned on the basis of cultural and religious issues because no matter how at odds with themselves German immigrants might have been, the protection of Old World habits and customs provided a common denominator for them. Thus, the politicized ethnic group became a defender of the autonomy of an ethnic, group life rooted in home, community, and neighborhood, with their various constellations of ethnocultural habits, values, and symbols. Of course, as we noted in examining the functional segmentation of Buffalo's labor along ethnic lines, the worlds of work and ethnicity might overlap considerably. But the need to forge coalitions led politicians to keep class grievances and prescriptions for radical change in the ownership or relations of production out of politics. The parties instead generally addressed issues of work and of the distribution of wealth in ways that sought to unify, not divide, men. Hence, they rejected redistribution of economic power and profit, and developed policies to stimulate growth powerful enough to bring prosperity to millionaire and wage earner alike. They emphasized the interdependence and common interests of classes, not the conflicts inherent in an economy rooted in inequality.[28]

It is doubtful that many native-born, white Americans understood the long-term implications of these emergent political processes. Convinced as many were by a Whiggish view of unilinear progress in history and a messianic, providential view of their national history, they saw democracy not as a process, but a set of institutions and procedures fixed in constitutional arrangements. These were legitimized by the symbolic texts of the Revolution and the period of constitution-making and by the imprimatur of the Founding Fathers.[29] Their own links with the Fathers gave them, they felt, the authority to dictate precisely what the nature and purposes of these arrangements should be. The possibility that republican institutions and democratic political methods would continue to evolve, that they were not merely a matter for rote learning by young people and foreigners, but subject to innovation and reinterpretation, was a shock. And all the more when that innovation was inspired by "ignorant" Irishmen and "lymphatic" Germans. Yet immigrants were nearly present at the creation of mass politics in northern cities. While the direction of the basic processes of politics was determined before they arrived, their grassroots activities and the politicians' need to include them gave character to this emergent political system. In the next chapter we shall see how vote-hungry American politicians, in the formative decade (1843–53) of local ethnic politics, accommodated themselves to the growing immigrant presence. In the final chapter we shall trace the course and consequences of these accommodations during the national crises and partisan realignments of the 1850s.

CHAPTER 11

Immigrant Political and Civic Integration: The Formative Decade, 1843–53

As Buffalo emerged from the 1837–43 depression, striking changes in politics and government were occurring. The expansion of population and enterprise put a strain on the city's crude infrastructure and necessitated an expansion and improvement of the functions of government. The subsequent growth of taxation, municipal debt, and public employment brought controversies and helped set a new agenda of concerns for citizens and voters. Along with economic and political crises in Europe, American prosperity stimulated immigration and immigrant residential stability, and hence immigrant political power. By late 1844 local and state politicians had begun to comment on the growing diversity of the electorate. Millard Fillmore attributed his loss of Erie County in the 1844 gubernatorial contest to the swelling of the Democratic immigrant vote. This election was just the beginning of Whig tribulations. Neighborhood after neighborhood in Buffalo fell to the Democrats as Irish and German voting increased.[1]

With the growth of the electorate and the rise of increasingly competitive political parties came another transformation of key importance. In the 1830s and early 1840s the new national parties—Whigs and Democrats—had only a shadow existence in municipal affairs. Mayors were chosen by the Common Council on the basis of personal qualities and social prestige. Councilmen were elected, but their manners, morals, and reputations for dispensing charity and comradery had as much to do with victory and defeat as did ideology or stands on issues. ("Politics had nothing to do with votes," said Dr. Burwell of the 1837 councilmanic elections in three of the five wards; charges of personal immorality had decided each contest.) When issues did arise, they were not framed in a partisan context. Indeed party identification is largely absent from reporting on the local politics of the time. After 1840, however, partisanship and party organization took hold, and elections were hotly contested. While in 1841 two Whigs opposed one another for mayor, by mid-decade party differences were an established fact in local contests. Now, too, as the mayor and councilmen of his party increasingly coordinated their policy initiatives, council elections became partisan. Simultaneously the national parties became established locally. After the 1840 presidential contest, in which the parties spent more money locally and generated unprecedented excitement, local party organizations routinely organized to fight for national and state candidates.[2] Partisanship now pervaded politics.

The political context formed by these developments began to unravel a decade later. The year 1853 found the second-party system in the North in crisis. Its stability was shaken by nativism, slavery, and temperance, all of which conspired to weaken the Democrats, destroy the Whigs, give brief life to the nativist Americans, and provide success for the new Republicans.[3] The local burden of economic crisis was added to these grave national and state issues. As the fortunes of Buffalo's waterborne commerce declined before the advance of railroads, the dislocations experienced by capital and labor became part of political debate and partisan calculation. Local politics and government were also being transformed by changes in the physical boundaries and formal processes of the polity. In 1853 Black Rock was annexed, the city's wards were reorganized, and the charter was rewritten. The city now had thirteen rather than four wards. This greatly increased the number of territorially based elected offices and patronage jobs and hence opportunities for ethnics. In 1843–53 nine foreign-born men (five Germans, three Irishmen, and a Scot) held ward and citywide elective or appointive office; after 1853 almost that many would routinely be elected from one of the city's new ethnic wards in each municipal contest.[4] Thus, the city that faced the various national and local crises of the 1850s did so in a greatly altered political context of weakened or dying parties, new political solidarities, and an enhanced ethnic political presence.

Immigrants of the formative 1843–53 decade came with no experience of participatory, democratic politics or of representative government. There was not as yet a mass electorate anywhere in Europe, and hence there were no mass political parties. Parties were still mostly assemblies of notables from the aristocracy and upper bourgeoisie. Equality of all citizens before the law and in dealings with government was only just emerging, as were: the uniform state incorporating, while subordinating, regional and communal structures; the replacement of estates by classes and localities in political representation; the precedence of nation-state over dynastic state; and the emergence of both influential private political circles and citizen voluntary associations capable of preparing people for political participation. The degree of political and civic modernization, however, was not uniform across Europe. Most advanced in Britain and France, it had hardly begun in Ireland, a captive nation with a state apparatus tightly controlled by Britain through the narrow Anglo-Irish establishment, or in the German states, where the divided, popular forces of democratization faced the greater power of a deeply entrenched Old Order.[5]

Yet both Irish and German immigrants had had political histories in Europe that variously provided an experiential basis for participation in American politics, especially when past experience could be complemented by the exigencies of their new American lives. While the German peasantry and residents of unincorporated towns had enjoyed no opportunities for sustained involvement in politics or government, the same could not be said of the *Heimat* residents of southern and western German states. It is true that *Heimat* governments were not chosen democratically, let alone conducted in direct response to the wishes of constituents. As vacancies appeared on local councils, new members were coopted from the ranks of older men, who were chosen on the basis of family name, kinship, business ties, and personal qualities. But the goal of these governments is instructive. The councils and *Bürgermeisters* sought to maintain fiscal integrity and social stability by controlling formal admissions to legal residence. In pursuit of order they worked alongside the guilds, which regulated the crafts by controlling admission of journeymen into local employment and conferral of the status of master. Power over the process of admission to legal residence and to a guild was the key to social stability.[6] Such a politics differed greatly from the American system: most residents had no role in decision making and the purpose of government was little more than to freeze the status quo. Yet the passion for security and order was not to be restricted to the Germans' Old World experience. In America Germans had crafts to defend against proletarianization, wages against the order system, entrepreneurial activities against costly licensing requirements and cumbersome regulations, small parcels of property against tax collectors, and popular cultures of recreation against Sabbatarians and prohibitionists. Municipal government again became a means for defending the fragile order of daily life. This was often, especially in its defense of small property, a politics of narrowly defined individual and group interests without the pretensions to speak for the common good that bourgeois Americans professed. But its legitimacy in a culture valuing craft and property was beyond a doubt.

What was needed to connect Germans with politics and government were processes of popular participation and mobilization. Energies liberating these processes were to be found within the emerging group. First, as we observed in the group that founded the *Weltbürger*, there was an ambitious ethnic leadership, which seized on political and civic participation as the means for unifying a fragmented people. Second, there was the popular, participatory experience gained by creating and maintaining ethnic institutions and *Vereine*. In Europe churches, guilds, and singing societies had often been part of the established order of things predating the life of the oldest resident, and their rules and methods were prescribed by custom.[7] In America, what had been taken for granted had to be voluntarily reestablished in a new environment, in which tradition was weak and authority constantly subject to questioning. The organization of *Vereine*, some of which drafted constitutions and sought charters from the state,[8] encouraged habits of participation, and provided an opportunity for dealings with government. The bitter intracommunal struggles among Old Lutherans and St. Louis parish Catholics also suggest, from another direction, the dynamics of this shadowy world of intraethnic immigrant political socialization.

Habits of civic and political mobilization, participation, and innovation were only slowly and sometimes painfully acquired by Germans. In contrast the Irish brought them from Europe. To be sure, taken on its own terms the British colonial system would have produced little more than the experience of powerlessness. But the Irish hardly took their situation on British terms. They developed a deep, amoral appreciation for the uses of power and a cynicism about the moral claims of Anglo-Saxon political institutions. In the parish church they forged a countervailing system of authority and communal solidarity, and a quasi-government that settled intracommunal disputes through the parish priest's harmonizing offices. Priests also negotiated with officials and landlords in behalf of parishioners.[9] Largely because of the centrality of the church in their affairs and the underdevelopment of the countryside, the Irish lacked what the Germans had in the Old World—a pattern of secular associations that created a broad range of opportunities for exercising communal leadership and the responsibility for maintaining order. But there were Irish experiences analogous to the organized, popular participation of the Germans, and these had the virtue of being political. Through local and regional secret societies, bound by oaths and headed by strong, ruthless men, the Irish dispensed rough justice to landlords, colonial officials, and collaborators, and periodically mounted uprisings.[10] In Daniel O'Connell's

Catholic Association (1823-29), they developed a national mass movement, which sought to end all discrimination against the church. A mix of popular and elite influences, it was supported at the grass roots through contributions, rallies, and petitions, but it was controlled in a disciplined fashion from above by an urban, intellectual leadership and the parish clergy.[11] Variously serving to create foundations for public organization were extensive, informal networks of mutual support and communication based on family, kinship, and godparentage. These were strong in direct proportion to the universal distrust of public, governmental authority.[12]

The Irish immigrated, therefore, with feelings of national identification that served as a counterpoint to regional animosities, an experience of disciplined activity bound by codes of honor and solidarity, a capacity for innovation and organization in the management of their own affairs, and an appreciation for the uses of power. American influences on Irish politics reinforced these. The church, which continued to pervade all aspects of group life, still provided authoritative models of discipline and obedience, while the parish priest, still a communal diplomat and arbitrator, doubtless was one inspiration for the neighborhood political operative.[13] As in Ireland, moreover, mobilizations to protect the church continued to encourage activism, and to make maintenance of the church's rights essential to the agenda of secular politics. On a deeper, psychological level, too, the Jansenist ethos of Irish Catholicism, which construed the cause of social evil to be original sin, helped create distrust of the reform currents that pulsed through American politics. In turn, legitimacy was given to politics bent less on perfecting society than on power for limited group, family, and individual needs.[14] What gave special salience to this orientation for the Irish was the chronic poverty and unemployment of the majority of the group, for whom the power to bargain for patronage, offices, cash, and contracts was a more important consideration than it was for the more prosperous, skilled Germans. But the same habit of looking to politics for individual alternatives to low-wage, unskilled work conditioned the Irish in times of economic crisis to demand that government provide for the unemployed poor. Another formative influence on Irish politics was the reconstruction of strong family and friendship networks, which along with the parish church and neighborhood tavern, facilitated political communication. These networks also were an informal and highly personalized political recruiting mechanism for staffing party organizations and determining the distribution of patronage within the group.[15]

In contrast to the Germans, the Irish, with their capacity for solidarity and their political acumen, seemed ready to begin the effective practice of American politics soon after their arrival. Indeed their success would be one of the causes of the hatred many Americans had for them. The Irish needed only a mechanism for establishing themselves politically and for putting forward claims to power and rewards. Like the Germans, only more intensely and effectively, they found it in the Democratic party.

The Democrats' ability to win immigrant allegiances was a product of two distinct achievements. First, though neither party was ideologically consistent in its approach to specific issues, the Democrats projected ideological messages compelling to working-class immigrants. The second was the party's skill in integrating these immigrants into the daily round of partisan activities—electioneering, governing the party, and distributing political resources and rewards.

Even prior to mass immigration, northern Democrats were successful in preempting claims to represent the welfare of the ordinary white working-class man. This claim was a part of the received wisdom all immigrants assimilated when they began to be informed about political affairs. Democrats called their party the "Democracy," as if to identify it, as Jean Baker has said, not as a mere organization, but as a mass movement personifying the people's own will.[16]

Most important in putting forward this claim was the party's political economy, which grew in importance because of the economic processes of the period in which immigrant politics took shape. Voters lived with painful memories of economic collapse. Some local Germans, for example, lost their savings in broken banks during the era's financial panics, but saw few bankers ruined and most of them rise to affluence again.[17] On the other hand, flush times raised questions about the morality of the acquisition and distribution of vast wealth. Founded upon a suspicion of power and belief in both human corruptibility and the inevitability of conflict over the world's goods, the Democracy's political economy had two articles of faith. Public welfare and social progress were founded upon the efforts of sturdy, self-reliant workingmen, who asked for no special favors from government and wished to be unhindered by government-protected private monopolies. Ideal government was frugal and decentralized. Its power was distributed in a carefully balanced federal system and limited to ensuring fairness and equality through legislation rather than through regulation. Essentially conservative, the Democracy's vision did not call for leveling social differences or redistributing wealth, but for protecting the legal balance between labor and capital, while maintaining the rights of both parties. But it was couched in egalitarian rhetoric, which not only gave it luster, but worked to the detriment of the Whigs.[18]

Proceeding on the premises that government inaction produced stagnation, that class differences were eradicable, and that in America individuals gained or lost in social competition through character and education rather than through privilege or wealth, Whigs favored government involvement in the economy. They advocated subsidies and legal assistance to corporations developing transportation to consolidate national markets, and manipulation of tariff and the money supply to stimulate growth. They were not worried about favoritism, because their mutualistic view of class relations dictated that what was good for capital was in the long run also good for labor. (A very large percentage of American entrepreneurs were Whigs, said the *Commercial Advertiser* in 1844: "Their interests are identical to those of the adopted citizens to whom they give employment.")[19] But the average immigrant workingman hardly perceived his interests and those of large employers, bankers, and real-estate owners as the same. Democratic politicians took full advantage of this visceral suspicion of affluence and privilege, and continually excoriated Whigs for disregard for the interests of the average person and ties to banks and corporations, which profited inordinately from the party's money and tariff policies.[20]

Just as Democrats resisted the full implications of capitalist economics in the name of traditional republican values, they opposed imposition of behavioral standards promulgated by a capitalist social revolution. In resisting the politicization of temperance and Sabbatarianism, they laid claims from their earliest days to be protectors of relaxed, premodern folk habits against those who would make bourgeois manners and morals a legal obligation for the reluctant masses. The party's stance was pluralist in its embrace of cultural diversity, and thus was attractive to immigrants with Old World habits of sociability to defend.[21] Whigs were far less comfortable with diversity, and embraced Anglo conformity for immigrants and bourgeois social behavior for the masses. This discomfort with pluralism was largely a consequence of the Whigs' special relationship to evangelical religion. Through evangelical Protestantism Whigs shared a concept of respectability founded upon pious obeisance to such bourgeois values as thrift, hard work, and sobriety. As individuals American Democrats belonged to evangelical churches and expressed respect for the same values. But they objected to a notion of moral stewardship that led Whigs to use law to impose their concepts of morality on others.[22] The Whigs' special relationship to evangelical religion and their recent roots in anti-Masonry,[23] especially in western New York, also had an impact on their party's perceptions of Catholicism. As members of churches that saw themselves as the vanguard of the Reformation, which was widely perceived by Americans to be the source of republican liberties, and of the party that had inherited the responsibility to safeguard American political institutions against conspiracies, Whigs were psychologically drawn to anti-Catholicism.[24] Democrats had no special liking for Catholicism, and would seek to distance themselves from the hierarchy on such questions as the right of parishes to control their property. But their espousal of pluralism and opposition to the politicization of religion, as well as eventual dependence on immigrant votes, led to a defense of the church, particularly when it was attacked by Whigs.

The Democracy's manipulation of the issues of race and slavery was the third source of its attraction for the average white workingman. Its racist approach had complex sources, which blended expediency with a conservative quest for order and a passionate embrace of American egalitarianism. Dependent on southern support, the party defended slavery. But Democratic racism also had ideological roots. Proceeding from the premise of black racial inferiority, Democrats reasoned that any effort to free the slaves or to end discrimination against northern blacks jeopardized not only the status of the ordinary white man, but the fragile, natural order of all human relations.[25] Especially in northern cities such as Buffalo where black populations were very small and could hardly threaten white interests, Democratic racist rhetoric accounts greatly for the feeling of white "skin-privilege" that adult white men, including the party's foreigners, came to value. The party taught foreigners to think of themselves as white, an identity outside their European experience. It made them a powerful force for the preservation of the racial status quo. (This much was evident in the 1846 state referendum on black enfranchisement: the Irish First Ward and the German Fourth both scored 87 percent majorities, by far the city's largest, against the measure.)[26] Whigs hardly offered a confident alternative. Usually accepting black inferiority as an inborn fate, they were nonetheless led by religious identification, evangelical benevolence, and mutualist ideas to improve the condition of the Protestant blacks. In contrast to the *Courier*, for example, the *Commercial Advertiser* gave cautious assent to school integration in the case of higher-status black children.[27] But in matters such as the 1846 referendum, their support was halfhearted. They opened themselves to charges of hypocrisy and political opportunism in expectation of winning the black vote, and they did little to challenge the Democrats' self-assured racism.[28]

Democrats also proved considerably more effective than Whigs in creating disciplined party structures and mobilizing campaign machinery that brought the average voter into politics. Whigs were ill at ease with the centralized mass politics, party building, and imposition of party discipline that the second-party system, with its frequent caucuses, delegate conventions, and elections, and its growing number of resources and rewards for partisans, required.[29] Moreover, as editorials in the *Commercial Advertiser* and the Whig's evangelical fellow traveler, the *Christian Advocate*, make clear, Whigs lived with much antiparty sentiment, even while functioning successfully as a party. The presence of many bourgeois commercial and professional men with disdain for ordinary folk, the evangelically conditioned moral seriousness that made pragmatic compromise difficult, and the passion for cultural homogeneity that made it difficult to approach foreigners on their own terms, all made partisan calculation and discipline more onerous for Whigs.[30]

The Buffalo Democracy was a loose coalition of neighborhood organizations that used the city's school districts as the territorial base for campaigning. During 1843–53, these organizations cooperated closely and accepted centralized direction, usually with little public dissent. Even though the party did have its competing factions, with the exception of the free soil insurgency of 1848 and several weak local workingmen's tickets, it experienced few open conflicts in its ranks in 1843–53. Neighborhood organizations united in ward caucuses to choose delegates to nominating conventions, to ratify slates of candidates, and to nominate men for ward offices (constables, election inspectors, tax assessors, and councilmen). Not until 1860 did the party govern itself through permanent ward committees elected by party members. Before that what coordination of activities existed at the ward level was accomplished on an ad hoc basis by a caucus-selected committee. Ward committees were coordinated by a city central committee, a self-selected body of leading party men, until 1860, when its members, too, began to be elected. More activist and tightly organized than its Whig counterpart, the Democratic central committee linked neighborhood and ward efforts to citywide, county, state, and national campaigns. Some members were state and federal patronage appointees, of whom there were a large number in Buffalo because of the customs house and the canal. Their dependence provided a special incentive to seek to improve the party's position. The central committee had at least three ways of financing its activities: cash contributions, assessments on candidates to pay for printing ballots, and assessments on the salaries of patronage appointees.[31]

Democrats maintained an active press. In the 1840s they had two English-language dailies and one semiweekly, the *Weltbürger*; and in the 1850s, when the latter became a daily, they added three more American dailies, not all of which, however, were long-lived. In contrast Whigs had only two American dailies before 1861, and no German daily until 1853. The Democracy also profited from the existence of the Irish and German diocesan papers, for however veiled their partisanship, both were Democratic in principles. In a similar way, Whigs gained from the *Christian Advocate*. Both parties could discipline dissident publishers and reward party regularity by withdrawing municipal printing contracts, which until 1857 were granted on a strictly partisan basis. Only Democrats, however, had occasion during the decade to use this mechanism for discipline. They penalized the *Republic* for supporting the Free Soil party. Usually both parties rotated contracts among their English-language dailies, and regularly gave their German papers contracts to print the city business in German.[32]

The use to which Democrats put this partisan machinery in integrating the foreign voter is clear in the assistance they gave immigrants who wished to be naturalized and to vote. The *Commercial Advertiser* maintained that in 1840 the Democracy began systematically to help foreigners file their naturalization papers, pay fees, and go into court for citizenship examinations and oaths. By the 1844 presidential election, the paper claimed, some 1,400 immigrant voters had been added to the Democracy's rosters. The *Courier* regularly implored those whom it called "our friends" (neighborhood party operatives) to see to it that foreigners had their citizenship papers and residency requirements in line by election day. Democratic municipal judges maintained a special pre-election schedule, when they heard only naturalization petitions. It was not unusual for local courts to process 200 new citizens a week, almost all of them Democrats, before spring and fall elections.[33]

Democrats were also skilled at involving partisans in campaigns and at maximizing the thrills of participation. The party's view, the *Republic* said, was that campaigns should be "people's festivals, democratic and boisterous."[34] In the evenings, just before elections, Democratic bands, accompanied by fireworks and marchers carrying torches, marched through Irish and German neighborhoods on their way to campaign rallies. Whig campaigns were considerably more subdued. Whigs had nothing quite like the Democrat's election-eve bonfire. Whigs sometimes would forego the conflagration, and their rallies always eschewed whiskey and beer.[35] The Democracy maintained dramatic tension on election day. Until the nativist campaigns of the mid-1850s, political rallies and polling places were peaceful, with the exception of an occasional fistfight and some drunken revelry. But Democratic editors and party leaders spoke as if the party were besieged by unscrupulous, potentially disruptive Whig legions, though there is ample room for doubt. Democrats established massive vigilance committees, by far the city's largest, in the First and Fourth wards. In 1851, for example, 100 Irishmen and 225 Germans were recruited to enhance their role in the electoral drama as pollwatchers—in precincts too overwhelmingly Democratic really to need their services.[36]

Democrats were slower to nominate foreigners to elective office than to integrate them into party machinery. This was not due to a shortage of able people, though in the case of individual Germans, language was a barrier. Party and ward officials usually came out of the ranks of the same occupations (artisans and craftsmen, owners of small industrial shops, storekeepers) which could be found to a greater (German) or lesser (Irish) extent among immigrant partisans.[37] Americans doubtless wished to hang on to the most prestigious, lucrative opportunities. Their resolve was probably strengthened by the fact that the small number of wards created a dearth of such opportunities. By 1844, therefore, immigrant Irish and Germans were thoroughly involved in First and Fourth ward meetings, caucuses and committees, and foreign operatives such as Patrick Short were present on central committees. But nominations lagged. In wards that were usually Democratic, by 1846 there had been only three ethnic councilmen (Patrick Smith, Dr. Dellenbaugh and Karl Esslinger).[38] A change, however, resulted from the Free Soil insurgency. Party leaders worried about a loss, perhaps permanent, to the new radicalism, and they attempted to hold on to the immigrant vote by presenting more balanced tickets. Insofar as names are a clue to ethnicity, in the 1848 spring municipal campaign, the Irish and Germans were no more than one of seven, and two of nine nominees in the First and Fourth wards. The next year's municipal campaign, however, found three Irish and one German on the First's ballot, and three Germans on the Fourth's. Thereafter, the numbers did not fall below this level for either group, and indeed somewhat improved. As a consequence, ethnic representation on the council grew: between 1849 and 1853 three Germans (Abram Swartz, Dr. Daniel Devening and Solomon Scheu) and one Irishman (John Walsh) served there. Swartz would serve two, and Walsh three, terms.[39]

The expansion of municipal services and hence of public employment contributed to the Democrat's new willingness to share patronage across ethnic lines. The police department, the largest source of municipal patronage, provides the clearest illustration. As population grew, and the docks became congested, said the *Commercial Advertiser*, with "a large floating population of sailors and boatmen who need to be controlled,"[40] all influential segments of private opinion favored increasing the size of the force. So, too, did the parties, which saw new opportunities to reward their friends. For them the first session of each newly elected council became a veritable celebration of partisanship, for here the police were nominated, either by the mayor or from within the council majority when the mayor was of the other party. In the

1840s there were some thirty police, then forty by 1851, and sixty by 1854, where the number would remain for the balance of the period. The conduct of the police was frequently a source of controversy in the partisan press, but neither party questioned publicly the use of police appointments to reward partisans. Indeed, in 1853 they agreed to secure the partisan nature of the appointments process. The new charter allowed the council's majority party two-thirds and the minority one-third of police appointments.[41]

In January, 1854, when both parties simultaneously appointed police for the first time, only ten of forty for the Whig majority were ethnics, while ten of twenty Democratic ones appear to have been.[42] Because most police served only for a year before being replaced, there were annually ample rewards to be distributed. The force, therefore, offered short-term relief from the rigors of the job market. Most appointees, however, were not in desperate need. A sample of twenty-six appointees in the 1850s reveals men in midlife with residential stability, some property, and modest affluence. Much patronage was probably a useful subsidy to those receiving it. But it rewarded those who had the relative material security in the first place, to give years of voluntary party service.[43]

Part of the Democrats' skill in integrating immigrants lay in the fact that the party did not approach them as an undifferentiated mass, but developed specific appeals and techniques geared to the Irish and Germans as unique peoples. Democrats quickly learned that anti-British sentiment, empathy with suffering Ireland, and defense of the church against nativists had powerful emotional appeal to Irish voters. The local Democratic press began in the 1844 presidential campaign to make such appeals routine parts of their approach to Irish voters. Moreover, it was usually such prominent Democrats as the *Courier*'s editor, Joseph Stringham, or Mayor George Clinton who led local mass meetings in support of Irish causes, such as repeal of the Act of Union. The Democratic press adopted a similar stance toward the political crises in the German states during the 1840s and 1850s, and expressed sympathy and support for Louis Kossuth and for such '48er refugees as Dr. Gottfried Kinkel. (Both men came to Buffalo in the early 1850s.) The American party press stopped short of endorsing U.S. intervention in Europe, and thus expressed reservations about the effort of men such as Kinkel to raise money to revivify the republican cause. The *Weltbürger*, however, supported both intervention and funding.[44]

The party's attention to ethnic needs extended to campaigning, and here it showed that capacity for tactical innovation for which it became widely reputed in Buffalo. A problem for the Irish and the party alike was the instability of the Irishmen's employment, which made it difficult to be home to vote or even to establish residence anywhere long enough to become voters. Whether elections were, as during 1843–53, in March, June, or November, laborers were often on the road. In response to the employment problems, when in power in Albany, Democrats offered work on the canal. For the mutual inconvenience of de facto disfranchisement, it offered "colonization," flooding electoral districts with mobile workers at election time.

Paired together, patronage and colonization could be a powerful tool. The Democracy's colonization efforts, about which Whigs constantly complained during 1842–48, focused on the Fifth Ward, the city's swing ward. While the First and Fourth were usually Democratic and the Second and Third usually Whig, the Fifth, with its growing German population, had too narrow an American majority to be entirely safely Whig.[45] The tactic worked like this: when they had power over the operation of the canal, Democrats timed canal improvements so that on election day large numbers of Irish laborers were at work on the sections of the canal running through the Fifth.[46] In order to combat Fifth Ward Whig pollwatchers' demands that Irishmen produce citizenship papers (which many did not possess), Democrats perfected a process of passing papers from ward to ward on election day.[47] Too, by the early 1850s railroads were available to bring Irish laborers, far and near, to targeted precincts. Patrick Short proved a master at this game, not only making arrangements for railroad transportation, room, and board for large numbers of men, but even staging a prizefight to entertain them.[48]

Short's own political career illustrates another accommodation between the Democracy and its Irish constituency. Family, kinship, and godparentage networks, which were central to Irish village life, were often reconstituted in America. Politicians seized on them because they were efficient mechanisms for political communication and mobilization. As a consequence, there was a peculiarly skewed, nepotistic distribution of political rewards among the Buffalo Irish. Along with a handful of other Irishmen, whose names repeatedly appear in lists of delegates, nominees, and appointees, Short proved extremely successful at cornering jobs for his family. During most of the 1850s he was both a federal mail agent and the local agent of the state immigration commissioners, while his son John had a position in the city controller's office and his brother James, a customshouse clerk, was also at various times a policeman.[49] By 1859, twenty-five of the sixty police were said to be Irishmen who were the cousins or sons of a few prominent Irish Democratic appointees or elected officials. It was charged, too, in that year that "three or four Irish families monopolized" as many as forty-five local offices and jobs, worth $38,000 a year.[50]

The Democracy did not find Germans as digestible as the Irish. It was not always clear what resources Germans wanted from the party, nor how they wished to be integrated into its structure. Moreover, the Germans occasionally divided on these matters, sometimes in ways overlapping with intragroup social and ideological divisions.

The first and least pressing of the two sources of difficulty concerned language. Because of the Germans' distinctive language, large numbers, and agitation for recognition of their language in the public sphere, American Democrats resolved early on that the group required some separate campaign efforts in the form of a subsidized German press and speeches in their own tongue. The problem lay in determining just how far this linguistic recognition and accommodation would be allowed to isolate Germans within the party. In sharp contrast to the Irish, who were integrated into regular ward organizations, the answer at first seemed, "Quite far"—to the point of separate organization. The formal entrance of Germans into the party came in 1840 with the creation of the German Democratic Association, which united Buffalo's Germans in that fall's presidential campaign. German party operatives seemed pleased with the arrangement, which made them the liaisons between their people and the party structure. But by the 1844 campaign this situation, which once had been perceived as opportunity, now was conceived as ghettoization. German Democrats charged that separate organization among the handful of German Whigs in the German Clay Club was merely a device to marginalize them and deny them access to party rewards.[51] Perhaps, too, though they did not say so, this was their experience in the Democracy. Whatever the case, after 1844 they requested, and received, complete integration into all ward organizations and vigilance committees. (Only in 1848, when a German workers' association was established within the party to counter that year's radical organizations and parties, would a citywide German Democracy again appear.) After 1844 language needs would be filled both in integrated and separate rallies and in German publications, which often were direct translations of English ones. Much informal translation must have been made at party meetings.[52]

The second problem, the distribution of nominations and patronage among Germans, was more complicated, and evaded a completely satisfactory resolution. Unlike the Irish, the Germans did not routinely make group representations demanding offices and jobs, for they were collectively sufficiently skilled and prosperous and did not need to depend on public employment.[53] But they did want symbolic recognition of their contributions to the party and the power and prestige of office, and doubtless some money-minded individuals wanted offices. How Germans were to be rewarded, therefore, was more problematic than was the case for the Irish, who wanted everything and constantly strained against what they were given to understand were the limits. The potential for friction in the German situation was deepened in several ways. Their concentration in the Fourth Ward until late 1853 placed structural limits on their access to office. Their lack of competitive political experience, internal disunity, and imperfect mastery of English within the integrated party apparatus they demanded also probably held them back. Throughout 1843–53, they believed they were neglected. The record bears them out except in appointments to the police force, on which they were well represented. They had the chance to elect a German councilman only in 1838 and 1845. But in those years the other councilman from the ward was American, as were both councilmen at other times, even though most voters in the ward were German. (Fifth Ward nominations were tokens, since, for all the Democracy's colonization efforts, the ward was usually Whig.) Germans received no nominations for citywide office, nor for the legislature. The one significant office they received was Philip Dorsheimer's appointment in 1838 and again in 1845 as postmaster. A consensus developed in the mid-1840s among German politicians: they wanted more and better rewards.[54]

To be sure, Dorsheimer's appointment was prestigious, and with it came control of many clerkships. But the reaction of German politicians to the appointment suggests internal divisions that further complicated matters. By 1838 Dorsheimer had been in America many years, grown rich managing a nationally renowned hotel, done years of service as a party operative, and not only mastered English, but had an extensive network of American contacts. In short, he had the prerequisites for the important post to which President Van Buren named him. But he was not an intimate of the more recently arrived German communal leaders, as the *Weltbürger* inadvertently proved in calling this "well-known" and "very respectable" German "Peter," in announcing his appointment. When the second appointment was announced, confusion gave way to public grumbling. Dorsheimer, it was now said, was unrepresentative of the mass of German party workers, and should not have received an appointment in their name.[55]

As feelings intensified, another consensus developed among German politicians: they must have greater control over which Germans obtained party rewards. They had some resources for achieving their desires, but only slowly did they move to use them. The results were unimpressive. After years of discontent about Americans obtaining Fourth Ward nominations, in February, 1846, German politicians bolted a caucus-fashioned ward ticket. In a rare public display of anger, thirty-eight of them met to pass resolutions endorsing the party's mayoral candidate, but dissenting on one of two councilmanic nominations, both of which had gone to Americans, and on the nomination for tax collector, which went to a German considered unacceptable. They asked German voters to write in the names of two Germans defeated in the caucus. But the regular candidates were overwhelmingly elected.[56] Though no more revolts of this type took place, discontent remained, and in contrast to its staunch partisanship in state and national elections, the Fourth would demonstrate more independence than any other ward in local contests. As the increase in German nominations and elections to the council after 1848 suggests, the party was responsive. Moreover, the situation partly took care of itself when the ward was broken up into four wards, three of them massively German, and the group's opportunities dramatically rose.[57] Yet as German complaints in the late 1850s about Irish domination of rewards demonstrate, there were Germans who continued to feel they were not getting a fair share of party rewards.[58]

That Democrats usually succeeded in diffusing such tensions and in mobilizing the Irish and German vote, just as Whigs dominated the American poll, is apparent from an analysis of elections during 1843–53. While turnout data for the decade are problematic, the available data do indicate what we might have anticipated: higher than average American turnouts; Irish turnouts at the mean; and German turnouts below, which indicate the difficulties of mobilizing a fragmented, foreign-speaking constituency. In three hotly contested races (the 1848 and 1852 presidential and 1850 gubernatorial), the approximate average aggregate turnout for all voters in the city's five wards was 73.5 percent. That for Americans, as indicated by the Second Ward, averaged 79.3 percent; for the Irish, as indicated by the First, 72.9 percent; and for the Germans of the Fourth, 62.9 percent.[59]

The data are much better for measuring partisanship. This is done in Table 1.

Buffalo's least volatile wards were the American Second and Third, which consistently voted Whig by predictable, similar majorities in elections at all levels. Indeed, only once in seventeen elections did either ward deliver less than a majority for the Whigs. (In both instances, the party received a winning plurality.) In these wards Whiggery was a cross-class American coalition. The party's political economy was obviously attractive to the commercial elite and its many legal retainers, with their interest in nationalizing markets and in a flexible, national currency. Furthermore, New York Whigs, especially

TABLE 1. Ward voting in seventeen elections, 1843–53.*

Ward	1	2	3	4	5
Winning party in majority of elections	DM	WH	WH	DM	WH
Average median percentage of vote, given victor	59%	58%	58%	53%	50%
Average mean percentage of vote, given victor	61%	60%	60%	59%	52%
Instances of defeat of usual winning party	2	0	0	6	6
Instances of usual winning party obtaining winning plurality (less than 50%)	0	0	1	1	0

*Only ticket heads analyzed. The elections are: three presidential, four state, and ten local contests.

Sources: Buffalo *Commercial Advertiser*, March 10, 1843; November 6, 1844; March 5, 1845; November 4, 1846; March 3, 1847; March 9, 1848; Buffalo *Courier*, November 5, 1845; March 4, 1846; November 8, 10, 1848; March 8, November 8, 1849; March 6, 1850; November 6, 1851; March 4, November 4, 1852; March 9, 1853; Buffalo *Weltbürger*, November 11, 1850, March 8, 1851.

in the western counties, were the leading exponents of canal improvement at the public expense, rather than through user's fees. (Dependence on fees was perceived in the early 1850s to hinder the canal in its competitive struggle with railroads.)[60] Whigs were particularly well represented in the wealthiest neighborhoods. The seventh and fourteenth school districts, which had a large number of American children in high-status private schools, were located in the western district of the Second and eastern district of the Fifth.[61] Both are distinguished for their high percentage of Whig voting (60 percent and 59.5 percent respectively) in elections during 1843–53 for which we have returns for districts within wards. Yet Buffalo Whigs were hardly the bloated plutocrats of Democratic propaganda. Often themselves employers, American and British artisans and craftsmen who were providing services at the docks and who were members of evangelical churches could also respond favorably to the party's ideology. Whig hostility to the Catholic church and to the Irish doubtless had special attractions to many British immigrants.[62] Whiggery's nonelite constituency was evident in both the Third Ward, where many American skilled workers lived, and in the industrial, eastern district of the Second, where the Hydraulics was located. In each, Whigs received 53 percent of the vote during the decade.

The Democracy had a firm, if minority, base in American wards. Skilled Americans could find Democratic political economy and egalitarian rhetoric attractive. If they were cultural traditionalists, its laissez faire response to calls for Sabbatarian and temperance legislation was correct. But the Democracy also contained a number of "gentlemen Democrats," such as Oliver Steele, George Clinton, Joseph Masten, Eli Cook, Timothy Lockwood, Isaac Vanderpoel, and James S. Wadsworth, all members of the bourgeois commercial and professional elite. Although men like Steele and Vanderpoel had been radical Jacksonians, by 1850 their politics seemed more sentimental than ideological. But men like Wadsworth of Genesee County, who was influential in Buffalo party affairs largely because he owned much of the land that comprised the docks, had never spoken in radical tones.[63] Democratic ideology promised such men fairness to all, without attacks on individual fortunes, and low-tax government. (In practice, several of the Democratic city administrations were among the decade's least thrifty.) Moreover, in the 1840s the local Democracy and most canal corridor Democrats found various convenient formulae by which to demand that the state improve the canal and that the federal government improve Great Lakes harbors, so Buffalo's bourgeois Democrats could have their principles and the self-interested exception. When it came to a vote, however, the national and much of the state party usually belied the hollowness of the local Democrats' position, leaving them to protest on grounds very similar to those of their Whig adversaries.[64] After the 1851–52 legislative session, moreover, the balance of New York State Democratic opinion swung increasingly against canal improvement not simply for ideological reasons, but in the belief that railroads were rendering the canal obsolete. At the same time, the Democracy became attractive to a new economic interest—those railroad men, such as Buffalo's Dean Richmond of the New York Central, and their retainers who wanted to see an end to subsidies to canal shippers.[65] After years of suffering charges that they were prisoners of special interests, local Whigs, who remained loyal to the canal, and then Republicans, too, could throw the same charge at the Democrats. They could also effectively associate Democrats with destruction of the city's economy. In this way an increasingly significant economic fissure within the local bourgeoisie came to have partisan overtones.

In its partisanship, the Democratic First Ward resembled the American wards. The aggregate ward data underestimate the extent of Irish partisanship: if we compare the particularly heavily Irish and proletarian western district for the years for which we have district tallies with the more ethnically mixed and somewhat more skilled eastern district, we find Democratic averages of 66 percent and 60 percent, respectively. The German Fourth and the mostly American Fifth were the most volatile wards. Though usually Democratic, the Fourth did not have predictably sized majorities, as the difference between its mean and median percentages establishes. Furthermore, on six occasions the Fourth voted against the Democracy, while giving it merely a plurality on another. The pivotal Fifth has a profile much like the Fourth, but favoring the Whigs.

The fortunes of the parties in citywide contests changed frequently during the decade, but less as a consequence of fluctuations in particular wards than of the changing population balance between Whiggish natives in wards Two and Three and Democratic foreigners in One and Four. This electoral volatility could not have been predicted at the start of the decade, which began with three consecutive victories by Democrats, an unprecedented run of good fortune for the party. The year 1844 saw the Democracy's first local presidential triumph. The *Courier* gloated, and the *Weltbürger* attributed success to the growth of the East Side German population. Both predicted that Whig control of the city was at an end.[66] But neither paper reckoned on two facts. First, new immigrants would have to wait five years before becoming naturalized. As Democrats were aware, many had to be prodded into becoming naturalized and then into voting. Democrats had their work cut out for them, for while the ratio of voters to population in 1844 was one in seven in Two and Three, and one in eight in One and Five, it was one in twelve in Four, where, according to 1844 estimates, there were 700 unnaturalized Germans of voting age.[67] Second, American in-migration was a significant factor in local population growth. American men could vote soon after establishing legal residence. Between 1844 and 1850 wards Two and Three increased in population by 87.5 and 81 percent respectively, while the First and Fourth increased by 65 and 91.5 percent with men who seldom could immediately vote.[68]

These factors sorted themselves out such that during the decade Whigs won nine of the seventeen elections analyzed. On closer inspection, however, the Whigs' total average winning margin was just under 50 percent, which suggests the party's fluctuating fortunes as the native and foreign balance shifted from year to year. On three occasions, third parties cut into the tallies of established ones. Both parties dominated the mayor's office five times, Democrats won two of three presidential contests, and Whigs won three of four gubernatorial ones. Control of the council also fluctuated. During the decade's ten councils, the ten seats per session were divided evenly three times, and each party had a six-to-four majority three times. Only in 1849 was there an election of a vastly lopsided (eight-to-two) council, a consequence of a pro-Whig protest over high taxes and increased municipal spending and debt under the Democratic regime of Mayor Joseph Masten and his council.[69] In the decade's final years, however, Whigs had increasing reasons to worry. As immigrants who streamed into Buffalo in the 1840s began to vote in the 1850s, American population growth was outpaced and the Whigs fell behind. In seven elections between 1850 and fall, 1853, Whigs won only twice and their percentage of the vote fell by the spring, 1853, mayoral contest to the lowest point (43 percent) in ten years.

Yet Democrats also had reasons for insecurity. Their ethnic, especially German, constituency showed disturbing signs of independence. During 1843–53, the Fourth dealt the Democracy six losses and one plurality. Ideological, material, and partisan factors provide the explanation. In 1839 and 1852, popular Whigs were elected councilmen in the ward by taking advantage of discontent about American domination of Democratic party resources and making promises of better treatment. More often, however, issues caused a portion of the German Democracy to shift to the opposition. With small parcels of property to protect, Germans were sensitive to shifts in tax rates and to assessments for neighborhood improvements. Taxation, too, inevitably raised ideological questions of fairness and of the boundaries of the legitimate activities of government. On two occasions (the 1846 and 1849 municipal elections), Fourth Ward voters crossed party lines to express themselves on just these issues.[70] On two other occasions, however, class protest and ideology, ultimately mixed with antislavery feeling, caused a shift away from the Democracy. In the spring, 1848, municipal election, a local workingmen's ticket won 15 percent (178) of the ward's vote attacking the order system. In that fall's presidential poll, which was held at the end of a period of intense protest against orders, the free soil movement put forward its own ticket, and won 18 percent (264). Democrats did poorer than usual that fall in the First, where Free Soilers got 15 percent (135), though it is difficult to isolate these as Irish votes. In a decade of fierce partisanship, these percentages are impressive. They boded ill for the stability of the second-party system, because they suggested the extent to which working-class resentments and aspirations approached obliquely through the slavery issue could destabilize alignments. By contrast the bourgeois, abolitionist Liberty party of the early 1840s was so marginal that its leading canvasser, George Washington Johnson, could confidently name the sixty-odd men who were likely to vote for its various tickets.[71] Yet after 1853, in the context of national crisis, both bourgeois and working-class antislavery grew; and joined together, they shook the party system to its roots.

Faced with a precarious situation that offered little hope for optimism as immigrant voting increased, the Whigs opted for contradictory strategies. During the decade Whigs tried to neutralize and suppress the immigrant vote *and* to win it over.

They tried to neutralize immigrant power through maintenance of vastly oversized wards. As population grew, the ward boundaries fixed by the 1832 charter proved obsolete. German political power was effectually halved by the decade's close. The Fourth had 9,051 residents in 1845, fully 30 percent of the city's total, while the First, the next-largest ward in population, had 7,107 (24 percent). In contrast the third-largest, the Second, had 5,877 people (20 percent). By 1850 the gap between the Fourth, which now had 15,711 (37 percent), and the other wards was even greater. The Third, now the second most populous ward, had only 8,534 (20 percent).[72] Neutralizing of the immigrant vote was also accomplished in apportionment of the county's state assembly seats by the County Board of Supervisors, the constant Whig domination of which was due to the overwhelmingly American population of most of the city's hinterland. The majority of supervisors distrusted Buffalo's growing power, resented its increasing welfare bill at the poorhouse, and feared the political potential of its immigrant Democracy. In creating the county's two assembly districts that included Buffalo, the First was attached to the city's Whig, American wards, and the Fourth to three overwhelmingly Whig towns north of Buffalo.[73]

Erie County was the Whig's fiefdom to run as they wished, for Democrats had little power outside Buffalo. But in seeking to preserve the municipal situation, Whigs profited from the collusion of Buffalo Democrats and their allies in Albany. The charter could be amended only by the legislature, which depended on a prior resolution by the city council, where the parties debated redistricting the Fourth in 1845, 1846, 1848, and 1851. (The status of the First was debated less frequently.) The terms of the debate were always the same. Whigs argued that numbers alone should not entitle voters to representation and frequently compared the large amounts of commercial and industrial property owned by Third Ward residents with the Germans' small homes and lots—to the disadvantage of the latter. Whigs coupled demands to divide the Fourth, with their own proposals to divide Whig wards like the Third. Democrats scored points with their plebeian constituency by denouncing the Whigs' elitist theory of representation. But they knew that the process of redistricting could get out of hand, and perhaps come to favor the Whigs. Though they marshalled a majority in favor of redistricting when they controlled the council, they refused to force the issue in Albany.[74] Only in the early 1850s, when politicians of both parties and leading commercial and professional men came to feel that municipal finances and services were hopelessly antiquated, was a city convention called and charter revision undertaken. In the process of revision, it was now agreed that the five wards and the newly annexed town of Black Rock would become thirteen wards at the time of the fall, 1853, election.[75]

Whigs simultaneously attempted to create a German Whiggery through subsidizing ethnic newspapers and political associations and through patronage and nominations. The effort was pursued most energetically in the early 1840s, when local Whigs still could hope that ethnic voting alignments were not firmly fixed, and it was made at the very time when, after reaching the opposite conclusion, Whigs in eastern cities were allying with nativists. The motives of Buffalo Whigs were largely, though not exclusively, opportunistic. As early as 1838 Whigs gave evidence of understanding that nativist rhetoric would not win them immigrant votes, while symbolic gestures that cost them little might. In that year they appointed a German constable, a Whig councilman was overheard to tell a colleague, in order "to catch the Germans."[76] Whigs probably knew that they could not capture the German vote en bloc, but hoped to get the Democratic vote in the Fourth down just enough that the American wards could carry citywide contests. Whigs did not make the same efforts among the Irish, because they were deemed less respectable and less approachable ideologically, and because there were so many fewer of them.

Systematic Whig efforts began in 1840 with the establishment of the *Volksfreund*. Like similar ventures that followed (the *Freimüthige* in 1843 and *Die Telegraph* in 1845), this short-lived paper was little more in conception than a campaign sheet. (*Die Telegraph* would eventually become a real newspaper.) Though it did not at first proclaim its Whiggery, opting instead to call itself independent, it usually grew more partisan as election day approached. But while election-oriented, these papers did not restrict themselves to endorsing Whig candidates or exposing Democratic double-dealing. Millard Fillmore, one of the handful of subsidizers of the *Freimüthige*, said that the larger purpose of such papers should be to provide Germans with a "proper introduction to American life." This meant, in practice, teaching them Whig principles, and criticizing as contrary to American values the immigrants' tendency to vote as a bloc, while obscuring both the party's position on ethnocultural issues and its occasional alliances with nativists.[77] Journalistic efforts were ultimately part of a larger effort that climaxed in 1844, when a new Whig council made three eye-catching German appointments and established a well-subsidized German Clay Club.[78]

The opportunism of American Whigs in seeking immigrant allies was transparent. They showcased their token German appointments, while making little effort to create a permanent, popularly based party structure in ethnic wards. Much of the copy for the *Freimüthige* was written at the *Commercial Advertiser* and translated by its German editor, Alexander Krause. The paper had few subscribers other than the Whig central committee, which distributed it gratis.[79] Yet it hardly follows that all German Whigs were dupes or mercenaries. To be sure, German Whigs were sometimes disgruntled Democrats who had not gotten what they wanted from their party and hoped to make the point with an act of independence. One suspects this, for example, of Dr. Dellenbaugh, who changed parties in 1844—and would do so repeatedly in the next decade. Too, German Whigs were often isolated, in background, status, and behavior, from the immigrant mainstream. They were more assimilated and more respectable in American terms. Dr. Dellenbaugh (formerly "Dellenbach") and Dr. Ernest Gray (formerly "Kreh"), for example, were long-established residents, Protestants, and by their professions and affluence, respectable men. Gray lived comfortably in both the American and German worlds, as did *Die Telegraph* editor Henry B. Miller, who was as fluent in English as in German. It was for men such as these that the *Volksfreund* regularly published articles in English as well as German.[80]

But it was precisely the assimilation of these men that made their attraction to Whiggery ominous for Democrats, because it suggested that as Germans gained experience in America, some could be expected to wander away from Democratic principles. Whig political economy probably had its attractions for some German professionals and merchants. Moreover, though slavery was not the major issue of the 1840s, the Democracy's close association with its defense bothered some Germans greatly. Krause and Miller both eventually entered antislavery politics, and Miller became a prominent German Republican.[81] Had the Whigs found a way to emphasize their political economy and sharpen their reservations about slavery, while detaching themselves from nativism and coercive moral reform, they might well have made effective allies of such Germans. That they did not, but that the Republicans would, is one reason why the Whigs perished and the Republicans prospered in Buffalo.

In the mid-1840s Whigs drew back from their overture to German immigrants. The turning point came in the wake of the 1844 fall elections. Local Whig politicians assessed the defeat of both Clay and, in the gubernatorial race, Fillmore. Fillmore was representative in his belief that the growth of immigrant voting, coupled with the Democrats' skill in linking Whigs with elitism and nativism, had so reduced the party's majority in its western New York heartland that statewide victory became impossible.[82] In Erie County the Whig majority had dropped from its usual 3,000–3,500 vote range to 1,878, while in Buffalo Polk succeeded in obtaining a sixty-seven-vote majority. The Fifth

Ward, where Fillmore resided and where his various candidacies had usually obtained immense, 300-vote majorities, gave him a mere four-vote plurality—he believed, because of an increase of Germans. Fillmore's organ, the *Commercial Advertiser*, was blunt in assessing the returns, "We have been overwhelmed by the alien vote in the country. Controlled by artful demagogues, it has been brought to bear almost as the vote of one man against us."[83]

Bitter resentment soon took hold. Fillmore's own minister, the respected George Hosmer, delivered a blistering attack on Roman Catholic political influence from the pulpit several weeks after the election.[84] A number of Whig zealots went beyond words. Planning began during the campaign itself as Whig prospects dimmed. After the election they announced the creation of a branch of the eastern, nativist American Republican Association. While a few big names from the local mercantile and professional elite were affiliated, the majority of the sixty-two founders were obscure men who were under thirty and employed as skilled workers, clerks, and shopkeepers. The ARA marked the rise of yet another Whig strategy toward immigrant political power. In conceiving of its goal as the extension of the period of residence for naturalization to twenty-one years, the ARA advocated suppression.[85]

Perhaps because Whig leaders such as Fillmore and papers such as the *Commercial Advertiser* kept their distance from it out of fear of social disorder, the ARA in Buffalo, as elsewhere, did not last long. But the principle of suppression gradually became an article of faith for many local Whigs as immigrant political power greatly increased and as the founders of the ARA chapter rose to prominence in the local party. Whigs did not give up entirely on their efforts to attract Germans. Patronage and nominations declined after 1844, but never completely disappeared. Though the *Freimüthige* was allowed to fold, *Die Telegraph* took its place in 1845.[86] But there could be no doubt that within the dominant, Fillmore wing of the local party, prejudices were increasingly being concretized into prescriptions for suppression. After 1844, the *Commercial Advertiser* routinely called for extension of the period of naturalization, firmer monitoring by courts of the naturalization process, and literacy tests for prospective voters.[87]

The consequences for the party were largely negative. The gulf between Whigs and immigrant voters grew, and so, too, eventually did the gulf between Whigs. To the long-standing animosities over the distribution of patronage and nominations between the Fillmore (or "Silver Gray") wing, and the wing controlled by Thurlow Weed and William Henry Seward, there was added disagreement over the problem presented by immigrant political power. Seward had made statements favorable to the employment of German-speaking teachers in immigrant neighborhoods. Moreover, Seward and Weed briefly courted Irish Catholic voters and Archbishop Hughes through a plan to give public funds to Catholic schools, an idea unacceptable to Silver Grays. Then, too, there were the quiet gestures taken on behalf of immigrants and their institutions, such as the assistance the Seward forces in the legislature initially rendered in gaining public funds for Sisters of Charity Hospital. Seward and Weed, whose forces were weak in Buffalo during the 1840s but stronger than the Silver Grays elsewhere in the state, never completely gave up on the possibility of winning large numbers of immigrant votes. Nativism, on the other hand, increasingly became a core belief among Silver Grays.[88] Along with their disagreements over slavery, which emerged during the Crisis of 1850, the contrary responses of Seward and Fillmore to the era's emergent pluralism and to immigrant political power ensured the death of the party in New York State in the early 1850s.

Before that, however, the gap between Whigs and immigrants would broaden yet further, both because of the party's guarded stand on European events and its association with coercive moral reform.

In sharp contrast to Democrats, Whigs, especially Silver Grays, disliked the stirring up of passions about Old World affairs, which, they felt, stalled the process of Americanization. Moreover, Whig Anglophilia and anti-Catholicism made it difficult to express deep sympathy with the Irish, just as their reluctance to become involved in foreign conflicts and fear of disorder made them distrustful of all romantic nationalist and revolutionary movements. The effort of such exiles as Kossuth, Kinkel, and William Smith O'Brien to inflame American opinion in favor of intervention and raise money here to revivify failed rebellions reinforced these fears. (As president, Fillmore publicly expressed reservations about these efforts in the early 1850s.) Whig fears also had a local cause. Britain, an important trading partner and source of investment capital, and potentially a dangerous adversary, was a neighbor across the Niagara. Buffalo Whigs, therefore, were in a poor position to take advantage of European events to win immigrant adherents. While they participated in protest rallies, mass assemblies, and reception committees for touring exiles, and helped organize famine relief, they usually took a backseat to Democrats. When for a time they made a point of claiming they gave more time and money to famine relief than Democrats, they found themselves making the same sort of ethnic appeals they professed to be wrong. While the Seward organ, the *Express*, was pro-Kossuth, the dominant Fillmore Whigs opposed using municipal funds to entertain Kossuth in 1851 when he visited the city, because he was raising money for revolutionary causes. Moreover, the *Commercial Advertiser* believed, Kossuth and other revolutionists had "wildly impractical notions of liberty which cannot be sustained," and would fail, if given the opportunity, to establish viable governments. No more eager for intervention, Democrats frequently expressed sympathies and moral support, and they usually succeeded in making Whigs, especially the highly visible Fillmore, seem allies of European reactionaries.[89]

But Kossuth and the others came and, however much they quickened republican hearts, they soon left. Temperance and Sabbatarianism grew in significance, and became inextricably intertwined. The availability of alcohol on what many evangelical Protestants considered a holy day became the symbolic embodiment of the alcohol issue, and a highly visible target for politicians seeking to get the most credit from moral reformers for the least amount of action. Local temperance and Sabbatarianism began as a largely personal and individual matter in the 1830s. During the 1837–43 depression, it became a small, largely elite, but formally organized movement, which used moral suasion to effect a voluntary reform of social conduct. Thereafter moral reform increasingly became a variegated movement active at many social levels along two lines—one still voluntarist and employing suasion; the other working politically for legal prohibition of alcohol. As reform became more political, it grew divisive, separating, somewhat imperfectly, native and foreigner and Whig and Democrat.[90]

Americans were not completely united on temperance, in any of its various manifestations. As the *Christian Advocate*, a strong advocate of suppression of alcohol, was quick to point out, there was much private drinking, especially during the winter social season, among the same respectable, bourgeois Americans who publicly condemned alcohol.[91] Then, too, as the center of the national grain trade and a gathering place for such reputedly heavy drinkers as immigrants, sailors, canallers, and public works laborers, Buffalo was an ideal location to establish distilling operations. While Germans dominated local brewing, it was Americans who controlled the smaller, but highly lucrative distilling business. Retailing and wholesaling liquor were also frequently American enterprises. One-third of the fifteen liquor dealers in 1855 were Americans, and American grocers and innkeepers doubtless profited from the drinks they sold. Americans, such as the artisan contractor Danforth Franklin, from time to time speculated in wholesale wine and spirit imports.[92]

Because temperance threatened established political alignments, American politicians, Whigs and Democrats alike, could hardly be enthusiastic about it. Of the city's five English-language dailies in the early 1850s, only the *Democracy* advocated making alcohol a political issue and mustered any enthusiasm at the prospect of a prohibitory law. Both parties seem to have agreed with the *Courier*'s 1850 injunction: "Temperance and politics should not be mixed."[93] But there were crucial differences in the extent to which the parties sought to avoid the issue. Democrats were freighted, as Whigs were not, with the burden of a heavily immigrant constituency. While immigrant leaders denounced drunkenness, there was a general rejection of coercive temperance among immigrants, especially Germans. Moreover, Germans regularly and publicly questioned whether the motives of American temperance advocates were benign. Germans saw antialcohol crusaders as meddling, desexed women, repression-bent fanatics, and base hypocrites, who secretly drank. Most Democratic politicians, therefore, felt comfortable going no further than symbolic pronouncements and highly publicized inductions into temperance societies of the sort accomplished by Mayor H. K. Smith when he joined the Sons of Temperance in 1850.[94] By such means Democrats hoped to mollify those among American supporters who were reform-minded, while keeping immigrant voters in line.

As elsewhere, therefore, temperance had a heavily Whig cast in Buffalo, not only because the social basis of both the party and the movement were the same, but also because Whig politicians had less to lose by identifying with moral reform. Yet they, too, would have been happy to substitute symbolism for substance, and get as much mileage as possible from events such as John B. Gough's 1844 visit. The great temperance orator administered "the pledge" not only at First Baptist and First and Central Presbyterian, but also at Whig campaign headquarters.[95] That Whigs eventually went further than symbols was less the result of enthusiasm than pressure from activists. Many local Whig politicians feared that strife over prohibition, which they saw as unenforceable and likely to bring the law into contempt, could rip the party apart. It was because of such twisting and turning by politicians that the Sons of Temperance concluded in 1852 that neither party was reliable enough on the question, and urged members to vote for individuals rather than parties if they wished to use their votes to further reform.[96]

If Whigs had to be pushed, it was bourgeois women, using moral suasion and petitions, who did the pushing, with their less active male allies following at a distance. Never before had these women taken so assertive a public role. They were reacting to the changed, and they felt ominous, context of the alcohol question in the mid-1840s. With the growth of the local economy and of the population of such groups as immigrants and sailors and boatmen, the number of places serving liquor and beer grew dramatically, and strained the municipal licensing mechanism. The authorities discovered that unlike the highly visible saloons, the ubiquitous groceries, which were fully 40 percent of all local businesses by 1845, frequently violated the law. In doing so, as both public officials and some local women temperance reformers bitterly complained in 1845 and 1846, they were assisted by the neighborhood ethnic population, including the police, which often disapproved of such laws. But for their part, temperance-minded Americans themselves were not prone to go into such neighborhoods to see that the law was enforced, so groceries continued their practices with impunity. In turn, lawbreaking as such became an issue, for even Americans willing to make allowance for less harmful German lager were angered by what seemed so clearly to them to be the German grocers' lawlessness.[97]

During the next seven years there was growing militance among American women and increasing ethnic polarization over the issue. Though an element of the local Whigs grew more firmly reform-oriented, little decisive action was taken by the majority of politicians, who felt themselves caught in the middle between the contending sides. In 1846 the state legislature approved a referendum on whether localities should be allowed to cease licensing liquor sales, because of complaints from around the state that licensing laws had become useless. Elite women were, said the *Weltbürger* "extraordinarily active" in getting out the antilicensing American vote. Immigrant wards, however, showed apathy, and there was confusion over the language of the proposition. With turnouts low in the First and Fourth and high in the Second and Third, where there was an aggregate 81 percent antilicensing vote, that position gathered a 257-vote majority.[98] But the narrow Whig council majority could not garner the two-thirds vote needed to recommend a change in the city charter, and the Democratic municipal judiciary ruled licensing must continue until a higher court resolved against it. Then, in 1847, another referendum on licensing established, on the basis of greatly enlarged First and Fourth Ward voting, a 1,160 majority *for* licensing.[99]

The impasse frustrated moral reformers, who believed they had three options. In the short run, they could monitor the activities of local liquor dealers to catch lawbreakers, and oppose on a case-by-case basis granting new licenses. Because of the failure of the licensing mechanism, however, in the long run, only prohibition seemed a real solution. Both these goals, in turn, would require an active citizens' lobby in Albany, and an active temperance wing in the local Whig party. Inspired directly by an emotional reappearance of Gough at Lafayette Presbyterian Church, both the women's temperance organizations and the all-male City Temperance Society reorganized in the spring of 1850 to achieve these goals. (Within the year, too, a branch of the semisecretive Carson League was founded to make war on liquor dealers.)[100] In 1850, the council received a petition from 1,469 American women demanding an end to licensing and full prosecution of lawbreakers.[101] A council equally divided between the parties had responded hesitantly to growing pressure in 1850, but the 1851 elections saw a decided shift toward greater American militance. Although the partisan deadlock in the council remained, temperance had become stronger among Whigs. Whigs elected to the council were now eager to see a crackdown on licensing, and a continuing flood of American petitions added force to their resolve. Believing now that American opinion favored action, American Democrats decided to cooperate with Whigs on the license committee. New applications for licenses were denied and existing ones taken away from proprietors violating closing hours regulations. Fourth Ward grocers were hit hard by the crackdown.[102]

Immigrants now mobilized against what they saw as a nativist attack on their cultures. This counterthrust was largely in the hands of Germans. They were most hurt by the actions of the license committee. Moreover, unlike the Irish, who had a serious group drinking problem and their own intragroup antialcohol efforts, and whose leaders resented American temperance activism but were ambivalent about opposing it publicly, Germans had no communal alcohol problem and were completely united, as they were on little else, against temperance. German leadership now sought to block the power of temperance forces within the Democracy, and demanded the party oppose all temperance initiatives. Skillfully tying together temperance and Whig nativism and elitism, the *Weltbürger* pressed readers to make themselves heard at Democratic caucuses and conventions and at the polls.[103] Fourth Ward residents petitioned the council in 1851 to protest denials and removals of licenses. That same year an Anti-Temperance Association was created to stimulate further agitation among Germans. These counter pressures raised German unity to unprecedented heights. They also had some effect on the alcohol issue. Fourth Ward councilman Harrison Park fought energetically and with some success to increase the number of licenses granted to the ward.[104] As the game of thrust and counterthrust escalated, within a year the women's temperance organization was again demanding that licensing end and lawbreakers be prosecuted.[105] Meanwhile, both sides increasingly looked to Albany and the battle shaping up in the legislature over prohibition.

As their militance grew, American moral reformers joined temperance and Sabbatarianism together. In doing so they created a convenient middle ground for politicians. American Sabbatarian activism was not new. Since the 1820s, trade unionists, principally printers, had struck for a workless Sunday; individual businessmen, such as George Tifft, had closed their enterprises on Sunday and attempted to convince others to so; and evangelical preachers had been proclaiming Sunday not merely a day of rest, but a holy day, respect for which was a religious obligation.[106] But local triumph of these principles, and municipal enforcement of the feeble state and local Sunday closing laws, ran headlong into several obstacles. Dock merchants, service business owners, and retailers catering to travelers were loath to close during the season of navigation, and opposed all calls to shut down the Erie Canal on Sundays. Workingmen opposed closing public markets and barbershops on the one day when they could conveniently attend to personal needs. Immigrants, especially Germans, dedicated the day to worship and convivial recreation and drinking, and were opposed to any effort to curb their weekend pleasures. In 1850 the New York *Herald*'s traveling correspondent concluded that Buffalo, especially around the docks, was even less observant of the Sabbath than Gotham.[107]

Temperance women and others demanded action, and politicians unenthusiastic about wholesale assaults on alcohol were willing to give it to them. In 1851, both parties in an evenly divided council contributed to the majority that strengthened the laws banning Sunday alcohol sales. Germans reacted bitterly to police efforts to enforce the new law, and within weeks three Democratic councilmen (two from the Fourth and one from the Fifth) had introduced legislation to legalize Sunday sales. Five Whigs and two Democrats united to defeat the measure. Yet within a year temperance women complained that regardless of the law, Sunday sales were proceeding as before. For the militant women, this was further proof of the necessity of prohibition.[108] Meanwhile, ethnic polarization and political conflict within and between the parties on the alcohol question continued, not to be resolved until the next decade.

Naturalization and the broad spectrum of partisan activity were accomplished often through the mechanisms of the Democracy, which guided many foreigners through the citizenship proceedings and then walked them to the polls. Little initiative was required on the part of immigrants, though in spite of itself, the situation did encourage them to regard themselves as citizens possessing rights and to have a positive orientation toward government. For all its manipulative aspects, therefore, political integration did encourage civic integration—daily dealings with government, not merely in the role of subject, but as a petitioner exerting pressure for favorable treatment, and as a participant in the practical tasks undertaken by, and the symbolic activities of, the corporate, civic community. Civic integration encompassed the voluntary or obligatory public service of militiamen, firemen, jurors, and those marching in the annual July Fourth parade, and the activities of those in ad hoc, grass-roots mobilizations of taxpayers, neighborhood residents, and occupational groups wanting to change the nature of the laws affecting their lives. Civic integration required citizen and group initiative. This civic voluntarism was strongly reinforced by the frequent absence of top-down party initiatives in the civic order. As politicians interpreted them, municipal issues often lacked sufficient ideological import to be resolved on any but a nonpartisan basis satisfying to the largest possible number of voters. The parties tended toward similar positions and patterns of behavior. On taxation and infrastructural development, both conformed to the logic of taxing and spending in good times, in response to constituency demands and perceptions of the common good, and retrenching in bad times. Disagreements between them were limited to the issues of which projects should be taken on, who should be taxed for them, and how high municipal debt should be allowed to climb. Even these questions, however, did not always provoke debate. Party positions on such matters were defined not by differing principles, but by whether a party was in or out of power. The guardian of the public purse in opposition became the improvement-conscious spender in power. This depoliticization of issues encouraged citizens to define their relations to government outside a partisan context.

The pace of civic integration was like that of political integration in that it was not only uneven and gradual, but varied from group to group. The determinants of the process lay in forces that were internal and external to the Irish and German populations. As the gatekeepers of civic opportunity, Americans were slow to allow full ethnic participation in leadership and sometimes, too, membership in prestigious civic bodies. Like political integration, therefore, civic integration was accomplished most successfully at the bottom of the structure of public life. Only the most widely respected and longest resident (and then very few indeed) ethnics were asked to serve on a grand jury. Up to 1852 none at all served on the committee that planned the annual Fourth of July ceremonies, though ethnic organizations participated for years in the parade that marked the day. Ethnic militia and volunteer fire companies existed for many years, but with very few exceptions, the officers of the Firemen's Benevolent Association and the high command of the militia were Americans.[109]

Historical experience, cultural traditions, habits of voluntary association formation, and socioeconomic position and aspirations account for differences in the nature and extent of civic integration. For example, a European legacy of popular military training and of enthusiasm of soldiering, a propensity for forming *Vereine*, and a desire to impress Americans led Germans as early as 1838 to form the first of the four militia companies they would control by 1853. In the latter year Germans had four of the eight community-based volunteer companies in Buffalo, while Americans had three and the Irish one. The German capacity for forming voluntary associations was also seen in the creation of fire companies. Of the twelve in 1853, Germans had five and the Irish only one, even more out of proportion to the Irish percentage in the population (18 percent) than the extent of their militia participation. In contrast, in both instances German percentages (50 and 41) were greater than, or roughly proportional to, the percentage of Germans in the population.[110]

Socioeconomic position and aspirations were especially significant in shaping daily relations with government. As a people with a relatively high incidence of property ownership and hence of taxpaying, Germans took a keen interest in the constantly debated questions of the costs of welfare and infrastructure. They not only used the poorhouse, sidewalks, and streets, but played an important role in financing them. As skilled workers and shopkeepers they were regulated—they often felt, at their inconvenience—by the municipality, while as consumers they profited from that regulation. Having a vital interest, like Americans, in both the production and consumption of municipal services, they experienced not only constant pressure to involve themselves in government activities, but also the opportunity to enter into constantly shifting coalitions with like-minded, self-interested people, mostly Americans, who tried to influence government decisions. The result was that German civic integration took place along a wide front of public concerns.

Moreover, in the relations of Americans and Germans, these joint civic mobilizations provided a counterweight to the tensions caused by divisive German initiatives over language. Indeed, while the latter declined in the 1850s, the former, with their potential for interethnic cooperation, would increase in frequency and intensity. The Irish, among whom property ownership, skills, and inclusion on the tax rolls were considerably rarer, had a quite different experience. They more frequently consumed government services than paid for them. In addition to truncating their civic involvement, this gave them little opportunity to present themselves as productive citizens. Indeed, it helped seal on them a reputation for civic parasitism. Moreover, the civic conflicts in which the Irish were engaged usually involved defense of the rights of *Catholic* consumers of services. Campaigns for Catholic rights tapped a rich vein of Old World Irish experience, but this activity reinforced their reputation as advanced agents of the papacy, who would never be Americanized. (The pope's "American children," said the *Commercial Advertiser*, quoting a phrase from a letter supporting Catholic rights, "sign themselves Patrick McGroarty, Donald McLeod, Charles O'Leary, and Patrick Cody.... These names do not grow naturally in America.")[111] While the Irish, therefore, were quicker than the Germans to experience political integration, their civic integration was slower and uneven. Finding power in the city's politics, they were isolated in its civic order.

These varying orientations toward government were apparent in the relationship of both groups to the era's most costly and systematized municipal services—public schools, the poorhouse, and the police. Both groups had less than total involvement with the public schools, because of attendance at sectarian schools and low rates of retention through the grades. Yet Catholic schools could not accommodate all immigrant children, and in the case of the German Protestants, only some Lutheran synods regularly sustained sectarian education, so both groups—and the Germans more so—depended on public schools. The Germans entered into positive, supportive relations with public education, which their taxes did much to sustain. Though critical of public spending in many areas, the *Weltbürger* and German political leaders supported adequate funds for schooling. On one occasion, when German aldermen voted against providing funds to sustain the city's first high school, 2,600 Germans criticized them sternly in a public petition.[112] German mobilizations for language rights in the schools might have disturbed this interethnic consensus on public education, but they were actually evidence of positive support. They suggest a desire not to abandon the public schools, but to improve them, on German terms, hence widening their appeal and diversifying their curriculum. To the extent the Irish were dependent on public schools, they felt captive of them. This was evident in public attacks by Timon, the parish clergy, and D'Arcy McGee and other secular leaders on "Godless" and "proselytizing" public schools, and in their calls for division of the taxes that supported education. German Catholics and Lutherans gave some support to these calls.[113] But as a body the tradition-minded majority of Lutherans also feared state regulation of sectarian schools, and were wary of providing any opening for it.[114] Under any circumstance, the Lutheran synods played little role in public affairs. Furthermore, as was true of all questions involving public defense of the Catholic church, the Irish, not the Germans, led the way.

A similar situation existed in the case of the poorhouse. Its inmates were very largely those foreigners—mostly Irish—who were set adrift from traditional communal and familial networks, and had to fall back on charity. Though unfortunate individuals among the Germans ended up there, Germans were never represented in proportion to their percentage in the total population. As its principal users, the Irish were the most frequent victims of the horrid physical conditions prevailing there and the religious bigotry that was often the policy of the Protestant administration. In 1849, 1852, and 1858, Irish church and secular leadership protested these conditions. They clashed bitterly with Americans, who, while divided over what material level inmates should be kept at, appeared united in opposing equality for the Catholic priesthood in public institutions. A prominent German Catholic close to the bishop, usually the wealthy merchant Stephen Bettinger, would occasionally join these efforts, which, however, remained almost exclusively an Irish matter, and a source of both Irish civic integration and conflict with Americans.[115]

Contemporary urban police had two principal functions—formally, crime control and informally, welfare (principally sheltering transients, lost children, and drunks.) Both ethnic groups had a stake in the former, as was clear in the frequent, sometimes cooperative, calls of their leaders for prosecution of dock runners.[116] Yet while crime and vice plagued the First Ward, there were no grass-roots mobilizations against them. Perhaps partly because residents knew the police tried to segregate vice there, residents might have felt the task hopeless. What crackdowns there were came because of elite concerns for the city's image among travelers. The circumstances of Irish life did lead to greater interest in police welfare activities, for the Irish were frequently in need of them. Not only the stranded condition of many traveling immigrants, but the extreme deprivation of the dockside Irish made it necessary for the First Police District's officers to provide food and sleeping quarters at the neighborhood station house. Thus, in winter the station house was filled with the unemployed and their families, and in summer, with stranded immigrants.[117]

German relations with the police, however, were principally about law enforcement. In 1846, 1851, and 1853, many Fourth Ward residents protested against prostitution, which the police had allowed to move into the East Side following an elite-inspired campaign against First Ward vice. In 1851 representatives of both the Germans and the ward's minority American population formed a permanent committee to monitor the situation and report to the police.[118] Interest in law enforcement led the German press to support various proposals made by American opinion leaders for the professionalization of the police. At first the proposals encompassed simply the wearing of badges and uniforms, but soon training and better screening of political appointees were urged. The Irish press opposed all these proposals in fear that patronage opportunities might be lost. The *Weltbürger* supported them, even though a uniformed, disciplined police would be a painful reminder, it said, of "the red-collared, saber-rattling gendarmerie" of Europe. The paper recognized that Germans were not dependent on patronage, and that uniforms and training would have a deterrent effect and perhaps make the police more responsible.[119] There was a limit—the laws regulating alcohol—to German support for tough law enforcement. But Germans never accepted the premise that beer drinking needed regulation, and, if the complaints of American temperance women are to be believed, neither did the German police. Moreover, the alcohol question became so suffused with politics and cultural prejudice that its law enforcement aspects were elusive for many Germans.

Social and economic regulation was another area of civic life that found Germans deeply and routinely engaged, along with Americans, in efforts to affect government. The Irish were largely marginal participants because of a lack of skills and property.

Buffalo's municipal government was heir to eighteenth-century ideas that government should be a guardian of the public good. While these ideas suffered criticism as free-market ideology gained credibility, they were sustained, and expanded upon, down to 1861. Both the 1832 and 1853 city charters provided for municipal licensing, inspection, and fines to protect the public from contaminated food and fraud by food sellers. Also subject to regulation because of epidemiological concerns, which grew stronger with successive cholera infestations, were various forms of environmental pollution, principally animal wastes. The city's desire for additional revenue from licenses and fines bolstered the case of those who argued for regulation. Above all, however, such regulation was popular among consumers and property-owning householders concerned about pollution, sanitation, and fraud.[120]

But regulation raised problems for the various groups to be regulated or otherwise inconvenienced by it, and for those who understood its costs. Prominent among the latter were such increasingly vocal American exponents of cheap, minimal government as the Whig politician, inventor, and entrepreneur William Ketchum, who denounced the growth of taxes for expenditures he believed inessential. These men were not entirely consistent, and self-interest had much to do with what they defined as essential. Thus, public markets and parks were frivolous, but harbor improvement at the public expense was not. These Americans were joined by many German shopkeepers and artisans who emphasized the biases of regulation. They and Dr. Brunck argued that regulation indirectly added to the cost of basic services and goods, was subject to partisan abuses, and contained an element of class oppression, because artisanal occupations, such as butchering, and small shops, such as groceries, were licensed and regulated, but few mercantile businesses and professions were. By the early 1850s, both Ketchum and Brunck had come to believe that the local passion for regulation was out of control. But Brunck, who tied this passion to the compulsive pursuit by the American evangelical conscience of social improvement and control was not optimistic that such a mentality could ever accept the disorder that accompanied freedom.[121]

The municipality sought to regulate food production and sales by maintaining public markets housed in municipally owned buildings. Public markets had existed before incorporation, and provision for them was contained in the 1832 charter. They existed primarily for the regulation of the sale of meat, but they also accommodated other food sellers, principally bakers, whose bread was subject to weight regulations. These markets, supervised by an inspector employed by the council, made practical sense in the small town of 1832, in which the city's two markets had been located in such a way that they were convenient to everyone. But they were difficult to maintain in the vastly expanded city of 1850, at which time there were still only two of them. Both were dirty and crowded, and far from the principal vectors of the city's expansion.[122]

The desire to maintain public markets precipitated major debates in two distinct connections. First, there was the continuing effort to regulate butchers, some two-thirds of whom were German by the mid-1850s. Possessing strong ethnic identity and pride of craft as well as entrepreneurial aspirations, butchers grew restive under laws requiring them annually to renew costly licenses and limiting their trade to public markets. Anomalies in the law added to their anger. Farmers could sell meat everywhere from wagons, so urban farmers had rights that their butcher neighbors lacked. Many German butchers broke the law by practicing their trade in unlicensed East Side shops. But they and the market butchers also engaged in years of protest. They exerted political pressure through Fourth Ward councilmen, who, from Dellenbaugh in 1839 on, made it their task to be the butchers' spokesmen. In response to this largely German pressure and to consumer complaints about the inconvenient location of public markets, an indecisive council alternately licensed retail butchers for neighborhood shops, and then did an about-face and licensed them only for public markets. At still other times only wholesale butchers were licensed for private shops. But the cost of licenses kept growing whatever the current policy, and it was this that eventually led the butchers to new tactics. Unionization and law suits came to supplement their customary reliance, now exerted effectively by one of their own, butcher and councilman Franklin Allberger, on political pressure. Such efforts would succeed in the 1850s in bringing down licensing costs.[123]

A second connection was the effort to expand the system of public markets to keep pace with spatial and population expansion. Though the question of whether markets should exist at all was discussed, the public accepted their utility. Instead, what preoccupied local debate was the problem of who should pay for these expensive services: neighborhood residents living right around markets, or the entire city, which could also draw benefits from them. Germans were especially agitated by this issue, and in consequence, they initiated and participated in some of the period's largest civic mobilizations.

A number of the issues involved were larger than the question of markets, though in the early 1850s this was the principal focus for their public discussion. Some context, therefore, is needed to understand the Germans' stance. From the 1830s on, the pace of infrastructure development proceeded almost without letup, as a wide array of individuals and groups proposed projects they believed would stimulate economic development and enhance the quality of life. Across party lines councilmen tried to please all these various constituencies. Only depressions caused a slackening of their efforts. Under normal circumstances, only when spending and, in train, debt and taxation reached burdensome levels, did mayors of both parties call for restraint, in the form of either slowing down the pace of development or making more efficient use of existing facilities, a favorite Democratic argument. Also urged upon the council was the creation of semipublic corporations, which could make use of private investments as well as public monies. Gas lighting (1848) and drinking water (1852) were developed by such corporations, but they could not provide a practical way for dealing with such incremental, routine improvements as paving and sewers, for which taxes were levied and neighborhood assessments made.[124]

Beyond constant griping about high rates, taxation and assessment prompted various complaints. Until 1844 the council could initiate any improvement, large or small, without approval of the residents affected, and this made it easy to approve inessential neighborhood paving projects as a way of rewarding political allies among contractors. In that year, however, while serving as mayor, William Ketchum pushed through the council legislation requiring that assessments be levied and collected before any work could commence. The purpose was to stop the growth of municipal debt, but the law also left an opening for residents to block work they did not want. Because ways were found, however, to pressure residents, especially foreign ones who did not know their rights, into paying assessments, many unpopular and unneeded projects continued to be executed. The 1853 charter, as a result, provided that a majority of neighborhood residents had to petition the council before any project could be undertaken.[125]

Perhaps no group felt as aggrieved by this situation as the Germans. The improvements accomplished by the council often favored the docks, central business district, and elite American neighborhoods. Thus, in water, gas lighting and waste removal, the East Side lagged far behind, even though it had miles of sidewalks residents often felt were unneeded, or at the least, too expensive for the benefits obtained.[126] Moreover, work ordered for the East Side commenced slowly, and frequently was done poorly. Fourth Ward Germans and Americans saw the council draw up sixteen different contracts for paving Genesee Street before the much needed job was done. Then, they protested, the work was done so poorly, it had to be redone.[127] But apart from how the work was done, there was the problem of the effects of tax increases and assessments on a struggling but thrifty people such as the Germans, whose little parcels of property were often their sole source of security. It did no good to tell a hard-pressed German that the improvements for which he was being assessed might raise the value of his property. (In fact, property values were more sluggish in the relatively unimproved East Side than elsewhere.) Some did not own the land their cottages sat atop, while others considered themselves settled for life and had no desire to sell their property. That tax increases and assessments hurt German householders is apparent in the number who lost their homes or lots because of nonpayment of taxes. The *Weltbürger* often complained that the large majority of those appearing on the list of forced sales were German. The assessors compounded the problem. For many years they did not publish lists of tax delinquents in the German press, and they failed to search for delinquents before auctioning off property some could have saved at the last minute.[128]

The problem was essentially one of dollars and cents, but it was continually crystallized in ideological form by the *Weltbürger* in the questions: What improvements should be undertaken? Who should pay for them? Many Americans and some Germans, too, would have said that all one had to know about Germans to guess their answers was that they were cheap. "You Germans of Buffalo," said one of them in 1848 protesting their lack of contributions to aid European revolutionaries, "it is like getting you to amputate a little finger before you will spend a cent for the common good." Americans, who used such words as "lymphatic" to characterize the Germans' response to civic projects, were probably not surprised on election day in 1852 when the Fourth Ward made the lowest prorated contribution to the collection for a monument to Washington—at three cents per voter, half what the rest of the city averaged.[129]

Germans, however, possessed their own priorities and principles for evaluating what was good for them and for the public. Within the ideological context of Democratic political economy and with allowance made for unique local problems, the *Weltbürger* developed a stance on infrastructure development with which many Germans seemed to have agreed. The paper deemed water supply and waste removal essential to the common good and strongly backed such projects, even though East Side neighborhoods were slow to profit from them. It believed water so important it opposed creating a semipublic corporation to develop it, and called instead, against its Democratic principles, for total municipalization. For the less essential gaslight service, it favored such a corporation.[130] The paper carefully sorted its way through infrastructural projects pertaining to interregional commerce. It supported widening the Erie Canal at state expense, because the canal sustained the prosperity of everyone in upstate New York. It agreed that the city should widen Buffalo harbor and create a ship basin, but it opposed the levying of a general assessment for the work on the grounds that only wealthy dock merchants would directly profit from it.[131] Concern about public subsidies to private interests in the name of the common good governed the paper's response to proposals for funding various railroads to enhance the city's competitive position. In each case the railroads were deemed necessary; it was the funding arrangements that caused dissent. It opposed large municipal loans to the Buffalo and Attica Railroad in 1842, and was unenthusiastic a decade later about a $400,000 loan and other guarantees to the Buffalo and Pittsburgh Railroad. In the latter case, it feared that the interest of householders, whose property would in effect be mortgaged by the city's new obligations, were not protected, while a few wealthy men stood to get wealthier from the project. (One German householder posted a sign on his little cottage—"A Mortgage of $400,000 on This Property"—during the public debate.) But in 1853 it supported a $150,000 loan to the Buffalo and Brantford Railroad (part of a planned line to Lake Huron), because it felt the arrangement equitable.[132] German voters agreed with these positions when they had the opportunity to express themselves. The Fourth Ward cast a 1,193 to 14 vote for the Buffalo and Brantford loan, but a 1,023 to 336 vote against the Buffalo and Pittsburgh, a large enough negative vote that the proposal achieved only a 37-vote majority.[133]

At no point was the popular basis for these civic priorities clearer than in debates about public markets. The battle around markets began, indirectly, with a debate over parks, and the two issues continued to be curiously intertwined as symbols of the conflict between necessary and unnecessary civic priorities. In the early 1850s a wide spectrum of bourgeois opinion, across party lines, began to complain about the central business district's raw, functional look and the lack of opportunities throughout Buffalo for outdoor recreation. The answer, many felt, lay in developing parks, of which there were only a few quite small ones. The most popular, opened in 1851 in front of the courthouse, was no more than a lawn. Hogs and cattle roamed the premises, and servants shook out rugs there. Thus, when that same year the wealthy politician Edward Bennett donated a large piece of land in the Fourth Ward, the council eagerly announced plans for a park, which was to be financed by small assessments on many Fourth and some Second Ward residents.[134]

Germans were unenthusiastic. They had their own places of recreation, and they and most Americans in the Fourth resented being assessed for a park that would be available to the entire city. At a large meeting, strong resolutions were passed. The proposal was denounced as a waste of money, and the meeting demanded instead that a public market be constructed in the upper part of the Fourth Ward. Led by Dellenbaugh and a largely German committee, a massive petition was gotten up in the Fourth to inform the council of the ward's sentiment.[135]

The demand for a new market in that neighborhood had precedent. In 1849 and again in 1850, many Fourth and Fifth Ward residents and the German-American Workingmen's Union had petitioned for one and asked that it be paid for by a general assessment, because, they claimed, they were already too highly taxed.[136] Now, however, the pleas for a market complemented the growing consciousness among council members that if the market system were not rejuvenated, it would die. After the council defeated the park proposal in a nonpartisan vote, it moved slowly to act on the market issue. It closed one dilapidated market, and projected plans to create three new ones, two of them on the East Side, that would be paid for by a combination of bonds, general taxes, and neighborhood assessments. These assessments were steep, however, because, the council maintained, the land was inexpensive, prime locations and it was only right that those whose property would grow in value because of proximity to the new markets should foot much of the bill.[137]

Thus began the period's most prolonged and intense civic controversy. Proposed locations shifted and technical legal issues entered the debate. But the forces engaged remained the same throughout. Across party lines council members hoped to accomplish their goals without political risk: all favored reinvigorating the market system, but at the least cost to constituents. Next there was a bipartisan American pressure group that took form around William Ketchum and was encouraged by cost-conscious Democratic Mayor Eli Cook. Opposed to increasing municipal expenditures and debts, it called for an end to the public market system and for its replacement by private enterprise, and took the issue into the courts. Finally there were a large number of German and some American householders who wanted markets and a general tax or a bond issue to pay for them. A compromise was reached.[138] Protecting its own, unassessed constituencies, the council majority confirmed unpopular, neighborhood assessments for one East Side market. In the case of the other, however, a site change was effected by appropriating the Bennett land and thus doing away with the need for a neighborhood assessment.[139]

This struggle and its outcome have a twofold significance. The shift in the function of the Bennett land on terms favorable to the priorities and material interests of German and American householders is noteworthy. It suggests that in a delicately balanced system in which politicians sought compromises acceptable to all of the varied, organized interests they represented, a coalition of foreign and native property owners could exert a powerful role in local affairs. Second, it is equally clear that the civic community demonstrated the capacity to absorb new groups, when constituted in particular ways, into its public life. In this case property-owning, taxpaying Germans were slowly but surely arriving as a factor in the civic community in a manner that eluded the politically powerful but propertyless Irish.

CHAPTER 12

From Ethnic Polarization to Social and Political Realignment, 1854–60

ETHNIC and religious tensions gathered ominously in 1853 and 1854. During the summer of 1853 a large group of Irishmen attacked Baptist missionaries proselytizing about the docks. Not long after, several of the principal Presbyterian ministers invited the controversial apostate priest, Alessandro Gavazzi, to speak at their churches. Clad in monk's robes, he delivered four sensational exposures of "papal aggression," and he took the opportunity to air the long-standing charges of sadism and repression against Archbishop Bedini, who everyone knew was soon to arrive in Buffalo. The extent to which Gavazzi's massive audience believed him was evident in the refusal of city officials to extend a formal welcome to Bedini that October. The following February Dr. Lord's lecture on the same themes drew 3,000, probably the largest audience ever in attendance at a local public lecture. When the weather improved, public animosities again shifted to the streets. Itinerant Protestant preachers harangued hostile First Ward Irishmen on the corruption of their religion, while American crowds threatened violence if the preachers were harmed. For the first time, the Fourth of July celebrations were scenes of street violence, as Irishmen and Americans randomly clashed throughout the day.[1]

Few observers, however, were probably prepared for the emergence of the mass nativist movement that materialized in June of 1854. Within weeks the otherwise secretive Know Nothings were publicly boasting that they had 1,478 members. In the next two years lodges were formed in all thirteen wards.[2] As impressive was the fact that many leading men were joining the order, and letting it be publicly known. The roster of the fourteen founders of Lodge #107, the first and most prestigious, was published in the sympathetic *Commercial*

Advertiser. It reads like a register of the most affluent, politically influential, and socially well-connected men. They crossed party lines, too, tending to be Silver Gray Whigs and Hard Democrats, who turned toward nativism to a greater extent than their intraparty, Soft foes. Eight were lawyers, including the Fillmore allies George Babcock and the deeply anti-Catholic James Putnam, both of whom served in the state senate. (It was said that 75 percent of the city's bar eventually was in the order.) Three of the others were merchants, and another was Dr. Lord himself. The presence of both local militia commanders, Nelson Randall and Gustavus Adolphus Scroggs, lent an ominous military cast to local nativism.[3] Soon Fillmore and his former law partners and current political advisors, Solomon Haven and Nathan K. Hall, entered Lodge #107.[4] This and the other local lodges would also come to count among their members such prominent men as Dr. Josiah Trowbridge, William Ketchum, Orlando Allen, and Elam Jewett, the publisher of the *Commercial Advertiser*, which soon went from being a coy fellow traveler to one of the foremost voices of northern nativism.[5]

The movement's political arm, the American party, made an equally dramatic first appearance, capturing 47 percent of the vote in the fall 1854 gubernatorial election. It then went on to vitalize and to consolidate the native vote, which had always been divided between two parties. Turnout in the American wards increased to its highest level, 81.5 percent during 1854–58, under the impact of nativism's issues. In the hotly contested spring, 1855, race for superior court judge, the party captured absolute majorities in all four wards (Two, Three, Nine, and Ten) in which native-born Americans were dominant. There was only an 8.6 percent average difference in all thirteen of the city's wards between the percentage of Americans of voting age and the percentage of the total vote given the American party that fall. In seven of the wards that difference was 5 percent or less, and in the Third, which had the largest percentage of native-born voters, the difference completely disappeared. Even in contests in 1856 and 1857, by which time the American party was in decline, it was capable of capturing about half of the native vote.[6]

The threat of nativism prompted polarization on the other side of the ethnic equation. Between 1854 and 1858 nativism, aided by temperance and Sabbatarianism, brought about to an unprecedented degree the Know Nothing activist's political nightmare—an unyielding immigrant Democratic vote swelled by exceptionally large turnouts. Irish turnouts increased from 74 percent in the previous decade to 80 percent during 1854–58, and German turnouts from 63 percent to 74 percent. As Americans left the Democracy to vote nativist, ethnics came to account for a growing percentage of its vote. In 1855, six of the seven most ethnic wards (One, Four, Five, Six, Seven, and Eight) had at least 60 percent of their voting populations composed of naturalized citizens, while the Twelfth, which had been part of Black Rock and had a large German population, had 54 percent. These wards accounted for 64 percent of the Democratic vote in 1853. The percentage jumped to 75 in the 1854 race for governor and 74.5 in the 1855 race for superior court judge. While the share of the most Irish wards (One and Eight) of the Democratic vote lingered around 21 percent in the three contests, the German wards' percentage jumped from 44 to 54.5, fueled by massive German turnouts. The German wards (Four, Five, Six, Seven, and now Twelve) alone produced either almost all (e.g., 80 percent in the 1856 presidential election) of the Democracy's majority, or more than its total majority, as in the 1855 municipal election in which the German wards *alone* could have elected the Democratic candidates. Correlation coefficients (.819, .913, .928, .733) for selected 1854-57 elections demonstrate the firm relationship between the Irish and the Democracy and the extent of Irish unity in the face of an increasing external threat. German coefficients (.546, .744, .743, .670) are also quite high, but do not suggest the same degree of single-mindedness.[7] Much more vocally than the Irish, Germans expressed outrage at temperance and Sabbatarianism, which threatened their way of life and violated their understanding of communal liberty. Moreover, they saw these causes as of a piece with nativism, both in the identity of their advocates and in their ethnocentric, repressive purposes. In spite of such common perceptions and evidence of greater unity of public purpose, Germans were unable to overcome completely their traditional divisions. Sectarian tension continued to be influential among them, and helped shape their responses to nativism and their voting. Out of this profound tension between unity and segmentation, a new, intragroup order would begin to emerge among Germans in the late 1850s.

The rapid rise of organized nativism and the great degree of ethnic political polarization accompanying it masked for a time not only divisions among Germans, but also weaknesses and contradictions within the nativist movement itself. In enhancing the authority of the Catholic church and giving the immigrant vote unprecedented power, the massive immigration of the late 1840s and early 1850s gave nativist ideology and purposes considerable popular credibility, which made it easy for contemporaries to overlook the derivative, shallow nature of nativist ideas. There was nothing new about the stereotypes, accusations, or fears articulated by 1850s nativists. The drunken, violent, impoverished Irishman; the lymphatic, miserly, unprogressive German; the devious, subversive Catholic priest—all had long been staple items of American popular thinking. Nor was there anything original about either nativism's critique of immigrant politics or its reform program. The complaint that immigrant voters lacked independent judgment, were herded to the polls like cattle, and voted unthinkingly as a unit had informed Whig attitudes for years. The goal of curbing the corrupting influences of immigrant politics was articulated in the mid-1840s by such nativist organizations as the American Republican Association, from which the nativists of the 1850s took their principal and most radical goal—the extension of the period of naturalization to twenty-one years. That at least four of the founders of the 1844 ARA chapter rose high in the councils of the local Know Nothing movement is evidence of the continuity of these ideas and proscriptions.[8] The movement's emphasis in New York State on demanding an end to routine abuses of the naturalization process by a partisan municipal judiciary also echoed a constant Whig complaint of previous years.[9] Even the secret signs and codes of the 1850s found precedent in the rituals of small, nativist organizations that existed in northeastern states in the late 1840s.[10]

Nativist ideas and behavior were also riddled with semiconscious, unrationalized elements and even some glaring contradictions. The movement doubtless contained genuine bigots with a deep hatred of foreigners and the Catholic church. There were those bullies who sought confrontation with Irishmen hooting Protestant street preachers.[11] Representative of them was John Carpenter, an American harnessmaker living around the docks, of whom it was said in 1856, "His chief business is to knock down and drag out Irishmen at our elections."[12] But simultaneously Americans of Carpenter's and other classes, higher and lower, often acted upon other premises. They sought medical attention at Sisters of Charity Hospital. The American poor stood in line next to Irish and Germans to obtain free food from the Sisters of Charity, especially in the wintry depths of the 1857–58 depression, when many respectable, skilled American workers were brought low by sudden unemployment. Affluent Americans, including Fillmore, gave money for the construction of the cathedral, and praised the Catholic clergy for its charitable work and its contributions to raising Buffalo's cultural level. During the height of nativism, too, Americans in ever growing numbers attended St. John's Day festivities and other German communal activities.

The inconsistency of nativist daily behavior was matched by the internal tensions in the ideas put forward by the movement's ideologists. For all its emphasis on immigrant crime, poverty, and moral and physical ills, the *Commercial Advertiser* felt a need to refute the *Courier*'s charges that nativism was responsible for the decrease in immigration in the mid-1850s. The editor knew, as did American employers, that the nation was profiting from the availability of cheap immigrant labor, and neither the *Commercial Advertiser* nor any local nativist spokesman advocated cutting off the supply. "We approve of immigration," the paper said flatly in 1854, "It builds up the country."[13] Even the proposal to adopt a literacy test to curb, rather than completely stop, the flow of immigrants, which was briefly advocated by the *Republic*, a Democratic but independent-minded paper, was never a formal part of the nativist program.[14] It was not in fact even discussed in the *Commercial Advertiser*. Nativists concentrated solely on limiting immigrant political rights, and thus implicitly accepted that it was in their own interest to continue to live among foreigners.

The embrace of immigrants was also extended to them in their particularity, especially in the case of the Germans—and with no serious effort made to separate Protestant from Catholic Germans. While striving to further American party interests, the *Commercial Advertiser* simultaneously praised German ethnic culture for its "life, spirit and fun," and the German character for valuing hard work, craft, and property. While sympathizing with the nativist movement and charging that German habits were "not always the best or purest," the *Christian Advocate* also stated that local Germans were "staunch, persevering and honest" people on whom "the city is dependent . . . for its improvement and extension." While the German character could profit from assimilation of American refinement and initiative, it possessed "a stability," Rev. John Robie said at another time, that even in its raw form lent itself to "the most permanent and lasting good."[15] Comments such as these sometimes reflected the nativists' largely opportunistic quest for the German vote, which the Buffalo American party never completely abandoned. But they also reflected a long-felt ambivalence toward Germans, and this ambivalence even led to awkward but no less sincere efforts to make room for German Protestants within the Know Nothing order itself.

Nativists had little ambivalence about the Irish, but here they were hardly unique. Even the Democratic press often proved reluctant to defend the Irish. Neither the *Courier*, which was tied to the wing of the local Democracy most dependent on the Irish, nor the *Republic* went beyond advocating justice for a vaguely defined "adopted citizenry" in answering attacks on the Irish. Irish poverty, crude peasant ways, hard drinking, violence, and single-minded unity in pursuing group interests troubled Americans, across partisan lines. Perhaps nothing was more disturbing than the intimate relationship between the Irish and the Catholic church, even to those who proclaimed themselves friends of the group. Timon's pressure on St. Louis parish, the church's role in the suppression of the 1848 revolutions and of Protestants in Catholic lands, and the intensification of the Catholic critique of the public schools, all were denounced by Democratic papers.[16] For Democratic papers, the uncompromising support the Irish gave coethnic Catholic clergymen in the face of these reactionary activities formed the essence of their quarrel with the Irish. No immigrant people, the *Republic* stated in 1854, "fuses so freely with American society and becomes so soon and so fully Americanized as the Irish." But "let the same peaceable, orderly, and easily affiliating or assimilating Irishman [settle] where there is a Roman Catholic bishop and a priest or two to stir all the worst passions of their nature, and he will find nothing American to please him, unless it be timber to make bludgeons and skulls susceptible to being fractured by them."[17] It is no wonder that the Democratic press could at times admit the validity of some aspects of the nativist critique, which was often pointed principally at the Irish. Of course there were limits on the expression of these sentiments by Democrats. All of the derangements of the political system, said the *Courier* with considerable candor, were due to "the premature conferment upon foreigners of the rights of suffrage."[18] However evident the reference might have been for nativists, the *Courier* could not single out the Irish as particularly ill-prepared to vote. To do so would be to divide the local Democracy. This partisan need for caution made impossible the public expression of the harshest nativist attitudes by Democratic editors and politicians, even as some of them were being secretly inducted into nativist lodges.[19]

Contradictory in its approach to solving problems, unoriginal in its ideas, weak on practical proposals, frightened of the radical potential of what ideas it did advance, and possessed of views that its adversaries could agree with and still successfully oppose at the polls, we should not be surprised that nativism was pushed aside quickly by the much more powerful issues of slavery and sectionalism. Indeed perhaps the most remarkable aspect of the development of nativism in the 1850s was not its rapid rise or its wholesale polarizing effect, but instead how short was its essentially four-year season, how complete its political collapse, and how few its institutional and programmatic legacies. Its decline began locally and nationally only two years after it first fielded separate electoral tickets, when Fillmore made a dismal showing in the 1856 presidential contest. As a separate entity, the American party made its final local appearance in the 1858 fall elections. Prominent individual nativists became both Democrats and much more often Republicans. But the party itself was never formally incorporated by the Republicans and the terms Republicans offered Know Nothings were highly unfavorable to the nativist program. Republicans conceded almost nothing to nativist concerns in forming their party at the state level. In this they had the support of local party leaders who were actively courting Germans. The party merely accepted Putnam's church property law, which was already on the books when Republicans began to contest elections. Republicans proposed, and in 1859 when they controlled the legislature, passed, a voter registration law in answer to complaints about the corruption of voting lists. While such immigrant leaders as Dr. Brunck saw the voter registration law as the start of a nativist-inspired disfranchisement campaign against naturalized voters, the law was, in fact, quite moderate. German Republicans praised it as a much-needed reform, and found it impartial.[20]

In terms of longevity and fulfillment of its programmatic aspirations, therefore, nativism was a failure, and seems easily dismissed as a transitory phenomenon. But this is likely to appear the case only if we insist on seeing nativism as nothing more than a reaction—and a weak one at that—to pressing social problems. There may be no doubt that nativism was partly a reactive and defensive phenomenon, which was precipitated by the suspicion that immigration was causing both a decline in American power and cultural authority and pervasive political corruption. Nativism exacerbated these anxieties, however, for its programmatic inertia and its short, frustrated career could only demonstrate to Americans that it was impossible for them to lead the way back to the simpler, homogeneous society of a half century before.

Yet for all its apparent failures, and even in light of its bigotry, nativism must also be said to have served a positive function for Americans. Under its influence, for the first time, politics functioned to create communal feeling among Americans, who had always divided their vote, as it had always done among the Irish and Germans. Its rhetorical strategy of incessantly comparing Americans with foreigners, moreover, led Americans to attempt to define not only who they were not, but also who they were. While it was a painful new experience to think of themselves merely as one people among many, they were led nonetheless to identify themselves as a group, which produced greater confidence, solidarity, and communality, if not the intense, comprehensive and often intimate group life enjoyed by the Irish and Germans. Nativism was not all there was impelling Americans toward ethnicization. It was joined by such proactive efforts as the formation of historical societies and interdenominational Protestant societies. Having assisted in accomplishing this American cultural renewal, nativism grew irrelevant as larger sectional issues overtook it. In its wake Americans were left more self-confident. They were better able to revive a faltering political system and to confront the need for a strategy for local economic redevelopment, both of which required interethnic, and particularly German, cooperation, and hence made bigotry self-defeating. This enhanced confidence also aided Americans in facing the crisis of the Union. No simple equation may help us to understand the results, however, since the revitalization of American identity lent itself variously to a commitment to order in the form of conservative unionism and to freedom in the form of antislavery.

The sources of the bitter, xenophobic side of nativism, which will be analyzed first, are clear in places such as Buffalo, with their large immigrant populations. By 1850 Americans understood that they soon might become a permanent minority in local politics. In that year, the massive Whig majority (1,157) of the previous mayoral contest had been overturned, and Democrats emerged with a 287-vote victory. While divisions over temperance had weakened them, Whigs like *Express* editor Almon Clapp believed that it was the vote of immigrant workingmen who were being naturalized in unprecedented numbers that was threatening "an overturn in the affairs of the city."[21] The political revolution Clapp feared did not happen immediately, for Whigs scored decisive victories in local contests in 1851 and 1852.[22] But the breakup of their party under the pressure of slavery and sectionalism, the polarizing effects of nativism, and the massiveness of the new immigrant vote all combined to produce immense Democratic majorities, averaging 1,166, in eight contests between 1853 and 1858.[23]

Democratic majorities and the concurrent growth of immigrant officeholding resulting from the revised charter of 1853 need not necessarily have produced the intense American alienation evident in nativism. After all, Americans continued to control the machinery of the Democracy in city, county, state, and nation. The Democratic mayors and judges the immigrants elected were, with the exception of a few Irish judges, Americans. Moreover, Whig, Know Nothing, and Democrat alike, Americans and their naturalized British allies were present in sufficient numbers in enough wards that Americans were actually the largest single group in the new, twenty-six-seat council.[24]

But a political presence of even this magnitude did not mean that Americans had the cultural authority to establish the agenda for, and style of, public discourse and the terms of public behavior. More than the changing fortunes of parties and candidates, this probably weighed most heavily on their minds. Authority is the didactic exercise, particularly dear to the evangelically conditioned conscience, of prescribing ethical principles and models of correct, moral behavior. Authority, therefore, is a noncoercive basis of hegemony, and as such, it is hollow if there is no one who pays attention to its commands or acts in harmony with its dictates. Americans felt that their claim to authority lay not merely in native birth, but in direct descent from the Founding Fathers. Moreover, American elites felt that they themselves had earned respect. Their ranks, they believed, were comprised of men who had achieved personal success by their own hard work, not through a title or massive inheritance, in a society with a democratic constitution.[25] Yet immigrants did not seem to listen to them, let alone act as they wished. Immigrants had their own press, churches, communal leadership, and often schools, which exercised authority in their communities.

Americans came up against two distinct but equally frustrating circumstances in which their claims to exercise authority were spurned by immigrants. One involved the questions both of the legitimacy of the legal regulation of public behavior and of obedience to laws passed to accomplish such regulation. Its fields of most intense combat were alcohol and the Sabbath. At the moment of its greatest success (prohibition, which was passed by the legislature in 1855), temperance would find itself defeated so soundly by public opinion and practice that even the Sabbath would not be free of alcohol. To be sure, not all Americans were prohibitionists. In its sole appearance, in the 1853 mayoral contest, a local prohibition party polled 163 votes.[26] But temperance forces had grown more active, bulked larger within the Whig electorate, and become more outspoken in their claims about how cleansing an effect prohibition would have. Even the *Republic*, *Express*, and *Commercial Advertiser*, which contrasted sharply with the *Democracy* and *Christian Advocate* in refusing to make glowing claims about the prospects of an alcohol-free world, believed that after years of debate it was time to give prohibition a chance. Under any circumstance, all agreed, a law must be obeyed.[27]

But in the brief period before state courts declared prohibition unconstitutional in March, 1856, in spite of the massive financial backing George Tifft and other leading men gave the Carson League to see that the law was understood and enforced, it encountered bitter criticism and was widely disobeyed.[28] While prohibition legislation was still being debated in Albany, a largely German coalition of drinkers, dealers, grocers, brewers, and tavern keepers opened the campaign with a 10,847-signature petition. After passage, joined by American distillers and liquor dealers, the antiprohibitionists began to amass a legal defense fund to defend violators of the law. More than anything else what galled those Americans who wished to give prohibition a chance was that from the start such actions revealed a purposeful, unapologetic intention to disobey an act of a democratically elected body of government. Moreover, they were appalled that the municipal administration did nothing in response to such lawbreaking but episodically enforce the law on Sunday. Well before its demise, the *Christian Advocate* admitted, the law was being disobeyed with "brazen effrontery" in immigrant neighborhoods—and this in spite of "the good people" who demanded respect for it.[29] As a fallback position, Rev. John Robie and others advocated a more rigorous licensing law, which the legislature passed in 1857. This, too, was soon openly disobeyed, and the cycle of Sunday crackdowns and police inactivity recommenced. By 1859 the situation was the same as a decade before—with one exception. Temperance forces had come to feel so hopeless that all of their associations had been disbanded.[30]

A second context in which the assertion of American authority proved to be futile was the ongoing conflict with the Catholic clergy over what were to be the limits of clerical involvement in those secular matters and public affairs Americans believed to have no spiritual meaning. The American position was value-laden and contradictory. Few Americans were prepared to accept from Timon the outspoken public pronouncements on such issues as slavery that many of them tolerated from Rev. John Lord. But Americans felt that their leaders labored at a disadvantage in competition with the Catholic clergy, and this allowed them to rationalize tensions in their position. Armed with both the charisma of an unbroken line of apostolic descent over nearly two millenia and the canon law, with its ultimate penalty of denial of the sacraments, the Catholic clergy seemed to command authority. In contrast, Lord could only speak and hope that Protestants, who were conditioned, as he was proud to acknowledge, to exercise independent and critical judgment, would listen.

Almon Clapp put his finger on the source of American discomfort with Catholic authority in discussing Timon's efforts to discipline Irish funerals. These reforms were needed, said Clapp, but from whence came the bishop's right to interfere? "It is difficult for us Americans, with our jealous notions of personal rights and personal independence, to understand the authority by which anyone can prescribe a rigid rule like that promulgated by Bishop Timon, and still more difficult for us to recognize that authority in a spiritual minister."[31] Such ruminations help explain Americans' outrage at the pressures Timon exerted against St. Louis parish and their profound disappointment and surprise when the parish compromised its position. Americans had never understood that republican ideology was only one element in the parish's dissent, and was balanced off uneasily against a desire to maintain traditional prerogatives within the church's system of authority. But Americans did know that even with its secular implications (growing out of the dispute over property ownership), the St. Louis affair was internal to the church. More dangerous from their point of view was the bishop's ability to mobilize large numbers of prominent Catholic laymen to exert pressure upon parties, government, and public opinion on such issues as priestly visitation at the poorhouse, and, in 1857, the effort of prominent Protestants to use public funds to open a local juvenile asylum for delinquent and homeless youth, which Timon feared was a device for alienating Catholic youth from their religion. These Catholic efforts were often successful. Priests were eventually admitted to the poorhouse and the asylum idea was blocked by the Common Council and the legislature, both of which responded to Catholic pressure as well as the tightness of money during the depression. Such defeats convinced Americans that they now lacked the ability to define what was best for their country.[32]

This realization was deepened by the perception that the political parties, though headed by Americans, were no longer dependable instruments for protecting republican principles and institutions, and served only selfish partisan interests. The picture of politics that emerges constantly in editorials in the *Christian Advocate*, *Commercial Advertiser*, and especially *Republic* in the 1850s is dismal. Politics seems little more than endless plotting by partisan wire-pullers, spineless conformity by placemen, and pervasive corruption. Much of this, it was believed even by the *Courier*, was a consequence of the massive incursion of immigrants into politics.[33] Anxieties about the decay of politics were reinforced by what in 1854 the *Republic* described as "the disjointed state of political organizations."[34] Divisions over resources and ideology and the constant quest for votes had weakened the will of the Whigs, Democrats, and even ultimately the new American party, to fight corruption and increased the temptation to employ it to gain advantage over rivals. Only the Republicans, vitalized by antislavery idealism, would escape this political debilitation, and consequently they would capture the vote of most Americans in the late 1850s.

Both from within and beyond its ranks the Democracy came in for the major share of such criticisms. The party was badly divided in the state between the Hards and Softs. The conflict had taken on ideological dimensions after the Kansas-Nebraska debate began, for the Hards favored accommodating the South, while their opponents espoused free soil. But at the local level the rivalry was less about principle than power. The tactics employed were tough and unscrupulous, which provides an explanation for the fierce criticism of the party in its most principled local journal, the *Republic*. The Hards had little popular support when they put forward separate local tickets in 1853 and 1854, but they were gaining control of the local party machinery. When the Pierce administration sought to unify party ranks behind conciliation of the South, it turned logically to the Hards, and threw a good deal of federal patronage their way. Armed with these resources of party discipline and blessed with a nativist opposition, the city's principal Hard politician, Dr. Timothy Lockwood, gathered together a group of Irish politicians and reputedly some of the Irish parish clergy. They successfully mobilized the Irish vote in unprecedented numbers behind a program the *Express* contemptuously called "pewter-mug democracy," i.e., spoils and payoffs.[35] When Lockwood ran for mayor in 1857 against a reform candidate backed by leading entrepreneurs and many nativist politicians, the First and Eighth wards alone produced almost half of his 1,336-vote majority. With a boldness that must have made Americans shudder, the *Sentinel* announced that "the Catholic vote" had given Lockwood his victory, and would now insist on recognition. Within a few months, however, the Irish were publicly charging they had not gotten their just reward, and the alliance suffered a setback.[36] But the career of men like Lockwood, scion of an old and wealthy family, could hardly provide solace for Americans worried about the decay of political morality and American authority. It is easy to see why disaffected Democrats, including such principled Hard politicians as General Scroggs and Elijah Ford, were becoming Know Nothings in the mid-1850s.[37]

The Whig party, which most Americans looked to for over a decade for principled politics, was in dissolution over the slavery issue in 1854, when it contested its last election in Buffalo, and this doubtless provided one impetus for the formation of the local American party that same year. But the nativists, who absorbed the vast majority of Whigs, did not intend to become the Whigs by another name. The old party had been riven by factions, and its conventions and caucuses had seen their share of deals. In line with their reform mission nativists hoped to purge politics of corruption, not only by curbing immigrant political power and carrying on unrestrained ideological battle with the Catholic clergy, but also by creating ethical intraparty and intramovement procedures and by making leadership opportunities available to new, uncorrupted men. While the movement used secrecy to consolidate its ranks and protect itself from the subversive machinations it assumed its Catholic enemies employed, it took pride in the democratic, open standards reigning at its early nominating caucuses and conventions. The movement brought new men into politics, probably less as a consequence of ideology than of having to duplicate the political structures, especially candidate rosters, of existing party politics. Nothing very much distinguished American party ward nominees in the 1855 local elections, relative to their Democratic opponents, except that they were obscure men. They had seldom, if ever, been active in politics before, either because they were blocked by party professionals in efforts to seek office, or because they were too disgusted by the maneuvering around them to try.[38]

Largely because Whig politicians now had to use another party to advance their fortunes, the American party did not escape the ills that nativist true-believers hoped to keep from their ranks. As Whig politicians scrambled to find a new home in 1854 and 1855 the nativist movement became the ground on which the Seward-Fillmore rivalry was fought. The Seward forces used nativism and the American party to advance both Seward's career and antislavery politics. Led locally by Almon Clapp and the banker and former congressman Elbridge Spaulding, they employed three different tactics. First, the *Express* increasingly denounced the Catholic church and immigrant—especially Irish—bloc voting, while simultaneously condemning the nativist movement for its antirepublican use of secrecy. Second, in 1854 Seward loyalists throughout the state created a shadowy "Know Something" organization, which also employed secrecy, to compete with the Know Nothings. Its stated purpose was to curb Catholic political power. Third, Seward's followers made secret alliances with antislavery Know Nothings, who, along with the Know Somethings subverted nativist lodges by publicizing embarrassing information about the inner life of the order. These ties paid off for Seward. Just as Seward loyalists in the legislature arranged to back prohibition in exchange for temperance votes for his reelection to the Senate, so they agreed to back the church property bill for the same payoff from nativist legislators. Seward's four-vote majority in the legislature ensured his return to Washington. It also marked the high point of cooperation between his men and the nativists. As the Republican party grew stronger, Seward forces distanced themselves from the Know Nothings in the belief that without a strong position on slavery, northern nativism was doomed. The prediction proved correct, and nativist politicians were soon seeking admission to Republican ranks.[39]

Fillmore and the Silver Grays also opportunistically used the nativist movement, but they had larger goals. The American party had a national organization and a southern wing, and was firmly unionist, so Silver Grays hoped to mold it into a Whiggish national union party. With the presidential contest of 1856 before them, Fillmore's confidants (Foote, Jewett, Babcock, Putnam, Haven, Hall, and the New York City patrician politicians Erastus Brooks and James Beekman) joined lodges. From within the order they spread word that Fillmore was available and the logical choice to be the party's first national standard-bearer. These men were not nativist ideologues. While they distrusted the Catholic church and had condescending attitudes to immigrants, there were few among them besides Putnam and Brooks, the authors of the church property law, for whom anti-Catholicism was an obsession and outlasted the movement. Nor does one sense any long-term commitment to either the American party or Know Nothing order. Their attitude was typified by Haven, who called the movement narrow in its ideas and "puerile" in its rituals. But, he said when urging Fillmore to join Lodge #107, "the material can be worked into a national fabric which could be of service."[40]

Fillmore was reluctant. He was not a nativist, scorned the apparatus of secrecy and oaths, and felt the American party could never form a viable national government. Personal and partisan ambition alone led him in January, 1855, to accept the pleadings of Haven, Hall, and the Massachusetts Whig Edward Everett, and seek induction into the order—and then on the condition that the oaths be administered in the privacy of his parlor. He left immediately for an extended European trip, which included a well-publicized audience with the pope and tour of various Vatican Jesuit facilities.[41] After he obtained the American nomination in 1856, his course continued to raise the anxieties of nativist true believers. While in the most general way endorsing the nativist principles, he was continually evasive about any goal other than maintenance of the Union.[42]

Nowhere were the ambiguities of the Fillmore campaign more in evidence for a nativist looking to reform politics and restore American authority than in the candidate's hometown. His friends actively solicited German Protestant and even Catholic votes in the belief that only by building an immigrant constituency could they be victorious in western New York and hence in the state. Implementation of this strategy, which was based on the lesson of Fillmore's failed 1844 gubernatorial campaign, began shortly after his January, 1855, induction. The intention in the short term was to facilitate the fall gubernatorial campaign and in the long-run the anticipated Fillmore run for the presidency. A local Fillmore operative, Charles G. Irish, Jr., founded the American Protestant Assembly, a secret nativist organization open to all Protestant citizens, native and naturalized alike. Some 100 immigrant Germans quickly joined the APA, which became self-sustaining and added the word "German" to its title.[43] After Fillmore's nomination, by which time the Know Nothing's vote-hungry state and national councils resolved to admit immigrant Protestants and native-born Catholics, local efforts to gain foreign support intensified. Nativist lodges were formed in the German wards. Composed of Protestant laymen, such as the congregants of St. Paul's Reformed (who gave Fillmore a 44 percent plurality in a pre-election straw vote), Whig operatives, '48er anticlericals, and men with militia ties to Scroggs and

Randall, the lodges were allowed to conduct their business in German and to name themselves after German Protestant heroes. German delegates began to show up at local American caucuses and conventions, and Germans were nominated for ward and even citywide offices. German Fillmore-Donelson clubs were formed on the East Side.[44] The *Commercial Advertiser* editorialized lovingly about the Germans, whom it contrasted favorably with the Irish.[45] Yet the Fillmore people privately sought Irish Catholic votes, too. Timon was approached twice, once by Haven himself, and was promised a large contribution to the church if he would endorse Fillmore. The bishop refused.[46] Fillmore's local campaign nonetheless had an ecumenical, polyglot character. As the *Republic*'s editor said of one Fillmore rally: "We found 200 persons, composed of all classes . . . Jews, Gentiles, Christians, and pagans of both native and foreign birth, who appeared to commingle harmoniously as if no such thing as proscription on account of birth were ever dreamed of."[47]

Local nativism had accepted ideological bankruptcy in pursuit of votes and in obeisance to a prestigious candidate. Yet the results, which embittered nativist ideologues, could not have pleased the Silver Grays. Fillmore failed to break the Democracy's hold on the foreign vote. In the five wards where 50 or more percent of the voters were German, he obtained only 15 percent (601), well behind his equally disappointing 26.5 percent in the city at-large. Even in those five wards, it is not clear Fillmore's votes were German, for in the two most German wards (Six and Seven) he received only 8 percent (118).[48] Whatever the appeal of an anti-Democratic politics for immigrants, clearly it would have to be repackaged to remove the taint of nativism, even the tepid Buffalo variety. Meanwhile organized nativism had reached a dead end. It had exhausted its usefulness, not only to politicians, but to all those Americans who had looked to it for guidance in a time characterized by economic decline, the social crisis of American authority, and the "disjointed state" of political parties.

That local antiforeignism was in decline is demonstrated not only by the American party's failure to recover from Fillmore's defeat, and by the gradual rise of the Republicans, but also by the extraordinary amount of proactive effort Americans were undertaking to cultivate group consciousness and unity. While American nativists were asking foreigners to shed ethnic allegiances and interests as principles of social identity and action, they themselves were preoccupied with forging an ethnic way of looking at and organizing themselves. The function of this ethnicization process was somewhat contradictory. On the one hand, ethnicity undeniably had compensatory and therapeutic value for a provincial bourgeoisie, which suffered from the feeling of living at the fringes of its civilization and was now seeing its authority decline, its economic position erode, and its political power stymied by forces, such as immigration or the New York Central, that were beyond local control. On the other hand, ethnic consciousness and unity provided Americans with the confidence they needed to reassert their claims to be masters in their own house and to reform and renew their institutions.

In contrast to group formation among Irish and Germans, American ethnicization was more a conscious than an existential activity. Americans were aware of the extent to which they were driven by, and even modeled their efforts after, the group life of others. The sting Americans felt when confronted by their situation would not have been so painful had they been in less of a position to compare themselves unfavorably with local foreigners, whose solidarity was evident in so many public contexts. Americans watched St. Patrick's Day parades and St. George's Day banquets with admiration and apparently not a little envy. The *Commercial Advertiser* praised the Irish in 1855 for the "virtuous sentiment of love of the land they were driven from by poverty and despotism" that they had recently demonstrated on St. Patrick's Day, and in 1857 praised St. George's Day celebrants for "the natural and praiseworthy sentiment" of love of homeland. Americans, the paper lamented on the first occasion, were too restless, mobile, and preoccupied with business to cultivate these emotions. By 1857 the paper had come to believe Americans were cultivating group feeling and pride. But it nonetheless felt compelled to implore them to work at cultivating those group feelings that came so easily to foreigners.[49]

In this emotional state Americans became sensitive to any sign of indifference to group welfare or national symbols. By 1854 Buffalo's Sixty-fifth Regiment had been suffering a decade of declining American interest. The international border was quiet, and military service interfered with earning a living. Most men in the ranks and middle and lower officers were Germans. Some American militiamen served under German, and in a few cases Irish, officers. "The Germans have companies full and overflowing, and it is to their credit that their spirit has been a means of keeping up the organization," said Scroggs. Nonetheless he felt the need "to infuse into the breasts of Americans a desire to keep up efficient military organizations of their own," and led a successful effort to form a new American company.[50] After years of false starts, the same competitive, prideful emotions led Americans in 1858 to raise enough money to open Buffalo General Hospital, which they saw as their ethnic alternative to Sisters of Charity Hospital.[51]

An even more intense feeling, akin to shame, was voiced about the state of the July Fourth celebration. German bands, militia, and *Vereine* had so come to dominate the annual procession that while viewing it in 1857 an American "gentleman" was overheard to remark bitterly, "The Germans take care of our celebrations and the Irish take care of our elections." Americans complained that they seemed too immersed in "commerce and speculation and steamboats and railroads and canal enlargements and arrivals of gold and all the moneymaking devices" to plan the day properly.[52] In the mid-1850s, however, even as the arrangements committee for the official celebration grew more ethnically diverse, Americans were insisting on revitalizing the Fourth with American meanings. Americans chose keynote speakers such as Dr. Lord, and these orators adopted an explicitly filiopietistic tone. ("Too much twaddle about Plymouth rock," said the *Sentinel*.)[53] Also, after complaints that too little was done to keep Washington's memory alive, a campaign for more deliberate celebration of his birthday began in 1856.[54]

Faced with recognition of the weakness of their group life, Americans undertook two types of proactive ethnicization activities. They attempted, as labors in behalf of their holidays suggest, to strengthen the expressive symbols of their history and culture; and they sought to overcome disunity.

Because class distinctions among Americans were not large compared to those separating most Americans and foreigners, political and denominational, rather than class, cleavages bulked largest in American minds as sources of group weakness. As the *Commercial Advertiser* stressed, the Know Nothings and the American party were seeking to unify Americans, not simply to curb immigrant power, and to lay foundations for revitalizing Americans' identity and sense of group political interests.[55] Though attracting less space in the press, efforts to mend denominational cleavages were also conceived with the desirability of American unity in mind. The *Christian Advocate*, which had long criticized "denominational landmarks and peculiarities" among Americans, evolved two arguments against sectarianism.[56] At first it sought to convince its American readers that whatever divided them as Protestants was minor compared to their differences with Catholics. But after the emergence of the nativist movement and the new American ethnic consciousness, Rev. John Robie's grounds for criticizing denominationalism shifted and became less defensive. In their intolerance of one another, he said in 1856, American Protestants had become "proud and aristocratic," and forgotten the good they might accomplish together.[57]

By the mid-1850s an American ecumenical movement was developing in several directions. Occasional snipes at the Episcopal church were still found in the *Christian Advocate*, but the paper now advocated cooperation with that denomination, and it praised those Episcopalians urging a similar course on coreligionists.[58] Now, too, conflicts among Presbyterians that had long threatened to precipitate organization of a Congregational church were pacified in 1859 when an influential Presbyterian minister appealed for "Christian cooperation."[59] No more significant effort against denominationalism was made than the establishment in 1857 of the Erie County Sunday School Association, which sought to improve Protestant Sunday school instruction. Though organized by the evangelical clergy, it included the balance of American Christendom (Episcopalians, Unitarians, and Universalists) as well the few German churches affiliated with American evangelicalism. (Some German Lutheran churches would participate occasionally, too.)[60] Sunday school activism was a substitute for, rather than an adjunct to, Sabbatarian political activism, which many Americans increasingly recognized as potentially socially divisive for their own group. The *Commercial Advertiser* acknowledged in 1859 that especially among the working classes, even committed American Protestants were divided on what their Sabbath obligations were. At any rate, workingmen and their families, the paper said, needed a day of leisure and recreation as well as worship.[61] The desire to include a few Germans also curbed whatever thought existed about turning the association into a vehicle for Sabbatarian politics.

Americans revitalized the symbols of Americanism through propagating the study of American history, folk traditions, and literature. This quest had deeper emotional and psychological roots than the conscious effort to create bases of ethnic bonding and identity, in which interest was frequently expressed. From the vantage point of the troubled 1850s, Americans had come to feel a sense of discontinuity, which made the uncertainty of the future even more burdensome. "It is sad," said the *Republic* in 1859, "to reflect how quickly the old families are passing away."[62] As the remnant of pioneers died, there was growing interest in those who, Rev. John Robie stated, "figured in the scenes which brought the old village of Buffalo into being . . . and have looked upon all the transitions connected with our history and progress." This interest soon extended to preserving old buildings and placing commemorative plaques. The Indians, too, were being memorialized, now that local contact with them had all but ended, for stoicism, dignity, and bravery. Out of all these diverse elements, there was developing a romantic pioneering legend of bold men and sustaining women who "broke the still of the forest depths."[63] In addition to its nostalgic and identity-enhancing functions, the pioneer myth served inspirational and therapeutic purposes. Local history, the *Commercial Advertiser* said in 1859, "will drive away the blues" from those preoccupied with the commercial "ruination of Buffalo." Had not Buffalo "been ruined no less than half a dozen times during the last fifty years," only to be revived?[64]

The ways in which history was clarifying an identity for Americans are evident in their engagement with British and New England roots in the mid-1850s. Britain was on the mind of many Americans. They were now reevaluating their debt, as well as historical antagonism, to the ancestral motherland. Conservatives, who feared social disorder and radicalism, such as the *Commercial Advertiser*'s editor, had begun to redefine the meaning of the American Revolution. The Founding Fathers were not revolutionists, said the paper in 1855, but proud Englishmen wishing to hold on to their substantial rights in a then thoughtlessly oppressive empire. They knowingly built upon the best of their British heritage, and, said the paper from its nativist viewpoint, left it to later generations to create an American nationality.[65] Conservatives were not alone in rethinking the British legacy. The effort to find good in that legacy crossed partisan lines and had a popular basis, too. Democrats, whose party had long been critical of Britain's role in Ireland, were involved. Britain had its faults, said leading Democrat James Wadsworth, a featured speaker at the 1853 St. George's Day celebration, but Americans owed their legal, political, and humanitarian traditions to it. The *Republic* agreed, attributing the American conception of liberty not only to the Reformation and the Pilgrims, but to British political culture.[66] These themes were sounded repeatedly at the 1858 St. George's Day banquet, which was formally dedicated to British-American friendship and attended by every major American politician and editor in Buffalo, and at the ceremonies accompanying both the opening of British consular offices and the completion of the trans-Atlantic cable.[67] Perhaps as significant a sign of reconciliation was evident in 1860 when the Prince of Wales visited Fort Erie. Americans demonstrated their peculiar fascination with British royalty even in the midst of an epic presidential campaign. The *Republic*, explaining that its readers had "Prince on the brain," devoted a great deal of space to his activities.[68]

Americans were also using Britain to define what they were not. They were not, said the *Commercial Advertiser*, like the leisured aristocrats who populated British novels. Thus, their passion for British literature, the editor continued, retarded the rise of their own national literature and taught them to view themselves through false lenses.[69]

A similar but informal effort to clarify identity took place in the context of the competition between cricket and baseball. For years American editors had been lamenting that while the Germans had gymnastics and the Irish had prizefighting, Americans had no national sport. They were addicted to work. Hence, "the feeble American physique" needed improvement.[70] Both cricket and baseball might correct the situation, and, as both grew in popularity, several clubs were founded in the 1850s. Composed of young merchants and lower white-collar workers, cricket clubs had British and American members, while baseball teams had only the latter. The two games were compared, and the differences between them, including the greater drawing power of baseball, inevitably attributed to national character. "Cricket," said the *Commercial Advertiser* in 1859, explaining the ascendence of baseball, "is a very slow game to anyone but an Englishman. It is not the equal of baseball, which is livelier and more energetic."[71]

Far more formal assertions of identity were the filiopietistic societies created in the 1850s. After a lapse of several years, the Young Men's Association in 1851 reactivated and broadened the mission of its committee on local history. With the aid of individual antiquarians, the committee now collected "frail and perishable records," through which it hoped to understand "local traditions," and restored local monuments, such as the grave of Red Jacket, the Seneca chief.[72] When it became known that Washington's home at Mount Vernon was decaying, an ad hoc committee, composed of the most prestigious families, was formed to get up a collection.[73] Equally prestigious was the New England Society, which was founded by seventy-five merchants and professionals in 1853 "to cultivate friendly feeling" among the descendants of that section and keep alive knowledge of the Pilgrims' contributions to the history of liberty.[74] The same elite background characterized the founders of the Pioneer Association, but because it was from the beginning in 1858 open to all, independent of class or denomination, who could lay claim to roots in western New York before 1820, it became a popular organization.[75] Not all of these endeavors proved long lasting, and Americans still occasionally said that too little was being done and charged that they were preoccupied with the workaday world. But all these activities contributed to the realization that a permanent historical society, "to commemorate the virtues of those who built up the city and its noble institutions," was needed, and one was founded, with Millard Fillmore as president, in 1862.[76]

This ethnicization process would not produce the intense group life that the Irish and Germans enjoyed. In comparison American ethnicity remained weak. But ethnicization had a vitalizing impact on Americans. In the public sphere it helped provide the bourgeoisie and its allies with the confidence to move forward in the 1850s with political reform and economic reconstruction. To be sure, self-interest was one cause of American activism, certainly evident in the unapologetically opportunistic manner in which Americans sought German cooperation. Organized nativism in the 1850s began amidst deep, general prosperity, but as the city's economy declined, nativism diverted the attention of Americans from reform and reconstruction, and poisoned their relations with the city's largest group, the Germans. Yet calculated self-interest alone could not have sufficed to lead so many Americans to surrender nativism. The turnabout of these Americans makes no sense unless we understand that ethnicization, even if partly fueled by nativism, gave them the confidence to abandon nativism, attempt to reassert their authority, and reach out to seek German allies in ways that would significantly broaden the social and political mainstreams.

The subsequent realignment of local groups was uneven and at times contradictory. It succeeded first in the civic not the political realm, because while many Germans had begun to rethink their partisan assumptions, they were not yet ready in 1855 and 1856 to desert the Democrats for the new Republican party. Because of the entrance of some nativists into Republican ranks, and Republican espousal of voter registration and vagueness about the alcohol question, there was, in fact, fear among Germans that the Republicans were heirs to the nativist legacy.[77]

Instead, growing civic cooperation between Germans and Americans grew out of mutually shared concerns about rising taxes and corrupt, inefficient government. These same issues had been of great importance in the gathering of the bipartisan, elite coalition which, in convention and with little ethnic representation, revised the city charter in 1852. The new charter, which was approved by both the legislature and local voters the next year, contained extensive cost-cutting and streamlining provisions intended to reform the administration of schools, police, and fire department and the execution of municipal infrastructure projects.[78]

Yet questions of overspending and corrupt, inefficient administration were soon raising tempers once more. Times were prosperous, and the new charter seemed to ensure that infrastructure could be expanded without corruption. In 1853 the council began an ambitious, comprehensive program of improvement, which peaked in 1856–57, when the Democratic majority appropriated $300,000 for streets, sidewalks, gaslights, and sewers. In addition, expensive public markets were under construction.[79] Many political abuses—cost overruns, inadequate evaluations of contractors' bills of expense, contractor profits of as much as 150 percent, contracts given to city officers, and unnecessary work—accompanied this expansion. Facilitating this vast pork barrel were seemingly innocent loopholes in the new charter. In the name of flexibility the council was allowed both to undertake work under $200 without a taxpayer-resident petition and assess property owners for it, and to establish annually a $5,000 fund out of general property taxes to do work valued at less than fifty dollars without having to levy an assessment.[80] In consequence of this expansion, by April, 1857, the city's per capita property tax rate was the nation's highest.[81] Businessmen feared this would retard investment, and impair the development of a more diversified, industrially based local economy.[82]

In the spring of 1857 a coalition of 150 American entrepreneurs, lawyers, and senior clerks resolved to bring about governmental reform and tax relief. Among them were active, wealthy capitalists such as real-estate magnate S. V. R. Watson, Board of Trade President George Hazard, industrialist Aaron Rumsey, and the protean businessman, George Tifft. These men usually had elite disdain (or were simply too busy) for politics and partisanship. They restricted their local political, and especially partisan, activity, as the *Republic* said in their praise, to voting. Furthermore, though active in the charter revision process out of a concern for institutionalizing cheap, efficient administration, and in attempts to get the city to contribute to financing needed railroad links, their local involvement was episodic. Economic interests usually led them to develop their most intense political contacts not at City Hall, but in Albany and Washington.[83] If one of them ventured into local party politics, he soon found himself in a humiliating position, beginning with the necessity of denying he was a snob and plutocrat. When the Whig dock merchant James Harrison ran unsuccessfully for mayor in 1853, the *Commercial Advertiser* felt compelled to begin its endorsement by admitting defensively that Harrison "[is] connected to the lake trade, it is true," but said that he had used this convenient location to engage in random acts of charity to "suffering emigrants."[84] In 1857, however, those whom the *Republic* called "our very best citizens"[85] had no Whig party to fight their battles against the Lockwood machine. Moreover, they refused to tie themselves to the declining American party, because they needed the votes of taxpaying Germans. Then, too, they were critical of the party system itself. Seeking to substitute good will and spotless reputations for party structure and professional political talent, they organized a nonpartisan "People's Ticket." They rejected systematic canvassing and tried to win voters, including Germans, through appeals to morality and low taxes.[86] A decade before, the *Commercial Advertiser* had denounced proposals to split the old Fourth Ward because there was too little property ownership there to legitimize the principle of one man, one vote. It now approached Germans as property owners and taxpayers, "stockholders," it said, in the municipal corporation, a theme reformers struck constantly.[87]

The *Commercial Advertiser*'s new attitude to the Germans reflected both calculation that the reform coalition would fail without the traditionally Democratic Germans, and the realization of the improved material circumstances of many immigrant Germans. That realization had been heightened by German civic activism around the issue of taxes. Because of distrust of the exclusive circle of Americans controlling charter revision, Germans had voted against revision. The old Fourth was the only ward to refuse to approve the new basic law.[88] But when reforms intended to lessen the burdens of taxation and protect the small property owner were enacted, Germans embraced them. The new charter (with additional amendments in the next few years) contained reforms—decentralization of tax collection; election of the city receiver; creation of five, elected, neighborhood tax assessor-collector positions; more frequent publication and wider distribution of lists of tax delinquents; and a longer period before forced sales of property commenced—that for years had been recommended by the *Weltbürger*.[89] With greater single-mindedness than was characteristic of them, Germans moved to take control of the tax collection process. At the fall, 1853, Democratic city convention they demanded, and received, the nomination for the first elected receiver, and their man was elected. By 1856 they had also succeeded in obtaining two of the five neighborhood assessor-collector posts. The first German assessor-collectors, Solomon Scheu and Michael Danner, initiated more innovations to aid German householders, such as preliminary lists of delinquents, which were posted prior to official ones and contained instructions in German about where to pay taxes and how to avoid fines.[90]

To their surprise, the reformers failed to get German votes. By themselves the most German wards supplied Lockwood with a combined majority that was actually larger than his citywide margin. At first the *Commercial Advertiser* attributed German voting to "clannishness" and indifference to their own, let alone, the common, good. But soon the paper admitted Democratic charges that nativists, who did not put up their own ticket but desperately wished to stop Lockwood and his Irish allies, had obtained People's Ticket ward nominations and some citywide nominations. Nor did it help that many reformers were Republicans. Most Germans still had little trust in the new party, which they believed would absorb the Know Nothings. That Lockwood's opponent, the incumbent Frederick Stevens, had deserted the Democracy in the middle of his first term for the Republicans, casting aside the voters who elected him, did not spread trust in the reform ticket. Even the Republican German *Telegraph* would not endorse the reformers in the belief that, though correct on taxation, they had inadvertently become a vehicle for nativism.[91] Yet the election was not completely an occasion for despair for reformers who desired a German-American alliance. The only Democratic defeat was in the race for streets commissioner, the official who approved and made assessments for all paving projects. So much scandal attached to the incumbent, Patrick Smith, the Democracy dared not renominate him. But Patrick Walsh, head of one of the other Irish patronage clans, fared poorly. He ran 490 votes behind Lockwood in the German wards, allowing the People's candidate to win a narrow, twenty-vote majority.[92]

With the onset of the depression later that year American businessmen and civic boosters intensified their activism. They again sought and, to an extent that surprised them, now received German support. Key to the American program for economic reconstruction was building a railroad bridge over the Niagara at Fort Erie that would link Buffalo with the routes to the upper Midwest via Canada. The proposal was not new, but it took on urgency after 1853. In that year the Great Western Railroad established links with Canada and the West via the new Suspension Bridge just north of Niagara Falls, and thus blocked the city's access to a good deal of western trade. A bridge at Buffalo, it was argued, would divert trade away from the northerly route. The *Express* was probably correct that 95 percent of the voters approved of public subsidization of construction of a bridge, which every local opinion leader believed vital to its survival.[93] But the plan the council put before voters in November, 1858, was controversial. It had been drafted by British and Canadian capitalists, whose good will and money were required to gain Canadian government cooperation and to finance construction. At $2,500,000 the bridge was expensive, largely because it was to be built of imported British iron rather than American metal or timber. A municipal obligation of $750,000, to be paid out of taxes over fifteen years, would be incurred to pay interest on bonds.[94]

It was the sort of proposal Germans usually opposed. The old Fourth Ward had almost single-handedly killed a similar package in 1853. Its 687-vote majority against municipal guarantees to the corporation creating rail links to the Pennsylvania coal mines had allowed the proposal only a thirty-seven-vote victory.[95] American boosters feared Germans would defeat the even more controversial bridge proposal, and devoted themselves to courting the German vote. In 1858, however, Germans did not completely fulfill the pessimistic expectations of these Americans. Of late, there was growing evidence of German interest in Buffalo's external trade. Commercial news was now featured prominently, along with for the first time weekly market data, in the *Weltbürger*. Too, some Germans were now in a position to gain inside information about and a broader picture of the local economy. Affluent Germans sat on the boards of directors of savings banks and others owned large amounts of real estate. Across the lines of religion and party, men such as the merchants Stephen Bettinger and Frank and Charles Georger were canvassing the East Side for the bridge. Brunck marshalled German antimonopoly feeling for the plan, arguing that while it was far from perfect, its chief opponent was the hated New York Central, which hoped to see defeat of the proposal and hence a further weakening of Buffalo's position. The size of the majority (1,716) for the proposal surprised even its proponents, as did the results of the German poll. In contrast to the overwhelmingly negative poll in 1853, the same neighborhoods now registered a margin of opposition of only 210 votes in an electorate almost two and a half times larger. Brunck was certain, he said, that another week of debate and canvassing the East Side would have massively swayed Germans behind the plan.[96] Fears for the future, individual and collective alike, were leading to unprecedented civic cooperation between Germans and Americans. The new Republican party now began to extend this cooperation into politics.

After five years of massive Democratic majorities and ethnic political polarization, a striking reversal of recent partisan alignments occurred in the 1858 fall elections. Composed largely of Republicans, with some American and Democratic participants, a local fusion ticket won an overwhelming victory: eleven of thirteen county supervisors, thirteen of fourteen councilmen, both local assembly seats, and the city's congressional seat. Only the failure to merge the American and Republican state tickets allowed the Democrats to eke out a 41.5 percent local plurality in the gubernatorial race, but they saw a 2,546-vote decline from the size of their winning margin in the 1857 state contest. The trend continued in 1859, when a Republican ticket headed by Franklin Allberger swept the municipal elections, and in 1860 when Lincoln and other Republicans scored victories. As the Republicans prospered, ethnic political polarization declined, largely because of a growing alliance between Germans and Americans outside the Democracy. In 1858–60 contests the German vote, which by itself was sufficient to constitute Lockwood's 1857 majority, fell to less than 50 percent of the total Democratic vote. In 1860 Republican margins in the German wards were 38 percent of Lincoln's majority. Lincoln won wards Seven and Twelve, and came within forty-two, seventy-four, and twenty-eight votes of taking the Fourth, Fifth, and Sixth wards. As the American party declined, American voters simultaneously were showing a preference for the Republicans. In 1860 Lincoln swept all of the American wards. Correlations between American and Democratic voting for selected contests in 1858, 1859, and 1860 were but −.711, −.266, −.831, and −.325.[97]

The Democracy's decline is attributable to the conjunction of several developments. Throughout the North the national party was seen as southern-dominated and was blamed for the repeal of the Missouri Compromise, which set the stage for violence in Kansas. In New York sectional issues and intraparty rivalries fragmented the state organization.[98] The party was divided and criticized in Buffalo for reasons that were local and regional. The tax-and-spend policies of Democratic municipal administrations differed little from those of previous Whig administrations, but in a context of economic crisis, they now appeared profligate. The opposition of Democrats elsewhere in the state to canal improvement and the close relations of prominent Democrats to the New York Central did not enhance the party's local standing. In addition, charges of bossism and corruption were made against the Lockwood machine. German Democrats felt they had been frozen out of the distribution of party rewards by clever Irishmen, even as Timothy Lockwood's Irish and American allies were fighting with one another over patronage. The growing openness with which the *Sentinel* and the *Aurora* boasted of the Democracy's indebtedness to Catholics did not help it with German and American Protestants.[99]

The difficulties faced by Democrats and Know Nothings did not necessarily add up to Republican gains. In a political system in which many voters were habituated to opting for the lesser of evils, Republicans could still have been construed as unworthy of support, and customary partisanship been maintained. Republicans, however, showed a genius for organization that allowed them to benefit from unsettled political conditions. They quickly converted their narrow political and ethnic bases into a complex, winning coalition, which, in contrast to the old Whigs, was well established at the grass roots in both German and American neighborhoods. The new party's popular character was revealed in 1860. Republicans called upon their neighborhood operatives, as Whigs had never been able to do, to follow the Democratic practice of naturalizing and registering immigrant allies in time for the fall elections.[100]

After organization by Seward Whigs and a much smaller number of Free Soil Democrats in September, 1855, the local Republican party spent three years expanding its American constituency by adding temperance advocates, Know Nothings, Silver Grays, and Democrats. From their first local statement of principles, Republicans skillfully packaged the messages of renewal and progress they directed at these groupings. They combined a moral condemnation of slavery and the power of slaveholders in the federal government with calls, in the name of opportunity, for low-cost homesteads in the West exclusively for free white labor—a nod to racism, without overt race-baiting. They called for public subsidies for improvement of Great Lakes harbors and rivers. Soon, too, they were advocating a protective tariff, which in the language of Whig mutualism, they defended as the only way to boost local industry and absorb the unemployed. The party also took a strong procanal position, and called for tax-supported enlargement of the canal and tolls for competing railroads. Its official positions on nativism and prohibition were framed to allow, at the least risk to itself, absorption of Know Nothings and antialcohol reformers, for whom the Democracy would have been an impossible choice, anyway. Republicans went no further than endorsing voter registration, the church property law, and the established practice of liquor licensing. Official party statements avoided anti-immigrant and antialcohol rhetoric.[101]

Assisted by events far from the city, in Kansas and Washington, the party profited from its antislavery stance. There had been little but apathy and conservatism on slavery in the past. But the growth of local antislavery feeling in the mid-1850s was dramatic. A wide spectrum of influential men from all parties and groups met in 1854 to denounce the Kansas-Nebraska Act. So, too, did twenty-seven local Protestant clergymen meeting separately. Similar, widely based protests followed the assault on Charles Sumner at the Senate. By late 1855 the Fugitive Slave Act was so unpopular that federal judge Nathan K. Hall warned a slaveowner from the bench that any attempt to capture his runaway would cause a riot. No local attorney would represent this southerner, and the U.S. Attorney refused to draw up the legal papers.[102] Yet abolitionism was almost nonexistent in local political circles. Almon Clapp, who went further than any local editor in expressing moral condemnation of slavery, espoused a tepid gradualism and preferred, for its partisan value, to emphasize the slaveholders' power in the Democracy. This moderate antislavery of Republicans attracted growing numbers of prominent free soil Democrats, such as Michael Danner, Frederick Stevens and Samuel Wilkeson, Jr., each of whom defected to the new party in 1856.[103]

Republicans began to court nativists after the 1856 presidential election. The local party's tactics for most of 1857 involved unleashing Clapp, the most prominent Republican nativist. While party pronouncements rejected nativism, Clapp's *Express* indulged in the bigotry it employed several years before to advance Seward's fortunes among nativists. It assaulted the Irish and the Catholic church, and denounced the ways in which the Irish vote had corrupted politics.[104] Yet neither Clapp nor certainly his party made important programmatic concessions, whether prohibition or political proscription, to temperance and nativism. This campaign was not particularly successful, whether in Buffalo or elsewhere in the state where similar tactics were employed. It backfired with some antislavery, antinativist Democrats. Disaffected from the Democracy by corruption and concessions to slavery, Brunck and successive editors of the *Republic*, Guy Salisbury and C. C. Bristol, were close to joining the new party, but came to see Clapp's bigotry and Republican support for liquor licensing and voter registration as evidence of unreliability. They remained in the Democracy and worked for its renewal.[105] Republican nods to nativism yielded little at the polls. Nowhere was this more apparent than in Clapp's failed race for secretary of state in 1857. While he sought to make canal improvement and railroad greed the issues, Democrats throughout the state made Clapp, who lost by 20,000 votes, the issue. They questioned whether a bigot should hold office, and whether Clapp's preoccupation with nativist concerns had prepared him to deal with the economic consequences of the recent money panic. At Buffalo he received a mere 20 percent of the vote, exactly what the candidate of the moribund American party received, and well below John C. Frémont's 1856 vote. Clapp did poorly in German wards. In the Seventh the Republican vote fell 71 percent. But Clapp's total in the American wards was also down, 35 percent below Frémont's, demonstrating the declining power of nativism before the force of other issues.[106]

Local Republicans took an uncompromising, consistent antinativist stance after Clapp's defeat, which thus became only a temporary setback. The county and city fusion tickets they worked out with the American party in 1858 and 1859 conceded nothing ideologically and little in terms of party rewards to nativists. Of the many nominations decided at the 1859 county convention Know Nothings got five, none of which, the *Express* said, involved influence or power. Their takings at the city convention, the *Commercial Advertiser* lamented, were as paltry.[107] Then in 1860 the Republican national convention decisively rejected a nativist-inspired platform plank promising a more rigorous naturalization law.[108] Nativist aspirations to enter Republican ranks as equals seemed blocked at every level. But as the *Commercial Advertiser* had already conceded, antislavery Silver Grays and Know Nothings had no alternative. Putting the best construction on the situation, the paper delivered a post mortem on the American party, explaining that the church property and registration laws, the increased circumspection of immigrants and the Catholic clergy about their duties to America, and the elevation of American group consciousness would have to suffice as the legacy of this generation of nativists. In 1860 the local American party formally dissolved. In its place, nativists founded a league open to all citizens and opposed to proscription on the basis of national origin, while upholding patriotic values and the purity of elections.[109]

Buffalo Republicans now concentrated on intensifying efforts they had been making perfunctorily since the party was established to attract Germans. Republicans knew that to triumph locally they would have to break out of the ethnic isolation that eventually reduced the Whigs to a minority. In 1855 there were 3,426 naturalized citizens in the five German wards, where they were an average 77 percent of the voting population. These voters were nearly a third of Buffalo's electorate. The same wards also had 1,926 unnaturalized male adults, who when registered would enhance any majority.[110]

Republicans approached the ordinary northern voter with promises of opportunity through economic growth directed by an active state. With their skills, passion for property acquisition, and capacity for steady work, Germans were perceived, as the Irish were not, to be open to this message and able to contribute a great deal to bring about national economic development. Germans were also believed, as the Irish again were not, to have independent tendencies of mind that facilitated breaking with past loyalties. They had never been as unflinchingly partisan as the Irish, and had manifested free soil inclinations in 1848. But perceptions of German independence went deeper. Republicans never publicly made a distinction between Protestant and Catholic in canvassing local Germans. Elsewhere, too, Republicans of a nativist bent might have justified dealing with the former; even Know Nothings eventually did. But were not Catholics tarnished by ecclesiastical ties, and were not their clergy conservative on sectional issues, to a significant extent because of a theologically influenced belief in the morality of southern slavery? In Buffalo, however, American perceptions of German Catholics were not wholly negative. The German-speaking laity at St. Louis Church had challenged their clergy, as the Irish never seemed to do. In the process, these laymen initiated legislative efforts culminating in the church property law. The parish was hardly representative of German Catholicism, and even it eventually made its peace with the church. But the conflict nonetheless helped create the local reputation of Germans—even German Catholics—for independent thinking.

Independent though Germans were believed to be, Republicans approached them not as individuals, but as a group, within the established pluralistic traditions of the second-party system. Beginning in the 1856 presidential campaign, the party used German-speaking notables to address rallies in German neighborhoods. It took full advantage of the German love of processions with musical accompaniment, and staged massive torchlight parades that surpassed the Democracy's. It subsidized its own German press by breathing life into the *Telegraph*. It did not at first seek to change the dispensation of ethnic nominations the Democrats had gradually established. In 1856 Republicans nominated Germans to office only in the five German wards, and for no more than two or three of the five ward positions, no matter how massive the ward's German majority. Also, Republicans accepted as "German" only certain German-held citywide positions, such as tax receiver, and did not extend German nominations beyond them.[111]

But as Republicans intensified their quest for German votes, they blazed new trails in ethnic politics, and opened important positions to Germans. In their first fusion convention with Know Nothings in 1858 Republicans engineered, to the nativists' horror, the nomination of a German for superintendent of the poorhouse. This successful candidacy was a subtle challenge to the nativist belief that most immigrants were content to live off public welfare. It was all the more noteworthy in a year in which, after a bitter Irish-German conflict at the Democratic local convention, Germans failed to obtain the nomination for the same post.[112] The next year saw the unprecedented and successful nominations by the state convention of Philip Dorsheimer for state treasurer and by the local convention of the butchers' friend, Franklin Allberger, for mayor. Allberger's candidacy was controversial. Nativist politicians opposed him for his foreign ancestry, and German politicians for his American birth, accented German, and Eleventh Ward residence. The nomination was a calculated response to a political challenge. The *Weltbürger* had recently expressed the hope local Democrats would emulate their party at Pittsburgh and nominate a German for mayor; and it added, "It is impossible to imagine the Republican–Know Nothings doing it." In spite of German pressure the Democratic convention actually nominated an ex–Know Nothing in a bid for former American party supporters. Allberger went on to outpoll the European-born Dorsheimer.[113] Once in power, local Republicans rewarded German operatives more liberally than the Democracy had. Also, as prosperity gained momentum late in 1860 Allberger and his Republican council initiated some sizable infrastructure projects, and, the *Weltbürger* admitted, Germans got many lucrative municipal contracts.[114]

Such efforts went far to prove that Republicans were not the Know Nothing "decoys" Brunck branded them. So, too, did the aggressiveness and good will Republicans brought to gaining German support for the party's political economy and antislavery. The *Telegraph* and the national German trade union figures among the party's orators tied together workers' anxieties about the slowness of the recovery with Republican support for a protective tariff, which, they argued, would give capitalists assurance of the markets and profits they required before they expanded employment and increased wages.[115] The Republicans also sought to emerge as defenders of the beleaguered fragment of the working class caught in the throes of industrialization. In April, 1860, the Fifth Ward Republican Club passed resolutions supporting striking German iron molders at the Jewett and Root Stove Works, and denounced, in a rhetoric long associated exclusively with German Democrats, all those newspapers, whatever their party, supporting the tyranny of "money-worshipping employers."[116] Republican concern and promises of relief soon began to have an effect on German opinion. German workers were so worried about unemployment, Brunck, a free trader, said in 1860, that many were now grasping at the protective tariff "just as drowning men reach for a root under the water." But Brunck had nothing better to offer. Calling the Republicans "the party of Biddle's bank" was surely evidence that he was out of touch with the times. Moreover, the *Weltbürger* fell into the trap of the party in power during a depression by denying times were really that bad. Many German wage earners apparently disagreed.[117]

Free soil and western homesteads were even more persistent themes in the Republican approach to the material concerns of Germans. The message was the same one employed when Republicans approached the average American voter, but German Republicans packaged it somewhat differently. To denounce the Slave Power, they appropriated the strong, direct language that '48er polemicists, many of whom became Republicans, had once directed at the European Reaction. Moreover, they rejected the race-baiting to which both the *Weltbürger*, in efforts to tie Republican antislavery to support of black equality, and an occasional American Republican, in order to shake off just such charges, descended. To be sure, like the large majority of American Republican politicians, German Republican spokesmen did not necessarily embrace racial equality. Free soil was a doctrine to benefit white men, not slaves. When the Republican state assembly mandated a referendum on black suffrage for 1860, most German politicians were reluctant to endorse the measure on any ground other than the need for uniform criteria for voting. (Blacks alone had to meet a property qualification at the time.) Yet, in spite of this stance, German Republican leaders eschewed the rhetoric of racial chauvinism. Moreover, rank-and-file ethnic organizations actually backed the measure on egalitarian grounds. Throughout the North, this was the official position of the staunchly Republican, radical Turner organizations. This stance had some noteworthy popular support. Black suffrage gathered only 22.4 percent approval in Buffalo, but in the Seventh Ward, which was the most German ward and which gave Lincoln a strong 57 percent majority, 42 percent of the voters approved the measure. Only the American Ninth, with 34 percent approval, came close.[118]

Clearly the Republicans were challenging the German political consensus of the past several decades. In doing so, they precipitated a major social and ideological debate with the group. Though the direction of this divisive debate was determined by the national struggle over slavery, the contending sides tended to replicate such preexisting intragroup divisions as Protestant versus Catholic and Gray versus Green that had been partly submerged by German political unity in the mid-1850s, antinativism electoral campaigns. But it went beyond those divisions, and revealed new fault lines and alliances, too. Prominent Germans denouncing antislavery and urging loyalty to the Democrats came to a common stance from quite distinct perspectives. The traditionally hostile religious forces—clergy and prominent laity of the Catholic Church and the Buffalo and Missouri Lutheran synods—denied that slavery was a moral wrong. They denounced the natural-rights doctrine that underlay the moral critique of slavery as a secular notion, which denied the hopelessness of the human position, whether as slave or master, without God. No matter how moderate, abolitionism, both the *Aurora* and the *Sentinel* contended, was proof that a fanatical, godless spirit, of which nativism was another, prominent sign, was loose in the land. Catholic papers predicted this spirit would cause an apocalyptic war.[119] The other body of prominent anti-Republicans was composed of secular moderates, such as Brunck, who rejected slavery on moral grounds, but saw no way to attack it without a dangerous centralization of federal power and, ultimately, civil war and racial anarchy. While they saw danger in the extent of southern influence over the Democracy, they had intense fears about the Republicans, whom they saw as prisoners of a fanaticism born of "good intentions." Brunck had long feared the emotional convictions generated by the enraged, ethnocentric Puritan moral conscience. Brunck saw these passions, with their divisive potential, already manifest in temperance, Sabbatarianism, and particularly nativism, none of which Republicans, to his mind, had unequivocally renounced.[120] Underlying both of these conservative perspectives, therefore, was an anxiety about any significant political change initiated by the secular, moralistic, reform spirit growing out of evangelical Protestant culture. Such anxiety had probably been at least a semiconscious part of the mentality of many immigrants for years. But in the ominous national political climate of the late 1850s it became central to and explicit in the public discourse of German leaders. Among them it created an enclave mood that logically sought safety in the tradition-bound, pluralistically inclined Democracy.

In contrast to the narrow, if complex, social and political bases of German anti-Republicanism, German Republican leadership crossed class, age, partisan, confessional, and Gray-Green lines. The party drew together German Democrats, Whigs, and Know Nothings. It united not only diverse Protestant denominations, especially the more liberal ones, but Protestants and some Catholics, such as St. Louis parishioners Frank Georger, Francis Kraft, and the former trustees John Chretien, Jacob Benziger, and Georg Richerte. It drew heavily from occupations typical of the ethnic elite—retail merchants, doctors, and small manufacturers—but it included less affluent and entrepreneurially inclined men. The antislavery Turners, almost all artisans and small shopkeepers, had affiliated en bloc in 1856 with their endorsement of Frémont. Intellectuals, such as the political writers and language teachers connected with the *Telegraph*, were among the chief Republican propagandists. Finally, far from being the party of Green "philosophes" and "beer hall revolutionists, third class" (Brunck's characterization of '48er intellectual and *Telegraph* editor, Christian Esselen), the Republicans attracted in Dr. Dellenbaugh, Philip Dorsheimer, and others some of the longest-resident, most respectable Grays. These men had been in America for many years and while closely identifying with the ethnic group, also showed (in anglicized names, American clients and friends, and membership in American churches) evidence of assimilation.[121]

Whatever the precise route by which men such as the wealthy miller George Urban, the '48er physician Edward Storck, the Catholic merchant Frank Georger, and the innkeeper and veteran politician Philip Dorsheimer came into the party, they demonstrated an aggressive, confident style of leadership that refused to shrink from confrontation, and which contrasted sharply with Dr. Brunck's cautious temperament. This was evident in the extent to which they politicized previously neutral ethnic ground. Like the radicals in the local Turner organization in 1856, they sought to win antislavery positions from the *Vereine* and they injected politics into civic festivals, such as the 1859 *Schillerfest*, at which prominent Republicans on the organization committee made speeches tying together antislavery and Schiller's humanism.[122] It was apparent, too, in the confident assertiveness with which the *Telegraph* tried to change American political thinking. The German paper issued an open editorial challenge to nativists to surrender the politics of ethnic polarization and prejudice in favor of a crusade for free soil and opportunity. The editors published these editorials, and then translated and circulated them to the appropriate American papers.[123]

Such confidence was also evident in their evaluation of nativism. Brunck, who would not consider any conciliation with nativists and saw American prejudice as ineradicable, did not understand, he said in 1860, how German Republicans could be so indifferent to nativism.[124] In truth, they were concerned. But they understood the context of American prejudice enough to put themselves at some ease, and they even shared some of the same prejudices. Many Germans had just as negative views of the Irish as Americans did, and looked unfavorably on a politically active Catholic clergy. The *Telegraph*, in fact, often took the Irish and their church to task. To be sure, Germans agreeing with the *Telegraph* could not accept the proscriptive aspects of the nativist agenda and sharply rejected bigoted characterizations of German immigrants. They were solidly antinativist in the electoral campaigns of the mid-1850s. But as the political power of nativism waned, they felt secure enough to conciliate the less cruel impulses behind nativism, and to hope that the bigoted impulses might be replaced by antislavery idealism. German Republicans probably found merit in the explanation of and antidote to nativism offered by Carl Schurz in a well-publicized local campaign speech in October, 1860. Schurz recognized Americans' desire for authority in the public affairs of their own land. He asked his German audience if they, too, would not have acted defensively before a flood of new immigrants who had united against them election after election. As a proud German speaking their language, he nonetheless saw fit to implore them to "Americanize." By this Schurz meant not the abandonment of ethnic culture, but rather its enrichment through study of the language, literature, and political institutions of their adopted country. Moreover, they would come to understand the aspirations of its founders and their descendants. Once they demonstrated such understanding, nativism would disappear, and they would be "taken at once into fellowship and welcomed by the warm American heart."[125] German Republicans, therefore, saw nativism as defensive and compensatory. On the other hand, they saw in the antislavery struggle evidence of an American yearning to live up to cherished, universalistic ideals. To revitalize those ideals these Germans, who themselves had been profoundly touched in 1848 by a wave of idealism that helped put them on the path to an antislavery alliance with Americans, were willing to a point to propitiate nativism. To this end, German Republicans such as Esselen embraced voter registration, not only because it helped to clear the field of nativist issues and to combat the corruption that they acknowledged existed in immigrant politics, but also because it was a way of demonstrating immigrant concern for the integrity of the political system.[126] This conscious effort to assist in creating preconditions for national action on the momentous issue of slavery was unprecedented at a time when ethnic politics was typically defensive in its concerns. It demonstrated that many Germans, while remaining distinctively ethnic, were coming to feel at home in and at one with America.

The 1860 election saw the further unfolding of the process of social and political realignment. Backing Stephen Douglas and formally known as the Union party, the Democrats gathered support from diverse sources. In addition to the usual constituencies, there were some unionist Silver Grays, led by Fillmore and Haven, who began by favoring the John Bell–Everett ticket, but switched when it became clear the Constitutional Unionists could not win. The party gave Haven the congressional nomination as an incentive. The small John Breckinridge movement, which owed its existence less to proslavery sentiment than local partisan wrangling, maintained a ticket until just before the election when it collapsed and entered Union ranks. Unionists ran a desperate, negative campaign, which manipulated racial anxieties and warned that after a national victory Republicans would emerge as nativists. In contrast, their own numbers swelling with the antislavery majority of the Silver Grays led by Putnam and Babcock and with Know Nothings, Republicans sensed victory. While skirting the race issue, they campaigned aggressively on the theme of opportunity and opposition to the Slave Power.[127]

Republicans swept all the county races, including the congressional contest won by Elbridge G. Spaulding. In Buffalo they elected eight of thirteen councilmen, seven of thirteen county supervisors, and a number of municipal officers, and took the city's two assembly seats. Lincoln's 438-vote majority (52 percent) illustrates the social nature of the realignment. Class interests and aspirations and ethnic and sectarian prejudices and preferences figured significantly in the formation of the multiethnic coalition that supported Lincoln. It was composed of a large majority of American voters and between 40 and 50 percent of the Germans, without whom Lincoln's victory would have been impossible.[128] Republicans were especially strong in the broad middle ranks of the population among those aspiring and security-conscious Americans and Germans, generally Protestants, but some Catholics too, most likely to find hope in the rhetoric of opportunity. Especially among the Germans, some minority of incalculable size among Republican voters was composed of those who had previously tended not to vote, content to see the Democracy win, but who now were being made partisans and voters by the Republican response to the political and economic crises of the late 1850s. Democrats did well particularly at the two poles of the social structure: among Irish and German proletarian Catholics, who were voting as they had always voted, and a minority group of affluent Americans, whose fears about the fate of the Union led them briefly into a party few would ever have imagined voting for in the past. This was an unwieldy coalition, and it would not survive the election.

Douglas received absolute majorities in only four of thirteen wards: the First and the Eighth, where largely Irish naturalized voters were some 70 and 61 percent of the voting population in 1855, and the Fifth and Sixth, where overwhelmingly German naturalized voters were about 82 and 92 percent of the electorate that same year. The First gave Douglas a strong 67 percent majority, and the Eighth a more modest 53 percent. Both wards acted as contemporaries predicted: Irish Catholics remained loyal to the party that provided them with jobs, defended their church, and promised to keep blacks in their place. Habituated to poverty and unemployment, it was difficult for the average Irish voter, a common outdoor laborer, to respond to the rhetoric of individual opportunity, whether it promised homesteads in the distant West or tariff-created, industrial jobs in Buffalo. Instead, as the 1858 Work or Bread protests demonstrate, the Irish looked to the Democratic party to help them through hard times. In better times, too, both white- and blue-collar Irishmen sought the party-sponsored public employment that had become the most dependable source of stable livelihoods that existed for the group. There was no greater measure of the depth of Irish partisanship than Haven's vote. In spite of a few angry, public Irish defections, the former nativist politician and now reluctant Democrat trailed Douglas by only twenty-two votes (2 percent) in the First and thirteen (0.3 percent) in the Eighth.[129]

The German Fifth and Sixth wards, in which Douglas received 53 and 51 percent, present a more complex picture. While the First was uniformly Democratic across the neighborhood divisions created by election officials (the Eighth was too small for such a division), tallies in the German wards did vary, and in telling ways, across neighborhood lines. The Democrats captured only Five A and Six B, both of which were heavily populated by the poorer German Catholics of, respectively, St. Mary's and St. Ann's. The latter was a new parish composed of many more recently arrived immigrants who were taking advantage of the opportunities for urban homesteading offered by the

East Side's rural precincts, with their low land prices. St. Mary's, long reputed the city's poorest German parish, lay far to the east, on the fringe of the central business district.[130]

In the American Second and Ninth, Democrats lost, yet were able to increase their vote over Buchanan's 1856 totals by 94 percent and 85 percent. They did so by adding the votes of affluent former Whigs and nativists, whose choices in 1860 were based on a combination of unionism, nationalism, and fear that disruption of national trade following a sectional Republican victory would propel the city and its enterprises into deeper economic crisis. These fears were profound enough that momentarily they outweighed both hatred of the state Democracy as the anticanal, prorailroad party, and the attractiveness of the Republican economic policy, especially the tariff, which promised to assist Buffalo to fulfill its long-term industrial development goals. Ward Two provides a clear example because its political and social boundaries closely overlapped. Its A section was the one elite enclave east of Main. Though shrinking in size, it was still the most convenient residential location for dockside businessmen and their white-collar employees. It contained the second ranked of twenty school districts in both real and personal property assessments in the late 1850s. Here Douglas received 54 percent of the vote. Further to the east, the ward's B section contained a variegated population of artisans, industrial workers, and shopkeepers. Largely American and neither poor nor affluent, it ranked eighth among school districts in real, and twelfth in personal, property assessments. Here Douglas received only 39 percent of the vote.[131]

That the strength of the Republican coalition lay in the middle levels of the social structure is further confirmed by analysis of those constituencies in which the party achieved its greatest gains between 1855 and 1860. No Buffalo ward gave Lincoln a greater majority (62 percent) than the Eleventh, one of the three wards (along with the more proletarian Third and the rural, underpopulated Thirteenth) that were thoroughly ethnically diverse. It was populated by Americans (29 percent) and British, Irish, and Germans, each of which contributed about 20 percent. The ward had a distinctively middling socioeconomic profile. It was located in recently annexed "lower" Black Rock, now a West Side residential area experiencing rapid growth as the neighborhoods around the central business district taken over by commerce and industry gradually lost population. The ward, which ranked first of thirteen in 1855 in the percentage of population owning property, was filled with unimposing one-and-a-half story frame cottages and somewhat more substantial two-story frame houses on small parcels of land. It ranked fourth of thirteen in per capita real and personal property in 1860, but its occupational structure was distinctly middling in the late 1850s: it was sixth in owners of businesses and fifth in blue-collar workers.[132]

German Republican voting reveals a similar profile, but one that must be understood in the context of the immigrant experience. In wards Six and Seven the Democracy lost fully 70 and 87 percent of its vote between 1855 and 1860. Buchanan had captured 68.5 percent of the Sixth's vote in 1856, but Douglas managed only a 51 percent, twenty-eight-vote majority and lost the ward's more populous A section. The Seventh went from one of the most Democratic to one of the most Republican wards. It was the Democrats' "banner ward" in the 1855 local judicial campaign, the first to pit a Know Nothing against an avowed antinativist. Democratic Judge Joseph Masten received a 93 percent, 688-vote majority in the Seventh, a quarter of his citywide majority. The ward now gave Lincoln a 57 percent, 157-vote edge. The Seventh's 1855 poll book and state census manuscripts assist us in establishing both a middling socioeconomic profile and an impressive record of immigrant achievement among its voters. Some 83 percent of the ward's voters in 1855 were German. Of these German voters, 95 percent lived in modest cottages, valued at slightly above $1,000. Seventy four percent owned land. Fully 58 percent were skilled, and only 6 percent unskilled. The Seventh, and the Sixth, which had a similar profile, had more skilled workers and property owners among German voters than did the Fourth and Fifth. Yet the Seventh's socioeconomic status was humble. In per capita assessed real and personal property it ranked, respectively, seventh and tenth of thirteen wards in 1860; and this even though it had more property owners as a percentage of its total population than the wealthier American wards. In its relative property-owning standing, the Sixth stood in almost the same position. Both wards, therefore, shared with the Republican Eleventh a middling status.[133] Interested in maintaining their modest material achievement and security, many voters in such constituencies looked anxiously back to a time of privation. All hoped to keep the option open to continue to improve themselves. Free soil, western homesteads, the prospect of economic growth through the protective tariff, and the rhetoric of opportunity itself were attractive to these individuals anxious over their long-term prospects. But such individual hopes might also be filtered through the normative framework of a universalistic egalitarian ideology, as the significant vote in the Seventh for black suffrage demonstrates.

Sectarian considerations also played a role in determining the vote in the Seventh and in Six A. The Sixth and Seventh had Buffalo's densest concentrations of northern, and hence probably Protestant,

Germans. Here one found resident most of the 1855 household heads from Hanover (74 percent), Mecklenburg (100 percent), Prussia (69.5 percent), and Saxony (56 percent). Within their borders were eight Protestant churches, including such large, prestigious congregations as United Evangelical St. Peter's and the Buffalo Synod's Trinity Lutheran Church, but only one Catholic parish, St. Boniface. In absolute numbers, southern, and thus probably Catholic, Germans from Baden, Bavaria, and Württemberg were larger in population. But the combination of deeply felt denominationalism of the sort that characterized the Buffalo Synod Lutherans, minority status, and anti-Catholicism may well have produced both considerable political solidarity among these Protestants and a disposition to vote *against* the pro-Catholic Democracy as well as *for* the Republicans. Mecklenburgers, for example, were two decades later described as long having been "Republican, to a man." As the Old Lutherans demonstrate, German Protestants did not necessarily think about politics as their preachers wished them to. Pastor Grabau was hostile to American reformism, antislavery, and eventually emancipation. But so numerous were his parishioners in the Fruit Belt section of the Seventh that Republicans could not have taken the ward without a significant percentage of their vote.[134]

It would be hasty, however, to assume that such a pattern of sectarian-influenced, Republican voting existed only among Protestants. Though it is likely that most German Catholics voted Democratic, German Catholicism was not monolithic, as the troubled history of St. Louis Church suggests. A large number of the Alsatians and other German-speakers affiliated with that parish lived in the Seventh, and the former especially were among the most affluent and residentially persistent people there.[135] If the activities of the several prestigious former trustees who became Republican leaders are representative, a shared history of anticlerical struggle, embrace of American republican ideology, and material achievement, different only in its particularities from that of the Buffalo Synod Lutherans, led a number of the parish's voters to leave the Democracy. The entrance of sections of these two historic antagonists—German Catholics and Lutherans—into the Republican coalition was a tribute to the dynamic capacity of the immigrants' new American reality to move them to reshape their thought. It was equally a tribute to the immigrants' own capacity to understand themselves as active agents in making the future of their new American home.

Epilogue

IN the late 1850s American nativists, such as Dr. Foote, who became Republicans contemplated the quickening pace of social and political realignment with pleasure. They envisioned a new social unity along terms dictated by Americans. Their vision was based on the assumption that Germans had begun to abandon the habits of group solidarity prompted by ethnic consciousness.[1] Deepening such impressions, after the attack on Fort Sumter, were the heartening, patriotic demonstrations of unity of national purpose by all segments of the population, but especially by Germans, who exercised their genius for martial display to its fullest. Then, too, Foote must have been pleased that the war effort broadened the interethnic, Republican coalition, which soon came to include the elite merchants and professionals who had voted for Douglas.[2] Patriotism and eventually the consciousness that the Republican economic program, particularly the protective tariff, was beneficial to the city's commerce and nascent industry made their entrance into Republican ranks both compelling and practical.

What Foote could not know was that the assimilation he detected in influential segments of the German population would hardly prove a unilinear, lockstep process that would rapidly eventuate in ethnic oblivion. The recent *Schillerfest* and *Sängerbundfest* had shown German ethnic culture at the height of its confidence and organizational sophistication. Among the organizers of both festivals were those self-possessed men, such as Dr. Storck, who showed such skill in their interactions with Americans and American institutions, and who became Republicans in the late 1850s. But deep involvement with this new party did not, as Foote and others hoped, sever the ties between

Storck and others like him and the ethnic group, let alone lessen the ethnic identification and involvement of the many ordinary Germans who also had changed parties. Instead the new partisan diversity among Germans widened the scope of intraethnic debate and intensified the involvement of the various segments of German political opinion with one another, a process of ethnic interaction and consolidation that had long been one source of whatever group coherence Germans were able to achieve.

This, however, would not be the only centripetal process that was at work among Germans. The sense of ethnic interests and the habits of ethnic mobilization Germans had acquired in the 1850s were too well-entrenched to disappear. They would be deeply reinforced, too, to the extent that the ethnocultural and sectarian conflicts—over public schools, language, alcohol, the Sabbath, and the disposition of public monies to the church-related institutions—that had torn society apart before the Civil War would continue after 1865. American animus toward foreigners and their native-born, ethnically identifying descendants provided the emotional context that gave these conflicts their continuing power to bring Germans together. For fed as nativism was by continuing disagreement on the character of the public sphere and by anxieties about the ability of American authority to define that sphere, nativism could hardly die. The Know Nothing movement was now gone, said an ethnic chronicler of the history of Buffalo Germans in 1898, but "its principles were too firmly fixed in the minds of many narrow-minded Americans" to expire with it. Indeed they would live on uneasily within the local Republican party itself, not, to be sure, as official policy, but, among individual Americans, as the emotional reflex of a pluralism that continues to this day to contain within it the seeds of many of the same conflicts that embittered intergroup relations in the nineteenth century. Because of nativism and ethnocultural conflict, and because of charges of bossism and corruption that Democrats eventually were able to use effectively against Republicans, the alliance of large numbers of Germans and Americans within the Republican party at times experienced setbacks after 1865. Germans would thus occasionally massively return to their tenuous alliance with the Irish within a Democratic party that continued in such cities as Buffalo to defend ethnic traditionalism and cultural pluralism. At these times Germans were impelled toward that ethnic unity of purpose they had experienced before the realignment of the late 1850s. These occasions worked to counteract the still powerful centrifugal forces that continued to exist among Germans, especially the class and ideological tensions that were intensifying with large-scale industrialization and the rise of a mass German socialist movement.[3]

But the antebellum legacy for the shape of American social pluralism was no less profound because such conflicts continued, or because they rendered interethnic alliances unstable. It was the management of such conflicts within the framework of democracy and capitalism that constituted this legacy. Before 1861 American urban society in the northern immigrant receiving centers had begun to acquire a distinctive capacity in the closely related political and civic realms to counter social polarization and threats to the existence of capitalism with appeals to common interests in opportunity, in all of its varied aspects from jobs to low taxes. Simultaneously the divisive potentials of both class and ethnicity were mitigated by coalition politics, which brought together diverse and competing groups in ways that contained or channeled conflict. This pluralistic social system was hardly static, and in this lay much of its enormous strength and resiliency in the midst of the ceaseless, deeply unsettling changes that characterize a society founded on capitalism. In developing its formidable absorptive processes, it had created mechanisms for transforming the whole, even as it grew more inclusive of its singular, emerging parts.

Ahead in the nineteenth and early twentieth centuries lay the even more massive immigrations from central, eastern, and southern Europe and the even greater dislocations that accompanied large-scale industrialization. Yet while the immigrants grew in number and changed in origin and culture, and while socioeconomic crises intensified, the capacity of American social pluralism to preserve order by balancing competing claims and interests, and by holding out visions of a good life in a just society to those allowed, willing, and able to take advantage of opportunity, remained an ultimate source of internal stability. Whether in this welter of competing claims and interests and unifying but vague visions of personal security and affluence a shared standard of the common good and the substance of social justice could be achieved has remained entirely another matter.

Notes

Key to Abbreviations in the Notes

AAS	American Antiquarian Association, Worcester, Massachusetts
ABA	Archdiocese of Baltimore, Archives, Baltimore, Maryland
BECHS	Buffalo and Erie County Historical Society, Buffalo, New York
BL	Baker Library, Harvard University Graduate School of Business Administration, Boston, Massachusetts
CCA	Canisius College, Archives, Buffalo, New York
DBA	Diocese of Buffalo, Archives, Buffalo, New York
DC	Dartmouth College, Archives, Hanover, New Hampshire
LC	Library of Congress, Manuscripts Division, Washington, D.C.
ML	Milne Library, State University of New York College at Geneseo
NUL	Niagara University Library, Niagara University, Niagara Falls, New York
NYHS	New York Historical Society, New York City
NYSA	New York State Archives, Albany
OC	Oberlin College, Archives, Oberlin, Ohio
PAC	Public Archives of Canada, Ottawa, Ontario
PFVL	Propaganda Fide Archives, Vatican Library, Rome, Italy (microfilm collections)
SUNYAB	State University of New York at Buffalo, Archives, Libraries, Departments, Amherst
UND	University of Notre Dame, Archives, Notre Dame, Indiana
UR	University of Rochester, Archives, Rochester, New York

Introduction

1. Michael Novak, *The Rise of the Unmeltable Ethnics* (New York, 1972). See also Richard Gambino, *Blood of My Blood* (New York, 1974).

2. Some of these points are summarized in Thomas Bender, "Wholes and Parts: The Need for Synthesis in American History," *Journal of American History*, 73 (June, 1986), 120–36.

3. Oscar Handlin, *Boston's Immigrants: A Study in Acculturation* (Cambridge, Mass., 1941); and idem, *The Uprooted* (Boston, 1973, 2d ed. enl.); Robert Wiebe, *The Segmented Society* (New York, 1975), and idem, *The Opening of American Society* (New York, 1984); Rowland Berthoff, *An Unsettled People: Social Order and Disorder in American History* (New York, 1971). Also, Bender, "Wholes and Parts," 120–36.

4. Ira Katznelson, *Black Men, White Cities* (New York, 1973); and idem, *City Trenches: Urban Politics and the Patterning of Class in the United States* (New York, 1981); Amy Bridges, *A City in the Republic: Antebellum New York and the Origins of Machine Politics* (New York, 1984).

5. Eugene Genovese, *The Political Economy of Slavery* (New York, 1965); *The World the Slaveholders Made: Two Essays in Interpretation* (New York, 1969); and idem, *Roll, Jordan, Roll: The World the Slaves Made* (New York, 1984).

Chapter 1. From Frontier Village to Continental Entrepôt

1. Ellicott quoted in John T. Horton, Edward T. Williams, and Harry S. Douglass, *History of Northwestern New York*, vol. 1 (New York, 1947), p. 30.

2. Rev. Timothy Dwight quoted in Truman C. White, *Our County and Its People: Descriptive Work on Erie County*, vol. 1 (Buffalo, 1898), p. 147.

3. Horton, et al., *History of Northwestern New York*, vol. 1, pp. 30–31; William Chazenoff, *Joseph Ellicott and the Holland Land Company: The Opening of Western New York* (Syracuse, 1970), pp. 33, 36–9, 42.

4. Horton, et al., *History of Northwestern New York*, vol. 1, p. 32; Chazenoff, *Joseph Ellicott and the Holland Land Company*, pp. 75–6, 83, 98–9.

5. Horton, et al., *History of Northwestern New York*, vol. 1, pp. 17–8, 43–55; David M. Ellis, "Rise of the Empire State, 1783–1825," *New York History*, 56 (1975), 5–28.

6. Ronald E. Shaw, *Erie Water West: A History of the Erie Canal, 1792–1854* (Lexington, 1966), pp. 14–83, 134–58; Marvin A. Rapp, "The Port of Buffalo, 1825–1880" (Ph.D. dissertation, Duke University, 1947), 9–13; Lewis F. Allen, "Recollections of Early Forwarding on the Lakes and Canals," Buffalo Historical Society *Publications*, 13 (1909), 377–9.

7. "The Great Lakes—Their Cities and Trade," *DeBow's Review*, 40, New Series 1 (1853), 381–2.

8. Rapp, "The Port of Buffalo," 24–5, 45; Shaw, *Erie Water West*, pp. 264–7; James F. W. Johnston, *Notes on North America: Agricultural, Economical, and Social*, vol. 1 (Edinburgh, 1851), pp. 222–3.

9. Dan Morgan, *Merchants of Grain* (New York, 1979), p. 57.

10. John G. Clark, *The Grain Trade of the Old Northwest* (Urbana, 1966), pp. 9–59.

11. George Rogers Taylor, *The Transportation Revolution, 1815–1860* (New York, 1951), pp. 162–3; Hugh G. J. Aitken, *The Welland Canal Company: A Study in Canadian Enterprise* (Cambridge, Mass., 1954), pp. 23–49; Gilbert N. Tucker, *The Canadian Commercial Revolution, 1845–1851* (Toronto, 1964), pp. 38–44.

12. Allen Pred, *Urban Growth and the Circulation of Information: The U.S. System of Cities* (Cambridge, 1973), pp. 43, 50, 137–9; Rapp, "The Port of Buffalo," 34; Clark, *The Grain Trade of the Old Northwest*, pp. 117–23, 179; Buffalo *Commercial Advertiser*, January 15, 1855.

13. "The Great Lakes—Their Cities and Trade," 381; Laurence A. Glasco, *Ethnicity and Social Structure: Irish, Germans, and Native-Born of Buffalo, N.Y., 1850–1860* (New York, 1980), p. 15.

14. Tyrone Power, *Impressions of America during the Years 1833, 1834, and 1835*, vol. 1 (London, 1836), pp. 388–9.

15. Glasco, *Ethnicity and Social Structure*, pp. 84–6, 90; *The Manufacturing Interests of the City of Buffalo* (Buffalo, 1866), pp. 36–50; Buffalo *Commercial Advertiser*, September 8, 1856; March 7, 25, 1857.

16. Buffalo *Courier*, November 3, 1847; Horton, et al., *History of Northwestern New York*, vol. 1, p. 91; Clark, *The Grain Trade of the Old Northwest*, pp. 111–4, 117–20; Allen Pred, *Urban Growth and City Systems in the U.S., 1840–1860* (Cambridge, 1980), p. 101.

17. *Directory for the City of Buffalo, 1836* (Buffalo, 1836), p. 8.

18. Mary P. Ryan, *Cradle of the Middle Class: The Family in Oneida County, New York, 1790–1865* (New York, 1981), p. 10.

19. *The Manufacturing Interests of the City of Buffalo*, pp. 36–62; Buffalo *Express*, May 19, 20, 1857; Glenn Porter and Harold Livesay, *Merchants and Manufacturers: Studies in the Changing Structure of Nineteenth Century Marketing* (Baltimore, 1971), pp. 62–70; Buffalo *Commercial Advertiser*, December 9, 1853; January 15, 1855; December 20, 22, 27, 1859; March 24, 1860.

20. Clark, *The Grain Trade of the Old Northwest*, pp. 250–83; Thomas D. Odle, "The American Grain Trade of the Great Lakes, 1825–1873," *Inland Seas*, 9 (Spring, 1953), 109, 162–6, 256–61; David M. Ellis, "The Rivalry between the New York Central and the Erie Canal," *New York History*, 29 (July, 1948), 268–88.

21. Buffalo *Commercial Advertiser*, March 24, 1860; Sandford B. Hunt, "Buffalo: A Glance at Its Progress down to the Present Time," in *The Manufacturing Interests of the City of Buffalo*, pp. 13–7.

22. Peter Heller, "Trade and Development at Buffalo from 1815 to 1863," (paper, 1968, BECHS), 19–21; Theresa L. Wolfe, *Tifft Farm: A History of Man and Nature* (Buffalo, 1984), pp. 9, 16; Buffalo *Courier*, April 22, 1844; March 17, 26, 1853; March 25, 1857.

23. Glasco, *Ethnicity and Social Structure*, p. 87; *Manufacturing Interests of the City of Buffalo*, pp. 36–62.

24. Glasco, *Ethnicity and Social Structure*, p. 87; *Manufacturing Interests of the City of Buffalo*, pp. 63–4; Henry Weyland Hill, editor in chief, *Municipality of Buffalo: A History, 1720–1923*, vol. 2 (New York, 1923), pp. 727–30.

25. Richard Larry Ehrlich, "The Development of Manufacturing in Selected Counties in the Erie Canal Corridor, 1815–1860" (Ph.D. dissertation, SUNYAB, 1972), 271, 323, 330.

26. Buffalo *Commercial Advertiser*, January 15, 1855, summarizes canal closings and openings, 1844–54.

27. Buffalo *Courier*, April 22, 1844; Buffalo *Commercial Advertiser*, February 21, September 8, 1855. On winter suffering: Buffalo *Courier*, December 1, 1842; January 10, 1844; September 15, 1847; December 18, 1851; Buffalo *Commercial Advertiser*, October 21, 1846; February 9, 1857; February 14, 1859; January 14, 1861; Buffalo *Sentinel*, February 23, 1856.

28. Buffalo *Commercial Advertiser*, November 22, 1855; Buffalo *Demokrat und Weltburger*, July 15, 1858; July 30, October 4, November 17, 1860; Buffalo *Christian Advocate*, October 11, 1860.

29. Susan E. Hirsch, *Roots of the American Working Class: The Industrialization of Crafts in Newark, 1800–1860* (Philadelphia, 1978), pp. 109–38.

30. Glasco, *Ethnicity and Social Structure*, pp. 90, 94, 97.

31. *Biographical Dictionary of American Mayors*.

32. Buffalo *Demokrat und Weltbürger*, February 16, 23, 1854; see also chapters 5, 9, 10 and 11, below.

33. Buffalo *Courier*, August 21, 1844; Buffalo *Republic*, August 21, 1855; Buffalo *Commercial Advertiser*, January 15, 1855; February 2, 1856; February 1, 1859; *Map of the City of Buffalo, Surveyed under the Direction of Quackenboss and Kennedy, Insurance Agents* (New York, 1854); Rapp, "The Port of Buffalo," 93–99.

34. Rapp, "The Port of Buffalo," 93–113, 195–217; Buffalo *Commercial Advertiser*, April 25, 1844; February 2, 1856; July 15, 1858; Merwin S. Hawley to Mary Hawley, May 8, 17, June 24, 1840, Merwin S. Hawley Papers, BECHS.

35. Rapp, "The Port of Buffalo," 74, 99; Merwin S. Hawley to Mary Hawley, May 17, 1840, Hawley Papers, BECHS.

36. Herman Melville, *Moby Dick* (1851; reprint, New York: Penguin Books, 1972), p. 353; Buffalo *Commercial Advertiser*, November 25, 1843; January 13, 1846; May 13, 1851; June 4, 1857; Buffalo *Republic*, February 22, 1859; Lionel Wyld, *Low Bridge: Folklore and the Erie Canal* (Syracuse, 1962).

37. New York *Herald*, n.d., quoted in Buffalo *Courier*, August 23, 1850.

38. Rapp, "The Port of Buffalo," 219–44. Charles Termini, "The Sailortown of Buffalo" (seminar paper, 1983, SUNYAB); Buffalo *Commercial Advertiser*, March 29, April 23, September 23, 1841; January 22, September 29, 1851; August 7, November 6, 1855; August 31, 1860; Buffalo *Courier*, December 21, 1847, August 11, 1851; Neil Larry Shumsky, "Tacit Acceptance: Respectable Americans and Segregated Prostitution, 1870–1910," *Journal of Social History*, 19 (Summer, 1986), 665–79.

39. Buffalo *Christian Advocate*, October 2, 1851; September 30, 1852; Buffalo *Commercial Advertiser*, October 5, 1853; March 1, 27, 1854; August 17, 1855.

40. Buffalo *Courier*, October 21, 1844; December 22, 1847; July 28, 1852; Buffalo *Commercial Advertiser*, October 22, 1844; April 11, 1856; December 16, 1857; Wyld, *Low Bridge*, p. 52; Samuel M. Welch, *Home History: Recollections of Buffalo, or Fifty Years Since* (Buffalo, 1891), p. 11; *Semi-Centennial Celebration of the City of Buffalo* (Buffalo, 1882), pp. 40-3; *Buffalo Medical Journal*, 8 (1852-53), 333.

41. *Map of the City of Buffalo*; Rev. G. Lewis, *Impressions of America and the American Churches* (Edinburgh, 1848), p. 333; James Silk Buckingham, *America: Historical, Statistical and Descriptive*, vol. 3 (London, 1841), pp. 1-4; Merwin S. Hawley to Mary Hawley, May 8, 1840, Hawley Papers, BECHS; "Buffalo City Advertisements," *Commercial Advertiser Directory for the City of Buffalo* (Buffalo, 1851), pp. 63-98; "Buffalo Business Directory," *Commercial Advertiser Directory for the City of Buffalo* (Buffalo, 1855), pp. 269-95; Buffalo *Republic*, November 3, 1860; Welch, *Home History*, pp. 61-110.

42. *Map of the City of Buffalo*; Welch, *Home History*, pp. 44-60; "Property of School Districts," Buffalo *Commercial Advertiser*, December 14, 1858; and also January 25, 1860; Buffalo *Christian Advocate*, March 15, 1855; May 5, 1859; Buffalo *Courier*, June 12, 1852.

43. Glasco, *Ethnicity and Social Structure*, pp. 60-1; Sandford B. Hunt, *Methodism in Buffalo* (Buffalo, 1893), p. 121; *Map of the City of Buffalo*; Buffalo *Christian Advocate*, July 5, 1855; July 24, 1857; March 25, 1858; December 1, 1859; Buffalo *Commercial Advertiser*, December 14, 1858.

44. Buffalo *Commercial Advertiser*, June 12, 1857; *Map of the City of Buffalo*; Glasco, *Ethnicity and Social Structure*, pp. 60-1; *Geschichte der Deutschen in Buffalo und Erie County, New York* (Buffalo, 1898), vol. 1, pp. 31-56; vol. 2, pp. 15-109; Deutsch-Amerikanische Historische und Biographische Gesellschaft, *Buffalo und Sein Deutschthum* (Buffalo, 1912), pp. 57-77.

45. Herbert Gutman and Laurence A. Glasco, "The Buffalo, New York Negro, 1855-1875" (manuscript, 1968, SUNYAB); Glasco, *Ethnicity and Social Structure*, pp. 60-1; Hildegard Graff, "Abolitionism and Anti-Slavery in Buffalo and Erie County" (Master's thesis, University of Buffalo, 1951); Arthur O. White, "School Segregation and its Critics: Buffalo, 1837-1880" (seminar paper, 1966, SUNYAB).

46. Frank Manual, "The Tenements of Buffalo" (paper, n.d., BECHS), 5; Buffalo *Commercial Advertiser*, September 2, 1856; Michael Katz, "Fathers and Sons: A Comparison of Occupations—Hamilton, 1851 and 1871; Buffalo, 1855," Working Paper #15, York Social History Project (Toronto, 1976), 305.

47. Welch, *Home History*, p. 77.

48. Lieselotte Clemens, *Old Lutheran Emigration from Pomerania to the U.S.A.: History and Motivation, 1839-1843*, trans. Joachim Peters (Kiel, West Germany, 1976), pp. 33-4, 60-5; Buffalo *Weltbürger*, September 14, 28, 1839.

49. *The Centenary of St. Mary's Church, 1844-1944* (Buffalo, 1944), p. 17. The same conditions existed still further east, almost two decades later: Johann Roth, "Wie es im Anfange um die St. Anna Kirche herum aussah," in "Die

Geschichte der St. Anna Gemeinde, 1858–1908," *St. Anna Bote* (Buffalo, 1908), pp. 101–3.

50. Buffalo *Commercial Advertiser*, July 31, October 14, December 12, 1854; Buffalo *Medical Journal*, 10 (1854–55), 373–81.

51. Buffalo *Commercial Advertiser*, July 14, 1858; Buffalo *Demokrat und Weltbürger*, July 15, 1858; Buffalo *Christian Advocate*, October 11, 1860.

52. *Map of the City of Buffalo, 1854*; *An Act to Incorporate the City of Buffalo, 1832* (Buffalo, 1837); Buffalo *Courier*, July 1, 1853.

53. Buffalo *Commercial Advertiser*, November 7, 1846; July 25, 1857; Buffalo *Courier*, November 3, 1847; Mark Goldman, "Buffalo's Black Rock: Neighborhood Identity and the Metropolitan Relationship" (Ph.D. dissertation, SUNYAB, 1973), 16, 22, 30.

54. Roger Whitman, "Queen's Epic: Benjamin Rathbun and His Times" (typescript, 1942, BECHS), 79; Horton, et al., *History of Northwestern New York*, vol. 1, pp. 33–4; Buffalo *Courier*, January 17, 1849; *Map of the City of Buffalo, 1854*.

55. Buffalo *Courier*, May 15, 1851; Buffalo *Commercial Advertiser*, July 31, 1854; April 28, December 16, 1856; August 29, 1857; Wolfe, *Tifft Farm*, p. 7; Fred Francis Jablonski, "The Dynamics of an East Buffalo Ethnic Neighborhood—Old (1846), New (1976)" (Master's thesis, SUNYAB, 1976), 2–8.

56. George Washington Johnson, Diary, 1849, entry of September 12, 1849, p. 400, DC.

57. Stanley Lieberson, *Ethnic Patterns in American Cities* (Glenco, 1963), p. 206; Kathleen Neils Conzen, *Immigrant Milwaukee, 1836–1860: Accommodation and Community in a Frontier City* (Cambridge, Mass., 1976), p. 132.

Chapter 2. Expansion, Speculation, and Collapse, 1825–38

1. Samuel M. Welch, *Home History: Recollections of Buffalo, or Fifty Years Since* (Buffalo, 1891), p. 3; Rev. John Timon, *Missions in Western New York and Church History of the Diocese of Buffalo* (Buffalo, 1862), p. 215 (for estimates of immigrant population); *Semi-Centennial Celebration of the City of Buffalo* (Buffalo, 1882), p. 24. In a theoretical discussion of the development of modern anomie, Elwin H. Powell uses the communal atmosphere of 1830s village Buffalo as a historical baseline. See his *The Design of Discord: Studies of Anomie* (New York, 1970), pp. 60–64, for analysis of the "strong sense of social solidarity" he discovers.

2. *Fifth Annual Festival of the Old Settlers of Buffalo* (Buffalo, 1868), pp. 9–12.

3. Powell, *The Design of Discord*, p. 63; Welch, *Home History*, pp. 209–26.

4. Sandford B. Hunt, *Methodism in Buffalo* (Buffalo, 1893), p. 30; Whitney Cross, *The Burned-Over District: The Social and Intellectual History of Enthusiastic Religion in Western New York, 1800–1850* (Ithaca, 1950), p. 45; *Biographical Dictionary of American Mayors* (Westport, 1981), pp. 8, 292, 360; Buffalo *Commercial Advertiser*, March 16, 1836; Tyrone Power, *Impressions of America during the Years 1833, 1834, and 1835*, vol. 1 (London, 1836), pp.

388–9. For the communal atmosphere of village July Fourth celebrations: Buffalo *Patriot*, July 3, 20, 1821; Buffalo *Emporium*, July 29, 1826.

5. *An Act to Incorporate the City of Buffalo, 1832* (Buffalo, 1837); Buffalo *Courier*, July 1, 1853.

6. Hosmer quoted in John N. Larned, *A History of Buffalo, Delineating the Evolution of the City*, vol. 2 (New York, 1911), p. 46.

7. Paul E. Johnson, *A Shopkeeper's Millennium: Society and Revivals in Rochester, New York, 1815–1837* (New York, 1978); Cross, *The Burned-Over District*, pp. 66, 72–6; Sylvester Eaton to Charles Grandison Finney, January 9, 1831, Charles Grandison Finney Papers, OC.

8. Harriet Martineau, *Retrospect of Western Travel*, vol. 1 (London, 1838), pp. 90–1.

9. Buffalo *Weltbürger*, March 24, 1838.

10. Detroit *Tribune* quoted in Buffalo *Republic*, October 15, 1855.

11. Mark Goldman, *High Hopes: The Rise and Decline of Buffalo, New York* (Albany, 1983), p. 36.

12. Rochester *Advertiser*, January 1, 1834; Johnson, *A Shopkeeper's Millennium*, p. 114. *Buffalo City Directory, 1835* (Buffalo, 1835), p. 100.

13. Ira Blossom to H. J. Huidekoper, August 10, 1827, Ira Blossom Papers, BECHS.

14. Frances Trollope, *Domestic Manners of the Americans*, vol. 2 (London, 1832), p. 271. See also James Stuart, *Three Years in North America*, vol. 1 (New York, 1833), p. 96; and C. D. Arfwedson, *The United States and Canada in 1832, 1833, and 1834*, vol. 2 (London, 1834), pp. 307–8.

15. John T. Horton, Edward T. Williams, and Harry S. Douglass, *History of Northwestern New York*, vol. 1 (New York, 1947), p. 75; James Silk Buckingham, *America: Historical, Statistical, and Descriptive*, vol. 3 (London, 1841), pp. 1–4; Larned, *A History of Buffalo*, p. 46.

16. Welch, *Home History*, pp. 203–8; Horton, et al., *History of Northwestern New York*, vol. 1, p. 75; Larned, *A History of Buffalo*, vol. 2, p. 50; H. Perry Smith, *History of the City of Buffalo and Erie County, New York*, vol. 2 (Syracuse, 1884), p. 57; David Grimsted, review of Karen Halttunen, *Confidence Men and Painted Women: A Study of Middle-Class Culture in America*, in *Journal of American History*, 70 (December, 1983), 666.

17. Larned, *A History of Buffalo*, vol. 2, p. 50; Roger Whitman, "Queen's Epic: Benjamin Rathbun and His Times" (typescript, 1942, BECHS), 156–7.

18. Guy Salisbury, "The Speculative Craze of 1836," Buffalo Historical Society *Publications*, 4 (1896), 317–37; and idem, "Buffalo in 1836 and 1862: A Paper Read before the Buffalo Historical Society," in *Thomas' City Directory, 1863* (Buffalo, 1864), pp. 13–28; Larned, *A History of Buffalo*, vol. 2, p. 46 (quotation).

19. Thomas D. Odle, "The American Grain Trade of the Great Lakes, 1825–1873," pt. 2, *Inland Seas*, 9 (Spring, 1953), 53–5; John G. Clark, *The Grain Trade of the Old Northwest* (Urbana, 1966), pp. 117–9.

20. Verna G. Walker, "Banking in Buffalo before the Civil War" (Master's thesis, University of Buffalo, 1933), 30–51; Welch, *Home History*, p. 199; Salisbury, "The Speculative Craze of 1836," 317–37.

21. Welch, *Home History*, pp. 172–99; Walker, "Banking in Buffalo before the Civil War," 40.

22. Whitman, "Queen's Epic," 158–9; Horton, et al., *History of Northwestern New York*, vol. 1, p. 87; Walter Buckingham Smith and Arthur H. Cole, *Fluctuations in American Business, 1790–1860* (Cambridge, Mass., 1935), pp. 66, 83.

23. Horton, et al., *History of Northwestern New York*, vol. 1, p. 82, 86–7; John G. Ramsey, "From Self-Educating Boosters to Stewards of Culture: Buffalo's Friends of Education," vol. 1 (Ph.D. dissertation, SUNYAB, 1984), pp. 31–2, 40.

24. Dr. Bryant Burwell, Diary, January 1, 1837–February 15, 1839, entry of March 7, 1837, BECHS.

25. Sylvester Eaton to Charles Grandison Finney, February 9, 28, 1831, Finney Papers, OC.

26. Horton, et al., *History of Northwestern New York*, vol. 1, pp. 120, 126–7; Sylvester Eaton to Charles Grandison Finney, February 21, 1831; Busby Torrey and S. Eaton to Finney, February 28, 1831; John Wadsworth to Finney, April 4, 1831; S. Eaton to Finney, April 15, 1831, Finney Papers, OC.

27. Buffalo *Courier*, July 24, 1848; Horton, et al., *History of Northwestern New York*, vol. 1, pp. 126–32; Lloyd Graham and Frank Severance, *The First Hundred Years of the Buffalo Chamber of Commerce* (Buffalo, 1945), p. 12 (quotation); *Biographical Dictionary of American Mayors*, s.v., "Samuel Wilkeson"; John Chase Lord, *"The Valiant Man": A Discourse on the Death of the Honorable Samuel Wilkeson of Buffalo* (Buffalo, 1848), pp. 11–34 (p. 23, quotation); Samuel Wilkeson to Sons, December 24, 1834, Wilkeson-Berringer Collection, BECHS.

28. Horton, et al., *History of Northwestern New York*, vol. 1, pp. 65–7, 97, 98; Boxes 5, 6, 7 (business papers), Samuel Wilkeson Papers, BECHS; Samuel Wilkeson, Jr. to "Friend" Stone, September 18, 1833, Wilkeson-Berringer Collection, BECHS.

29. *Memoir of John C. Lord, D.D. Pastor of Central Presbyterian Church for Thirty-eight Years* (Buffalo, 1878), pp. 5–43; Lord, *"The Valiant Man,"* pp. 6–7; Rev. Charles Wood, "Memorial Sermon," in *Semi-Centennial, Central Presbyterian Church: Addresses and Discourse, 1835–1885* (Buffalo, 1886), pp. 65–7.

30. Welch, *Home History*, pp. 244–8; "Historical Discourse," in *Semi-Centennial, Central Presbyterian Church*, pp. 26–36.

31. Charles Brooks, "John C. Lord and Old School Presbyterian Thought in Buffalo, 1837–1864" (seminar paper, SUNYAB, 1980), 1–10; Horton, et al., *History of Northwestern New York*, vol. 1, pp. 123, 127–9, 153–4; Buffalo *Courier*, July 22, December 16, 1846; September 6, 1850; Buffalo *American Celt and Catholic Citizen*, April 23, 1853; Buffalo *Express*, November 22, 1861.

32. Buffalo *Courier*, February 7, 18, 19, 20, 23, 25, March 2, 1850; Buffalo *Weltbürger*, January 20, March 17, 1838; "Historical Discourse," *Semi-Centennial, Central Presbyterian Church*, p. 30; Brooks, "John C. Lord and Old School Presbyterian Thought," 10–7; Horton, et al., *History of Northwestern New York*, vol. 1, pp. 153–4; Buffalo *Christian Advocate*, January 17, 1861.

Lord is an excellent example of what Lois Banner calls "Christian republicanism," in "Religious Benevolence as Social Control: A Critique of an Interpretation," *Journal of American History*, 60 (June, 1973), 23–41.

33. Horton, et al., *History of Northwestern New York*, vol. 1, pp. 128–31; Brooks, "John C. Lord and Old School Presbyterian Thought," 20–3. James O. Putnam, "Memorial Paper," in *Semi-Centennial, Central Presbyterian Church*, pp. 21–5. Lord's defense of the South and of slavery ended with the outbreak of civil war; see his *The Justice of Our National Cause: A Sermon, September 26, 1861* (Buffalo, 1861).

34. Horton, et al., *History of Northwestern New York*, vol. 1, pp. 127–32; Buffalo *Commercial Advertiser*, June 14, 1842; Lord, *"The Valiant Man,"* pp. 22, 44–6.

35. Horton, et al., *History of Northwestern New York*, vol. 1, p. 129.

36. Frederick Marryat, *A Diary in America with Remarks on Its Inhabitants*, ed. Sydney Jackson (New York, 1962), p. 91; Whitman, "Queen's Epic," 3–71.

37. Marryat, *A Diary in America*, p. 91; Whitman, "Queen's Epic," 71–99, 103, 123–6, 138–73; Horton, et al., *History of Northwestern New York*, vol. 1, pp. 74–5; Larned, *A History of Buffalo*, vol. 2, pp. 50–1.

38. Whitman, "Queen's Epic," 174–86; Welch, *Home History*, pp. 174–87; Bond, November 9, 1835, Samuel Wilkeson Papers, BECHS.

39. Whitman, "Queen's Epic," 191–229; George Rogers Taylor, *The Transportation Revolution, 1815–1860* (New York, 1951), pp. 341–3; Reginald C. McGrane, *The Panic of 1837* (Chicago, 1963).

40. Whitman, "Queen's Epic," 229–81.

41. Ira Blossom to H. J. Huidekoper, August 4, 1838, Blossom Papers, BECHS.

42. Buffalo *Weltbürger*, July 21, 1838.

43. Whitman, "Queen's Epic," 282–321; Welch, *Home History*, pp. 2, 4; Buffalo *Weltbürger*, June 6, 1840.

44. Whitman, "Queen's Epic," 282–303; James Barton, "Early Reminiscences of Buffalo," Buffalo Historical Society *Publications*, 1 (1879), 172–3; Samuel Rezneck, "The Social History of an American Depression," *American Historical Review*, 40 (July, 1935), 662–87; New York *Journal of Commerce*, May 10, 1837.

45. Dr. Bryant Burwell, Dairy, 1837–39, entry of May [?], 1837, BECHS.

46. Ira Blossom to H. J. Huidekoper, February 8, 1838, Blossom Papers, BECHS.

47. Walker, "Banking in Buffalo before the Civil War," 52–76 (60, 72, quotations); "Lewis Allen Petitions," n.d., William L. Marcy Papers, folder #554, NYSA; New York *Journal of Commerce*, May 10, 1837.

48. Dr. Bryant Burwell, Diary, 1840–41, entry of January 15, 1840, BECHS.

49. Whitman, "Queen's Epic," 316–21; Dr. Bryant Burwell, Diary, 1839, entries of January 5 (quotation); June 24 (suicide and debts), and passim, BECHS; *Biographical Dictionary of American Mayors*, s.v., "Hiram Pratt"; Millard Fillmore to J. C. Wright, November 2, 1853, Millard Fillmore Papers, LC (microfilm); Samuel Wilkeson to John Wilkeson, October 18, 31, 1837;

February 17, March 22, May 12, 23, November 2, 1838; Heman P. Potter to Samuel Wilkeson, May 12, 1838, Wilkeson-Berringer Collection, BECHS.

50. Hugh Honour, *The New Golden Land: European Images of America from the Discoveries to the Present Time* (New York, 1975), pp. 202 (painting), 202–3 (text); Whitman, "Queen's Epic," 316.

Chapter 3. Commerce and Class Formation

1. Rev. John Chase Lord, *"Pride, Fullness of Bread, and Abundance of Idleness": The Prominent Causes of the Present Pecuniary Distress of the Country* (Buffalo, 1839).

2. Rev. George W. Hosmer, *Address* (Buffalo, 1840), p. 40.

3. *Semi-Centennial of the City of Buffalo* (Buffalo, 1882), p. 39.

4. Ronald E. Shaw, *Erie Water West: A History of the Erie Canal, 1792–1854* (Lexington, 1966), p. 229; Charles L. Bland, "Institutions of Charity in Jacksonian Erie County: 1829–1861" (seminar paper, SUNYAB, 1975), 35, 46.

5. Buffalo *Courier*, March 17, 1843; January 3, April 11, 1844; *Buffalo City Directory, 1842* (Buffalo, 1842); Bryant Burwell, Diary, July 1, 1841–May 10, 1843, entry of August 23, 1841, BECHS.

6. John T. Horton, Edward T. Williams, and Harry S. Douglass, *History of Northwestern New York*, vol. 1 (New York, 1947), pp. 112–3; Buffalo *Courier*, August 28, 1846.

7. Hosmer, *Address*, pp. 2–4; Horton, et al., *History of Northwestern New York*, vol. 1, pp. 82–3; John G. Ramsey, "From Self-Educating Boosters to Stewards of Culture: Buffalo's Friends of Education," vol. 1 (Ph.D. dissertation, SUNYAB, 1984), pp. 48–92, 94–120.

8. Buffalo *Courier*, April 13, May 20, August 11, September 20, December 30, 1843; John G. Clark, *The Grain Trade of the Old Northwest* (Urbana, 1966), p. 117.

9. Oliver G. Steele, *Memorial of the Late Walter Joy* (Buffalo, 1864), p. 1.

10. Roger Whitman, "Queen's Epic: Benjamin Rathbun and His Times" (typescript, 1942, BECHS), 318–9; Buffalo *Commercial Advertiser*, June 14, 15, November 14, 1858; Buffalo *Christian Advocate*, January 20, 1859; Bishop John Timon to Counseil, February 20, 1859 (with undated clipping from Buffalo *Express*), Society for the Propagation of the Faith, Lyons, UND (microfilms).

11. Daniel Walker Howe, *The Political Culture of American Whigs* (Chicago, 1979), p. 106; Paul Boyer, *Urban Masses and Moral Order in America, 1820–1920* (Cambridge, Mass., 1978), pp. viii–ix, 1–119; Mary P. Ryan, *Cradle of the Middle Class: The Family in Oneida County, New York, 1790–1865* (New York, 1981); and Frederick Cople Jaher, *The Urban Establishment: Upper Strata in Boston, New York, Charleston, Chicago and Los Angeles* (Urbana, 1982).

12. George B. Forgie, *Patricide in the House Divided: A Psychological Portrait of Lincoln and His Age* (New York, 1979), pp. 13–53.

13. Maurice Dobb, *Studies in the Development of Capitalism* (London, 1946), pp. 177–220; also, see Ryan, *Cradle of the Middle Class*, p. 114.

14. Buffalo *Mercantile Courier*, November 11, 1842.

15. Note 8, above; George Rogers Taylor, *The Transportation Revolution, 1815–1860* (New York, 1951), pp. 342–51; Peter Heller, "Trade and Development at Buffalo from 1815 to 1863" (typescript, 1968, BECHS), 32–9, 55; Buffalo *Courier and Pilot*, November 28, 1846; Buffalo *Courier*, October 7, November 8, 1847.

16. Marvin A. Rapp, "The Port of Buffalo: 1825–1880" (Ph.D. dissertation, Duke University, 1947), 30–1; Thomas D. Odle, "The Grain Trade of the Great Lakes, 1825–1873," pt. 1, *Inland Seas*, 7–8 (1951–52), 176–7; Arthur Markowitz, "Joseph Dart and the Emergence of Buffalo as a Grain Port, 1820–1860," *Inland Seas*, 25 (Fall, 1969), 183–4.

17. Patricia Therre Harris, "The Rise of the Grain Trade and the Grain Merchant in Buffalo in the Mid-Nineteenth Century" (seminar paper, SUNYAB, 1981), 28–53; Fred Mitchell Jones, *Middlemen in the Domestic Trade of the United States, 1800–1860* (Urbana, 1937), pp. 10–1, 19–29; Buffalo *Commercial Advertiser*, November 27, 1858; "Buffalo Business Directory," *Commercial Advertiser Directory for the City of Buffalo, 1855* (Buffalo, 1855), pp. 276, 279–80.

18. Clark, *The Grain Trade of the Old Northwest*, pp. 117–8; Merwin S. Hawley, "Merwin Spencer Hawley—Autobiography" (manuscript, 1872, Merwin S. Hawley Papers, BECHS), 24. The affluent millwright Danforth Franklin provides an example in 1842 of grain purchases by someone outside the ranks of the commission merchants: Private Account Book, 1842, Danforth Franklin Papers, BECHS. But the established commission merchants, the Hollister brothers, provide an example of occasional speculation by respectable dockside entrepreneurs. At the first word of the Irish potato famine they dispatched an agent to the West to buy grain in enormous quantities. While he was in the field, wheat prices rose from $.50 cents to $1.50 per barrel in anticipation of Irish needs. Samuel M. Welch, *Home History: Recollections of Buffalo, or Fifty Years Since* (Buffalo, 1891), p. 93.

19. Jones, *Middlemen in the Domestic Trade*, pp. 11, 33–43; "Buffalo Business Directory" (1855), 278, 280–2, 282–3, 284 (for iron, dry goods, hardware, and grocery wholesalers), and 269 (auctioneers).

20. Taylor, *The Transportation Revolution*, pp. 10–4.

21. "Insurance Companies," *Commercial Advertiser Directory for the City of Buffalo, 1850* (Buffalo, 1850), pp. 31–2; Buffalo *Courier*, December 4, 1850; Harris, "The Rise of the Grain Trade and Grain Merchant," 34.

22. "Buffalo Business Directory" (1855), 271, 277, 280, 283, 285, 289, 291.

23. Verna G. Walker, "Banking in Buffalo before the Civil War" (Master's thesis, University of Buffalo, 1933), 89–99; Thomas D. Odle, "The American Grain Trade of the Great Lakes," *Inland Seas*, 9 (Spring, 1953), 54–8.

24. Merwin S. Hawley to Elijah Hawley, January 25, April 1, 1851; March 18, 1852, Hawley Papers, BECHS; Horton, et al., *History of Northwestern New York*, vol. 1, pp. 106–8.

25. Peter Emslie, *Atlas of the City of Buffalo, Showing Original Lots and Subdivisions, Also the Names of Present Owners*, vol. 1 (Buffalo, 1866); "Maps and Tax Records of James S. Wadsworth's Holdings in Buffalo, 1856–9," James S. Wadsworth Papers, ML; Boxes 5 and 6, George Hunter Bartlett Papers, BECHS; "List of Lands Owned by Family," Samuel Wilkeson Papers, BECHS; Buffalo *Courier*, September 2, 1850. For legal work in managing property: William Wadsworth to James S. Wadsworth, September 20, 1847, Angus Cameron to D. H. Fitzhugh, October 10, 1853; May 16, 1855, Wadsworth Papers, ML; Rapp, "The Port of Buffalo," 252.

26. "Buffalo Business Directory" (1855), 270–95; Laurence A. Glasco, *Ethnicity and Social Structure: Irish, Germans, and Native-Born of Buffalo, N.Y., 1850–1860* (New York, 1980), pp. 92, 94, 97; Taylor, *The Transportation Revolution*, pp. 10–4.

27. Buffalo *Commercial Advertiser*, August 5, 1858, *Buffalo City Directory*, 1858, (for identities of committee members). Also, Buffalo *Courier*, December 10, 1850.

28. Hawley, "Merwin Spencer Hawley—Autobiography," 16, 24, 28–9; Odle, "The Grain Trade of the Great Lakes, 1825–1873," pt. 2, p. 56; Welch, *Home History*, p. 170; Allen Pred, *Urban Growth and City Systems in the U.S., 1840–1860* (Cambridge, Mass., 1980), p. 101; Rapp, "The Port of Buffalo," 149.

29. Odle, "The American Grain Trade of the Great Lakes, 1825–1873," 108–9, 162–3; Pred, Urban Growth and City Systems, p. 97; and idem, *Urban Growth and the Circulation of Information: The U.S. System of Cities, 1790–1840* (Cambridge, Mass., 1973), p. 50.

30. Suzanne T. Lach, "The Railroads Come to Buffalo: A Study of the Railroads before 1860" (typescript, 1963, BECHS); Taylor, *The Transportation Revolution*, pp. 61–2; Odle, "The Grain Trade of the Great Lakes, 1825–1873," 178, 187; Horton, et al., *History of Northwestern New York*, vol. 1, pp. 99–100; Marvin Rapp, "Buffalo and the Great Lakes Trade, 1825–1900," *Inland Seas*, 25 (Fall, 1969), 21–2.

31. Markowitz, "Joseph Dart and the Emergence of Buffalo," 183–5; Joseph Dart, "The Grain Elevators of Buffalo," Buffalo Historical Society *Publications*, 1 (1879), 399.

32. John Storck and Walter Teague, *Flour for Man's Bread: A History of Milling* (Minneapolis, 1952), pp. 165–6, 180–3; Markowitz, "Joseph Dart and the Emergence of Buffalo," 185–92; Buffalo *Commercial Advertiser*, July 18, 1860.

33. Markowitz, "Joseph Dart and the Emergence of Buffalo," 192.

34. "Agreement" [April 27, 1850], and [bill, 1851], James D. Sawyer Papers, BECHS; "Agreement" [April 2, 1859], "Agreement" [June 1, 1861], and "Western Elevating Company Statement of December 16, 1861," Bartlett Papers, BECHS; "Amounts Paid the Wadsworth Elevator by the Wadsworth Elevating Company" [1864–68], and [rental agreement, 1853–58], Wadsworth Papers, BECHS; Markowitz, "Joseph Dart and the Emergence of Buffalo," 192; Buffalo *Express*, January 6, 1860.

35. Rapp, "The Port of Buffalo," 45–50; Buffalo *Mercantile Courier*, January 19, May 3, 1844; George Clinton, "Historical Sketch," in *The Manufacturing*

Interests of the City of Buffalo (Buffalo, 1866), p. 11; Merwin S. Hawley to Elijah Hawley, November 18, 1851, Hawley Papers, BECHS.

36. Harris, "The Rise of the Grain Trade," 25–8; Rapp, "The Port of Buffalo," 256–62; Buffalo *Courier*, June 16, September 17, 1847.

37. On the seawall: "Undersigned Forwarders and Merchants of the City of Buffalo" (petition, June 9, 1843), "Miscellaneous Manuscripts, Buffalo, N.Y. (Harbor Construction)," NYHS. On the Wilkeson proposals, "Citizens of Buffalo," [1843?] Buffalo *Whig and Journal, Extra* (map and text), Wilkeson Papers, BECHS.

38. Clinton, "Historical Sketch," 11–2; Horton, et al., *History of Northwestern New York*, vol. 1, pp. 103–4; Buffalo *Courier*, May 25, 1847.

39. Rapp, "The Port of Buffalo," 65–70; Horton, et al., *History of Northwestern New York*, vol. 1, pp. 103–4; Buffalo *Courier*, December 8, 1847.

40. Shaw, *Erie Water West*, pp. 311–96; Buffalo *Courier*, April 23, 1851.

41. Horton, et al., *History of Northwestern New York*, vol. 1, pp. 103–4, 170–1; Rapp, "The Port of Buffalo," 60–4, 71; Buffalo *Courier*, June 21, 1847; Buffalo *Commercial Advertiser*, September 25, 1852.

42. Rapp, "The Port of Buffalo," 73–4, 99; Buffalo *Commercial Advertiser*, February 2, 1856; Port improvement may be traced in the six maps (1804–66) in Henry H. Baxter and Erik Heyl, eds., *Maps, Buffalo Harbor, 1804–1964* (Buffalo, 1965), pp. 10–9, 30–1.

43. Horton, et al., *History of Northwestern New York*, vol. 1, p. 104; Rapp, "The Port of Buffalo," 162; Buffalo *Courier*, January 9, 1844; Buffalo *Weltbürger*, June 7, 1845.

44. Rapp, "The Port of Buffalo," 172, 188, 265–7; Lloyd Graham and Frank Severance, *The First Hundred Years of the Buffalo Chamber of Commerce* (Buffalo, 1945), pp. 44–5, 57–65.

45. Buffalo *Courier*, April 25, 1844; Buffalo *Republic*, December 16, 1853; January 11, 1854; Buffalo *Demokrat und Weltbürger*, November 5, 1855; L. Porter Smith, "Notes on the Canal Forwarding Trade," Buffalo Historical Society *Publications*, 13 (1909), 383; Lloyd Graham, "Western New York: Innovators and Entrepreneurs," *Western New York* (April, 1976), 37–8; *Hunt's Merchants' Magazine and Commercial Review*, March, 1854, 321; Hugh G. J. Aitken, *The Welland Canal Company: A Study in Canadian Enterprise* (Cambridge, Mass., 1954), p. 23.

46. Graham and Severance, *The First Hundred Years of the Buffalo Chamber of Commerce*, p. 22.

47. Ibid., pp. 22–3 (quotation), 42–3; Buffalo *Republic*, June 5, 1854; Frank Severance, "Historical Sketch of the Board of Trade, the Merchant's Exchange, and the Chamber of Commerce, Buffalo," Buffalo Historical Society *Publications*, 13 (1909), 242–9, 257–8.

48. George S. Hazard, untitled remarks on assuming presidency of the Board of Trade, *Hunt's Merchants' Magazine and Commercial Review*, April, 1855, 38–9. See Thomas L. Haskell, "Capitalism and the Origins of the Humanitarian Sensibility," pt. 2, *American Historical Review*, 90 (June, 1985), 549–56.

49. Shaw, *Erie Water West*, pp. 225–6; "Indenture," February 8, 1848, Sawyer Family Papers, BECHS; Buffalo *Commercial Advertiser*, December 11, 1857; March 23, 1859.

50. Buffalo *Christian Advocate*, May 11, 1854.

51. Saul Engelbourg, *Power and Morality: American Business Ethics, 1840–1914* (Westport, 1980), p. 7; James D. Norris, *R. G. Dun and Co., 1841–1900: The Development of Credit-Reporting in the Nineteenth Century* (Westport, 1978), pp. 3–23; Bertram Wyatt-Brown, "God and Dun and Bradstreet, 1841–1851," *Business History Review*, 40 (Winter, 1966), 432–50; James H. Madison, "The Credit Reports of R. G. Dun and Co. as Historical Sources," *Historical Methods Newsletter*, 8 (September, 1975), 128–31.

52. Norris, *R. G. Dun and Co., 1841–1900*, pp. 25–69, 84–7.

53. David A. Gerber, "Ethnics, Enterprise, and Middle Class Formation: Using the Dun and Bradstreet Collection for Research in Ethnic History," *Immigration History Newsletter*, 12 (May, 1980), 1–7. (The correct title for this collection is the "R. G. Dun and Company Collection.") Idem, "Cutting Out Shylock: Elite Anti-Semitism and the Quest for Moral Order in the Mid-Nineteenth Century American Market Place," *Journal of American History*, 69 (December, 1982), 615–37.

54. Buffalo *Christian Advocate*, April 5, 1855; March 1, 1860; Buffalo *Republic*, November 5, 1857.

55. Stow Persons, *The Decline of American Gentility* (New York, 1973), p. 41. Also see Haskell, "Capitalism and the Origins of the Humanitarian Sensibility," pt. 2, pp. 560–3; and Edward A. Rotundo, "Body and Soul: Changing Ideals of American Middle Class Manhood," *Journal of Social History*, 16 (Summer, 1983), 23–8.

56. "Indenture," February 8, 1848, Sawyer Family Papers, BECHS.

57. "Jacob Barker," unidentified clipping [1859 obituary?], Burgess Scrapbook, 1863–75, BECHS.

58. H. Perry Smith, *History of the City of Buffalo and Erie County, New York*, vol. 2 (Syracuse, 1884), p. 91 (of appended biographical section).

59. Hawley, "Merwin Spencer Hawley—Autobiography," 24, 26, 30, Hawley Papers, BECHS.

60. Smith, *History of the City of Buffalo and Erie County, New York*, vol. 2, p. 106 (of appended biographical section).

61. Buffalo *Commercial Advertiser*, September 11, 1856; Dan Morgan, *Merchants of Grain* (New York, 1979), pp. 95–7.

62. Morgan, *Merchants of Grain*, p. 97; Clark, *The Grain Trade of the Old Northwest*, pp. 117–20; Markowitz, "Joseph Dart and the Emergence of Buffalo as a Grain Port," 94.

63. Hawley, "Merwin Spencer Hawley—Autobiography," 46, 53, Hawley Papers, BECHS.

64. Smith, *History of Buffalo and Erie County*, vol. 2, pp. 534, 537, 541–2; *Fifth Annual Festival of the Old Settlers of Buffalo* (Buffalo, 1868), pp. 28–32; "First Annual Opening of the Buffalo Fine Arts Academy," clipping [1864?], George S. Hazard Scrapbook, BECHS.

Chapter 4. Culture, Ethos, and Ideology in Class Formation

1. On the problem of class terminology, see Raymond Williams's discussion of "bourgeois" in his *Keywords: A Vocabulary of Culture and Society* (New York, 1976), pp. 37–40. Also, Daniel Walker Howe, *The Political Culture of American Whigs* (Chicago, 1979), p. 106.

2. The term "old settler" is employed frequently in Dr. Bryant Burwell's diary (see, e.g., Diary, 1839, entry of January 5, BECHS) and later became the basis for the name of the "Old Settlers of Buffalo," an association of the descendants of the old settlers. For the passing of this generation, see chapter 2, note 49, above, and "Necrology of Our Early Settlers," Buffalo *Commercial Advertiser*, January 22, 1869.

3. Biographical information on Samuel Wilkeson's three sons may be found in the unpublished guide to the Samuel Wilkeson Papers, BECHS.

4. H. Perry Smith, *History of the City of Buffalo and Erie County, New York*, vol. 2 (Syracuse, 1884), pp. 87–8 (biographical section); John T. Horton, Edward T. Williams, and Harry S. Douglass, *History of Northwestern New York*, vol. 1 (New York, 1947), p. 230.

5. Michael B. Katz, Michael J. Doucet, and Mark J. Stern, "Migration and the Social Order in Erie County, New York, 1855," *Journal of Interdisciplinary History*, 8 (Spring, 1978), 684.

6. The sample is drawn from Smith, *History of the City of Buffalo and Erie County, New York*, vol. 2, (biographical section); with supplementary data provided by the Biographical Files, (n.d.), BECHS.

7. Edward Pessen, "The Lifestyle of the Antebellum Urban Elite," *Mid-America*, 55 (July, 1973), 163–79; Frederic Cople Jaher, *The Urban Establishment: Upper Strata in Boston, New York, Charleston, Chicago and Los Angeles* (Urbana, 1982).

8. Samuel M. Welch, *Home History: Recollections of Buffalo, or Fifty Years Since* (Buffalo, 1891), pp. 164–5 (quotation), 185, 328–406; Smith, *History of the City of Buffalo and Erie County, New York*, vol. 2, pp. 468–70.

9. Steward H. Holbrook, *The Yankee Exodus: An Account of Migration from New England* (New York, 1950); David M. Ellis, "The Yankee Invasion of New York, 1783–1850," *New York History*, 32 (January, 1951), 3–17; Welch, *Home History*, pp. 185–91.

10. Ivan Light, "Immigrant and Ethnic Enterprise in North America," *Ethnic and Racial Studies*, 7 (April, 1984), 205–6. On white-collar apprenticeship: Margery Davis, *Woman's Place Is at the Typewriter: Office Work and Office Workers, 1870–1900* (Philadelphia, 1982), chapter 1.

11. Laurence A. Glasco, *Ethnicity and Social Structure: Irish, Germans, and Native-Born of Buffalo, N.Y., 1850–1860*, (New York, 1980), p. 134.

12. Merwin S. Hawley, "Merwin Spencer Hawley: Autobiography," (manuscript, 1872) 1–15, 19–20; and letters to Mary Hawley, May 8, 17, June 24, 1840, Merwin S. Hawley Papers, BECHS.

13. Glasco, *Ethnicity and Social Structure*, p. 157.

14. Ibid., pp. 161, 163.

15. Hawley, "Merwin Spencer Hawley: Autobiography," 15, 28–9.

16. Glasco, *Ethnicity and Social Structure*, pp. 144–5, 193–203. For marriages, see clippings in the Burgess Scrapbook, 1863–75, BECHS.

17. Richard M. Bernard, *The Melting Pot and the Altar: Marital Assimilation in Early Twentieth Century Wisconsin* (Minneapolis, 1980), pp. 90–5; Charles Hirschman and Judah Matras, "A New Look at the Marriage Market and Nuptiality Rates, 1915–1958," *Demography* 8 (November, 1971), 549–69.

18. Glasco, *Ethnicity and Social Structure*, p. 123; Michael B. Katz, "The Structure of Inequality and Length of Residence in Buffalo, New York, 1855," Working Paper #13, of the York Social History Project (Toronto, 1976), 109; Michael B. Katz, Michael J. Doucet, and Mark J. Stern, *The Social Organization of Early Industrial Capitalism* (Cambridge, Mass., 1982), pp. 57–8.

19. Horton, et al., *History of Northwestern New York*, vol. 1, p. 106; Buffalo *Courier*, June 12, 1852; Buffalo *Commercial Advertiser*, April 28, 1854; January 25, 1860; Buffalo *Christian Advocate*, March 15, 1855; May 5, 1859.

20. Buffalo *Courier*, February 5, 1853.

21. J. W. Hill and J. H. Colen, artists, *Buffalo*, lithograph, 1853; and Charles Magnus, publisher, *Buffalo*, lithograph, [1863?] (Historic Urban Plans: Ithaca, N.Y., reproductions); *City of Buffalo*, undated lithograph (probably 1850s) in the author's possession; Peter Emslie, "Map of a Part of the City of Buffalo" (Philadelphia, 1866); Gwendolyn Wright, *Building the Dream: A Social History of Housing in America* (New York, 1981); David Handlin, *The American Home: Architecture and Society, 1815–1915* (Boston, 1979).

22. Kirk Jeffrey, "The Family as Utopian Retreat from the City," in Sallie TeSelle, ed., *The Family, Communes, and Utopian Societies* (New York, 1972), pp. 21–39.

23. Barbara Welter, "The Cult of True Womanhood: 1820–1860," *American Quarterly*, 18 (Summer, 1966), 151–74.

24. Glasco, *Ethnicity and Social Structure*, pp. 158–9.

25. Mary P. Ryan, *Cradle of the Middle Class: The Family in Oneida County, New York, 1790–1865* (New York, 1981), pp. 160–1, 177.

26. Buffalo *Courier*, November 28, 1848. The absence of this scene from his home after the death of his first wife in 1838 was an ever present theme in the diary of Dr. Bryant Burwell until his 1845 remarriage.

27. Glasco, *Ethnicity and Social Structure*, pp. 193–9, 203–10. Age nineteen was the last age at which more than 50 percent of American men and women resided in their parental household. An interethnic comparison of those living at home at nineteen yields, for women, 51.5 percent (American), 10.5 percent (Irish), 22.2 percent (German); for men, 59.2 percent (American); 50 percent (Irish); 45 percent (German). There are no data dividing ethnic groups by class, but inferences may be made on the basis of the fact that ethnic youth often left home to become servants and apprentices, patterns absent among bourgeois families.

28. Smith, *History of the City of Buffalo and Erie County, New York*, vol. 2, p. 323; Buffalo *Courier*, August 6, 1851; *Register, Buffalo Female Academy, 1857–1858*, NYHS; Oliver G. Steele, "The Buffalo Common Schools," Buffalo Historical Society *Publications*, 1 (1879), 418.

29. Rev. John Chase Lord, *An Address to Young Women* (Newburyport, Mass., 1837), p. 11; Buffalo *Commercial Advertiser*, September 13, 1852. Charles West, *Address* (New York, 1851), pp. 3–4; *First Annual Circular and Catalogue, Buffalo Female Academy* (Buffalo, 1852), p.10; *An Address Delivered before the Patrons and Pupils of the Buffalo Female Academy* (Buffalo, 1852), p. 25.

30. Carroll Smith-Rosenberg's "Beauty, the Beast, and the Militant Woman: A Case Study in Sex Roles and Social Stress in Jacksonian America," *American Quarterly*, 23 (1971), 562–84.

31. Katz, et al., "Migration and the Social Order," 690–1.

32. E.g., Buffalo *Christian Advocate*, March 14, 1850.

33. Note 27, above.

34. Nancy Ciliberti, "Irish Domestic Servants in Buffalo, New York during the Nineteenth Century" (seminar paper, SUNYAB, 1981), 28.

35. Welch, *Home History*, p. 170; Hawley, "Merwin Spencer Hawley: Autobiography," 16–18 and passim.

36. Buffalo *Commercial Advertiser*, October 7, 1859.

37. "From late November to March or April, Buffalo was virtually isolated. It lapsed into the character of a winter-bound, remote country village," said two historians of the Buffalo of the 1840s and 1850s. "Men whose business drove them mercilessly during the summer months had little to do in the winter months but prepare for the coming season." Lloyd Graham and Frank Severance, *The First Hundred Years of the Buffalo Chamber of Commerce* (Buffalo, 1945), p. 31.

38. Buffalo, *Commercial Advertiser*, October 7, 1859; Merwin S. Hawley to Elijah Hawley, January 25, 1851; February 24, 1852, Hawley Papers, BECHS.

39. Buffalo *Commercial Advertiser*, October 7, 1859; Rev. Grosvenor Heacock, *Sermon Preached at Central Presbyterian Church, March 20, 1859—Subject: The Christian Law of Amusements* (Buffalo, 1859).

40. Merwin S. Hawley to Elijah Hawley, February 24, 1852, Hawley Papers, BECHS; Carroll Smith-Rosenberg, "The Female World of Love and Ritual: Relations between Women in Nineteenth-Century America," *Signs*, 1 (Autumn, 1975), 1–29.

41. James Silk Buckingham, *America: Historical, Statistical, and Descriptive*, vol. 3 (London, 1841), pp. 38–9; Busby Torrey to Charles Grandison Finney, February 28, 1831, quoted in Whitney Cross, *The Burned-Over District: The Social and Intellectual History of Enthusiastic Religion in Western New York, 1800–1850* (Ithaca, 1950), p. 155.

42. Buffalo *Christian Advocate*, February 6, 1851; February 24, 1853; April 3, 1856; January 14, 28, February 4, 18, March 11, 18, 25, July 15, 1858.

43. Ibid., April 1, 1858.

44. Ibid., November 13, 1851. For such expressions of bourgeois piety, see Hawley, "Merwin S. Hawley: Autobiography," 14; and Hawley to Mary Hawley, July 28, 1843, Hawley Papers, BECHS; "George Tifft," in Smith, *History of Buffalo and Erie County, New York*, vol. 2, pp. 104–8 (biographical section).

45. Smith, *History of Buffalo and Erie County, New York*, vol. 2, pp. 276–81, 285–9, 291–301; Horton, et al., *History of Northwestern New York*, vol. 1, pp. 121–2; Buffalo *Courier*, December 29, 1847.

46. Buffalo *Christian Advocate*, December 5, 1850.

47. Max Weber, *The Protestant Ethic and the Spirit of Capitalism* (Chicago, n.d.); R. H. Tawney, *Religion and the Rise of Capitalism* (London, 1926); Charles Brooks, "John C. Lord and Old School Presbyterian Thought in Buffalo, 1837-1864" (seminar paper, SUNYAB, 1980), 10-7.

48. Horton, et al., *History of Northwestern New York*, vol. 1, p. 121; George E. DeMille, *St. Paul's Cathedral, Buffalo, 1817-1867: A Brief History* (Buffalo, 1966), pp. 48, 208-9; Buffalo *Courier*, April 2, 1850; Buffalo *Commercial Advertiser*, April 9, 1855; April 14, 1857; April 9, 10, 11, 1860; Buffalo *Christian Advocate*, April 19, 1855; April 4, 1860; "Pew Owners, 1850," St. Paul's Protestant Episcopal Church Collection, BECHS.

49. Burwell, Diary, 1846, entry of March 18, 1846, BECHS; Buffalo *Christian Advocate*, September 25, 1856; May 7, 1857; September 2 (quotation), November 11, 1858.

50. DeMille, *St. Paul's Cathedral, Buffalo*, pp. 38, 42, 46-7, 49; Buffalo *Christian Advocate*, July 15, 1858; [declarations of intentions to form congregations, February 10, 1817], St. Paul's Episcopal Church, Scrapbook, 1817-1830; and February 19, 1845, St. John's Protestant Episcopal Church Collection, BECHS. All of the city's Episcopal churches held elections annually for wardens and vestrymen, and these were reported in the daily and evangelical press; see note 48, above.

51. Sandford B. Hunt, *Methodism in Buffalo* (Buffalo, 1893), p. 30; Cross, *The Burned-Over District*, p. 45; Buffalo *Commercial Advertiser*, March 18, 1836; *Memorial to George W. Hosmer* (Buffalo, 1882), p. 83; Rev. J. H. Martyn, *A Narrative of the Origin and Progress of the First Free Congregational Church in Buffalo, N.Y.* (Buffalo, 1834); Ellis, "The Yankee Invasion of New York," 14-5.

52. John G. Ramsey, "From Self-Educating Boosters to Stewards of Culture: Buffalo's Friends of Education," vol. 1 (Ph.D. dissertation, SUNYAB, 1984), pp. 40, 137-40.

53. Buffalo *Commercial Advertiser*, January 13, 1847; Buffalo *Courier*, February 17, December 5, June 19, 1852.

54. Ryan, *Cradle of the Middle Class*, p. 129.

55. Welch, *Home History*, pp. 340-7 (quotation); Horton, et al., *History of Northwestern New York*, vol. 1, p. 112; Ramsey, "From Self-Educating Boosters to Stewards of Culture," vol. 1, pp. 250-2; Buffalo *Mercantile Courier*, November 16, 1842; Buffalo *Courier*, February 10, 1848.

56. Smith, *History of Buffalo and Erie County, New York*, vol. 2, pp. 411-2; Buffalo *Courier*, July 18, 1849; February 2, 1852; Ryan, *Cradle of the Middle Class*, p. 177.

57. Welch, *Home History*, p. 84; *Semi-Centennial, Central Presbyterian Church: Addresses and Discourse, 1835-1885* (Buffalo, 1886), p. 30; Buffalo *Courier*, December 3, 1850; August 27, 1852.

58. Paul Boyer, *Urban Masses and Moral Order in America, 1820-1920* (Cambridge, Mass., 1978), pp. 108-19; Smith, *History of Buffalo and Erie County, New York*, vol. 2, pp. 537-8; Young Men's Christian Association,

Third Annual Report, 1855 (Buffalo, 1855), p. 138; Buffalo *Christian Advocate*, March 6, 1856; March 5, 1857; March 11, 1858; January 27, 1859.

59. Smith, *History of Buffalo and Erie County, New York*, vol. 2, pp. 351–412.

60. Buffalo *Courier*, January 29, 1849 (Seamen's Bethel); February 13, 1850 (poor relief); Buffalo *Commercial Advertiser*, January 13, 1847 (orphanage); March 13, 1854 (hospital); Buffalo *Christian Advocate*, December 25, 1856 (Bible); *Commercial Advertiser Directory of Buffalo, 1850* (Buffalo, 1850), pp. 37 (university), 44 (temperance).

61. Buffalo *Courier*, March 18, April 10, December 19, 1850; April 12, 1852; Buffalo *Commercial Advertiser*, January 22, 1851. Calculations of the number of those deriving income from alcohol production or trade are based on: "Buffalo Business Directory," *Commercial Advertiser Directory of Buffalo, 1855* (Buffalo, 1855), pp. 269–95, passim; New York State, *Manufacturing Census of Buffalo, 1855* (in Laurence A. Glasco's possession).

62. Paula Baker, "The Domestication of Politics: Women and American Political Society, 1780–1920," *American Historical Review*, 89 (June, 1984), 621, 647, is right in suggesting that whatever the outcome of particular struggles, the larger historical importance of these women's activities was that they pioneered in developing political tactics for disfranchised people.

63. *Commercial Advertiser Directory of Buffalo, 1850*, p. 41.

64. Buffalo *Courier*, January 18, 1850; Buffalo *Commercial Advertiser*, April 10, June 12, 1854; November 7, December 16, 1856; March 27, October 8, 1857; January 15, March 8, April 20, 1858; April 11, 1859.

65. Ryan, *Cradle of the Middle Class*, p. 215.

66. Buffalo *Courier*, June 25, 1847. Also Buffalo *Commercial Advertiser*, January 25, 1840 (for the look of "Our Fifth Avenue," Delaware Avenue).

67. Ibid., May 27, 1847.

68. Buffalo *Courier*, January 4, April 28, 1851; Buffalo *Commercial Advertiser*, November 28, 1853; Robert J. Rayback, *Millard Fillmore: Biography of a President* (Buffalo, 1959), p. 407; Rev. Thomas Donohue, *History of the Catholic Church in Western New York* (Buffalo, 1904), pp. 200-1, 319–24.

69. Buffalo *Commercial Advertiser*, June 4, 1857; Horton, et al., *History of Northwestern New York*, vol. 1, p. 164; *Fifth Annual Festival of the Old Settlers of Buffalo* (Buffalo, 1868), p. 13.

70. Buffalo *Commercial Advertiser*, June 4, 1857. (Ibid., February 2, 1854, for a similar defense of elite cultural aspirations.)

71. *Fifth Annual Festival of the Old Settlers of Buffalo*, p. 13.

72. Buffalo *Republic*, July 31, 1855.

73. Buffalo *Commercial Advertiser*, December 7, 1844; Buffalo *Courier*, January 4, 1848.

74. This pride was evident, for example, in the pleasure taken in the large number of patents owned by local manufacturers and craftsmen; *Manufacturing Interests of the City of Buffalo* (Buffalo, 1866), pp. 94–6.

75. Buffalo *Commercial Advertiser*, December 7, 1844; Buffalo *Courier*, January 4, 1848.

76. On the "revolutionary" nature of capitalism, see Sheldon S. Wolin, "Editorial," *democracy*, 2 (Fall, 1982), 3; and Charles Douglass Lummis, "The Radicalism of Democracy," ibid., 13; as well as Peter L. Berger, *The Capitalist Revolution: Fifty Propositions about Prosperity, Equality, and Liberty* (New York, 1986), p. 3 and passim.

77. Buffalo *Courier*, March 15, 1850; June 21, 1851; Buffalo *Commercial Advertiser*, December 31, 1857; February 10, 14, 15, 17, 1860.

78. Buffalo *Christian Advocate*, January 10, 1850; June 17, 1858.

79. Dr. Austin Flint, "The Principles of Public and Private Charity," quoted extensively in Buffalo *Mercantile Courier*, February 6, 1844; Buffalo *Commercial Advertiser*, November 14, 1857; John Garraty, *Unemployment in History* (New York, 1978), pp. 114–6.

80. The *Commercial Advertiser*, November 14, 1857, carefully outlined the principles of this political economy during the gloomy days of the 1857–58 depression.

81. Horton, et al., *History of Northwestern New York*, vol. 1, p. 126; Buffalo *Commercial Advertiser*, August 17, 21, 1844; January 14, 1847; Buffalo *Courier*, September 6, 1851.

82. Buffalo *Courier*, January 18, 1850.

83. Buffalo *Commercial Advertiser*, December 23, 27, 29, 31, 1856; Buffalo *Courier*, January 7, 1857; Buffalo *Demokrat und Weltbürger*, December 24, 27, 29, 1856.

84. Buffalo *Commercial Advertiser*, October 17, 1844; October 31, 1846; February 24, March 6, July 21, December 4, 1854; November 30, 1859; November 22, 1860; Buffalo *Courier*, February 6, 1844; October 16, 1849; July 28, September 20, 1852. See also Joan Underhill Hannon, "Poor Policy in Antebellum New York State: The Rise and Decline of the Poorhouse," *Explorations in Economic History*, 22 (1985), 233–56.

85. Buffalo *Commercial Advertiser*, December 24, 1856. For the same point—wealth and its redemption: the *Christian Advocate*, April 11, 1850; March 4, 1852; September 14, 1854; July 2, 1857. See also the concise statement in John Higham, "The Immigrant in American History," in *Send These to Me*, ed. idem (Baltimore, 1984), p. 24.

86. Ramsey, "From Self-Educating Boosters to Stewards of Culture," vol. 2, p. 204. Lord later changed his mind in the belief that a common public school system was required in a society as pluralistic as the United States; Buffalo *Express*, November 22, 1861.

87. Ramsey, "From Self-Educating Boosters to Stewards of Culture," vol. 1, pp. 94–163, 202ff.; Horton, et al., *History of Northwestern New York*, vol. 1, pp. 83–4; Oliver G. Steele, "The Buffalo Common Schools," Buffalo Historical Society *Publications*, 1 (1879), 408–31.

88. Subjects to be dealt with extensively in Part Four. The outlines of this tension have been set down with skill in Marvin Myers, *The Jacksonian Persuasion: Politics and Belief* (Stanford, 1957); and David Brion Davis, "Some Themes of Counter-Subversion: An Analysis of Anti-Masonic, Anti-Catholic, and Anti-Mormon Literature," *Mississippi Valley Historical Review*, 47 (September, 1960), 205–24.

89. Buffalo *Christian Advocate*, December 20, 1855; and also, March 6, 1856.
90. Ralph Barton Perry, *Puritanism and Democracy* (New York, 1944), pp. 247-9, 259-63, 283-5, and passim.
91. Buffalo *Courier and Pilot*, July 22, 1846.
92. Buffalo *Republic*, May 22, 1854, endorsed "female suffrage" on the well-charted ground of contemporary gender ideology: its potential "purifying effect." But under different editorship (August 18, 1858) it withdrew its support. The paper consistently supported women entering the medical profession, but would limit their practice to obstetrics and women's diseases (May 22, 1854; July 11, 1857; August 18, 1858).
93. Horton, et al., *History of Northwestern New York*, vol. 1, p. 105; Smith, *History of Buffalo and Erie County, New York*, vol. 2, p. 332. Buffalo's Democratic mainstream conformed to the ideology of the party statewide, except in regard to government funding of internal improvements; see Judah B. Ginsberg, "The Tangled Web: The New York State Democratic Party and the Slavery Controversy, 1844-1860" (Ph.D. dissertation, University of Wisconsin, 1974), 1-26, 326-30.
94. Horton, et al., *History of Northwestern New York*, vol. 1, pp. 128-42; Buffalo *Christian Advocate*, March 4, 1852.
95. Horton, et al., *History of Northwestern New York*, vol. 1, pp. 109, 126, 133, 141; Smith, *History of the City of Buffalo and Erie County, New York*, vol. 2, p. 458; Samuel Wilkeson, Jr., to John W. Wilkeson, September 19, 1853, Wilkeson-Berringer Collection, BECHS.
96. Elwin H. Powell, "Street as School: Ideas and Assembly in Buffalo, Seen through the Diary of George Washington Johnson (1835-1849)," *Urban Education*, 18 (January, 1984), 413-25; Buffalo *Republic*, November 22, 1853; Buffalo *Republic and Times*, January 22, 23, 25-29, February 1, 2, 4, 6, 1858; George Washington Johnson, Diary, 1841, entry of November 30; Diary, 1858, entries of January-April passim (anti-Sabbatarian and antirevival thoughts and activities); Diary, 1859, entries of April 2, September 18, DC.

Chapter 5. Clerks, Shopkeepers, and Artisans: Americans, Canadians, and Britons

1. Laurence A. Glasco, *Ethnicity and Social Structure: Irish, Germans, and Native-Born of Buffalo, N.Y. 1850-1860* (New York, 1980), p. 20. In addition, there were seventeen Welsh-born heads of households and six more for whom "Great Britain" was given as a birthplace.
2. Ibid., p. 94; Roland Berthoff, *British Immigrants in Industrial America, 1790-1950* (Cambridge, Mass., 1953), p. 21; Michael B. Katz, "The Structure of Inequality and Length of Residence in Buffalo, New York, 1855," Working Paper #13, of the York Social History Project (Toronto, 1976), 98-9; R. G. Dun and Co., New York, vol. 80, pp. 6 (Tho.), 30 (Jam.), 47 (Row.), 81 (McC.), 148 (Had.), 234 (Mur.), 360 (Gle.), 396 (Mur.); and vol. 81, p. 42 (Gle.), R. G. Dun and Company Collection, BL.
3. Berthoff, *British Immigrants in Industrial America*, pp. 184-5; Leon E. Truesdell, *The Canadian-Born in the United States: An Analysis of the Ca-*

nadian Element in the Population of the United States, 1850–1930 (New Haven, 1943).

4. Buffalo *Commercial Advertiser*, June 14, 1858; Buffalo *Express*, June 14, 1858; Christopher McGimpsey, "Internal Ethnic Conflict: Orange and Green in Nineteenth Century New York, 1868–1872," *Immigrants and Minorities*, 1 (March, 1982), 42–3. The very largely Catholic, Friendly Sons of St. Patrick appears to have had a few Scots-Irish members, on the basis of such surnames as "Rose," "Hamilton," and "Butler" on its rosters (Buffalo *Sentinel*, February 25, 1860; March 23, 1861), just as this fraternal lodge did in other American cities (Joan Gosnell, Irish-American Historical Society to author, April 5, 1984). Also see John Higham, "Les Deux Irlandes en Amerique," *Critique* (June–July, 1982), 619–20.

5. The social bases of these societies were determined by tracing in annual city directories and the 1855 state census alphabetized printout (SUNYAB) lists of officers, managers, and participants found in Buffalo *Courier*, November 16, December 7, 1850; November 13, December 8, 1852; Buffalo *Commercial Advertiser*, April 19, 1855; March 29, 1856.

6. The annual April St. George's Day and December St. Andrew's Day banquets were reported in remarkable detail for many years; see, e.g., Buffalo *Commercial Advertiser*, December 2, 1844; December 3, April 24, 1846; Buffalo *Courier*, February 20, 1847; April 28, 1849; December 7, 1850; December 8, 1852. For the other activities of these societies: *Commercial Advertiser*, February 17, 1847; January 22, 1856; July 31, August 3, 1857; January 25, March 3, January 26, May 29, 1859.

7. James McKay, "An Exploratory Synthesis of Primordial and Mobilizationist Approaches to Ethnic Phenomena," *Ethnic and Racial Studies*, 5 (October, 1982), 407–8.

8. See note 6, above, for dates of representative banquets and reporting of the toasts. For one of the examples of politicization—over the Scottish established church—see Buffalo *Commercial Advertiser*, December 2, 4, 1844.

9. Buffalo *Mercantile Courier*, December 6, 1842; December 11, 1843. As memories of the Old World dimmed, so, too, perhaps did the possibilities for conjuring up the state of mind the evening required. Thus, a few ethnic symbols eventually might become the substance of such ethnicity: it would not be long before these Scots and their American children, now in the ranks of "old settlers," would be showing up at their *American* communal festivities in kilts to sing "Auld Lang Syne"; *Fifth Annual Festival of the Old Settlers of Buffalo* (Buffalo, 1868), p. 12.

10. Berthoff, *British Immigrants in Industrial America*, pp. 184–5.

11. Glasco, *Ethnicity and Social Structure*, pp. 64–7. On the cultural adjustment of British and Canadian immigrants, see Berthoff, *British Immigrants in Industrial America*, pp. 127–34.

12. George E. DeMille, *St. Paul's Cathedral, Buffalo, 1817–1967: A Brief History* (Buffalo, 1966), pp. 46–7; Berthoff, *British Immigrants in Industrial America*, pp. 151–6.

13. Buffalo *Mercantile Courier*, August 4, 1843; Buffalo *Commercial Advertiser*, April 10, July 20, 1844; Berthoff, *British Immigrants in Industrial America*, pp. 133, 156–7.

14. See note 6, above (for Americans at banquets); Buffalo *Commercial Advertiser*, July 31, August 3, 1857; March 3, 1858; May 26, 1859; Berthoff, *British Immigrants in Industrial America*, p. 179; William J. Baker, *Sports in the Western World* (Totowa, N.J., 1982), pp. 138–43.

15. Buffalo *Mercantile Courier*, January 5, March 1, 1844.

16. Berthoff, *British Immigrants in Industrial America*, p. 131; Buffalo *Courier*, June 26, 1847; Buffalo *Republic*, June 20, 1853. For a guardedly positive characterization of the English in the German press (the only one found for the entire period), see Buffalo *Demokrat und Weltbürger*, April 26, 1854.

17. Buffalo *Express*, June 14, 1858; Berthoff, *British Immigrants in Industrial America*, pp. 133, 188–94.

18. Arthur Mann, *The One and the Many: Reflections on the American Identity* (Chicago, 1979), p. 55.

19. Ibid., pp. 56–7.

20. John Higham, "The Immigrant in American History," in *Send These to Me*, ed. idem (Baltimore, 1984), p. 20.

21. Dr. Bryant Burwell, Diary, 1838, entry of October 28, Burwell-Glenny Collection, BECHS.

22. Buffalo *Courier*, April 3, 1849; February 14, 1851.

23. Ibid., December 18, 1846; September 20, 1847; October 29, 1849; February 12, 27, 1851; Buffalo *Republic*, June 8, 1853; March 17, 1854; Buffalo *Christian Advocate*, May 30, July 27, 1858; November 8, 1860; Buffalo *Commercial Advertiser*, December 29, 1859.

24. Buffalo *Courier*, November 28, 1853; Buffalo *Commercial Advertiser*, November 30, December 22, 1853; December 20, 1856; June 9, December 4, 1858; December 31, 1859; New England Society of Buffalo, "Constitution and Members," vol. 1 [1853], BECHS; "Old Settlers Festival," January 6, 1865 [announcement], James D. Sawyer Papers, BECHS; *Seventy-fifth Anniversary of the Founding of the Buffalo Historical Society* (Buffalo, 1937), pp. 1–27.

25. Buffalo *Commercial Advertiser*, October 6, 1857; January 23, 1858; Buffalo *Republic and Times*, August 11–18, 23, September 2, 1858; Buffalo *Republic*, September 15, 17, 1860.

26. Buffalo *Republic*, June 9, 1853; Buffalo *Commercial Advertiser*, February 22, 1856; June 16, 21, 1860. The second annual banquet of the New England Society was canceled, the *Commercial Advertiser* (December 19, 1854) said, because of "the unusual absorption of the community in business," even after the close of the navigation season. In addition, no one had been chosen to find an orator, in spite there of having been a year to do so.

27. See below, chapter 11.

28. In Buffalo and New York State, this Whig viewpoint was first articulated in the late 1830s, and reached its earliest crescendo during and after the 1844 election. Its resurgence in the mid-1850s was related to the rise of political nativism. Buffalo *Weltbürger*, June 30, 1838; Buffalo *Commercial Advertiser and Journal*, October 18, 1842; Buffalo *Commercial Advertiser*, May 13, October 22, 30, 1844; Louis D. Scisco, *Political Nativism in New York State* (New York, 1901), pp. 39–58.

29. See chapter 12, pp. 386–90, below.

30. John T. Horton, Edward T. Williams, and Harry S. Douglass, *History of Northwestern New York*, vol. 1 (New York, 1947), pp. 149–50; Buffalo *Courier*, June 15, 1854.

31. See, chapter 12, pp. 372, 377–83, below.

32. Horton, et al., *History of Northwestern New York*, vol. 1, p. 190; Glasco, *Ethnicity and Social Structure*, pp. 226–318; chapter 12, below.

33. Glasco, *Ethnicity and Social Structure*, pp. 92, 94, 97; Stuart Blumin, "The Hypothesis of Middle Class Formation in Nineteenth Century America: A Critique and Some Proposals," *American Historical Review*, 90 (April, 1985), 312–8.

34. Buffalo *Courier*, December 10, 1850; May 6, 1851; Buffalo *Commercial Advertiser*, April 9, 1857; August 5, 1858; *Commercial Advertiser City Directory of Buffalo, 1855* (Buffalo, 1855), pp. 16–7 (banks) and passim. The 1851, 1857, and 1858 directories were also used to identify names.

35. *The Manufacturing Interests of the City of Buffalo* (Buffalo, 1866), pp. 36–62, passim.

36. John G. Ramsey, "From Self-Educating Boosters to Stewards of Culture: Buffalo's Friends of Education," vol. 1 (Ph.D. dissertation, SUNYAB, 1984), pp. 31–2; Buffalo *Courier*, May 29, 1852.

37. Buffalo *Commercial Advertiser*, March 18, 1844.

38. H. Perry Smith, ed., *History of the City of Buffalo and Erie County, New York* (Syracuse, 1884), vol. 2, p. 324; Buffalo *Christian Advocate*, April 16, 1856.

39. Glasco, *Ethnicity and Social Structure*, p. 68.

40. *Commercial Advertiser Directory of Buffalo, 1855*, pp. 17, 19, 20, 22, 23–25; Blumin, "The Hypothesis of Middle Class Formation," 332–3.

41. Buffalo *Commercial Advertiser*, December 10, 1846; December 13, 1855; December 10, 1857; December 15, 1859; Buffalo *Courier*, December 15, 1843; *Commercial Advertiser Directory of Buffalo, 1850* (Buffalo, 1850); alphabetized printout, *New York State Census, 1855*, SUNYAB.

42. The relief association: Buffalo *Courier*, January 17, February 13, 1850; December 27, 1851; August 6, 1852; January 10, 1853; Buffalo *Commercial Advertiser*, January 17, 1857; *Buffalo City Directory, 1857* (Buffalo, 1857); the temperance society: Buffalo *Republic*, September 10, 1853; *Commercial Advertiser Directory of Buffalo, 1850*, pp. 44–6.

43. Every alderman in the city's history, up to 1883, is listed in Smith, *History of Buffalo and Erie County, New York*, vol. 2, pp. 133–47, and these lists for the American wards were checked against city directories in search of the identities of more obscure individuals. See also: Ryrie E. MacTaggart, "A Labor History of Buffalo (1846–1917), Containing an Introduction Consisting of Conditions Prior to '46" (Master's thesis, Canisius College, 1940), 19–20.

44. See above, note 34; Buffalo *Commercial Advertiser and Journal*, February 18, 1843; Buffalo *Commercial Advertiser*, March 1, 1844; March 6, 1856; March 5, 1857; Buffalo *Courier*, January 19, 1847; July 10, 1849; May 14, 1851; *Commercial Advertiser Directory of Buffalo, 1855*, pp. 19–20, 22–3, and passim. City directories were consulted for 1843, 1844, 1847, 1849, and 1851 to establish individual identities; also used was the alphabetized printout of

the *New York State Census, 1855* (SUNYAB). See, too, Blumin, "The Hypothesis of Middle Class Formation," 334–5.

45. Glasco, *Ethnicity and Social Structure*, pp. 133, 137; Michael B. Katz, Michael J. Doucet, and Mark J. Stern, *The Social Organization of Early Industrial Capitalism* (Cambridge, Mass., 1982), pp. 106, 147.

46. Buffalo *Commercial Advertiser*, May 17, 21, 1844; Susan E. Hirsch, *The Roots of the American Working Class: The Industrialization of Crafts in Newark, 1800–1860* (Philadelphia, 1978), pp. 8–10, 43–7, 74–5.

47. Glasco, *Ethnicity and Social Structure*, p. 61.

48. Ibid., pp. 165–78.

49. Not until the late 1850s was extensive erosion of the traditional pattern of separation of work and home among blue-collar workers noted: Buffalo *Commercial Advertiser*, n.d., in Buffalo *Demokrat und Weltbürger*, July 15, 1858; Buffalo *Christian Advocate*, October 11, 1860.

50. A concise analysis of this culture is found in Richard J. Oestreicher, "Industrialization, Class, and Competing Cultural Systems: Detroit Workers, 1875–1900," in *German Workers in Industrial Chicago, 1850–1910: A Comparative Perspective*, ed. Hartmut Keil and John B. Jentz (DeKalb, Ill., 1983), pp. 61–7.

51. Verna G. Walker, "Banking in Buffalo before the Civil War" (Master's thesis, University of Buffalo, 1933), 89, 105–10; Buffalo *Commercial Advertiser*, March 17, 1858. As Walker demonstrates from available data, these banks were mostly successful from the start on the basis of small and moderate accounts. Three of them became permanent fixtures in local banking. A fourth, founded by and for Catholic immigrants, soon failed.

52. Horton, et al., *History of Northwestern New York*, vol. 1, pp. 81–2; Welch, *Home History*, pp. 209–18; Buffalo *Mercantile Courier*, March 20, 1848; Buffalo *Courier*, March 14, 22, 1849.

53. Buffalo *Commercial Advertiser*, January 17, 18, 1842; January 11, 1843; July 12, 1844; January 9, 1845; August 24, 1854; Buffalo *Mercantile Courier*, July 17, 1844; Buffalo *Courier*, January 10, April 29 (quotation), 1847; Mark Goldman, *High Hopes: The Rise and Decline of Buffalo, New York* (Albany, 1983), pp. 39–40, 42–4.

54. Ramsey, "From Self-Educating Boosters to Stewards of Culture," vol. 1, pp. 48–92; Horton, et al., *History of Northwestern New York*, vol. 1, pp. 82–3; Goldman, *High Hopes*, p. 40.

55. Ramsey, "From Self-Educating Boosters to Stewards of Culture," 19.

56. Ibid., 53–4, 123.

57. Buffalo *Christian Advocate*, February 6, 1851; April 3, 1856; January 14, February 18, March 18, 1858. The evangelical paper (July 15, 1858) reported, on the basis of data provided by the individual congregations at the end of the 1858 revival, 358 conversions for the American Methodists, 251 for the Presbyterians, and 135 for the Baptists. Though I disagree with some of it, a well-argued interpretation of revivalism as social control imposed by a socioeconomic elite is found in Paul E. Johnson, *A Shopkeeper's Millennium: Society and Revivals in Rochester, New York, 1815–1837* (New York, 1978).

58. Buffalo *Christian Advocate*, February 28, 1850; *Commercial Advertiser Directory of Buffalo, 1850*, pp. 45-6; *Commercial Advertiser Directory of Buffalo, 1855*, pp. 21-2.

59. Buffalo *Christian Advocate*, February 28, October 17, November 28, 1850; Buffalo *Courier*, February 21, 1850; March 2, 1854; *Commercial Advertiser Directory of Buffalo, 1850*, pp. 45-6 and passim (for occupations and identities).

60. Signers, with pledge, dated February 21, 1850, John B. Gough Papers, AAS. Names were checked in the local returns of the 1850 federal census, for which there is an alphabetized typescript, NYSA.

61. Mary P. Ryan, *Cradle of the Middle Class: The Family in Oneida County, New York, 1790-1865* (New York, 1981), p. 135; and Peter Bailey, "Will the Real Bill Banks Please Stand Up?: Towards a Role Analysis of Mid-Victorian Working Class Respectability," *Journal of Social History*, 12 (1979), 336-52, whose analysis is closely confirmed by the Buffalo *Commercial Advertiser*, September 8, 1856, portrait of the life-style and workaday values of perhaps the most elite craftsmen, the ship carpenters, the majority of whom were American, British, or Canadian.

62. Ryan, *Cradle of the Middle Class*, p. 135.

63. Buffalo *Courier*, November 28, 1853; Buffalo *Commercial Advertiser*, September 2, 1858.

64. Two of the six were born in Ireland, but had what seem to be Anglo-Saxon names—P. E. Camp and George Wilson. The seventh was born in Germany.

65. Buffalo *Courier*, June 16, 24, 1851; Buffalo *Christian Advocate*, July 2, 1851; Welch, *Home History*, pp. 353-4.

66. Buffalo *Courier*, June 10, 1847; July 27, 1850; July 24, 1854; Buffalo *Christian Advocate*, June 24, 1852.

67. Bailey, "Will the Real Bill Banks Please Stand Up?" 337.

Part Three. Introduction: Mass Immigration, Ethnicity, and Group Formation

1. For discussions of the relations between ethnicity and pluralistic society, see Pierre Van den Berghe, *Race and Ethnicity* (New York, 1970), especially pp. 14, 16; and Milton Yinger, "Ethnicity and Social Change: The Interaction of Structural, Cultural, and Personality Factors," *Ethnic and Racial Studies*, 6 (October, 1983), 395. On the evolution of Buffalo's Fourth of July celebration, see Buffalo *Patriot*, July 3, 20, 1821; Buffalo *Emporium*, July 29, 1826; Buffalo *Daily Buffalonian*, June 12, 1839; Buffalo *Weltbürger*, July 4, 1840; April 27, 1844; June 30, 1847; Buffalo *Courier*, July 3, 13, 1847; June 30, 1849; June 29, July 1, 1850; June 21, 1851; June 4, July 5, 1852; June 23, 1853; Buffalo *Sentinel*, July 11, 1857; Buffalo *Commercial Advertiser*, June 16, 26, July 3, 1858; July 5, 1859; July 2, 1860; Buffalo *Demokrat und Weltbürger*, June 17, 21, 1859.

2. Of the many surveys, see Marcus Lee Hansen, *The Atlantic Migration, 1607-1860* (New York, 1961, paperback ed.); Maldwyn Allen Jones, *American*

Immigration (Chicago, 1960), pp. 92–146; Philip Taylor, *The Distant Magnet: European Emigration to the U.S.A.* (New York, 1971), pp. 1–47; Terry Coleman, *Going to America* (New York, 1973).

3. Rev. John Timon, *Missions in Western New York and Church History of the Diocese of Buffalo* (Buffalo, 1862), p. 215.

4. Laurence A. Glasco, *Ethnicity and Social Structure: Irish, Germans, and Native-Born of Buffalo, N.Y., 1850–1860* (New York, 1980), pp. 20, 60; Buffalo *Courier and Pilot*, November 25, 1846.

5. See, for example, Ulf Beijbom, *Swedes in Chicago: A Demographic and Social Study of the 1846–1880 Immigration* (Vaxjo, Sweden, 1971); Kathleen Neils Conzen, *Immigrant Milwaukee, 1836–1860: Accommodation and Community in a Frontier City* (Cambridge, Mass., 1976).

6. Buffalo *Commercial Advertiser*, July 11, 1844; August 21, 1846; *Proceedings of the Erie County Board of Supervisors, 1855* (Buffalo, 1855), March 2, 1855; New York *Old Countrymen*, May 10, 1832; Glasco, *Ethnicity and Social Structure*, pp. 52–4.

7. Buffalo *Commercial Advertiser*, March 26, 1844; Buffalo *Daily Morning Courier*, December 5, 1844; Buffalo *Courier*, May 3, 1849; April 9, 1852; October 19, 1853.

8. On the stranded immigrant and the problem of runners: Samuel M. Welch, *Home History: Recollections of Buffalo, or Fifty Years Since* (Buffalo, 1891), p. 158; Buffalo *Daily Morning Courier*, May 12, June 20, July 1, 1843; Buffalo *Courier and Pilot*, August 28, September 15, 1846; Buffalo *Courier*, August 14, 25, 1847; March 26, April 10, May 2, 1849; May 9, 1851; March 12, April 3, 5, 1852; February 7, June 4, 7, 1853; Buffalo *Commercial Advertiser*, March 1, 1854; April 24, 1858; *Buffalo Medical Journal*, 3 (1847–48), 502.

9. Buffalo *Sentinel*, February 2, 1856; Buffalo *Commercial Advertiser*, January 13, 1848; January 12, 1857.

10. E.g., Buffalo *Commercial Advertiser and Journal*, June 25, September 8, 1842; Buffalo *Commercial Advertiser*, January 17, 1847; Buffalo *Courier*, March 3, 1847; November 19, 1849; August 24, 1850.

11. Buffalo *Courier*, July 14, August 28, 1849; September 6, 16, 25, 1852; Buffalo *Commercial Advertiser*, February 9, June 19, July 31, August 22, December 12, 1854.

12. New York *Irish-American*, July 28, 1855, quoting Sharp from the New York *Herald* (n.d.); Richard H. Leach, "The Impact of Immigration on New York, 1840–1860," *New York History*, 31 (1950), 15–30; Marvin A. Rapp, "The Port of Buffalo, 1825–1880" (Ph.D. dissertation, Duke University, 1947), 216–7; Buffalo *Courier*, October 15, 1847; January 17, February 28, April 24, July 13, 1848; June 19, 27, 30, 1851; Buffalo *Commercial Advertiser*, August 13, 1855; April 24, 1858.

13. The activities of the Commissioners of Immigration are summarized in Leach, "The Impact of Immigration on New York, 1840–1860," 15–30. Also, see David M. Schneider, *The History of Public Welfare in New York State, 1609–1866* (Montclair, 1969), pp. 126–36.

14. Buffalo *Sentinel*, February 2, 1856.

15. See chapter 10, below, pp. 300–302.

16. See chapter 7, below, p. 203.
17. Milton Yinger, "Ethnicity in Complex Societies," in *The Uses of Controversy in Sociology*, ed. Lewis Coser and Otto N. Larsen (New York, 1977), p. 200.
18. On ethnicization: Victor Greene, *For God and Country: The Rise of Polish and Lithuanian Ethnic Consciousness in America, 1860–1910* (Madison, 1975), pp. 1–13; Jonathan Sarna, "From Immigrants to Ethnics: Toward a New Theory of 'Ethnicization,' " *Ethnicity* 5 (December, 1978), 370–8; Andrew M. Greeley, *Ethnicity in the United States: A Preliminary Reconnaissance* (New York, 1974), pp. 297, 301–2, 308–12, 320. For the critique of "primordialism," see Edna Bonacich, "Class Approaches to Ethnicity and Race," *Insurgent Sociologist*, 10 (Fall, 1980), 9–11, and W. L. Yancey, et al., "Emergent Ethnicity: A Review and Reformulation," *American Sociological Review*, 41 (June, 1976), 391–2. My understanding of culture has been informed by Richard A. Peterson, "Revitalizing the Culture Concept," *Annual Review of Sociology*, 5 (1979), 137–66.
19. Yancey, et al., "Emergent Ethnicity," 391–403; Bonacich, "Class Approachs to Ethnicity and Race," 9–23; Allan Dawley, "E. P. Thompson and the Peculiarities of the Americans," *Radical History Review*, 19 (Winter, 1978–79), 40–1.
20. On stereotypes, see Sander L. Gilman, *Difference and Pathology: Stereotypes of Sexuality, Race and Madness* (Ithaca, 1985), pp. 15–29.
21. Raymond Breton, "Institutional Completeness of Ethnic Communities and the Personal Relations of Immigrants," *American Journal of Sociology*, 70 (1964), 193–205; Edward O. Lauman, "The Social Structure of Religious and Ethnoreligious Groups in a Metropolitan Community," *American Sociological Review*, 34 (April, 1969), 182–97; Don Doyle, *The Social Order of a Frontier Community: Jacksonville, Illinois, 1825–1870* (Urbana, 1978), p. 178; Dawley, "E. P. Thompson and the Peculiarities of Americans," 40–1; Harold Abramson, "On the Sociology of Ethnicity and Social Change," *Economic and Social Review*, 8 (1976), 47–8.
22. Abner Cohen, *Two Dimensional Man* (Berkeley, 1974); Leon A. Despres, *Ethnicity and Resource Competition in Plural Societies* (The Hague, 1975), pp. 87–117, 188–204; Daniel Patrick Moynihan and Nathan Glazer, *Beyond the Melting Pot* (Cambridge, Mass., 1963); A. Strauss, *Negotiations—Varieties, Contexts, Processes, and Social Order* (San Francisco, 1978).
23. C. J. Calhoun, "Community: Toward a Variable Conceptualization for Comparative Research," *Social History*, 5 (1980), 105–29; Robert V. Hine, *Community on the American Frontier* (Norman, 1980); Charles Abrams, *The Language of Cities* (New York, 1971), p. 60.
24. John Higham, "Introduction: The Forms of Ethnic Leadership," in *Ethnic Leadership in America*, ed. idem (Baltimore, 1978), pp. 1–18; Penina Werbner, "The Organization of Giving and Ethnic Elites: Voluntary Associations amongst Manchester Pakistanis," *Ethnic and Racial Studies*, 8 (July, 1985), 368–85.
25. Breton, "Institutional Completeness of Ethnic Communities," 193–205; Yancey, et al., "Emergent Ethnicity," 394–9; Kathleen Neils Conzen, "Im-

migrants, Immigrant Neighborhoods, and Ethnic Identity: Historical Issues," *Journal of American History*, 66 (December, 1979), 603–15; Frederick Barth, *Ethnic Groups and Boundaries: The Social Organization of Cultural Difference* (Boston, 1969), pp. 13–6, 19–20. K. S. Nair, "Structural Pluralism and Ethnic Boundaries: An Empirical Analysis in an Indian City," *Ethnic and Racial Studies*, 6 (October, 1983), 410–1, 432, 436.

26. Oscar Handlin, *Boston's Immigrants: A Study in Acculturation* (Cambridge, Mass., 1941); idem, *The Uprooted* (Boston, 1973, 2d ed. enl.); idem, "The Social System," in *The Future Metropolis*, ed. Lloyd Rodwin (New York, 1961), p. 22; and idem, "The Modern City as a Field for Historical Study," in *The Historian and the City*, ed. Handlin and John Burchard (Cambridge, Mass., 1963), pp. 15–7.

27. Yinger, "Ethnicity and Social Change," 395.

Chapter 6. Poverty, Catholicism, and Solidarity: The Formation of Irish Ethnicity

1. Kenneth H. Connell, *Irish Peasant Society* (Oxford, 1968); and idem, "The Potato in Ireland," *Past and Present*, 40 (1968), 72–83; R. Theodore Hoppen, *Elections, Politics and Society in Ireland, 1832–1885* (New York, 1984); Kevin O'Neill, *Family and Farm in Pre-Famine Ireland: The Parish of Killshandra* (Madison, 1984); Gearoid O'Tauthaigh, *Ireland before the Famine, 1798–1848* (Dublin, 1972); Cecil Woodham-Smith, *The Great Hunger, 1845–1849* (New York, 1962); Daniel J. Casey and Robert E. Rhodes, eds., *Views of the Irish Peasantry, 1800–1916* (Hamden, Conn., 1977).

2. Patrick Carey, "Voluntaryism: An Irish Catholic Tradition," *Church History*, 48 (March, 1979), 49–62; S. J. Connolly, *Priests and People in Pre-Famine Ireland, 1780–1845* (New York, 1982); Gearoid O'Tauthaigh, "The Role of Women in Ireland under the New English Order," and J. J. Lee, "Women and the Church since the Famine," in *Women in Irish Society: The Historical Dimension*, ed. Margaret MacCurtain and Donncha O'Corrain (Westport, 1979); T. D. Williams, *Secret Societies in Ireland* (Dublin, 1973); Fergus O'Ferrall, *Catholic Emancipation: Daniel O'Connell and the Birth of Irish Democracy, 1820–30* (London, 1985).

3. Robert Kennedy, *The Irish: Emigration, Marriage, and Fertility* (Berkeley, 1973); Oliver MacDonagh, "The Irish Famine Emigration to the United States," *Perspectives in American History*, 10 (1976), 357–446; W. F. Adams, *Ireland and Irish Immigration to the New World from 1815 to the Famine* (New Haven, 1932).

4. How many Irish Protestants there were in Buffalo at any time before 1860 we shall never know, because censuses did not ask people to name their religions, only their places of birth. As was noted in chapter 5, tracings of such a population may be found. The American press used the term "Catholic Irish" frequently enough to reveal that it knew the difference between the two types of Irish. Whether it did so in recognition of a local body of "Protestant Irish,"

we do not know. It appears, however, from the absence of an organized Irish Protestant communal life that this population was quite small. Certainly *as a group*, it had no visibility in the city's public life.

5. Rev. Thomas Donohue, *History of the Diocese of Buffalo* (Buffalo, 1929), pp. 250–1, 258–9; Rev. John Timon, *Missions in Western New York and Church History of the Diocese of Buffalo* (Buffalo, 1862), p. 215; Laurence A. Glasco, *Ethnicity and Social Structure: Irish, Germans, and Native-Born of Buffalo, New York, 1850–1860* (New York, 1980), p. 41. Ronald E. Shaw, *Erie Water West: A History of the Erie Canal, 1792–1854* (Lexington, 1966), pp. 90–2, disputes this oral tradition. So did nativists in the mid-nineteenth century who considered it mere "trucking and toadying" to the Irish Catholic vote; Buffalo *Commercial Advertiser*, July 24, 1854.

6. Glasco, *Ethnicity and Social Structure*, p. 41.

7. Ibid., p. 52.

8. Ibid., p. 131.

9. The term "tragic era" is coined by R. A. Burchell in "The Historiography of the American Irish," *Immigrants and Minorities*, 1 (November, 1982), 281–94. My perspective contrasts with that of the well-conceived work of Kirby Miller, *Emigrants and Exiles: Ireland and the Irish Exodus to North America* (New York, 1985).

10. Glasco, *Ethnicity and Social Structure*, p. 60; Buffalo *Express*, June 17, 1857; Ellen Taussig, "The Irish," Buffalo *Evening News*, May 13, 1972; Buffalo *Commercial Advertiser*, October 31, 1860.

11. Mary Catherine Mattis, "The Irish Catholic Family in Buffalo, N.Y., 1855–1875: A Socio-Historical Analysis" (Ph.D. dissertation, Washington University, 1975), 101, 113; Lionel Wyld, *Low Bridge: Folklore and the Erie Canal* (Syracuse, 1962), p. 52; Buffalo *Courier*, October 21, 1844; December 22, 1847; April 10, 1850; April 26, September 27, 1851; Buffalo *Commercial Advertiser*, April 8, 11, May 2, December 16, 1856; December 16, 1857; Samuel M. Welch, *Home History: Recollections of Buffalo, or Fifty Years Since* (Buffalo, 1891), p. 11.

12. Mattis, "The Irish Catholic Family in Buffalo," 111; Glasco, *Ethnicity and Social Structure*, p. 131.

13. Dr. Bryant Burwell, Diary, 1842–1843, entry of June 14, 1843, BECHS; Buffalo *Weltbürger*, June 12, 1847; Buffalo *Commercial Advertiser*, July 14, 1857; July 12, 19, August 5, 1859; Theresa L. Wolfe, *Tifft Farm: A History of Man and Nature* (Buffalo, 1984), p. 7.

14. Mattis, "The Irish Catholic Family in Buffalo," 129, 132; H. M. Gitelman, "'No Irish Need Apply': Patterns of and Responses to Ethnic Discrimination in the Labor Market," *Labor History*, 8 (Fall, 1967), 60–1.

15. Mattis, "The Irish Catholic Family in Buffalo," 136–7; Buffalo *Commercial Advertiser*, May 30, July 5, 1844; Buffalo *Courier*, December 2, 1851; January 21, May 20, 1852; William V. Shannon, *The American Irish: A Social and Political Portrait* (New York, 1966, 2d ed.), p. 41; Gitelman, "'No Irish Need Apply,'" 63–5.

16. Mattis, "The Irish Catholic Family in Buffalo," 129–31; Glasco, *Ethnicity and Social Structure*, p. 94; John R. Commons, *Labor and Administration* (New York, 1913), pp. 269–70; Sidney H. Levy, "The Grain Scoopers of

Buffalo: An Essay in Local Labor History" (Master's thesis, University of Buffalo, 1940), 1–9; Walter B. Smith, "Wage Rates on the Erie Canal, 1828–1881," *Journal of Economic History*, 23 (1963), 298–301, 306; Buffalo *Commercial Advertiser*, December 13, 1855; contracts for canal improvements at Buffalo in the names of engineers F. D. Barton, November, 1854–May 1855; Abraham Van Slyke, November, 1854–December, 1855; C. C. Whallon, February, 1856–?, Erie Canal Records, NYSA.

17. Levy, "The Grain Scoopers of Buffalo," 4; Smith, "Wage Rates on the Erie Canal," 302–9; Mattis, "The Irish Catholic Family in Buffalo," 130; Buffalo *Courier*, February 9, 1849; John T. Horton, Edward T. Williams, and Harry S. Douglass, *History of Northwestern New York*, vol. 1 (New York, 1947), p. 87; Joseph Dart, "Ship Canal Excavation" (February 28–May 2, 1846), Day Book, n.p., BECHS; "Check Roll for October, George W. Rector, Foreman," [1856], Erie Canal Records, NYSA.

18. Buffalo *Commercial Advertiser*, October 14, 15, 1846; Buffalo *Courier and Pilot*, October 15, 1846; Buffalo *Courier*, May 23, 1848; May 13, 1853.

19. Buffalo *Commercial Advertiser and Journal*, May 4, 1841; Buffalo *Courier*, September 2, November 23, 1847; June 24, 1848; April 17, June 17, July 29, 1851; May 3, 1852; December 14, 1853; Buffalo *Commercial Advertiser*, February 3, 1855; December 12, 1856; January 7, 1858; July 23, 1859; New York *Irish-American*, May 22, 1852; Buffalo *Weltbürger*, December 7, 1850; C. H. Mason to V. S. Benton, October 31, 1857, Erie Canal Records, NYSA.

20. Mattis, "The Irish Catholic Family in Buffalo," 136–7, Hasia Diner, *Erin's Daughters in America: Irish Immigrant Women in the Nineteenth Century* (Baltimore, 1983), pp. 70–105, 115; Nancy Ciliberti, "Irish Domestic Servants in Buffalo, N.Y. during the Nineteenth Century" (seminar paper, SUNYAB, 1981), 5–9. Forty percent of American households employed servants; Glasco, *Ethnicity and Social Structure*, pp. 158–9. By contrast, only 10 percent of Irish households did.

21. Of 1,427 manufacturing jobs in wards One and Eight in 1855, 178 went to boys and in many fewer cases, girls, and forty-two to women. Data on manufactures in wards One and Eight, *New York State Census of Manufactures, 1855*. I want to thank Laurence A. Glasco for supplying me with a computer-processed rendering of these data, which are in my possession.

22. Glasco, *Ethnicity and Social Structure*, pp. 201–11; Mattis, "The Irish Catholic Family in Buffalo," 176, 188; Diner, *Erin's Daughters in America*, p. 26; Michael B. Katz, Michael J. Doucet, and Mark J. Stern, *The Social Organization of Early Industrial Capitalism* (Cambridge, Mass., 1982), pp. 263–4, 276; Ellen Horgan Biddle, "The American Catholic Irish Family," in *Ethnic Families in America: Patterns and Variations*, by Charles H. Mindel, et al. (New York, 1981, 2d ed.), pp. 91, 101.

23. Glasco, *Ethnicity and Social Structure*, pp. 212–9, 220–1; Katz, et al., *The Social Organization of Early Industrial Capitalism*, p. 276; George Washington Johnson, Diary, 1849, entry of October 23; and Diary, 1858, entries of January 2, May 24, DC; Buffalo *Commercial Advertiser*, July 12, 19, 1859.

24. Biddle, "The American Catholic Irish Family," 91, 101; Mattis, "The Irish Catholic Family in Buffalo," 36–57, 176–95; Kerby A. Miller, with Bruce

Boling and David N. Doyle, "Emigrants and Exiles: Irish Cultures and Irish Emigration to North America, 1790–1822," *Irish Historical Studies*, 22 (September, 1980), 105–8.

25. Glasco, *Ethnicity and Social Structure*, p. 152–7; St. Patrick's Church, "Baptisms, 1841–1844," CAA (microfilms); St. Joseph's Cathedral, "Baptisms, 1854–1855" at St. Joseph's, Buffalo; St. Bridget's Church, "Baptisms, 1855," CAA (microfilms).

26. Michael Drake, "Marriage and Population Growth in Ireland, 1750–1845," *Economic History Review*, 2d series, 16 (1963), 307–13; Connell, "Catholicism and Marriage in the Century after the Famine," *Irish Peasant Society*, pp. 113–61; Mattis, "The Irish Catholic Family in Buffalo," 176; Glasco, *Ethnicity and Social Structure*, p. 179.

27. Michael B. Katz, *Poverty and Policy in American History* (New York, 1983), pp. 76–7; Charles L. Bland, "Institutions of Charity in Jacksonian Erie County: 1829–61" (seminar paper, SUNYAB, 1975), table 1.

28. Buffalo *Commercial Advertiser*, June 2, 1855.

29. Katz, *Poverty and Policy in American History*, p. 86; Buffalo *Commercial Advertiser*, April 1, 1855.

30. Buffalo *Commercial Advertiser*, March 9, 1854; June 2, 1855; April 23, 1856; April 3, 1858.

31. Katz, *Poverty and Policy in American History*, p. 76; Glasco, *Ethnicity and Social Structure*, p. 34. To some extent, this sex ratio is accounted for by the relative absence of mobile laborers when the count was done by census takers. Since the absence of men was a contributing factor to family poverty, however, the skewed sex ratio might have social significance, even if to a degree an artifact of the data-gathering process. The harshness of the 1854–55 winter, in which there was a steep, temporary rise in unemployment, was also a stimulus for even more men than usual to seek work outside the city; Buffalo *Commercial Advertiser*, April 1, 1855.

32. Glasco, *Ethnicity and Social Structure*, p. 147; Diner, *Erin's Daughters in America*, pp. 46, 47, 50, 54, 55–7, 59, 64, 67.

33. Katz, *Poverty and Policy in American History*, pp. 76–7.

34. Diner, *Erin's Daughters in America*, pp. 59–64, 92–3, 113–5; Connell, *Irish Peasant Society*, pp. 51–86; Richard J. Stivers, *A Hair of the Dog: Irish Drinking and American Stereotype* (University Park, 1976), p. 109; Buffalo *Commercial Advertiser*, March 12, 18, May 15, July 21, 1846; May 12, 1856; February 24, 1857; July 29, 1858. Illegitimacy data are extremely difficult to come by, let alone interpret. Still there seems something suggestive about the fact that of 697 baptisms analyzed in three parishes, in only nine (1.4 percent) do the facts, as recorded in sacramental books by the parish priest, suggest illegitimacy. These are cases in which there was no male sponsor for a baptism and/or no natural parents' names given at the time an infant was presented for baptism. Source: $n = 269$ (1855), St. Bridget's Church, "1853–1871, Baptisms," CAA (microfilms); $n = 290$ (1855), St. Joseph's Cathedral, "Baptisms," at St. Joseph's, Buffalo; $n = 138$ (1841–44), St. Patrick's Church, "Baptisms," CAA (microfilms).

35. Buffalo *Commercial Advertiser*, February 10, 1847; November 9, 1852; October 10, 1853; October 19, 1854; October 13, 1855; October 18, 1858.

36. Robert Bales, "Attitudes toward Drinking in Irish Culture," in *Society, Culture, and Drinking Patterns*, ed. David J. Pittman and Charles R. Snyder (New York, 1962), pp. 157–87; J. R. Barrett, "Why Paddy Drank: The Social Importance of Whiskey in Pre-Famine Ireland," *Journal of Popular Culture*, 11 (April, 1977), 155–66; Stivers, *A Hair of the Dog*, pp. 15–33; Connell, "Illicit Distillation," *Irish Peasant Society*, pp. 1–50; Elizabeth Malcolm, *Ireland Sober, Ireland Free: Drink and Temperance in Nineteenth Century Ireland* (Syracuse, 1986).

37. Stivers, *A Hair of the Dog*, pp. 101–63; William J. Rorabaugh, *The Alcoholic Republic* (New York, 1979), p. 144; New York *Irish-American*, November 22, 29, December 20, 1851.

38. Samuel Clark and James Donnelly, Jr., eds., *Irish Peasants: Violence and Political Unrest, 1780-1914* (Madison, 1983); Edward M. Levine, *The Irish and Irish Politicians: A Study of Cultural and Social Alienation* (Notre Dame, 1966), pp. 66–7; David Grimsted, "Ante-bellum Labor: Violence, Strikes, and Communal Arbitration," *Journal of Social History*, 19 (Fall, 1985), 9–10; R. E. Swift, " 'Another Stafford Street Row': Law, Order, and the Irish Presence in Mid-Victorian Wolverhampton," *Immigrants and Minorities*, 3 (March, 1984), 5–29.

39. Buffalo *Commercial Advertiser and Journal*, November 25, 1842; March 14, 1843; Buffalo *Courier and Pilot*, September 25, 1846; Buffalo *Commercial Advertiser*, September 23, 1844; August 26, 1851; May 6, June 5, 21, July 3, 5, 1854; March 31, 1857; October 24, 1860; Buffalo *Courier*, July 26, 1844; June 1, 1848; August 27, 1851; March 25, April 3, 1852; Buffalo *Republic*, July 5, 1853; June 5, 1854; New York *Irish-American*, November 22, 29, December 20, 1851, February 21, 1852.

40. E.g., the conflicted municipal contest of June, 1857; Buffalo *Commercial Advertiser*, June 9, 10, 1857; Buffalo *Sentinel*, July 4, 1857.

41. Buffalo *Commercial Advertiser*, September 20, 1853. For local reporting of Orange versus Green rioting in Canada, ibid., July 13, 1844; August 4, 1846; Buffalo *Courier*, July 17, 1849.

42. Buffalo *Courier*, August 21, 1854.

43. Buffalo *Commercial Advertiser*, October 23, 1854; February 5, 1857; Buffalo *Christian Advocate*, October 26, 1854.

44. Stivers, *A Hair of the Dog*, pp. 142–63; Buffalo *Courier*, June 19, 1843; June 29, 1849; July 9, November 12, 1850, June 3, 1857; L. Perry Curtis, Jr., *Apes and Angels: The Irishman in Victorian Caricature* (Washington, 1971); Richard Ned Lebow, *White Britain and Black Ireland: The Influence of Stereotypes on Colonial Policy* (Philadelphia, 1976).

45. Buffalo *Commercial Advertiser*, April 19, May 1, 1854; Buffalo *Express*, July 11, 1857; Buffalo *Sentinel*, July 18, 1857. The presidents of the St. George's and St. Andrew's societies, for example, attended the St. Patrick's Day banquet in their official capacities in the 1840s. But beginning in 1849, just after the worst of the famine and in the midst of political turmoil in Ireland, St. George's president stopped participating, and several years later, St. Andrew's did, too.

Buffalo *Commercial Advertiser*, March 19, 1846; Buffalo *Courier*, March 23, 1847; March 21, 1848; March 22, 1849.

46. Buffalo *Courier*, March 23, April 20, 1843; January 5, July 4, 1844; June 22, 24, 1848; Buffalo *Commercial Advertiser*, July 25, 27, November 14, 1844; January 4, February 2, 13, 16, March 1, 2, 1847; August 11, 16, 1848.

47. For praise of the Irish, Buffalo *Courier*, January 27, 1847; April 28, 1852 (for generosity to family in Ireland); Buffalo *Republic*, June 8, 1853; August 14, 1854 (for being ideal material for American citizenship, but only in places where the Catholic clergy was nonexistent). More common were the generalized praise for immigrant labor and calls for justice for all foreigners: *Courier*, June 14, December 19, 1847; December 21, 1851; April 3, 1852; September 16, October 5, 1854; October 23, 1858; and *Republic*, June 11, 1855; June 13, 1857. The *Courier*'s tepidness in defense of the Irish led it to come out on the short end of a number of polemical battles with its chief journalistic rival, the *Commercial Advertiser*; see ibid., September 6, 1850; January 9, 12, 1857.

48. "Pat" was so widely conceived that a sketch of him can be drawn from all of the city's major newspapers, Democratic and Whig-Republican, not to mention nativist: Buffalo *Courier*, September 30, 1843; January 13, 1844; March 27, 28, 1846; September 2, 1850; September 22, 1851; Buffalo *Commercial Advertiser*, July 9, 1842; December 9, 1844; September 18, 25, 1846; May 4, December 5, 1848; March 6, June 4, July 4, 7, 1854; March 8, 17, April 18, 21, May 5, November 15, 25, 1856; February 2, July 14, 1857, March 8, 1859; October 31, 1860; Buffalo *Republic*, June 13, 24, 1853; June 12, August 11, 1855; Buffalo *Express*, June 12, 1857. The evolution of the Irish stereotype in America is traced in Dale T. Knobel, *Paddy and the Republic: Ethnicity and Nationality in Antebellum America* (Middletown, 1986).

49. Buffalo *Commercial Advertiser*, January 10, 1849.

50. *Niles Weekly Register*, 18 (August 22, 1835), 440.

51. Buffalo *Christian Advocate*, February 13, 1851.

52. Buffalo *Republic*, November 25, 1853.

53. Buffalo *Commercial Advertiser*, February 19, 1856, in which the *Demokrat* is quoted.

54. Buffalo *Republic*, August 22, 1853.

55. Buffalo *Commercial Advertiser*, July 22, 1856.

56. R. G. Dun and Co., New York, vol. 80, pp. 13 (Cov.) quotation, 50 (Coo.), 173 (S), 184 (R), 341 (Coo); and vol. 81, pp. 72 (B), 182 (Cov.), R. G. Dun and Company Collection, BL.

57. Buffalo *Commercial Advertiser*, March 18, 1857; George Washington Johnson, Diary, 1856, entry of January 22, p. 42, DC.

58. Diner, *Erin's Daughters in America*, p. xiii.

59. Buffalo *Commercial Advertiser*, March 22, 1856; July 26, 1858; Harriet Prescott Spofford, *The Servant Girl Question* (Boston, 1881), pp. 66, 74–5.

60. Nancy Spaulding to E. G. Spaulding, August 29, 1850, Elbridge Gerry Spaulding Papers, BECHS. On the Hawley's experience, see above, p. 72.

61. Buffalo *Commercial Advertiser*, January 19, 1856. This proposal apparently was not acted upon, and it was introduced again five years later; ibid. January 23, 1861.

62. Ibid., January 23, 1861.
63. Spofford, *The Servant Girl Question*, pp. 19, 37-8, 44, 74-5, 136.
64. Ibid., pp. 87-9. Spofford mistakenly sees this transition in the Irish servant girl as a generational phenomenon that took fifty years to occur. One sees the same complaints about "Bridget's" uppity, arrogant behavior in the 1850s as three decades later, when Spofford wrote.
65. Ibid., pp. 18-9.
66. Mary T. C. McGee to "Aunt," August 2, 1852, Thomas D'Arcy McGee letters, PAC.
67. Surname analysis of the priests at the 1852 diocesan synod suggests that thirty-five of sixty-five priests (54 percent) had Irish names while another nine had Anglo-American names that were perhaps Irish, bringing the figure to 68 percent. Two years before, Bishop Timon had estimated that twenty-one of fifty-two priests (40 percent) were German, from which one may well infer most of the balance were Irish. *Synodus Dioceseana Buffalensis Quarta, Anno MDCCCLII*, Progaganda Fide Collection, UND (microfilms); Bishop John Timon to Leopoldine Society, Vienna, 1850, Leopoldine Stiftung Collection, UND (microfilms).
68. Buffalo *Commercial Advertiser*, November 1, 1859.
69. R. G. Dun and Co., New York, vol. 80, pp. 13 (Coo.), 44 (Va.), 71 (McC.), 132 (Fie.), 163 (Ken.), 173 (Sh.), 184 (Ril.), 279 (Cal.), 349 (Sho.), 352 (Swe.); and vol. 81, p. 72 (Bam.), R. G. Dun and Company Collection, BL; Glasco, *Ethnicity and Social Structure*, p. 97. The range of Irish enterprise and presence in the professions is suggested by advertisements in the Irish press; see, e.g., Buffalo *American Celt and Catholic Citizen*, June 12, 1852; Buffalo *Sentinel*, July 4, 1847; and the list in Jeremiah O'Donovan, *A Brief Account of the Author's Interviews with his Countrymen . . . 1854 and 1855* (Pittsburgh, 1864), pp. 340-3. On Keogh, Buffalo *Sentinel*, July 12, 1856 and R. G. Dun and Co., New York vol. 80, p. 106, R. G. Dun and Company Collection, BL; on Carland, Buffalo *American Celt and Catholic Citizen*, May 22, 1852.
70. R. G. Dun and Co., New York, vol. 80 p. 150 (Coo.), R. G. Dun and Company Collection, BL; David A. Gerber, "Ethnics, Enterprise, and Middle Class Formation: Using the Dun and Bradstreet Collection for Research in Ethnic History," *Immigration History Newsletter*, 12 (May, 1980), 3, 5-6. (The correct name is the "R. G. Dun and Company Collection.")
71. Glasco, *Ethnicity and Social Structure*, p. 94.
72. The sample was taken from the *New York State Census, 1855* manuscripts, from which data was collected on persistence. Surname analysis is hardly scientific, especially in light of the interpenetration of Protestant and Catholic Irish populations, but such names as "Brown," "Martin," "Bray," and "Beaker" seem to be more characteristic of the former than latter. The mean (8.4 years) and median (5.9 years) for the sample seem significant when we consider that in the same year 56 percent of all Irish household heads had been in the city between four and five years. Of the sample, however, 52 percent (fifty-seven) had been in the city six years or more, among whom thirty-one (28 percent) had been present eleven or more years. See, also, Buffalo *Commercial Advertiser*, September 8, 1856.

73. Michael B. Katz, "The Structure of Inequality and Length of Residence in Buffalo, New York, 1855," Working Paper #13, of the York Social History Project (Toronto, 1976), 108–9.

74. Glasco, *Ethnicity and Social Structure*, p. 133; Katz, "The Structure of Inequality and Length of Residence in Buffalo," 109–10. Names for the samples were drawn from lists in: Buffalo *American Celt and Catholic Citizen*, October 16, 1852; Buffalo *Courier*, February 20, October 14, 1852; May 13, 1853; Buffalo *Commercial Advertiser*, October 23, 1855; February 25, 1856; December 13, 1858. These names were then traced in the *New York State Census, 1855*. James Henretta has raised the important question of whether this pattern of Irish property holding suggests cultural values rather than economic position. Irish cultural priorities may have placed contributing money to the church and, via remittances, to family in Ireland, over property acquisition. The problem here is that German immigrants also sent money to family in Europe and contributed not only to churches, but to a broad network of secular voluntary associations. Hence, relative economic position seems to explain differing ethnic patterns. See James Henretta, "The Study of Social Mobility: Ideological Assumptions and Conceptual Biases," *Labor History*, 18 (Spring, 1977), 165–78.

75. Buffalo *Commercial Advertiser*, February 10, 1854; Glasco, *Ethnicity and Social Structure*, pp. 69–107. For sample, see above, note 74.

76. Buffalo *Commercial Advertiser*, May 29, 1858; Buffalo *Christian Advocate*, October 27, 1859. This institution soon failed, however.

77. *Semi-Centennial Celebration of the City of Buffalo* (Buffalo, 1882), p. 45.

78. Connolly, *Priests and People in Pre-Famine Ireland*, pp. 1–13, 24–43, 56, 74–134, 135–71, 219–63; O'Ferrall, *Catholic Emancipation*; John A. Murphy, "Priests and People in Modern Irish History," *Christus Rex*, 23 (October, 1969), 235–59; Oliver MacDonagh, "The Irish Catholic Clergy and Emigration during the Great Famine," *Irish Historical Studies*, 5 (1946–47), 287–302; Emmet Larkin, "The Devotional Revolution in Ireland, 1850–1875," *American Historical Review*, 77 (June, 1972), 625–39.

79. John A. Murphy, "The Support of the Catholic Clergy in Ireland, 1750–1850," *Historical Studies*, 5 (1965), 103–19; Carey, "Voluntaryism," 49–51.

80. Carey, "Voluntaryism," 52–3; MacDonagh, "The Irish Catholic Clergy and Emigration," 289–300; Murphy, "The Support of the Catholic Clergy in Ireland," 109–19; Murphy, "Priests and People in Modern Irish History," 239–47; Connolly, *Priests and People in Pre-Famine Ireland*, pp. 239–55.

81. Carey, "Voluntaryism," 53–9; MacDonagh, "The Irish Catholic Clergy and Emigration," 301–2; Theodore Roemer, O.M., *The Leopoldine Foundation and the Church in the United States, 1829–1839* (New York, 1933), pp. 177–9.

82. John Higham, "Les Deux Irlandes en Amerique," *Critique* (June-July, 1982), 615; Jay Dolan, *The Immigrant Church: New York's Irish and German Catholics, 1815–1865* (Baltimore, 1975), p. 57. Connolly, *Priests and People in Pre-Famine Ireland*, pp. 83–120.

83. Connolly, *Priests and People in Pre-Famine Ireland*, pp. 135–71; Dolan, *The Immigrant Church*, pp. 60–2; Buffalo *American Celt and Catholic Citizen*, October 9, December 4, 1852; Buffalo *Sentinel*, October 10, 1857; Buffalo *Demokrat und Weltbürger*, April 18, 1859; Buffalo *Commercial Advertiser*, May 3, 1859.

84. Stivers, *A Hair of the Dog*, pp. 46–50, 95–8; Sister Joan Bland, *Hibernian Crusade: The Story of the Catholic Total Abstinence Union of America* (Washington, D.C., 1951), pp. 8–43; Malcolm, *Ireland Sober, Ireland Free*.

85. Donohue, *History of the Diocese of Buffalo*, p. 259.

86. Buffalo *Sentinel*, April 11, 25, 1857.

87. Buffalo *Commercial Advertiser*, August 26, September 1, 1851; Donohue, *History of the Diocese of Buffalo*, pp. 258–9.

88. Stivers, *A Hair of the Dog*, p. 170; Buffalo *Courier*, March 18, 1853; Buffalo *Commercial Advertiser*, March 17, 1856; March 20, 1857; Buffalo *American Celt and Catholic Citizen*, February 26, 1853; Buffalo *Sentinel*, March 15, 1856; March 9, 1857; March 3, 1860.

89. Buffalo *Commercial Advertiser*, March 20, 1857.

90. Buffalo *Commercial Advertiser and Journal*, March 16, 21, 1842; Buffalo *Courier*, March 15, 21, 22, 1843; March 20, 1846; March 19, 23, 1847; March 21, 1848; March 22, 1849; March 22, 1850; March 21, 1851; March 19, 1852; Buffalo *Commercial Advertiser*, March 19, 21, 1846; March 18, 1858; March 19, 1860; March 19, 1861; Buffalo *American Celt and Catholic Citizen*, March 26, 1853; Buffalo *Sentinel*, March 23, 1861.

91. Buffalo *Sentinel*, March 2, 1861; Buffalo *Commercial Advertiser*, March 6, 1861.

92. The bishop's appeals, which were most elaborate during the hotly contested nativist campaigns of the mid-1850s, combined rules for behavior at the polls with nonpartisan appeals to let Christian principle guide the voter's choices; see, e.g., Buffalo *Sentinel*, October 31, 1857.

93. Levine, *The Irish and Irish Politicians*, p. 196.

94. St. Bridget's Church, Buffalo, "Marriages, 1853–1856," CAA (microfilms).

95. Donohue, *History of the Diocese of Buffalo*, pp. 245–6, 250–1, 258–9, 259–60; Buffalo *American Celt and Catholic Citizen*, February 12, 1853; Buffalo *Commercial Advertiser*, October 19, 1859; Dolan, *The Immigrant Church*, pp. 51–2; Buffalo *Courier*, July 18, 1853.

96. *Twenty-Second Annual Report of the Superintendent of Public Schools, 1859* (Buffalo, 1860), p. 10; Ignatius Murphy, "Primary Education," in *A History of Irish Catholicism*, ed. Patrick Cornish (Dublin, 1970), vol. 5, *The Church since Emancipation*, part 6, "Catholic Education," pp. 1–52; Donohue, *History of the Diocese of Buffalo*, pp. 200–1, 245–6; Rev. William B. Smith, "The History of the Diocese of Buffalo, 1847–1867" (Master's thesis, Catholic University, 1967), pp. 172–3; Buffalo *American Celt and Catholic Citizen*, January 8, 1853; Buffalo *Sentinel*, May 16, 1857; May 18, 1861; Bishop John Timon to Kirby, Congregation for the Propagation of the Faith, Rome, March 17, 1859, Propaganda Fide Collection UND (microfilms); Diner, *Erin's Daughters in America*, pp. 127, 129, 142, 145–6.

97. Donohue, *History of the Diocese of Buffalo*, p. 319; Thomas D'Arcy McGee to Sadler, May 9, 1853, Miscellaneous Letters, BECHS; Buffalo *American Celt and Catholic Citizen*, November 20, 1852; Buffalo *Courier*, June 17, 1854; Buffalo *Sentinel*, March 22, April 12, 1856.

98. Donohue, *History of the Diocese of Buffalo*, p. 323; Buffalo *American Celt and Catholic Citizen*, September 18, 25, October 16, November 13, 20, 1852; March 26, May 28, 1853; Buffalo *Sentinel*, December 19, 1857; December 15, 1860.

99. Donohue, *History of the Diocese of Buffalo*, pp. 190, 199; Buffalo *American Celt and Catholic Citizen*, October 16, 1852; Buffalo *Sentinel*, January 12, 1856; December 19, 1857; February 25, 1860; Buffalo *Commercial Advertiser*, April 12, 1856; February 21, 1859; Buffalo *Sentinel*, March 22, 1856 (quotation).

100. Buffalo *Commercial Advertiser*, October 23, 1855; May 9, 1859; Buffalo *Courier*, April 22, 1861; Buffalo *Sentinel*, June 22, 1861.

101. Michael Funchion, ed., *Irish-American Voluntary Organizations* (Westport, 1983), pp. 250-61; Sons of Erin, Minute Book, 1847, NUL; Buffalo *Commercial Advertiser*, December 8, 1846; Buffalo *Courier*, June 22, 1847; February 17, December 23, 1848; February 23, June 11, December 10, 1850; January 25, February 21, 1851; March 14, 1853; Diner, *Erin's Daughters in America*, pp. 28, 120-1, 123, 129, 130-4. The social bases of these societies were reconstructed by examining lists of members in the press, and tracing them in the 1855 state census: Buffalo *Courier*, February 20, October 14, 1852; May 13, 1853; Buffalo *Commercial Advertiser*, February 25, 1856; December 13, 1858.

102. Ira Katznelson, *City Trenches: Urban Politics and the Patterning of Class in the United States* (New York, 1981), p. 82.

103. Buffalo *American Celt and Catholic Citizen*, February 12, 1853.

104. James A. Reynolds, *The Catholic Emancipation Crisis in Ireland, 1823-1829* (New Haven, 1954), pp. 36-8.

105. Buffalo *Sentinel*, July 4, 1857. On Hughes: Buffalo *Demokrat und Weltbürger*, March 26, April 5, 1859; and R. G. Dun and Co., New York, vol. 1, p. B158, R. G. Dun and Company Collection, BL.

106. Reynolds, *The Catholic Emancipation Crisis in Ireland, 1823-1829*, p. 38; Lawrence J. McCaffrey, *The Irish Diaspora in America* (Bloomington, 1976), p. 58; Walter P. Zenner, "Lachrymosity: A Cultural Reinforcement of Minority Status," *Ethnicity* 4 (June, 1977), 156-66; Thomas N. Brown, *Irish-American Nationalism, 1870-1890* (Philadelphia, 1966), p. 23.

107. Buffalo *Commercial Advertiser*, April 19, 1854.

108. Buffalo *Commercial Advertiser and Journal*, March 21, 1842; March 19, 1846; Buffalo *Courier*, March 21, 1843; March 21, 1848; March 22, 1850. Joseph O'Grady, *How the Irish Became Americans* (New York, 1973) contains the basis of this argument, though in a rather different form.

109. Robin B. Burns, "Thomas D'Arcy McGee: A Biography" (Ph.D. dissertation, McGill University, 1976), 87-122; 214-24, 251-68; Buffalo *American Celt and Catholic Citizen*, May 8, 1852; Buffalo *Courier*, June 11, 1852.

110. Buffalo *American Celt and Catholic Citizen*, September 18, November 30, December 11, 1852; January 8, 29, February 5, 12, 26, March 19, April 2, 9, 1853; Buffalo *Courier*, November 30, 1852.

111. New York *Times*, April 27, 1853; Stivers, *A Hair of the Dog*, p. 157 (quoting McGee); Burns, "Thomas D'Arcy McGee: A Biography," 235–6.

112. Boston, *American Celt*, August 31, 1850; Buffalo *American Celt and Catholic Citizen*, September 18, 25, November 13, 20, 1852; March 26, May 28, 1853.

113. James P. Shannon, *Catholic Colonization on the Western Frontier* (New Haven, 1957), pp. 15–9; Buffalo *Sentinel*, February 2, 1856; Buffalo *Commercial Advertiser*, February 13, 14, 15, 16, 23, 1856; New York *Irish-American*, February 23, March 1, 1856; Diner, *Erin's Daughters in America*, p. 126.

114. Shannon, *Catholic Colonization on the Western Frontier*, pp. 20–2. Priests in several states also founded societies to encourage settlement in the West, but these efforts, too, soon collapsed; New York *Irish-American*, May 17, 31, 1856.

115. Buffalo *Courier*, May 3, 1853; Buffalo *Commercial Advertiser*, November 30, 1857; Burns, "Thomas D'Arcy McGee: A Biography," 251–68, 300–1; Buffalo *American Celt and Catholic Citizen*, February 26, 1853; Buffalo *Sentinel*, May 30, 1857.

116. Buffalo *Commercial Advertiser*, March 26, 1859.

117. Charles G. Deuther, *The Life and Times of the Right Reverend John Timon, D.D., the First Roman Catholic Bishop of the Diocese of Buffalo* (Buffalo, 1870), p. 269, 284; Bishop John Timon to Archbishop Francis Kenrick, February 11, 1861, Francis Kenrick Papers, AAB.

118. Buffalo *Sentinel*, March 8, April 26, December 27, 1856; January 10, 17, February 7, July 18, 25, August 8, 29, 1857; December 5, 1857, January 9, 30, 1858. On Hagan, R. G. Dun and Co., New York, vol. 81, p. 74, R. G. Dun and Company Collection, BL; Buffalo *Commercial Advertiser*, June 24, 1854.

119. Buffalo *Sentinel*, February 23, March 22, 1856; July 11, 1857.

120. Ibid., February 9, 1856.

121. Ibid., July 25, 1857; January 2, 1858.

122. Ibid., February 23, 1856; May 30, December 5, 1857; January 2, 16, 25, February 13, 1858.

123. Buffalo *Sentinel*, September 17, October 3, 10, 1857.

124. Ibid., November 14, 21, 28, December 5, 1857.

125. Ibid., May 10, August 3, 1856; October 10, 1857; Buffalo *Express*, November 7, 1855, quoting the Buffalo *Sentinel* (n.d.) as saying that "the hearts of Catholics are anti-slavery to the last shred." Also, Buffalo *Christian Advocate*, March 4, 1852; Jean H. Baker, *Affairs of Party: The Political Culture of Northern Democrats in the Mid-Nineteenth Century* (Ithaca, 1983); Madeleine Hooke Rice, *American Catholic Opinion in the Slavery Controversy* (New York, 1944).

Chapter 7. Buffalo's Germans: Foundations in Diversity

1. Laurence A. Glasco, *Ethnicity and Social Structure: Irish, Germans and Native-Born of Buffalo, N.Y., 1850–1860* (New York, 1980), p. 20.

2. *New York State Census, 1855*, p. 63, SUNYAB. On subregional identities: St. Michael's Church, "Part I, Marriages from 1851–1873"; St. Mary's Church, "Baptisms, III"; St. Anne's Church, "Baptisms, 1858–1873" (All sacramental records were consulted at the individual parish); Buffalo *Demokrat und Weltbürger*, May 28, 1859.

3. The mixing of people in church congregations is established by sacramental records such as those cited above in note 2. On these two examples of intracongregational hostility, see, Rev. Paul Theodore Burger, *Chronik der Ersten Evangelischen Lutherischen Dreifaltigkeits Gemeinde, U.A.C., in Buffalo, New York* (Buffalo, 1889), pp. 7–20; Selig Adler and Thomas E. Connolly, *From Ararat to Suburbia: History of the Jewish Community of Buffalo* (Philadelphia, 1960), pp. 64–7.

4. Glasco, *Ethnicity and Social Structure*, pp. 92–4.

5. Heinz Kloss, "German as an Immigrant, Indigenous, Foreign, and Second Language," in *The German Language in America: A Symposium*, ed. Glenn Gilbert (Austin, 1971), pp. 114–5; Jurgen Eichoff, "The German Language in America," in *America and the Germans: An Assessment of a Three-Hundred-Year History*, ed. Frank Trommler and Joseph McVeigh, vol. 1, *Immigration, Language, and Ethnicity* (Philadelphia, 1985), pp. 224–39; Buffalo *Weltbürger*, January 26, 1839; February 13, 1841; May 7, 1842; Buffalo *Demokrat und Weltbürger*, May 28, 1859.

6. Albert Bernhardt Faust, *The German Element in the United States* (New York, 1927); John Hawgood, *The Tragedy of German-America: The Germans in the United States during the Nineteenth Century and After* (New York, 1940). This usage is still sometimes employed in the literature.

7. *Geschichte der Deutschen in Buffalo und Erie County, New York*, vol. 1 (Buffalo, 1898), pp. 92–6, 115–6; H. Perry Smith, *History of the City of Buffalo and Erie County, New York*, vol. 2 (Syracuse, 1884), pp. 157–8. On diversity and unity as a problem in the analysis of German ethnicization: James Berquist, "German Communities in American Cities: An Interpretation of the Nineteenth Century Experience," *Journal of American Ethnic History*, 4 (Fall, 1984), 12–13, 24, and passim; and Kathleen Neils Conzen, "The Paradox of German-American Assimilation," *Yearbook for German-American Studies*, 16 (1981), 153–9.

8. Harold Abramson, "On the Sociology of Ethnicity and Social Change: A Model of Rootedness and Rootlessness," *Economic and Social Review*, 8 (1976), 50–1.

9. U.S. Bureau of the Census, *Historical Statistics of the United States: Colonial Times to 1970* (Washington, D.C., 1976), pp. 105–6; Mack Walker, *Germany and the Emigration, 1816–1855* (Cambridge, Mass., 1964), pp. 42–174; Louis Chevalier, "L'Emigration Française au XIXe Siècle," *Etudes d'Histoire Moderne et Contemporaine*, 1 (1947), 131, 147–8, 156–8, 162; Takenori Inoki, "Aspects of German Peasant Emigration to the United States, 1815–1914: A Reexamination of Some Behavioral Hypotheses in Migration Theory" (Ph.D. dissertation, Massachusetts Institute of Technology, 1974), 51–87; P. Leuilliot, "L'Emigration Alsacienne sous l'Empire et au Début de la Restauration," *Revue Historique*, 165 (September–December 1930), 254–79.

10. Walker, *Germany and the Emigration*, pp. 240–1, and idem, *German Home Towns: Community, State, and General Estate, 1648–1871* (Ithaca, 1971); Peter Marschalck, *Deutsche Überseewanderung in 19 Jahrhunderts* (Stuttgart, 1973), pp. 72–83, 84.

11. John G. Gagliardo, *From Pariah to Patriot: The Changing Image of the German Peasant, 1770–1840* (Lexington, 1969), pp. 3–22, 134–5, 196–218; Walker, *Germany and the Emigration*, pp. 240–1; Inoki, "Aspects of the German Peasant Emigration," 105–33, 142–66; Gunter Moltmann, "The Pattern of German Emigration," in *America and the Germans*, ed. Trommler and McVeigh, pp. 17–8; Walter D. Kamphoefner, *Westfalen in der Neuen Welt* (Munster, 1982), pp. 22–56, 75–85.

12. The story of these obscure '48er artisans is told in Bruce Carlan Levine, " 'In the Spirit of 1848': German-Americans and the Fight over Slavery's Expansion" (Ph.D. dissertation, University of Rochester, 1980). On the more well-known refugee intellectuals in Buffalo, see Carl Wittke, *Refugees of Revolution: The German 48ers in America* (Philadelphia, 1952), pp. 12, 62, 188, 200, 205, 211, 213, 254.

13. Wilhelm Iwan, *Geschichte der Altlutherischen Auswanderung um die Mitte des 19. Jahrhunderts*, 2 vols. (Breslau, 1943); Lieselotte Clemens, *Old Lutheran Emigration from Pomerania to the U.S.A.: History and Motivation, 1839–1843*, trans. Joachim Peters (Kiel, 1976), pp. 79–81. Eugene W. Camann, *Land Use and Early Structures of the North German Settlements in Wheatfield, New York* (Buffalo, 1983); and *Occupations and Craftsmanship of the Prussian Settlers in Wheatfield, New York* (Buffalo, 1983). Buffalo *Weltbürger*, September 14, 28, 1839; Philip von Rohr Sauer, "Heinrich von Rohr and the Great Emigration of 1839," *Concordia Historical Quarterly*, 56 (Summer, 1983), 63–4; *Kirchliches Informatorium*, May 1, 1853, 111.

14. Glasco, *Ethnicity and Social Structure*, p. 50; Smith, *History of Buffalo and Erie County*, vol. 2, pp. 151–2; Ismar Ellison, "An Historical Essay: The Germans of Buffalo," Buffalo Historical Society *Publications*, 2 (1880), 121; Andrew Yox, "The Decline of the German-American Community in Buffalo, 1855–1925" (Ph.D. dissertation, University of Chicago, 1983), 33; *Geschichte der Deutschen*, pp. 31–47.

15. Buffalo *Republican*, August 1, 1839.

16. Buffalo *Weltbürger*, December 19, 1840.

17. Glasco, *Ethnicity and Social Structure*, pp. 40–2, 44–5, 50, 52–3; Yox, "Decline of the German-American Community in Buffalo," 33; Inoki, "Aspects of German Peasant Emigration," 59–61; Buffalo *Demokrat und Weltbürger*, March 20, 1854.

18. Glasco, *Ethnicity and Social Structure*, p. 19–21; Yox, "Decline of the German-American Community in Buffalo," 34.

19. Above, chapter 1, p. 18. For the text of the letter, see Iwan, *Geschichte der Altlutherische Auswanderung*, vol. 1, p. 48. Yox, "Decline of the German-American Community," 16.

20. Glasco, *Ethnicity and Social Structure*, p. 94; Ellen Taussig, "The German Community," Buffalo *Evening News*, October 21, 1972; Johann Roth, "Wie es im Anfange um die St. Anna Kirche herum aussah," in "Die Ges-

chichte der St. Anna Gemeinde, 1858–1908," *St. Anna Bote* (Buffalo, 1908), pp. 101–3.

21. This usage is employed, e.g., in *Geschichte der Deutschen*, passim. Berquist, "German Communities in American Cities," 9–11, makes the same observation about the spatial dispersion of German settlement in cities with very large German populations.

22. Glasco, *Ethnicity and Social Structure*, pp. 60, 64–6; Yox, "Decline of the German-American Community in Buffalo," 28.

23. Buffalo *Courier*, December 3, 1845; March 21, 1846; November 20, 1848; Buffalo *Weltbürger*, December 6, 1845; March 25, 1846; October 14, 1848; April 14, 1849; November 9, 1850; February 12, 1851.

24. Glasco, *Ethnicity and Social Structure*, p. 60; Buffalo *Commercial Advertiser*, September 2, 1855; City of Buffalo, *Census of Children, 1 January 1845*; Buffalo *Christian Advocate*, October 25, 1860; *Map of the City of Buffalo, Surveyed under the Direction of Quackenboss and Kennedy, Insurance Agents* (New York, 1854).

25. *Buffalo Medical Journal*, 10 (1854–55), 373–81.

26. *Map of the City of Buffalo*; Roth, "Wie es im Anfange um die St. Anna Kirche," pp. 101–3; Frank Manual, "The Tenements of Buffalo" (seminar paper, n.d., BECHS), 5.

27. Glasco, *Ethnicity and Social Structure*, pp. 63, 70, 72; Andrew Yox, "Bonds of Community: Buffalo's German Element, 1853–1871," *New York History*, 66 (April, 1985), 158; and idem, "Ethnic Loyalties of the Alsatians in Buffalo, 1829–1855," *Yearbook of German-American Studies*, 20 (1985), 107–8, 112–3.

28. Andrew Yox, "The Myth of Persistence of Families in the Orchard: An East Buffalo Neighborhood," *New York Folklore*, 10 (Summer-Fall, 1984), 89–103.

29. Glasco, *Ethnicity and Social Structure*, pp. 77–8.

30. Ibid., pp. 153, 156–7.

31. The date here is based on ibid., pp. 144–5, 146; and general trends are confirmed by both Yox, "Decline of the German-American Community in Buffalo," 38, and my own research in sacramental records at St. Michael's, St. Mary's, and St. Anne's parishes. These records establish, in samples drawn for 1851–63, six examples in 234 (2.5 percent) of religious intermarriage, three (1.2 percent) of marriage between language groups with one partner German, and 82 (35 percent) of marriage between members of one German state or German-speaking nation and another. Such parish baptismal records also establish the universality of godparentage, though neither the godparent's precise relation to the baby's family nor place of origin are recorded.

32. Buffalo *Commercial Advertiser*, September 2, 1855.

33. Ibid., June 12, 1857.

34. Ibid., September 19, 1856.

35. Walker, *German Home Towns*, pp. 52–5, 88–9, 330–1; Gagliardo, *From Pariah to Patriot*, pp. 101–2; Jerome Blum, *The End of the Old Order in Rural Europe* (Princeton, 1978), pp. 178–93.

36. Glasco, *Ethnicity and Social Structure*, p. 94; Buffalo *Commercial Advertiser*, September 2, 1855. On German occupational structure in American cities, see Nora Faires, "Occupational Patterns of German-Americans in Nineteenth Century Cities," in *German Workers in Industrial Chicago, 1850–1910: A Comparative Perspective*, ed. Hartmut Keil and John B. Jentz (DeKalb, 1983), pp. 37–51.

37. Glasco, *Ethnicity and Social Structure*, p. 94.

38. Buffalo *Weltbürger*, September 17, 1845.

39. Buffalo *Demokrat und Weltbürger*, May 26, 1857. Before this, the *Weltbürger* had published only one short article (June 7, 1845): when the board's building was dedicated. But on that occasion it did not discuss what the board's function was.

40. Glasco, *Ethnicity and Social Structure*, pp. 94–7; *Buffalo Commercial Advertiser City Directory, 1855* (Buffalo, 1855), pp. 270, 272–3, 276; *New York State Census of Manufactures, 1855* (printout for Buffalo in author's possession); Michael B. Katz, "The Structure of Inequality and Length of Residence in Buffalo, New York, 1855," Working Paper #13, of the York Social History Project (Toronto, 1976), 105.

41. *New York State Census of Manufactures, 1855*. For evidence of German factory employment, see Buffalo *Courier*, November 15, 1851; Buffalo *Demokrat und Weltbürger*, September 30, 1856; January 2, April 20, 1857; June 25, 1859; December 15, 1860; Buffalo *Commercial Advertiser*, June 23, 1857; *Map of The City of Buffalo*.

42. For German factory ownership outside brewing, see Smith, *History of Buffalo and Erie County*, vol. 2 (biographical section), pp. 57, 95, 109, 388 (text); *The Manufacturing Interests of the City of Buffalo* (Buffalo, 1866), p. 77.

43. Glasco, *Ethnicity and Social Structure*, pp. 97, 101.

44. Ibid., pp. 90, 94, 102–3, 121; Buffalo *Commercial Advertiser*, December 15, 1855; Bruce Laurie, George Alter, and Theodore Hershberg, "Immigrants and Industry: The Philadelphia Experience, 1850–1880," in *Philadelphia: Work, Space, Family, and Group Experience in the Nineteenth Century*, ed. Theodore Hershberg, (New York, 1981), pp. 93–116 (on the decline of the traditional crafts); Michael B. Katz, Michael J. Doucet, and Mark J. Stern, *The Social Organization of Early Industrial Capitalism* (Cambridge, Mass., 1982), p. 192; Katz, "The Structure of Inequality and Length of Residence," 108. A measure of how seldom Germans did the sort of outdoor public works and railroad construction labor done by the Irish was the infrequency with which contractors advertised for labor in the German-speaking press. I found but one example: Buffalo *Demokrat und Weltbürger*, May 25, 1853.

45. Glasco, *Ethnicity and Social Structure*, p. 199; *New York State Census of Manufactures, 1855*; Walker, *German Home Towns*, p. 334.

46. Glasco, *Ethnicity and Social Structure*, p. 94.

47. *Buffalo Commercial Advertiser City Directory, 1855*, pp. 269–96, especially pp. 277–8, 282–3, 291–2; Buffalo *Mercantile Courier*, July 17, December 5 (advertisement), 1844; Buffalo *Weltbürger*, January 6 (adv.), August 25 (adv.), 1838; March 16, 1844; R. G. Dun and Co., New York, vol. 80, pp. 41 (Sch.),

109 (Dev.), 235 (Del.), 272 (Hae.); and vol. 81, pp. 4 (Lei.), 6 (Bes.), and 53 (Sam., et al.), R. G. Dun and Company Collection, BL.

48. *Buffalo Medical Journal*, 1 (1845–47), 162–3; Buffalo *Demokrat und Weltbürger*, May 7, 1855; Buffalo *Commercial Advertiser*, August 28, 1860; *Buffalo Commercial Advertiser City Directory, 1855*, pp. 288–9. LaVern Ripley, *Of German Ways* (Minneapolis, 1970), p. 184.

49. Buffalo *Commercial Advertiser*, April 16, 1856 (quotation); R. G. Dun and Co., New York, vol. 81, p. 39 (Alb.); and vol. 82, pp. 117 (Hab.), 149 (Jos.), R. G. Dun and Company Collection, BL; *New York State Census of Manufactures, 1855*; *Buffalo Commercial Advertiser City Directory, 1855*, p. 272; Stanley Baron, *Brewed in America: A History of Beer and Ale in the United States* (Boston, 1962), pp. 166–98; William J. Rorabaugh, *The Alcoholic Republic* (New York, 1979), pp. 106–8; Buffalo *Demokrat und Weltbürger*, August 8, 1860; Buffalo *Courier*, August 1, 1850.

50. Buffalo *Demokrat und Weltbürger*, June 3, 1854; January 25, 1860; Buffalo *Express*, August 1, 1857; *Buffalo Commercial Advertiser City Directory, 1855*, pp. 280–2; R. G. Dun and Co., New York, e.g., vol. 80, pp. 22 (Fou.), 67 (Wei.), 99 (Hot.), 113 (Goo.), 137 (Hel.), 142 (Dol.), 163 (Hei.), 164 (Ble.); and vol. 81, p. 42 (Bue.), R. G. Dun and Company Collection, BL. For Old World drinking habits, see James S. Roberts, "Drink and Industrial Work Discipline in Nineteenth Century Germany," *Journal of Social History*, 15 (September, 1981), 26.

51. *Buffalo Commercial Advertiser City Directory, 1855*, pp. 272–3; Glasco, *Ethnicity and Social Structure*, p. 94.

52. *Buffalo Commercial Advertiser City Directory, 1855*, pp. 269–95; Buffalo *Courier*, October 21, 1850 (adv.); June 29, 1852 (quotation); Buffalo *American Celt and Catholic Citizen*, December 24, 1852 (adv.), Buffalo *Commercial Advertiser*, June 4, 1858; Buffalo *Weltbürger*, June 2, (adv.), August 25 (adv.), 1838; Buffalo *Demokrat und Weltbürger*, March 11, 1854; April 8, 1857 (advs.); December 3, 1860 (adv.).

53. Buffalo *Courier*, August 1, 1850; Buffalo *Commercial Advertiser*, March 8, 1858; June 21, 1859; June 26, July 20, August 2, 1860; Buffalo *Demokrat und Weltbürger*, January 26, 1859.

54. *Buffalo Medical Journal*, 11 (1855–56), 63; Buffalo *Courier*, February 2, 1850; April 28, 1853; Buffalo *Commercial Advertiser*, November 18, 1853; February 24, May 12, 1859; *Buffalo Commercial Advertiser City Directory, 1855*, pp. 288–9; Buffalo *Weltbürger*, April 6, 1839.

55. *Geschichte der Deutschen* (biographical section), pp. 8, 15, 22, 24, 30–1, 36, 45, 53–4, 54–5, 59–60, 63, 70, 73, 80, 82, 90, 96, 109; Smith, *History of Buffalo and Erie County*, vol. 2, pp. 153–4, 388 and (biographical section), pp. 57, 95, 109; Elaine Roszak, "The George Urban Family, 1820–1896" (seminar paper, D'Youville College, 1969), 3–21; R.G. Dun and Co., New York, vol. 80, pp. 10 (Dor.), 16A (Has.), 39 (F. Geo.), 42 (Sch.), 50 (Sie.), 59 (Bet.), 87 (Swa.), 90 (C. Geo.), 103 (Ott.), 159 (Bey.), 229 (Bec.), 264–5 (Urb.), 302 (Bec.), 338 (C. Geo.), 442 (Urb.); vol. 81, pp. 11 (All.), 30 (Roo.), 35 (Zei.), 56 (All.), 87 (Sch.), 196 (Bet.); and vol. 82, p. 109 (Dol.), R. G. Dun and Company Collection, BL.

56. Smith, *History of Buffalo and Erie County*, vol. 2, pp. 161-2; *Semi-Centennial of the City of Buffalo* (Buffalo, 1882), p. 45; *Geschichte der Deutschen*, pp. 258-66. There were also several smaller insurance companies established to serve the local market for home fire protection. The idea of a German bank appears as early as 1857, but the depression ultimately, it seems, overtook the planners; Buffalo *Commercial Advertiser*, July 16, 1857.

57. Buffalo *Courier*, July 23, 1847.

58. Dorothee Schneider, "For Whom Are All the Good Things in Life?: German-American Housewives Discuss Their Budgets," in *German Workers in Industrial Chicago*, ed. Keil and Jentz, p. 151.

59. Glasco, *Ethnicity and Social Structure*, pp. 122-34; Yox, "Decline of the German-American Community of Buffalo," 36, 121-2, 123; Buffalo *Commercial Advertiser*, July 15, 1844; Katz, et al., *The Social Organization of Early Industrial Capitalism*, p. 147; and "The Structure of Inequality and Length of Residence," 103, 110.

60. Glasco, *Ethnicity and Social Structure*, pp. 33-5, 147-57, 161-5.

61. Ibid., pp. 210-1; Buffalo *Commercial Advertiser*, March 20, 1857; Buffalo *Republic*, September 24, 1857; *New York State Census of Manufactures, 1855*; Robert Lee, "Family and Modernization: The Peasant Family and Social Change in Nineteenth Century Bavaria," in *The German Family: Essays on the Social History of the Family in Nineteenth and Twentieth Century Germany*, ed. Richard Evans and W. R. Lee (London, 1981), p. 95; and Arthur Imhof, "Women, Family and Death: Excess Mortality of Women of Child-Bearing Age in Four Communities in Nineteenth Century Germany," in ibid., pp. 153, 172; Martha Kaarsberg Wallach, "German Immigrant Women," *German-American Studies*, 13, (1978), 100-3.

62. *Seventeenth Annual Report of the Superintendent of Public Schools, 1853* (Buffalo, 1854), p. 69. In 1859 the most German public school districts, while ahead of the most Irish in the percentage of school-age children in public schools, were still under 50 percent, by from 2 percent to 10 percent. Some of the remaining 40 percent to 60 percent of these school-age Germans were in sectarian schools; *Twenty-Second Annual Report of the Superintendent of Public Schools, 1859* (Buffalo, 1860), p. 10.

63. Glasco, *Ethnicity and Social Structure*, pp. 199, 212-6; *New York State Census of Manufactures, 1855*.

64. Lee, "Family and Modernization," in *The German Family*, ed. Evans and Lee, p. 97; Glasco, *Ethnicity and Social Structure*, pp. 201-11; Buffalo *Weltbürger*, August 18, 1838 (adv.); Buffalo *Commercial Advertiser*, May 30, 1844 (adv.); Buffalo *Courier*, May 20, 1852 (adv.).

65. *Seventeenth Annual Report of the Superintendent of Public Schools, 1853*, p. 69.

66. Buffalo *Weltbürger*, December 16 (adv.), 20 (adv.), 1837; January 9, 1841 (adv.); November 1, 1851; Buffalo *Demokrat und Weltbürger*, October 7, 1854 (adv.); December 1, 1855; October 4, 1856; Buffalo *Courier*, January 13, 1848; October 29, 1851; Buffalo *Commercial Advertiser*, October 28, 1856 (adv.); July 1, 1857; *Thirteenth Annual Report of the Superintendent of Public*

Schools, 1849 (Buffalo, 1850), p. 21; *Sixteenth Annual Report of the Superintendent of Public Schools, 1852* (Buffalo, 1853), pp. 24–6, 29, 33–43.

67. Wallach, "German Immigrant Women," 99–106; *Thirteenth Annual Report of the Superintendent of Public Schools, 1849*, p. 21; *Sixteenth Annual Report of the Superintendent of Public Schools, 1852*, pp. 33–43.

68. Charles Bland, "Institutions of Charity in Jacksonian Erie County, 1829–61" (seminar paper, SUNYAB, 1975), table 1.

69. Glasco, *Ethnicity and Social Structure*, p. 147.

70. John Knodel, "Two Hundred Fifty Years of Demographic History in a Bavarian Village," *Population Studies*, 24 (November, 1970), 365–6; St. Mary's Church, "Baptisms" (1855), vol. 3, pp. 120–46; St. Michael's Church, "Baptisms from 1851 to 1882," 1855, n.p.

71. Buffalo *Commercial Advertiser*, February 10, 1847; October 10, 1853; April 12, July 18, October 11, 19, 1854; October 13, 1855; July 22, 1856; July 21, 22, 1857; April 13, July 13, October 15, 18, 1858; April 12, July 12, October 11, 1859; January 10, 1860; Buffalo *Courier*, November 19, 1852; January 5, 1856. The German press took pride in these low incarceration rates; see, e.g., Buffalo *Weltbürger*, February 11, 1846.

72. Ripley, *Of German Ways*, p. 263; James S. Roberts, *Drink, Temperance, and the German Working Class in Nineteenth Century Germany* (Boston, 1984).

73. Baron, *Brewed in America*, pp. 192–3.

74. Christiane Harzig, "Chicago's German North Side, 1880–1900: The Structure of a Gilded Age Ethnic Neighborhood," in *German Workers in Industrial Chicago*, ed. Keil and Jentz, p. 141; R. G. Dun and Co., New York [reports], vols. 80, 81, passim, R. G. Dun and Company Collection, BL; Buffalo *Demokrat und Weltbürger*, July 12, 1856.

75. Buffalo *Weltbürger*, July 16, August 23, 1845; January 10, July 18, 1846; *Der Lutheraner*, March 12, 1850; 118–9; Ripley, *Of German Ways*, p. 274.

76. Buffalo *Weltbürger*, September 29, 1838; November 23, December 21, 1839; Buffalo *Demokrat und Weltbürger*, December 29, 1860 (quotation). On German antivice efforts, see Buffalo *Weltbürger*, August 20, 1842; September 14, 1844; September 6, October 1, November 15, 1851; and Buffalo *Courier*, August 19, 26, October 22, 1851.

77. Buffalo *Weltbürger*, November 21, 1840; July 11, 1846 (quotation); July 28, 1847; January 29, 1848; June 4, 1851; Buffalo *Demokrat und Weltbürger*, February 5, 11, 1857; July 19, 1860. The *Weltbürger*, however, was always sympathetic to Ireland's national aspirations; see, e.g., October 23, 1841; June 17, 1843; June 26, 1847; April 2, 1851.

78. Buffalo *Commercial Advertiser*, September 19, 1856.

79. Smith, *History of Buffalo and Erie County*, vol. 2, p. 160; Buffalo *Demokrat und Weltbürger*, April 20, November 15, 1860.

80. Buffalo *Weltbürger*, January 29, February 2, 1839.

81. *Geschichte der Deutschen*, pp. 51–6, 57–62, 62–4, 70–6, 83–5.

82. Ellison, "An Historical Essay: The Germans of Buffalo," 134–5.

83. *Der Lutheraner*, February 19, 1850, 97–9; Buffalo *Weltbürger*, May 21, 1851; Buffalo *Christian Advocate*, May 29, 1851; *Kirchliches Informatorium*,

December 1, 1852, 108; Buffalo *Republic,* May 18, 1854; Buffalo *Evening Post,* October 6, 1873.

84. Peter Burke, *Popular Culture in Early Modern Europe* (New York, 1978), pp. 182–91; Ripley, *Of German Ways,* pp. 193–205, 206–9; Buffalo *Weltbürger,* December 28, 1839; January 25, 1840; Buffalo *Courier,* December 22, 1851; Buffalo *Demokrat und Weltbürger,* February 4, 1856; Buffalo *Commercial Advertiser,* January 11, 1861.

85. Walker, *German Home Towns,* pp. 33–43, 56–64, 88–9, 106, 110–2, 202, 327.

86. Mary Jane Corry, "The Role of German Singing Societies in Nineteenth Century America," in *Germans in America: Aspects of German-American Relations in the 19th Century,* ed. E. Allen McCormick (New York, 1983), pp. 155–6.

87. New England Society of Buffalo, "Constitution and Members," vol. 1 (1853), BECHS; *Geschichte der Deutschen,* pp. 116–8 (on the *Leidertafel*).

88. *Constitution und Nebengesetze des Gesangvereins Buffalo Leidertafel, Amendirt und Verbessert den 12 Dec. 1879* (Buffalo, 1880), NYSL; *Geschichte der Deutschen,* pp. 116–28, for the activities of the German singing societies. The Turners' constitution also begins with a grand statement of philosophy and aspirations: *Constitution des Buffalo Turn-Vereins, Gegrundet am 29 Marz 1853, Incorporirt am 12 Mai 1869* (Buffalo, 1871), NYSL.

89. Smith, *History of Buffalo and Erie County,* vol. 2, pp. 157–8; Buffalo *Courier,* September 23, 1857.

90. Adler and Connolly, *From Ararat to Suburbia: History of the Jewish Community of Buffalo,* pp. 46–50; and *Geschichte der Deutschen,* pp. 268–311, for an overview of all Christian churches.

91. Buffalo *Commercial Advertiser,* July 18, 1857.

92. Joseph White, "Religion and Community: Cincinnati's Germans, 1814–1870" (Ph.D. dissertation, University of Notre Dame, 1980), 3.

93. Jonathan Sperber, *Popular Catholicism in Nineteenth Century Germany* (Princeton, 1984); White, "Religion and Community," 271–4; Michael Paul Fogarty, *Christian Democracy in Western Europe, 1820–1953* (London, 1957), p. 7; Edgar Alexander, "Church and Society in Germany," in *Church and Society: Catholic Social and Political Thought and Movements, 1789–1950,* ed. Joseph N. Moody (New York, 1953), pp. 331–65. Ernst Anton Reiter, *Schematismus der Katholischen Deutschen Geistlichkeit* (New York, 1869), pp. 111–2, estimates the total number of congregants in all five Buffalo German parishes at 24,600 in the late 1860s.

94. Rev. Emmet H. Rothan, *The German Catholic Immigrant in the United States (1830–1860)* (Washington, D.C., 1946); Rev. V. J. Fecher, *A Study of the Movement for German National Parishes in Philadelphia and Baltimore, 1787–1802* (Rome, 1955); Jay Dolan, *The Immigrant Church: New York's Irish and German Catholics, 1815–1865* (Baltimore, 1975).

95. Rev. Thomas Donohue, *History of the Catholic Church in Western New York* (Buffalo, 1904), pp. 242–3, 245, 248, 256–7; Yox, "Decline of the German-American Community in Buffalo," 72; *The Centenary of St. Mary's Church, 1844–1944* (Buffalo, 1944), pp. 17–9; Buffalo *Courier-Express,* May 3, 1942;

"St. Michael's Bazar [sic] Papers," nos. 1–10 (July 22 to August 14, 1889), n.p. (typescript at St. Michael's Church); *St. Anne's Apostle*, 1858–1908 (Buffalo, 1908), pp. 2–25.

96. David A. Gerber, "Modernity in the Service of Tradition: Ante-Bellum Catholic Lay Trustees at Buffalo's St. Louis Church and the Transformation of European Communal Traditions, 1829–1855," *Journal of Social History*, 15 (June, 1982), 655–89.

97. White, "Religion and Community," 159–60, 188, 230–46; Rev. John Timon to Bishop Francis Kenrick, July 14, 1857; March 6, 1857, Kenrick Papers, AAB; Buffalo *Courier*, April 26, 1848; "Synodus Dioceseana Buffalensis Quarta, Anno MDCCCLII," Congregation of the Propaganda Fide Collection, UND (microfilms); Donohue, *History of the Catholic Church in Western New York*, pp. 114–27, 212–32; Buffalo *Weltbürger*, April 8, 1843; Rev. John Timon to Archbishop Milde, Vienna, December 16, 1849, Leopoldine Foundation Collection UND (microfilms); Buffalo *Demokrat und Weltbürger*, November 8, 1854.

98. Archbishop Gaetano Bedini to Propaganda Fide, Rome, October 22, 1853, Congregation of the Propaganda Fide Collection, UND (microfilms).

99. Donohue, *History of the Catholic Church in Western New York*, p. 241; Buffalo *Die Aurora*, November 15, 16, 1853; R. G. Dun and Co., New York, vol. 80, p. 294, R. G. Dun and Company Collection, BL.

100. Buffalo *Commercial Advertiser*, July 9, 1856; July 3, 1860; Buffalo *Sentinel*, August 24, 1861; Donohue, *History of the Catholic Church in Western New York*, pp. 254–6; *St. Anne's Apostle*, pp. 2–25; Alfred Steckel, "German Roman Catholic Central Society of the U.S.A.," *Records of the American Catholic Historical Society*, 6 (1895), 252–5; White, "Religion and Community," 216–8.

101. *Twenty-Second Annual Report of the Superintendent of Public Schools, 1859*, p. 10; Donohue, *History of the Catholic Church in Western New York*, pp. 200, 254–6; "St. Michael's Bazar" [sic], n.p.; *St. Michael's Parish Centennial, 1851–1951*, (Buffalo, 1951), pp. 9–10; Buffalo *American Celt and Catholic Citizen*, July 17, 1852.

102. Smith, *History of Buffalo and Erie County*, vol. 2, pp. 168–9, 175–6, 177, 177–8; Buffalo *Daily Mercantile Courier*, May 24, 1843; Buffalo *Courier*, October 9, 1847; Buffalo *Commercial Advertiser*, August 21, 1857; Buffalo *Demokrat und Weltbürger*, July 14, 1859. Burger, *Chronik der Ersten Evangelischen Lutherischen Dreifaltigkeits Gemeinde*, pp. 7–20.

103. Vergilius Ferm, *The Crisis in American Lutheran Theology: A Study in the Issue between American Lutheranism and Old Lutheranism* (New York, 1927); and idem, *The Formation of the American Lutheran Church: A Case Study in Lutheran Unity* (Columbus, 1958); White, "Religion and Community," 92–100, 261; Ellison, "An Historical Essay: The Germans of Buffalo," 141; Buffalo *Commercial Advertiser*, October 7, 1854; July 24, 1857; October 5, 1860.

104. White, "Religion and Community," 247–60, 291–332; *Geschichte der Deutschen*, 40–7, 294–5, 295–7; Yox, "Decline of the German-American Community in Buffalo," 75; Smith, *History of Buffalo and Erie County*, vol. 2, pp.

169, 169–70, 172, 174–5; Buffalo *Weltbürger*, June 22, 1844; Buffalo *Commercial Advertiser*, August 8, 1857; September 18, 1858; Walter Beck, *Lutheran Elementary Schools in the U.S.* (St. Louis, 1939), pp. 5–84, 110–7, 124–6; Eichoff, "The German Language in America," 235–6.

105. Smith, *History of Buffalo and Erie County*, vol. 2, pp. 170–1, 178–9, 179; Yox, "Decline of the German-American Community in Buffalo," 45–6; *Geschichte der Deutschen*, pp. 307–8; Buffalo *Weltbürger*, March 10, 1838; January 6, April 6, 1844; August 21, 1850; Buffalo *Courier*, March 17, 1850; March 1, 1853; Buffalo *Christian Advocate*, September 2, December 9, 1852; Buffalo *Commercial Advertiser*, August 25, 1860; [signers of temperance pledge, 21 February 1850], Octavo volume 13, John B. Gough Papers, AAS; White, "Religion and Community," 101–52, 247–60, 291–332.

106. Buffalo *Christian Advocate*, September 12, 1850; February 24, 1859; Buffalo *Courier*, July 19, 1853; Buffalo *Commercial Advertiser*, September 30, 1856; Buffalo *Die Aurora*, June 27, November 11, 1856; Buffalo *Demokrat und Weltbürger*, July 11, 1859; *Kirchliches Informatorium*, July 1, 1852, 126; July 15, 1852, 7; October 15, 1852, 55; August 15, 1853, 15; March 1, 1854, 113; August 15, 1855, 6; Buffalo *Weltbürger*, December 24, 1842.

107. Smith, *History of Buffalo and Erie County*, vol. 1, pp. 160–1; Buffalo *Demokrat und Weltbürger*, May 1, 1854; Yox, "Decline of the German-American Community in Buffalo," 48–52.

108. Buffalo *Courier*, September 11, October 23, November 15, 17, 18, December 8, 10, 17, 23, 24, 1851; *Geschichte der Deutschen*, 103, 106.

109. Buffalo *Weltbürger*, June 18, 1851; Burke, *Popular Culture in Early Modern Europe*, p. 195.

110. *Geschichte der Deutschen*, pp. 141–4; Bruce Carlan Levine, " 'In the Spirit of 1848': German-Americans and the Fight over Slavery's Expansion" (Ph.D. dissertation, University of Rochester, 1980), 40–3; Buffalo *Weltbürger*, January 9, 1847; May 27, 1849; June 28, August 27, 1851; Albert Post, *Popular Free Thought in America, 1825–1850* (New York, 1943), p. 198; chapter 8, below, pp. 231–33; and chapter 10, pp. 264–71.

111. Wittke, *Refugees of Revolution*, pp. 147–8; Augustus J. Prahl, "The Turners," in *The Forty-Eighters*, ed. A. E. Zucker (New York, 1950), pp. 79–90; Faust, *The German Element*, vol. 2, pp. 387–8.

112. Noel Iverson, *Germania, U.S.A.: Social Change in New Ulm, Minnesota* (Minneapolis, 1966), pp. 33–52; Levine, " 'In the Spirit of 1848,' " 87.

113. Wittke, *Refugees of Revolution*, p. 195; Buffalo *Demokrat und Weltbürger*, August 27, September 8, 11, October 1, 3, 8, 1856; August 27, 1859.

114. *Geschichte der Deutschen*, pp. 144–8; Carol Poore, "An Alternative Tradition: The Nineteenth Century German-American Socialists," *Yearbook for German-American Studies*, 16 (1981), 131–40; Klaus Ensselin and Heinz Ickstadt, "German Working Class Culture in Chicago," in *German Workers in Industrial Chicago*, ed. Keil and Jentz, pp. 242–51; Yox, "Decline of the German Community in Buffalo," 80.

115. Buffalo, *Demokrat und Weltbürger*, March 9, 1860.

116. Buffalo *Weltbürger*, May 27, 1849; *Journal des Deutschen Singervereins von Buffalo, 1844–1848*, BECHS.

117. Yox, "Ethnic Loyalties of the Alsatians in Buffalo," 118–9; Smith, *History of Buffalo and Erie County*, vol. 2, pp. 368–9, 397–8, 412. For Bishop Timon, these particular secular affiliations went a long way to explain the parish's rebellion; see Rev. John Timon to Propaganda Fide, Rome, July 1, 1852; and March 19, 1854, Congregation of the Propaganda Fide Collection, UND (microfilms).

118. *Geschichte der Deutschen* (biographical section), pp. 8, 30–1 (Free Thinker's Society), 36, 53–4, 59–60, 163. Unfortunately the records of many of these institutions and organizations no longer exist, so cross-referencing individuals and relevant substructures is difficult; hence, the tentative tone.

119. Ibid. (biographical section), pp. 8, 15, 36; Smith, *History of Buffalo and Erie County*, vol. 2, pp. 397–8; Yox, "Ethnic Loyalties of the Alsatians in Buffalo," 113–4, 118–9.

120. Buffalo *Weltbürger*, March 4, 1843; January 31, 1846; Buffalo *Commercial Advertiser*, October 18, 1860; Philip Dorsheimer to Thurlow Weed, October 29, 1861, Seward-Weed Collection, UR; Yox, "Decline of the German-American Community in Buffalo," 39, 87; *Geschichte der Deutschen*, p. 35; Ellison, "The Germans of Buffalo," 125; Roszak, "The George Urban Family," 3–21.

121. Buffalo *Courier*, August 23, 1843; Buffalo *Commercial Advertiser*, February 12, 1855; November 14, 1857 (quotation); August 22, 1859.

122. R. G. Dun and Co., New York, vol. 80, pp. 61 (Vol.), 64 (Ste.), 80 (Wei.), 167–8 (Koc.), 169 (Meu.), 169 (Mun.), 173 (Ube.), 174 (Wec.), 204 (Muh.), 228 (Rod.), 264 (Wil.); vol. 81, pp. 45 (Per.), 172 (Sch.); and vol. 82, pp. 30 (Kna.), 91 (Wel.), R. G. Dun and Company Collection, BL.

123. Buffalo *Commercial Advertiser*, March 20, 1857; Wallach, "German Immigrant Women," 101.

124. R. G. Dun and Co., New York, vol. 80, p. 64, R. G. Dun and Company Collection, BL.

125. Buffalo *Commercial Advertiser*, January 28, July 22, 1856.

126. Buffalo *Courier*, October 2, 1850; Buffalo *Commercial Advertiser*, April 20, 1854; May 22, 1856; March 3, 1857. As we shall see in chapter 8, the German ethnic leadership often joined Americans in describing their people as apathetic in public affairs. However, as we shall also see, the different goals and strategies of leaders and ordinary folk go a long way toward explaining the perceptions of the former.

127. Buffalo *Commercial Advertiser*, November 14, 1857.

128. Buffalo *Weltbürger*, January 20, 1838; May 19, 1859; Buffalo *Christian Advocate*, August 7, 1851; April 27, 1854; March 22, 1855; July 14, 1859; Buffalo *Commercial Advertiser*, March 21, 1846; November 27, 1855; Buffalo *Republic*, May 18, 20, 1854.

129. Buffalo *Weltbürger*, November 10, 1838.

130. Ibid., June 6, 1848; Buffalo *Demokrat und Weltbürger*, December 5, 8, 20, 1854; May 5, 1856; June 22, 1857; March 19, 1858 (quotation).

131. Buffalo *Weltbürger*, December 22, 1838; July 13, 1839; June 26, 1842; March 20, 1850; Buffalo *Demokrat und Weltbürger*, July 2, 1853; April 15

(quotation), May 3, 19, 1854; August 21, 1855; March 15, 1858; December 19, 1859.

132. Buffalo *Weltbürger*, June 12, 1847.

133. Buffalo *Weltbürger*, March 20, 1850; Buffalo *Demokrat und Weltbürger*, December 22, 1856; Wallach, "German Immigrant Women," 102-3.

134. *Kirchliches Informatorium*, March 1, 1857, 103; Buffalo *Weltbürger*, February 5, 1842; August 21, 1850; March 5, 1851.

135. Buffalo *Demokrat und Weltbürger*, July 7, 1855.

136. For Germans in the construction of elite homes, see e.g., ibid., March 28, 1859; *Buffalo Commercial Advertiser City Directory, 1855*, pp. 289-95; Glasco *Ethnicity and Social Structure*, p. 94.

137. Buffalo *Commercial Advertiser*, July 22, 1876 (quotation). Ibid., December 9, 1853; and Buffalo *Courier*, April 29, 1843, for similar remarks.

138. Yox, "Decline of the German-American Community in Buffalo," 26; Smith, *History of Buffalo and Erie County*, vol. 2, p. 118; Buffalo *Weltbürger*, May 13, 1843; May 17, 1848 (adv.); Buffalo *Demokrat und Weltbürger*, December 11, 1856; October 27, 1857; "Lot Book Containing Maps and Descriptions of Lots in Buffalo, N.Y."; and James S. Wadsworth to Nelson James, June 8, 1859, James S. Wadsworth Papers, ML.

139. Buffalo *Weltbürger*, April 18, 25, 1840; January 31, 1846; February 24, 1847; December 25, 1849; *Täglicher Buffalo Demokrat*, September 17, 1851.

140. Buffalo *Weltbürger*, January 24, July 22, 1846; January 18, May 7, March 24, April 14, 1852; Buffalo *Demokrat und Weltbürger*, June 21, September 1, 1854; September 2, 1857; March 19, 1858; December 9, 1859; Buffalo *Commercial Advertiser*, April 9, 1857; *Buffalo Commercial Advertiser City Directory, 1855*, pp. 16-17; Manufacturers and Traders Trust Company, *Seventy-Five Years of Sound Conservative Banking* (Buffalo, 1931), p. 4.

141. R. G. Dun and Co., New York, vol. 80, pp. 59 (Bey.), 59 (Bet.), 103 (Ot.), 137 (Hel.), 141 (Deb.), 163 (Heim.), 167-8 (Koc.), 169 (Men.), 181 (Wac.), 234 (Geo.), 280 (Deu.); and vol. 81, p. 58 (Hau.), R. G. Dun and Company Collection, BL. Also, see Buffalo *Republic*, October 5, 1857; Buffalo *Christian Advocate*, February 6, 1859. Because of the patterns of a distinctive business culture and of traditional anti-Semitism, the credit reports on German Jews are much different and highly negative; see David A. Gerber, "Cutting out Shylock: Elite Anti-Semitism and the Quest for Moral Order in the Mid-Nineteenth Century American Market Place," *Journal of American History* 69 (December, 1982), 615-37.

142. "No Ragged Schools in Buffalo," *New York Teacher*, 3 (March, 1855), 364-5; Buffalo *Courier*, July 28, 1853; Buffalo *Commercial Advertiser*, April 30, 1859. Also, see notes 65, 66, above.

143. Buffalo *Courier*, October 1, 1844; August 26, 28, December 23, 1852; Buffalo *Commercial Advertiser*, September 8, 1858; *Buffalo Commercial Advertiser City Directory, 1855*, pp. 21-2.

144. Yox, "Decline of the German-American Community in Buffalo," 26; Buffalo *Courier*, December 29, 1847; June 2, August 26, 1852; April 12, July 14, 1853; Buffalo *Christian Advocate*, July 15, 1858; Buffalo *Commercial Advertiser*, March 10, April 23, 1860.

145. Buffalo *Weltbürger*, August 21, 1847; April 4, 1849; Buffalo *Christian Advocate*, October 19, 1854; November 17, 1859; R. G. Dun and Co., New York, vol. 80, p. 298, R. G. Dun and Company Collection, BL.

146. Gerber, "Modernity in the Service of Tradition," 655–89; Buffalo *Demokrat und Weltbürger*, September 8, 17, 1853; Buffalo *Express*, June 21, 1851; Buffalo *Courier*, February 23, October 8, 1852; June 30, September 14, October 31, November 19, 1853; Buffalo *Christian Advocate*, July 6, 20, 1853; Buffalo *Commercial Advertiser*, June 27, 30, July 5, 12, August 28, September 12, October 3, 1854; February 2, March 5, May 24, 29, June 23, 1855; W. S. Tisdale, ed., *The Controversy between Senator Brooks and John, Archbishop of New York* (New York, 1855).

147. Buffalo *Commercial Advertiser*, June 27, 1854.

148. Buffalo *Commercial Advertiser*, June 24, 1854; Buffalo *Weltbürger*, June 18, 28, 1851; Buffalo *Demokrat und Weltbürger*, June 24, 1853; June 3, 1854; June 30, 1855; June 24, 1856; June 18, 1859; June 23, 1860.

149. Buffalo *Commercial Advertiser*, June 23, 1855; June 26, 1857; June 24, 1858 (quotation); June 26, 1860; Buffalo *Demokrat und Weltbürger*, June 24, 1853; June 30, 1855; June 18, 1859.

150. Buffalo *Commercial Advertiser*, July 16, 1856. Also, Buffalo *Republic*, July 19, 1856.

151. Buffalo *Commercial Advertiser*, July 16, 1856.

152. Ibid., June 24, 1857; Buffalo *Weltbürger*, June 28, 1851; Buffalo *Demokrat und Weltbürger*, June 3, 1854; June 30, 1855.

153. Buffalo *Commercial Advertiser*, June 21, 1859.

154. Ibid., August 14, 1856. The paper was enthusiastic about the 1860 "Grand Lager Bier Festival," at which free samples were provided by brewers hoping to develop a market among those seeking alternatives to liquor; see July 20, 1860.

155. Ibid., August 29, 1859; January 6, 1860. The Buffalo *Republic* agreed with this assessment, based on its belief that lager "is not really liquor"; see July 17, 1855; August 4, 1858 (quotation).

156. Buffalo *Christian Advocate*, August 27, 1854.

157. Buffalo *Courier*, April 8, 1853; Buffalo *Demokrat und Weltbürger*, July 5, 1855; March 26, 1858; Buffalo *Commercial Advertiser*, March 8, 1858.

158. Buffalo *Commercial Advertiser*, January 5, 1847; February 9, 1854; January 22, March 13, 31, April 6, 1857; January 7, March 10, November 24, 1858; May 8, October 29, 1860; Buffalo *Courier*, February 25, March 16, 1850; June 6, 1851; March 14, April 7, June 23, 1853; Buffalo *Demokrat und Weltbürger*, January 2, September 14, 1857.

159. Buffalo *Commercial Advertiser*, November 8, 1859; July 11, 22, 23, 24, 26, 1860; Buffalo *Christian Advocate*, November 17, 1859; July 26, 1860; Buffalo *Demokrat und Weltbürger*, November 2, 7, 11, 1859; January 19, 20, February 17, April 23, July 18, 23, 24, 25, 26, 1860.

160. Buffalo *Demokrat und Weltbürger*, July 18, 1860; Buffalo *Commercial Advertiser*, July 21, 25, 1860.

161. Buffalo *Commercial Advertiser*, June 22, 1858.

162. "Payroll, August 10, 1839, Buffalo Harbor," in Miscellaneous Manuscripts, Buffalo, New York, Harbor Construction, NYHS, in which the paymaster of a surveying party changed the signatures of, for example, "Ambs," "Diehl," and "Vollmer," to "Ames," "Peel," and "Fuller."

163. Buffalo Common Council, *Proceedings*, November 5, 1839, BECHS (microfilm); Buffalo *Courier*, January 11, 1849. Americans continued to be helpless when confronted with some German surnames, as in 1854 when "a German, whose name it is impossible to give in English" was reported arrested by the Buffalo *Republic*, February 27, 1854.

164. Buffalo *Commercial Advertiser*, September 23, 1856; Buffalo *Demokrat und Weltbürger*, November 22, 1858; May 3, 1859.

165. *Geschichte der Deutschen*, pp. 118–20.

166. Buffalo *Weltbürger*, February 24, 1847; March 27, 1852; Buffalo *Republic*, October 4, 1855; Buffalo *Commercial Advertiser*, November 21, 1844; October 17, 1855; George Washington Johnson, Diary, 1849, entry of November 5, 488.

167. *Geschichte der Deutschen*, p. 78.

Chapter 8. Buffalo's Germans: Leadership, Ideology, and the Struggle for Unity

1. Frederick Luebke, "The Germans," in *Ethnic Leadership in America*, ed. John Higham (Baltimore, 1978), pp. 67–8; Kathleen Neils Conzen, "German-Americans and the Invention of Ethnicity"; and Willie Paul Adams, "Ethnic Leadership and the German-Americans," both in *America and the Germans: An Assessment of a Three-Hundred-Year History*, ed. Frank Trommler and Joseph McVeigh, vol. 1, *Immigration, Language, and Ethnicity* (Philadelphia, 1985), pp. 131–47, 148–59.

2. Buffalo *Weltbürger*, December 2, 1837; March 23, April 29, July 6, 1839; Buffalo *Courier*, September 30, 1844, June 1, 1846; Norbert Fullington, "The *Weltbürger-Demokrat*: Mirror of the Political Opinion of Buffalo's *Deutschthum*, 1837–1860" (M.A. thesis, University of Buffalo, 1951); Carl Wittke, *The German Language Press in America* (Lexington, 1957), p. 46; *Geschichte der Deutschen in Buffalo und Erie County, New York*, vol. 1 (Buffalo, 1898), p. 54.

3. *Geschichte der Deutschen*, vol. 2, p. 2; Buffalo *Courier*, March 10, 1887; R. G. Dun and Co., New York [reports], vol. 80, p. 123 (Bru., et al.).

4. Buffalo *Weltbürger*, December 2, 1837; January 13, March 31, April 7, June 30, 1838; *Geschichte der Deutschen*, vol. 1, pp. 62–3; Ismar Ellison, "An Historical Essay: The Germans of Buffalo," Buffalo Historical Society *Publications*, 2 (1880), 129–30.

5. Robert J. Rayback, *Millard Fillmore: Biography of a President* (Buffalo, 1959), pp. 156–7; R. G. Dun and Co., New York [reports], vol. 81, p. 56 (Ben.); *Geschichte der Deutschen*, vol. 1, pp. 70–2.

6. Buffalo *Weltbürger*, January 20, 1838; December 24, 1841; April 9, 1842; April 27, August 17, 1844; November 26, 1845.

7. Ibid., July 21, 1838.

8. Ibid., July 11, 1846.
9. Buffalo *Commercial Advertiser*, May 22, 1856, and above, p. 201.
10. See above, pp. 176-77, and extended analysis in chapters 11 and 12, below.
11. Mack Walker, *German Home Towns: Community, State, and General Estate, 1648-1871* (Ithaca, 1971), pp. 34-71, 198-202; John G. Gagliardo, *From Pariah to Patriot: The Changing Image of the German Peasant, 1770-1840* (Lexington, 1969), p. 176; Leonard Krieger, *The German Idea of Freedom* (Boston, 1957). The same apathy has been noted among German immigrants in a very different setting—Brazil; see Frederick C. Luebke, "A Prelude to Conflict: The German Ethnic Group in Brazilian Society, 1890-1917," *Ethnic and Racial Studies*, 6 (January, 1983), 3.
12. Buffalo *Weltbürger*, December 2, 1837; February 24, August 11, 1838; September 25, 1841; February 19, 1842; November 16, 1853.
13. Ibid., June 30, 1838.
14. Ibid., February 21, 1846. See also December 17, 1842, for a similar injunction in regard to a proposed revision of the city's charter.
15. Ibid., March 21, 1840; March 19, 1845.
16. Ibid., January 13, March 17, July 28, November 10, 1838; October 10, 17, 1840; September 21, November 2, 1844.
17. John T. Horton, Edward T. Williams, and Harry S. Douglass, *History of Northwestern New York*, vol. 1 (New York, 1947), pp. 77-8.
18. Buffalo *Weltbürger*, December 9, 1837; August 4, 1838; February 2 (quotation), 16, May 25, 1839; January 16, 19, October 23, 1841; *Geschichte der Deutschen*, pp. 57-60; Buffalo *Courier*, January 9, 1843; December 29, 1848; Buffalo *Commercial Advertiser*, November 30, December 15, 1846.
19. Buffalo *Weltbürger*, December 2, 1837; February 24, June 30, July 14, August 11, December 8, 29, 1838; January 19, April 20, June 22, September 14, 1839; September 25, 1841, February 19, December 17, 1842; February 21, 1846.
20. Vladimir Nahirny and Joshua A. Fishman, "American Immigrant Groups: Ethnic Identification and the Problem of Generations," *Sociological Review*, 13 (November, 1965), 311-26. Also, see Stanley Lieberson and Timothy Curry, "Language Shift in the U.S.: Some Demographic Clues," *International Migration Review*, 5 (Summer, 1971), 125-37; and Heinz Kloss, "German-American Language Maintenance Efforts," in *Language Loyalty in the United States*, ed. Joshua Fishman (The Hague, 1966), pp. 206-52, especially 206-12.
21. *Geschichte der Deutschen*, vol. 1, p. 56; Buffalo *Weltbürger*, March 3, 23, April 20, 29, May 4, July 6, 1839; Buffalo Common Council, "Minutes" (Reel 4), November 5, 1839, BECHS; Buffalo *Courier*, December 11, 1844; July 14, 1846; January 19, 1847; July 10, November 20, 1849.
22. Rayback, *Millard Fillmore: Biography of a President*, pp. 156-7; R. G. Dun and Co., New York, vol. 81, p. 56 (Ben.), R. G. Dun and Company Collection, BL; Buffalo *Commercial Advertiser*, June 20, 1854; March 20, 1860; Buffalo *Weltbürger*, July 6, 1839; February 17, 1844.
23. Buffalo *Weltbürger*, February 17, 1844; and 1852-54 passim; Buffalo *Courier*, August 23, 1853; Buffalo *Commercial Advertiser*, April 25, June 13, 1854; May 1, 1860.

24. Buffalo *Weltbürger*, September 10, 1842; Buffalo *Demokrat und Weltbürger*, November 2, 1853; Buffalo *Commercial Advertiser*, January 19, 1859.

25. Buffalo *Commercial Advertiser*, June 11, 13, 1846; January 28, 1847; January 12, 14, 1854; April 24, 1855; March 9, September 28, 1854; Buffalo *Courier*, May 30, 1850; May 14, 1851.

26. Prior to the 1854 celebration a translation of the Declaration was reprinted in the *Weltbürger*, but not read at the official celebration. In that year, however, public reading of a German translation began. Buffalo *Weltbürger*, June 29, 1839; July 3, 1841; Buffalo *Demokrat und Weltbürger*, July 3, 1854; Buffalo *Courier*, July 4, 1854.

27. Buffalo *Weltbürger*, July 14, December 19, 1838; Melvin George Deck, "Buffalo's Early Struggle for Free Public Schools" (M.A. thesis, University of Buffalo, 1949).

28. Buffalo *Weltbürger*, March 24, April 21, July 14, 21, September 29, 1838; March 2, September 14, 1839; Buffalo Common Council, "Minutes," (Reel 3), May 14, 1839.

29. Buffalo *Weltbürger*, July 21, December 29, 1838; February 2, 1839.

30. Ibid., April 7, 1838.

31. Ibid., February 9, March 2, 9, 1839; *Geschichte der Deutschen*, vol. 1, pp. 11, 65, 70.

32. Buffalo *Weltbürger*, December 16, 30, 1837; March 10, 1838; Rev. Paul Theodore Burger, *Chronik der Ersten Evangelischen Lutherischen Dreifaltigkeits Gemeinde U.A.C., in Buffalo, New York* (Buffalo, 1889), p. 19; Walter Beck, *Lutheran Elementary Schools in the U.S.* (St. Louis, 1939), pp. 124–6.

33. Buffalo *Weltbürger*, December 8, 1838; January 29, 1839. Enough money was raised to grant free schooling to the poor.

34. *Geschichte der Deutschen*, vol. 1, pp. 77–8 (for the story of this school and the men who founded it), and vol. 2, pp. 8, 45 (on these two individuals). Also, Andrew Yox, "Bonds of Community: Buffalo's German Element, 1853–1871," *New York History*, 66 (April, 1985), 157, for a similar observation on acculturation and retention of ancestral culture.

35. Nahirny and Fishman, "American Ethnic Groups: Ethnic Identification and the Problem of Generations," 311–26.

36. Buffalo *Weltbürger*, November 17, 1838; January 19, 26, April 20, 1839.

37. Ibid., September 14, 1839.

38. In 1860, twelve of ninety-one teachers had German names and presumably were capable of speaking the language to students, though not allowed to teach in it; Andrew Trusz, "The Public School Teachers of Buffalo, 1854–1864" (seminar paper, SUNYAB, n.d.). For other citations on German enrollments, see Buffalo Superintendent of Schools, *Third Annual Report, 1839* (Buffalo, 1840), p. 5; City of Buffalo, *Census of Children (ages 5–16), 1 January 1845* (Manuscript, BECHS); Buffalo Superintendent of Schools, *Tenth Annual Report, 1846* (Buffalo, 1847), p. 4.

39. Buffalo Superintendent of Schools, *Annual Report*, 1840–1850, passim. The anxieties school officials had about German enrollments were probably partly allayed by the large number of German young men in night school; see above, p. 184.

40. Beck, *Lutheran Elementary Schools in the U.S.*, pp. 5-8, 78-84; Rev. John Timon, *Missions in Western New York and Church History of the Diocese of Buffalo* (Buffalo, 1862), pp. 235-40; Vincent P. Lannie, *Public Money and Parochial Education: Bishop Hughes, Governor Seward, and the New York School Controversy* (Cleveland, 1968); Neil G. McCluskey, S.J., *Catholic Education in America: A Documentary History* (New York, 1964), pp. 51-81.

41. Buffalo *Courier*, October 2, 1850.

42. Ibid. (for report of the council school committee on the trustees' petition and for reference to antitrustee, German petitions). See also the remarks of the Buffalo Superintendent of Schools, *Fourteenth Annual Report of the Superintendent of Schools, 1850* (Buffalo, 1851), pp. 17-8.

43. Buffalo *Courier*, October 2, 1850; Buffalo *Weltbürger*, October 5, 1850.

44. Buffalo *Weltbürger*, October 26, 1850.

45. Buffalo *Courier*, October 2, 1850.

46. Ibid., On the district-option method and other methods by which German entered public schools, see L. Viereck, "German Instruction in American Schools," U.S. Commissioner of Education, *Report, 1900-1* (Washington, D.C., 1902), pp. 531-708.

47. Buffalo *Weltbürger*, October 26, November 2, 9, 1850.

48. Buffalo *Courier*, November 7, 28, 1850; Buffalo *Weltbürger*, November 9, 1850.

49. Buffalo *Weltbürger*, November 9, December 11, 1850.

50. Ibid., November 9, 1850.

51. Ibid.

52. Ibid., December 11, 1850; January 18, 1851.

53. Buffalo *Courier*, January 15, 1851.

54. Ibid., January 9, 1851, for the text of the minority proposal.

55. Ibid.

56. Buffalo *Demokrat und Weltbürger*, December 13, 1859; Buffalo *Courier*, February 28, 1860; Buffalo *Die Aurora*, June 15, 1860. German finally entered the local public school curriculum in 1866; see David A. Gerber, "Language Maintenance, Ethnic Group Formation, and Public Schools: Changing Patterns of German Concern, Buffalo, 1837-1874," *Journal of American Ethnic History*, 4 (Fall, 1984), 45-6.

57. Buffalo *Weltbürger*, March 25, 29, April 1, 15, 19, 1848.

58. Ibid., June 28, 1851.

59. Ibid.; *Geschichte der Deutschen*, vol. 1, pp. 92-4.

60. Buffalo *Weltbürger*, June 21, 25, 1851; February 4, 1852; Buffalo *Demokrat und Weltbürger*, May 2 (quotation), 31, September 8, 1853; February 14, 18, 1856.

61. R. G. Dun and Co., New York [reports], vol. 80, p. 123 (Bru., et al.); Buffalo *Courier*, April 7, 1853; Buffalo *Demokrat und Weltbürger*, May 2, 1853; Deutsch-Amerikanische Historische und Biographische Gesellschaft, *Buffalo und Sein Deutschtum* (Buffalo, 1912), p. 55.

62. Buffalo *Demokrat und Weltbürger*, May 31, September 8, 17, 20, December 27, 1853; June 7, 13, 26, 1854; January 9, 11, 1855. On the anti-Catholicism of the Whig and later Republican *Die Telegraph*, of which no

copies exist: Buffalo *Commercial Advertiser*, November 10, 12, December 12, 1855; October 15, 1857; Buffalo *Die Aurora*, December 16, 1859.

63. For an overview of Gray-Green conflict, see Carl Wittke, *Refugees of Revolution: the German 48ers in America* (Philadelphia, 1952); and idem, *The German Language Press in America*, pp. 63–79.

64. Buffalo *Weltbürger*, January 9, 1847; May 27, 1849; August 10, 1850; March 8, 1851; April 27, 1853.

65. Buffalo *Demokrat und Weltbürger*, September 9, 1853.

66. Bruce Carlan Levine, " 'In the Spirit of 1848': German-Americans and the Fight over Slavery's Expansion" (Ph.D. dissertation, University of Rochester, 1980), 186, 264; Conzen, "German-Americans and the Invention of Ethnicity," 136–9.

67. Buffalo *Weltbürger*, April 19, 1848; June 28 (quotation), October 16, 1850; August 27, November 20, 1850; August 27, October 15, 1851.

68. Ibid., January 26 (quotation), 30 (quotation), February 2, 1850; March 8, 1951; *Der Pionier*, August 1, 1853 (Heinzen).

69. Wittke, *Refugees of Revolution*; and idem, *The German Language Press in America*, pp. 63–79; Levine, " 'In the Spirit of 48,' " 43–6, 87, 188, 220; Buffalo *Weltbürger*, November 13, 1850; July 26, 1851; Albert Post, *Popular Free Thought in America, 1825–1850* (New York, 1943), pp. 197–8; Buffalo *Demokrat und Weltbürger*, June 2, 1853; June 22, 1854; November 21, December 31, 1857; *Buffalo Commercial Advertiser City Directory, 1855*; *New York State Census, 1855*, alphabetized printout, SUNYAB.

70. Levine, " 'In the Spirit of 48,' " 97–8, 106, 108–10, 143, and *Geschichte der Deutschen*, vol. 1, pp. 62–3, 154–9.

71. *Geschichte der Deutschen*, vol. 2, pp. 59–60; Gerber, "Language Maintenance, Ethnic Group Formation, and Public Schools," 48–51.

72. E. J. Hobsbawm, *The Age of Revolution, 1789–1848* (New York, 1964), pp. 85–6, 141, 154, 249–54; Levine, " 'In the Spirit of 48,' " 40–51.

73. Levine, " 'In the Spirit of 48,' " 64; below, pp. 265–69.

74. Levine, " 'In the Spirit of 48,' " 85; *Geschichte der Deutschen*, pp. 144–50; Buffalo *Weltbürger*, May 23, 27, 1849; November 13, 1850.

75. Buffalo *Weltbürger*, July 7, 1849; March 2, June 8, 19, August 7, 10, 14, 17, 1850; February 19, 1851.

76. *Geschichte der Deutschen*, vol. 1, p. 142.

77. Ibid., pp. 141–3; *Die Republik der Arbeiter*, 1 (November, 1850), 174.

78. *Die Republik der Arbeiter*, 1 (November, 1850), 174.

79. Buffalo *Weltbürger*, July 31, August 3, 7, September 21, 1850; January 1, 1851; Buffalo *Demokrat und Weltbürger*, March 12, 1855.

80. *Die Republik der Arbeiter*, 1 (December, 1850), 186–7, 187–9; Buffalo *Weltbürger*, November 23, 1850; Carol Poore, *German-American Socialist Literature* (Bern, 1982), pp. 31–5.

81. David A. Gerber, "The Pathos of Exile: Old Lutheran Refugees in the United States and South Australia," *Comparative Studies in Society and History* 26, (July, 1984), 510–3; *Kirchliches Informatorium*, December 1, 1852; William O. Shanahan, *German Protestants Face the Social Question*, vol. 1,

The Conservative Phase, 1815–1871 (Notre Dame, 1954), pp. 39–49, 97, 135–6.

82. Gerber, "The Pathos of Exile: Old Lutheran Refugees in the United States and South Australia," 512–4.

83. Rev. John Timon to Propaganda Fide, Rome, July 1, 1852; and March 19, 1854, Congregation of the Propaganda Fide Collection, UND (microfilms).

84. Rev. Thomas Donohue, *History of the Catholic Church in Western New York* (Buffalo, 1904), p. 241; R. G. Dun and Co., New York, vol. 80, p. 294, R. G. Dun and Company Collection, BL.

85. Buffalo *Die Aurora*, November 15, 16, 1853; November 11, 18, December 9, 16, 23, 1859; March 16, June 15, 1860; March 19, 1861.

86. Philip Gleason, *The Conservative Reformers: German-American Catholics and the Social Order* (Notre Dame, 1968), pp. 22–3.

Chapter 9. Class and Ethnicity in the Rise of Labor

1. Susan E. Hirsch, *The Roots of the American Working Class: The Industrialization of Crafts in Newark, 1800–1860* (Philadelphia, 1978); David M. Gordon, Richard Edwards, and Michael Reich, *Segmented Work, Divided Workers: The Historical Transformation of Labor in the United States* (New York, 1982), chapters 1, 2, 3; Bruce Laurie, George Alter, and Theodore Hershberg, "Immigrants and Industry: The Philadelphia Experience, 1850–1880," in *Philadelphia: Work, Space, Family, and Group Experience in the Nineteenth Century*, ed. Theodore Hershberg (New York, 1981), pp. 93–119; Bruce Laurie and Mark Schmitz, "Manufacturing and Productivity: The Making of an Industrial Base, Philadelphia, 1850–1880," ibid., pp. 43–92.

2. Laurence A. Glasco, *Ethnicity and Social Structure: Irish, Germans, and Native-Born of Buffalo, N.Y., 1850–1860* (New York, 1980), p. 90; Buffalo *Commercial Advertiser*, June 22, 1859. On the relatively large number of the unskilled in Buffalo, see Theodore Hershberg, et al., "Occupation and Ethnicity in Five Nineteenth Century Cities," *Historical Methods Newsletter* 7 (1974), 174–216.

3. Glasco, *Ethnicity and Social Structure*, pp. 92–7.

4. Ibid., p. 87; Richard Larry Ehrlich, "The Development of Manufacturing in Selected Counties in the Erie Canal Corridor, 1815–1860" (Ph.D. dissertation, SUNYAB, 1972), 271–314; Buffalo *Courier*, September 27, 1852; Buffalo *Commercial Advertiser*, February 10, 1854; January 15, 1855; March 7, 1857; February 27, 1858; Buffalo *Republic*, June 9, 1855.

5. On Carland: Buffalo *Republic*, February 21, 1854; Buffalo *Commercial Advertiser*, November 10, 1860. On other large firms, see the series in the *Commercial Advertiser*, January 10, 13, 14, 20, 21, 24, 25, 27, 29, February 3, 8, 9, 14, 15, May 28, 30, 1859.

6. Buffalo *Commercial Advertiser*, March 17, 24, October 18, December 20, 22, 23, 27, 1859; February 23, 25, March 3, 24, 1860; February 21, March 22, 1861; Buffalo *Christian Advocate*, March 1, 29, June 21, 1860; March 21, 1861; Henry Wayland Hill, *The Municipality of Buffalo: A History*, vol. 2, (New York, 1923), p. 791; Sandford B. Hunt, "Buffalo: A Glance at Its Progress

down to the Present Time," in n.a., *The Manufacturing Interests of the City of Buffalo* (Buffalo, 1866), pp. 13–7 (quotation), and in the general text of ibid., p. 51.

7. Buffalo *Demokrat und Weltbürger*, March 22, 1861; Ehrlich, "The Development of Manufacturing in Selected Counties in the Erie Canal Corridor," 312–4, 323. On the pessimism of the time, see, "Buffalo: A Finished City," Buffalo *Christian Advocate*, August 5, 1858.

8. Buffalo *Commercial Advertiser*, September 10, 21, 1858; February 18, 1859; March 24, August 1, 1860; March 5, 1861; Buffalo *Christian Advocate*, November 22, 1860; Buffalo *Courier*, April 19, 1861.

9. Ehrlich, "The Development of Manufacturing in Selected Counties in the Erie Canal Corridor," 312–4, 323; Buffalo *Commercial Advertiser*, January 10, 13, 20, 21, 27, February 8, 9, 1859; March 24, 1860.

10. Buffalo *Demokrat und Weltbürger*, February 15, 1854; July 15, 1858; July 30, October 4, November 17, 1860; Buffalo *Commercial Advertiser*, November 22, 1855; July 14, 1858; Buffalo *Christian Advocate*, October 11, 1860.

11. Hirsch, *The Roots of the American Working Class*, pp. 21–2, 24–7; David Grimsted, "Ante-Bellum Labor: Violence, Strikes, and Communal Arbitration," *Journal of Social History* 19 (Fall, 1985), 7–8; Gordon, et al., *Segmented Work, Divided Workers*, p. 64.

12. Gordon, et al., *Segmented Work, Divided Workers*, pp. 65–7; Buffalo *Courier*, May 8, August 30, 1850; December 22, 1852; Buffalo *Demokrat und Weltbürger*, February 15, 1854; Buffalo *Commercial Advertiser*, March 28, 1856; February 8, May 17, 1859; John T. Horton, Edward T. Williams, and Harry S. Douglass, *History of Northwestern New York*, vol. 1 (New York, 1947), pp. 96–9.

13. Hirsch, *The Roots of the American Working Class*, pp. 22–3, 24–36; Gordon, et al., *Segmented Work, Divided Workers*, pp. 89–90; Laurie and Schmitz, "Manufacturing and Productivity," 58–65; Clyde Griffen and Sally Griffen, *Natives and Newcomers: The Ordering of Opportunity in Mid-Nineteenth Century Poughkeepsie* (Cambridge, Mass., 1978), pp. 139–65.

14. Hirsch, *The Roots of the American Working Class*, pp. 23, 24–36; Laurie and Schmitz, "Manufacturing and Productivity," 47–58; Griffen and Griffen, *Natives and Newcomers*, pp. 139–65.

15. Hirsch, *The Roots of the American Working Class*, pp. 24–36; Griffen and Griffen, *Natives and Newcomers*, pp. 139–65; Gordon, et al., *Segmented Work, Divided Workers*, pp. 64–7, 89–90; Buffalo *Courier*, May 25, 1852; Buffalo *Commercial Advertiser*, December 9, 1853; April 29, 1854; January 24, February 8, 18, March 8, May 10, June 9, 14, 1859; *New York State Census of Manufactures, 1855*, printout in the possession of the author.

16. Ehrlich, "The Development of Manufacturing in Selected Counties in the Erie Canal Corridor," 312–4, 323; Gordon, et al., *Segmented Work, Divided Workers*, pp. 79–88; Laurie, et al., "Immigrants and Industry," 114–5; Mark Goldman, *High Hopes: The Rise and Decline of Buffalo, New York* (Albany, 1983), p. 67; Buffalo *Commercial Advertiser*, April 29, 1854; Buffalo *Courier*, July 20, 23, 1853.

17. *New York State Census of Manufactures, 1855*, printout; Glasco, *Ethnicity and Social Structure*, pp. 201–9; Hirsch, *The Roots of the American Working Class*, pp. 38–41; Gordon, et al., *Segmented Work, Divided Workers*, pp. 69–71, 93–4; Buffalo *Republic*, June 21, 1853; Buffalo *Commercial Advertiser*, March 25, 1858; Buffalo *Demokrat und Weltbürger*, March 22, 1861; Goldman, *High Hopes*, p. 68; Jeanne Boydston, "To Earn Her Daily Bread: Housework and Antebellum Working Class Subsistence," *Radical History Review*, no. 35 (1986), pp. 7–25.

18. *New York State Census of Manufactures, 1855*, printout; Glasco, *Ethnicity and Social Structure*, pp. 201–19; Gordon, et al., *Segmented Work, Divided Workers*, pp. 68–73.

19. *New York State Census of Manufactures, 1855*, printout; Glasco, *Ethnicity and Social Structure*, pp. 189–201; Hirsch, *The Roots of the American Working Class*, pp. 8–10, 41–7, 74–5; Gordon, et al., *Segmented Work, Divided Workers*, pp. 64, 68–73; Buffalo *Commercial Advertiser*, May 17, 1844; February 2, 1861; Buffalo *Courier*, July 20, 28, 1853; William R. Rorabaugh, *The Craft Apprentice: From Franklin to the Machine Age in America* (New York, 1986).

20. Michael B. Katz, Michael J. Doucet, and Mark J. Stern, "Migration and the Social Order in Erie County, New York: 1855," *Journal of Interdisciplinary History*, 8 (Spring, 1978), 698–9; Stephan Thernstrom, *The Other Bostonians: Poverty and Progress in the American Metropolis, 1880–1970* (Cambridge, Mass., 1973), pp. 231–2.

21. Buffalo *Weltbürger*, January 9, 1847 (quotation); November 15, 1848; Buffalo *Courier*, June 3, 1847 (quotation).

22. Hirsch, *The Roots of the American Working Class*, pp. 88–9; Lloyd Graham and Frank Severance, *The First Hundred Years of the Buffalo Chamber of Commerce* (Buffalo, 1945), pp. 32, 37; Buffalo *Courier*, April 22, 1844; April 1, November 24, 1847; September 7, 1849; April 13, 1852; Buffalo *Republic*, October 19, 1853; January 12, April 25, June 22, 26, 1854; March 24, August 25, 1855; May 30, September 29, October 29, 1857; October 1, 5, 10, November 4, 1859; Buffalo *Express*, May 27, November 3, September 8, 1859; Buffalo *Commercial Advertiser*, April 21, 1858; May 5, 1859.

23. Samuel M. Welch, *Home History: Recollections of Buffalo, or Fifty Years Since* (Buffalo, 1891), pp. 353–4; [orders on "Mr. Taylor's Store"], March and April, 1843; Samuel Wilkeson Papers, BECHS; Buffalo *Weltbürger*, March 16, 1844; Buffalo *Demokrat und Weltbürger*, December 5, 8, 20, 1854; November 15, 1859; Buffalo *Commercial Advertiser*, January 15, 1855; March 3, 1857; March 22, 1858; February 26, 1861; Buffalo *Courier*, March 13, 1858; Buffalo *Sentinel*, October 17, 1857.

24. Buffalo *American Celt and Catholic Citizen*, June 12, 1852; Buffalo *Commercial Advertiser*, July 5, 1859; Glasco, *Ethnicity and Social Structure*, p. 94. For evidence of the domination of the period's only butchers' union by Germans, see Buffalo *Republic and Times*, July 26, 1858.

25. On British immigrants and the American labor movement, see Roland Berthoff, *British Immigrants in Industrial America, 1790–1950* (Cambridge, Mass., 1953), pp. 88–106. Also, E. P. Thompson, *The Making of the English*

Working Class (New York, 1966, paperback ed.), pp. 55–185; Ray Boston, *British Chartists in America, 1839–1900* (Manchester, England, 1971). On the Jacksonian workingmen's movement in Buffalo, see Goldman, *High Hopes*, pp. 39–45; and Ryrie E. MacTaggart, "A Labor History of Buffalo (1846–1917), Containing an Introduction Consisting of Conditions Prior to 1846" (M.A. thesis, Canisius College, 1940), 6–9.

26. Hirsch, *The Roots of the American Working Class*, pp. 53–66, 115, 123–4, 127; Amy Bridges, *A City in the Republic: Antebellum New York and the Origins of Machine Politics* (New York, 1984), pp. 103–24; Alan Dawley, *Class and Community: The Industrial Revolution in Lynn* (Cambridge, Mass., 1976), Bruce Laurie, *Working People of Philadelphia, 1800–1850* (Philadelphia, 1980); Sean Wilentz, *Chants Democratic: New York City and the Rise of the American Working Class, 1788–1850* (New York, 1984).

27. Buffalo *Weltbürger*, May 4, 1839 (German translation of these resolutions).

28. Buffalo *Courier*, June 10, 1847.

29. Jean H. Baker, *Affairs of Party: The Political Culture of Northern Democrats in the Mid-Nineteenth Century* (Ithaca, 1983), pp. 101–7.

30. Buffalo *Weltbürger*, May 4, 1839.

31. Ibid.

32. Buffalo *Commercial Advertiser*, January 17, 18 (quotation), 1842.

33. Ibid., May 21, 1844.

34. Horton, et al., *History of Northwestern New York*, vol. 1, p. 81.

35. Buffalo *Commercial Advertiser*, January 17, 18 (quotation), 1842; December 22, 1856; January, 8, 1858; December 7, 1859; Buffalo *Courier*, January 12, 1850; January 12, October 15 (quotation), 1852; Buffalo *American Celt and Catholic Citizen*, June 12, 1852; January 29, 1853; Buffalo *Demokrat und Weltbürger*, January 12, 1861.

36. Danforth Franklin, "Timebook," 1853–54, vol. 1, BECHS. Twenty-seven of thirty-one men missed at least one and as many as five whole, half, or quarter Mondays during terms of employment averaging 5.5 weeks. Some of Franklin's highest paid—and hence, most skilled and senior—men were the most delinquent.

37. Buffalo *Weltbürger*, May 4, 1839.

38. Hirsch, *The Roots of the American Working Class*, p. 91; Bridges, *A City in the Republic*, p. 53; Buffalo *Commercial Advertiser*, May 23, 1859; H. Perry Smith, ed., *History of the City of Buffalo and Erie County*, vol. 2 (Syracuse, 1884), pp. 40–1 (biographical section). Forty-four of forty-nine men listed themselves as "builders" and "contractors" in the *Buffalo Commercial Advertiser City Directory, 1855* (Buffalo, 1855), pp. 272, 276–7.

39. Buffalo *Weltbürger*, May 4, 1839.

40. Buffalo *Courier*, June 10, 1847.

41. Ibid., June 10, 1847; March 30, 1852.

42. Buffalo *Commercial Advertiser*, February 2, 1854.

43. Buffalo *Weltbürger*, January 15, 1842; Buffalo *Commercial Advertiser and Journal*, January 11, 1843; Buffalo *Commercial Advertiser*, July 12, 1844; January 9, 1845; December 7, 1846; January 16, December 22, 1856; Buffalo

Courier, January 27, May 6, July 17, 1844; January 10, April 29, 1847; March 1, July 1, 1850; February 2, 1853; Goldman, *High Hopes*, pp. 39–40.

44. Buffalo *Commercial Advertiser*, January 17, 18, 1842; Oliver G. Steele, "Address," *Twenty-Ninth Annual Report of the Young Men's Association* (Buffalo, New York), p. 52; John G. Ramsey, "From Self-Educating Boosters to Stewards of Culture: Buffalo's Friends of Education," vol. 1 (Ph.D. dissertation, SUNYAB, 1984), pp. 31–2, 40, 261–2.

45. Buffalo *Commercial Advertiser*, June 7, August 24, 1854; Buffalo *Courier*, March 30, May 3, October 15, 1852; April 5, May 7, 10, 1853.

46. Buffalo *Commercial Advertiser*, February 14, 1856.

47. Buffalo *Courier*, January 27, May 6, 1844; January 10, April 29, 1847; February 2, 1853; Buffalo *Commercial Advertiser*, August 24, 1854.

48. Buffalo *Courier*, July 17, 1844; June 10, 1847; July 27, 1850; May 2, 1852; July 24, 1854; Buffalo *Christian Advocate*, June 24, 1852; Buffalo *Commercial Advertiser*, August 24, 1854.

49. Buffalo *Weltbürger*, September 4, 1841; Buffalo *Courier*, January 27, May 6, 1844; August 6, 1847; Goldman, *High Hopes*, pp. 39–44.

50. Buffalo *Courier*, August 6, 1847; Buffalo *Commercial Advertiser*, February 2, 1861; Rorabaugh, *The Craft Apprentice*.

51. Buffalo *Weltbürger*, May 4, 1839.

52. Buffalo *Courier*, February 5, 1853; Buffalo *Commercial Advertiser*, August 24, 1854.

53. Buffalo *Commercial Advertiser*, January 16, 1856; January 30, 1861; Buffalo *Demokrat und Weltbürger*, February 13, 1861; Buffalo United Trades and Labor Council of Erie County, *Illustrated History of the United Trades and Labor Council of Buffalo and Erie County* (Syracuse, 1897), pp. 239–40.

54. John R. Commons, *History of Labor in the United States*, vol. 1 (New York, 1926), pp. 444–5; Buffalo *Courier*, June 10, 1847; March 30, May 3, 1852; Buffalo *Commercial Advertiser*, August 28, 1851; February 2, 1861; Buffalo *Demokrat und Weltbürger*, April 18, 1859.

55. Buffalo *Commercial Advertiser*, October 10, 17, 20, 1859; Buffalo *Demokrat und Weltbürger*, October 10, 17, November 23, 26, December 5, 1859; Buffalo *Christian Advocate*, October 20, 27, 1859; Buffalo *Republic*, September 11, 1860.

56. Buffalo *Courier*, January 9, 10, 11, 12, 16, February 2, October 13, 16, 1849; March 16, 1850; Buffalo *Weltbürger*, March 20, December 1, 1850; Buffalo *Demokrat und Weltbürger*, January 11, 1955, December 17, 1858; Buffalo *Commercial Advertiser*, January 22, 24, 25, 29, February 5, March 7, 8, 31, 1855; April 2, 1858; James Swinnich, "Strike and Rebellion upon the Towpath" (seminar paper, SUNYAB, 1983).

57. Buffalo *Republic and Times*, June 12, 14, 15, 1858; Buffalo *Commercial Advertiser*, June 14, 15, 16, 17, July 14, 1858; Buffalo *Demokrat und Weltbürger*, June 14, 15, 1858; Buffalo *Express*, June 15, 1858; Buffalo *Christian Advocate*, June 17, 1858.

58. MacTaggart, "A Labor History of Buffalo (1846–1917)," 22; Walter B. Smith, "Wage Rates on the Erie Canal, 1828–1881," *Journal of Economic History*, 23 (1963), 298–311; Peter De Lottinville, "Joe Beef of Montreal:

Working Class Culture and the Tavern, 1869–1889," *Labor/Le Travailleur*, 8/9 (Autumn-Spring, 1981–82), 32–3; Ruth Bleasdale, "Class Conflict on the Canals of Upper Canada in the 1840s," *Labor/Le Travailleur*, 7 (Spring, 1981), 9–39.

59. David Montgomery, "The Irish and the American Labor Movement," in *America and Ireland, 1776–1976: The American Identity and the Irish Connection*, ed. David Doyle (Westport, 1980), pp. 205–14; Buffalo *Courier*, January 9, 10, 1849; Buffalo *Weltbürger*, March 20, 1850; Buffalo *Commercial Advertiser*, January 22, 1855; New York *Irish-American*, November 22, 29, December 20, 1851; February 21, 1852.

60. Buffalo *Sentinel*, November 21, 28, December 5, 1857.

61. Buffalo *Courier*, January 9, 1849; March 16, 18, 1850; Buffalo *Republic and Times*, June 14, 15, 1858; Buffalo *Commercial Advertiser*, June 14, 15, 1858; Buffalo *Express*, June 15, 1858.

62. Buffalo *Republic and Times*, June 14, 15, 1858; Buffalo *Commercial Advertiser*, June 14, 1858.

63. Buffalo *Demokrat und Weltbürger*, October 31, 1854.

64. Buffalo *Courier*, January 10, 1849; Swinnich, "Strike and Rebellion upon the Towpath," 10, 11. In this dependence on the community-at-large, the Irish alone embody the primary characteristic of pre-1861 labor struggle, applied to *all* workers, in Grimsted, "Ante-Bellum Labor: Violence, Strikes, and Communal Arbitration," 5–19.

65. Buffalo *Sentinel*, November, 14, 21, 28, 1857.

66. Smith, "Wage Rates on the Erie Canal," 300; Buffalo *Courier*, January 10, 1849.

67. Buffalo *Courier*, September 16, 17, 1857; Buffalo *Commercial Advertiser*, September 17, 1857; Buffalo *Sentinel*, October 3, 10, 24, 1957.

68. Buffalo *Commercial Advertiser*, June 15, 16, 17, 1858.

69. Ibid., October 15, 20, 1857; Buffalo *Courier*, October 31, 1857; Buffalo *Sentinel*, November 14, 28, 1857.

70. Buffalo *Republic and Times*, June 15, 1858. The Buffalo *Express*, June 15, 1858, agreed.

71. Buffalo *Sentinel*, October 3, 10, 1857. In ibid., February 13, 1858, editor Hagan outlined views interweaving these ideas.

72. Buffalo *Weltbürger*, January 10, 1849.

73. The best analysis of antebellum German class politics is Bruce Carlan Levine, " 'In the Spirit of 1848': German-Americans and the Fight over Slavery's Expansion" (Ph.D. dissertation, University of Rochester, 1980).

74. Buffalo *Weltbürger*, August 21, 1850.

75. Ibid., November 30, 1839.

76. Buffalo *Demokrat und Weltbürger*, April 18, 1860. For an earlier example of the one-set-of-masters theme, see Buffalo *Weltbürger*, October 27, 1838.

77. Buffalo *Weltbürger*, January 10, 1849.

78. Buffalo *Demokrat und Weltbürger*, April 18, 1860.

79. Buffalo *Weltbürger*, January 9, 1847; August 21, 1850; October 15, 1851; Levine, " 'In the Spirit of 1848,' " 186, 264.

80. Buffalo *Weltbürger*, January 9, 1847 (quotation); and August 21, 1850, for very similar remarks.

81. Ibid., August 10, 1850; Buffalo *Demokrat und Weltbürger*, April 18, October 8, 1860.

82. *Geschichte der Deutschen in Buffalo und Erie County, New York* (Buffalo, 1898), vol. 1, pp. 141–2; Buffalo *Weltbürger*, August 7, 10, 14, 17, 1850.

83. See above, pp. 232–33, and note 72.

84. Buffalo *Demokrat und Weltbürger*, October 8, 1860.

85. E. J. Hobsbawm, *The Age of Revolution, 1789–1848* (New York, 1964), pp. 85–6, 141, 154, 249–54; Levine, " 'In the Spirit of 1848,' " pp. 40–51; Gwyn Williams, *Artisans and Sans-Culottes* (New York, 1969), pp. 18, 32; John Garraty, *Unemployment in History* (New York, 1978), p. 16; Hirsch, *The Roots of the American Working Class*, p. 8. For struggles around taxation and property, see chapters 11 and 12, below.

86. On the relations between German culture and class politics, see Hartmut Keil, "German Immigrants in Nineteenth Century America: Working Class Culture and Everyday Life in an Urban Industrial Setting," in *America and the Germans, An Assessment of a Three Hundred-Year History*, vol. 1, *Immigration, Language, and Ethnicity*, ed. Frank Trommler and Joseph McVeigh (Philadelphia, 1985), pp. 199–201.

87. On the ideology and tactics of antebellum German trade unions in America, see, Levine " 'In the Spirit of 1848,' " 85.

88. Buffalo *Weltbürger*, August 28, 1850. For the butchers' interests and organizations, see Buffalo *Weltbürger*, December 31, 1842; August 24, 1844; Buffalo *Courier*, December 20, 1853; Buffalo *Demokrat und Weltbürger*, March 30, 31, April 6, 22, May 26, July 24, August 24, 1858; March 9, 17, April 5, June 7, 1859; Buffalo *Republic and Times*, June 12, 1858.

89. Glasco, *Ethnicity and Social Structure*, p. 94; Hirsch, *The Roots of the American Working Class*, pp. 27–8, 38; Griffen and Griffen, *Natives and Newcomers*, pp. 170–4; Laurie and Schmitz, "Manufacture and Productivity," 47–64; Laurie, et al., "Immigrants and Industry," 96–106; Buffalo *Weltbürger*, July 31, August 3, 7, September 21, 1850.

90. Buffalo *Weltbürger*, June 17, August 3, 7, 14, 28, 1850; January 1, 1851; Buffalo *Demokrat und Weltbürger*, October 31, 1854; *Die Republik der Arbeiter*, 1 (November, 1850), 174, 176.

91. Buffalo *Weltbürger*, January 18, April 5, 21, 1851; Buffalo *Demokrat*, September 17, 1851; *Die Republik der Arbeiter*, 2 (February, 1851), 4.

92. Buffalo *Weltbürger*, March 12, 1855; R. G. Dun and Co., New York, vol. 80, pp. 86, 129, 248, R. G. Dun and Company Collection, BL; Levine, " 'In the Spirit of 1848,' " 81–2; Hirsch, *The Roots of the American Working Class*, p. 86. *Geschichte der Deutschen*, p. 144.

93. Buffalo *Demokrat und Weltbürger*, March 12, 1855.

94. Buffalo *Demokrat und Weltbürger*, September 14, 1854; Buffalo *Commercial Advertiser*, September 24, 1860.

95. Buffalo *Demokrat und Weltbürger*, April 13, 1859; May 14, September 25, 27, 28, 29, October 2, 8, December 15, 1860; Buffalo *Republic*, September

22, 1860; Buffalo *Commercial Advertiser*, September 24, 1860; Buffalo United Trades, *Illustrated History*, pp. 240–3.

96. *New York State Census of Manufacturers, 1855*, printout; Jacqueline C. Simon, "The Iron Molders' Strike, April, 1860" (seminar paper, SUNYAB, 1984).

97. Simon, "The Iron Molders' Strike, April, 1860"; Buffalo *Demokrat und Weltbürger*, January 9, April 2, 12, 20, 1860; Buffalo *Commercial Advertiser*, April 12, 13, 1860.

98. Buffalo *Demokrat und Weltbürger*, April 12, 20, 1860; Buffalo *Commercial Advertiser*, April 12, 1860.

99. Buffalo *Demokrat und Weltbürger*, April 12, 18 (quotation), 20, 21, 1860; Buffalo *Commercial Advertiser*, April 12, 1860; Buffalo *Christian Advocate*, April 19, 1860; Simon, "The Iron Molders' Strike, April, 1860," 14–6.

100. *Die Republik der Arbeiter*, 1 (November, 1850), 174; Buffalo *Weltbürger*, July 7, 1849; March 2, June 8, 19, 1850; February 19, 1851; *Geschichte der Deutschen*, pp. 141–2; Hermann Schluter, *Die Anfange der Deutschen Arbeiterbewegung in Amerika* (Stuttgart, 1907), pp. 83–5.

101. Buffalo *Demokrat*, September 17, 1851; Buffalo *Weltbürger*, June 11, 1853; *Geschichte der Deutschen*, p. 142; Schluter, *Die Anfange der Deutschen Arbeiterbewegung*, p. 85.

102. Carl Wittke, *Refugees of Revolution: The German 48ers in America* (Philadelphia, 1952), pp. 147–8, 195; Levine, "'In the Spirit of 1848,'" 87; Buffalo *Demokrat und Weltbürger*, August 27, September 8, 11, October 1, 3, 8, 1856; August 27, 1859.

103. Buffalo *Weltbürger*, May 23, 27, 1849.

104. Carl Wittke, *The Utopian Communist: A Biography of Wilhelm Weitling, Nineteenth Century Reformer* (Baton Rouge, 1950), pp. 204–30; Carol Poore, *German-American Socialist Literature* (Bern, 1982), pp. 27–35; William O. Shanahan, *German Protestants Face the Social Question*, vol. 1, *The Conservative Phase, 1815–1871* (Notre Dame, 1954), pp. 169–84.

105. *Die Republik der Arbeiter*, 1 (November, 1850), 174, 176; 2 (January, 1851), 16; and 2 (April 18, 1851), 4; Buffalo *Weltbürger*, March 12, November 14, 1855.

106. Wittke, *The Utopian Communist*, pp. 230–3; Karl Obermann, *Joseph Weydemeyer: Pioneer American Socialist* (New York, 1947), pp. 186–7, 187–9; Poore, *German-American Literature*, pp. 31–5; Buffalo *Weltbürger*, November 23, 1850.

107. MacTaggart, "A Labor History of Buffalo (1846–1917)," chapters 2, 3, 4; Buffalo *Die Arbeiterstimme am Erie*, May-November, 1878; Buffalo *Arbeiter-Zeitung*, 1887–97; Buffalo United Trades, *Ilustrated History*.

108. Buffalo *Weltbürger*, December 24, 1841; February 3, 1844; Buffalo *Mercantile Courier*, April 15, 1844.

109. Buffalo *Courier*, May 11, 17, 18, June 1, 3, 18, July 7, 1847; Buffalo *Weltbürger*, May 19, 1847; August 7, 10, 14, 17, 1850; Buffalo *Republic*, June 1, 1847.

110. Buffalo *Weltbürger*, May 19, 1847; August 14, 17, 1850; Buffalo *Courier*, June 3, 18, July 7, 1847.

111. Buffalo *Courier*, June 1, 1847; Buffalo *Weltbürger*, August 14, 1850.

112. Buffalo *Courier*, October 16, 22, November 4, 13, 1847; March 9, 1848; Buffalo *Commercial Advertiser*, November 4, 1847; Buffalo *Weltbürger*, October 27, December 20, 1847; March 4, 11, 1848.

113. Above, pp. 232–33.

114. Buffalo *Courier*, April 6, 1850; February 25, 1853; Buffalo *Demokrat und Weltbürger*, January 13, March 19, 1861.

115. I. H. Walton, "Sailor Lore of the Great Lakes," *Michigan History Magazine*, 18–19 (1934–35), 356–9.

116. Buffalo *Express*, April 26, 1855; Buffalo *Commercial Advertiser*, April 17, 24, 27, 1855; April 5, August 20, 28, 29, 31, September 1, 11, 1860; Buffalo *Demokrat und Weltbürger*, April 25, 28, May 4, 1855; Buffalo *Courier*, April 28, 1855; MacTaggart, "A Labor History of Buffalo (1846–1917)," 24–5.

117. MacTaggart, "A Labor History of Buffalo (1846–1917)," 24, 26; Buffalo *Express*, April 18, March 31, June 15, 1858; Buffalo *Commercial Advertiser* March 31, 1858; May 3, August 28, 30, 1860; March 18, 1861; Buffalo *Demokrat und Weltbürger*, March 9, 19, 20, 1860.

118. Buffalo *Commercial Advertiser*, April 30, 1860; Buffalo *Courier*, April 20, 1861.

119. Walton, "Sailor Lore of the Great Lakes," 356–9; Glasco, *Ethnicity and Social Structure*, pp. 90, 94; Charles Termini, "The Sailortown of Buffalo" (seminar paper, 1983, SUNYAB).

120. Buffalo *Demokrat und Weltbürger*, April 25, 1855; Buffalo *Express*, April 26, 1855; Buffalo *Commercial Advertiser*, August 28, 1860.

121. Buffalo *Courier*, January 29, 1849; August 9, 1851; April 28, 1855; Buffalo *Commercial Advertiser*, April 24, 1855; August 28, 29, 31, 1860; Buffalo *Republic*, September 1, 1860.

122. Buffalo *Commercial Advertiser*, April 27, 1855.

123. Glasco, *Ethnicity and Social Structure*, pp. 90, 94; *New York State Census, 1855*, alphabetized printout, SUNYAB; Buffalo *Commercial Advertiser*, March 7, 1857.

124. *Hunt's Merchants' Magazine and Commercial Review* (March, 1853), 307; Buffalo *Courier*, April 10, December 20, 1852; Buffalo *Commercial Advertiser*, January 15, 1855; September 8, 1856; March 7, 1857; February 8, 1858; Buffalo *Demokrat und Weltbürger*, March 9, 1861.

125. *New York State Census, 1855*, alphabetized printout, SUNYAB; Glasco, *Ethnicity and Social Structure*, p. 45.

126. Buffalo *Commercial Advertiser*, February 2, September 8, 1856 (quotation); *New York State Census, 1855*, alphabetized printout, SUNYAB; *Map of the City of Buffalo, Surveyed under the Direction of Quackenboss and Kennedy, Insurance Agents* (New York, 1854).

127. Buffalo *Commercial Advertiser*, September 8, 1856.

128. Ibid., October 4, 1860.

129. Buffalo *Evening Post*, October 3, 1860.

130. Buffalo *Commercial Advertiser*, September 8, 1856.

131. Ibid., March 31, 1858; May 3, August 28, October 4, 1860; March 18, 1861; Buffalo *Demokrat und Weltbürger*, March 19, 20, 1860.

Chapter 10. The Catholic Church and the Emergence of a New Interconfessional Order

1. Buffalo *Courier*, October 5, 21, 23, 25, 1847; Buffalo *Weltbürger*, October 27, 1847; Rev. John Timon, *Missions in Western New York and Church History of the Diocese of Buffalo* (Buffalo, 1862), pp. 216, 239–40.

2. Rev. John Hughes to Propaganda Fide, Rome, January 24, 1845; Congregation of the Propaganda Fide, Rome, Collection, UND (microfilms).

3. Timon, *Missions in Western New York*, pp. 236, 240.

4. For the ideas of antebellum anti-Catholicism, see: Ray Allen Billington, *The Protestant Crusade, 1800–1860* (New York, 1938); David Brion Davis, ed., *The Fear of Conspiracy: Images of Un-American Subversion from the Revolution to the Present* (Ithaca, 1971), pp. 1–22; Michael F. Holt, *The Political Crisis of the 1850s* (New York, 1978), pp. 101–38, 139–81. For these themes in local anti-Catholic writing, see Buffalo *Courier*, November 21, 1851; Buffalo *Commercial Advertiser*, December 20, 1853; July 12, September 8, 1854; February 1, April 23, October 15, 1856; April 27, 1858; August 23, 1859 (quotation); Buffalo *Christian Advocate*, December 20, 1853; Buffalo *American Celt and Catholic Citizen*, February 26, 1853.

5. Buffalo *Christian Advocate*, September 26, 1850; February 13, 1851; December 25, 1856; November 26, 1857; November 10, 1859; October 11, 1860; Buffalo *Courier*, October 26, 1850; Buffalo *Commercial Advertiser*, March 13, 1854; Buffalo *American Celt and Catholic Citizen*, February 19, 1853.

6. Buffalo *Courier*, January 18, 1851; November 9, 1853; September 16, 1854; November 24, 1857; Buffalo *Christian Advocate*, January 1, April 8, September 23, 1852; March 24, June 29, October 27, 1853; April 27, 1854; November 15, 1855; December 25, 1856; November 26, 1857; March 18, 1858; Buffalo *Commercial Advertiser*, October 10, 1853; June 20, 1854; May 24, 28, 1855; August 30, 1856 (quotation); January 9, 26, March 19, 1857; January 22, June 7, 1858; February 7, December 27, 1859.

7. Almost any editorial written by D'Arcy McGee would qualify as evidence, but even the moderate Michael Hagan at times indulged in anti-Protestant, "triumphalist" editorializing; see Buffalo *Sentinel,* March 8, 29, April 26, 1856; July 18, August 8, 1857; Buffalo *Commercial Advertiser*, April 13, 1854; June 22, 1857; Buffalo *Courier*, May 28, 1851; January 10, 1853.

8. I have discussed this matter in "Ambivalent Anti-Catholicism: Buffalo's American Protestant Elite Faces the Challenge of the Catholic Church, 1850–1860," *Civil War History*, 30 (June, 1984), 120–43, which includes a brief discussion (120–1) of the relevant historiography.

9. Buffalo *Commercial Advertiser*, January 31, June 8, October 14, December 19, 1854; November 14, 1856; January 22, March 13, 31, April 6, 1857; January 7, March 10, November 24, 1858; June 14, 15, 21, July 22, August 29, November 8, 1859; May 8, 10, June 28, October 29, 1860.

10. Rev. Thomas Donohue, *History of the Catholic Church in Western New York* (Buffalo, 1904), pp. 105–13, 134–5; Timon, *Missions in Western New York*, pp. 60, 147–9.

11. Donohue, *History of the Catholic Church in Western New York*, pp. 214–5.

12. Buffalo *Journal*, July 21, 1829; Martha J. F. Murray, "Memoir of Stephen Louis Le Couteulx de Caumont," Buffalo Historical Society *Publications*, 9 (1906), 433-53; Donohue, *History of the Catholic Church in Western New York*, p. 212.

13. Buffalo *Weltbürger*, January 29, 1839; Rev. Joseph Salzbacher, *Meine Reise nach Nord-Amerika* (Vienna, 1845), p. 260; Donohue, *History of the Catholic Church in Western New York*, pp. 114-27, 253-4; Anita Louise Beaudette, "A Man and a Church Named Louis" (undated typescript at St. Louis Church, Buffalo), 2, 15-6, 25, 28-9; Murray, "Memoir of Stephen Louis Le Couteulx de Caumont," 449; Buffalo *Journal*, July 21, 1829.

14. Rev. John Hughes, "Archepiscopal Reminiscences of the Diocese of New York for the Past Twenty Years" (manuscript, 1858), n.p., Congregation of the Propaganda Fide, Rome, Collection, UND; Father John Neumann to Fr. Dichtl, May 31, 1839, and to Archbishop Milde, 1843-5[?], Leopoldine Foundation Collection, UND (microfilms).

15. Hughes, "Archepiscopal Reminiscences of the Diocese of New York," n.p.; Donohue, *History of the Catholic Church in Western New York*, pp. 141-89. The interpretation here follows my "Modernity in the Service of Tradition: Ante-Bellum Catholic Laymen and the Transformation of European Communal Traditions at Buffalo's St. Louis Church, 1829-1855" *Journal of Social History*, 15 (June, 1982), 655-84.

16. L. Pfleger, "Untersuchungen zur Geschichte des Pfarrei-Institute in Elsass," part 3, "Die Einkommensquellen, 1. Das Kirchenvermogen," *Archiv für Elsassiche Kirchengeschichte*, 8 (1932), 13-4; Andre Schaer, "Le Chapitre Rural Ultra Colles Ottinis en Haute-Alsace: Après la Guerre de Trente Ans jusque à Le Revolution. La Vie Paroissiale (1648-1789)," *Archiv de l'Eglise d'Alsace*, part 1, New Series 16 (1967-68), 168, 197, 200-6, and ibid., part 3, New Series 18 (1970), 174-5; P. Leuilliot, *L'Alsace au Debut du XIXe Siècle: Essais d'Histoire Politique, Economique, et Religieuse, 1815-1830*, vol. 3 (Paris, 1959), pp. 1-17.

17. Pierre Basile Mignault, *Le Droit Paroissiale: Etant Une Etude Historique et Legale de la Paroisse Catholique, de Sa Creation, de Son Gouvernment, et de Ses Biens* (Montreal, 1893), pp. vi-viii, 44, 210-25, 234-46, 260-4, 272-3, 308-11; George Pare, *The Catholic Church in Detroit, 1701-1888* (Detroit, 1951), pp. 199-200, 339-40, 443-4; Roger Baudier, *The Catholic Church in Louisiana* (New Orleans, 1939), pp. 91, 121, 158, 255-8, 335, 348; Richard Shaw, *Dagger John: The Life and Unquiet Times of Archbishop John Hughes of New York* (New York, 1977), pp. 115-37.

18. Patrick J. Dignan, *A History of the Legal Incorporation of Church Property in the United States, 1784-1932* (Washington, D.C., 1933), pp. 52-4, 64-7, 129-32, 148; Rev. Peter Guilday, *A History of the Councils of Baltimore, 1791-1884* (New York, 1932), pp. 87, 90-1; Shaw, *Dagger John*, pp. 129-32.

19. Shaw, *Dagger John*, p. 181; Jay Dolan, *The Immigrant Church: New York's Irish and German Catholics, 1815-1865* (Baltimore, 1975), pp. 47-8, 90-1; Donohue, *History of the Catholic Church in Western New York*, pp. 144-55, 222-30.

20. Timon, *Missions in Western New York*, pp. 215-6; Donohue, *History of the Catholic Church in Western New York*, pp. 229-57 passim, 258-61; Rev. Robert T. Bapst, "A Brief History of St. Louis Church," in *125th Anniversary, 1829-1954, St. Louis Church, Buffalo*, ed. idem (Buffalo, 1954), pp. 13-4; Buffalo *Commercial Advertiser*, February 10, 1854.

21. Samuel M. Welch, *Home History: Recollections of Buffalo, or Fifty Years Since* (Buffalo, 1891), p. 261; N.a., *The Centenary of St. Mary's Church, 1844-1944* (Buffalo, 1944), p. 17; Donohue, *The History of the Catholic Church in Western New York*, pp. 254-6; Gerber, "Modernity in the Service of Tradition," 662-3 (on the relative affluence of St. Louis parishioners).

22. Donohue, *History of the Catholic Church in Western New York*, pp. 136-8; Timon, *Missions in Western New York*, pp. 235-7 (quotation, p. 235).

23. Charles G. Deuther, *The Life and Times of the Right Reverend John Timon, D.D., the First Roman Catholic Bishop of the Diocese of Buffalo* (Buffalo, 1870), pp. 17-55.

24. Ibid., pp. 55-89; Rev. William B. Smith, "The History of the Diocese of Buffalo, 1847-1867" (Master's thesis, Catholic University of America, 1967), 56-7; *New Catholic Encyclopedia*, s.v., "Timon, John."

25. For Timon's complaints on these matters, see, Rev. John Timon to Archbishop Francis Kenrick, December 30, 1851; May 29, November 23, 30, December 5, 21, 1852; September 27, 1853; February 19, 1856; Kenrick Collection, AAB; and Rev. John Timon to Bishop Peter Paul Lerevere, September 7, 1851, Detroit (1843-52), Collection, UND; and Buffalo *Die Aurora*, December 19, 1859.

26. General Congregation, Acta S.C., December 7, 1846, Congregation of the Propaganda Fide, Rome, Collection, UND (microfilms).

27. Donohue, *History of the Catholic Church in Western New York*, pp. 136-8; Rev. John Timon to Archbishop Francis Kenrick, July 14, 1857; March 6, 1852, Kenrick Collection, AAB.

28. Donohue, *History of the Catholic Church in Western New York*, pp. 156-61.

29. Buffalo *Courier*, December 6, 1847. Timon later reorganized the diocese, so that there was one vicar general and two pro-vicars general, one each for the two principal ethnic groups; Buffalo *Sentinel*, September 13, 1856.

30. Donohue, *History of the Catholic Church in Western New York*, pp. 242-3, 248, 256-7; Smith, "The History of the Diocese of Buffalo, 1847-1867," 152-3.

31. Rev. John Timon to Ludwigmissionsverein, n.d., 1848, Ludwigmissionsverein collection, UND (microfilms); Donohue, *History of the Catholic Church in Western New York*, p. 241.

32. Donohue, *History of the Catholic Church in Western New York*, pp. 159, 260-1.

33. Hughes, "Archepiscopal Reminiscences of the Diocese of New York," n.p.; William Le Couteulx, "To the Right Rev. John Hughes" and letters to Propaganda Fide, Rome, April 20, December 18, 1853, Congregation of the Propaganda Fide, Rome, Collection UND (microfilms); Gerber, "Modernity in the Service of Tradition," 663-6 (on residential persistence); above, chapter

7, note 146, p. 464. The turning point for the *Weltbürger* (June 21, 25, 1851) was an 1851 clash between Timon and the trustees, after which the paper grew hostile; e.g., see ibid., April 11, 1854.

34. Rev. Patrick Cronin, *Life and Labors: Rt. Rev. Stephen Vincent Ryan, D.D., C.M.* (Buffalo, 1896), pp. 24, 26–7. Also, Deuther, *The Life and Times of the Right Reverend John Timon*, pp. 34, 90, 312–8.

35. Buffalo *Christian Advocate*, September 26, 1850; Buffalo *Courier*, January 4 (quoting Philadelphia *North American*), June 19, 1851; Buffalo *Republic*, June 13, 1854; Buffalo *Demokrat und Weltbürger*, June 26, 1854; Buffalo *Sentinel*, February 7, 1857; Mary T. C. McGee to [Aunt], August 2, 1852, Thomas D'Arcy McGee Papers, PAC; Rev. John Timon, Diary, entries for December 27, 28, 1860, ADB.

36. Cronin, *Life and Labors*, pp. 24, 26–7.

37. Deuther, *The Life and Times of the Right Reverend John Timon*, pp. 267, 271–6; Buffalo *Courier*, October 28, 1848; Buffalo *American Celt and Catholic Citizen* and Buffalo *Die Aurora*, November 25, 1859 ("Pastoral Letter"); Buffalo *Sentinel*, June 29, 1861; Rev. John Timon to "Hon. Monsieur," February 5, 1863, Society for the Propagation of the Faith, Lyons, Collection UND (microfilms); and to Archbishop Francis Kenrick, February 11, 1861, Kenrick Papers, AAB. Also, Ralph Barton Perry, *Puritanism and Democracy* (New York, 1944), p. 188; C. J. Nuesse, *The Social Thought of American Catholics, 1634–1829* (Westminster, Md., 1945), pp. 179–80, 281–6; Vincent P. Lannie, "Alienation in America: The Immigrant Catholic and Public Education in Pre-Civil War America," *Review of Politics*, (1970), 503–21.

38. The one exception, about which Timon doubtless had mixed feelings, was Rome's dispatching Italian Archbishop Gaetano Bedini to Buffalo to mediate the St. Louis conflict. Timon did not ask for the mediation, and probably was aware of Bedini's unpopularity with American and German Protestants. Yet Bedini sustained Timon's course in dealing with St. Louis parish. See below.

39. E.g., Rev. John Timon to Directors, December 28, 1849, Society for the Propagation of the Faith, Lyons, Collection, UND (microfilms).

40. Smith, "The History of the Diocese of Buffalo, 1847–1867," pp. 192–3; Buffalo *Courier*, October 11, 16, November 8, 1849.

41. Buffalo *Die Aurora*, November 2, 1860; Smith, "The History of the Diocese of Buffalo, 1847–1867," 192–4. Even D'Arcy McGee upheld this code of conduct; Buffalo *American Celt and Catholic Citizen*, June 26, 1852. Also, Buffalo *Christian Advocate*, October 30, 1856, for praise of Timon's record of encouraging peace at the polls.

42. Smith, "The History of the Diocese of Buffalo, 1847–1867," 192–4; Buffalo *Sentinel*, May 23, 1857.

43. Smith, "The History of the Diocese of Buffalo, 1847–1867," 192–4; Buffalo *Republic*, November 19, 1856; Buffalo *Sentinel*, November 15, 1856; May 23, 1857.

44. Buffalo *Sentinel*, January 19, July 12, November 8, 1856; April 25, 1857; Buffalo *Commercial Advertiser*, October 30, 1855; November 24, 1856; Smith, "The History of the Diocese of Buffalo, 1847–1867," 194; above pp. 160–62,

234–35. The *Sentinel* endorsed Horatio Seymour for governor, with great apologies for feeling the need to do so, in the midst of the heated nativist campaign of 1855; Buffalo *Sentinel*, November [?], 1855, clipping, Scrapbook 1, Horatio Seymour Papers, NYSA.

45. James Hannon, "The Catholic Church and Desegregation" (paper presented at the 1984 Toronto meeting of the Social Science History Association).

46. N.a., "A Notre Saint Père, La Pape Pie IX" (petition, 1852), Propaganda Fide, Rome, Collection UND (microfilms); Rev. James F. Connelly, *The Visit of Archbishop Gaetano Bedini to the United States of America (June, 1853–February, 1854)* (Rome, 1960), pp. 3, 13, 163; Donohue, *History of the Catholic Church in Western New York*, pp. 156–75, Buffalo *Courier*, October 8, 1852; September 22, 1853; Buffalo *Commercial Advertiser*, June 5, 1854; Rev. John Timon to Archbishop Francis Kenrick, July 10, September 27, 1853, Kenrick Papers, AAB.

47. Connelly, *The Visit of Archbishop Gaetano Bedini*, pp. 32–5, 92–163; Billington, *The Protestant Crusade*, pp. 300–1.

48. Buffalo *Demokrat und Weltbürger*, August 12, 19, October 24, 25, 30, 31, November 1, 1853; Buffalo *Christian Advocate*, October 27, 1853; Buffalo *Commercial Advertiser*, October 22, 1853; Donohue, *History of the Catholic Church in Western New York*, pp. 176–9, 180–1, 188–9; Connelly, *The Visit of Archbishop Gaetano Bedini*, pp. 50–73; n.a. *Affairs of St. Louis Church* (Buffalo, 1853), p. 19.

49. Buffalo *Courier*, October 31, 1853; June 30, 1854; Buffalo *Christian Advocate*, July 6 (quoting and commenting on a Buffalo *Democracy* editorial, n.d.), 20, 1854; Buffalo *Commercial Advertiser*, July 27, August 28, 1854. Cf. earlier and much more moderate commentary: Buffalo *Mercantile Courier*, October 2, 1843; Buffalo *Christian Advocate*, May 15, 1851; Buffalo *Express*, June 21, 1851; Buffalo *Courier*, September 14, 1853.

50. Rev. Joseph P. Murphy, *The Laws of the State of New York Affecting Church Property* (Washington, D.C., 1957), pp. 45–50; Shaw, *Dagger John*, pp. 294–7; Donohue, *History of the Catholic Church in Western New York*, p. 179; John, Cardinal Farley, *The Life of John Cardinal McCloskey: First Prince of the Church in America, 1810–1885* (New York, 1918), pp. 184–94. As Murphy makes clear, the Putnam law was never enforced, and seems, therefore, to have been merely a symbolic nod to anti-Catholicism. It was repealed in 1863 and replaced by a statute accommodating Catholic practice.

51. Rev. John Timon to Archbishop Francis Kenrick, July 10, 1852, Kenrick Papers, AAB; "A Notre Saint Père"; Buffalo *Courier*, August 27, 1853; Buffalo *Commercial Advertiser*, June 24, 1854; June 23, 1855; William P. Le Couteulx to Propaganda Fide, Rome, March 31, 1852; February 2, 1853; September 20, 1854; and "To the Right Reverend John Hughes" (typescript, 1852), Archbishop Gaetano Bedini to Propaganda Fide, Rome, April 2, 1854, Congregation of the Propaganda Fide, Rome, Collection, UND (microfilms).

52. Deuther, *The Life and Times of the Right Reverend John Timon*, pp. 210–2; Donohue, *History of the Catholic Church in Western New York*, pp. 188–9; Buffalo *Commercial Advertiser*, September 12, 1854; June 23, 1855; "Proclamation, John, Bishop of Buffalo," September 28, 1854, at St. Michael's

Church, Buffalo; Rev. John Timon to Propaganda Fide, Rome, July 5, 1855, Congregation of the Propaganda Fide, Rome, Collection, UND (microfilms); Buffalo *Sentinel*, August 30, 1856.

53. Donohue, *History of the Catholic Church in Western New York*, pp. 136-8; Buffalo *American Celt and Catholic Citizen*, August 21, 1852; Rev. John Timon to Mon. Choiselat Gallien, September 5, 1849, Society for the Propagation of the Faith, Lyons, Collection; and to Rev. Joseph Salzbacher, November 29, 1850, Leopoldine Society Collection, UND (microfilms).

54. Rev. John Timon to "Monsieur Les Directeurs," December 10, 1847; to Mon. Choiselat Gallien, September 5, 1849, Society for the Propagation of the Faith, Lyons, Collection; and to Archbishop Milde, September [?], 1849; June 30, 1851; and Joseph Salzbacher, November 29, 1850, Leopoldine Foundation Collection, UND (microfilms).

55. Donohue, *History of the Catholic Church in Western New York*, p. 127; Hughes, *Archepiscopal Reminiscences of the Diocese of New York*, n.p.; Rev. John Timon to Cardinal Joseph Othmar von Rauscher, October 29, 1856, Leopoldine Foundation Collection, UND (microfilms).

56. Rev. John Timon to Bishop Samuel Eccleston, September 19, 1849, Eccleston Papers, AAB; Buffalo *Courier*, December 19, 1849; Buffalo *American Celt and Catholic Citizen*, November 20, December 24, 1852; Smith, "The History of the Diocese of Buffalo, 1847-1867," 96; Donohue, *History of the Catholic Church in Western New York,* pp. 202-4; Buffalo *Commercial Advertiser*, April 24, 1860; Buffalo *Sentinel*, August 3, 1861.

57. This accounts for why the question of debt was second only to that of obedience in Timon's confrontation with lay trustees; see Smith, "The History of the Diocese of Buffalo, 1847-1867," 104-5; Donohue, *History of the Catholic Church in Western New York*, pp. 141-89, passim; Buffalo *Commercial Advertiser*, May 26, June 16, 1857.

58. N.a., *To the Right Reverend Bishop Timon* (Buffalo, 1864), Hartford Diocese Collection, UND; Smith, "The History of the Diocese of Buffalo, 1847-1867," 110-1, 208-14; Rochester *Union and Advertiser*, November 5, 1864; Deuther, *The Life and Times of the Right Reverend John Timon*, pp. 294-312; Buffalo *American Celt and Catholic Citizen*, November 20, 1852; Rev. John Timon to Archbishop Francis Kenrick, September 20, 1856; June 21, 1860, Kenrick Papers, AAB.

59. Deuther, *The Life and Times of the Right Rev. John Timon*, pp. 271-6; Buffalo *Sentinel*, August 29, 1857; January 16, February 6, 1858; n.a., *Discussion Relative to the Buffalo Hospital of the Sisters of Charity* (Buffalo, 1850), pp. 6-7, 12-3, 28-9. Vincent P. Lannie, *Public Money and Parochial Schools: Bishop Hughes, Governor Seward, and the New York School Controversy* (Cleveland, 1968); Timon, *Missions in Western New York*, pp. 235-40.

60. On Catholic conceptions of the ideal woman, mother, and wife, see Buffalo *Sentinel*, May 17, 1856; May 9, December 19, 1857; Catherine Mc Dannell, *The Christian Home in Victorian America, 1840-1900* (Bloomington, 1986), which finds considerable difference between Catholics and Protestants in regard to domestic ideology.

61. Buffalo *Courier*, October 2, 1850; Buffalo *Sentinel*, August 29, 1857; Buffalo Superintendent of Schools, *Fourteenth Annual Report of the Superintendent of Public Schools, 1850* (Buffalo, 1851), pp. 17–8; Timothy L. Smith, "Protestant Schooling and American Nationality, 1800–1850," *Journal of American History*, 63 (March, 1967), 679–95; Buffalo *Christian Advocate*, September 23, 1852.

62. Buffalo *Courier*, July 22, December 16, 1846; October 2, 1850; Buffalo *Commercial Advertiser*, March 18, 1858; Buffalo *Christian Advocate*, March 18, 1858; Deuther, *The Life and Times of the Right Reverend John Timon*, p. 273 (quoting Timon's November, 1859, "Pastoral Letter" on the public schools, in which he speaks of how often over many years "we have warned the faithful ... not to send their children to 'Godless schools.'")

63. John Webb Pratt, *Religion, Politics, and Diversity: The Church-State Theme in New York History* (Ithaca, 1967), pp. 191–2; Deuther, *The Life and Times of the Right Reverend John Timon*, pp. 291–2; Buffalo *Commercial Advertiser*, October 10, 1853; "W. W. N." (Buffalo), "Sectarian Schools," *New York Teacher*, 1 (June, 1853), 276–9. Nowhere was the contradictory nature of the Catholic indictment of the public schools more evident than in Timon's 1859 "Pastoral Letter," in which in the same paragraph he calls the public schools "Godless" and charges them with a "proselytizing, sectarian spirit"; Deuther, *The Life and Times of the Right Reverend John Timon*, p. 273.

64. Buffalo *Christian Advocate*, May 9, 1851; March 23, 1853; Buffalo *Commercial Advertiser*, October 10, 1853; April 27, 1858; February 7, 1859.

65. Pratt, *Religion, Politics, and Diversity*, pp. 204–11; David M. Schneider, *The History of Public Welfare in New York State, 1609–1866* (Montclair, N.J., 1969), pp. 311–2, 334–6; Richard H. Leach, "The Impact of Immigration in New York State, 1840–1860," *New York History*, 31 (1950), 15–30; Buffalo *Commercial Advertiser*, December 6, 1853; June 3, August 12, 1856; January 16, April 14, 1857; April 20, 1858; Buffalo *Republic*, August 12, 1856.

66. Rev. Bernard O'Reilly to Thurlow Weed, March 19, 1849, Thurlow Weed Papers, UR.

67. Deuther, *The Life and Times of the Right Reverend John Timon*, p. 220.

68. Buffalo *Commercial Advertiser*, October 2, 1856; April 2, 1858; January 25, 1860; New York State Senate, *Documents*, 75th Session, 1852, vol. 2, p. 48; 76th Session, 1853, vol. 2, pp. 38–9; 77th Session, 1854, vol. 2, p. 36; 81st Session, 1858, vol. 3, p. 40.

69. Charles L. Bland, "Institutions of Charity in Jacksonian Erie County: 1829–61" (research paper, SUNYAB, 1975), 27, 38–9; Buffalo *Courier*, April 30, May 1, 1849.

70. These letters, which appeared in the *Express*, and occasionally in the *Courier*, are brought together in *Discussion Relative to the Buffalo Hospital of the Sisters of Charity*, passim, and pp. 8–9, 14 (quotations).

71. Ibid., passim, has O'Reilly's replies and, on pp. 24–25, affidavits refuting charges of proselytizing.

72. Buffalo *Commercial Advertiser*, March 1, 2, 1850.

73. Deuther, *The Life and Times of the Right Reverend John Timon*, p. 168. Apparently the two men also clashed over the handling of diocesan funds; see *To the Right Reverend John Timon*.

74. Rev. John Timon to Archbishop Francis Kenrick, July 17, 1852, Kenrick Collection, AAB.

75. Ibid.; and in the same collection, Timon to Kenrick, December 9, 21, 1852; Rev. Bernard O'Reilly to Propaganda Fide, Rome, Congregation of the Propaganda Fide, Rome, Collection, UND (microfilms).

76. Timon to "Membres du Conseil," September 17, 1847, Society for the Propagation of the Faith, Lyons, Collection, UND (microfilms); Donohue, *History of the Catholic Church in Western New York*, pp. 139–40; Buffalo *Courier*, August 30, 1851; Edward John Hickey, *The Society for the Propagation of the Faith: Its Foundation, Organization, and Success (1822–1922)* (Washington, D.C., 1922); Rev. Theodore Roemer, *The Leopoldine Foundation and the Church in the United States (1829–1839)* (New York, 1933); idem, *The Ludwigs-Missionsverein and the Church in the United States, 1838–1918* (Washington, D.C., 1933); idem, *Ten Decades of Alms* (St. Louis, 1942).

77. Rev. John Timon to "Monsieur Les Directeurs," December 10, 1847; November 3, 1848; to Mon. Choiselat Gallien, September 5, 1849; January 1, 1853 (quotation); to [unnamed priest], February 3, 1860, Society for the Propagation of the Faith, Lyons, Collection; to Archbishop Milde, September [?], 1849; June 30, 1851; Leopoldine Foundation Collection; to Archbishop Anselm von Gebsattel, December 24, 1848; to Ludwig Ignatz Lebling, December 27, 1848; to Bishop von Oberkamp, August 10, 1855, Ludwigmissionsverein Collection, UND (microfilms).

78. Buffalo *Courier*, August 10, 1847; November 24, 1849; Buffalo *Christian Advocate*, May 23, August 15, 1850; September 4, 1856; n.a., "Missionary Intelligence," *American Protestant*, 5 (July, 1849), 44–50; "Mission among the Roman Catholic Germans at Buffalo," ibid., 5 (October, 1849), 145; Buffalo *Commercial Advertiser*, March 1, 1844; December 12, 1846.

79. Rev. John Timon to "M. Les Directeurs," November 3, 1848; and to "Counseil," July 8, 1858 (quotation), Society for the Propagation of the Faith, Lyons, Collection; and to Leopoldine Foundation, November 29, 1850, Leopoldine Foundation Collection, UND (microfilms).

80. Roemer, *Ten Decades of Alms*, pp. 100, 111, 121, 124; Donohue, *History of the Catholic Church in Western New York*, pp. 139–40.

81. Buffalo *Commercial Advertiser*, June 7, 1858; Billington, *The Protestant Crusade*, pp. 121–5, 127, 178; Roemer, *The Leopoldine Foundation*, p. 143.

82. *To the Right Reverend Bishop Timon*; Smith, "The History of the Diocese of Buffalo, 1847–1867," 208–14.

83. Emmet Larkin, "The Devotional Revolution in Ireland, 1850–1875," *American Historical Review*, 77 (June, 1972), 625–52; Edgar Alexander, "Church and Society in Germany," in *Church and Society: Catholic Social and Political Thought and Movements, 1789–1850*, ed. Joseph N. Moody (New York, 1953), pp. 331–65; Joseph White, "Religion and Community: Cincinnati's Germans, 1814–1870" (Ph.D. dissertation, University of Notre Dame, 1980), 261–74; Roemer, *The Ludwig-Missionsverein*, pp. 143–6; Hughes, *Archepiscopal Reminiscences of the Diocese of New York*, n.p.; Rev. John Timon to Ludwig Ignatz Lebling, December 27, 1848, Ludwigmissionsverein Collection, UND (microfilms).

84. Rev. John Timon to Propaganda Fide, Rome, June 5, 1852, Congregation of the Propaganda Fide, Rome; and to Archbishop Milde, December 16, 1849, Leopoldine Foundation Collection, UND (microfilms).

85. Donohue, *History of the Catholic Church in Western New York*, p. 319; Buffalo *Courier*, June 20, November 10, 1849; Buffalo *Sentinel*, May 9, 1857; Buffalo *Commercial Advertiser*, May 5, 1860; Rev. John Timon to Propaganda Fide, Rome, July 19, August 26, 1851; August 29, 1857; August 16, 1861; February 11, October 11, 1862; and Propaganda Fide, Rome to J. C. Villavecchia, C.M., July 28, 1858; and to Rev. John Timon, September 17, 1861, Congregation of the Propaganda Fide, Rome, Collection, UND (microfilms).

86. E.g., Rev. John Timon to Bishop John Purcell, July 4, August 1, 1855, Cincinnati, 1854–56, Collection, UND (microfilms). On this occasion Timon succeeded in obtaining a priest for the difficult assignment at St. Louis Church.

87. Rev. John Timon to Leopoldine Foundation, October 20, 1850, in Leopoldine Foundation, *Berichte* 3 (1852), 7–15; Donohue, *History of the Catholic Church in Western New York*, pp. 190, 199, 200–1, 242–3, 248, 256–7. By 1858, the number of clergy reached eighty-five; Buffalo *Commercial Advertiser*, March 15, 1858.

88. For a general survey of relations between priests and bishops, see Robert Trisco, "Bishops and Their Priests in America," in *The Catholic Priest in America: Historical Investigations*, ed. John Tracy Ellis (Collegeville, Minn., 1971), pp. 111–41, 270–3.

89. Smith, "The History of the Diocese of Buffalo, 1847–1867," pp. 56–7, 208–14.

90. Ibid., pp. 186–9; Deuther, *The Life and Times of the Right Reverend John Timon*, pp. 262–8; Buffalo *American Celt and Catholic Citizen*, December 4, 19, 1852; n.a., *Acts and Decrees of the Fourth Synod of Buffalo* (Buffalo, 1852), Congregation of the Propaganda Fide, Rome, Collection, UND (microfilms); Rev. John Timon to Archbishop Samuel Eccleston, July [21?], 1849, Eccleston Papers, AAB; Rev. John Timon to Archbishop Francis Kenrick, September 20, 1856; May 21, 1860, Kenrick Papers, AAB; Rev. John Timon to Propaganda Fide, Rome, September 8, 1851; June 5, 1852, Congregation of the Propaganda Fide, Rome, Collection, UND (microfilms).

91. Buffalo *Commercial Advertiser*, May 13, 1859; Rev. George Pax, untitled circular on cemeteries and burials [August, 1860]; Rev. John Timon to Guarini, February 4, 1861; Rev. E. Chevalier to Propaganda Fide, Rome, October 11, 1861; November 27, 1861; September 10, 1862, Congregation of the Propaganda Fide, Rome, Collection, UND (microfilms).

92. Deuther, *The Life and Times of the Right Reverend John Timon*, pp. 312–8; *To the Right Reverend John Timon*.

93. Buffalo *Commercial Advertiser*, January 22, 1858.

94. In fact, I have found only two newspaper items for the entire period in which individual members of the local Catholic clergy are charged with immorality. Both concern the use of a parishioner's money. One (Buffalo *Weltbürger*, September 29, 1849), however, explicitly identifies its own printed story as "gossip." The other (Buffalo *Christian Advocate*, July 27, 1854) states that a priest allowed a young woman to leave her savings with him, but he provided

no interest, no records, and no passbook. For praise of Catholic temperance activity, undertaken by both Father Mathew and Timon, see Buffalo *Christian Advocate*, August 28, 1851; March 14, 1861.

95. Buffalo *Commercial Advertiser*, January 12 (quotation), March 18, 1858; Buffalo *Christian Advocate*, January 12, March 18, 1858; February 1, 17, 1861.

96. Rev. John Timon to "M. Les Directeurs," March 22, 1849, Society for the Propagation of the Faith, Lyons, Collection; and to Propaganda Fide, June 5, 1852, Congregation of the Propaganda Fide, Rome, Collection, UND (microfilms).

97. Smith, "The History of the Diocese of Buffalo, 1847-1867," 172-3; Rev. John Timon to Ludwig Ignatz Lebling, December 27, 1848, Ludwigmissionsverein Collection, UND (microfilms).

98. Buffalo *Courier*, November 28, 1850.

99. Donahue, *History of the Catholic Church in Western New York*, pp. 200-1, 320-4; Smith, "The History of the Diocese of Buffalo," 172-3; Buffalo *Sentinel*, December 5, 1857; Bishop J. Timon, Diary, entry of November 12, 1859; Buffalo *Die Aurora*, November 25, 1859; Buffalo *American Celt and Catholic Citizen*, July 17, 1852; Mc Dannell, *The Christian Home in Victorian America, 1840-1900*.

100. Donahue, *History of the Catholic Church in Western New York*, pp. 200-1, 319-24; Buffalo *Courier*, June 29, 1849; January 4, April 28, August 22, 1851; Buffalo *Commercial Advertiser*, November 28, 1853; Robert J. Rayback, *Millard Fillmore: Biography of a President* (Buffalo, 1959), p. 407.

101. Donahue, *History of the Catholic Church in Western New York*, p. 259.

102. Ibid., pp. 202-4, 239-40; Buffalo *Courier*, February 5, 7, 1851.

103. Mark Goldman, *High Hopes: The Rise and Decline of Buffalo, New York* (Albany, 1983), pp. 96-7; Smith, "The History of the Diocese of Buffalo, 1847-1867," 87; Buffalo *Courier*, October 4, 1850.

104. Buffalo *Christian Advocate*, February 13, 1851; December 25, 1856; November 26, 1857; Buffalo *Courier*, November 24, 1857 (response to the *Express*, n.d.); Buffalo *Commercial Advertiser*, June 7, 1858.

105. Donahue, *History of the Catholic Church in Western New York*, pp. 202-4; Rayback, *Millard Fillmore*, p. 407; Buffalo *Courier*, November 24, 1857; Buffalo *American Celt and Catholic Citizen*, December 24, 1852.

106. On bourgeois travel to Europe, Buffalo *Commercial Advertiser*, June 4, 1857; *Fifth Annual Festival of the Old Settlers of Buffalo* (Buffalo, 1868), p. 13; Rayback, *Millard Fillmore*, pp. 396-407.

107. Frances Trollope, *Domestic Manners of the Americans*, vol. 2 (London, 1832), pp. 270-3; Harriet Martineau, *Retrospect of Western Travel*, vol. 1 (London, 1838), pp. 90-1; *Map of the City of Buffalo, Surveyed under the Direction of Quackenboss and Kennedy, Insurance Agents* (New York, 1854); Buffalo *Commercial Advertiser*, March 27, 1854; April 8, 11, 1856; October 31, 1860; Buffalo *Republic and Times*, June 15, 1858; Buffalo *Express*, April 22, 1859; undated petition to Buffalo Common Council, Box 1, Buffalo Collection, BECHS.

108. Buffalo *Republic*, September 7, 1853; Buffalo *Commercial Advertiser*, May 17, 1856.

109. Buffalo *Courier*, December 16, 1851; Buffalo *Commercial Advertiser*, May 17, 1856; August 3, 1857; January 30, April 13, 1858; June 29, 1859. For similar, favorable comments on both the design of, and activities at, other Buffalo Catholic churches, see Buffalo *Courier*, September 26, 1850; Buffalo *Commercial Advertiser*, November 1, 1854; August 23, 1856; February 23, 1857; March 26, May 17, 1858. Also, Buffalo *Demokrat und Weltbürger*, June 29, 1855.

110. Jackson Lears, *No Place of Grace: Antimodernism and the Transformation of American Culture* (New York, 1981), p. 194.

111. John O'Grady, *Catholic Charities in the United States: History and Problems* (Washington, D.C.), passim, especially pp. 129–31, 217.

112. Buffalo *Commercial Advertiser*, January 10, April 18, December 18, 1853; January 8, June 20, 1855; January 24, 28, February 16, April 23, 1856; January 17, 1857; February 17, 1858; February 14, March 2, 1859.

113. John Garraty, *Unemployment in History* (New York, 1978); Michael B. Katz, *Poverty and Policy in American History* (New York, 1983); Gertrude Himmelfarb, *The Idea of Poverty: England in the Early Industrial Age* (New York, 1983).

114. Buffalo *Commercial Advertiser*, January 22, 1858.

115. Buffalo *Christian Advocate*, January 10, March 14, April 11, May 9, 1850; February 18, 1851; April 15, September 23, November 18, 1852; October 29, 1857; April 29, 1858; Buffalo *Commercial Advertiser*, June 15, 1858; August 22, 1859; January 27, 29, February 15, 1860; Schneider, *The History of Public Welfare in New York State, 1609–1866*, pp. 226–9.

116. Robert H. Bremner, *From the Depths: The Discovery of Poverty in the United States* (New York, 1956), p. 28; John Duffy Ibson, "Will the World Break Your Heart?: A Historical Analysis of the Dimensions and Consequences of Irish-American Assimilation" (Ph.D. dissertation, Brandeis University, 1976), 46–50.

117. Donohue, *History of the Catholic Church in Western New York*, pp. 322–3; Bland, "Institutions of Charity in Jacksonian Erie County," 36–40; Buffalo Medical Society, *Buffalo Medical Journal*, 5 (1849–50), 424–8; Buffalo *Courier*, October 11, 16, 1849; July 28, September 17, 20, 22, 24, 1852; January 9, 1858.

118. Donohue, *History of the Catholic Church in Western New York*, p. 209.

119. Ibid., pp. 190, 199, 321–2; Murray, "Memoir of Stephen Louis Le Couteulx de Caumont," 449.

120. O'Grady, *Catholic Charities*, pp. 73–82, 120–2, 129–31, 173, 208, 217, 352, 382; Donohue, *History of the Catholic Church in Western New York*, pp. 190, 199, 321–4; Buffalo *Courier*, December 9, 1851; August 12, 1852; Buffalo *Commercial Advertiser*, January 18, 1856; May 3, 1859; Buffalo *Sentinel*, January 26, October 11, 1856; July 4, November 7, 1857; February 16, 1861.

121. Buffalo *Sentinel*, January 26, February 2, 1856; January 2, 1858; February 16, 1861; Buffalo *Commercial Advertiser*, November 7, 1857; January 29, February 6, 9, 17, April 3, June 14–17, October 10, December 24, 1859; Buffalo *Express*, February 19, 1859; Timon to "Conseil," February 20, 1859, Society for the Propagation of the Faith, Lyons, Collection, UND.

122. Buffalo *Sentinel*, July 4, 1857; New York State Senate, New York State Senate Committee to Visit the Charitable and Penal Institutions of the State, *Report*, 80th Session, vol. 1, 1857, pp. 127–33.

123. Buffalo *Commercial Advertiser*, October 2, 1856; March 22, 1858; January 25, 1860.

124. Buffalo Medical Society, *Buffalo Medical Journal*, 5 (1849–50), 373.

125. John T. Horton, Edward T. Williams, and Harry S. Douglass, *History of Northwestern New York*, vol. 1 (New York, 1947), p. 113; W. G. Rothstein, *American Physicians in the Nineteenth Century: From Sects to Science* (Baltimore, 1972); Buffalo *Courier*, July 31, November 2, 17, December 9, 1850; January 9, 30, 1852; Buffalo *Commercial Advertiser*, November 23, 1853; June 7, 1854; Buffalo Medical Society, *Buffalo Medical Journal*, 4 (1848–49), 659–61; 5 (1849–50), 434; 8 (1852–53), 255.

126. Buffalo Medical Society, *Buffalo Medical Journal*, 4 (1848–49), 775–6; 5 (1849–50), 255, 373, 574; Buffalo *Courier*, April 30, 1849.

127. Horton, et al., *History of Northwestern New York*, vol. 1, p. 163; Buffalo Medical Society, *Buffalo Medical Journal*, 4 (1848–49), 326; 5 (1849–50), 433–4; 6 (1850–51), 574.

128. Nathan K. Hall to Millard Fillmore, August 12, 1854, Millard Fillmore Papers, BECHS (microfilms).

129. Buffalo *Commercial Advertiser*, February 2, 1854; March 19, 1858; November 16, 1859; August 6, 1860; Buffalo *Christian Advocate*, August 23, 1860.

130. Buffalo *Express*, February 21, 1850.

131. Buffalo *Commercial Advertiser*, February 1, June 12, September 26, 1854; March 19, 1858; March 1, 1860; Buffalo *Christian Advocate*, December 2, 1858; December 8, 1859; October 11, November 15, 1860; Evelyn Hawes, *Proud Vision: A History of Buffalo General Hospital* (New York, 1964), pp. 1–13; n.a., *Semi-Centennial Celebration: The Buffalo Orphan Asylum, April 26, 1887* (Buffalo, 1887), pp. 1, 22, 38–9.

132. Rev. John Timon, Diary, entries of June 11, 12, 1861, ADB; Leonard R. Riforgiato, "Bishop Timon, Buffalo, and the Civil War," *Civil War History*, 73 (January, 1987), 62–80.

Part Four. Introduction: Politics, Pluralism, and Social Integration

1. Robert E. Shalhope, "Toward a Republican Synthesis: The Emergence of an Understanding of Republicanism in American Historiography," *William and Mary Quarterly*, 3d series, 31 (January, 1974), 48–65; Isaac Kramnick, "Republican Revisionism Revisited," *American Historical Review*, 77 (June, 1982), 629–64. Also, see Rowland Berthoff, "Peasant and Artisans, Puritans and Republics: Personal Liberty and Communal Equality in American History," *Journal of American History*, 69 (December, 1982), 579–98; and Eric Foner, *Free Soil, Free Labor, Free Men: The Ideology of the Republican Party before the Civil War* (New York, 1970), pp. 9–13.

2. Edward Pessen, *Jacksonian America: Society, Personality, and Politics* (Homewood, Ill., 1978, rev. ed.), pp. 149–59; Chilton Williamson, *American*

Suffrage from Property to Democracy, 1760–1860 (Princeton, 1960); T. Scott Miyakawa, *Protestants and Pioneers: Individualism and Conformity on the American Frontier* (Chicago, 1964), pp. 3–9. Donald G. Mathews, "The Second Great Awakening as an Organizing Process, 1780–1830," *American Quarterly*, 21 (Spring, 1969), 23–43.

3. Richard P. McCormick, *The Second American Party System: Party Formation in the Jacksonian Era* (Chapel Hill, 1966); Ronald P. Formisano, *The Birth of Mass Political Parties: Michigan, 1827–1861* (Princeton, 1971); Jean H. Baker, *Affairs of Party: The Political Culture of Northern Democrats in the Mid-Nineteenth Century* (Ithaca, 1983); Daniel Walker Howe, *The Political Culture of American Whigs* (Chicago, 1979), pp. 12–21; Amy Bridges, *A City in the Republic: Antebellum New York and the Origins of Machine Politics* (New York, 1984), pp. 61–82, 132–5; L. E. Fredman, *The Australian Ballot: The Story of An American Reform* (East Lansing, 1968), pp. 21–5, 28.

4. Bridges, *A City in the Republic*, pp. 72–3, 129–32; Sam Bass Warner, Jr., *The Private City: Philadelphia in Three Periods of Its Growth* (Philadelphia, 1968), pp. 152–3; Ronald Formisano, "Deferential-Participant Politics: The Early Republic's Political Culture, 1789–1840," *American Political Science Review*, 68 (June, 1974), 473–87; and idem, "Political Character, Antipartyism, and the Second Party System," *American Quarterly*, 21 (Winter, 1969), 683–709.

5. Baker, *Affairs of Party*, pp. 71–107; Gabriel A. Almond and Sidney Verba, *The Civic Culture: Political Attitudes and Democracy in Five Nations* (Princeton, 1963), passim, especially pp. 6, 27, 149, 169, 218, 280, 305–22.

6. Baker, *Affairs of Party*, pp. 177–258, 261–316; Bridges, *A City in the Republic*, pp. 103–61; Oscar Handlin and Mary L. Handlin, *Commonwealth: A Study of the Role of Government in the American Economy: Massachusetts, 1774–1861* (New York, 1947); Harry N. Scheiber, "Government and the Economy: Studies of the 'Commonwealth' Policy in Nineteenth-Century America," *Journal of Interdisciplinary History*, 3 (Summer, 1972), 135–54; Sheldon S. Wolin, "The New Public Philosophy," *democracy* 1 (October, 1981), 23–31, and idem, "Revolutionary Action Today," ibid., 2 (Fall, 1982), 20–3; Laurence Goodwyn, "Organizing Democracy: The Limits of Theory and Practice," ibid., 1 (January, 1981), 47; Hanna Fenichel Pitkin and Sara M. Shumer, "On Participation," ibid., 2 (Fall, 1982), 52.

7. Bridges, *A City in the Republic*, pp. 149–60.

8. William E. Gienapp, " 'Politics Seem to Enter into Everything': Political Culture in the North, 1840–1860," in *Essays on American Antebellum Politics, 1840–1860*, ed. Stephen E. Maizlich and John J. Kushma (College Station, Tex., 1982), pp. 15–40.

9. See, for example, Jack S. Blocker, Jr., *"Give to the Winds Thy Fears": The Women's Temperance Crusade, 1873–1874* (Westport, 1985); Ellen Carol DuBois, *Feminism and Suffrage: The Emergence of an Independent Women's Movement in America, 1848–1869* (Ithaca, 1978); Leon Litwack, *North of Slavery: The Negro in the Free States, 1790–1860* (Chicago, 1961).

10. Bridges, *A City in the Republic*, pp. 8, 11; Alan Dawley, *Class and Community: The Industrial Revolution in Lynn* (Cambridge, Mass., 1976), pp.

66–72; Seymour Martin Lipset, *The First New Nation: The United States in Historical and Comparative Perspective* (New York, 1963), pp. 174–5, 341–2.

11. Alan Dawley, "E. P. Thompson and the Peculiarities of the Americans," *Radical History Review* 19 (Winter, 1978–79), 52; and idem, "Death and Rebirth of the American Milltown," *Labour/Le Travailleur*, 8/9 (Autumn-Spring, 1981–82), 146. Also, Dawley, *Class and Community*, 66–72.

12. David Montgomery, "Strikes in Nineteenth Century America," *Social Science History*, 4 (February, 1980), 81–104; Ira Katznelson, *City Trenches: Urban Politics and the Patterning of Class in the United States* (New York, 1981), pp. 45–72.

13. Bridges, *A City in the Republic*, pp. 130–1, 143–4; Marvin Myers, *The Jacksonian Persuasian: Politics and Belief* (Stanford, 1957), passim; Pessen, *Jacksonian America*, pp. 86–99, 251–3.

14. Bridges, *A City in the Republic*, pp. 146–61.

15. Ira Katznelson, *Black Men, White Cities* (New York, 1973), pp. 111–3; Edgar Litt, *Beyond Pluralism: Ethnic Politics in America* (Glenview, 1970); John M. Allswang, *Bosses, Machines, and Urban Voters: An American Symbiosis* (Port Washington, 1977); Nathan Glazer and Daniel Patrick Moynihan, *Beyond the Melting Pot: The Negroes, Puerto Ricans, Jews, Italians, and Irish of New York City* (Cambridge, Mass., 1963); Edward M. Levine, *The Irish and Irish Politicians: A Study of Cultural and Social Alienation* (Notre Dame, 1966), pp. 69–142.

16. See below, chapter 11, p. 345, and chapter 12, pp. 372–73.

17. John Higham, "The Immigrant in American History," in *Send These to Me: Immigrants in Urban America*, ed. idem (Baltimore, 1984), p. 20.

18. James H. Kettner, *The Development of American Citizenship, 1608–1870* (Chapel Hill, 1978), pp. 225–37.

19. Ibid., pp. 245–7; Arthur Mann, *The One and the Many: Reflections on the American Identity* (Chicago, 1979), pp. 80–1, 89–90.

20. Kettner, *The Development of American Citizenship*, p. 247.

21. Ibid., p. 246.

22. New York *Old Countryman*, December 29, 1831. One could not, however, lease or will that property until one became a citizen. Furthermore, if one had not naturalized six years after the declaration of intention, the right to hold and dispose was lost.

23. Ibid., November 15, 1832; Buffalo *Daily Mercantile Courier*, April 17, 1844; Buffalo *Courier*, March 1, 1847; Buffalo *Commercial Advertiser*, September 26, 1859; Buffalo *Demokrat und Weltbürger*, October 24, 1859; Buffalo *Republic*, October 18, 1860; Joseph Harris, *Registration of Voters in the United States* (Washington, D.C., 1929), pp. 69–71, 72–4.

24. Lance Liebman, "Ethnic Groups and the Legal System," in *Ethnic Relations in America*, ed. idem (Englewood Cliffs, 1982), pp. 153–5; Katznelson, *Black Men, White Cities*, pp. 64–6; and idem, *City Trenches*, pp. 55–8; Levine, *The Irish and Irish Politicians*, p. 119; John Higham, "Introduction: The Forms of Ethnic Leadership," in *Ethnic Leadership in America*, ed. idem (Baltimore, 1978), pp. 1–16; Almond and Verba, *The Civic Culture*, p. 216.

25. Katznelson, *Black Men, White Cities*, pp. 64–6, 73–9, 83–5.

26. Katznelson, *City Trenches*, pp. 56–8; Almond and Verba, *The Civic Culture*, pp. 122–3; Sheldon S. Wolin, "The People's Two Bodies," *democracy*, 1 (January, 1981), 12–6; David Montgomery, *Beyond Equality: Labor and the Radical Republicans, 1862–1872* (New York, 1967), p. 215.

27. Katznelson, *City Trenches*, p. 19. Also, see Susan E. Hirsch, *The Roots of the American Working Class: The Industrialization of Crafts in Newark, 1800–1860* (Philadelphia, 1978), pp. 77–8; and Aileen S. Kraditor, *The Radical Persuasion: Aspects of the Intellectual History and the Historiography of Three American Radical Organizations* (Baton Rouge, 1981).

28. Bridges, *A City in the Republic,* pp. 121–4, 154–7; Howe, *The Political Culture of American Whigs*, pp. 16, 98–122, 182–92, 276–91.

29. Goodwyn, "Organizing Democracy," 45.

Chapter 11. Immigrant Political and Civic Integration: The Formative Decade, 1843–53

1. Millard Fillmore to Thurlow Weed, November 6, 1844, Millard Fillmore Papers, BECHS; Robert J. Rayback, *Millard Fillmore: Biography of a President* (Buffalo, 1959), pp. 158–60; Lee Benson, *The Concept of Jacksonian Democracy: New York as a Test Case* (Princeton, 1961), p. 139.

2. David M. Ellis, et al., *A History of New York State* (Ithaca, 1973), pp. 144–9, 211–24; Dr. Bryant Burwell, Diary, January 1, 1837–February 15, 1839, entry of March 7, 1837; Diary, 1840, entries of March 3, October 30; and Diary, 1846, entry for March 3, BECHS; Buffalo *Weltbürger*, March 6, 1841; *Biographical Dictionary of American Mayors*, s.v. "Andrews, Andre," "Barker, Pierre," "Harrington, Isaac," "Johnson, Ebenezer," "Thompson, Sheldon," "Trowbridge, Josiah," and "Walden, Ebenezer."

3. Michael F. Holt, *The Political Crisis of the 1850s* (New York, 1978).

4. *Geschichte der Deutschen in Buffalo und Erie County, New York*, vol. 1 (Buffalo, 1898), pp. 68–9; Samuel M. Welch, *Home History: Recollections of Buffalo, or Fifty Years Since* (Buffalo, 1891), p. 100; and below, p. 340.

5. Dietrich Gerhard, *Old Europe: A Study in Continuity, 1000–1800* (New York, 1981), pp. 123–47.

6. Mack Walker, *German Home Towns: Community, State, and General Estate, 1648–1871* (Ithaca, 1971), 34–64, 76–107, 110–3.

7. Ibid., pp. 33, 36, 76.

8. Buffalo Turnverein, *Constitution* (Buffalo, 1871); Buffalo Liedertafel, *Constitution und Nebengesetze* (Buffalo, 1880). (Both are amended versions of antebellum documents I have not been able to locate.)

9. Edward M. Levine, *The Irish and Irish Politicians: A Study of Cultural and Social Alienation* (Notre Dame, 1966), pp. 5, 32–8, 39–51, 116, 127, 129; Gabriel A. Almond and Sidney Verba, *The Civic Culture: Political Attitudes and Democracy in Five Nations* (Princeton, 1963), pp. 17–8; S. J. Connolly, *Priests and People in Pre-Famine Ireland, 1780–1845* (New York, 1982).

10. Samuel Clark and James Donnelly, Jr., eds., *Irish Peasants: Violence and Political Unrest, 1780–1914* (Madison, 1983); T. D. Williams, *Secret Societies in Ireland* (Dublin, 1973).

11. James A. Reynolds, *The Catholic Emancipation Crisis in Ireland, 1823–1829* (New Haven, 1959).

12. Kevin O'Neill, *Family and Farm in Pre-Famine Ireland: The Parish of Killshandra* (Madison, 1984); Kenneth H. Connell, *Irish Peasant Society* (Oxford, 1968).

13. Levine, *The Irish and Irish Politicians*, pp. 73–106, 127, 129, 200; Almond and Verba, *The Civic Culture*, pp. 366–8.

14. Levine, *The Irish and Irish Politicians*, pp. 91–2, 155–202; William V. Shannon, *The American Irish: A Political and Social Portrait* (New York, 1963), pp. 60–7.

15. Levine, *The Irish and Irish Politicians*, pp. 132–5, 147–8, 152; Laurence A. Glasco, *Ethnicity and Social Structure: Irish, Germans, and Native-Born in Buffalo, New York, 1850–60* (New York, 1980), pp. 152–7; Shannon, *The American Irish*, pp. 63, 65–6.

16. Jean H. Baker, *Affairs of Party: The Political Culture of Northern Democrats in the Mid-Nineteenth Century* (Ithaca, 1983), p. 114.

17. *Geschichte der Deutschen*, vol. 1, pp. 62, 87–91.

18. Baker, *Affairs of Party*, pp. 147, 317–21; Amy Bridges, *A City in the Republic: Antebellum New York and the Origins of Machine Politics* (New York, 1984), pp. 23, 106–7; W. R. Brock, *Parties and Political Conscience: American Dilemmas, 1840–1850* (New York, 1979), pp. 11, 57–70; Judah B. Ginsberg, "The Tangled Web: The New York State Democratic Party and the Slavery Controversy, 1844–1860" (Ph.D. dissertation, University of Wisconsin, 1974), 1–26, 326–30, 337–46; Edward Pessen, *Jacksonian America: Society, Personality, and Politics* (Homewood, Ill., 1978, rev. ed.), pp. 225–6.

19. Buffalo *Commercial Advertiser*, November 6, 1844; Bridges, *A City in the Republic*, pp. 21, 69; Brock, *Parties and Political Conscience*, pp. 12–21, 52–3, 65, 68; David Walker Howe, *The Political Culture of American Whigs* (Chicago, 1979), pp. 4, 9, 12–36, 98–122, 181–202, 210–25.

20. E.g., Buffalo *Weltbürger*, February 24, April 7, 14, September 29, October 27, December 1, 1838; May 29, 1839; May 2, July 25, 1840; March 24, April 7, 1849.

21. Bridges, *A City in the Republic*, p. 98; Howe, *The Political Culture of American Whigs*, pp. 38, 300; Paul Kleppner, *The Cross of Culture: A Social Analysis of Midwestern Politics, 1850–1900* (New York, 1970), p. 70.

22. Howe, *The Political Culture of American Whigs*, pp. 18–19, 32, 150–75, 202.

23. Kathleen Smith Kutolowski, "Antimasonry Reexamined: Social Bases of the Grass-Roots Party," *Journal of American History*, 71 (September, 1984), 277, 290; Holt, *The Political Crisis of the 1850s*, pp. 21–2.

24. Howe, *The Political Culture of American Whigs*, pp. 163–5.

25. Ginsberg, "The Tangled Web," 104–6; Baker, *Affairs of Party*, pp. 178–9, 214–58. For representative local examples of Democratic racial ideology and manipulation of race, Buffalo *Courier*, February 28, 1844; June 12, 1846.

26. Buffalo *Courier and Pilot*, November 4, 1846; Phyllis F. Field, *The Politics of Race in New York: The Struggle for Black Suffrage in the Civil War*

Era (Ithaca, 1982), p. 61. The American Whig Second and Third wards voted against the proposition by a 72 percent majority.

27. Howe, *The Political Culture of American Whigs*, p. 38; Buffalo *Commercial Advertiser*, April 27, 28, 1842.

28. Field, *The Politics of Race in New York*, pp. 61–3; Buffalo *Commercial Advertiser*, April 30, May 6, 1846.

29. Ronald P. Formisano, "Political Character, Antipartyism, and the Second Party System," *American Quarterly*, 21 (Winter, 1969), 683–709; William E. Gienapp, " 'Politics Seem to Enter into Everything': Political Culture in the North, 1840–1860," in *Essays on American Antebellum Politics, 1840–1860*, ed. Stephen E. Maizlish and John J. Kushma (College Station, Tex., 1982), pp. 45–6; Lynn L. Marshall, "The Strange Stillbirth of the Whig Party," *American Historical Review*, 72 (January, 1967), 445–68.

30. E.g., Buffalo *Christian Advocate*, May 9, 1850; Buffalo *Christian Advocate*, October 26, 1852. Also, see Gienapp, " 'Politics Seem to Enter into Everything,' " 45. Brock, *Parties and Political Conscience*, pp. 8–9. The *Commercial Advertiser* frequently criticized the Democrats for "flattering the people": see Buffalo *Courier*, January 12, 13, 1844.

31. Buffalo *Commercial Advertiser*, March 3, 1847; Buffalo *Express*, June 12, 1857; Buffalo *Demokrat und Weltbürger*, November 1, 1860; Ginsburg, "The Tangled Web," 229–97; Baker, *Affairs of Party*, p. 21; L. E. Fredman, *The Australian Ballot: The Story of an American Reform* (East Lansing, 1968), p. 27.

32. Buffalo *Commercial Advertiser*, August 30, 1842; Buffalo *Courier*, May 18, 1843; March 18, 1845; April 7, 1852; Buffalo *Express*, October 16, December 30, 1857; Common Council, *Proceedings*, July 2, 1839, BECHS; John T. Horton, Edward T. Williams, and Harry S. Douglass, *History of Northwestern New York*, vol. 1 (New York, 1947), pp. 85–6, 105; *Geschichte der Deutschen*, pp. 70–1.

33. Buffalo *Commercial Advertiser*, October 12, 1842; November 7, 1844; September 8, 19, October 22, November 1, 1856; October 20, 1857; October 18, 20, 1858; Buffalo *Courier*, December 23, 1842; September 21, 1844; October 19, 1849; September 19, 1857; Buffalo *Express*, October 21, 1858.

34. Buffalo *Republic*, June 9, 1857.

35. Ibid., and the press for any campaign during 1843–53.

36. Buffalo *Courier*, February 28, October 31, November 2, 1846; November 2, 1849; February 27, March 3, 1851; Buffalo *Weltbürger*, November 3, 1838; October 28, 1848; March 10, 1849.

37. John G. Ramsey, "From Self-Educating Boosters to Stewards of Culture: Buffalo's Friends of Education," vol. 1 (Ph.D. dissertation, SUNYAB, 1984), pp. 105–7 (for analysis of the social basis of the Common Council). Credit reports on politicians confirm this pattern: R. G. Dun and Co., New York, vol. 81, pp. 42 (Clo.), 73 (Web.), 74 (Hag.), 126 (Bey.), 187 (Kra.), 249 (Die.), 299 (Reh.), R. G. Dun and Company Collection, BL. Also, see Mark Goldman, *High Hopes: The Rise and Decline of Buffalo, New York* (Albany, 1983), p. 103.

38. Buffalo *Courier*, September 21, 25, 1844; September 22, 1846; February 16, March 1, 1848; October 2, 30, 1849; February 18, March 7, 1850; October 9, 1850; March 9, 1853; Buffalo *Weltbürger*, August 18, September 29, 1838; October 10, 1840; January 27, 1844; October 11, 1848; March 8, 1849; February 26, 1851; March 3, 1852; Buffalo *Commercial Advertiser*, November 10, 1853.

39. Buffalo *Courier*, March 2, 1848; February 26, 1849; February 26, 1850; February 18, 22, 1851; February 17, 1853; Buffalo *Weltbürger*, February 28, 1849; March 2, 1850; November 1, 1853.

40. Buffalo *Commercial Advertiser*, September 23, 1841.

41. Buffalo *Courier*, February 4, 1846; May 21, 1847; July 30, 1850; March 19, 1851; March 17, 1852; January 15, 1856; Buffalo *Commercial Advertiser*, January 10, 1854; January 17, 1855; January 15, 16, 1856; July 29, 1857; August 24, 1860; Buffalo *Demokrat und Weltbürger*, January 10, 1854.

42. Buffalo *Commercial Advertiser*, January 10, 1854.

43. Ibid., January 17, 1855; *New York State Census, 1855*, alphabetized printout, SUNYAB; *Buffalo Commercial Advertiser City Directory, 1855* (Buffalo, 1855). (Average age = 35.6; average residence = 16.3 years; owning land = 10 years; average value of real estate = $3,224; average value of personal estate = $4,836; number of individuals residing in dwellings valued under $1,000 = 6, or 23 percent.)

44. Buffalo *Courier*, June 17, 19, 26, 27, 28, November 18, 1843; February 9, 10, July 4, August 31, October 11, 1844; June 1, 6, 1847; April 4, November 4, 1848; October 29, 1850; July 30, September 15, November 19, 1851; Buffalo *Weltbürger*, January 24, July 24, 1852.

45. Buffalo *Courier*, March 1, 1843; February 27, 1846; February 25, 1847; Buffalo *Commercial Advertiser*, February 27, 28, 1843; March 3, 1844; February 24, March 5, 1845; March 12, April 29, 1846.

46. Buffalo *Courier*, March 1, 18, 1843; February 27, 1846; Buffalo *Commercial Advertiser*, February 27, 28, 1843; March 3, 1844; February 24, 1845; March 12, 1846.

47. Buffalo *Commercial Advertiser*, March 3, 1844.

48. Buffalo *Express*, June 13, 1857.

49. Buffalo *Courier*, March 27, 1852; Buffalo *Commercial Advertiser*, November 1, 1859; Almon Clapp to Edward D. Morgan, April 21, 1857, E. D. Morgan Papers, NYSA.

50. Buffalo *Commercial Advertiser*, November 1, 1859.

51. *Geschichte der Deutschen*, p. 62; Buffalo *Courier*, September 3, October 28, November 4, 1844; February 21, 1846; Buffalo *Weltbürger*, February 9, 1839; April 25, May 2, 1840; July 16, October 8, 1842.

52. Buffalo *Weltbürger*, March 28, 1846; June 28, September 20, 1848; Buffalo *Courier*, October 7, 1848; February 21, 1849.

53. In a sample of twenty-one German Democrats who obtained prestigious party positions or nominations and patronage appointments, fourteen (67 percent) came to America with education, including, in two cases, university attendance. Nine (43 percent) had been apprenticed in Europe and developed their skills into businesses in Buffalo. Moreover, in addition, fully sixteen (76 percent) had professions or businesses they were identified with for at least

five years during 1840–60. *Geschichte der Deutschen* (biographical section), passim.

54. Buffalo *Weltbürger*, March 31, June 9, October 20, 1838; March 6, 1841; February 26, 1842; March 19, 1846; Buffalo *Courier*, April 17, 1844; April 15, 1845.

55. *Geschichte der Deutschen* (biographical section), p. 24; Buffalo *Weltbürger*, June 9, 16, 1838; April 9, 1845; and, for other evidence of grumbling over patronage and appointments, March 3, 1843; September 22, 1845.

56. Buffalo *Weltbürger*, February 28, March 4, 1846.

57. Buffalo *Courier*, August 20, 1853; *Geschichte der Deutschen*, vol. 1, pp. 69–70.

58. Buffalo *Commercial Advertiser*, November 1, 1859.

59. I want to thank Professor William E. Gienapp of the University of Wyoming, who generously shared his data with me. (Turnouts for each of the three contests were: Second Ward, 81.1, 71.4, 85.4 percent; First Ward, 80.5, 62.6, 75.6 percent; Fourth Ward, 70.3, 54.6, 63.6 percent).

60. Horton, et al., *History of Northwestern New York*, vol. 1, pp. 35, 70, 71; Ronald E. Shaw, *Erie Water West: A History of the Erie Canal, 1792–1854* (Lexington, 1966), pp. 311–75.

61. Buffalo Superintendent of Schools, *Eighth Annual Report of the Superintendent of Common Schools, 1844* (Buffalo, 1845), p. 1; and *Fourteenth Annual Report of the Superintendent of Public Schools, 1850* (Buffalo, 1851), pp. 17–8; Buffalo *Commercial Advertiser*, October 26, 1842.

62. Benson, *The Concept of Jacksonian Democracy*, pp. 169–70, estimates that in New York State Whigs received 90 percent of the vote of both naturalized Scots and Irish Protestants and 75 per cent of the vote of naturalized Englishmen.

63. Ramsey, "From Self-Educating Boosters to Stewards of Culture," vol. 1, pp. 261–2; Horton, et al., *History of Northwestern New York*, vol. 1, p. 108; Buffalo *Weltbürger*, August 7, 1850. "Maps and Tax Records of James S. Wadsworth's Holdings in Buffalo, New York, 1856–1859," James S. Wadsworth Collection, ML; Fred T. Stevens to James S. Wadsworth, January 7, 1847; Isaac Sherman to James S. Wadsworth, January 3, 1848; James S. Wadsworth Papers, LC.

64. Shaw, *Erie Water West*, pp. 318–59, 375, 391; Marvin A. Rapp, "The Port of Buffalo, 1825–1880" (Ph.D. dissertation, Duke University, 1947), pp. 60–71; Buffalo *Weltbürger*, August 12, 1846; June 19, 1847.

65. Shaw, *Erie Water West*, pp. 375–91; Edward Hungerford, *Men and Iron: The History of the New York Central Railroad* (New York, 1938), pp. 73, 189, 193–209; David M. Ellis, "Rivalry between the New York Central and the Erie Canal," *New York History*, 29 (July, 1948), 272–84; Buffalo *Express*, September 4, 1855; July 6, 17, 28, August 2, 3, October 5, 13, 1859; January 6, 30, February 20, 24, 1860.

66. Buffalo *Weltbürger*, November 6, 1841; March 5, November 12, 1842; March 11, 1843; March 9, 1844; Buffalo *Courier*, March 8, 1843; November 6, 1844.

67. Buffalo *Courier*, July 11, 12, 1844; February 25, 1847.

68. Buffalo *Commercial Advertiser*, September 30, 1844; Buffalo *Courier*, February 25, 1847; Buffalo *Weltbürger*, October 23, 1850.

69. Buffalo *Weltbürger*, March 3, 10, 1849. The Free Soil party put up a city slate and a few ward slates in that municipal campaign, but seems to have made no difference in any ward but the Fourth. There, however, the *Weltbürger* contended, taxation, not antislavery ideology, was the source of the narrow victory of the Whig mayoral candidate. The Free Soilers had little impact on the mayoral contest, which the Whig candidate won by one of the greatest majorities (1,157) in the city's pre-1861 history; Buffalo *Courier*, March 8, 1849.

70. Buffalo *Weltbürger*, November 16, 1839; February 28, March 4, 1846; March 3, 10, 1849; March 3, 1852.

71. George Washington Johnson, Diary, 1841, entry of October 29, DC; Ginsberg, "The Tangled Web," 135–228; Buffalo *Weltbürger*, November 11, 1848; Buffalo *Republic*, August 11, 1848.

72. Buffalo *Courier*, September 10, December 3, 1845; Buffalo *Weltbürger*, October 23, 1850.

73. Buffalo *Courier*, February 10, December 16, 1846; November 3, 1849; Buffalo *Weltbürger*, November 9, 1850; Horton, et al., *History of Northwestern New York*, vol. 1, pp. 93–7.

74. Buffalo *Courier*, December 3, 10, 1845; March 21, November 18, 1846; February 2, 1848; Buffalo *Commercial Advertiser*, March 21, 1846; Buffalo *Weltbürger*, December 6, 1845; March 25, 1846; October 14, November 20, 1848; April 14, 1849; March 9, 1850; February 12, 1851; Buffalo *Republic*, June 15, 1853.

75. Buffalo *Weltbürger*, March 9, 1850; Buffalo *Courier*, July 19, 24, 27, 30, August 2, 5, 20, 23, 24, 30, September 23, 1852; August 20, 23, 29, 1853.

76. Buffalo *Weltbürger*, March 31, 1838. The man was soon canvassing for the Whigs; ibid., October 13, 1838.

77. Rayback, *Millard Fillmore*, pp. 156–7 (quotation); Buffalo *Weltbürger*, July 25, August 1, September 5, 1840; March 11, April 8, June 17, 1843; February 3, March 16, June 15, August 10, 1844; Buffalo *Courier*, December 23, 1842; January 6, 29, March 7, 1844; Buffalo *Commercial Advertiser*, July 10, October 5, 11, 22, 30, 1844; Buffalo *Demokrat und Weltbürger*, May 4, 1854.

78. Buffalo *Weltbürger*, March 2, 9, 23, 1839; March 16, August 10, November 9, 1844; Buffalo *Commercial Advertiser*, October 12, November 4, 1842; August 5, 21, October 23, November 4, 1844.

79. Buffalo *Weltbürger*, October 13, 1838; February 27, 1841; Buffalo *Courier*, January 6, 29, 1844.

80. Buffalo *Weltbürger*, August 1, 1840; February 27, 1841; March 4, 1843; *Geschichte der Deutschen* (biographical section), p. 70; Buffalo *Courier*, November, 1849; February 18, 1850; Buffalo *Commercial Advertiser*, November 7, 1853.

81. Buffalo *Weltbürger*, September 13, 1848; Henry B. Miller to Thurlow Weed, July 5, August 27, 1856, Seward-Weed Collection, UR.

82. Millard Fillmore to Thurlow Weed, November 6, 1844; Millard Fillmore to Henry Clay, November 11, 1844, Millard Fillmore Papers, BECHS.
83. Rayback, *Millard Fillmore*, pp. 158–60; Buffalo *Commercial Advertiser*, November 8, 16 (quotation), 1844; Buffalo *Courier*, November 16, 21, 1844.
84. Buffalo *Gazette*, December 27, 1844; Buffalo *Courier*, November 9, 1844.
85. Scisco, *Political Nativism in New York State*, pp. 39–44; American Republican Association, "Subscription of Names, September 27, 1844," BECHS; and *Preamble and Constitution* (Buffalo, 1845), *Buffalo City Directory, 1844* (Buffalo, 1844), passim; Buffalo *Courier*, July 9, 1844.
86. Louis D. Scisco, *Political Nativism in New York State* (New York, 1901), pp. 45–58. On these reservations about allying with nativists, see Rayback, *Millard Fillmore*, pp. 156–7, 187; Buffalo *Commercial Advertiser*, November 16, 1844; March 13, 20, 1847; November 7, 1853; Buffalo *Weltbürger*, September 3, 1845; August 30, 1848; March 17, April 10, 1849; Deutsch-Amerikanische Historische und Biographische Gesellschaft, *Buffalo und Sein Deutschtum* (Buffalo, 1912), p. 55.
87. Buffalo *Commercial Advertiser*, November 22, 27, 1844; February 6, 1845; March 23, April 8, October 13, 1846; and, with unbroken thematic continuity in the 1850s, at the height of organized nativism, December 14, 1854; February 24, 1855; May 8, 1856; May 8, 1857.
88. Harry J. Carmen, "The Seward-Fillmore Feud and the Disruption of the Whig Party," *New York History*, 24 (June, 1943), 335–7; Rayback, *Millard Fillmore*, pp. 108–13, 143, 204; Lee Howland Warner, "The Silver Grays: New York State Conservative Whigs, 1846–1856" (Ph.D. dissertation, University of Wisconsin, 1971), 1–148, 185–97; Vincent P. Lannie, *Public Money and Parochial Education: Bishop Hughes, Governor Seward, and the New York School Controversy* (Cleveland, 1968); Buffalo *Commercial Advertiser*, November 5, 1842; May 13, August 16, 1844; Buffalo *Weltbürger*, September 22, 1849.
89. Buffalo *Commercial Advertiser*, March 20, 1855, retrospectively summarizes its response to Kossuth and other European revolutionaries. Also, see Buffalo *Weltbürger*, December 20, 24, 27, 1851; Buffalo *Christian Advocate*, February 12, June 3, 1852; Buffalo *Express*, May 22, 1852; Rayback, *Millard Fillmore*, pp. 329–31.
90. In this evolution local temperance followed the national pattern; see Ian R. Tyrell, *Sobering Up: From Temperance to Prohibition in Antebellum America, 1800–1860* (Westport, 1979).
91. Buffalo *Christian Advocate*, March 14, 1850; February 21, 1856; November 1, 1860.
92. *New York State Census of Manufactures, 1855*; *Buffalo Commercial Advertiser City Directory, 1855* (Buffalo, 1855), pp. 272, 277, 280–2, 283, 290; William J. Rorabaugh, *The Alcoholic Republic* (New York, 1979), pp. 69–75, 84–7, 140–5; Danforth Franklin, Private account book, 1842, BECHS.
93. Buffalo *Courier*, March 12, 1850. The Buffalo *Christian Advocate*, October 18, 1854, criticized these dailies for their attitude on the alcohol question. Also, Buffalo *Democracy*, n.d., clipping in Scrapbook, vol. 1, Horatio Seymour Papers, NYSA.

94. *Geschichte der Deutschen*, vol. 1, pp. 64-8; Buffalo *Weltbürger*, December 24, 1842; January 10, February 21, May 13, 1846; January 31, 1849; February 23, March 12, 20, 1850; May 28, 1851; Buffalo *Courier*, April 10, 1852; Tyrell, *Sobering Up*, pp. 261-3.

95. Dr. Bryant Burwell, Diary, 1844, entry of July 11, BECHS.

96. Tyrell, *Sobering Up*, pp. 261-3; Buffalo *Christian Advocate*, August 5, 1852; October 18, 1854. The *Commercial Advertiser* and the *Express* met the alcohol question largely with silence—much to the frustration of the *Christian Advocate*.

97. Rorabaugh, *The Alcoholic Republic*, pp. 140-50; Buffalo *Commercial Advertiser*, January 17, 1845; Buffalo *Weltbürger*, November 22, 1845; Buffalo *Courier*, January 16, 1846; Ian R. Tyrell, "Women and Temperance in Ante-Bellum America, 1830-1860," *Civil War History*, 28 (June, 1982), 140-1; "Ladies Temperance Society," *Buffalo Commercial Advertiser City Directory, 1850-1* (Buffalo, 1851), p. 31.

98. Buffalo *Weltbürger*, February 21, May 13, 16, 23, 1846; Buffalo *Commercial Advertiser*, May 12, 20, 1846; William J. Rorabaugh, "Prohibition as Progress: New York State's License Elections, 1846," *Journal of Social History*, 14 (Spring, 1981), 425-43.

99. Buffalo *Commercial Advertiser*, August 17, September 18, 1846; Buffalo *Courier*, October 7, 1846; April 28, 1847; Buffalo *Weltbürger*, September 19, 1846; February 20, April 17, 28, 1847.

100. Buffalo *Christian Advocate*, March 6, 14, November 14, December 19, 1850; April 3, 17, 1851; Buffalo *Courier*, March 12, 18, 1850; Buffalo *Weltbürger*, March 13, 1850.

101. Buffalo *Courier*, April 10, 1850; Buffalo *Weltbürger*, April 13, 27, 1850.

102. Buffalo *Courier*, April 10, 1850; April 17, 1851; Buffalo *Weltbürger*, May 21, June 18, 1851.

103. *Geschichte der Deutschen*, vol. 1, pp. 64-6; Buffalo *Weltbürger*, April-May, 1851.

104. Buffalo *Courier*, May 14, 28, 30, 1851; April 12, 1852; Buffalo *Christian Advocate*, May 22, 29, 1851.

105. Buffalo *Courier*, April 12, 1852.

106. Shaw, *Erie Water West*, pp. 225-6; Buffalo *Commercial Advertiser*, July 14, 1842; December 11, 1857; Buffalo *Courier*, May 29, 1847; July 2, 1849; Buffalo *Christian Advocate*, February 12, June 24, 1852; March 3, 1853; John Chase Lord, *Medical Science and Materialism* (Buffalo, 1854); Theresa L. Wolfe, *Tifft Farm: A History of Man and Nature* (Buffalo, 1984), pp. 15, 16; Melvin Hyman, "Sabbatarianism and Sunday Blue Law Controversies in New York State" (Ph.D. dissertation, New York University, 1973), 9-24.

107. Buffalo *Courier*, August 1, 1844; June 4, 1846; March 16, 1849; August 23, 1850; Buffalo *Weltbürger*, June 26, 1842; January 13, 1847; April 22, 1848; Buffalo *Christian Advocate*, February 25, November 27, 1851; March 25, 1852; Buffalo *Commercial Advertiser*, April 17, June 12, 1855.

108. Buffalo *Courier*, October 30, 1847; May 14, 1851; April 12, June 20, 1852; Buffalo *Christian Advocate*, January 3, 1850; July 14, 1853.

109. Buffalo *Commercial Advertiser*, February 18, 1843; December 10, 1846; December 13, 1855; December 10, 1857; November 25, 1858; December 15, 1859; Buffalo *Courier*, January 19, 1847; July 10, September 12, 1849; July 1, August 15, 1850; May 14, 1851; June 4, 1852; June 23, 1853.

110. *Geschichte der Deutschen*, vol. 1, pp. 57–62, 83–5; *Buffalo Commercial Advertiser City Directory, 1854* (Buffalo, 1854), p. 99; *Buffalo Commercial Advertiser*, October 23, 1855. "We doubt," said the *Christian Advocate* (June 19, 1856), "Yankees evince anything like the spirit which animates our German soldiery."

111. Buffalo *Commercial Advertiser*, March 15, 1860; Fergus O'Ferrall, *Catholic Emancipation: Daniel O'Connell and the Birth of Irish Democracy, 1820–30* (London, 1985).

112. Buffalo *Demokrat und Weltbürger*, March 10, 12, 19, 23, 1860. Not surprisingly the German aldermen (with one exception) voted differently when the question came up for reconsideration two weeks later.

113. Buffalo *Courier*, October 2, 1850; Buffalo *Weltbürger*, October 25, 1850.

114. Walter H. Beck, *Lutheran Elementary Schools in the United States* (St. Louis, 1939), pp. 5–8, 78–84, 124–6, and passim.

115. Buffalo Courier, October 11, 16, 1849; July 20, 28, September 17, 20, 22, 24, 25, 1852; Buffalo *American Celt and Catholic Citizen*, July 31, August 7, 21, September 25, October 9, 1852; Buffalo *Sentinel*, January 9, March 25, 1858; *Buffalo Medical Journal*, 5 (1849–50), 424–8.

116. Erik H. Monkonnen, *Police in Urban America, 1860–1920* (Cambridge, Mass., 1981). For demands to suppress dock runners: Buffalo *Commercial Advertiser*, June 4, 1846; April 28, June 1, July 18, December 15, 1854; Buffalo *Weltbürger*, April 29, May 6, 1848; Buffalo *Courier*, August 21, 23, 1850.

117. Marvin A. Rapp, "The Port of Buffalo, 1825–1880" (Ph.D. dissertation, Duke University, 1947), 219–51; Buffalo *Courier and Pilot*, September 11, 1846; Buffalo *Commercial Advertiser*, April 12, July 18, 20, October 11, 1854; July 22, October 10, 1856; July 21, November 12, December 1, 11, 1857; April 13, July 13, October 10, 1858; April 12, July 12, December 24, 1859.

118. Buffalo *Commercial Advertiser*, October 24, 1846; Buffalo *Courier*, October 24, 1846; April 12, 1853; Buffalo *Weltbürger*, August 23, 27, 1851.

119. Buffalo *Courier*, September 23, 1852; Buffalo *Demokrat und Weltbürger*, December 2, 1853; Buffalo *Sentinel*, April 25, 1857.

120. *An Act to Incorporate the City of Buffalo* (Buffalo, 1832), pp. 21–5; Buffalo *Weltbürger*, May 11, June 22, 1844; Buffalo *Republic*, August 6, 1853; April 13, October 1, 1857; Buffalo *Commercial Advertiser*, June 19, July 20, 1854; July 12, 16, 19, August 5, 1859; Joel A. Tarr, "Building the Urban Infrastructure in the Nineteenth Century: An Introduction," in Public Works Historical Society, *Infrastructure and Urban Growth in the Nineteenth Century* (Chicago, 1985), pp. 62–4.

121. Buffalo *Weltbürger*, December 24, 31, 1842; May 11, 1842; June 12, 1847; *Biographical Dictionary of American Mayors*, s.v. "Ketchum, William." Ketchum laid out his public philosophy in a series of letters, explaining what for many years had been and would remain his position on municipal finances; see Buffalo *Commercial Advertiser*, March 8, 9, 16, 1854.

122. *An Act to Incorporate the City of Buffalo*, pp. 21-5; George Clinton, "Historical Sketch," in *The Manufacturing Interests of the City of Buffalo* (Buffalo, 1866), pp. 5-7; *Biographical Dictionary of American Mayors*, s.v. "Pratt, Hiram"; Buffalo *Courier*, February 18, 1850; July 1, 1853; Buffalo *Weltbürger*, December 16, 1848; Buffalo *Republic*, June 28, 1856; Common Council, *Proceedings*, May 2, 1856, BECHS.

123. Buffalo *Weltbürger*, December 31, 1842; August 24, 1844; Buffalo *Courier*, December 20, 1853; Buffalo *Demokrat und Weltbürger*, April 14, 15, 1857; March 30, 31, April 6, 22, 1858; March 9, 17, April 5, June 7, 1859; March 6, 1860; Buffalo *Republic*, June 12, 1858; Common Council, *Proceedings*, November 5, 1839, BECHS; *An Act to Incorporate the City of Buffalo*, pp. 21-5; *Revised Charter of the City of Buffalo* (Buffalo, 1856).

124. Ramsey, "From Self-Educating Boosters to Stewards of Culture," vol. 1, pp. 94-163; *Biographical Dictionary of American Mayors*, s.v. "Allen, Orlando," "Burton, Hiram K.," "Clinton, George W.," "Harrington, Isaac," "Ketchum, William," "Masten, Joseph," "Pratt, Hiram," "Spaulding, E. G.," "Trowbridge, Josiah"; Buffalo *Commercial Advertiser*, March 8, 1842; March 14, 1843; February 3, 1857; Buffalo *Weltbürger*, June 30, 1847; January 26, March 29, 1848; February 27, 1850; February 26, March 15, 1851; Buffalo *Demokrat und Weltbürger*, January 12, 1854; Buffalo *Courier*, May 6, 8, 1851; Buffalo *Republic*, June 30, 1853; March 3, 1855; Tarr, "Building the Urban Infrastructure," 69.

125. *Biographical Dictionary of American Mayors*, s.v. "Ketchum, William"; Buffalo *Demokrat und Weltbürger*, January 12, 1854; March 3, 1856; Glyndon Van Deusen, *William Henry Seward* (New York, 1967), p. 134.

126. Buffalo *Demokrat und Weltbürger*, March 3, 1856; Buffalo *Commercial Advertiser*, March 7, 1857.

127. Buffalo *Weltbürger*, April 8, June 13, August 8, 1846.

128. Ibid., December 24, 1841; July 21, August 23, 1849; Buffalo *Demokrat und Weltbürger*, November 22, 1853; April 10, 14, May 6, 1856; Buffalo *Commercial Advertiser*, March 7, 1857.

129. Buffalo *Weltbürger*, June 24, 26, 1848; Buffalo *Courier*, November 4, 1852; Buffalo *Commercial Advertiser*, June 22, 1856.

130. Buffalo *Weltbürger*, May 18, 1844; May 24, August 16, 1845; February 21, 1846; February 23, 1848; February 13, July 24, 1850.

131. Ibid., January 27, February 17, March 2, 1844; April 9, September 17, 1845; December 18, 1847; February 7, 10, 21, 1849; Buffalo *Demokrat und Weltbürger*, February 9, 10, 13, 1854. The German wards along with the rest of the city, gave 99 percent support for canal enlargement in an 1854 state referendum; Buffalo *Commercial Advertiser*, February 16, 1854.

132. Buffalo *Weltbürger*, July 30, December 2, 1843; Buffalo *Demokrat und Weltbürger*, May 10, 20, 21, 30, June 13, 14, 15, 1853.

133. Buffalo *Express*, May 4, 1852; Buffalo *Courier*, June 17, 1853.

134. Buffalo *Commercial Advertiser*, July 16, 1851; August 4, 1856; Buffalo *Weltbürger*, August 23, 1851; Buffalo *Courier*, June 17, July 31, 1852; Buffalo *Republic*, August 24, 1853; September 9, 1854; July 19, 1856; Buffalo *Express*, May 13, 1857; January 19, 1858.

135. Buffalo *Weltbürger*, August 23, 1851; Buffalo *Commercial Advertiser*, August 19, 27, September 3, 8, 9, 1851; Buffalo *Courier*, August 19, 22, 23, September 10, 1851.

136. Buffalo *Courier*, December 19, 1849; Buffalo *Weltbürger*, December 15, 1849; January 1, March 2, 1850.

137. Buffalo *Republic*, August 22, December 30, 1853; January 3, 1854; May 8, 1854; Buffalo *Courier*, December 27, 1853.

138. Buffalo *Demokrat und Weltbürger*, February 16, March 18, 24, October 23, 1854; July 8, August 15, 18, 1856; Buffalo *Courier*, March 8, 9, 16, 29, November 22, 1854; January 31, 1855; Buffalo *Commercial Advertiser*, November 16, 17, 21, 22, 1854; Buffalo *Republic*, November 21, 1854; August 14, 15, 18, September 6, 1856; and for motives and actions of council members, see below, note 139.

139. Buffalo *Demokrat und Weltbürger*, September 20, 1853; December 27, 1855; January 2, March 25, September 9, 10, 26, December 16, 1856; September 15, 23, 1858; Buffalo *Courier*, February 21, March 1, 14, 1854; Buffalo *Republic*, June 8, 1854; May 27, 1856; Buffalo *Commercial Advertiser*, December 12, 1854; February 21, 1855; August 18, September 9, 29, 1856. Both markets opened in October, 1857; Buffalo *Republic*, October 3, 1857.

Chapter 12. From Ethnic Polarization to Social and Political Realignment, 1854–60

1. Buffalo *Commercial Advertiser*, September 15, October 10, 11, November 3, 9, 1853; May 11, July 5, 12, 13, 14, 1854; Buffalo *Christian Advocate*, September 22, 1853; *Buffalo Republic*, October 12, 1853; February 12, 1854.

2. Buffalo *Republic*, June 6, 10, 1854; Buffalo *Commercial Advertiser*, September 2, October 9, 28, 1854.

3. Buffalo *Commercial Advertiser*, April 17, July 20, October 9, 1854; February 26, May 26, November 2, 1857; Buffalo *Courier*, June 9, 1854; John T. Horton, Edward T. Williams, and Harry S. Douglass, *History of Northwestern New York*, vol. 1 (New York, 1947), pp. 163–7; *Buffalo Commercial Advertiser Directory for 1855* (Buffalo, 1855); Buffalo *Demokrat und Weltbürger*, October 10, 1854.

4. Below, pp, 383–84.

5. Louis D. Scisco, *Political Nativism in New York State* (New York, 1901), p. 185; Horton, et al., *History of Northwestern New York*, vol. 1, p. 163; Buffalo *Express*, June 13, 1855; Buffalo *Commercial Advertiser*, November 2, 1857.

6. Buffalo *Commercial Advertiser*, November 8, 1854; September 2, 1855; June 10, 1857; Buffalo *Demokrat und Weltbürger*, June 6, 7, 14, 1855; Buffalo *Republic*, November 5, 1856; Andrew Yox, "The Decline of the German-American Community in Buffalo, 1855–1925" (Ph.D. dissertation, University of Chicago, 1983), 47. Professor William E. Gienapp shared his data on election turnouts with me; they are also used in note 7, below.

7. Buffalo *Demokrat und Weltbürger*, June 6, 7, 14, 1855; Buffalo *Commercial Advertiser*, September 2, 1855; Buffalo *Republic*, November 5, 1856. Edward Fries, "Buffalo, New York, 1854–1860: A Multivariate Analysis of

Voting Behavior" (M.A. thesis, State University of New York College at Fredonia, 1978), 25, 57, 66, 74, 87 (the four elections are the 1854 and 1856 congressional and 1855 and 1857 state senate contests, which are analyzed by Fries); Andrew Yox, "Bonds of Community: Buffalo's German Element, 1853–1871," *New York History*, 66 (April, 1985), 152.

8. The four men—David Cooper, C. J. Wells, Edward Hulbert, and Charles McComber—are listed in Buffalo *Commercial Advertiser*, September 22, 1855; August 22, 1859; and American Republican Association, "Subscription of Names, September 27, 1844," BECHS.

9. Buffalo *Commercial Advertiser*, December 7, 1855; January 14, 1856.

10. Scisco, *Political Nativism in New York State*, pp. 62–82. It is not clear whether organizations such as the Order of United Americans or the Order of United American Mechanics were present in Buffalo; the latter were not as of September 25, 1851, according to the Rhinebeck, New York, *American Mechanic* of that date.

11. Buffalo *Commercial Advertiser*, July 5, 12, 1854.

12. R. G. Dun and Co., New York, vol. 80, p. 306 (Car.), R. G. Dun and Company Collection, BL.

13. Buffalo *Commercial Advertiser*, June 30, August 3 (quotation), 1854; July 13, 1855; Buffalo *Courier*, December 18, 1855.

14. Buffalo *Republic and Times*, June 8, 1858.

15. Buffalo *Commercial Advertiser*, June 24, 1854; Buffalo *Christian Advocate*, October 19, 1854; February 6, 1857.

16. Buffalo *Courier*, October 7, 11, 1848; November 17, 26, 1849; August 13, 1851; March 29, April 30, May 3, November 9, 11, 1853; March 24, October 5, 1854; February 2, 1855; October 23, 1858; Buffalo *Republic*, June 8, 13, 22, 23, 27, 1853; January 25, May 11, June 20, 27, 28, August 14, November 14, 1854; June 11, 1855; June 13, 1857.

17. Buffalo *Republic*, August 14, 1854.

18. Buffalo *Courier*, n.d., quoted in Buffalo *Republic*, November 14, 1854.

19. Charges frequently were made that Democratic candidates had once been or continued to be Know Nothings: Buffalo *Demokrat und Weltbürger*, November 9, 1855; Buffalo *Courier*, September 19, 1857; Buffalo *Express*, November 2, 1857; Buffalo *Evening Post*, October 16, 1858; Buffalo *Commercial Advertiser*, November 2, 1859.

20. Hendrik Booream, IV, *The Formation of the Republican Party in New York: Politics and Conscience in the Antebellum North* (New York, 1983), pp. 212–8; Thomas J. Curran, "The Know Nothings of New York State" (Ph.D. dissertation, Columbia University, 1963), viii, 272; Eric Foner, *Free Soil, Free Labor, Free Men: The Ideology of the Republican Party before the Civil War* (New York, 1970), pp. 227–59; Scisco, *Political Nativism in New York State*, pp. 226–43; Buffalo *Express*, December 31, 1857; Buffalo *Demokrat und Weltbürger*, November 19, 1856.

21. Buffalo *Express*, March 7, 1850, clipping in Seward-Weed Collection, UR.

22. Buffalo *Courier*, November 6, 1851; March 4, 1852.

23. Ibid., March 9, 1853; Buffalo *Commercial Advertiser*, November 8, 1854; November 7, 1855; June 10, 1857; November 5, 1857; November 3, 1858; Buffalo *Demokrat und Weltbürger*, June 6, 7, 14, 1855; Buffalo *Republic*, November 5, 1856.

24. Buffalo *Commercial Advertiser*, November 8, 1854; June 6, November 7, 1855; April 8, 1856; *New York State Census of 1855*, alphabetized printout, SUNYAB.

25. Amy Bridges, *A City in the Republic: Antebellum New York and the Origins of Machine Politics* (New York, 1984), pp. 101-2; John P. Diggins and Mark E. Kann, "Authority in America: The Crisis of Legitimacy"; John P. Diggins, "The Three Faces of Authority in American History"; and Mark E. Kann, "Consent and Authority in America," in *The Problem of Authority in America*, ed. John P. Diggins and Mark E. Kann (Philadelphia, 1981), pp. 3-9, 17-39, 59-83.

26. Buffalo *Commercial Advertiser*, November 10, 1853.

27. Buffalo *Republic*, June 18, 1853; Buffalo *Express*, March 3, 1854; February 14, September 21, 1855; Buffalo *Christian Advocate*, March 30, April 13, November 2, 1854; July 26, August 16, 1855; July 19, 1856; Buffalo *Demokrat und Weltbürger*, June 20, 1855; Buffalo *Democracy* [1854?], clipping in Scrapbook, vol. 1, Horatio Seymour Papers, NYSA; Buffalo *Commercial Advertiser*, January 31, 1856; John A. Krout, "The Maine Law in New York Politics," *New York History*, 17 (1935), 264-5.

28. Buffalo *Demokrat und Weltbürger*, June 20, 23, 25, 27, 1855; Buffalo *Christian Advocate*, June 28, 1855.

29. Buffalo *Demokrat und Weltbürger*, March 16, 23, 1854; April 11, 16, 19, May 1, 9, 11, June 6-28, 1855; Buffalo *Commercial Advertiser*, June 25, 28, July 6, 25, 1855; January 26, 1856; Buffalo *Christian Advocate*, February 7 (quotation), April 3, 1856.

30. Buffalo *Commercial Advertiser*, April 16, 1856; November 21, 1859; Buffalo *Demokrat und Weltbürger*, May 26, 1857; February 13, 15, 17, 1857; May 28, July 2, 23, 27, August 30, 1858; June 2, 1860; Buffalo *Christian Advocate*, June 4, 25, July 30, 1857; July 1, 8, 1858; March 17, 1859; August 30, 1860; July 21, 1861.

31. Buffalo *Express*, May 23, 1859.

32. On the juvenile asylum controversy: Buffalo *Commercial Advertiser*, December 4, 1855; January 18, May 9, 18, December 3, 23, 27, 29, 1856; January 12, 1857; Buffalo *Sentinel*, December 27, 1856; January 10, 17, February 7, March 7, 1857; January 30, 1858. On the poorhouse: Buffalo *Courier*, October 11, 16, 1849; September 17, 20, 22, 24, 1852; January 9, 1858.

33. E.g., Buffalo *Republic*, July 25, October 13, 1853; June 8, 9, 20, November 16, 1854; January 29, 1855; November 4, 5, 6, 1856; Buffalo *Commercial Advertiser*, October 22, 1853; April 20, July 24, 1854; Buffalo *Christian Advocate*, June 12, 1856; November 3, 1859; Michael F. Holt, "The Politics of Impatience: The Origins of Know Nothingism," *Journal of American History*, 60 (September, 1973), 315-22.

34. Buffalo *Republic*, June 10, 1854.

35. Buffalo *Demokrat und Weltbürger*, August 17, 1854; Buffalo *Commercial Advertiser*, January 24, 1856; Buffalo *Republic*, October 8, 1856; June 10, 1857; September 18, 1858; Buffalo *Express*, May 28, 1857.

36. Buffalo *Sentinel*, June 13, October 3, 10, 24, 1857; Buffalo *Commercial Advertiser*, June 8, 1857.

37. Scisco, *Political Nativism in New York State*, p. 112; Buffalo *Republic*, October 9, 1854.

38. Holt, "The Politics of Impatience," 315–22; Scisco, *Political Nativism in New York State*, pp. 103, 113, 194–7: Buffalo *Commercial Advertiser*, April 5, October 17, 19, November 5, 1855; *Buffalo Commercial Advertiser Directory for 1855* (Buffalo, 1855).

39. Buffalo *Commercial Advertiser*, December 4, 1854; January 16, 1855; Buffalo *Demokrat und Weltbürger*, August 3, 1854; Buffalo *Republic*, October 12, 18, 1854; September 17, 1855; Buffalo *Express*, January 4, 9, February 8, 9, May 4, 14, 15, 1855; Scisco, *Political Nativism in New York State*, pp. 130–1, 141, 157–60; Krout, "The Maine Law in New York Politics," 267–8.

40. Lee Howland Warner, "The Silver Grays: New York State Conservative Whigs, 1846–1856" (Ph.D. dissertation, University of Wisconsin, 1971), 145–81; Horton, et al., *History of Northwestern New York*, vol. 1, pp. 164–7; Buffalo *Commercial Advertiser*, September 2, November 7, 1854; Solomon G. Haven to Millard Fillmore, June 29, December 9 (quotation), 1854; and Edward Everett to MF, November 10, 1854, Millard Fillmore Papers, BECHS (microfilms). Putnam was still an anti-Catholic crusader thirty years later; see John Hay to James O. Putnam, March 28, 1883, Miscellaneous Papers, BECHS.

41. Robert J. Rayback, *Millard Fillmore: Biography of a President* (Buffalo, 1959), pp. 387–96; Buffalo *Express*, March 4, 1856; Elbridge Spaulding to William Henry Seward, August 2, 1856, Seward-Weed Papers, UR; Millard Fillmore to Edward Everett, December 13, 1854; April 7, 1855; and to Alexander H. H. Stuart, January 15, 1855; Nathan K. Hall to Millard Fillmore, December 14, 1854; Edward Everett to MF, December 16, 1854; Solomon G. Haven to MF, December 20, 22, 1854; January 10, 1855, Millard Fillmore Papers, BECHS (microfilms).

42. Rayback, *Millard Fillmore*, pp. 407–8; "Campaign of 1856," *Millard Fillmore Papers*, ed. Frank H. Severance, vol. 2 (Buffalo, 1907), pp. 16–7; Horton, et al., *History of Northwestern New York*, vol. 1, pp. 164–5.

43. Buffalo *Express*, April 12, 1855; Buffalo *Demokrat und Weltbürger*, April 3, 1855; March 8, 29, 1856; Buffalo *Commercial Advertiser*, November 3, 1855; March 7, 1856; Charles G. Irish, "Dear Sir, March, 1855, Buffalo" (circular).

44. Buffalo *Demokrat und Weltbürger*, May 26, 28, 1855; February 20, August 28, 1856; Buffalo *Commercial Advertiser*, June 27, July 8, 30, October 9, 25, 28, 29, November 3, 1856; September 15, 1859; Curran, "The Know Nothings of New York State," 224–33.

45. Buffalo *Commercial Advertiser*, September 19, 1856.

46. Rev. John Timon, Diary, entry of October 31, 1856, DBA.

47. Buffalo *Republic*, July 11, 1856.

48. Ibid., November 5, 1856. Nativist charges that Fillmore was more unionist than nativist were loudly and widely made even before the campaign began;

Buffalo *Demokrat und Weltbürger*, February 27, 1856. Also, Booream, *The Formation of the Republican Party in New York*, pp. 180-1, for the issue during the campaign.

49. Buffalo *Commercial Advertiser*, March 19 (quotation), 1855; April 10, 28 (quotation), 1857.

50. Buffalo *Courier*, June 15, 1854; Horton, et al., *History of Northwestern New York*, vol. 1, pp. 149-50.

51. Buffalo *Commercial Advertiser*, February 3, March 13, December 30, 1854; February 16, 1856; January 20, March 27, 1857; June 22, 1858; Evelyn Hawes, *Proud Vision: A History of Buffalo General Hospital* (New York, 1964), pp. 1-13.

52. Buffalo *Express*, n.d., quoted in Buffalo *Sentinel*, July 11, 1857; Buffalo *Republic*, June 9, 1853. For similar complaints, see Buffalo *Courier*, June 21, 1851; Buffalo *Commercial Advertiser*, June 16, 1860.

53. Buffalo *Courier*, July 1, 1850; June 4, 1852; June 23, 1853; May 23, 1854; Buffalo *Sentinel*, July 11, 1857; Buffalo *Commercial Advertiser*, June 16, 26, 1858.

54. Buffalo *Commercial Advertiser*, February 22, 1856.

55. Ibid., March 10, 1855; April 10, 28, 1857.

56. Buffalo *Christian Advocate*, January 3, 1850.

57. Ibid., January 29, March 11, 1852; February 28, 1856 (quotation), September 9, 1858; September 12, 1861.

58. Ibid., September 25, 1856; May 7, 1857; September 2, November 11, 1858; April 17, 1859; October 18, 1860.

59. Ibid., February 10, 1859.

60. Harlan M. Frost, *An Ecumenical Wind in Buffalo: A History of the Local Council of Churches* (Buffalo, 1977), pp. 2-4; Buffalo *Christian Advocate*, March 8, 1860.

61. Buffalo *Commercial Advertiser*, April 18, 1859. The *Christian Advocate* reluctantly acknowledged the same, and fluctuated between calling on the denominations to get people into church and on government to enforce laws that it admitted no one showed any disposition to obey; ibid., December 30, 1858; May 29, 1859; July 19, August 2, November 6, 1860.

62. Buffalo *Republic*, September 29, 1859; Howe, *The Political Culture of American Whigs*, pp. 234-5.

63. Buffalo *Courier*, September 20, 1847; April 3, October 29, 1849; February 12, 14, 27, 1851; Buffalo *Republic*, June 8, 1853; March 17, 1854; Buffalo *Christian Advocate*, May 30 (quotation), July 27, 1858; Buffalo *Commercial Advertiser*, December 29, 1859; Buffalo *Express*, April 10, 1858; (undated obituaries), Burgess Scrapbook, 1853-1875, BECHS; H. Perry Smith, ed., *History of the City of Buffalo and Erie County, New York*, vol. 2 (Syracuse, 1884), p. 78.

64. Buffalo *Commercial Advertiser*, March 17, 1859.

65. Ibid., April 26, 1855. Also see December 22, 1853.

66. Buffalo *Courier*, April 29, 1853; Buffalo *Republic*, June 20, 1853.

67. Buffalo *Commercial Advertiser*, January 23, April 24, 1858; Buffalo *Republic and Times*, August 11-18, 23, September 2, 1858.

68. Buffalo *Republic*, September 15, 17 (quotation), 1860.
69. Buffalo *Commercial Advertiser*, April 26, 1855.
70. Ibid., June 24, 1858.
71. Buffalo *Republic and Times*, June 11, September 17, 25, 1858; Buffalo *Commercial Advertiser*, May 26, 1859; George B. Kirsch, "American Cricket: Players and Clubs before the Civil War," *Journal of Sports History*, 11 (Spring, 1984), 28–50. William Baker, *Sports in the Western World* (Totowa, 1982), pp. 138–43, charts this same competition for the nation-at-large.
72. Buffalo *Courier*, April 3, 1849; February 14, 27, 1851; Buffalo *Commercial Advertiser*, October 22, 1853; December 29, 1859; Buffalo *Republic*, March 17, 1854; Buffalo *Christian Advocate*, July 27, 1858.
73. Buffalo *Express*, February 21, 1859.
74. Buffalo *Courier*, November 28, 1853; Buffalo *Commercial Advertiser*, November 30, December 22, 1853; December 20, 1856; Buffalo *Christian Advocate*, December 4, 14, 22, 1858; New England Society of Buffalo, *Constitution and Members*, vol. 1, BECHS.
75. Buffalo *Commercial Advertiser*, June 9, 1858; December 31, 1859; Committee on Invitations, "Old Settlers' Festival," January 6, 1865, James D. Sawyer Papers, BECHS; n.a., *Fifth Annual Festival of the Old Settlers of Buffalo* (Buffalo, 1868).
76. Buffalo *Commercial Advertiser*, December 19, 1854; December 20, 1856; December 4, 1858; Millard Fillmore, "Inaugural Address," in *Seventy-Fifth Anniversary of the Founding of the Buffalo Historical Society* (Buffalo, 1937), p. 8 (quotation), 27.
77. Buffalo *Demokrat und Weltbürger*, October 18, 19, 21, 23, 24, 25, 1855; February 23, March 15, 26, May 27, June 20, 27, November 18, 1856.
78. Buffalo *Courier*, July 19, 24, 27, 30, August 2, 5, 20, 23, 24, 30, September 23, 1852.
79. Buffalo *Express*, September 26, 1857; *Biographical Dictionary of American Mayors*, s.v. "Barton, Hiram," "Cook, Eli, Jr.," "Stevens, Frederick P."
80. Buffalo *Demokrat und Weltbürger*, April 23, 1855; Buffalo *Express*, April 15, 16, 1857; Buffalo *Republic*, May 7, 1857; Buffalo *Commercial Advertiser*, May 27, 1857.
81. *Hunt's Merchants' Magazine*, n.d., quoted in Buffalo *Express*, April 13, 1857.
82. Buffalo *Express*, April 17, 18, 1857; Buffalo *Republic*, May 2, 1857.
83. Buffalo *Commercial Advertiser*, October 2, 1852; Buffalo *Demokrat und Weltbürger*, November 5, 1855; Buffalo *Express*, May 27, 1857; Buffalo *Republic*, June 5, 10, 1857; *Hunt's Merchants' Magazine*, (April, 1855), 38–9; Bridges, *A City in the Republic*, pp. 36–8, 137–45, 146–61.
84. Buffalo *Commercial Advertiser*, November 7, 1853.
85. Buffalo *Republic*, June 8, 1857.
86. Buffalo *Express*, June 1, 1857; Buffalo *Republic*, June 10, 1857.
87. Buffalo *Commercial Advertiser*, May 16, 1857.
88. Buffalo *Courier*, November 4, 1852.
89. Buffalo *Weltbürger*, July 21, 1849; Buffalo *Demokrat und Weltbürger*, November 22, 1853; April 10, 14, 1856.

90. Buffalo *Republic*, October 27, 1853; Buffalo *Demokrat und Weltbürger*, March 3, 1856.

91. Buffalo *Demokrat und Weltbürger*, May 30, June 5, 12, 1857; Buffalo *Express*, June 12, 1857; Buffalo *Courier*, June 8, 1857; Buffalo *Commercial Advertiser*, June 10, 12, 1857.

92. Buffalo *Commercial Advertiser*, June 10, 1857.

93. Ibid., August 10, 26, 1858; Buffalo *Courier*, August 26, 1858; Buffalo *Express*, November 12, 1858.

94. Buffalo *Commercial Advertiser*, August 10, 17, 25, 26, October 5, November 12, 1858; Buffalo *Republic and Times*, August 11, 20, 21, September 20, November 10, 12, 1858; Buffalo *Express*, November 12, 1858.

95. Buffalo *Courier*, June 17, 1853.

96. Buffalo *Demokrat und Weltbürger*, November 12, 13, 15, 17, 1858; Buffalo *Commercial Advertiser*, November 17, 1858.

97. Buffalo *Commercial Advertiser*, November 3, 1858; November 10, 1859; November 7, 1860; Fries, "Buffalo, New York, 1854–1860: A Multivariate Analysis of Voting Behavior," pp. 92, 96, 97, 108. As we have noted, Fries's selected elections are the 1858 and 1860 congressional and the 1859 secretary of state and state senate races.

98. Judah B. Ginsberg, "The Tangled Web: The New York State Democratic Party and the Slavery Controversy, 1844–1860" (Ph.D. dissertation, University of Wisconsin, 1974), 405–25, 436, 570–632.

99. Buffalo *Express*, September 4, November 10, 1855; January 3, July 6, 17, 28, August 2, 3, October 13, 1858; October 13, 1859; January 30, February 20, 24, 1860; Buffalo *Commercial Advertiser*, October 30, 1855; April 25, 1857; October 18, 1858; October 8, 10, November 1, 1859; Buffalo *Demokrat und Weltbürger*, May 16, 21, 1857; November 4, 6, 1858; August 15, 1859; Buffalo *Sentinel*, June 13, October 3, 24, 1857; Buffalo *Aurora*, December 23, 1859.

100. Buffalo *Express*, October 24, 1860; Booream, *The Formation of the Republican Party in New York*, pp. 225–7. William Gienapp's monumental *The Origins of the Republican Party, 1852–1865* (New York, 1987) appeared too late for me to make use of its findings in my conceptualization of the origins of the Republican party in Buffalo. I am impressed, however, by the extent to which my localized analysis of party formation in Buffalo has come to conclusions that agree with those I have found in Gienapp's macrocosmic analysis.

101. Buffalo *Express*, September 17, 21, 1855; Buffalo *Demokrat und Weltbürger*, March 23, April 22, 23, 24, 1857; Horton, et al., *History of Northwestern New York*, vol. 1, pp. 160–2; *Platform and Constitution of the Republican Association of the City of Buffalo, 1856* (Buffalo, 1856); Elbridge Spaulding to William Henry Seward, August 13, 1856, Seward-Weed Papers, UR; Buffalo *Commercial Advertiser*, March 8, 1859.

102. Buffalo *Christian Advocate*, April 20, 1854; Buffalo *Republic*, September 7, 1855; June 3, 1856; Horton, et al., *History of Northwestern New York*, vol. l, pp. 139–41, 158–9; Buffalo *Express*, March 1–5, 1854.

103. Buffalo *Express*, June 24, 1854; February 14, 1860; Buffalo *Demokrat und Weltbürger*, October 17, 1855; July 22, 23, August 5, 1856; Buffalo *Re-*

public, July 27, August 10, 11, 14, 1855; May 19, July 9, 17, 1856; Booream, *The Formation of the Republican Party in New York State*, pp. 76, 122, 130-1, 201-11.

104. Buffalo *Sentinel*, May 23, July 4, 11, 1857; Buffalo *Express*, June 8, 16, 25, 27, 30, September 28, 1857; William E. Gienapp, "Nativism and the Creation of a Republican Majority in the North before the Civil War," *Journal of American History*, 72 (December, 1985), 548-50.

105. Buffalo *Demokrat und Weltbürger*, August 17, September 1, October 6, 7, 13, 1854; March 29, 30, 1855; November 18, 1856; January 6, September 25, 1857; Buffalo *Republic*, February 27, March 6, 1854; February 3, June 13, 1855; June 7, September 9, 14, 15, 16, October 5, 19, 26, November 2, 1857.

106. Buffalo *Sentinel*, October 10, 17, 1857; Buffalo *Republic*, October 29, November 2, 1857; Buffalo *Express*, November 5, 6, 7, 1857; Buffalo *Commercial Advertiser*, November 5, 1857.

107. Buffalo *Express*, August 10, 1859; Buffalo *Commercial Advertiser*, October 24, 1859.

108. Buffalo *Commercial Advertiser*, May 22, 1860.

109. Ibid., January 5, 1859, and again, August 7, 1860, for a similar statement; *Declaration of Principles, Constitution, and Rules of Order of the Erie County American League* (Buffalo, 1860).

110. Buffalo *Commercial Advertiser*, September 2, 1855. As the Germans often contended, if the American-born children of immigrants were factored into projections of "the German vote," the latter would be larger still; ibid., August 30, 1855, quoting the *Demokrat und Weltbürger*, n.d.

111. Buffalo *Republic*, October 11, 13, 1855; July 3, 7, October 3, 31, November 1, 1856; Buffalo *Commercial Advertiser*, May 14, 1856; Buffalo *Demokrat und Weltbürger*, October 3, 29, 1856; February 18, 1861; Elbridge Spaulding to Thurlow Weed, August 27, 1856; and to William Henry Seward, September 25, 1856, Seward-Weed Papers, UR; Yox, "Bonds of Community," 155.

112. Buffalo *Commercial Advertiser*, September 29, 1858; Buffalo *Demokrat und Weltbürger*, September 29, 1858.

113. Buffalo *Demokrat und Weltbürger*, January 5, 1858 (quotation), September 21, 27, 1859; Buffalo *Express*, October 24, November 8, 9, 1859; Buffalo *Commercial Advertiser*, November 2, 1859; *Geschichte der Deutschen in Buffalo und Erie County, New York*, vol. 1 (Buffalo, 1898), p. 69 (for other nominations).

114. *Biographical Dictionary of American Mayors*, s.v. "Allberger, Franklin"; Buffalo *Demokrat und Weltbürger*, April 13, 1861.

115. Bruce Carlan Levine, "Free Soil, Free Labor, and *Freimanner*," in *German Workers in Industrial Chicago, 1850-1910: A Comparative Perspective*, ed. Hartmut Keil and John B. Jentz (DeKalb, 1983), pp. 165-78; Buffalo *Express*, October 13, 1857; February 15, 17, 1860; Buffalo *Demokrat und Weltbürger*, November 2, 1860; Buffalo *Commercial Advertiser*, November 3, 1860.

116. Buffalo *Demokrat und Weltbürger*, April 20, 1860; James L. Huston, *The Panic of 1857 and the Coming of the Civil War* (Baton Rouge, 1987).

117. Buffalo *Demokrat und Weltbürger*, October 7, 8, 19 (quotation), 24, 1859; April 20, September 13, October 8, 1860.

118. Ibid., June 23, 1856; August 22, 1857; April 10, 1858; December 22, 24, 1859; Buffalo *Express*, October 24, 1860; Bruce Carlan Levine, " 'In the Spirit of 1848': German-Americans and the Fight over Slavery's Expansion" (Ph.D. dissertation, University of Rochester, 1980), 106, 108–10, 143; Phyllis F. Field, *The Politics of Race in New York: The Struggle for Black Suffrage in the Civil War Era* (Ithaca, 1982), pp. 115–9, 135–7, 146; Buffalo *Republic*, November 16, 1860.

119. *Der Lutheraner*, 19 (1862), 1–3; 20 (1863), 115; n.a., "Der Geschichte der Buffalo Synode," *Wachende Kirche*, 60 (December, 1879), 7; Buffalo *Commercial Advertiser*, October 30, 1855; Buffalo *Aurora*, June 15, September 7, October 5, November 9, 1860; Madeleine Hooke Rice, *American Catholic Opinion in the Slavery Controversy* (New York, 1944), pp. 11–3, 63–82, 83–4, 103; Yox, "Decline of the German-American Community in Buffalo, 1855–1925," 84–5; Buffalo *Demokrat und Weltbürger*, September 19, 1855.

120. Buffalo *Demokrat und Weltbürger*, April 28, June 13, 15, 29, 30, July 14, 1854; April 14, September 12, 1855; May 5, November 15, 1856; September 25, 1857; August 6, October 8, 9, 10, December 8, 1859.

121. Yox, "Decline of the German-American Community in Buffalo, 1855–1925," pp. 84–5 and 88, note 2; *Geschichte der Deutschen* (biographical section), passim; *New York State Census of 1855*, alphabetized printout, SUN-YAB; *Buffalo Commercial Advertiser Directory for 1855*; Buffalo *Republic*, July 23, August 6, 12, 22, September 3, 1856; Buffalo *Commercial Advertiser*, September 27, October 11, 19, 30, 1858; July 7, August 15, September 6, October 20, 22, 1855; Buffalo *Demokrat und Weltbürger*, September 15, 1855; July 14, 18, 19, 21, September 12 (quotation), 1856; February 11 (quotation), October 16, 1857; November 3, 1860.

122. Buffalo *Demokrat und Weltbürger*, August 27, September 8, 11, October 1, 3, 8, 1856; March 30, April 10, 1858; November 19, 21, 1859; Yox, "Decline of the German-American Community in Buffalo, 1855–1925," 84–5.

123. Buffalo *Demokrat und Weltbürger*, May 18, June 15, October 16, 1857; Buffalo *Commercial Advertiser*, October 28, 1858.

124. Buffalo *Demokrat und Weltbürger*, October 19, 26, 1860.

125. Buffalo *Express*, August 10, 1856; Buffalo *Demokrat und Weltbürger*, May 21, 1857; Buffalo *Commercial Advertiser*, June 15, 1857; October 17, 1860; Buffalo *Aurora*, December 23, 1859; March 16, 1860.

126. Buffalo *Demokrat und Weltbürger*, November 19, 1856; Buffalo *Commercial Advertiser*, April 9, 1859.

127. Buffalo *Republic*, July 9, 20, August 2, 3, 4, 6, 10, 25, September 24, October 12, 16, 26, 27, 29, November 1, 2, 3, 1860; Buffalo *Evening Post*, October 15, 18, 27, 30, November 1, 6, 1860; Buffalo *Commercial Advertiser*, July 7, September 29, October 22, 30, 1860; Buffalo *Express*, August 15, 20, 28, 29, October 2, 1860; Buffalo *Demokrat und Weltbürger*, October 5, 1860.

128. Buffalo *Commercial Advertiser*, November 7, 1860; Buffalo *Demokrat und Weltbürger*, November 15, 1860. Fries, "Buffalo, New York, 1854–1860: A Multivariate Analysis of Voting Behavior," 107–11, charts the complexity

of 1860 alignments, but draws no conclusions. Estimates of the total German vote for Lincoln are based on Norbert L. Fullington, "The *Weltbürger-Demokrat*, Mirror of Political Opinion of Buffalo's Deutschtum, 1837–1860" (M.A. thesis, University of Buffalo, 1951), 104, note 11, whose estimate of one-third, which is based on assuming that all of the non-German minority in German wards were Republicans, is much too conservative. Laurence A. Glasco, *Ethnicity and Social Structure: Irish, Germans and Native-Born in Buffalo, N.Y., 1850–1860* (New York, 1980), pp. 246–76, offers conclusions which are similar, but less comprehensively conceived with respect to class and neighborhood as well as, though to a lesser extent, ethnicity.

129. Buffalo *Commercial Advertiser*, June 10, November 5, 1857; November 3, 1858; November 7, 1860; Fries, "Buffalo, New York, 1854–1860: A Multivariate Analysis of Voting Behavior," 87, 92, 108; Huston, *The Panic of 1857 and the Coming of the Civil War*.

130. Buffalo *Republic*, November 16, 1860; Peter Emslie, Surveyor, *Map of a Part of the City of Buffalo* (Philadelphia, 1866); Rev. Thomas Donohue, *History of the Catholic Church in Western New York* (Buffalo, 1904), pp. 242–3, 254–6; Yox, "Bonds of Community," map, 159.

131. Buffalo *Republic*, November 16, 1860; Emslie, *Map of a Part of the City of Buffalo*; Buffalo *Commercial Advertiser*, December 14, 1858. Philip S. Foner, *Business and Slavery: The New York Merchants and the Irrepressible Conflict* (Chapel Hill, 1941); Glasco, *Ethnicity and Social Structure*, pp. 60, 63, 68–70.

132. Buffalo *Republic*, November 16, 1860; *Map of the City of Buffalo, Surveyed under the Direction of Quackenboss and Kennedy, Insurance Agents* (New York, 1854); Sandford B. Hunt, *Methodism in Buffalo* (Buffalo, 1893), p. 121; Glasco, *Ethnicity and Social Structure*, pp. 60, 63, 68–70; U.S. Department of the Interior, *Population of the United States in 1860: The Eighth Census*, vol. 1 (Washington, D.C., 1864), p. 333; Buffalo *Commercial Advertiser*, September 2, 1855; October 27, 1860; Buffalo *Christian Advocate*, July 5, 1855; July 4, 1857; March 25, 1858.

133. U.S. Department of Interior, *Population, 1860*, vol. 1, p. 333; *New York State Census of 1855*, alphabetized printout, SUNYAB; *Ward Seven, Poll Book* (BECHS), sample = 96 of 660 (14.5%); Buffalo *Express*, June 8, 1855 (quotation); Buffalo *Commercial Advertiser*, November 7, 1855; June 10, November 5, 1857; November 3, 1858; November 10, 1859; October 27, 1860; Buffalo *Republic*, November 5, 1856; November 16, 1860.

134. Ismar Ellison, "An Historical Essay: The Germans of Buffalo. Read before the Buffalo Historical Society, April 27, 1880," Buffalo Historical Society *Publications*, vol. 2 (1880), p. 124 (quotation); Glasco, *Ethnicity and Social Structure*, pp. 20, 63; Andrew Yox, "The Myth of Persistence of Families in the Orchard, an East Buffalo Neighborhood," *New York Folklore*, 10 (Summer-Fall, 1984), 90, 95, 97.

135. David A. Gerber, "Modernity in the Service of Tradition: Catholic Lay Trustees at Buffalo's St. Louis Church and the Transformation of European Communal Traditions, 1829–1855," *Journal of Social History*, 15 (Summer, 1982), 663–64, 666; *A Notre Saint Père, le Pape Pie IX* (petition dated Sep-

tember 1, 1852), Congregation of the Propaganda Fide Collection, UND (microfilms); *New York State Census of 1855*, alphabetized printout, SUNYAB; *Buffalo Commercial Advertiser Directory for 1855*.

Epilogue

1. Buffalo *Commercial Advertiser*, November 6, 1858. Presuming this process was already underway, in a local speech that was intensely examined, Lincoln urged it be accelerated to the extent that immigrants forget "that they are foreigners as soon as possible." See ibid., February 18, 1861; and Buffalo *Demokrat und Weltbürger*, February 18, 1861.

2. Horton, et al., *History of Northwestern New York*, vol. 1, pp. 173–80, 210, 214; Buffalo *Demokrat und Weltbürger*, February 7, April 10, 20, 22, 23, 27, May 1, 4, 1861; Buffalo *Courier*, April 17, 23, 24, 25, 30, May 3, 6–11, 14, 17, 1861; Buffalo *Christian Advocate*, May 6, 7, December 5, 1861; Buffalo *Sentinel*, March 30, April 20, June 22, 1861.

3. Buffalo *Demokrat und Weltbürger*, March 5, 1866; David A. Gerber, "Language Maintenance, Ethnic Group Formation, and Public Schools; Changing Patterns of German Concern, Buffalo, 1837–1874," *Journal of American Ethnic History*, 4 (Fall, 1984), 45–54; *Geschichte der Deutschen*, vol. 1, p. 65; Andrew Yox, "Bonds of Community," 156, 162; and idem, "Decline of the German-American Community in Buffalo, 1855–1925."

Index

Abramson, Harold, 168
Adam, Karl, 208, 209
Alcohol. *See* Americans; *Christian Advocate;* Germans; Irish; Temperance
Allberger, Franklin, 12, 181, 201, 366, 395, 400
Allberger, Job, 181
Allberger, John, 181
Allen, Lewis, 138
Allen, Orlando, 372
Alsatians, 113, 171, 172; associations of, 187–88; and French, 287; location of, 174–75; number of, 114, 163; and religion, 190; and St. Louis church, 192, 285; and voting, 409
American Bible Society, 78
American Celt, 293
American Celt and Catholic Citizen, 153
American Hotel, 28
American Labor Union, 273
American party: emergence of, 372; decline of, 392, 396; collapse of, 398–99; and 1855 election, 382–83; and corruption, 381; and European affairs, 341; and Germans, 375; and nativism, 376–77; as vehicle for American ethnicization, 387
American Protestant Assembly, 384
American Protestant Buffalo Medical Society, 315
American Republican Association, 353, 374
American Seamen's Bethel Society, 78
American Temperance Union, 186
American Tract Society, 205, 302–3
Americans: and alcohol, 207; and authority, 378–79; and Catholic church, 281–84, 299, 380; church affiliation of, 101; and Democratic party, 346–47; and ecumenism, 388; and emulation of bourgeois life-style, 99–100, 103; and ethnic groups, 386; and ethnicity, 120; ethnicization of, 96–98, 99, 101–2, 377–78, 385–91; family structure of, 102–3; fertility rates of, 103; and filiopietistic societies, 390; and German Catholics, 205; and German language, 208–10, 218, 218–22; and German popular culture, 205–8; and Germans, 201–2, 391–95; and Great Britain, 97, 389–90; and historical awareness, 96–97, 388–89, 390; and lack of group consciousness, 96–98, 386–87, 388; marriage patterns of, 68; and militia, 98–99, 386; and music, 208; nonbourgeois, 99–100; occupations of, 99–100, 242; and ownership of property, 68, 102, 124, 182; and patriotism, 96; and political nativism, 98, 371–85; and prohibition, 379–80;

residential cohesiveness of, 101; social homogeneity of, 22–24; and temperance, 105–7, 355, 379; volunteer activities of, 101–2; voting patterns of, 98, 345–46, 406, 407

Amusements: American, 72–74, 390; early, 26–27; German, 205–8

Anti-Temperance Association, 358

Apprenticeships: change in structure of, 241–42; and labor unions, 252; decline of, among Americans, 102; collapse of, 104

Artisans
—associations of, 23, 104; effects of industrialization on, 238–39, 240; and home occupations, 19; and self-improvement ethic, 108; and slowness of industrialization, 11, 19
—American: anticapitalist ideology of, 248, 249; belief in superiority of, 247–48; class consciousness among, 108; and education, 105; as entrepreneurs, 100, 248–49; and moral reform, 105–7; occupational independence of, 103; organization of, 23, 250–51; political ideology of, 108, 246–47; printers, 247–48; and religion, 105; and self-improvement ethic, 104, 248, 251
—German: compared with Americans, 108; and ethnic culture, 198; and industrialization, 177–78; in Old World, 169, 170; organization of, 198

Attorneys. *See* Lawyers

Die Aurora, 153; emergence of, 234, 290; and Americans, 293; and Catholic church, 193, 234–35; and Democratic party, 396

Austrians, 163

Authority: definition of, 378–79; and Catholic church, 380–81; decline of American claim to, 379–81; and ethnic groups, 379; shifting of, following depression, 45

Babcock, George, 372, 383
Baer, Conrad, 202–3
Baker, Jean, 335
Banks and banking: by Germans, 181; collapse of, 38; and commerce, 49; credit practices, 29–30; savings banks, establishment of, 104, 144, 203–4. *See also* Credit-reporting

Baptist church, 195
Barker, Jacob, 59
Barker, P. A., 203, 205
Barton, James, 28
Baseball, 390
"The Beach," 123
Becker, Philip, 181
Bede, Patrick, Vicar General Rev., 150, 158
Bedini, Gaetano, Archbishop, 193, 294, 296, 371
Beekman, James, 383
Bell, David, 100
Bennett, Edward, 369, 370
Benziger, Jacob, 403
Bettinger, Stephen, 181, 363, 395
Beyer, Jacob, 181
Big Buffalo Creek, 20
Bingham, Robert, 100
Black Rock: and Erie Canal, 4–5; and industry, 20; merges with Buffalo, 17, 331, 351; as residential area, 407
Blacks, 17–18, 135, 401–2
Blossom, Ira, 38
Board of Trade, 53, 55–57
Boards, civic, 78
Bohemians, 163
Bourgeoisie: and antiradicalism, 89–90; characteristics of, 66–67; and charity, 311–12; and civic improvement, 87; conflict within, 88–89, 90; and domestics, 72; education of, 81; emergence of, 44–47, 55, 57, 62, 64–66; and European travel, 82; and external influences, 80–81; and familial roots, 67–68; family life of, 70; and government regulation, 86–87; housing of, 67–70; and immigrants, 116–17; inconsistencies within, 86–88; and individualism, 86–87; and marriage, 68; mentality of, 83; origins of, 66; and ownership of property, 68–69; and politics, 88, 90; and poverty, 84–86, 311–12; provinciality of, 82–83; and religion, 73–76; and slavery, 89–91; social life of, 72–74. *See also* Americans; Men, bourgeois; Women, bourgeois
Brace, Lester, 292
Braley and Pitts Agricultural Works, 267
Breckinridge, John, 405
Bridge to Canada, 394–95

Bridges, Amy, 324
Bristol, C. C., 398
British, 113, 114, 120, 137
Brooks, Alonzo, 249
Brooks, Erastus, 383, 384
Brunck, Francis, Dr.: background of, 213; and bridge to Canada, 395; and Democratic party, 230, 398; and Germans, 401; and government regulation, 364–65; and Grays, 197, 228–29, 233, 263; and nativism, 404; and Republican party, 402, 403; and voter registration law, 377; and *Weltbürger*, 214, 215, 225–26; and working classes, 273. See also *Weltbürger*
Bryant and Stratton Business College, 101
Buchanan, James, 408
Buffalo: establishment of, 3–4; growth of, 4–6, 24–26, 27, 65; advantages of, for German settlement, 18, 173; characteristics of early, 22–23; charter, 24; charter, revision of, 350–51, 391–92, 393; compared with industrial areas, 11; compared with Rochester, 7, 25–26; as immigration center, 114; pitfalls of, 7; population of, 6, 47; as principal port, 5–6; as transshipment center, 6–7, 114
Buffalo Apprentices Society, 23, 104, 250
Buffalo Association for the Encouragement of Manufactures, 9, 237–38
Buffalo Association for Relief of the Poor (BARP), 78, 80, 85, 86, 101, 116–17, 130, 311
Buffalo Catholic Institute, 153
Buffalo Female Academy, 70
Buffalo Fine Arts Academy, 62
Buffalo General Hospital, 78, 316, 386
Buffalo Historical Society, 62, 97
Buffalo Hotel, 23
Buffalo Hydraulics Association, 20
Buffalo Medical Journal, 315
Buffalo Medical Society, 315
Buffalo Mercantile College, 101
Buffalo Orphan Asylum, 77, 78, 80, 86
Buffalo Protestant Orphanage, 313
Buffalo Savings Bank, 204
Buffalo Scale Works, 238
Buffalo Seminary, 309

Buffalo Society of Natural Sciences, 62
Bulletin, 89
Burwell, Bryant, Dr., 30, 38, 76, 97, 124
Business district, 17, 19
Business ethics, origins of, 57, 59–61

Canadians, 113; and ethnicity, 120; integration with Americans, 94–96; lack of ethnic awareness among, 93; lack of political consciousness among, 94; number of, 92, 114; occupations of, 93; stereotypes of, 95; and temperance, 107
Capitalism, 46–47, 83–85
Carland, William, 143, 144, 237, 266–67, 271
Carpenter, John, 374
Carson League, 358, 379
Cary, Walter, Dr., 90
Catholic Association, 334
Catholic church: American attitude toward, 281–84; associations within, 152, 153; churches, increase in number of, 307–8; Diocese of Buffalo, 280–81; ethnic composition of, 284–85; financial problems of, 297–98; and German-Irish animosities, 191–92; and Germans, 191–93, 287, 309; growth of, 285; and Irish, 123, 150–54, 309; and lay management, 192, 285–87, 290; and nativism, 226–27, 376, 383; parishes, 152, 191–93, 284–85; and politics, 333–34; and poverty, 312–13; and the press, 153; priests, 145–48, 285, 304–7; problems of, 285, 287–88; Protestant attitudes toward, 281–84; and Protestantism, 154, 283; and public schools, 299–300; and public welfare, 313, 316; Putnam Law, 296; and radicalism, 234–35; and secular authority, 380–81; seminary, establishment of, 304; and slavery, 162; as vehicle for ethnicization, 123, 151, 172. *See also* Charity; Schools, Catholic
Catholic Repeal and Total Abstinence Association, 150
Catholics: marriage patterns of, 151–52; number of, 113
Central Presbyterian church, 33, 101
Central-Verein, 235

Chamberlain, Hunting, 249
Chapin, Cyrenius, Dr., 27
Charity: advent of, 86; after depression, 43–44; and American Protestants, 311–12; and bourgeoisie, 78–80, 86; and Catholic church, 153–54, 301, 313–15; early lack of, 27; and immigrants, 115–17. *See also* Public welfare
Chicago, 114
Children: bourgeois, 71; German, employment of, 183–84; in industry, 240–41; Irish, employment of, 128, 131–32; and public welfare, 85
Cholera epidemics, 19, 115
Chretien, John, 403
Christian Advocate: and alcohol, 207; and Bishop Timon, 290, 294; and bourgeoisie, 88; and Catholic church, 139, 282, 299, 303, 307; and commerce, 57; and credit-reporting, 59; and ecumenism, 388; and Episcopal church, 76; and Germans, 375; and industrialization, 238; and politics, 381; and port culture, 15; and poverty, 84; and priests, 307; and prohibition, 379, 380; and religion, 74; and St. Joseph's Cathedral, 309; and sectarianism, 387; and Sisters of Charity Hospital, 315–16; and temperance, 106, 355; and Whig party, 338, 339
Church of the Ascension, 76
"The Churches," 310
Ciolina, Dr., 199–200, 232, 270
City Dispensary, 101
City Missionary Society, 78, 102
City Temperance Society, 101, 357
City Temperance Union, 78, 79, 105
Civic improvement, movement for, 366–67. *See also* Municipal services
Civic integration: advent of, 359–61. *See also* Germans; Irish; *Weltbürger*
Civil War: growth of pluralism following, 412; unity triggered by, 410
Clapp, Almon: and immigrant vote, 378; and nativism, 155, 383, 397–98; and slavery, 90; and Bishop Timon, 380
Clark, John, Dr., 38
Class, concept of, 242. *See also* Social classes

Class struggle, 108, 243–44, 247. *See also* Social classes
Clay, Henry, 352
Cleveland, 114
Clinton, George, 53, 341, 347
Coffee, Patrick, 273–74
Colleges and universities: business colleges, establishment of, 100–101; first university, establishment of, 27–28. *See also names of specific colleges and universities*
Commerce: after depression, 44, 45–46; and bourgeois social life, 72–73; defended by broad spectrum of community, 50; effect on Buffalo, 13; expansion of, 27, 47–48, 51; numbers employed by, 50; and politics, 12, 331; and related services, 49–50; reliance upon, 7–8, 10, 11, 12–13. *See also* Grain trade; Board of Trade; Merchants
Commercial Advertiser, 73; and 1844 election, 353; and American ethnicization, 387; and American Revolution, 389; and bourgeoisie, 284, 392; and British, 389; and capitalism, 83–84; and Catholic church, 281–82, 283, 303, 362; and Catholic schools, 81; and charity, 86; and cricket, 390; and Democratic party, 339; and Erie Canal, 54; and European revolutionists, 355; and European travel, 82; and Dr. Thomas J. Foote, 35; and German popular culture, 206, 207; and Germans, 201–2, 375, 385, 392–93; and industrialization, 237, 238; and Irish, 137, 138, 139, 140, 150, 155, 257, 386; and labor, 89; and local history, 389; and merchants, 60; and nativism, 353, 371–72, 375, 398–99; and police department, 340; and politics, 381; and port culture, 15; and priests, 307; and prohibition, 379; and public welfare, 314; and racism, 337; and Sabbatarianism, 388; and sailors, 276; and St. Joseph's Cathedral, 309–11; and St. Louis Church, 294; and ship carpenters, 277, 278, 279; and Sisters of Charity, 306; and Sisters of Charity Hospital, 315–16; strike against, 253; and Whig party, 338; and Whig press, 352

Common Council: and bilingualism debate, 224; and civic improvement, 366-67, 391-92; and commerce, 52-53; and dock regulation, 115; and early politics, 330-31; and German language, 208-9, 217-18; and party fluctuations, 348; and public markets, 369-70; regulation by, 24-25, 364-66; and schools, 219, 222-23
Congregational church, 76-77
Cook, Elijah, 276, 347, 370
Corn Exchange, 55
County Board of Supervisors, 350
Courier: and capitalism, 83-84; and Democratic party, 348; and immigrant vote, 376; and Irish, 137, 256, 375; and labor unions, 251; and nativism, 375; and naturalization, 339; and politics, 381; and sailors' strike, 276; and St. Joseph's Cathedral, 310; and St. Louis Church, 294; and temperance, 356; and Bishop Timon, 290; and working classes, 89, 243
Craftsmen. *See* Artisans
Credit-reporting, 57-59
Cricket, 390
Cultural institutions: establishment of, 61-62, 97

Danner, Michael, 393, 397
Dart, Joseph, 52, 126
Daughters of Temperance, 105
Dawley, Alan, 325
De Haas, Karl, Dr., 226, 229, 230, 232
Dellenbach. *See* Dellenbaugh, Frederick, Dr.
Dellenbaugh, Frederick, Dr.: assimilated with Americans, 200, 352; elected to Common Council, 219, 340; and German butchers, 365; and Grays, 197; and public market, 369; and public schools, 221; and Republican party, 403
Democracy, 294, 355-56, 379
"The Democracy." *See* Democratic party
Democratic party: emergence of, 322; and bourgeoisie, 90; and campaigning, 339; and Catholic church, 337; and colonization, 342; decline of, 331, 381, 396; and elections (1854-58), 372-73; (1858), 395, 396; (1859), 396; (1860), 396, 405, 406-7, 408; and ethnic groups, 340, 341-42, 349, 372; and European affairs, 254, 355; and Germans, 213-14, 340, 343-45, 352; "Hards" and "Softs," 372, 381-82; and immigrants, 330, 335, 339, 359; and Irish, 162, 340, 341-43; and nativism, 372, 372-73; newspapers of, 338-39; and patronage, 340-41, 342; pluralistic nature of, 336; political economy of, 335; and population fluctuation, 348; and racism, 337; and slavery, 162; structure of, 338; and temperance, 356, 358; threats to, 331; and vigilance committees, 339-40; and Whig party, 336; and workingmen's movement, 23
Demokrat, 139, 213, 223, 226, 229, 233
Demokrat und Weltbürger, 213, 226
Depressions, economic: aftermath of, 43-45; and bourgeoisie, 64-65; and commerce, 10; impact of, 25, 37-39; and industrialization, 237, 238; and Irish, 259; and working classes, 213, 342
Detroit, 114
Devening, Daniel, Dr., 340
Diner, Hasia, 140
Dobinson, William, 75
Dock trade. *See* Commerce
Dolan, Jay, 147
Dold, Jacob, 181
Dorsheimer, Philip, 181, 201; and Democratic party, 213; and German National Loan, 197; nominated state treasurer, 400; and Republican party, 403; as postmaster, 344
Dorsheimer, William, 231
Douglas, Stephen, 405-10 passim
Druids, 204
DuBois, Jean, Bishop, 284-85, 286
Dutch, 163

Eagle Tavern, 23, 35
East Side: and civic improvement, 367, 368; description of, 173; foreign character of, 173; and Germans, 17, 18-19, 173, 187, 225; and prostitution, 363; and public market, 369; and working classes, 18
Eaton, Sylvester, Rev., 26, 31

Education. *See* Artisans; Bourgeoisie; Germans; Irish; Schools; Working classes, American
Eighth Ward Workingman's Club, 260
Elections: and American vote, 345–47; early, 322; and ethnic vote, 345; and Irish violence, 135, 150; presidential (1860), 405–9; results of (1843–53), 345–54; (1858–60), 395–96; Seward-Fillmore contest, 383–85; voter registration law, 377; voting, and naturalization, 326–27. *See also* Wards; People's Ticket (1857)
Elite: absence of, in early Buffalo, 65–66
Ellicott, Joseph, 3–4, 11, 13, 21, 49, 203
Emigrant Savings Bank, 144
Emmett, Robert, 156
English: economic status of, 93; ethnic awareness of, 93–94; integration with Americans, 94–96; lack of political consciousness among, 94; number of, 92; occupations of, 93; societies of, 93–94; stereotypes of, 95; and temperance, 107
Episcopal church: attitudes toward, 76; and bourgeoisie, 101; and charity, 77; relations with Presbyterians, 76; roots of, 95
Erie Canal: opening of, 4–5; decline of, 8–9; canallers, 14; and commerce, 237; and Democratic party, 342; effect on Buffalo, 25; enlargement of, 12; importance of, 3; improvement of, 53, 54; and Irish laborers, 127; as political issue, 54, 347; pollution of, 14; and the railroad, 50
Erie County Mechanics Association, 104, 250–51, 252
Erie County Penitentiary, 85
Erie County Sunday School Association, 388
Esselen, Christian, 403, 405
Esslinger, Karl, 340
Ethnic group, concept of, 117–18
Ethnic groups: American attitudes toward, 115; and class formation, 118; and credit-reporting, 58; as social and political subcultures, 119, 331; struggle within, 119
Ethnic identification. *See* Ethnicization
Ethnicity: definition of, 117; and class formation, 118; territoriality, 120

Ethnicization, 118–20; definition of, 118. *See also* Americans; Germans; Irish
Evans-Peacock family, 49
Everett, Edward, 384
Express: and bridge to Canada, 394; and Catholic church, 307; and European affairs, 354; and Irish, 138, 139, 160; and nativism, 398; and patronage, 382; and printers' strike, 253; and prohibition, 379; and St. Joseph's Cathedral, 309; and Seward campaign, 383; and slavery, 90; and working-class protest, 257

Fargo family, 49
Fifth Ward Republican Club, 401
Fillmore, Millard, 54, 90, 376; and Catholic church, 374; and Catholic schools, 81, 309; and economic depression, 38; and European travel, 82, 310; and *Die Freimüthige*, 214; and Germans, 351; and gubernatorial contest, 330, 352–53; and historical society, 390; and immigrants, 116; and nativism, 353, 354, 372, 384; and presidential campaign, 383–85; and Silver Grays, 405; and Young Men's Association, 77–78
Finney, Charles Grandison, 26, 31
Fire companies, volunteer: and bourgeois men, 78; and ethnic groups, 361; German, 188; as vehicle for class and ethnic distinction, 101
Firemen's Benevolent Association, 101, 360
First Presbyterian church, 17
First Trinity Evangelical Lutheran Church, 194
First Ward Workingman's Club, 258, 260
Fish, S. H., 75
Five Points, 14, 26
"The Flats," 15–16, 123
Flint, Austin, Dr., 85, 86
Fogarty, Lawrence, 139
Foote, Thomas J., Dr., 300, 383; and assimilation of ethnic groups, 410; and attitude toward women, 70; and Catholic church, 306, 307, 314; and conservatism, 35; and domestics, 140, 141

Forbush and Brown, 241
Ford, Elijah, 382
Forest Lawn Cemetery, 206
48'ers, 170, 198, 225; and anti-Americanism, 228; bourgeois, 229–31; and Grays, 227, 228; plebeian, 231–33; perceptions of Buffalo, 229. *See also* Greens
Forward, Oliver, 5
Forwarding Association, 55
Fourth of July, 96, 113, 207, 371, 387
Franco-German Society, 187–88
Franco-Germans. *See* Alsatians
Franklin, Benjamin, 247–48
Franklin, Danforth, 248, 249, 355
Free Soil party, 273, 340, 349
Free Thinker's Society, 227
Die Freimüthige, 214, 351–52, 353
Frémont, John C., 398, 403
French, 285, 287
Friendly Sons of St. Patrick, 150, 154
"Fruit Belt," 19, 175

Gavazzi, Alessandro, 371
Georger, Charles, 181, 197, 395
Georger, Frank, 181, 197, 395, 403
German-American Bank, 181
German-American Workingmen's Union (GAWU), 197–98, 232–33, 264–74 passim, 369
German Bank of Buffalo, 181
German Clay Club, 343, 351
German Democratic Association, 214, 343
German Free Christian Church, 195
German Insurance Company, 181
German Medical Association, 180
German National Loan, 197
German Singing Societies, 189, 208, 269. See also *Sängerbundfest*
German Steuben Guard, 216
German Young Men's Association, 166, 197, 200, 206, 208, 226, 230
Germans: and alcohol, 133, 167, 179–80, 185–86, 207, 357; American perceptions of, 187, 214; and Americans, 180, 202–3; and anticlericalism, 226–27, 229–30; apathy of, in political and civic affairs, 199, 214–15; and apprenticeships, 178–79, 183, 241–42; as artisans, 19, 177–78; assimilation of, 182, 187, 195–216 passim, 391; associations of, 166, 174, 187–90, 199–200; and banking, 204; beer gardens, 180, 186, 188; and brewing industry, 179; as butchers, 180, 244, 365–66; and Calvinism, 193, 195; and Catholic church, 113, 171, 172, 191–93, 227, 297; charitable assistance to, 130; churches, establishment of, 190–96; and civic improvement, 367–68; civic integration of, 167–68, 333, 361, 364; civic integration of, as vehicle for ethnicization, 215; and civil libertarianism, 229; and class, 164; and commerce, 12, 176–77, 395; and communal institutions, 187–90; compared with Irish, 176, 177; and crime, 185, 186; and cultural activities, 205–6; cultural advantages of, 176; and cultural nationalism, 197, 198–99, 225–26, 229, 230; and Democratic party, 98, 142–43, 188, 213, 219, 343–45, 372–73, 403, 411; diversity of, 163–66; and economic depression, 213; education of, 183, 184, 204; and English language, 204, 209; as entrepreneurs, 179, 180–81; and ethnicity, 120; ethnicization of, 163, 165–68, 182, 190–200 passim, 211–13, 214–15; and exercise, 208; family structure of, 182, 185; as farmers, 18–19, 173; and food trades, 177, 179–80; and Free Soil movement, 401–2, 404; as grocers, 179–80, 204; and group consciousness, lack of, 211–12, 217; and holidays, 188–89, 197; ideological conflict among, 164; and illegitimacy, 185; immigration of, 18–19, 169–71, 188, 189; inconsistencies among, 199–200; as independent community, 176, 177, 187; as independent thinkers, 399; and industrialization, 177–78; and internationalist class ethic, 260–61; and intraethnic conflict, 168, 410–11; and Irish, attitude toward, 186–87; and labor movement, 197–98, 232–33; and language, 164–65, 166, 184, 192, 212, 216–22; life-style as basis for ethnicization, 167–68, 188–89; and lodges, 196–97, 204–5; and lumbering, 173; and Lutheranism, 193–95;

marriage patterns of, 175; and militia, 188, 216, 361, 386; moral conditions of, 184–87; moral standards of, 189; and music, 189–90, 204, 208; and nativism, 167, 373, 384–85, 404–5; number of, 114, 163; occupations of, 125, 164, 176–77, 178, 242; Old World origins of, 163–64, 172; and Old World values, 217, 261, 328; and ownership of property, 124, 167, 181–83, 203–4; and parks, 369; and patriotism, 225; and patronage, 343–44; as physicians, 179, 180; and the police, 363–64; political activity of, 168, 230, 332–33, 400; and political appointments, 218; and popular culture, 167, 197, 205–8; and poverty, 185; and private schools, 219–20; and prostitution, 186, 363; and Protestantism, 170–71, 193–96; and public markets, 366, 368–70; and public schools, 221, 223–24, 299, 362; and public welfare, 363; and radicalism, 170, 196–99, 200, 225; and radicalism, bourgeois, 229–31; and radicalism, plebeian, 231–33; and railroads, 368; recreational activities of (*See* Popular culture); and religion, 191, 193–96; religious diversity of, 164, 194; and Republican party, 230, 391, 402–4, 409, 410–11; and Sabbatarianism, 359, 373; and the Sabbath, 167, 188; settlement by, 171–72, 173; as skilled workers, 177, 178; and slavery, 402; and socialism, 199–200; subgroups of, 172, 175; and taxation, 367–68, 393–94; and temperance, 107, 167, 196, 356, 358, 364, 373; voting patterns of, 395–96, 405–7, 408–9, 409; and Whig party, 343, 352. *See also* Old Lutherans

Goodell, Jabez, 203, 205
Gothic Hall, 143, 237, 266–67
Gough, John B., 106, 149, 196, 356, 357
Government, municipal: before rise of partisan politics, 330–31; in Germany, 332. *See also* Common Council; Elections
Grabau, Johannes A. A., Rev., 171, 194–95, 196, 233, 409
Grain trade: expansion of, 5–6, 47–48, 51; grain elevator, 6, 13–14, 48, 51–52; speculation in, 49, 61; decline of, 8

Grand Lager Beer *Fest*, 206
Gray, Ernest, Dr., 200–201, 213
Grays, 168; and Greens, 196–97, 228; ideology of, 212, 227, 228; and Republican party, 403; and working classes, 263
Greens, 168, 196–98, 212. *See also* 48'ers
Grosvenor Library, 62
Guistiniani, L., Rev., 195
Gumbell, Joseph, Rev., 195, 196
Guth, Francis, Rev., 289, 290, 302, 304

Haberstro, Joseph, 181, 273–74
Hagan, Michael, 153, 160–62, 258, 259, 293. See also *Sentinel*
Hall, Nathan K., Judge: and Millard Fillmore, 66, 384; and nativism, 372, 383; and Sisters of Charity Hospital, 315; and slavery, 397; and Young Men's Association, 77–78
Harbor: improvement of, 5, 53–55; inadequacies of, 14, 15–16, 52, 54–55; inner harbor, growth of, 13–14; waterfront as center of city, 13
Harrison, James, 392
Harugari, 197
Hauenstein, Joseph, Dr., 197
Haven, Solomon, 33, 66; and Irish vote, 406; and nativism, 372, 383–84; and Union party, 405; and Young Men's Association, 77–78
Hawley, Elijah, 68
Hawley, Merwin S., 51, 64, 67–68; business ethics of, 60; and cultural institutions, 61–62; and grain trade, 48–49
Hawley family, 51, 140
Hays, George, 203, 205
Hazard, George S., 56, 392
Heacock, Grosvenor, Rev., 73
Heacock, Reuben, 20, 33
Heimat, 169, 189, 265, 332
Heinzen, Karl, 229
Hellreigel, Conrad, 220
Hellreigel, Henry, 181
Helvetia Men's Choir, 187
Hersee, Thompson, 239
Heywood, Russell, 55–56
Higham, John, 147, 326
Hildebrandt, Edward, 39
Historical societies, establishment of, 96–97, 390

Holidays. *See names of specific holidays*
Holland Land Company, 3, 4, 13
Hollister family, 51
Holy Trinity Lutheran Church, 194
Honour, Hugh, 39
"The Hook," 123
Hosmer, George, Rev., 24–25, 43, 76, 77, 353
Hospitals: Catholic, 284, 314–15; Catholic, and public funds, 301–2, 306; public, 86, 316; and public funds, 300
Housing. *See* Bourgeoisie; Germans; Irish; Neighborhoods
Hughes, Bernard, 155
Hughes, John, Bishop, 214, 296; and public funds, 354; and St. Louis Church, 285–87, 295; and St. Mary's parish, 192–93
Hunt's Merchants' Magazine, 277
"The Hydraulics," 20–21, 101, 346

Immigrants. *See* Ethnic groups
Immigration and emigration: effect on Buffalo, 115–16; mass, 113–16
Industrial Association and School, 80
Industrialization: change in production methods, 239–40; effects of, on work force, 238–42; lack of, 7–8, 9–10; lack of, and artisans, 103; promotion of, 20, 32, 237–38
Industry: brewing, 179; distilling, 355; early, 8, 9–10, 20; furniture-making, 237; growth of, 20–21, 237–38; industrial systems, types of, 238–40; iron, 9, 11, 20, 238; location of, 20–21; meatpacking, 21, 48, 238; metal and machinery, 237; milling, 9; shipbuilding, 7, 9, 10, 11, 237; shoe factory, 9–10; slow growth of, 9–11; tanning, 9–10, 20, 237; types of, 237, 238
Inflation, 30
Irish: and alcohol, 133–34, 148–50; American attitudes toward, 136–38; and Americans, 135–36; assimilation of, 122–23, 144–45; associations of, 150, 154; and Catholic church, 113, 142, 143, 151–54, 361–62; and charitable activities, 153–54; charitable assistance to, 130; civic integration of, 361–62, 364; and colonization scheme, 158–59, 160–61; and crime, 132; and Democratic party, 98, 142–43, 162, 258–59, 372–73, 406; and employers, 125, 126; and ethnic consciousness, 120, 121; ethnicization of, 123, 136, 141–42, 150–56; family structure of, 129; and fertility, 129; funeral customs of, 147–48; and Germans, 136; and Great Britain, 155–56; housing of, 123–24; immigration of, 121, 122; leadership, 155; marriage patterns of, 129; migration of, serial, 122; and nativism, 161; number of, 92, 114, 122; occupations of, 124–27, 143–44, 242; and Old World values, 123, 129, 155; and ownership of property, 122, 124, 144; and patriotism, 156, 160–61; and patronage, 342–43; and police, 363–64; and politics, 142, 156, 161–62, 333–35; and poverty, 123–24, 129–30; and priests, 145–48; and public schools, 362; and public welfare, 362–63; and slavery, 162; social conditions of, 142; socioeconomic status of, 123, 142–45; and temperance, 107, 358; and unemployment, 257, 259; and upward mobility, 144–45; and violence, 132, 134–36, 187, 255–57; voting patterns of, 347, 406
Irish, Charles G., Jr., 384
Irish Archaeological Society of the United States, 153

Jewett, Elam R., 104, 372, 383
Jewett, Sherman S., 75, 100, 249, 250
Jewett and Root Stove Works, 240, 267, 401
Jews, 164, 190–91
Johnson, Ebenezer, Dr., 33, 36, 38
Johnson, George Washington, 21, 90–91, 140, 209, 349
Jones, George, 100
Journeymen Iron Molders Union, 268
Journeymen Operative Building Society, 30
Joy, Ira, 33
Jüngerich, Conrad, 271, 273

Katznelson, Ira, 328
Keogh, Augustine, 143

Ketchum, William, 64; and civic improvement, 366; and government regulation, 365; and nativism, 372; and public markets, 370; and taxes, 364
Kinkel, Gottfried, Dr., 197, 341, 354
Kirchliches Informatorium, 233
Klinck, Christian, 181
Know Nothing party: emergence of, 371; decline of, 398-99, 411; and American ethnicization, 387; and Democratic party, 382; and Germans, 375; and immigrant vote, 374; and Know Something party, 383; and nativism, 372, 384; and Republican party, 377, 396, 400
Know Something association, 383
Kossuth, Louis, 197, 341, 354-55
Kraffert, Andreas, 273
Kraft, Francis, 403
Krause, Alexander, 352
Kreh. *See* Gray, Ernest, Dr.
Krettner, Jacob, 201, 203

Labor unions.
—American: formation of, 250; carpenters' union, 30; conventions of, 246-47, 248, 252; and cooperative ventures, 253-54; effects of industrialization on, 252-53; growth of, 253; political lobbying by, 251-52; printers' union strikes, 107-8, 253; problems within, 251-52
—German: formation of, 197-98, 232-33, 264, 265-66, 267; and cooperative ventures, 267; and ethnic culture, 269, 270; and helpers, 267-68; internationalist class ethic within, 264; iron molders' union, 267-69; and socialism, 269-71; and strikebreaking, 268-69; tailors' strike, 266-67; and women, 264
—multiethnic: formation of, 274; sailors' strike, 274-75; ship carpenters' strike, 274-75
Ladies Temperance Union, 79, 105
Lafayette Guard, 216
Lake Erie, commercial navigation of, 51
Land. *See* Real-estate investment
Lawyers: and commercial law, 49-50; political importance of, 11-12

Le Couteulx de Caumont, Stephen Louis, 284-85
Le Couteulx de Caumont, William, 294
Le Couteulx family, 49, 313
Leidertafel. *See* German Singing Societies
Liberty party, 349
Liederkranzen. *See* German Singing Societies
Lincoln, Abraham, 395-96, 405, 407, 408
Little Buffalo Creek, 20
Lockwood, Stephen, 33
Lockwood, Timothy, Dr., 45; charges of corruption against, 396; and Democratic party, 347; and Germans, 393, 395; and Irish, 257, 259, 382
Lodge #107, 371-72
Lord, John Chase, Rev. Dr., 90, 214, 380, 387; conversion of, 31; career of, 33-35; and bourgeois attitudes, 89; and Catholic church, 301; and denominational hostility, 76, 371; and female education, 70; and immigrants, 95; and nativism, 372; and public schools, 87-88, 299-300; and Sisters of Charity Hospital, 315, 316
"Dr. Lord's Church." *See* Central Presbyterian Church
Love, Thomas C., 33, 90
Luther, Martin, 194
Lutheran church, 193-95; Buffalo Synod, creation of, 233; Evangelical, 194; and sectarian schools, 362; synods of, 194-95

McFarlane, Robert, 100
McGee, Mary T. C., 142, 290
McGee, Thomas D'Arcy, 283; arrival in Buffalo, 153; career of, 156-60; and Buffalo Catholic Institute, 153; polemical style of, 155; and public schools, 362; and Bishop Timon, 293
Main-Hamburgh Canal, 20, 53-54
Manufacturers and Traders Trust Company, 204
Martineau, Harriet, 26
Marxism, 271
Masons, 78, 95, 197, 204-5
Masten, Joseph, Judge, 347, 348, 408
Mathew, Theobold, Father, 148, 149, 307

Mattis, Mary Catherine, 129
Mechanics and Apprentices Association, 250
Mechanics' Institute, 250
Mechanics and Laboring Men's party, 273
Mechanics' Mutual Association, 250
Mechanics' Mutual Protection, 104, 106, 250, 251, 252
Men
—bourgeois: associations of, 77–78; and charitable institutions, 78; and religion, 74, 75; role of, 70; and women's rights, 89
—Irish: moral conditions of, 131–33; occupations of, 124–27; as priests, 146–47; stereotypes of, 138–40
Mendelssohn Association, 208
Men's Social *Turnverein*, 198
Mercantile Agency, 58
Merchants: credit practices of, 29–30; during depression, 38; formal organization of, 50–51, 53, 55; predominance of, 11–12, 47; types of, 48–49, 50
Merchants Exchange, 27, 38
Merrigan, Thomas, 161, 258
Mertz, Nicolas, Rev., 285
Mesmer, Michael, 176, 181
Methodist church, 76, 101, 195
Middle classes. *See* Bourgeoisie
Miller, Henry B., 352
Milwaukee, 114
Mollitor, Stephen, 213, 214, 218, 219
Moral conditions, 14–15, 30–31; and credit-reporting, 58–59
Morgan, Dan, 60
Morgenröthe, 227
Morning Express, 246
Municipal services, 368, 391; beginnings of, 46; and bourgeoisie, 87
Murray, John, Judge, 258, 259
Mutual Benefit Temperance Society, 150
Mutual Protection and Equal Rights Association, 258–59

Nativism, 331; emergence of, 353, 354, 371–72; decline of, 376–77, 385, 398; bases for, 88, 115, 135, 300, 301–2, 377; and bilingualism debate, 224; and Catholic church, 226–27, 376, 383; as entrenched attitude, 411; and Germans, 375, 384–85; and immigrants, 373–74, 375; inconsistencies within, 374; and Irish, 375–76; and lodges, 197, 371–72; lodges, German, 384–85; political, 97, 98, 371–85; and public welfare, 314; and Seward-Fillmore contest, 383–85; as vehicle for American ethnicization, 377–78
Naturalization, process of, 326–27
Needham, S. P., 26–27
Neighborhoods: American, 17; blacks in, 17–18; bourgeois, 16–17, 69; elite, 17; German, 17, 173–76; Irish, 123–24, 144; lower-class, 15–16, 18; and territoriality, 120; working-class, 15, 17–20, 101. *See also names of specific areas*
Newark, 11
New England Pioneers of Western New York, 97
New England Society, 189, 390
New York State Commissioners of Immigration, 115
Newspapers: Catholic, 160, 290, 293; German, 153, 188, 212–14, 218, 234; Irish, 153; political, 214, 338–39, 351; and temperance, 355–56. *See also names of individual newspapers*
Niagara Square, 17

O'Brien, Bridget, 72
O'Brien, William Smith, 354
O'Connell, Daniel, 156, 333–34
Odd Fellows, 78, 95, 102, 204
O'Farrell, Francis, Rev., 158
Old Lutherans, 188; emigration of, 18–19, 170–71; and antiradicalism, 233–34; beliefs of, 194; churches of, 194; and "Fruit Belt," 175; number of, 172; and Reformed church, opposition to merger of, 195; and St. Louis Church, 333; and schools, 220
Old settlers: decline of, 64–65; organizations, 62, 82, 97
O'Neall, Isaac J., 268
"Orange lodges," 93
Order system. *See* Wage-earning
O'Reilly, Bernard, Vicar General Rev., 298–304 passim

Orphanages, 300, 313–14
Oswego, 9
Ottenot, Nicholas, 181

Palmer, Lance, 43, 45, 61, 181; career of, 27–28; and economic depression, 64–65; death of, 38
Park, Harrison, 358
Parks, 368–69
Pastoral Letter, 286
"The Patch," 123
People's Ticket (1857), 392–94
Perry monument, 27
Perry's Coffee House, 23
Pioneer Association, 390
Pluralism, rise of, 119–20
Poles, 163
Police department: functions of, 363; and patronage, 340–41
Political parties: beginnings of, 322, 331; decline of American authority within, 381–82; and the elite, 322–23; fusion tickets, 395, 398; and patronage, 322; and working classes, 349. *See also* names of specific parties
Politics: and citizen participation, 323–24; democratization of, 117, 321–22, 329; depoliticization of municipal issues, 360; early, 24; and ethnicity, 328; in Europe, 331–32; and Germans, 326; and immigrants, 117, 326, 329; pluralistic nature of, 321, 324; and social conflict, 328; social functions of, 324–25; as vehicle for assimilation, 325; as vehicle for ethnicization, 325–26, 327–29. *See also* Political parties; and names of individual political parties
Polk, James, 352
Poorhouse. *See* Public welfare
Poor relief. *See* Charity; Public welfare
Poppenberg, Gustav, 208
Port culture, 14–15, 26
Porter, Augustus, 20
Porters, 36
Potter, Heman, 76
Power, Tyrone, 137
Pratt, Hiram, 38
Pratt family, 64, 239
Presbyterian church, 76, 95, 101, 195
Press. *See* Newspapers

Prohibition party, 379
Proletarian League, 271
Protestant churches, 17, 75
Protestant Orphanage, 102
Protestant Sunday School Association, 205
Protestantism: attempts to convert Catholics, 302–3; and bourgeoisie, 75; and Catholic church, 281–84, 299, 307; moral philosophy of, 89; and poverty, 311–12; sectarian rivalries within, 24, 76–77
Public markets, 20, 24, 365–66, 368–70, 391
Public sphere, scope of, 317
Public utilities. *See* Municipal services
Public welfare: advent of, 43–44, 85–86; and Catholic church, 313, 363; juvenile asylum, 85; poorhouse, 85–86, 313; workhouse, 32. *See also* Charity
Putnam, James O., 294–95, 372, 383, 384
Puttkamer, Alexander von, Rev., 196

Quebecers, 285

Railroads, 13; emergence of, 8–9, 54; effect on commerce, 52; feeder lines, 51; funding of, 368; and industry, 20–21; Buffalo and Attica Railroad, 368; Buffalo and Brantford Railroad, 368; Buffalo and Niagara Falls Railroad, 17, 36; Buffalo and Pittsburgh Railroad, 368; Great Western Railroad, 394; New York Central, 8, 9, 50, 52; New York and Erie, 9
Randall, Nelson, 104, 372, 385
Rathbun, Benjamin, 28, 61, 87; career of, 35–37; and bank notes, 29; and charity, 43, 45; and working classes, 213
Real-estate investment, 28–29, 203–4. *See also* Speculation
Red Jacket Engine Company #6, 78
Religion: ecumenical movement, 388; Sunday School activism, 388
Religious revivals, 25–26, 31, 73–74
Republic: and American ethnicity, 388; defends Buffalo, 82; and Democratic party, 381; and Fillmore campaign, 385; and Free Soil party, 339; and

Great Britain, 389; and immigrants, 375; and Irish, 138, 139, 257, 375, 376; and People's Ticket, 392; and politics, 381; and printers' strike, 253; and prohibition, 379; and Republican party, 398; and St. Joseph's Cathedral, 310; and Bishop Timon, 290; and woman suffrage, 89
Republican party: rise of, 331, 381, 396–97; and Civil War, 410; and elections (1855–60), 396, 405–6, 407–8; and Free Soil movement, 401; and Germans, 352, 377, 399–402, 403; and immigrants, 396; and nativism, 376–77, 383, 397–99, 404–5; platform of, 397; and slavery, 230, 397
Die Republik der Arbeiter, 270
Residential districts. *See* Neighborhoods
Revivals. *See* Religious revivals
Reynolds, James, 155
Richerte, Georg, 403
Richmond, Dean, 347
Rinck, Wilhelm, 220
Robie, John, Rev., 90; and American ethnicization, 388; and bourgeoisie, 75; and Catholic church, 307; and credit-reporting, 59; and Germans, 375; and Protestants, 387; and public schools, 299–300; and religion, 74; and temperance, 380. See also *Christian Advocate*
Rochester, 7, 9, 25–26, 297
Rohr, Carl von, Rev., 171
Roos, Jacob, 181
Root, Edward, 100
Root, Francis, 75, 104, 249, 250
Rumsey, Aaron, 392
Rumsey family, 49
Ryan, James, 161
Ryan, Mary, 77, 106

Sabbatarianism, 358–59, 388; and commerce on Sunday, 57; and labor unions, 251; and temperance, 355, 359; and working classes, 107–8, 359
Sailors' Home, 86
St. Andrew's Evangelical Lutheran Church, 194
St. Andrew's Society, 93–94, 107
St. Ann's parish, 174, 191, 193, 406–7
St. Boniface parish, 191, 192, 409
St. Clair Flats, 55
St. Francis Xavier parish, 191, 193
St. George's Day, 386, 389
St. George's Society, 93–94, 107
St. James Hall, 208
St. John's Day, 167, 197, 199, 206
St. John's Episcopal Church, 76
St. John's Evangelical Lutheran Church, 171, 194
St. John's parish, 222
St. John's Protectory, 314
St. John's United Evangelical Church, 195
St. Joseph's Cathedral, 297, 309–11
St. Joseph's College, 81
St. Joseph's Male Orphan Society, 314
St. Louis Catholic Church, 191, 200, 214, 226, 280; founding of, 171; and Alsatians, 192; and Americans' attitude toward, 380–81; and Democratic party, 409; and Irish, 122; and lay management, 205, 234, 235, 285–87, 293–96, 399; and Old Lutherans, 333; parish school at, 220; and Press Committee, 205; and Bishop Timon, 281, 309
St. Mary's Catholic Church, 19, 185, 191, 406; founding of, 287; and collections, 298; location of, 407; parish school, 222; taken over by Redemptorists, 192–93
St. Mary's of the Lake, 122
St. Michael's parish, 185, 191, 192, 193
St. Patrick's Church, 122, 281
St. Patrick's Day, 149–50, 386
St. Paul's Episcopal Church, 17, 76, 310
St. Paul's Evangelical Lutheran Church, 194, 195
St. Paul's Reformed Church, 384
St. Peter's German Evangelical Church, 195, 287
St. Stephen's United Evangelical Church, 195
St. Vincent de Paul societies, 152, 153, 313, 314
St. Vincent's Female Orphan Asylum, 314
Salisbury, Guy, 28–29, 398
"Sandytown," 123
Sängerbundfest, 197, 208, 410
Sawyer, James D., 57, 59, 61
Sawyers Association, 262, 265

Scajaquada Creek, 20
Scheu, Solomon, 260, 340, 393
Schillerfest, 197, 208, 403, 410
Schoellkopf, Jacob, 181, 197
Schools
—Catholic: and bourgeoisie, 81; and classical education, 308–9; demand for, 222; and education of girls, 81, 152–53, 193, 308–9; establishment of, 81, 152–53, 308–9; German parish schools, 193; and public funds, 222–23, 299–300
—public: and bilingualism debate, 218–22; Catholic view of, 152–53, 222, 285, 299–300; establishment of, 219; evening schools, 184; free public-school system established, 30, 44, 105; and Germans, 195, 219–25; supported by bourgeoisie, 87–88; as vehicle for assimilation, 317
Schurz, Carl, 231, 404
Scots: attitudes toward Irish, 137; economic status of, 93; ethnic awareness of, 93–94; number of, 92; occupations of, 93; societies of, 93–94; stereotypes of, 95
Scots-Irish, 92, 93, 95–96
Scroggs, Gustavus Adolphus, Gen., 372, 382, 384, 386
Sentinel: and American patriotism, 387; and Catholic church, 160; and colonization, 161; and Democratic party, 396; and Germans, 153; and Irish, 161–62, 255–56; and nonpartisanship, 293; and unemployment, 258
Seward, William Henry, 353–54, 383
Short, James, 342
Short, John, 342
Short, Patrick, 115, 340, 342
Siebold, Jacob, 181
Silver Grays. *See* Whig party
Sisters of Charity, 152, 284, 306, 314, 315
Sisters of Charity Hospital, 297; establishment of, 284, 301, 313; and nativists, 306; nonsectarian character of, 315; and public funds, 301–2, 314–15, 354
Sisters of the Sacred Heart academy, 81
Sisters of St. Joseph, 314
Slums. *See* Neighborhoods, lower-class

Smith, H. K., 269, 356
Smith, Patrick, 273, 340, 394
Social classes: and credit-reporting, 58; emergence of, 83–85; in early Buffalo, 22–23; relationship to ethnicity, 242–44. *See also* Class; Class struggle
Socialism, 199–200, 269–71
Sons of Erin, 150, 154
Sons of Temperance, 105–6, 356
Spaulding, Elbridge G., 383, 405
Spaulding, Nancy, 140
Speculation, 29, 61. *See also* Real-estate investment
Spofford, Harriet Prescott, 141
Sprague, A. S., 33
Steamboat Owners Association, 55
Steele, Oliver G.: and Democratic party, 347; as entrepreneur, 100; and Erie County Mechanics Association, 250; and free evening schools, 184; and importance of skilled workers, 247; and Mechanics' Mutual Protection, 104; named first school superintendent, 105; on postdepression Buffalo, 44–45; and religious prejudice, 77; and self-cultivation, 248; and workingmen's movement, 30
Stereotypes, 118; development of, 136; of Americans, 202–3; of Anglo–Canadian groups, 95; of Germans, 201–2, 214; of Irish, 138–42
Sternberg, Pearl, 75
Stevens, Frederick, 394, 397
Stevenson, Edward L., 59–60
Storck, Edward, Dr., 230–31, 403, 410–11
Storepay system. *See* Wage-earning
Street railroads, 27, 174
Streets: establishment of, 3–4; development of, 16–17; boulevards, 21; Batavia Street, 17; Broadway, 174; Delaware Avenue, 17, 29, 69; East Seneca Street, 180; East Swan Street, 180; Ellicott Street, 17, 175; Franklin Street, 69; Genesee Street, 17, 174, 367; Main Street, 4, 16–17, 27, 39, 47, 69, 175, 180; Mechanic Street, 13; Michigan Street, 17, 175; Niagara Street, 101; Pearl Street, 69; Seneca Street, 16, 20; Swan Street, 16. *See also* Neighborhoods
Stringham, Joseph, 94, 341

Swartz, Abram, 181, 201, 340
Swartz, S., 239
Swartzenbaugh. *See* Swartz
Swiss, 163, 164, 187, 284–85

Tappan, Arthur, 58
Tappan, Lewis, 58
Tax reform movement, 392–94
Die Telegraph, 351; emergence of, 214, 353; and Irish, 404; and Republican party, 400; and tax reform movement, 394
Telegraphic communications: and commerce, 51
Temperance: inception of, 26–27, 31; growth of, 44; decline of, 380; and antilicensing laws, 357–58; and antiprohibitionists, 379–80; and bourgeoisie, 79, 105; and Catholic church, 148–50; and Germans, 186; and Irish use of alcohol, 134; as political movement, 355–59; prohibition law passed, 379; rallies, 106; social functions of, 106; societies, 79, 105–6, 150, 356, 357–58; as vehicle for American integration, 105–7. *See also names of individual temperance societies*
Tenements. See Neighborhoods, lower-class
The Terrace, 16
Thalia Theater Company, 269
Thompson, James, 100
Tifft, George, 33, 60, 359, 379, 392
Tifft family, 49
Timmerman, Benjamin, 181, 239
Timmerman, Joseph, 239
Timon, John, Bishop, 113, 156, 157, 158; arrival of, 280–81; career of, 288; goals of, 296–97, 304, 309; personality of, 290–91; and American Protestants, 291, 296; and antiradicalism, 234–35; and Catholic school system, 81, 308–9; and charity, 311, 313–14; and construction of churches, 307–8; and cultural activities, 284; and election violence, 150; and Fillmore campaign, 385; and financial matters, 297–98, 302–4; and funeral customs, 148, 380; and Germans, 186, 193, 289–90; and immigrants, 116; and Irish press, 153; and parish schools, 222; political attitudes of, 159–60, 291–93; and poverty, 312–13; and priests, 146, 291, 298, 303–4, 305–6; and public funds, 292, 298–99, 300–301; and public schools, 299–300, 362; and public welfare, 316; and St. Joseph's Cathedral, 309–11; and St. Louis Church, 285–96 passim, 380–81; and secret societies, 196; and seminary, establishment of, 304; and Sisters of Charity Hospital, 316; and temperance, 148–50; and working-class protest, 257–58
Toledo, 114
Townsend, Charles, 5
Towpath Rebellion, 135, 254, 256–57
Trade. *See* Commerce
Trade unions. *See* Labor unions
Tradesmen. *See* Artisans
Trinity Episcopal Church, 76
Trinity Lutheran Church, 409
Trollope, Frances, 27
Trowbridge, Josiah, Dr., 315, 316, 372
Turnerfesten, 206
Turners, 170, 174, 198–99, 200, 230, 269, 403

Unemployment: seasonal, 10
Union party, 405–6
Unitarian church, 76, 195
United Evangelical St. Peter's Church, 409
University of Buffalo, 44, 78
University of Western New York, 27–28, 105
Urban, George, 176, 181, 200, 201, 403
Urban agriculture, 18; and Germans, 173; and Irish, 124
Utica, 8

Vanderpoel, Isaac, 257, 347
Vaughan, Maurice, 158
Vereine, 174, 194, 196; activities of, 189–90; description of, 167; development of, 187–88; and radical culture, 200, 270; secular, 230; as vehicle for assimilation, 333
Vereinswesen, 167
Volksfreund, 351, 352
Voluntarism. *See* Civic integration

Voting. *See* Elections
Voting districts. *See* Wards

Wadsworth, James S., 203, 347, 389
Wadsworth family, 49
Wages-earning: advent of, 240; and laborers, 243; orders, or storepay system, 89, 243-44, 251; rallies against, 272-73; uncurrent specie, 243
Walhalla Odd Fellows Lodge, 196-97
Walsh, John, 340
Walsh, Patrick, 394
Wards: and ethnic vote, 373; size of, 350; increase in number of, 331; redistricting of, attempts at, 350-51; First Ward, 123-24, 150, 340-63 passim, 406; Second Ward, 123, 144, 342-50 passim, 372, 407; Third Ward, 123, 144, 342-50 passim, 372; Fourth Ward, 172, 174-75, 186, 340, 342-69 passim, 393; Fifth Ward, 174, 342-69 passim, 406; Sixth Ward, 124, 174, 175, 182, 406, 408-9; Seventh Ward, 124, 174, 175, 182, 408-9; Eighth Ward, 123-24, 144, 150, 406; Ninth Ward, 372, 407; Tenth Ward, 372; Eleventh Ward, 407-8; Twelfth Ward, 373
Washington Engine Company #5, 78
Waterfront. *See* Harbor
Watson, S. V.R., 203, 205, 392
Webb, George J., 250, 253
Weed, Thurlow, 301, 353-54
Weitling, Wilhelm, 198, 232, 233, 265, 269-71. *See also* Workingmen's League
Welch, Samuel, 18, 22, 65
Weltbürger, 209; emergence of, 212-15; and American stereotyping, 202-3; and anticlericalism, 226-27; and apathy, 199; and Archbishop Bedini, 294; and bilingualism debate, 220-21, 223-24, 225; and citizen participation, 333; and civic improvement, 367, 368; and civic integration, 189, 216-17, 235; and class distinction, 242-43; and commerce, 176, 395; and cultural nationalism, 225-26; and Democratic party, 338, 348; and depression, 401; as ethnic press, 188; and European affairs, 341; and German politics, 400; and Grays, 263; and industrialization, 238; and Irish, 187; and labor unions, 268; and lay management, 290; and organization of labor, 264; and the police, 364; and public schools, 362; and radicalism, 225; and schools, 219; and socialism, 227, 233; and taxation, 393; and temperance, 357, 358; and Bishop Timon, 291; and workers' strikes, 260
Weninger, F. X., Father, 295-96
West, Charles E., 70
Westphal's Gardens, 180, 206-7
West Side, 17, 18, 19, 20, 101
Whalen, William, Rev., 148-49
Whig party: rise of, 322, 330; decline of, 348-49, 352-54, 378, 381, 382; and campaigning, 339; and Catholic church, 336-37; and Catholic vote, 354; and Democratic party, 335; and elections (1843-53), 345-46; (1844), 352-53; and European affairs, 354-55; and evangelical religion, 336-37; and German vote, 349, 351-52; and immigrants, 301, 336, 349-53, 374; lack of discipline within, 337-38; and nativism, 213, 351, 372; newspapers of, 214, 218, 351; and patronage, 98, 218, 341; political economy of, 336; and population fluctuation, 348; and the press, 339; and racism, 337; Silver Grays, 353-54, 383, 385, 398, 405; and temperance, 356, 357, 358, 379; threats to, 331
Whitcomb, H. H., 248, 250
White's Corners, 136
Wieckmann, Charles, 234
Wilhelm Tell Society, 187
Wilkeson, John, 64
Wilkeson, Samuel: career of, 31-33; after economic depression, 38; and harbor, 5, 53; and public welfare, 85; and Rathbun, 36, 37
Wilkeson, Samuel, Jr., 64, 397
Wilkeson, William, 33, 64
Wilkeson family, 49, 66, 239
Wilkeson stove works, 9
Women: in industry, 240-41; and suffrage, opposition to, 89
—bourgeois: and charity, 78-80; and education, 81; and "gay season," 73; and religion, 75; role of, 70-71; and

temperance, 31, 79, 356–58; and women's rights, 89
—German: as domestics, 183–84; role of, 184; as service workers, 183
—Irish: marriage patterns of, 128; and milk business, 128; and poverty, 130–31; and prostitution, 131; role of, 152; as service workers, 125, 127–28, 131–32, 140; stereotypes of, 140–42
Women's Industrial School, 86
"Work or Bread" demonstrations, 254–59 passim, 406
Workhouse. *See* Public welfare
Working classes: and bourgeois values, 107; and cooperative ventures, 108; ethnicity within, 242–43; factory workers, 238; ideology of, 244–45; and industrialization, 238–39; lack of unity within, 236–42; organization of, 30, 108; organization of, and ethnicity, 244; organization of, multiethnic, 244, 272–73, 274; and politics, 12, 244, 271–72, 273–74; sailors, 274–76; semi-skilled workers, 237; ship carpenters, 274–75, 276–79; skilled workers, 237; social life of, 15; unskilled workers, 236–37; and wages, 243–44. *See also* Class struggle; Labor unions
—American: and advancement to bourgeois occupations, 100–101, 248–49; and bourgeois life-style, 100; and bourgeois values, 99, 103–4, 107, 248; and education, 105; fertility rates of, 103; and moral reform, 105–7; and nativism, 272; organization of, 107–8, 250–54; and ownership of property, 102; percentage of, 99; political ideology of, 108, 245–46; and self-improvement ethic, 248; values of, 103; and working conditions, 107–8
—Anglo-Canadian, 245–46
—German: and Americans, 261–63; class consciousness within, 261; and ethnicity, 265; ideology of, 262–63, 264–65; and Irish, compared with, 261; organization of, 260–61, 264, 272; and radicalism, 264
—Irish: and Americans, 255–57; ethnicity among, 256; lack of unity within, 255; organization of, 258, 259–60; and politicians, 258; protests and strikes by, 254–55, 256–57; strikebreakers, 255; and violence, 255–57
Workingmen's League, 198, 232–33, 269–71
Workingmen's movement, 23, 30, 161

Yinger, Milton, definition of ethnic group, 117–18, 119, 120
Young Men's Association, 77–78, 97, 104, 153, 190, 390
Young Men's Christian Union, 78, 102, 205
Young Men's Temperance Society, 31, 44

Zahm, Georg, 213–19 passim
Zahm, Jacob, 214
Ziegele, Albert, 181
Zion Evangelical Reformed Church, 195
Züngler, Johannes, 18, 173

Note on the Author

David A. Gerber received his B.A. degree from Northwestern University and his Ph.D. from Princeton University, and since 1971 has taught at the State University of New York at Buffalo in Amherst, New York, where he is Professor of History. Gerber is the author of *Black Ohio and the Color Line* (University of Illinois Press, 1976) and editor of *Anti-Semitism in American History* (University of Illinois Press, 1986). His most recent honors include a National Endowment for the Humanities Fellowship for Independent Study and Research (1986–87) and special recognition from the Gustavus Myers Center for Human Rights (1987) for his volume on anti-Semitism.